Printed in the United States
By Bookmasters

Lecture Notes in Computer Science 8407

Commenced Publication in 1973
Founding and Former Series Editors:
Gerhard Goos, Juris Hartmanis, and Jan van Leeuwen

Editorial Board

Linawati   Made Sudiana Mahendra
Erich J. Neuhold   A Min Tjoa   Ilsun You (Eds.)

Information and Communication Technology

Second IFIP TC5/8 International Conference
ICT-EurAsia 2014
Bali, Indonesia, April 14-17, 2014
Proceedings

 Springer

Volume Editors

Linawati
Made Sudiana Mahendra
Udayana University, Denpasar, Bali, Indonesia
E-mail: linawati@unud.ac.id
E-mail: mahendramade@yahoo.com

Erich J. Neuhold
University of Vienna, Austria
E-mail: erich.neuhold@univie.ac.at

A Min Tjoa
Vienna University of Technology, Austria
E-mail: amin@ifs.tuwien.ac.at

Ilsun You
Korean Bible University, Seoul, South Korea
E-mail: isyou@bible.ac.kr

ISSN 0302-9743   e-ISSN 1611-3349
ISBN 978-3-642-55031-7   e-ISBN 978-3-642-55032-4
DOI 10.1007/978-3-642-55032-4
Springer Heidelberg New York Dordrecht London

Library of Congress Control Number: 2014935887

LNCS Sublibrary: SL 3 – Information Systems and Application,
incl. Internet/Web and HCI

Typesetting: Camera-ready by author, data conversion by Scientific Publishing Services, Chennai, India

Printed on acid-free paper

Springer is part of Springer Science+Business Media (www.springer.com)

Preface

The ICT-EurAsia conference is thought as a platform for the exchange of ideas, experiences, and opinions among theoreticians and practitioners and for defining requirements of future systems in the area of ICT with a special focus on fostering long-term relationships among and with researchers and leading organizations in Eurasia.

On the one hand the idea of organizing this cross-domain scientific event came from the IFIP president Leon Strous at the IFIP 2010 World Computer Congress in Brisbane and on the other hand by the many activities of the ASEA-UNINET (ASEAN-European Academic University Network). This network was founded in 1994 especially to enhance scientific and research cooperation between ASEAN countries and Europe. The great success of ASEA-UNINET led to the foundation of the EPU-network (Eurasia Pacific University Network), which complements the geographic area of ASEA-UNINET covering the Eurasian super-continent. Both university networks have a strong focus on ICT.

The IFIP organizers of this event, especially the Technical Committees TC 5 (IT Applications) and TC 8 (Information Systems), very much welcome the fertilization of this event by the collocation of AsiaARES as a special track on Availability, Reliability and Security.

We would like to express our thanks to all institutions actively supporting this event:

- University Udayana, Indonesia
- International Federation for Information Processing (IFIP)
- ASEAN-European University Network
- Eurasia-Pacific University Network
- The Austrian Competence Centres for Excellent Technology SBA (Secure Business Austria)
- The Austrian Agency for International Cooperation in Education and Research
- The Austrian Embassy in Jakarta

The papers presented at this conference were selected after extensive reviews by the Program Committee and associated reviewers. We would like to thank all Program Committee members for their valuable advice, the chair of the special sessions, and the authors for their contributions.

Many persons contributed numerous hours to organize this conference. Their names will appear on the following pages as committee members of this scientific conference.

We are greatly indebted to the University of Udayana for the wholehearted support of its leaders. We would like to specifically mention the very significant support of President Prof. Ketut Suastika and Prof. I Made Suastra.

Last but not least, we want to thank Amin Anjomshoaa and Yvonne Poul for their contribution that made this edition of the conference proceedings possible.

January 2014

Linawati
Made Sudiana Mahendra
Erich Neuhold
A Min Tjoa
Ilsun You

Organization

Information and Communication Technology-EurAsia Conference 2014, ICT-EurAsia 2014

General Chairs

Stephane Bressan   National University of Singapore, Singapore
Erich Neuhold   Chair of IFIP Technical Committee on Information Technology Application

Program Committee Chairs

Ladjel Bellatreche   Laboratorie d'Informatique Scientifique et Industrielle, France
Lihua Chen   Peking University, China
Alfredo Cuzzocrea   University of Calabria, Italy
Tran Khanh Dang   National University of Ho Chi Minh City, Vietnam
Isao Echizen   National Institute of Informatics, Japan
Mukesh Mohania   IBM Research India
A Min Tjoa   Vienna University of Technology, Austria
Khabib Mustofa   Universitas Gadjah Mada, Indonesia

Special Session Chairs

Amin Anjomshoaa   Vienna University of Technology, Austria
Andreas Holzinger   University of Graz, Austria
Ilsun You   Korean Bible University, Korea

Steering Committee:

Masatoshi Arikawa   University of Tokyo, Japan
Wichian Chutimaskul   King Mongkut's University of Technology Thonburi, Thailand
Zainal A. Hasibuan   Universitas Indonesia, Indonesia
Hoang Huu Hanh   University of Hue, Vietnam
Josef Küng   University of Linz, Austria

Ismail Khalil	Johannes Kepler University Linz, Austria
Inggriani Liem	Institute of Technology Bandung, Indonesia
Made Sudiana Mahendra	Udayana University, Indonesia
Pavol Navrat	Slovak University of Technology Bratislava, Slovakia
Günther Pernul	University of Regensburg, Germany
Maria Raffai	University of Györ, Hungary
Ahmad Ashari	Universitas Gadjah Mada, Indonesia

Organizational Coordination Chairs

Yvonne Poul	SBA Research, Austria
Peter Wetz	University of Technology, Vienna

Senior Program Committee

Hamideh Afsarmanesh	University of Amsterdam, The Netherlands
Amin Anjomshoaa	Vienna University of Technology, Austria
Masatoshi Arikawa	University of Tokyo, Japan
Hyerim Bae	Pusan National University, Korea
Sourav S. Bhowmick	Nanyang Technological University, Singapore
Nguyen Thah Binh	IIASA, Austria
Robert P. Biuk-Aghai	University of Macau, China
Gerhard Budin	University of Vienna, Austria
Somchai Chatvichienchai	University of Nagasaki, Japan
Key Sun Choi	KAIST, Korea
Wichian Chutimaskul	KMUTT, Thailand
Hoang Xuan Dau	PTIT, Hanoi, Vietnam
Duong Anh Duc	University of Information Technology, Vietnam
Tetsuya Furukawa	University of Kyushu, Japan
Andrzej Gospodarowicz	Wroclaw University of Economics, Poland
Zainal Hasibuan	University of Indonesia, Indonesia
Christian Huemer	Vienna University of Technology, Austria
Mizuho Iwaihara	Faculty of Science and Engineering Waseda University, Japan
Gerti Kappel	Vienna University of Technology, Austria
Dimitris Karagiannis	University of Vienna, Austria
Shuaib Karim	Quaid-i-Azam University, Pakistan
Dieter Kranzlmüller	Ludwig-Maximilians-Universität München, Germany
Narayanan Kulathuramaiyer	Universiti Malaysia Sarawak, Malaysia
Josef Küng	Johannes Kepler Universität Linz, Austria

Khalid Latif	National University of Sciences and Technolgy, Pakistan
Lenka Lhotska	Czech Technical University, Czech Republic
Inggriani Liem	ITB-Institute of Technology Bandung, Indonesia
Vladimir Marik	Czech Technical University, Czech Republic
Luis M. Camarinha Matos	Universidade Nova de Lisboa, Portugal
Günter Müller	University of Freiburg, Germany
Thoai Nam	HCMC University of Technology, Vietnam
Bernardo Nugroho Yahya	Ulsan National Institute of Science and Technology, Korea
Günther Pernul	University of Regensburg, Germany
Geert Poels	Ghent University, Belgium
Gerald Quirchmayr	University of Vienna, Austria
Dana Indra Sensuse	University of Indonesia, Indonesia
Josaphat Tetuko Sri Sumantyo	Chiba University, Japan
Wikan Danar Sunindyo	Institute of Technology Bandung, Indonesia
Katsumi Tanaka	Kyoto University, Japan
Juan Trujillo	University of Alicante, Spain
Nguyen Tuan	Vietnam National University, Vietnam
Werner Winiwarter	University of Vienna, Austria

The 2014 Asian Conference on Availability, Reliability and Security, AsiaARES 2014

Program Committee Chair

Ilsun You	Korean Bible University, South Korea

Program Committee

Tsuyohsi Takagi	Kyushu University, Japan
Dong Seong Kim	University of Canterbury, New Zealand
Kyung-Hyune Rhee	Pukyong National University, Republic of Korea
Qin Xin	University of the Faroe Islands, Denmark
Marek R. Ogiela	AGH University of Science and Technology, Poland
Pandu Rangan Chandrasekaran	Indian Institute of Technology Madras, India
Shinsaku Kiyomoto	KDDI R&D Laboratories Inc., Japan
Atsuko Miyaji	JAIST, Japan
Willy Susilo	University of Wollongong, Australia

Xiaofeng Chen   Xidian University, China
Shuichiroh Yamamoto   Nagoya University, Japan
Fangguo Zhang   Sun Yan-Sen University, China
Xinyi Huang   Fujian normal university, China
Rana Barua   Indian Statistical Institute, India
Baokang Zhao   National University of Defense Technology,
                             China
Joonsang Baek   Khalifa University of Science, Technology &
                             Research (KUSTAR), UAE
Fang-Yie Leu   Tunghai University, Taiwan
Francesco Palmieri   Seconda Università di Napoli, Italy
Aniello Castiglione   Università degli Studi di Salerno, Italy
Ugo Fiore   Seconda Università di Napoli, Italy
Yizhi Ren   Hangzhou Dianzi University, China
Kirill Morozov   Kyushu University, Japan
Ren Junn Hwang   Tamkang University, Taiwan
Shiuh-Jeng Wang   Central Police University, Taiwan
Igor Kotenko   St. Petersburg Institute for Informatics and
                             Automation (SPIRAS), Russia
Shuhui Hou   University of Science and Technology Beijing,
                             China
Wolfgang Boehmer   Technische Universität Darmstadt, Germany
Akihiro Yamamura   Akita University, Japan
Mauro Migliardi   University of Padua, Italy
Adela Georgescu   University of Bucharest, Romania
Kensuke Baba   Kyushu University, Japan
Hiroaki Kikuchi   Meiji University, Japan
Zhenqian Feng   National University of Defense Technology,
                             China
Siuming Yiu   The Univeristy of Hong Kong, Hong Kong
Vaise Patu   Nagoya University, Japan
Kouichi Sakurai   Kyushu University, Japan
Masakatsu Nishigaki   Shizuoka University, Japan
Yuan Li   Lund University, Sweden
Xiaofeng Wang   National University of Defense Technology,
                             China

Invited Talks

Interoperability - Problems and Solutions

Erich J. Neuhold

University of Vienna, Austria
Research Group Multimedia Information Systems
erich.neuhold@univie.ac.at

Abstract. Interoperability is a qualitative property of computing infrastructures that denotes the ability of the sending and receiving systems to exchange and properly interpret information objects across system boundaries.

Since this property is not given by default, the interoperability problem involves the representation of meaning and has been an active research topic for approximately four decades. Early database models such as the Relational Model used schemas to express semantics and implicitly aimed at achieving interoperability by providing programming independence of data storage and access.

After a number of intermediate steps such as Object Oriented Data Bases and Semi – Structured Data such as hypertext and XML document models, the notions of semantics and interoperability became what they have been over the last ten years in the context of the World Wide Web and more recently the concept of Open Linked Data.

The talk will concentrate on the early history but also investigate the (reoccurring) problem of interoperability as it can be found in the massive data collections around the Open Linked Data concepts. We investigate semantics and interoperability research from the point of view of information systems. It should give an overview of existing old and new interoperability techniques and point out future research directions, especially for concepts found in Open Linked Data and the Semantic WEB.

Sifting through the Rubble of Big Data for the Human Face of Mobile

Ismail Khalil

Johannes Kepler University Linz, Austria
Institute of Telecooperation
ismail.khalil@jku.at

Abstract. As the landscape around Big data continues to exponentially evolve, the "big" facet of Big data is no more number one priority of researchers and IT professionals. The race has recently become more about how to sift through torrents of data to find the hidden diamond and engineer a better, smarter and healthier world. The ease with which our mobile captures daily data about ourselves makes it an exceptionally suitable means for ultimately improving the quality of our lives and gaining valuable insights into our affective, mental and physical state. This talk takes the first exploratory step into this direction by presenting motivating cases, discussing research directions and describing how to use mobiles to process and analyze the "digital exhaust" it collects about us to automatically recognize our emotional states and automatically respond to them in the most effective and "human" way possible. To achieve this we treat all theoretical, technical, psycho-somatic, and cognitive aspects of emotion observation and prediction, and repackage all these elements into a mobile multimodal emotion recognition system that can be used on any mobile device.

Table of Contents

Semantic Web and Knowledge Management

Cloud Computing

Image Processing

Software Engineering

Collaboration Technologies and Systems

E-Learning

Data Warehousing and Data Mining

E-Government and E-Health

Biometric and Bioinformatics Systems

The 2014 Asian Conference on Availability, Reliability and Security, AsiaARES 2014

Network Security

Dependable Systems and Applications

Privacy and Trust Management

Cryptography

Multimedia Security

Dependable Systems and Applications

The Human Face of Mobile

Hajar Mousannif[1] and Ismail Khalil[2]

[1] Cadi Ayyad University, LISI Laboratory, Faculty of Sciences Semlalia,
B.P. 2390, 40000, Marrakesh, Morocco
`mousannif@uca.ma`
[2] Johannes Kepler University, Institute of Telecooperation,
Altenberger Strasse 69, A-4040Linz, Austria
`Ismail.khalil@jku.at`

Abstract. As the landscape around Big data continues to exponentially evolve, the « big » facet of Big data is no more number one priority of researchers and IT professionals. The race has recently become more about how to sift through torrents of data to find the hidden diamond and engineer a better, smarter and healthier world. The ease with which our mobile captures daily data about ourselves makes it an exceptionally suitable means for ultimately improving the quality of our lives and gaining valuable insights into our affective, mental and physical state. This paper takes the first exploratory step into this direction by using the mobile to process and analyze the "digital exhaust" it collects to automatically recognize our emotional states and accordingly respond to them in the most effective and "human" way possible. To achieve this we treat all technical, psycho-somatic, and cognitive aspects of emotion observation and prediction, and repackage all these elements into a mobile multimodal emotion recognition system that can be used on any mobile device.[1]

Keywords: Emotion Recognition, Affective Computing, Context, Pattern Recognition, Machine Learning, Reality Mining, Intelligent Systems.

1   Introduction

Who among us never yelled at his/her mobile phone, and cried or laughed franticly at it? Who among us never wished his/her mobile phone was able to react in one way or another to his/her anger, sadness, disgust, fear, surprise or happiness? Sifting through the rubble of the huge amount of data (Big data) our mobiles are collecting about us to automatically recognize and predict our emotional states is definitely one of the very innovative fields of current research with many sorts of interesting implications.

Mobile phones are part of our everyday life. They have the ability to get inside our heads and position our bodies [1]. They can even impact the way we define our identity and therefore represent an exceptionally suitable means for improving the

---

[1] The system and method described in this work were registered as Patent Application Ref. 36049 at the Moroccan Office of Industrial and Commercial Property OMPIC (jun. 26th 2013).

Linawati et al. (Eds.): ICT-EurAsia 2014, LNCS 8407, pp. 1–20, 2014.

quality of our life. A broad range of functions are already available on mobile phones nowadays, ranging from the basic functions of calling and texting, to more advanced ones such as entertainment and personal assistance. Mobile phones also have many modalities that are equivalent to human senses, such as vision (through cameras), hearing (through microphones), and touch (through haptic sensors). They, however, lack the human ability of recognizing, understanding and expressing emotions in an effort to support humans emotionally whenever and wherever they need it.

A variety of technologies especially in the fields of artificial intelligence and human computer interaction consider and implement emotions as a necessary component of complex intelligent functioning. Many emotion recognition systems which process different communication channels (speech, image, text, etc.,) as well as the outputs from bio-sensors and off-the-shelf sensors of mobile terminals have been developed. Research on integrating many modalities into a single system for emotion recognition through mobile phones is still at a very early stage, not to mention a shortage of literature on real applications that target providing personalized services that fit users' current emotional states.

In this paper, we design a multimodal emotion recognition system that aims at integrating different modalities (audio, video, text and context) into a single system for emotion recognition using mobile devices. We also design a method, we refer to as EgoGenie, which automatically recognizes the emotional states of mobile phone users and reacts to them by serving up personalized and customized content and service offerings based on their emotional states.

While all agree that interpreting human emotional cues and responding accordingly would be highly beneficial, addressing the following problem areas is a challenging task:

1. How can we represent and model emotions?
2. How can we extract the valuable and insightful information that best conveys the emotional states of mobile phone users from the Big data they generate?
3. How can we process users' data despite the limitations and constraints of mobile technology?
4. How to accordingly and "humanly" respond to the identified emotional states of the users?

The rest of the paper is structured as follows. Section 2 presents the emotion-theoretical background and sheds light on the importance of emotions in human's way of reasoning and its decision-making activities. Section 3 reviews some related work in the area of emotion recognition using mobile technology. We classify it into 5 categories: 1°) Emotion recognition in speech, 2°) Facial emotion recognition, 3°) Affective information detection in text the user types, 4°) Emotion recognition from the context around the user, and 5°) Multimodal emotion recognition where many communication channels or modalities are used. In section 4, we describe our proposed multimodal system for emotion recognition. Section 5 introduces our proposed method for emotion recognition and personalized content/service delivery and presents some implementation examples. Conclusions and directions for future work are presented in section 6.

2   Theoretical Background

Over the last years, research on emotions has become a multidisciplinary research field of growing interest. For long, research on understanding and modeling human emotion has been predominantly dealt with in the fields of psychology and linguistics. The topic is now attracting an increasing attention within the engineering community as well. More particularly, emotion is now considered as a necessary component of complex intelligent functioning, especially in the fields of artificial intelligence and human computer interaction. It is well argued that for systems to adapt the human environment and to communicate with humans in a natural way, systems need to understand and also express emotions in a certain degree [2]. Of course, systems may never need to have all of the emotional skills that humans have but they will definitely require some of these skills to appear intelligent when interacting with humans.

Unlike physical phenomena such as time, location, and movement, human emotions are very difficult to measure with simple sensors. Extensive research has been conducted to understand and model emotions. Two famous models have been adopted by the scientific world in order to classify emotions and distinguish between them: the basic emotions model (or a mix of them) and the 2-dimensional Arousal-Valence classification model. While the former tends to classify emotions as a mix of some basic emotions (such as anger, sadness, disgust, fear, surprise and happiness), the latter aims at representing emotions on two axes: valence, ranging from "unpleasant" to "pleasant", and arousal, ranging from "calm" to "excited". We argue that an emotion cannot be properly investigated without the analysis of the following 3 components (Figure 1):

1. The cognitive component: which consists in classifying and understanding the environment, the context, and attended situations that triggered the emotion.
2. The physical component: which includes focusing on the physical response (facial expressions, speech, postures, verbal/non verbal behavior etc.) and physiological response (heartbeats, blood volume pressure, respiration, etc.) that co-occur with the emotion or immediately follow it.
3. The outcome component: This involves analyzing the impact of the emotion, e.g. on behavior, on social communications, on decision making, on performance, on activities, etc.

Additionally, emotion assessment can be exploited in at least two levels: Either as a tool in evaluating attractiveness, appreciation and user experience of a service or product or in bringing the machine closer to the human by making the machine recognize, understand and express emotions in an effort to naturally interact with humans. Many real life applications are making use of emotion assessment in both levels. One could refer to [3] for some examples. Those incorporating mobile technology are the ones that are of much interest to us. Examples include improving mobile education and learning [4], mobile healthcare [5], stress detection [6], predicting and preventing task performance degradation [7] and avatar realism [8] among many others.

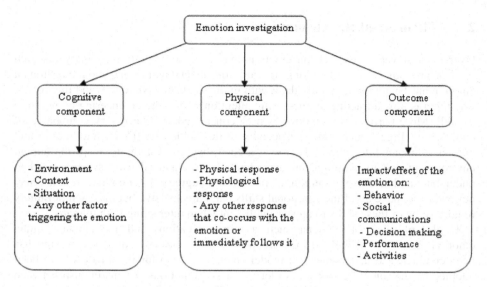

Fig. 1. The three essential components for a better investigation of emotions

3   Emotion Recognition

While general research on Automatic Emotion Recognition (AER) has matured over the last decades especially in the fields of affective computing and Human-Computer Interaction (HCI), research on emotion recognition and processing using mobile technology is still at a very early stage.

Most (if not all) emotion recognition systems are based on either a rule-based system or on a well-trained system that decides which emotion category, dimension or label fits the best. From a scientific perspective, emotion recognition is nothing more than a mapping function from a feature space to emotion descriptors or labels space using solid and analytically-founded machine learning algorithms [9]. Theoretically, any type of information, such as audio, visual, written, mental or even physiological [10], can be used for an accurate selection of features and emotional labels. In practice, integrating all these modalities into a single system for emotion-sensitive analysis is still a very challenging issue. In this section, we start by presenting the most recent state of the art in the field of emotion recognition using mobile technology. We classify it into 5 categories: 1°) Emotion recognition in speech, 2°) Facial emotion recognition, 3°) Affective information detection in text, 4°) Emotion recognition from the context around the user, and 5°) Multimodal emotion recognition. We also describe the challenges related to adopting a multimodal emotion recognition approach and highlight our contribution.

3.1   Emotion Recognition in Speech

In any speech emotion recognition system, three crucial aspects are identified [11]. The first one is the extraction of a reasonably limited, meaningful, and informative set of features for speech representation. Some of these features might be speech pitch [12], spectra [13] and intensity contours. The second is the design of an appropriate classification scheme capable of distinguishing between the different emotional classes it was trained with. This design depends on many aspects such as finding the best machine learning algorithm (neural networks, support vector machines, etc.) to use in constructing the classifier [14], the suitable architecture for the classifier [15], [16], or the proper technique to use when extracting features [17]. The last aspect is the proper preparation of an emotional speech database for evaluating system performance [18]. The number and type of emotions included in the database as well as how well they simulate real-world environment are very important design factors.

Although many combinations of emotional features and classifiers have been presented and evaluated in the literature especially in the context of Human Computer Interaction, little attention has been paid to speech emotion recognition using mobile technology. In [19] for instance, authors propose a speech emotion recognition agent for mobile communication service. They argue that the agent is capable of determining the degree of affection (love, truthfulness, weariness, trick, friendship) of a person, in real-time conversation through a cellular phone, at an accuracy of 72.5 % over five predetermined emotional states (neutral, happiness, sadness, anger, and annoyance). The system alleviates the noises caused by the mobile network and the environment, and which might cause emotional features distortion, by adopting a Moving Average filter and a feature optimization method to improve the system performance.

Authors in [20] introduce an emotional speech recognition system for the applications on smartphones. The system uses support vector machines (SVM) and a trained hierarchical classifier to identify the major emotions of human speech, including happiness, anger, sadness and normal. Accent and intonation are recognized using a time-frequency parameter obtained by continuous wavelet transforms. Authors argue that their system achieves an average accuracy of 63.5% for the test set and 90.9% for the whole data set. As an application on smartphones, authors suggest to combine the system with social networking websites and the functions of micro blogging services in an effort to increase the interaction and care among people in community groups.

In [21], authors introduce EmotionSense, a mobile sensing platform for conducting social and psychological studies in an unobtrusive way. EmotionSense automatically recognizes speakers and emotions by means of classifiers running locally using Gaussian Mixture methods. According to authors, the platform is capable of collecting individual emotions as well as activities and location measures by processing the outputs from the sensors of off-the-shelf mobile phones. These sensors can be activated or deactivated using declarative rules social scientists express according to the user context. Authors claim that the framework is highly programmable and run-time adaptive.

In [20] and [21] emotion recognition is processed locally within the mobile phone, whereas in [19], the speech signal is transmitted to an emotion recognition server which performs all the computation and processing and reports back a classification result to the mobile agent based on the confidence probability of each emotional state.

3.2   Facial Emotion Recognition

Emotions are highly correlated with facial expressions. When we smile, frown or grimace, thousands of tiny facial muscles are at work making it almost impossible to express emotions without facial expressions.

A typical facial expression detection system would comprise of two essential blocks: the feature extraction block and the feature recognition block. The first block tries to extract some relevant patterns from the images (such as the shape, the texture composition, the movements of the lips, the eyebrows, etc,), and then feed them into either a rule-based or well-trained feature recognition block that is able to recognize the emotions based on the extracted features. A large variety of purely facial emotion recognition systems has been presented in recent years. A detailed overview of these techniques can be found in [22].

Processing images requires a considerable amount of computational resources (CPU) and it is highly time-consuming. If a visual emotion recognition system is to be implemented in mobile devices, it must definitely take into account their limited hardware performance. Very few works in the literature investigate visual emotion recognition using mobile devices. Authors in [23] for instance investigate the deployment of a face detection algorithm to identify facial features on an android mobile platform. The algorithm uses a mixture of statistical approaches to predict different facial regions (eyes, nose and mouth areas) and image processing techniques to accurately locate specific features. Authors claim that less than 3 sec is needed for accurate features detection. No emotion recognition, however, is investigated using the extracted features.

In [24], authors propose EmoSnaps, a mobile application that captures pictures of one's facial expressions throughout the day and uses them for later recall of momentary emotions. The photo captures are triggered by events where users are paying visual and mental attention to the device (e.g "screen unlock", "phone call answer" and "sms sent"). The photo shots are not used for real-time emotion recognition but for reconstructing one's momentary emotions by inferring them directly from facial expressions. Authors argue that EmoSnaps should better be used for experiences that lie further in the past rather than the recent ones.

A more market-oriented approach is presented in [25] where authors show how mobile devices could help in measuring the degree of people's response to the media. More specifically, authors document a process capable of assessing the emotional impact a given advertisement has on a group of people through Affectiva's facial coding platform Affdex [26]. Affdex provides real-time emotional states recognition by analyzing streamed webcam videos in Affectiva's cloud and tracking smirks, smiles, frowns and furrows to measure the consumer response to brands and media. Emotions are later aggregated across individuals and presented on a dashboard that allows playback of the ad synchronized with the emotion response. Authors also explore how this process can help in providing new insights into ad effectiveness and ad recall.

3.3 Context Emotion Recognition

It is very difficult even for humans to judge a person's emotional state from a short spoken sentence or from a captured image. To interpret an utterance or an observed facial expression, it is important to know the context in which they have been displayed. Therefore, modern Automatic Emotion Recognition systems are influenced by the growing awareness that long-range context modeling plays an important role in expressing and perceiving emotions [27]. Again, there are relatively few focused studies on retrieving emotional cues from the context around the user through mobile devices.

Motivated by the proliferation of social networks such as Facebook and MySpace, authors in [28] propose a mobile context sharing system capable of automatically sharing high-level contexts such as activity and emotion using Bayesian Networks based on collected mobile logs. Low-level contexts from sensors such as GPS coordinates, and call logs are collected and analyzed. Meaningful information is then being extracted through data revision and places annotation. To recognize high-level contexts, Bayesian Networks models are used to calculate the probability of activities (e.g. moving, sleeping, studying, etc.) according to predetermined factors: status factor, a spatial factor, a temporal factor, an environmental factor, and a social factor. Authors later derive specific emotions (e.g. bored, contented, excited, etc) directly from the activity arguing that activity has an influence on user's emotion directly, which, in our sense, might not be accurate since a user's specific activity can be associated with different types of emotion.

Authors in [29] propose a method for generating behaviors of a synthetic character for smartphones. Like in 28, user contexts are also inferred using Bayesian networks to deal with information insufficiency and situations uncertainty. Authors deploy two types of Bayesian networks: one infers valence and arousal states of the user and the other infers the business state of the user by gathering and analyzing information available in smartphones such as contact information, schedules, call logs, and device states. Their work, however, focuses more on how to create the emotions of the synthetic character rather than inferring the emotional state of the user from the context around him/her.

In [30], authors introduce a machine learning approach to recognize the emotional states of a smartphone user in an unobtrusive way using the user-generated data from sensors on the smartphone. The data is first classified into two groups: behavior (e.g. typing speed, frequency of pressing a specific key, etc) and context of the user (location, time zone, weather condition, etc). Specific emotions are then identified using a Bayesian Network classifier and used for enhancing affective experience of Twitter users. Their experimental results, which were obtained using a developed Twitter client installed in the mobile device, showed an average classification accuracy of 67.52% for 7 different emotions. During the data collection process, participants are required to self-report their current emotion, whenever they feel it at the certain moment in their everyday life, via the Twitter client using some short text messages. This might not be practical in our sense since an emotion recognition system should be able to identify emotions in a more autonomous and stand-alone way.

3.4   Emotion Recognition from Text

It is generally rather difficult to extract the emotional value of a pure written text (whether it is containing emoticons or not). One reason could be the contextual ambiguity of sentences and their lack of subtleness. In fact, it is easier to express emotions through facial expressions rather than putting them into words. Authors in [31] showed how a banal conversation through instant messaging may turn into a fight by giving the example of someone who is getting increasingly annoyed in a conversation until he/she finally 'shouts' at the conversation partner that he/she had enough of it. The emotion detection system would suddenly change the perceived emotion from "neutral" to "outraged", making it difficult for the conversation partner to understand this sudden outburst of anger.

Emotion recognition from text involves concepts from the domains of both Natural Language Processing and Machine Learning. Text-based emotion recognition techniques can be classified into Keyword Spotting Techniques, Lexical Affinity Methods, Learning-based Methods and Hybrid Methods [32]. These techniques as well as their limitations are surveyed in [33].

We found no literature record of a mobile phone system or architecture that is able to recognize emotional states from pure textual data. Text input is usually combined in a multimodal setup with other communication channels such as audio, video or context.

3.5   Multimodal Emotion Recognition

A multimodal emotion recognition system is a system that responds to inputs in more than one modality or communication channel (e.g., speech, face, writing, linguistic content, context, etc.). Many earlier works have already proved that combining different modalities for emotion recognition provides complementary information that tends to improve recognition accuracy and performance. A comprehensive survey about these works in a HCI context can be found in [34].

Mobile phones have many modalities that are equivalent to human senses. They can see us through their cameras, hear us through their microphones, and touch us through their haptic sensors. Moreover, they are becoming more and more powerful since all sort of data are stored and accessed through them. The most surprising issue regarding multimodal emotion recognition is that despite the huge advances in processing modalities (audio, video, text, context, etc.) separately and despite the fact that great improvement of recognition performance could be achieved if these channels are used in a combined multimodal setup, there were only a few research efforts which tried to implement a multimodal emotion analyzer. Further, there is no record of a research effort that aims at integrating all modalities into a single system for emotion recognition through mobile devices.

In [35], authors propose a model that uses emotion-related data, obtained through biosensors, along with physical activity data, obtained through motion sensors integrated in the mobile phone, as input to determine the likely emotional state of the user. Authors claim that their model chooses an appropriate personalized service to provide based on the computed emotional state but, in the experimental prototype, only the mobile device ring tone is modified to match the user's current emotional state. Also, authors only vaguely describe how emotions are identified. The model has also the limitation that users should always wear a device in form of a glove for emotion-related data to be gathered, which can be quite intrusive.

A similar approach is presented in [36] where authors developed an emotion recognition engine for mobile phone. The engine uses a sensor enabled watch for the gathering of bio signals and environmental information. Compensation methods were applied for the sensor enabled watch to increase emotion decision accuracy. Based on one of the two identified emotional states: pleasant and unpleasant, differentiated multimedia contents, through IPTV, mobile social network service, and blog service, are provided to the user. However, practical limitations like in [35] are to be mentioned since wearing a biosensor watch all the time may cause inconvenience to users.

Authors in [37] propose an emotion recognition framework for smartphone applications. Using an emotional preference learning algorithm, the difference between two quantified (prior and posterior) behaviors is learnt for each entity in a mobile device (e.g. downloaded applications, media contents and contacts of people). Their conducted experiment showed that touching behavior (e.g. tapping, dragging, flicking, etc.) can also give clues about smartphone users' emotional states. No explicit response to predicted emotions is investigated by the authors.

3.6   Mobile Multimodal Emotion Recognition

With respect to all related efforts presented above, most authors focus on emotion recognition via mobile phones using only one communication channel (speech, image, context, etc.). The very few of them who tried to integrate many modalities into a single system desperately struggled with both hardware performance and energy limitations of mobile devices. As we mentioned earlier, processing many modalities locally within the mobile phones requires a considerable amount of computational resources and it is highly time and energy consuming. Moreover, most of them fail to provide immediate responses or reactions to recognized emotions in an effort to support mobile phones users emotionally.

The present work comes to overcome such limitations. The key contributions of this work can be summarized as follows:

- We design a multimodal emotion recognition system that aims at integrating different modalities into a single system for emotion recognition using mobile devices. All emotion recognition processing and their related computing complexity issues are dealt with in the cloud [38], while mobile devices simply transmit different inputs' data to the cloud which reports back the emotion recognition decision to the mobile device.
- We design a method, we refer to as EgoGenie, which automatically recognizes the emotional states of the user through his/her mobile phone and reacts to them accordingly by presenting personalized content and service offerings to support him/her emotionally and effectively, whenever and wherever the user needs it.

It is important to point out that both the proposed system and method could be implemented on any interactive device, PC or tablet, but since mobile phones are part of our everyday life and are almost all the times with us, the emotional impact of the proposed system and method on users is higher when deployed through mobile devices. Next sections provide extensive details about both the proposed system and method.

4   Mobile Multimodal Emotion Recognition System

This section explores the design of the mobile multimodal emotion recognition system and describes its major building blocks. The system is depicted in Figure 2. It includes client devices, a data collection engine, an emotion recognition engine, a content delivery engine, a network, an online service provider, an advertiser, and an input/output unit. The method which will be described in the next section, and which is illustrated in Figure 4, orchestrates the interaction between all the components in the system.

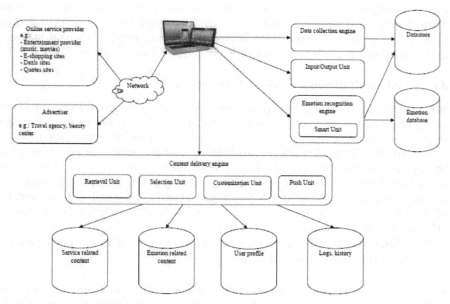

Fig. 2. Mobile Multimodal Emotion Recognition System Overview

The system comprises a data collection engine to collect expressive, behavioral and contextual data associated with an emotional state, analyze the collected data, and extract patterns associated with (or triggering) specific emotional states, an emotion recognition engine to map the patterns to different emotion categories and automatically recognize the emotional states, a content delivery engine to deliver to the user personalized content based on his/her emotional state, and an Input/output unit to interact with the user and the network. Some functions of the mentioned engines may be performed locally on the mobile phone or deported to the cloud for more convenience.

4.1   Data Collection Engine

The data collection engine may collect and analyze all types of data described in FIG. 3 including visual data, vocal data, written data, and contextual data. It also extracts relevant expressive, behavioral and contextual patterns and features to be used by the emotion recognition engine. Contextual data may include both low-level and high-level context. Low-level context is retrieved from both internal and external sensors.

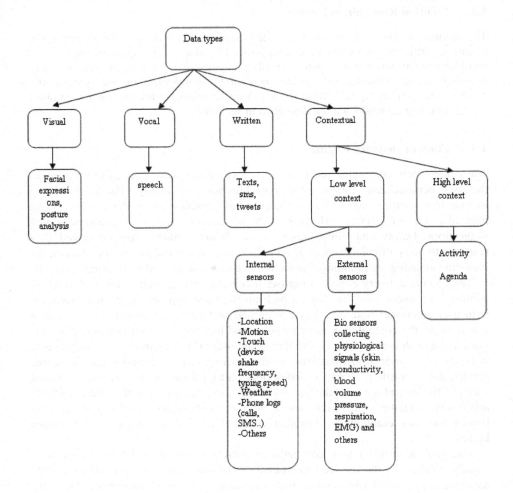

Fig. 3. Data types collected by the Data collection engine

Internal sensors may provide information about location (through GPS), motion (through accelerometer), touch behavior, e.g. device shake frequency, typing speed, etc. (through haptic sensors). Additional information may be provided by phone logs (e.g. call logs, SMS logs, tweets, etc.). External sensors may include bio sensors that collect physiological signals (such as skin conductivity, blood volume pressure, respiration, EMG, etc.). High-level context such as user activity is also collected. User agenda is used to determine user activity (e.g. in a meeting, exercising, etc.).

The data collection engine uses collected data to extract relevant expressive, behavioral and contextual patterns and features to be used by the emotion recognition engine.

4.2   Emotion Recognition Engine

The emotion recognition engine maps the patterns extracted by the data collection engine to different emotional state categories. The emotion recognition engine also includes a smart unit that may automatically recognize emotional states. The accuracy of automatic emotion recognition depends on the confidence on the patterns the emotion recognition engine is trained with. A detailed description on how the emotion recognition engine works will be described in section 5.

4.3   Content Delivery Engine

The content delivery engine reacts to the recognized emotional states by pushing to the user personalized content to support him/her emotionally. The content may include text, pictures, animations, videos or any combination of them. The content may also include service offerings such as vacation and SPA deals, shopping suggestions, beauty and fitness sessions, etc. Many contents may be served as a response to one particular emotional state. In neutral emotional states, specific content including amusing, entertaining, inspirational, ego-boosting, and motivating is served.

The content delivery engine comprises a content retrieval unit to retrieve different contents, a content selection unit to pick up the most appropriate content based on both user emotional state and user profile and preferences, a content customization unit to make the content look more personal and increase its emotional impact on the user, and a push unit to send the content to the user. The content delivery engine also interacts with a user profile database to store user-specific information such as name, gender, date of birth, preferences and hobbies, a logs database to store the emotional states of the user along with the pushed content, an emotion related content database and a service related content database to store contents or service offerings that may impact the user emotionally. Detailed description of these elements is provided bellow.

The content retrieval unit may retrieve content either from the emotion related content database or the service related content database. The emotion related content database is populated with content that may support the user emotionally, boost his ego, make him feel better about himself and cheer him up. An example of this content may be a quote, a poem, or a joke, retrieved from the online service provider.

The service related content database contains service offerings which may impact the user emotionally or improve his/her emotional state. Example of these services include dating websites (suggested by the system to people with broken hearts), travel offerings and SPA/massage sessions offerings (suggested to stressed people), beauty centers (suggested to women feeling ugly or in a bad mood), psychologists (suggested to very depressed people), and hospitals (in case the monitoring of the emotional states of some patients is critical like in cardio-vascular illnesses where patients should not get too angry to avoid heart attacks for example). These services are offered by the advertiser.

The content selection unit allows users to adjust both the nature and the frequency of the content to be served. It may also use the context around the user, retrieved through the method described in Figure 4, the user profile and preferences, and the user activity to refine content selection. For instance, a new hairstyle at a beauty center cannot be suggested to an old man.

The content customization unit uses user-specific information and preferences to customize the content in order to increase its emotional impact on the user. User-specific information may be retrieved from user profile database.

The push unit pushes content to users according to their emotional states. It also selects the most appropriate time to push the content based on the activity of the user, which is retrieved from the collected contextual data.

5   EgoGenie

In this section, we present a method we refer to as EgoGenie, and which can be built on top of the mobile multimodal emotion recognition system described in the previous section. EgoGenie automatically recognizes the emotional states of the mobile phone users with a certain confidence and reacts accordingly to them by pushing to the user personalized contents and service offerings. We start by presenting EgoGenie and then we provide some examples of its implementation.

5.1   Presentation

EgoGenie is a method to automatically recognize the current emotional states of the mobile phone user by analyzing different modalities such as: facial expressions (e.g. smiles, frowns or grimaces, etc.), speech (e.g. pitch, intensity contours, etc.), text the user types (e.g. instant messaging, tweets, etc.) and context around the user (e.g. location, weather condition, etc.). Once the method determines how the user is feeling, it will subsequently serve up personalized content and service offerings on his mobile phone to promote his well-being and boost his ego. Our idea is triggered by finding solutions to problems, such as daily life stresses, lack of productivity at work, task performance degradation, lack of self-confidence and self-esteem, and even more. The nature of the content pushed to the mobile phone varies according to the emotional state of the mobile phone user.

5.2   EgoGenie Logic

EgoGenie performs the following basic actions:

- Collecting contextual expressive and behavioral data and extracting patterns associated with an emotional state;
- Mapping expressive, behavioral and contextual patterns to an emotion category;
- Automatically deciding the emotional state of the user;
- Selecting and customizing the content or service offering, as a response to the recognized emotional state;
- Delivering the content or service offering.

The operating logic of EgoGenie is illustrated in Figure 4. Referring to Figure 4, upon method initialization, the emotional state is set to neutral. Neutral is the default emotional state in case no other emotional state is recognized.

The data collection engine starts by collecting contextual data. The main objective from collecting contextual data is to classify and understand the environmental, contextual, and attended situations that contributed or triggered the emotional state. A similar context is more likely to trigger the same emotional reaction from the user, in the future. Understanding the context allows the emotion recognition engine to automatically recognize the emotional state of the user without any self-reporting from the user himself.

After contextual data is collected, it needs to be analyzed. The data collection engine extracts contextual patterns. These patterns may include any pattern susceptible to be associated with (or trigger) an emotional state. For example, the approaching deadline for an exam or a project (provided through Agenda) is a pattern that is likely to generate a "stressed" emotional state. Period approaching for a female (also provided through Agenda) is a pattern that is likely to generate a "Fragile" emotional state. Being in a hospital or a cemetery (retrieved through location sensors of the client device) is a pattern that is likely to be associated with a "sad" emotional state. A user shouting during or after receiving a phone call (retrieved through the microphone of the client device) is a pattern that may indicate that the user is in "upset" or "angry" emotional state. Many patterns could be fed into the emotion recognition engine. The accuracy of emotion recognition depends on the degree of confidence in the patterns. This is obtained through the training of the emotion recognition engine during the self-reporting phase.

The client device allows the user, through the Input/output unit, to self-report his/her emotions very much like as if the user is talking or writing to a close friend and seeking comfort or advice. The progress of the algorithm will depend on whether the user self-reports his/her emotional state or not.

If the user self-reports the emotional state, the emotion recognition engine determines the emotion category by analyzing the written/vocal input stream. Concurrently, the data collection engine collects and extracts expressive and behavioral patterns associated with the emotion by analyzing data captured from the different sensors of the client device (e.g. camera, microphone, etc.). This consists in determining how the user expresses a specific emotion. Expressive patterns may include speech patterns (e.g. speech pitch, spectra, intensity contours, etc.), facial patterns (such as the shape, the texture composition, the movements of the lips, the eyebrows, etc.), or any combination of them (e.g. laughing, crying, shouting, etc.). Behavioral patterns may include body posture and attitude (e.g. holding head, hiding eyes, etc.). These patterns are used to train the smart unit to automatically detect the user's emotional state even if the user does not explicitly self-report it.

The data collection engine checks whether a new pattern is identified, by verifying whether the pattern has or has not been previously stored as associated with an emotion category in the emotion database. If the pattern is new, the emotion recognition engine maps it to the emotion category which was identified earlier and increases the confidence in that pattern. If the pattern is not new, the emotion recognition engine will simply increase confidence in the pattern. Let us assume, for example, that a person reported his sad emotional state to the client device, the emotion recognition engine analyzes what the user said and set the present emotional state of the user to "sad". The data collection engine collects expressive and behavioral patterns associated with the "sad" emotional state of the user, and concludes that the pattern:"In tears" is set. The emotion recognition engine checks whether that pattern is already associated with the "sad" emotional state in the emotion database. If not, it will map it along with the other patterns and increase confidence in that pattern. If yes, it will simply increase confidence in the pattern.

The content delivery engine retrieves and select appropriate content/service offering associated with the identified emotional state and customize it to increase its emotional impact on the user. Finally, the content delivery engine pushes the content or service offering to the user.

The extracted contextual patterns are periodically checked by the smart unit to identify any match with an already mapped emotional state. Since some contextual patterns can be associated with more than one emotional state, a high blood volume pressure for example can be associated with both "Angry" and "Happy" states, expressive and behavioral patterns are recollected by the data collection engine to better identify the emotion.   Hence, the smart unit identifies, with a certain confidence, the emotional state of the user based on contextual, expressive and behavioral patterns it was trained with during the self-reporting phase. The confidence in emotional state recognition is correlated with the confidence in the patterns.

In case no match between contextual patterns and emotion category is identified, the emotional state is maintained to "Neutral" and the content delivery engine serves up to the user specific content associated with "Neutral" states, including entertaining, amusing, inspirational, ego-boosting, and motivating.

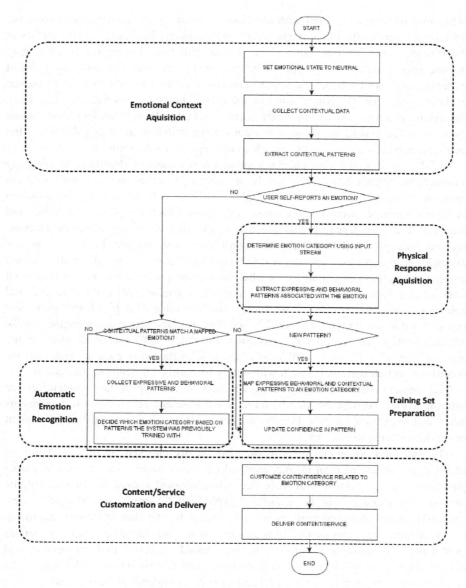

Fig. 4. EgoGenie operating logic

5.3   Implementation Examples

This section provides two implementation examples of EgoGenie: an example of content display based on emotion self-reporting and an example of content display based on automatic emotion recognition.

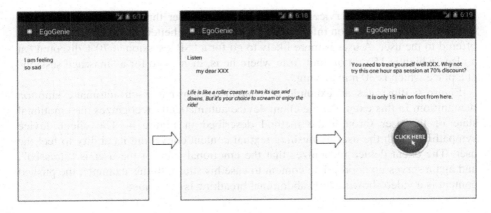

Fig. 5. Example of content display based on emotion self-reporting

As illustrated in (a) of Figure 5, the user of the client device self-reports his emotional state through a textual input. The client device analyzes the textual input and assigns a "sad" emotional state to the user based on the word "sad" used by the user in the text. In (b) of Figure 5, the client device reacts to the identified emotion by interacting in a friendly manner with the user through the sentence "my dear XXX" where XXX is the first name of the user obtained from the user profile database. The emotion-related content which corresponds in this example to a quote, retrieved from the online service provider through the emotion-related content database, is pushed to the user to support him/her emotionally. The pushed content, as illustrated in (c) of Figure 5, can also be a service-related content (SPA session in this example) retrieved

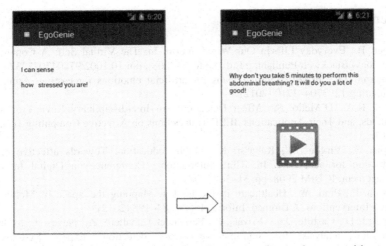

Fig. 6. Example of content display based on automatic emotion recognition

from either the online service provider or the advertiser through the service-related content database. Location information may be used to better select the services to be offered to the user. A user is more likely to go for a "SPA session at 70% discount" at a place which is 15 min on foot from where he is, than to go for a "massage session" at a place which is 30 min driving.

Figure 6 illustrates an example of content display based on automatic emotion recognition. In this example, the client device automatically recognizes the emotional state of the user through the method described in Figure 4. The client device sympathizes with the user by pushing textual content conveying its ability to feel the user. The client device recognizes that the emotional state of the user is "stressed", and again serves up appropriate content to ease his stress. In this example, the pushed content is a video showing how abdominal breathing is performed.

6   Conclusions and Future Work

In this paper, we showed how EgoGenie added a layer of emotional intelligence to mobile phones and made them go beyond the basic functions of calling and texting to fulfill more human and complex roles such those of recognizing, understanding and expressing emotions to support humans emotionally whenever and wherever they need it. We believe that the more mobile phones learn about us, the more they will become emotionally smart and the more they become emotionally smart, the more we will connect to them and maybe fall in love with them! We will work on making EgoGenie smarter while preserving the privacy and the autonomy of the psychic life of the user. We will also work on improving the interaction between the user and the mobile phone so it appears more natural and spontaneous.

References

1. Agger, B.: Everyday Life in Our Wired World. In: The Virtual Self: A Contemporary Sociology. Blackwell Publishing Ltd., Oxford (2008), doi:10.1002/9780470773376.ch1
2. Salmeron, J.L.: Fuzzy cognitive maps for artificial emotions forecasting. Applied Soft Computing 12, 3704–3710 (2012)
3. Calvo, R.A., D'Mello, S.: Affect Detection: An Interdisciplinary Review of Models, Methods, and Their Applications. IEEE Transactions on Affective Computing 1(1), 18–37 (2010)
4. Alepis, E., Virvou, M., Kabassi, K.: Mobile education: Towards affective bi-modal interaction for adaptivity. In: Third International Conference on Digital Information Management, ICDIM 2008, pp. 51–56 (2008)
5. Klasnja, P., Pratt, W.: Healthcare in the Pocket: Mapping the Space of Mobile-Phone Health Interventions. J. Biomed. Inform. 45(1), 184–198 (2012)
6. Carneiro, D., Castillo, J.C., Novais, P., Fernández-Caballero, A., Neves, J.: Multimodal behavioral analysis for non-invasive stress detection. Expert Systems with Applications 39, 13376–13389 (2012)
7. Cai, H., Lin, Y.: Modeling of operators' emotion and task performance in a virtual driving environment. Int. J. Human-Computer Studies 69, 571–586 (2011)

8. Kang, S.-H., Watt, J.H.: The impact of avatar realism and anonymity on effective communication via mobile devices. Computers in Human Behavior 29, 1169–1181 (2013)
9. Busso, C., Bulut, M., Narayanan, S.: Social emotions in nature and artifact: emotions in human and human-computer interaction. In: Marsella, S., Gratch, J. (eds.). Oxford University Press, New York (2012) (Press)
10. Quintana, D.S., Guastella, A.J., Outhred, T., Hickie, I.B., Kemp, A.H.: Heart rate variability is associated with emotion recognition: Direct evidence for a relationship between the autonomic nervous system and social cognition. International Journal of Psychophysiology 86, 168–172 (2012)
11. El Ayadi, M., Kamel, M.S., Karray, F.: Survey on speech emotion recognition: Features, classification schemes, and databases. Pattern Recogn. 44(3), 572–587 (2010), doi:10.1016/j.patcog.2010.09.020
12. Yang, B., Lugger, M.: Emotion recognition from speech signals using new harmony features. Signal Processing 90, 1415–1423 (2010)
13. Busso, C., Lee, S., Narayanan, S.: Analysis of emotionally salient aspects of fundamental frequency for emotion detection. IEEE Trans. Audio Speech Lang. Proc. 17, 582–596 (2009)
14. Pierre-Yves, O.: The production and recognition of emotions in speech: features and algorithms. Int. J. Human-Computer Studies 59, 157–183 (2003)
15. Albornoz, E.M., Milone, D.H., Rufiner, H.L.: Spoken emotion recognition using hierarchical classifier. Computer Speech and Language 25, 556–570 (2011)
16. Lee, C.-C., Mower, E., Busso, C., Lee, S., Narayanan, S.: Emotion recognition using a hierarchical binary decision tree approach. Speech Communication 53, 1162–1171 (2011)
17. Koolagudi, S.G., et al.: Real Life Emotion Classification using Spectral Features and Gaussian Mixture Models. Procedia Engineering 38, 3892–3899 (2012)
18. Ververidis, D., Kotropoulos, C.: A Review of Emotional Speech Databases, http://citeseerx.ist.psu.edu/viewdoc/summary?doi:10.1.1.98.9202
19. Yoon, W.-J., Cho, Y.-H., Park, K.-S.: A Study of Speech Emotion Recognition and Its Application to Mobile Services. In: Indulska, J., Ma, J., Yang, L.T., Ungerer, T., Cao, J. (eds.) UIC 2007. LNCS, vol. 4611, pp. 758–766. Springer, Heidelberg (2007)
20. Tarng, W., Chen, Y.-Y., Li, C.-L., Hsie, K.-R., Chen, M.: Applications of Support Vector Machines on SmartPhone Systems for Emotional Speech Recognition. World Academy of Science, Engineering and Technology 48 (2010)
21. Rachuri, K.K., Musolesi, M., Mascolo, C., Rentfrow, P.J., Longworth, C., Aucinas, A.: EmotionSense: A Mobile Phones based Adaptive Platform for Experimental Social Psychology Research. In: UbiComp 2010, Copenhagen, Denmark, September 26-29 (2010)
22. Tian, Y., Kanade, T., Cohn, J.F.: Facial Expression Analysis. In: Handbook of Face Recognition, pp. 487–519. Springer, London (2011)
23. Mawafo, J.C.T., Clarke, W.A., Robinson, P.E.: Identification of Facial Features on Android Platforms. In: Industrial Technology (ICIT), pp. 1872–1876 (2013)
24. Niforatos, E., Karapanos, E.: EmoSnaps: A Mobile Application for Emotion Recall from Facial Expressions. In: CHI 2013, Paris, France, April 27-May 2 (2013)
25. Swinton, R., El Kaliouby, R.: Measuring emotions through a mobile device across borders, ages, genders and more. In: ESOMAR 2012 (2012)
26. Affdex, http://www.affectiva.com/affdex/#pane_overview (accessed on May 9, 2013)

27. Barrett, L.F., Kensinger, E.A.: Context is routinely encoded during emotion perception. Psychol. Sci. 21, 595–599 (2010)
28. Oh, K., Park, H.-S., Cho, S.-B.: A Mobile Context Sharing System using Activity and Emotion Recognition with Bayesian Networks. In: 2010 Symposia and Workshops on Ubiquitous, Autonomic and Trusted Computing, pp. 244–249 (2010)
29. Yoon, J.-W., Cho, S.-B.: An intelligent synthetic character for smartphone with Bayesian networks and behavior selection networks. Expert Systems with Applications 39, 11284–11292 (2012)
30. Lee, H., Choi, Y.S., Lee, S., Park, I.P.: Towards Unobtrusive Emotion Recognition for Affective Social Communication. In: The 9th Annual IEEE Consumer Communications and Networking Conference-Special Session Affective Computing for Future Consumer Electronics, pp. 260–264.
31. Tetteroo, D.: Communicating emotions in instant messaging, an overview. In: The 9th Twente Student Conference on IT, Enschede (June 23, 2008)
32. Fragopanagos, N., Taylor, J.G.: Emotion recognition in human–computer interaction, Department of Mathematics, King's College, Strand, London WC2 R2LS. UK Neural Networks 18, 389–405 (2005)
33. Kao, E.C.-C., Liu, C.-C., Yang, T.-H., Hsieh, C.-T., Soo, V.-W.: Towards Text-based Emotion Detection A Survey and Possible Improvements. In: International Conference on Information Management and Engineering, ICIME 2009, April 3-5, pp. 70–74 (2009), doi:10.1109/ICIME.2009.113
34. Sebe, N., Cohen, I., Gevers, T., Huang, T.S.: Multimodal approaches for emotion recognition: a survey. In: Proc. SPIE, vol. 5670, pp. 56–67 (2005)
35. Hussain, S.S., Peter, C., Bieber, G.: Emotion Recognition on the Go: Providing Personalized Services Based on Emotional States. In: Proc. of the 2009 Workshop: Measuring Mobile Emotions: Measuring the Impossible?, Bonn, Germany (September 15, 2009)
36. Lee, S., Hong, C-S., Lee, Y. K., Shin, H.-S.: Experimental Emotion Recognition System and Services for Mobile Network Environments. In: Proc. of IEEE SENSORS 2010 Conference, pp. 136–139 (2010)
37. Kim, H.-J., Choi, Y.S.: Exploring Emotional Preference for Smartphone Applications. In: The 9th Annual IEEE Consumer Communications and Networking Conference - Special Session Affective Computing for Future Consumer Electronics, pp. 245–249 (2012)
38. Mousannif, H., Khalil, I., Kotsis, G.: The cloud is not "there", we are the cloud! International Journal of Web and Grid Services 9(1), 1–17 (2013)

Agent-Based Methods for Simulation of Epidemics with a Low Number of Infected Persons

Florian Miksch[1,3,*], Philipp Pichler[2], Kurt J. Espinosa[1], and Niki Popper[3]

[1] University of the Philippines Cebu, Department of Computer Science, Cebu City, Philippines
fmiksch.up@gmail.com, kpespinosa@up.edu.ph
[2] Vienna University of Technology,
Institute for Analysis and Scientific Computing, Vienna, Austria
philipp.pichler@tuwien.ac.at
[3] dwh Simulation Services, Vienna, Austria
niki.popper@dwh.at

Abstract. Modeling of infectious diseases with a low number of infections is a task that often arises since most real epidemics affect only a small fraction of the population. Agent-based methods simulate individuals and their behavior. When the model is simulated, the epidemic automatically arises without being explicitly defined. Surprisingly, it is not easy to produce such epidemics with small infection numbers. Instead, it needs model improvements to accomplish that task. In this paper, we show different extensions, addressing the person's behavior, the pathogen's behavior and the environmental impacts. It turns out that the discussed improvements have different consequences. Hence, they need to be used deliberately to overcome modeling issues of a specific epidemic in an appropriate and valid way. Even more, these improvements address the underlying behavior of epidemics and hence have the ability to provide a deeper insight into the real spreading process of a disease.

Keywords: Agent-based modeling, epidemic simulation, infectious disease modeling, infection numbers.

1 Introduction

Most epidemics that occur on a regular basis only affect a small part of the population. Public perception might draw a different picture due to reports and warnings in media, even though the number of infected people is very low compared to the whole population. Influenza and Dengue serve as examples for such situations [1–3]. Simple epidemic models, however, tend to simulate epidemics with higher fractions of affected persons. Thus, they are not able to simulate some real epidemics accordingly and need improvement. Recent publications also deal with that issue [4, 5]. This publication is going to show different approaches and techniques for such model improvements as well as their impacts.

---

* Corresponding author.

Linawati et al. (Eds.): ICT-EurAsia 2014, LNCS 8407, pp. 21–28, 2014.

2   Underlying Techniques

Ideas and approaches in this paper are based on a simple SIR epidemic. This model of a simplified epidemic has been introduced back in 1927 by Kermack and McKendrick [6]. Unlike them, thanks to available computational power today, we are going to compute SIR epidemics with agent-based models. This does not only provide higher modeling flexibility, it also allows clearer representation of produced effects and results.

2.1   Agent-Based Modeling

Agent-based modeling is a method that emerged in the 1990s. It tries to model the world as it is observed, based on individual entities, which are called agents. These agents exist within an in-silico environment; they have attributes and a behavior and also interact with each other [7–9]. For epidemics, this approach means to model single persons in their environment, give them the ability to be healthy or infected and assure that relevant contacts, which allow transferring the disease from infectious to susceptible persons, happen. Generally, it is important to incorporate all underlying causalities relevant for the spread of an infectious disease such as personal attributes, social behavior concerning contacts and aspects about the disease. Then, one can simulate the model and observe the propagation of the disease. Agent-based models do not directly provide results, instead statistical calculations on the simulated population are required. This needs more effort for evaluation but also leaves room for examining specific details. It should be clear that agent-based modeling is rather a general concept that provides freedom for the modeler but requires extended research [9].

2.2   SIR Epidemics

An SIR epidemic describes the spread of a simplified disease, which can be used to represent a wide class of diseases. The idea is to simulate a disease that can infect susceptible people and after a while they recover and become resistant. Hence, people are in one of the three states susceptible (S), infected (I) and resistant (R) (Fig. 1). To keep it simple, their approach assumes a homogenous population where every infected person can transmit the disease to any susceptible person with a given probability. Typically, initially most people are susceptible and a few are infected, then more people get infected – this means that the epidemic gets stronger. After a while, more people become resistant and, due to the smaller number of susceptible people -so the epidemic gets weaker, until it finally becomes extinct. Kermack and McKendrick [6] used differential equations for simulation; however, we are going to use an agent-based modeling approach.

2.3   The Agent-Based SIR Model

Following the simple SIR approach, we construct an agent-based model of n agents representing persons. The only attribute that persons have describes their disease state which can be susceptible (S), infected (I) or resistant (R). In each time step, random pairwise contacts are performed with an average of c contacts per person. This means that $\frac{2 \cdot total\ number\ of\ contacts}{number\ of\ persons} = c$. State changes happen for two reasons: First, a susceptible person becomes infected with probability α when they meet an infected person. Contacts are processed independently, which means that a person can get infected more than once. Computed infections always apply for the proceeding time step which grants the order of contacts of a time step is not important because persons cannot get infected and infect someone else in the same time step. And second, infected persons become resistant after being infected for r time steps. Hence, the resulting model contains four parameters: n, c, α and r.

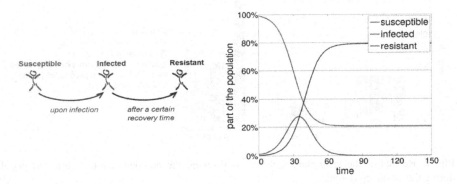

Fig. 1. Left: Disease state progression of an SIR epidemic. Right: Typical behavior of an SIR epidemic.

3   Methods

3.1   The Tasks

At first, the underlying SIR model will be analyzed and issues will be outlined. Then, strategies will be discussed that might help to overcome these issues. This includes methodological descriptions as well as general analyses of their impacts on simulations. Agent-based models do not allow analytic examinations and can only be simulated using concrete parameters. Thus, exemplarily, an epidemic will be simulated for each case. It should infect totally 5% of the population and has an average of 10 relevant contacts for transmission per person per day and a recovery time of 7 days. Additionally, the sensitivity of disturbances should be evaluated, represented by variation of the infection probability by ±5% (hence, it will be multiplied by 0.95 and 1.05).

3.2   The Basic SIR Model

Calibration leads to an infection probability of 0.015 so that the simulation results in an epidemic that totally infects 5% of the population. However, the system is extremely sensitive. Decreasing the infection probability causes the epidemic to become extinct while increase of 5% results in an epidemic that already infects 10% of the population. This makes it hard to parameterize and simulate such a system. Even more, it questions credibility and validity of the model unless the real epidemic reacts extremely sensitive to disturbances (Fig. 2).

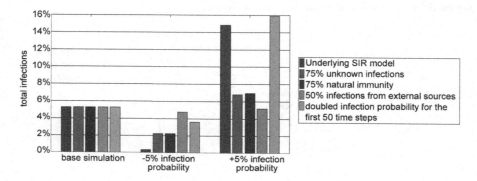

Fig. 2. Results of the exemplary simulations showing the number of totally infected people during the whole epidemic

3.3   Natural Immunity

The first attempt comes up with an explanation of the system behavior. It suggests that infections numbers are low because many people are resistant to the disease so they cannot get infected. These people can also be referred to as "naturally immune". This assumption can be explained with a strong immune system of some people, with past vaccinations, with immunity from past infections, with cross-protection from immunity against other strains, or with other predisposition. The intention is representing an unknown, prior to simulation start existing immunity. Hence, it should not be mixed up with vaccinations which might be known explicitly or even tested.

Such behavior is documented for several diseases. For example, infections with influenza might cause resistance to further infections or even provide cross-protection against other strains [10–12]. Also for Dengue it has been shown that the DENV causing secondary disease is always of a different serotype than the virus that induced immune responses during the earlier DENV infection [13].

From a system's point of view, this means that the actual number of people at risk is significantly smaller than the whole population. In other words, a higher fraction of people at risk get infected than among the whole population. Hence, the spread of the expected epidemic is limited and the system is expected to be more stable due to disturbances.

The exemplary simulation assuming 75% naturally immune people among the population clearly confirms this expectation (Fig. 2).

3.4 Infections from External Sources

The second attempt provides a different explanation why only a small number of people get infected. It proposes that the epidemic is generally weak, even too weak to survive. The reason why it does not become extinct is that people permanently get infected from an external source. This might be the case when the pathogen is found in the nature, in food, in garbage or in water. It is possible that animals carry the pathogen without getting sick and are able to transmit it to humans.

For example, lower primates infected with dengue viruses develop viremias of a magnitude sufficient to infect mosquitoes and mount an immune response but do not develop any detectable clinical signs [14]. Hence, via vectors they serve as an external source of transmissions for persons.

In the model, additionally to the regular transmissions from person to person upon contacts, every susceptible person can get infected from an external source with a given probability per time unit. Technically, this idea allows, at least to a certain extent, arbitrary steering of infections which makes it easier to reach a specific infection number. Hence, this approach should also lead to a system which is more stable due to disturbances. For the exemplary simulation, both infection probabilities are adjusted in a way so that half of all infections are from an external source. However, this epidemic would not end automatically since it only should affect a small part of the population, hence simulation time is strictly limited to the duration of the epidemic in the underlying SIR model. For simulation of disturbances, both infection probabilities are varied by 5%. Results show that this approach is extremely stabilizing and not prone to small disturbances (Fig. 2).

3.5 Unknown Infections

The third attempt suggests that unknown infections exist. This can be explained by asymptomatic infections, which means that people get infected and spread the pathogen but do not experience any symptoms. However, the modeler might also consider that people are sick but their cases are just not reported.

For example, estimates on the fraction of reported influenza cases, hospitalization rates or case fatalities are subject to uncertainty [15, 16]. Asymptomatic infections might also happen for influenza [17, 18]. For streptococcus pneumoniae, reported colonization rates differ a lot among studies [19]. And for dengue, primary infections are often mild or even inapparent [20, 21] so that modelers assume asymptomatic infections by "unnatural infection routes" [5].

In both situations, asymptomatic and unreported cases, the model needs to simulate higher infection numbers than originally proposed and distinguish between reported and unreported cases. This should lead to easier model handling and higher stability due to disturbances. The exemplary simulation assumes that 75% of the infections are unknown. Results clearly meet the expectations (Fig. 2).

3.6   Time-Dependent Impacts

The fourth and last presented attempt suggests that the epidemic is generally too weak to survive. But, due to external conditions, the risk of transmissions increases for a limited time. This is a possible explanation why an epidemic sometimes stops even though it did not affect large parts of the population yet. Such behavior might occur due to specific weather conditions like coldness or rain, due to events or media hypes that change the behavior of the people or due to contaminated food or water. However, this approach provides great freedom and needs to be handled with care since it does not specify how long these conditions exist, whether they are recurring or only single events, and to what extent they change the risk of transmissions. Also, it requires a justification why the pathogen does not become completely extinct already before the external conditions become true.

Seasonal epidemics caused by external conditions apply for several diseases. For example, influenza epidemics usually happen during winter time and stop by the beginning of spring [22, 23] and dengue epidemics reach their peak during rainy season [24].

In the model, this attempt is realized by a time-dependent infection probability. For the exemplary simulation, the infection probability is doubled from simulation start to the time when the underlying SIR model reaches the peak of infections. Results show that the model still reacts extremely sensitive to small disturbances (Fig. 2). However, since this approach has reasonable real interpretations it might be combined with other approaches for valid results.

4   Results

A simple SIR model has problems simulating epidemics with low infection numbers because it is so simple that the epidemic would not stop as long as there are enough susceptible people in the population. The presented model extensions have the ability to improve the quality of simulations and results and hence help to overcome these issues to some extent. If the fraction of unknown infections, infections from external sources or natural immunity is increased, then the result represented by the total number of infected people, reacts less sensitive to variations of the infection probability. However, implementation of time-dependent infection probability even increased the sensitivity of the infection probability in our case.

5   Discussion

The underlying issue is an unrealistic model behavior, hence solutions are motivated by real epidemiological mechanisms. Three of the four presented techniques clearly improve the model behavior while one fails in our test scenario. Still, one needs to be aware that the fourth method is extremely flexible so there might be different ways of applications that lead to different model behavior.

Even though the three successful methods significantly change the model behavior in a desired way, one has to justify that performed changes are valid [25, 26]. This means that the added structures must have meaningful interpretations which need to agree with knowledge on the real system. If this information on the real system is lacking, then the model can still be justified using inductive reasoning: The model behavior and the results agree with knowledge on the real system. Therefore, the updated model structure is likely to be correct and hence valid. In the context of inductive reasoning, the model structure might be used to obtain knowledge by having ideas how the real system might work.

In some situations it can be useful to combine two or more approaches to get even better results. For example, a part of the population might be naturally immune while others experience asymptomatic infections. Then, only checking for validity is not sufficient, it also requires specific testing on a technical level to understand the impact of the added structures.

References

1. Thompson, W.W., Comanor, L., Shay, D.K.: Epidemiology of Seasonal Influenza: Use of Surveillance Data and Statistical Models to Estimate the Burden of Disease. J. Infect. Dis. 194, S82–S91 (2006)
2. Arima, Y., Edelstein, Z.R., Hwi Kwang, H., Matsui, T.: Emerging Disease Surveillance and Response Team, Division of Health Security and Emergencies, World Health Organization Regional Office for the Western Pacific. Epidemiologic update on the dengue situation in the Western Pacific Region (2011); West. Pac. Surveill. Response J. 4, 51–58 (2013)
3. Viboud, C., Boëlle, P.-Y., Pakdaman, K., Carrat, F., Valleron, A.-J., Flahault, A.: Influenza epidemics in the United States, France, and Australia, 1972-1997. Emerg. Infect. Dis. 10, 32–39 (2004)
4. Coburn, B.J., Wagner, B.G., Blower, S.: Modeling influenza epidemics and pandemics: insights into the future of swine flu (H1N1). BMC Med. 7 (2009)
5. Chikaki, E., Ishikawa, H.: A dengue transmission model in Thailand considering sequential infections with all four serotypes. J. Infect. Dev. Ctries. 3, 711–722 (2009)
6. Kermack, W.O., McKendrick, A.G.: A Contribution to the Mathematical Theory of Epidemics. Proc. R. Soc. Math. Phys. Eng. Sci. 115, 700–721 (1927)
7. Wooldridge, M.: Agent-based software engineering. IEE Proc. Softw. Eng. 144, 26–37 (1997)
8. Casti, J.L.: Would-be worlds: how simulation is changing the frontiers of science. J. Wiley, New York (1997)
9. Macal, C.M., North, M.J.: Tutorial on agent-based modelling and simulation. J. Simul. 4, 151–162 (2010)
10. Tecle, T., White, M., Hartshorn, K.: Innate Immunity to Influenza A Virus Infection. Curr. Respir. Med. Rev. 1, 127–145 (2005)
11. Morris, K.: Influenza protection—natural immunity and new vaccines. Lancet Infect. Dis. 11, 268–269 (2011)
12. Joshi, S.R., Shaw, A.C., Quagliarello, V.J.: Pandemic Influenza H1N1 2009, Innate Immunity, and the Impact of Immunosenescence on Influenza Vaccine. Yale J. Biol. Med. 82, 143–151 (2009)

13. Rothman, A.L.: Dengue: defining protective versus pathologic immunity. J. Clin. Invest. 113, 946–951 (2004)
14. Henchal, E.A., Putnak, J.R.: The dengue viruses. Clin. Microbiol. Rev. 3, 376–396 (1990)
15. Fair, J.M., Powell, D.R., LeClaire, R.J., Moore, L.M., Wilson, M.L., Dauelsberg, L.R., Samsa, M.E., DeLand, S.M., Hirsch, G., Bush, B.W.: Measuring the uncertainties of pandemic influenza. Int. J. Risk Assess. Manag. 16, 1 (2012)
16. Carrat, F., Luong, J., Lao, H., Sallé, A.-V., Lajaunie, C., Wackernagel, H.: A "small-world-like" model for comparing interventions aimed at preventing and controlling influenza pandemics. BMC Med. 4, 26 (2006)
17. Lau, L.L.H., Cowling, B.J., Fang, V.J., Chan, K., Lau, E.H.Y., Lipsitch, M., Cheng, C.K.Y., Houck, P.M., Uyeki, T.M., Peiris, J.S.M., Leung, G.M.: Viral Shedding and Clinical Illness in Naturally Acquired Influenza Virus Infections. J. Infect. Dis. 201, 1509–1516 (2010)
18. Olalla Sierra, J., Ory Manchón, F., de Casas Flecha, I., Montiel Quezel-Guerraz, N., Salas Bravo, D.: Asymptomatic infection by influenza AH1N1 virus in healthcare workers: MARBEGRIP study, preliminary results. Rev. Esp. Salud Pública 85, 63–71 (2011)
19. Cardozo, D.M., Nascimento-Carvalho, C.M.C., Souza, F.R., Silva, N.M.S.: Nasopharyngeal colonization and penicillin resistance among pneumococcal strains: a worldwide 2004 update. Braz. J. Infect. Dis. Off. Publ. Braz. Soc. Infect. Dis. 10, 293–304 (2006)
20. Endy, T.P., Chunsuttiwat, S., Nisalak, A., Libraty, D.H., Green, S., Rothman, A.L., Vaughn, D.W., Ennis, F.A.: Epidemiology of inapparent and symptomatic acute dengue virus infection: a prospective study of primary school children in Kamphaeng Phet, Thailand. Am. J. Epidemiol. 156, 40–51 (2002)
21. Nisalak, A., Endy, T.P., Nimmannitya, S., Kalayanarooj, S., Thisayakorn, U., Scott, R.M., Burke, D.S., Hoke, C.H., Innis, B.L., Vaughn, D.W.: Serotype-specific dengue virus circulation and dengue disease in Bangkok, Thailand from 1973 to 1999. Am. J. Trop. Med. Hyg. 68, 191–202 (2003)
22. Fuhrmann, C.: The Effects of Weather and Climate on the Seasonality of Influenza: What We Know and What We Need to Know. Geogr. Compass. 4, 718–730 (2010)
23. Tang, J.W., Lai, F.Y.L., Nymadawa, P., Deng, Y.-M., Ratnamohan, M., Petric, M., Loh, T.P., Tee, N.W.S., Dwyer, D.E., Barr, I.G., Wong, F.Y.W.: Comparison of the incidence of influenza in relation to climate factors during 2000-2007 in five countries. J. Med. Virol. 82, 1958–1965 (2010)
24. Cuong, H.Q., Vu, N.T., Cazelles, B., Boni, M.F., Thai, K.T.D., Rabaa, M.A., Quang, L.C., Simmons, C.P., Huu, T.N., Anders, K.L.: Spatiotemporal Dynamics of Dengue Epidemics, Southern Vietnam. Emerg. Infect. Dis. 19, 945–953 (2013)
25. Balci, O.: Verification, Validation, and Testing. In: Banks, J. (ed.) Handbook of Simulation, pp. 335–393. John Wiley & Sons, Inc., Hoboken
26. Sargent, R.G.: Verification and validation of simulation models. In: Proceedings of the 2010 Winter Simulation Conference (WSC), pp. 166–183. IEEE (2010)

Cellular Automata Model of Urbanization in Camiguin, Philippines

Maria Isabel Beltran[1] and Guido David[2,*]

[1] Sea Oil, Philippines
[2] Institute of Mathematics &
Computational Science Research Center
University of the Philippines

Abstract. Monitoring and forecasting land use and change in the Philippines are necessary for urban planning, agricultural mapping, resource allocation and conservation. Land change studies are important in order to guide policymakers, government and private institutions. In this paper, 2-dimensional cellular automata using Markov chains is used to numerically simulate land change in Camiguin, an island province in the Philippines, over a period of 50 years. The preliminary findings of the study identify wooded areas that may be at risk of disappearing. The study also emphasizes the need for updated land cover data in the Philippines in order to improve land use forecasts.

Keywords: Cellular Automata, Markov chains, Monte Carlo simulation, land cover, maps.

1 Introduction

Since 1984, the Philippine population has been increasing at a rate of approximately 2% each year [1]. Roughly 13% of the national population live in the Metro Manila area [2]. Urbanization and development of the provincial regions of the Philippines, in part due to the flourishing tourism industry, would result in more people migrating to the provinces. Changes in land use are natural consequences of population growth. Cities have limited carrying capacity, and with time, more people would settle in neighboring areas. In this regard, it is important to study how land change could affect the nation's natural resources, including agriculture and forestry land. Grasslands are critical for farming and production of food resources, whereas forests and wooded areas preserve wildlife and endangered animal groups, and help control floods and reduce Carbon Dioxide in the atmosphere. Predicting how land is developed allows legislators to implement measures that may help prevent deforestation and maintain agricultural regions. Land cover simulations would also lead to improvements in strategic agriculture and mapping of farmlands to suitable crops. Moreover, land use

---

* Corresponding author.

Linawati et al. (Eds.): ICT-EurAsia 2014, LNCS 8407, pp. 29–35, 2014.

studies would also provide a guide to long term urban planning. Hence it is necessary to conduct land change forecasts in order to anticipate future problems in urban and farm management, and to take necessary steps in correcting problems before they arise. Previous studies on land use in the Philippines have focused mainly on deforestation [3], and a much more comprehensive study on urbanization and farming allocation is needed.

Camiguin is an island province in the Philippines in the Mindanao region. It has an area of 237.95km^2, and a population of 83,800 (as of 2010) which has been growing annually at a rate of 1.22% [4]. Its geographical features include volcanoes, waterfalls, and natural springs. It is home to a variety of aquatic habitats and corals. Camiguin has been advertised as a tourist destination for its beaches and diving attractions. In this study, a land development algorithm is implemented using Camiguin island as a model.

2   Methods

Two-dimensional cellular automata models have been used in analyzing transitions in land cover in other cities [5]. Examples include land change use in Dongguan, Southern China [6] and in the Istanbul Metropolitan Area [7]. In a Cellular Automata model, each cell, corresponding to a unit area of land, is assigned one of four possible states, given here by:

1. water: seas and inland bodies of water
2. forests and wooded land
3. open land: agricultural land, pastures and barren land
4. built-up areas: developed areas, residential or commercial

Other studies have used more than four states by further reclassifying each group. For example, open land may be divided into barren land, cultivated land and pastures. A unit area of land may include more than one of the above, for example a region which has both barren land and built-up sections. In such cases, the state of the land region is simply the state that comprises majority of the area.

A Cellular Automata model provides transition rules that prescribe how one state may change to another state. Although Cellular Automata models are typically deterministic, the uncertainty of land change requires Markov matrices to account for probability-based transitions. At least two land images are needed in order to compute transition probabilities. Unfortunately, forestry data for the Philippines was only available for the year 2003. The transition matrix obtained from Istanbul [7] was used, given by the matrix A below, which provided transition probabilities over an 11-year period.

$$A = \begin{pmatrix} 0.9967 & 0.0009 & 0.0017 & 0.0007 \\ 0.0016 & 0.8850 & 0.1076 & 0.0058 \\ 0.0135 & 0.0798 & 0.8590 & 0.0477 \\ 0.0054 & 0.0008 & 0.0004 & 0.9934 \end{pmatrix} \tag{1}$$

By convention, the A_{ij} entry of A denotes the probability that state i moves to state j after 11 years. An assumption used here was that the rate of urban development in a region is linearly correlated with the population growth rate in the region. In Istanbul, the population grew 1.68% annually. Over 11 years, this is roughly equivalent to 15 years under a growth rate of 1.22%, the annual population growth rate in Camiguin. The one year transition matrix for modeling Camiguin was then obtained using $T = \exp(\log A/15)$, where matrix logarithm and exponential was used. Due to the absence of inland water regions in the island, transitions from water to land or vice-versa were not considered. Thus,

$$
T = \begin{pmatrix} 1 & 0 & 0 & 0 \\ 0 & 0.9916 & 0.0082 & 0.0002 \\ 0 & 0.0061 & 0.9905 & 0.0034 \\ 0 & 0.0001 & 0.0000 & 0.9999 \end{pmatrix} \tag{2}
$$

The neighborhood of each cell was assumed to be a 9×9 Moore neighborhood, which included the 80 surrounding cells. This was roughly equivalent in area to the 5×5 neighborhood used in [7]. To obtain the actual one year transition probability for each cell, the following scheme was used:

$$
p_{ij} = \frac{w_j T_{ij}}{\sum_{k=1}^{4} w_k T_{ik}} \tag{3}
$$

where i is the current state of the cell ($i = 1, 2, 3, 4$), j is the target state ($j = 1, 2, 3, 4$), and w_j is the number of neighboring cells in state j [8]. The assumption here was that the future state of a cell of land is affected by the present state of surrounding cells of land. For example, open land surrounding an isolated developed area was less likely to become developed than a piece of open area surrounded mostly by built-up areas of land.

3   Results and Discussion

An image map of Camiguin in 2003, obtained from [9], is shown in Figure 1 as a Matlab® image file, with blue indicating water, dark green indicating forests and wooded areas (with broad-leaved trees, shrubs or wooded grasslands), light green for open land (barren or with crops) and red for built-up areas (residential or factory). The image was equivalent to about 20km along the vertical and 19km along the horizontal. The land mass image was made up of 242,154 pixels, thus each pixel was equivalent to 982.64m^2, or a square piece of land 31m on each side. The wooded areas comprised 101,388 pixels for a land cover of 99.63km^2, agricultural land comprised 137,986 pixels for a land cover of 135.59km^2, and built-up areas comprised 2,780 pixels, for a land cover of 2.73km^2. There were no inland water regions, and the coastline was assumed to be static. Changes in land cover after 20 years and 50 years are shown in Figures 2 and 3, respectively. Land development is a stochastic process, and random variations play a signifi-cant role in how land changes with time. Numerical forecasts are useful because

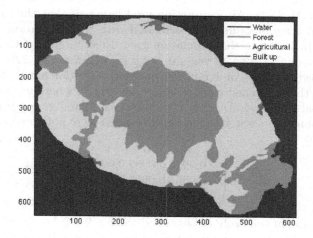

Fig. 1. Land cover of Camiguin, Philippines, based on 2003 data. Each pixel is equivalent to 982.64m². The box represents scaled dimensions of 19km × 20km.

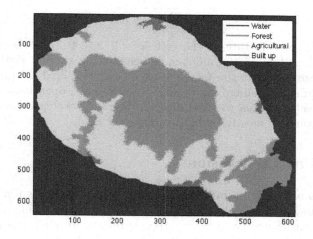

Fig. 2. Land cover of Camiguin, projected for 2023

they indicate likely trends in how land will develop in a geographical region. The forecast for 2023 (Figure 2) showed a 2.96% increase in built-up land from 2003. Most of this increase was at the expense of agricultural land. However, agricultural land also had an increase of 1.46% from 2003 to 2023. Agricultural land that was lost due to development was replaced by wooded land that had transitioned to grasslands. As a result, wooded land decreased by 2.80% from 2003 to 2023.

Longer term forecasts are causes for concern. According to Figure 3, in 2053, the built-up land would have increased by 263% from 2003. Most of this can be attributed to turnover of agricultural land. Agricultural land also increased by 4.39% due to conversion of wooded land. On the other hand, forests and wooded land decreased by 13.2%. Some of the forests in the island of Camiguin, such as those near the south and southwest, would be in danger of disappearing.

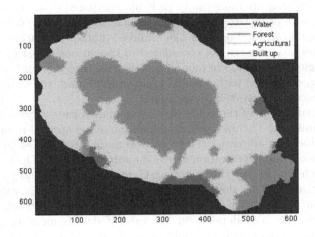

Fig. 3. Land cover of Camiguin, projected for 2053

4   Conclusion

A Markov-based cellular automata model of land change was used to numerically forecast land use in the island province of Camiguin. Land cover data in the Philippines was only available for 2003, and this served as a starting point for the simulations. With the lack of data, transition rates from Istanbul [7] were used. The Markov matrix was adjusted to match the population growth rate in the Philippines, assuming that urban development was proportional to population growth.

The results showed that in 2023, there would have been modest increases of 2.96% and 1.46% in built-up areas and agricultural land, respectively, while wooded land would have decreased by 2.80%. By 2053, the built-up land would have increased by 263%, agricultural land would have increased by 4.39% and wooded land would have decreased by 13.2%. Such changes are significant and pose a threat to the existence of some wooded areas. Policymakers might be best advised to come up with laws if they wish to protect some of the endangered wooded areas. Land development is a natural result of the increasing population, and planning is needed for the proper management of the country's natural resources.

In any mathematical model, long term forecasts should be regarded with caution. Firstly, the model incorporates randomness, hence forecasts only show some of the possible scenarios. Although the 50-year forecast may identify interesting trends and patterns, it is not as reliable as a shorter term forecast. Given a fixed geographic region, transition rates are not constant[7], and may vary significantly over long periods of time. Rates of development in Istanbul are likely to differ from those in the Philippines; even those from different regions in the Philippines are unlikely to be the same. Rates of urbanization are likely to be higher for regions that are moderately built-up, compared to areas that have few developments, such as isolated areas, or provinces that are close to saturation in terms of urbanization, e.g. big cities like Manila. Another limitation of the study is that elevation factors were not considered in transitions. Most of the wooded areas in the region are located in mountainous areas, thus it would be reasonable to assume that, compared with wooded areas in level land, the former would be less likely to become converted to open land.

The numerical results of the study serve as a guide for identifying land change patterns in Camiguin. The methods used herein may be applied to other regions in the Philippines, by adjusting the transition matrix to align with population growth rate, or obtaining transition values directly from data. The present study was made much simpler by the fact that Camiguin is an island province that is not directly affected by developments in its neighbors. This convenience is not possible for regions that are geographically connected. In such a case, the transition rates may also depend on the rate of development in neighboring regions, and adjustment factors would depend on available data. This study may also be expanded by using more land states, for example differentiating between wooded areas with broad-leaved trees, shrubs and grasslands. As more land use data becomes available, the specific classification of lands, as well as more precise transitions may be used to improve the cellular automata forecasts of land change. This would lead to more reliable forecasts of land cover in the Philippines.

Acknowledgments. This project was supported by the University of the Philippines Research and Creative Work Program and Neuroworks Inc.

References

1. David, G., Gomez, F.: Sexuality-based compartmental model of spread of HIV in the Philippines. Philippine Science Letters 7(1), 62–66 (2014)
2. The World Factbook 2013-14. Central Intelligence Agency, Washington, DC (2013), https://www.cia.gov/library/publications/the-world-factbook/index.html (retrieved from)
3. Verburg, P.H., Veldkamp, A.: Projecting land use transitions at forest fringes in the Philippines at two spatial scales. Landscape Ecology 19, 77–98 (2004)
4. Ericta, C.N.: 2010 Census of Population and Housing. National Statistics Office, Philippines (2010), http://www.census.gov.ph/statistics/census/population-and-housing (retrieved from)

5. O'Sullivan, D., Torrens, P.: Cellular automata and urban simulation: Where do we go from here? Environment and Planning B: Planning and Design 28, 163–168 (2007)
6. Li, X., Yeh, A.: Neural network-based cellular automata for simulating multiple land use changes using gis. International Journal of Geographical Information Science 16(4), 323–343 (2002)
7. Demirel, H., Cetin, M.: Modelling urban dynamics via cellular automata. ISPRS Archive 38(pt. 4-8-2-W9), 199–203 (2010)
8. Beltran, M.I.: A cellular automata model for land development and urbanization. Undergraduate Research Paper, University of the Philippines (2013)
9. Forest Management Bureau, Forest Cover, DENR, Quezon City, Philippines (2003), http://forestry.denr.gov.ph/landusereg.htm (retrieved from)

A Flexible Agent-Based Framework for Infectious Disease Modeling

Florian Miksch[1,2,*], Christoph Urach[3], Patrick Einzinger[2], and Günther Zauner[2]

[1] University of the Philippines Cebu, Department of Computer Science, Cebu City, Philippines
fmiksch.up@gmail.com
[2] dwh Simulation Services, Vienna, Austria
{florian.miksch,patrick.einzinger,guenther.zauner}@dwh.at
[3] Vienna University of Technology,
Institute for Analysis and Scientific Computing, Vienna, Austria
christoph.urach@tuwien.ac.at

Abstract. Agent-based modeling is a method to model a system by autonomous entities. The proposed framework models single persons with personal behavior, different health states and ability to spread the disease. Upon simulation, the epidemic emerges automatically. This approach is clear and easily understandable but requires extensive knowledge of the epidemic's background. Such real-world model structures produce realistic epidemics, allowing detailed examination of the transmission process or testing and analyzing the outcome of interventions like vaccinations. Due to changed epidemic propagation, effects like herd immunity or serotype shift arise automatically. Beyond that, a modular structure splits the model into parts, which can be developed and validated separately. This approach makes development more efficient, increases credibility of the results and allows reusability and exchangeability of existing modules. Thus, knowledge and models can be easily and efficiently transferred, for example to compute scenarios for different countries and similar diseases.

Keywords: epidemic simulation, modular concept, disease propagation.

1 Introduction

Simulation of epidemics has a long history in mathematics but also in medical fields. However, calculations vary a lot in addressed problems and accuracy. In the past years, new methods have emerged and became possible due to increasing computational power. The intention of this work is to integrate old and new methodologies in a newly developed framework to provide a flexible, standardized and easy-to-handle approach for modeling a wide class of infectious diseases. This framework consists of a model that relies on agent-based modeling, which is a promising young technique because it aims to simulate dynamic systems based on fundamental rules [1–3]. Its modular concept assures high flexibility. The approach should be able to produce accurate results by modeling epidemics in a realistic way, which helps to deal with uncertain dynamics and effects. It can be used for studies on a specific disease and is

---

* Corresponding author.

Linawati et al. (Eds.): ICT-EurAsia 2014, LNCS 8407, pp. 36–45, 2014.

suitable for current research on general issues concerning analysis of epidemics. The approach also supports handling of disputed effects like herd immunity [4, 5] and serotype shift [6–8], which make it hard to predict the outcomes of vaccination strategies. In an agent-based model they automatically occur upon the fundamental rules and are not part of the model structure.

2   Underlying Concepts

2.1   Epidemic Modeling

Classical approaches for epidemic modeling often use ordinary differential equation respectively system dynamics, where aggregated variables represent the population of interest that is being split by health and other attributes [9–13]. These models are easy to handle from a mathematical point of view but they are on a high abstraction level which makes it hard to go into details or calculate parameters from observed data. In contrast to that, another concept is simulating simplified individual people with their behavior and observing how an epidemic arises [3, 14, 15]. Such an approach is often referred to as agent-based modeling and creates an epidemic based on knowledge on individuals.

2.2   Agent-Based Modeling

Agent-based modeling is a method that emerged in the 1990s. It tries to model the world as it is observed, based on individual entities, which are called agents. These agents exist within an in-silico environment; they have attributes and behavior, can change themselves and also affect each other [1, 16–18]. For epidemics, this approach means to model single persons in their environment, give them the ability to be healthy or infected and assure that relevant contacts, which allow transferring the disease from infectious to susceptible persons, happen. Generally, it is important to incorporate all information relevant for the spread of an infectious disease such as personal attributes, social behavior concerning contacts and aspects about the disease. Then, one can simulate the model and observe the propagation of the disease. The outcome of single individuals in the model is usually not of interest which requires further computations. Results are commonly given by statistical analyses on the simulated population.

It should be clear that agent-based modeling is not a well-defined method. It is rather a general concept that provides freedom for the modeler but requires extended research for specific models addressing different problems [18].

3   The Model Framework

3.1   Aim

We intend building a framework for epidemic simulation that should be flexible enough to be applied on different populations, different situations and on different diseases with different transmission paths. To support this aim, we focus on a modular concept, introducing three different modules for population, contacts and disease, which can be developed and validated separately. Additionally, a protocol module tracks the agents and provides the results.

The following chapters show an approach how to set up such a framework and how to read results and to interpret the dynamics of the system. The aim is to show the ideas, structures, challenges and potentialities, but it is not a programming instruction.

3.2   The Population Module

The agents, which represent people, are the most fundamental part of the model. In a first step, the population module has to create these people and equip them with basic attributes like age and gender and other relevant information about personal background or previous medical history. They might have behavior like getting older, eventually die, and women might give birth to children. Considering immigration and emigration assures an accurate population structure over long simulation periods.

The module has to create the desired number of people and assign them these attributes according to their joint distribution. Additionally, it has to provide interfaces in a way that other modules can add more attributes and rules. Commonly, each interface is implemented as a reference to an object that handles all attributes and behavior assigned by a module.

3.3   The Contact Module

An infectious disease spreads by transmission from one person to another. It can be transmitted in various ways like for smear infections, sexually transmitted or airborne diseases. Pathogens can also be transmitted by food, water, or by animals like mosquitos. The duty of the contact module is to model all kind of events that can lead to transmission of the actual disease.

We are going to present a place-based approach to build a social contact system, which differs from partly used contact networks [14, 19, 20]. This is done in 3 steps and is mostly suitable for diseases that spread directly through airborne and smear transmissions. Figure 1 shows an exemplary visualization of such a structure.

(1) At first, all places where infectious contacts might happen need to be created. Studies often explicitly consider households, workplaces, schools, transportation and leisure places [21]. Based on national data, the modeler needs to identify how many places of each place type exist for the given population. Then, assignments to places indicate where people generally belong to. For example, each person gets assigned to exactly one household so that the household distribution by size and age of people is achieved [22]. Assignments to schools and workplaces tell where someone works or goes to school.

(2) Step two builds a system of daily routines. In a time step, each person visits one or more places. Parameterization of daily routines can be tough since it usually combines national data about places and social contact data. Time steps are considered to be atomic. This means that a person has only two options: Visiting a place within a time step or not. However, it makes sense to allow visiting multiple places during a

time step. For example, if a time step represents one day, then persons would visit all places of their whole daily routine. But then it is not possible any more to differentiate on a finer level when they go there or how much time they spend there. Desiring more detailed daily routines requires shorter time steps like hours or even minutes. The daily routine of a person depends on several factors: On personal attributes, if a person is feeling sick, on the day of the week. Assigned places assure that people always go to the same household, school or workplace where they meet the same colleagues and friends, and variations, especially for transport and leisure, provide a mixing of random people.

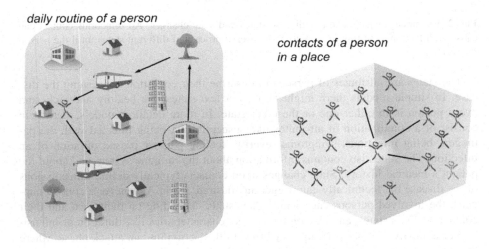

Fig. 1. Exemplary visualization of a person's daily routine and contacts within a place. A person visits several places each day, depending on many factors and influences. In places, contacts happen between present people; number and distribution of contacts are according to knowledge on social studies.

(3) This step finally creates contacts in every place between all present people within a time step. Social studies, often based on empirical research, serve as a basis for contact patterns [21]. This means to model contacts between random people in a place, so that contact numbers and age-distribution of studies are resembled. Depending on the place and the circumstances, contacts might be loose or close, short or long, physical or non-physical.

3.4 The Disease Module

The duty of the disease module is the handling of all aspects concerning the disease. An agent-based model involves information on an individual level, which can be split up into three parts: First, disease and health states of a person, second, state changes caused by contacts and third, state changes independent of contacts. Figure 2 shows an exemplary visualization of these tasks.

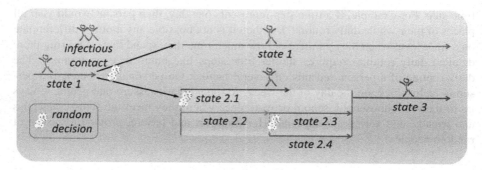

Fig. 2. Exemplary visualization of disease states and state changes. An infectious contact can cause an infection, resulting in an automatic disease process of different states until the person recovers.

The states are attributes of persons to describe their condition concerning the disease. In simple models there might be only a few states like healthy and sick, and every person is in either one or the other state. In more detailed models, states can consist of a combination of attributes like susceptibility, being infected with the pathogen, being infectious, symptoms severity, feeling pain or passed duration of an infection. The state also contains information about the immune system and about the patient's medical history. State changes upon contacts typically define transmissions of the disease but technically can trigger any desired action. Whenever a contact happens, the involved persons can change their state, depending on their own and their contact person's states, and also on the contact characteristics like duration or intensity. For complex diseases it is suggested to split this action into an attack phase, where the infected person transmits the disease with a probability, followed by a receive phase where the susceptible person either gets infected or defeats the disease. Often, transmission of a disease is not a deterministic process, but happens under special conditions with a certain probability. The other state changes might depend on the state of the person and their environment. They typically represent progression of a disease, recovery, or general changes of the personal health.

Disease states can also affect other modules. For example, a disease might affect the daily routine of persons so that they only stay at home and do not go to work or school. Disease might cause the death of a person which is handled by the population module.

3.5   The Protocol Module

The protocol module keeps track of all information of interest to generate the desired results. There are two possible approaches. The first possibility is that the protocol permanently checks everything that happens and stores the information of interest. This approach can be extended to a so called VOMAS (Virtual Overlay Multi-Agent System), a well-known method where an overlay is added to the model containing another type of agents that watch and log [23]. The other approach is having a listening protocol module while it is the agents' duty to report all information of interest.

After the simulation the protocol module usually provides statistical calculations as results based on all collected individual data.

Concerning epidemics, two classes of data that are evaluated by the protocol module are of particular interest: states of agents and changes of states. For example, one might be interested in the number of people that are infected but also in the number of people that get infected in a time step. More detailed analyses are able to reveal where and under what circumstances transmissions happen and help to indicate population subgroups that are particularly responsible for spreading the disease.

3.6   Simulating the Model

The following paragraph describes a proposed simulation strategy that splits up into three phases and is also shown in Figure 3. In the initialization phase, all modules initialize. They create the persons, equip them with all required attributes so that they represent the desired population and also set up the environment (e.g., the places). Then the simulation phase starts. The model simulates over time using time steps, which are by definition atomic and cannot be split up further. This means that they consist of several actions that are not temporally ordered. Instead, a smart collision handling is required, which decides upon logical rules what to do. It is highly suggested to preserve personal states during a whole time step, store proposed changes

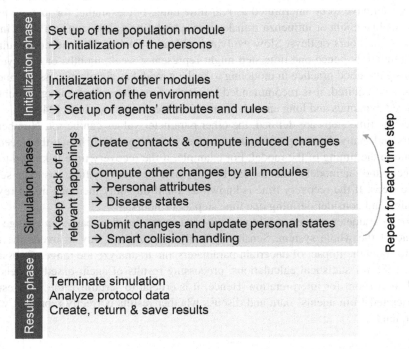

Fig. 3. Overview of phases and simulation of the agent-based epidemic framework

and perform changes only between time steps. At first, contacts are created and contact-based infections and changes are calculated. Then, other changes are created by the modules. Finally, every person has a set of proposed changes. The logical procedure of deciding the personal state for the next time step highly depends on the actual disease. Generally it makes sense to apply all attributes that do not affect each other, while competitive changes within one time step, for example new infections, recoveries, infections with different diseases or vaccinations, might be chosen case dependent. The only restriction is to find a well-defined state for every person for the next time step. The protocol module keeps track of the information of interest (e.g., personal states and proposed and performed state changes) and also of other relevant happenings (e.g., constructed contacts). This procedure is repeated for each time step and results in an evolving system. Finally, in the results phase the protocol module stores and represents the collected data in an appropriate format. Commonly this includes histograms and time series but, depending on the actual model, further statistical analyses and experimental visualizations might be possible and useful.

4   Parameter Settings and Interpretation of Results

Correct parameterization and interpretation of the model results are crucial aspects for modeling of epidemics. Most aspects are time related. The model itself does not provide any real timing like days, weeks or years. Instead, it calculates a number of time steps, which have to be interpreted as real time units. For example, for fast-evolving epidemics like ebola or influenza it makes sense to define a time step as a short interval like some hours or days. Slow-evolving epidemics such as HIV do not require a daily simulation, hence one time step might represent a week, months or even years. Following the good practice in modeling to make a model as simple as possible and as complex as required, it is recommended to set the time steps short enough to obtain all desired dynamics and long enough to prevent unnecessary overhead [24].

Once the time steps are defined, the other parameter values can be set. Number of contacts and many disease parameters are given time-dependent; hence they need to correlate to the timing of the model. For example, if the recovery time is known to be two weeks and the model simulates day by day, then the recovery time has to be set as 14 time steps. If the recovery time is known as a half day only then one might revise the timing and consider defining one time step as 12 hours.

Wrong parameter settings might not only distort results, they can even change the dynamic of the whole system. Sensitivity analysis is a good way to overcome this issue, to show the impact of uncertain parameters and to analyze the range of possible results. Like for statistical calculations, processing results of agent-based models always leaves room for interpretation. Hence, it is crucial to scrutinize the way results are generated from agents' data and discuss whether results correctly represent what they pretend.

5   Discussion and Outlook

The agent-based concept offers great benefits. Constructing a system that produces an epidemic in a similar way as it happens in reality produces reliable results and allows a wide range of testing assumptions. A real-looking structure leads to a better understanding of the model so that it is easier to communicate, gains a higher acceptance and allows non-modelers to comment on it, which helps improving it.

Consideration of vaccinations allows testing of various scenarios. In this context, a few interesting effects occur, which are represented accordingly in the agent-based model. Stochastic calculations and models are able to consider such effects only if they are known for every single parameter setting. Often, this is a severe issue because they cannot be measured for future scenarios and also cannot be extrapolated from available data. In the agent-based model, where the epidemic automatically emerges upon basic rules, herd immunity and serotype shift both occur and can even be examined without prior knowledge. This does not only make results more trustable, it even allows fundamental research on the spread of epidemics. Yet it is a matter of current research to find a definition and a standardized way for measurement of herd immunity and serotype shift [5]. Beyond that, observation and analysis of the basic reproduction rate R0, which commonly describes the strength of an epidemic, is possible [25].

However, the method also has an issue that requires additional effort: If a relevant basic factor is not considered or included in a wrong way, then the model might still produce epidemics, but the propagation of the disease will happen incorrectly. Hence, the results will be wrong. Validation is a term containing a wide class of methods to overcome this issue by asking whether the model is being developed according to the model question [26–28]. Hence, it helps to identify problems and errors and increases the credibility of the model.

Another key benefit is the modular structure, especially for well-planned interfaces between the modules. First, the modular approach allows independent development of the modules, reusability of modules, combinations of existing modules. Thus, a pool of modules can be developed to create specific models just by assembling them. For example, various population modules representing different societies allow efficient transferability of the model to other countries. Development of new disease modules makes it possible to use an existing model for simulating other diseases. Second, it assures that changes only affect one specific module, which makes changes, adoptions and improvements easier. This highly supports an iterative modeling process. A third benefit is that separate validation of the single modules supports validating the whole model. Hence, validated modules might be reused for other projects, which decreases effort and increases accuracy.

6   Conclusions

Agent-based modeling is a promising way to simulate epidemics. It models individual people, their contacts and transmissions. The global spread of the disease is not explicitly defined and happens automatically. Such a system has great benefits because it allows modeling complex dynamics based on simple rules. The structures, which finally lead to an epidemic, should correspond to reality. If these real-world structures incorporate all relevant basics then they result in a real-world behavior. This leads to direct calculation of different scenarios and high quality results and allows examination of widely disputed and unknown effects. Studying the infection and propagation process and its impact on the overall spread is also possible. From a technical point of view, it is generally simple to make changes for different assumptions in agent-based models, especially modular ones, because they only affect a small part of the model while other model parts remain unchanged.

References

1. Casti, J.L.: Would-be worlds: how simulation is changing the frontiers of science. J. Wiley, New York (1997)
2. Okhmatovskaia, A., Verma, A.D., Barbeau, B., Carriere, A., Pasquet, R., Buckeridge, D.L.: A simulation model of waterborne gastro-intestinal disease outbreaks: description and initial evaluation. In: AMIA. Annu. Symp. Proc., pp. 557–561 (2010)
3. Liccardo, A., Fierro, A.: A Lattice Model for Influenza Spreading. PLoS One 8, e63935 (2013)
4. Topley, W.W.C., Wilson, G.S.: The Spread of Bacterial Infection. The Problem of Herd-Immunity. J. Hyg (Lond.). 21, 243–249 (1923)
5. John, T.J., Reuben, S.: Herd immunity and herd effect: new insights and definitions. Eur. J. Epidemiol. 16, 601–606 (2000)
6. Lysenko, E.S., Lijek, R.S., Brown, S.P., Weiser, J.N.: Within-Host Competition Drives Selection for the Capsule Virulence Determinant of Streptococcus Pneumoniae. Curr. Biol. 20, 1222–1226 (2010)
7. Hsu, K.K., Shea, K.M., Stevenson, A.E., Pelton, S.I.: Changing Serotypes Causing Childhood Invasive Pneumococcal Disease. Pediatr. Infect. Dis. J. 29, 289–293 (2010)
8. WHO: Changing epidemiology of pneumococcal serotypes after introduction of conjugate vaccine: report. Wkly. Epidemiol Rec. 85, 434–436 (2010)
9. Kermack, W.O., McKendrick, A.G.: A Contribution to the Mathematical Theory of Epidemics. Proc. R. Soc. Math. Phys. Eng. Sci. 115, 700–721 (1927)
10. Dietz, K.: Epidemiologic interference of virus populations. J. Math. Biol. 8, 291–300 (1979)
11. Lipsitch, M.: Vaccination and Serotype Replacement. In: Dieckmann, U. (ed.) Adaptive Dynamics of Infectious Diseases: in Pursuit of Virulence Management, pp. 362–374. IIASA, Cambridge University Press, Cambridge, New York (2002)
12. Matrajt, L., Longini, I.M.: Critical immune and vaccination thresholds for determining multiple influenza epidemic waves. Epidemics 4, 22–32 (2012)
13. Xue, Y., Kristiansen, I., de Blasio, B.: Dynamic modelling of costs and health consequences of school closure during an influenza pandemic. BMC Public Health 12, 962 (2012)
14. Eubank, S., Kumar, V.S.A., Marathe, M.V., Srinivasan, A., Wang, N.: Structure of Social Contact Networks and Their Impact on Epidemics. AMS-DIMACS Spec. Vol. Epidemiol. 70, 181–213 (2006)

15. Bauer, A., Pöll, C., Winterer, N., Miksch, F., Breitenecker, F.: Analysis and comparison of different modelling approaches based on an SIS epidemic. In: Proceedings of the International Workshop on Innovative Simulation for Health Care 2012, Vienna, pp. 115–120 (2012)

16. Wooldridge, M.: Agent-based software engineering. IEE Proc. Softw. Eng. 144, 26–37 (1997)

17. Jennings, N.: On agent-based software engineering. Artif. Intell. 117, 277–296 (2000)

18. Macal, C.M., North, M.J.: Tutorial on agent-based modelling and simulation. J. Simul. 4, 151–162 (2010)

19. Blower, S., Go, M.-H.: The importance of including dynamic social networks when modeling epidemics of airborne infections: does increasing complexity increase accuracy? BMC Med. 9, 88 (2011)

20. Parker, J.: A Flexible, Large-Scale, Distributed Agent Based Epidemic Model. In: Proceedings of the 2007 Winter Simulation Conference (2007)

21. Mossong, J., Hens, N., Jit, M., Beutels, P., Auranen, K., Mikolajczyk, R., Massari, M., Salmaso, S., Tomba, G.S., Wallinga, J., Heijne, J., Sadkowska-Todys, M., Rosinska, M., Edmunds, W.J.: Social Contacts and Mixing Patterns Relevant to the Spread of Infectious Diseases. PLoS Med. 5, e74 (2008)

22. Miksch, F., Zauner, G., Popper, N., Breitenecker, F.: Agent-Based Population Models For Household Simulation. In: Snorek, M., Buk, Z., Cepek, M., Drchal, J. (eds.) Proceedings of the 7th EUROSIM Congress on Modelling and Simulation, Prague, Czech Republic, pp. 567–572 (2010)

23. Muaz, A.N., Hussain, A., Kolberg, M.: Verification & Validation of Agent Based Simulations using the VOMAS (Virtual Overlay Multi-agent System) approach. In: Proceedings of the Second Multi-Agent Logics, Languages, and Organisations Federated Workshops, Torino, Italy (2009)

24. Sánchez, P.C.: As simple as possible, but no simpler: a gentle introduction to simulation modeling. In: Proceedings of the 2006 Winter Simulation Conference, Monterey, CA, pp. 2–10 (2006)

25. Keeling, M.J., Grenfell, B.T.: Individual-based Perspectives on R0. J. Theor. Biol. 203, 51–61 (2000)

26. Balci, O.: Validation, verification, and testing techniques throughout the life cycle of a simulation study. Ann. Oper. Res. 53, 121–173 (1994)

27. Sargent, R.: Verification and validation of simulation models. In: Proceedings of the 2010 Winter Simulation Conference, Baltimore, MD, pp. 166–183 (2010)

28. Klügl, F.: A validation methodology for agent-based simulations. In: Proceedings of the 2008 ACM Symposium on Applied Computing, pp. 39–43. ACM Press, New York (2008)

Transformation of Digital Ecosystems: The Case of Digital Payments

Stefan Henningsson and Jonas Hedman

Department of IT Management, Copenhagen Business School, Denmark
{sh.itm,jh.itm}@cbs.dk

Abstract. In digital ecosystems, the fusion relation between business and technology means that the decision of technical compatibility of the offering is also the decision of how to position the firm relative to the coopetive relations that characterize business ecosystems. In this article we develop the Digital Ecosystem Technology Transformation (DETT) framework for explaining technology-based transformation of digital ecosystems by integrating theories of business and technology ecosystems. The framework depicts ecosystem transformation as distributed and emergent from micro-, meso-, and macro-level coopetition. The DETT framework consists an alternative to the existing explanations of digital ecosystem transformation as the rational management of one central actor balancing ecosystem tensions. We illustrate the use of the framework by a case study of transformation in the digital payment ecosystem.

Keywords: Digital ecosystem, Coopetition, Payments, Transformation.

1 Introduction

Digital artefacts, including music, books, tickets, social media and money, hold increasingly prominent positions in the life of individuals, organizations, and society at large. An ongoing digitalization makes more and more industries fused with digital technologies (henceforth referred to as digital industries) (Tilson et al., 2010).

Digital industries present typical characteristics that set them apart from other industries. Traditional metaphors such as the value chain (Porter 1985) have been found inadequate to capture the actor relationships of digital industries (Stabell and Fjeldstad 1998). Digital industries are characterized by tension between competition and collaboration among actors (Ghazawneh and Henfridsson 2012). While some of the actors are direct competitors, they are also mutually dependent on the success of the industry as a whole. Digital industries are therefore conceived as digital ecosystems (Basole and Karla 2011). A business ecosystem is a coopetitive environment in which symbiotic relationships are formed to create mutual value for its members (Walley, 2007; Moore, 1996). Digital ecosystems (Selander et al., 2013; Ghazawneh & Henfridsson, 2012; Yoo et al., 2012) are ecosystems characterized by a fusion-relation to digital technologies (c.f. Sawy 2003). The fusion of technology makes digital ecosystems transforming along with technological innovations that transforms the business landscape (Evans et al., 2006; Yoo et al., 2008).

Linawati et al. (Eds.): ICT-EurAsia 2014, LNCS 8407, pp. 46–55, 2014.

This paper contributes to the explanation of how the fusion-relationship between business and technology in digital ecosystems affects ecosystem transformation. Explicitly and implicitly, the extant literature on digital ecosystems has in general assumed a perspective on ecosystem transformation as the central actors' management of competitive and collaborative ecosystem tensions (e.g. Shane 2001; Ghazawneh and Henfridsson 2013). For some digital ecosystems, transformation is a much more distributed process, where transformation is emergent. Such transformation is, for example, much emphasized in the literature of digital infrastructures (Tilson et al., 2010; e.g Hanseth & Lyytinen, 2010; Henningsson & Zinner Henriksen, 2011) and the literature on technology ecosystems (Adomavicius et al., 2007). Addressing the need for a more distributed and emergent explanation to digital ecosystem transformation, we integrate ecosystems framework from the business and technology domains into a Digital Ecosystem Technology Transformation (DETT) framework. The result is a multi-level framework that depicts technology-based transformation as micro-, meso-, and macro-level business and technology innovation positioning.

To illustrate the framework's use, we apply it on one digital ecosystem which transformation cannot be understood from the position of one central actor's rational governance: the digital payment ecosystem. For centuries the evolution of payments was slow and strictly controlled. Now, partly due to the fusion with digital technologies, payments have become one of society's most innovative and dynamic sectors, with fierce technology-based competition. In this ecosystem, ecosystem transformation is the emerging result of strategic decisions from all ecosystems members on how to align technological innovations with the ecosystems installed base.

2   Related Literature and Framework Development

Taking departure in the view of digital industries as digital ecosystems, this section develops the DETT framework for explanation of technology-fused transformation of digital ecosystems. It is emphasised that the transformation cannot be fully conceived by approaching either business or technology strategy in isolation. Rather, both entities have to be conceived as the wider ecosystems of which they form part (Adomavicius et al. 2007).

At the core of our framework lies the notion of technical compatibility, where technical innovations form part of technical systems. In a market fused with digital technologies, the decision of compatibility borders becomes inseparable from business ecosystem positioning. Elaborating on this fundamental idea, we integrate the literature on business ecosystems (Moore 1996; Tansley 1935) with the literatures on compatibility and system-based competition (Adomavicius et al. 2007).

2.1   Business Ecosystems

We define an ecosystem as a coopetitive environment in which symbiotic relationships are formed to create mutual value for its members (Selander et al. 2010). In the literature, two features of ecosystems stand out (Selander et al. 2010). First, an ecosystem is characterized by simultaneous competition and cooperation, so called coopetition (Walley 2007). A micro-level of analysis depicts some actors as direct competitors, while a macro-level of analysis depicts the same actors as mutually dependent on the success of the ecosystem as a whole and are therefor forced into collaboration with other entities.

Ecosystems are not homogenous constructs. Within a business ecosystem, certain actors can have closer relations than other actors. One can even talk about ecosystems of ecosystems, or ecologies (García-Marco 2011). However, from this position the issue arises of how to handle the within-ecosystems clusters of actors that are more tightly connected than others. Within ecosystems, actors might form partnerships, alliances, networks and other formal and informal clusters that as a group have coopetive relations to other clusters. To capture this level of coopetive relations, a meso-level of analysis is required. The meso-level of analysis depicts situations where more than one, but not all, actors of an ecosystem form business clusters that have coopetive relations to other clusters.

The second typical characteristic of ecosystems is that ecosystems are dynamic entities that constantly evolve. Continuous re-adaptations in the relationships between ecosystem members across micro-, meso-, and macro-levels make ecosystems dynamic. The systemic properties of the ecosystem means that changes in one of the ecosystems entities will trigger response and changes in other entities in a constantly dynamic process (Selander et al. 2011).

2.2   Technology-Fused Business Ecosystems

Previous research has observed that digital ecosystems transform rapidly along with technological innovations that alter conditions for the business landscape (Evans et al. 2006; Yoo et al. 2008; Zammuto et al. 2007). New technology generations are fundamentally reshaping the traditional logic, as business processes become intertwined with surrounding technology ecosystems (Basole 2009).

A digital ecosystem is an ecosystem that exists in a fusion-relation (c.f. Sawy 2003) to mobile technologies, where digital technologies form part of a 'technology ecosystem'. Adomavivious et al. (2007 p. 201) define a technology ecosystem as *"A system of interrelated technologies that influence each other's evolution and development."* The definition is based on the view of evolving components of complex technologies as mutually interdependent (Iansiti et al. 1995). Consequently, from the consumer side, the selection of a specific technology is associated with a strategic decision to join a particular business network that operates in a specific technological 'regime' with interoperable technologies (Shane 2001). For the digital ecosystem actors, the fusion relation between business and strategy means that the collaborative and competitive strategies are inseparable from the strategic adoption of technology.

2.3   Technology-Based Transformation in Digital Ecosystems

The two sections above have established digital ecosystems as business ecosystems, and analysed the effects of technological compatibility on ecosystem positioning.

Here, we draw on the conclusions made to develop the integrative DETT framework. The developed framework is divided into micro-, meso- and macro-levels as presented in Figure 1. Competition and collaboration exist on all three levels, and so do classes of compatible and incompatible technology. Consequently, technology-based transformation in digital ecosystems can be understood as a three-levelled process based on technology positioning:

- Micro-level, individual business units compete through proprietary technologies.
- Meso-level, strategic clusters are formed through shared technologies.
- Macro-level, the ecosystem of interdependent members as a whole competes with other ecosystems through technology regimes.

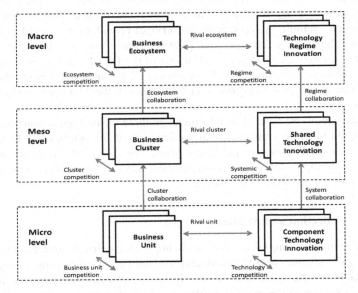

Fig. 1. Digital Ecosystem Technology Transformation Framework

Members contribute to the ecosystem technologies by innovation and adoption either in competitive or collaborative mode. In the collaborative mode, members on micro-, meso-, or macro-levels jointly innovate and/or adopt component, application, or support technologies that will benefit the members in the collaboration. Conversely, in the competitive mode members on the micro level innovate and/or adopt component, application, or support technologies that will benefit the specific member. The meso-level adoption is a situation of combined competition and collaboration mode.

3   Method

3.1   Research Approach and Case Selection

Empirically, this paper is based on a case study of the payment ecosystem in Denmark consisting of three embedded cases of digital payment innovations. The case study approach is suitable when studying contemporary phenomenon with unclear borders between phenomenon and its real-life (Yin 1984). Another important reason for applying the case study is that cases can be viewed as a series of experiments and thereby allowing for replication logic (Yin 1984). This is here achieved by three embedded cases that replicate findings across analytical levels. In practice, this means that each case is analysed in relationship to the initial framework and additional cases are used to challenge the insights gained from the previous cases. The insights grow with each case and allows for the emergence of theory and understanding.

There are two main reasons why we chose the digital payment ecosystem as empirical domain for illustrating our framework. First, the payment ecosystem is currently highly turbulent and unstable, as it searches for a new equilibrium as technology-fused ecosystem. Payments, with increasing frequency, consist of digital representations of money that are transferred in a global intertwined system that involve multiple parties, including payers, payment services providers, banks, telecom operators, mobile phone manufactures, and payees. This allows for identification and investigation of ongoing strategies on all levels of the DETT framework. Second, the payment ecosystem is central in today's society. This makes payments the battleground for one of the most important societal clashes of the 21st century (Ondrus and Lyytinen 2011).

In our case study, we have chosen to focus on three technological innovations, and their associated business strategies, that are being used for entering the Danish payment market on micro-, meso-, and macro level. They are iZettle (a payment dongle invented by a startup), SMS payments (a payment service from mobile operators), and PayPal (a potential ecosystem contender).

3.2   Data Collection and Analysis

We used documents, interviews and workshops as empirical sources. Documents were official documents from Denmark and the European Union on the payment ecosystem (Danmarks-Nationalbank, 2005; Kokkola, 2010), and publicly available sources, such as annual reports, press releases, research articles, and web pages. One of the authors took part in six workshops on future payment technologies, organized by the financial industry in Denmark. Notes were taken during the workshops, which were later expanded after the session. Interviews with eight representatives from various ecosystem members were conducted. Interviews were recorded and transcribed.

When analysing the cases, the empirical observations were matched and compared with the DETT framework and its concepts, cf. Yin's (1984) pattern-matching technique. Being a case study, we aimed for generalizing towards theory (rather than population) and used the empirical findings to challenge existing frameworks and concepts related to evolution of payment ecosystem.

4   Framework Illustration

The introduction of the Eurozone, SEPA (Kokkola 2010), and changing payment behaviour (Evans and Schmalensee 2005) has drastically changed the payment landscape over the last decade (Garcia-Swartz et al. 2006). The main current development in the payment market is the replacement of the physical payment infrastructures with a digital payment infrastructure. This process started with payment cards and continued with internet and mobile banks. The digitalization of payments has changed the previously stable market. New actors emerge competing with technological innovations. Telecom operators are aggressively trying to get mobile payments onto their technical infrastructure. Many of these innovations are tied to new technologies. Banks all over the world are talking about "the new normal" or "the new standards". For centuries the evolution of payments was slow and strictly controlled. Now, payments have become one of society's most innovative and dynamic sectors.

4.1   Micro Level Competition - iZettle

Starting at the micro level, the payment ecosystem is experiencing the introduction of new technological innovations, including smartphone payment card dongles. This technology competes with card terminals or electronic funds transfer at point of sale (EFTPOS) that has existed since the mid 1980s. Traditionally payment card clearinghouses, such as Nets and Point, offer card terminals to merchants against a monthly fee and percentage of the transaction volume. Nets defend its market position through its monopoly. They are the only one allowed, by law, to process Dankort transactions and they invest heavily in their payment infrastructure. The merchant provides the payer with a terminal, provided by Nets or Point, so they can swipe their card. The EFTPOS establish a link to the payment card clearinghouse, which checks whether the card is valid and if there are any available funds. Then the payer approves the transaction through a pin code. There were about 220.000 card terminals that managed close to one billion card transaction in 2010.

Over the past few years a contender to the EFTPOS has emerged from startups in USA and Sweden, including companies such as Square from the USA (www.square.com) and iZettle from Sweden (www.izettle.com). iZettle entered the Danish market in 2011 and offers smartphones owners a dongle, which converts smartphones into EFTPOS. iZettle is registered as payment service providers, but not as a financial institution. Consequently, they do not work under the same laws and rules as, for instance, a bank. iZettle applies a battering ram strategy by offering similar functionality as a traditional EFTPOS, but with a low fixed costs to small businesses and private persons and charges 2.75% of each transaction. The offering disrupts the market by providing functionality to new market segments. For small merchants they offer a small point of sale system (POS). Nets and Point do not provide this service to is customers.

The dongle is compatible with existing smartphone communication ports. It uses the same installation procedure as for any software on a smartphone (AppStore or Goggle Play). The startup exploits the diffusion and the capabilities of smartphones. Howeverm this requires collaboration and partnership with Apple and Google to deploy the applications to the smartphone. Furthermore they collaborate with the Mastercard and VISA to accept these cards. They also collaborate with payment clearinghouses to verify the card and transaction. As a response the establishment,

Nets, has launched MobilePenge – person-to-person account transfers through SMS – with a 7% transaction fee. Nets draw upon its existing network of banks and its control of NEM-Konto to increase the barriers of entry on this market.

4.2   Meso Level Competition - SMS Payments

At the meso level we find the mobile operators who provide SMS payments. This type of payment is based on text messaging service in mobile communication systems. The SMS standard is part of the Global System for Mobile Communications (GSM) series of standards. The problem that SMSs solved was to send notifications to and from mobile phones, e.g. to inform of voice mail messages. Nokia was the first phone manufacturer to implement the standard back in 1993. Since then, the use of SMS has exploded in volume, in 2010, 6.1 trillion SMS were sent, and the roles have changed from notifications to a tool for personal communication, accessing digital content, and making payment.

The Finnish mobile operator Saunalahti (now part of Elisa Group) introduced SMS payments in 1998, when they offered the world's first downloadable ring tones. Today it is used for online payments, mobile application stores, bus tickets, and parking tickets. SMS payments use premium-rate telephone numbers for which prices are higher than normal. The provider of SMS payments uses either the telecom operators, such TDC, TeliaSonera, 3 or Telenore, directly or through a payment gateway provider, such as Unwire. The cost of the premium SMS are billed to the customers by the mobile operator. Unlike a normal SMS, part of the charge is paid to the service or content provider. The payout to the service provider varies between SMS number and operator, but up to 45% of the price is kept by the operator.

SMS payments compete with payment cards cash payment and they are based on the collaboration between mobile operators and content providers or service providers. This is an example of how industries can enter a new market and compete with business clusters. The existing ecosystem has not come up with a directly competing technology, but is defending the market position through lobbing. Furthermore, SMS payments actually solves a bank issue, namely it reduces the use of coins in vending and parking machines.

4.3   Macro Level Competition - PayPal

PayPal might be a possible contender of the established payment ecosystem. PayPal was founded in 1998 and has over 120 million active accounts. PayPal accepts payments in 25 currencies, including the Danish Krone. They registered as a bank in Luxembourg. PayPal provide the basic bank services of setting up accounts both for individuals and merchants. It is possible to make payments and financial transactions through web interfaces, mobile interfaces, and e-mail. The growth and expansion of PayPal is based on three-phase strategy. "First, PayPal focused on expanding its service among eBay users in the U.S. Second, we began expanding PayPal to eBay's international sites. And third, we started to build PayPal's business off eBay" (former eBay CEO Meg Whitman). On example, of the expansion strategy is that PayPal are providing an API for third party software developers. This is build and defends strategy by PayPal. They are expanding their payment function from the eBay ecosystem to become a global payment provider.

The functionality found in PayPal is making up a technology regime. Similar to payment dongles and SMS payments, PayPal utilizes existing technology components and systems. However, they adopt their offerings to different platforms, from eBay, to the ecommerce sites to mobile ecosystems, such as iPhone and Android. They grow organically and have slowly begun to attack the payment ecosystem. As said before they are collaborating and partnering with different actors in the payment market. For instance, they collaborate with all the major payment cards companies (business clusters), such as VISA, MasterCard. In Denmark they collaborate with a foreign small bank (SEB) to allow PayPal users to transfer money to their PayPal account. Furthermore, they are collaborating with e-commerce firms, by having an API to enable integration between PayPal and e-commerce sites. The current business models of PayPal have components that could challenge existing payment ecosystems.

The reaction towards this potential enemy has been indirect. The established payment ecosystem continues to invest in their existing infrastructure to provide the users with better services than PayPal. For instance, the launch of mobile banks has been huge successes. Dansk Bank used Facebook to involve its customers in the development of their mobile bank. A key resource for the banks in this battle might actually be there local presence and the trust they have built with their customers.

5   Discussion and Conclusion

Building on the existing literature on digital ecosystems, this paper develops a complementary perspective on transformation of digital ecosystems by regarding ecosystem transformation as a distributed and emergent process. We illustrate the use of the framework by a study of the digital payment ecosystem.

In the case of the digital payment ecosystem, no single actor holds a position that allows them to rationally design ecosystem transformation. Instead ecosystem transformation can be seen as emerging from the collective positioning of technological innovations in relation to the micro-, meso- and macro-level positioning

Starting at the micro unit level, the payment ecosystem is experiencing the introduction of new technological innovations which challenge the individual members and existing payment technologies. At this level, actors draw on existing technological systems and regimes with compatible technology innovations.

On the meso level, new technologies that are incompatible with existing technologies, but still existing within the same technological ecosystem lead to rival technological systems. This leads to competition between business clusters, as in the case where banks competes against telecom providers with rival SMS payment innovations.

Finally, on the macro level, new technology regimes may emerge that challenge the existing ecosystem. This leads to competition among the ecosystems. PayPal's ecosystem based on internet-technologies rather than the traditional payment IT infrastructure consist an ecosystem challenge to the traditional payment ecosystem.

5.1   Theoretical Contribution

This paper contributes towards the explanation of how the fusion-relationship between business and technology in digital ecosystems affects ecosystem transformation. The DETT framework explains the effects of technological compatibility on ecosystem positioning. The horizontal dimension of the framework shows the competitive dimension of ecosystems as rivalry between existing businesses, with its installed base of technology, and new entrants with technological innovations that are trying to enter the market.

The vertical dimension shows the collaborative dimension of digital ecosystems, depicting collaboration between actors on two levels: meso (collaboration in cluster), and macro (collaboration as ecosystem). On the micro-level, individual business units compete with incompatible technologies. On the meso-level, formal and informal strategic networks and alliances are formed as a result of members joining forces in clusters to compete with other clusters of members. On the macro-level, the ecosystem of interdependent members as whole competes with other ecosystems through market collusion strategies based on technology regimes. The vertical dimension also shows how collaboration occurs between the levels through system-, cluster-, regime-, and ecosystem collaboration.

5.2   Practical Implications

For the growing number of industries being fused with digital technologies, exploiting the specific characteristics of these industries becomes a key challenge for firm success. Here we discuss the implications of our findings on two distinct actors related to digital ecosystem transformation: new entrants and existing members.

In the payment ecosystem case, new entrants come from two distinct sources: start-ups, and from adjacent industries, such as telecom. The case suggests that traditional members, to a greater extent than new entrants, approach technologies that are compatible with existing technology clusters (systems). New entrants seek to make their entries with technological solutions that are incompatible with existing technology systems, which creates rival competitive systems.

Existing members can take two positions in the blocking of new entrants: to face them on the micro- or meso level. Facing the new actors on a micro-level leads to the acceptance of rival competitive systems. This can be motivated by that new entrants are not direct competitors. Facing new entrants on the meso level yields two options: systemic competition or inclusion in clusters. An example of the first is Danske Bank's collaboration with an external provider for their iPhone application. An example of the latter is the clustered competition of rival systems for SMS payments. Traditional actors (banks) are forced to collaborate to face off a rival system that indirectly threatens existing business. Regardless of level of encounter, the market entry is blocked by increasing level of capital investment in technology required to enter, or by restraining access to specific technology that complements the entrants offering.

Acknowledgements. This work was in part carried out with the support of Copenhagen Finance IT Region (www.cfir.dk) and was funded by the Danish Enterprise and Construction Authority grant number ERDFH-09-0026.

References

Adomavicius, G., Bockstedt, J.C., Gupta, A., Kauffman, R.J.: Technology Roles and Paths of Influence. Information Technology and Management 8(2) (2007)

Basole, R.C., Karla, J.: On the Evolution of Mobile Platform Ecosystem Structure and Strategy. Business & Information Systems Engineering 3(5), 313–322 (2011)

Danmarks-Nationalbank. Betalningsformidling i Danmark. Danmarks Nationalbank, København (2005)

Evans, D.S., Hagiu, A., Schmalensee, R.: Invisible Engines: How Software Platforms Drive Innovation and Transform Industries. The MIT Press, Boston (2006)

García-Marco, F.J.: Libraries in the Digital Ecology: Reflections and Trends. The Electronic Library 29(1), 105–120 (2011)

Garcia-Swartz, D., Hahn, R., Layne-Farrar, A.: The Move toward a Cashless Society. Review of Network Economics 5(2), 175–197 (2006)

Ghazawneh, A., Henfridsson, O.: Balancing Platform Control and External Contribution in Third Party Development. Information Systems Journal (2012)

Hanseth, O., Lyytinen, K.: Design Theory for Dynamic Complexity in Information Infrastructures. Journal of Information Technology 25(1), 1–19 (2010)

Henningsson, S., Zinner Henriksen, H.: Inscription of Behaviour and Flexible Interpretation in Information Infrastructures. JSIS 20(4), 355–372 (2011)

Iansiti, M., Levien, R.: The Keystone Advantage. HBSP, Boston (2004)

Kokkola, T. (ed.): The payment system. European Central Bank, Frankfurt (2010)

Moore, J.: The Death of Competition: Leadership and Strategy in the Age of Business Ecosystems. Harper Business, New York (1996)

Ondrus, J., Lyytinen, K.: Mobile Payments Market: Towards Another Clash of the Titans? In: The 10th ICMB, Como, Italy (2011)

Porter, M.E.: Competitive Advantage: Creating and Sustaining Superior Performance. Free Press, Boston (1985)

Sawy, O.A.E.: The 3 Faces of Is Identity: Connection, Immersion, and Fusion. Communications of the Association for Information Systems 12(1), 588–598 (2003)

Selander, L., Henfridsson, O., Svahn, F.: Transforming Ecosystem Relationships in Digital Innovation. In: 31st ICIS, St. Louis (2010)

Selander, L., Henfridsson, O., Svahn, F.: Capability Search and Redeem across Digital Ecosystems. Journal of Information Technology (2013)

Shane, S.: Technology Regimes and New Firm Formation. Management Science, 1173–1190 (2001)

Stabell, C.B., Fjeldstad, D.: Configuring Value for Competitive Advantage. Strategic Management Journal 19(5), 413–437 (1998)

Tilson, D., Lyytinen, K., Sørensen, C.: Digital Infrastructures: The Missing IS Research Agenda. Information Systems Research 21(4), 748–759 (2010)

Walley, K.: Coopetition. International Studies of Management and Organization 37(2), 11–31 (2007)

Yin, R.K.: Case Study Research: Design and Methods. SAGE, Thousand Oaks (1984)

Yoo, Y., Lyytinen, K., Boland, R.: Innovation in the Digital Era: Digitization and Four Classes of Innovation Networks (2008)

Zammuto, R.F., Griffith, T.L., Dougherty, D.J., Faraj, S.: Information Technology and the Changing Fabric of Organization. Org. Sci. 18(5), 749–762 (2007)

Do Personality Traits Work as Moderator on the Intention to Purchase Mobile Applications Work? - A Pilot Study

Charnsak Srisawatsakul[1,*], Gerald Quirchmayr[2], and Borworn Papasratorn[1]

[1] Requirement Engineering Laboratory, School Of Information Technology
King Mongkut's University of Technology Thonburi, Bangkok, Thailand
charnsak.sri@st.sit.kmutt.ac.th, borworn@sit.kmutt.ac.th
[2] Faculty of Computer Science, University of Vienna, Vienna, Austria
gerald.quirchmayr@univie.ac.at

Abstract. Mobile application markets are now transforming into a multibillion-dollar business. Understanding the consumer's intention to purchase them and the moderating factors of individual differences – personality traits – allowed us to know more about consumers. The objectives of this research are to determine whether personality traits have any moderating effect with the consumer's intention to purchase mobile application. Our preliminary data for the pilot study consists of 147 participants, who are office workers and students who use smart devices and live in Bangkok, Thailand. Hierarchical multiple regression was used to analyze the data. The results from our pilot study indicate that personality traits did not show a significant moderating effect. However, the result supported the original Theory Reasoned Action. It demonstrates that there are differences in attitudes toward the purchase of mobile applications between office workers and students. Therefore, this research has thrown up many questions in need of further investigation. As the initial data was only 147 respondents, a more extensive study will have to follow up our preliminary results.

Keywords: Intention to Purchase, Mobile Applications, Personality traits, Theory of Reasoned Action.

1 Introduction

Recently, the mobile apps (short for applications) market has been growing rapidly. According to ABI Research, the overall market value of mobile apps will reach $27 billion [1]. Furthermore, the prices of those devices have dropped dramatically, which makes them affordable to average consumers while becoming increasingly powerful in terms of computation, sensing, and interaction capabilities. Gartner has forecast that by the end of 2013 the worldwide device shipment of smartphones and tablets will reach 181 and 18 billion [2], respectively. Mobile apps in the market were acquired from two dominant stores. First, Apple have their ecosystem for iOS users called Apple App Store, which holds more than 850,000 apps [3] to download. Second, Google has more than 700,000 apps on their Play Store for Android

---

* Corresponding author.

Linawati et al. (Eds.): ICT-EurAsia 2014, LNCS 8407, pp. 56–65, 2014.
© IFIP International Federation for Information Processing 2014

users. There is evidence suggesting that personality play a role in determining the satisfaction [4] and usages preference of mobile apps [5, 6]. This paper tries to inspect the moderating effect of the individual differences on the purchase intention of mobile apps. Our model is based on the Theory of Reasoned Action (TRA) [7] which we use to predict the intention to purchase mobile apps. We use the big five-personality traits [8, 9] to categorize the individual differences. It measured by the Mini International Personality Item Pool (Mini-IPIP) questionnaires instrument [10].

The major outcome of our pilot examination enhances understanding of the moderating effect between personality traits and mobile apps purchase intention. It also expectantly eagerly is a great starting indication and will subsequently be used for empirical research in the future.

2   Literature Review

2.1   Theory of Reasoned Action

Fishbein and Ajzen [7] introduced TRA in 1975. The conceptual model of TRA is shown in figure 1. It proposed fundamental and influential factors to understand the behavioral intention. According to the TRA, attitude toward the behavior and subjective norm (or, social influence) are two factors that mainly determine a person's behavioral intention to perform a specified behavior. Moreover, behavioral intention will lead to actual performance of that behavior. "The stronger the intention, the more likely the performance of behavior" [7]. Attitude toward behavior is defined as "an individual's positive or negative feelings (evaluative affect) about performing the target behavior" [7]. Subjective norm can be explained as "the person's perception that most people who are important to him think he should or should not perform the behavior in question" [7]. TRA have been applied for predicting a wide range of behaviors. For example, it has been used to understand behavioral intention in context of mobile marketing including Thailand [11, 12]. The theories also seem suited for the purpose of investigating and predicting consumer purchase intentions of mobile apps.

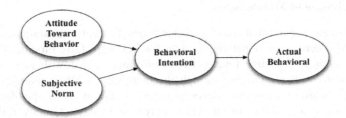

Fig. 1. Original Theory of Reasoned Action [7]

2.2   Personality Traits

The conceptualization of the Big Five personality traits, based on enduring characteristics of the individual that summarize trans-situational consistencies in characteristic styles of responding to the environment [8], proposes a framework that organized personality into 5 groups known as Big Five traits (Neuroticism, Extraversion, Openness, Conscientiousness, and Agreeableness), which explain much of the shared variance of human personality. There is a number of free and commercial scales designed questionnaires to measure Big Five personality traits. One of the most famous inventories is the International Personality Item Pool (IPIP). It is a free construct items for questionnaires, proposed by Goldberg et al [13] in 1996. It consists of 50 and 100 items. Many researchers studied on reducing the number of questionnaires from using an extremely brief measure of the Big-Five personality dimensions to 100 items. To illustrate this, the revised NEO Five-Factor Inventory is a 60 items questionnaire proposed by Costa et al [14]; Donnellan [10] proposed 20 questions items called Mini-IPIP, 40 items Mini Markers of Big Five [15], 44-item Big Five Inventory [16], 75 items Traits Personality Questionnaire 5 (TPQue5) [17].

In this study, Mini-IPIP 20 questions scale was used to measure the personality traits of the participants. There are 5 reasons that support the use of Mini-IPIP. First of all, the most limiting disadvantage of the IPIP are the huge questionnaires items [10]. Participants may respond carelessly due to annoyance with the length of assessment. Second, the result from studies conclude that Mini-IPIP is a psychometrically acceptable and practically useful short measure of the Big Five personality traits in the term of reliability and validity and comparable to IPIP [10, 18]. Third, Mini-IPIP is not the shortest instrument for investigate the Big Five personality traits. There are shorter version such as 5 items [19–21] and 10 items [22] inventories. However, the shorter instrument is not the better. The use of very short instruments of personality traits may significantly affect the validity and reliability [23]. Besides, Baldasaro et al [24] argued that the result from TIPI is not adequately reliable. Moreover, the items are having a relatively high correlation between each other. Fourth, Shafer [25] proposed a 30 items inventory for measuring the personality traits. However, the results suggested that the 30 items have lower or equal validity scores than Mini-IPIP. Finally, many studies discovered that Mini-IPIP shows the reliability and validity as well as the 50 items IPIP [10, 18, 23, 24]. For those reasons, Mini-IPIP was used as an instrument to measure the Big Five personality traits in this study.

2.3   Purchasing of Mobile Apps

Mobile apps can be classified into 3 sub-categories, content-, marketing-, or service-oriented [26]. There are 3 monetizing options for B2C apps [26]. First of all, developers sell the apps as one-time loyalty free. Consumers can download re-install and update it for free after purchase through the ecosystem of their platform. Second, freemium applications allow consumers to download and use their apps for free with limitation such as a permit to use its full features for 15 days. Moreover, developers may allow users to use their "lite" versions, which have only basic feature available. Also, they can make money from advertising space in their apps; if consumers need more advance functionality or don't want to see the advertising, they can purchase an upgrade it directly from in-app purchase. Third, developers focus on offering premium content inside the apps. For example, users could buy new tool in a game; they can subscribe to their favorite magazine, newspaper or books.

3   Approach

3.1   Model-Based Investigations

The conceptual model in this study shows in figure 2. The model is based on TRA. The Big five personality traits have been added to investigate the moderating effect within the TRA factors. We now try to answer the following questions:

Question 1: Do the Big Five Personality traits have a moderating effect between the attitude toward purchase of mobile applications and the intention to purchase mobile applications in office workers and students in Bangkok, Thailand?

Question 2: Do Big Five Personality traits have a moderating effect between Subjective Norm and the intention to purchase mobile applications in office workers and students in Bangkok, Thailand?

Question 3: Do Big Five Personality traits have a moderating effect between the intention to purchase mobile applications and an Actual Purchase of Mobile Applications in office workers and students in Bangkok, Thailand?

Fig. 2. Proposed model for measuring the moderating effect of personality traits

3.2   Initial Data Used in a First Test of the Model

The pilot study was conducted on a sample of 149 participants (n=149) who live in Bangkok, Thailand, 62 and 87 of them are students and office workers, respectively. Of these, 59.7% were female and 39.6% were male (0.7% of the participants chose not to answer this question). Participants use a diversity of mobile operating systems. Specifically, Apple iOS for 47.5%, Android for 42.1%, Microsoft Windows Phone for 4.4%, Black Berry for 4.4% and other operating system for 1.6%. Data was collected using self-report web-based and paper-based questionnaires. The design of the questionnaires items was based on questions developed by TRA [7] and Mini-IPIP [10]. Participants indicate their level of agreement with each item on a 5 point Likert scale (1 = strongly disagree, 5 = strongly agree). The Cronbach's Alpha of over all questions in TRA and Mini-IPIP question is 0.92 and 0.61, respectively.

4   Preliminary Results

The correlation matrix of variables is demonstration in Table.1. (ATT=Attitude Toward Purchase of Mobile Apps, SUB=Subjective Norm, INT=Intention To Purchase,
EXT=Extraversion, AGR=Agreeableness, CONS=Consciousness, NEU=Neuroticism,
OPEN=Openness to Experience). Attitude toward purchase of mobile apps and subjective norm are significantly correlated with intention to purchase (r = 0.74 and r =
0.47, p < 0.01). Moreover, Intention to purchase is highly correlated with actual purchase (r = 0.81, p < 0.01). Hence, this confirms the original conclusions of TRA. The
Big Five personality traits did not show a significant correlation with our predictor's
variables. Openness to experience was positively correlated with extraversion (r =
0.29, p < 0.01), agreeableness(r = 0.48, p < 0.01), consciousness(r = 0.26, p < 0.01)
and negative correlated with neuroticism (r = -0.19, p< 0.01).

Table 1. Correlation matrix of all variables

	1	2	3	4	5	6	7	8	9
1.ATT	1	.37**	.74**	.69**	0.06	.175	0.10	0.08	0.07
2.SUB	.37**	1	.47**	.39**	.17	.189	0.08	0.09	0.06
3.INT	.74**	.47**	1	.81**	0.05	.162	0.14	-0.05	0.11
4.ACT	.69**	.39**	.81**	1	0.04	.161	0.14	0.05	0.05
5.EXT	0.06	.17	0.05	0.04	1	.37**	.30**	0.10	.29**
6.AGR	.18	.19	.16	.16	.37**	1	.44**	-0.14	.48**
7.CON	0.10	0.08	0.14	0.14	.30**	.44**	1	-0.06	.26**
8.NEU	0.08	0.09	-0.05	0.05	0.10	-0.14	-0.06	1	-.19**
9.OPEN	0.07	0.06	0.11	0.05	.29**	.48**	.26**	-.19**	1

** Correlation is significant at the 0.01 level (2-tailed).

4.1   Moderating Role of Personality Traits

To investigate the prediction that personality traits moderate intention to purchase and
actual purchase, 2 hierarchical multiple regression models were established. First, in
step 1, Intention to purchase served as dependent variable. It was tested by attitude
toward purchase of mobile apps and subjective norms as predictors. In step 2, personality traits were entered as interaction effect with attitude toward purchase of mobile
apps and subjective norms. For the second model, in step 1 we added actual purchase
as dependent variable along with intention to purchase as predictor. Also, the interaction between personality traits and intention to purchase were entered in step 2. We
separate data from participants based on their occupation into 2 groups "Office Worker" and "Student". All predictors' variables were centered by mean to reduce multi-
collinearity effects. The results of model 1 and 2 show in table 2 and 3, respectively.

The cumulative percentage of explained variance of attitude toward purchase of
mobile apps in office workers is 66% (adjusted R square = 0.66); Student is 41%
(adjusted R square = 0.41). For the subjective norms, it can explain variance of 28%
(adjusted R square = 0.28); for office workers and 26% (adjusted R square = 0.26);
for students. In Table 2, show the value of standardized coefficient (β) and R square
change of the model that have intention to purchase as dependent variable.

Table 2. Hierarchical regression result of "Attitude Toward Purchase of Mobile Apps" and "Subjective Norm" as predictors to Intention to purchase

		Office Worker		Student	
		INT		INT	
		ΔR^2	β	ΔR^2	β
Attitude Toward Purchase of Mobile Apps					
Step 1:	ATT	0.67*	0.81*	0.42*	0.66*
	EXT		0.023		-0.12
Step 2:	ATT X EXT	0	-0.14	0.01	-0.14
Step 1:	ATT	0.67*	0.80*	0.42*	0.66*
	AGR		0.66		-0.42
Step 2:	ATT X AGR	0	0.15	0	0.14
Step 1:	ATT	0.67*	0.81*	0.45*	0.62*
	OPEN		0.03		0.16
Step 2:	ATT X OPEN	0.01	0.154	0.15	-0.287
Step 1:	ATT	0.67*	0.80*	0.42*	0.62*
	CON		0.7		-0.06
Step 2:	ATT X CON	0.005	0.78	0.02	-1.1
Step 1:	ATT	0.67*	0.81*	0.50*	0.70*
	NEU		-0.05		-0.29*
Step 2:	ATT X NEU	0	0.11	0	-0.133
Subjective Norm					
Step 1:	SUB	0.30*	0.54*	0.29*	0.52*
	EXT		-0.01		-0.06
Step 2:	SUB X EXT	0.01	0.27	0.03	-1.35
Step 1:	SUB	0.30*	0.50*	0.29*	0.52*
	AGR		0.11		0.1
Step 2:	SUB X AGR	0.01	0.5	0.01	0.61
Step 1:	SUB	0.30*	0.54*	0.33*	0.52*
	OPEN		0.13		0.24*
Step 2:	SUB X OPEN	0.01	-0.43	0.01	-0.3
Step 1:	SUB	0.32*	0.54*	0.29*	0.52*
	CON		0.16		-0.075
Step 2:	SUB X CON	0.01	0.44	0.02	1.72
Step 1:	SUB	0.34*	0.57*	0.33*	0.55*
	NEU		-0.22		-0.21*
Step 2:	SUB X NEU	0	-0.64	0.02	-0.78

Note: * = $p<0.05$

We analyzed all the variables and interaction term in our study. The R square changes in all steps are relatively low. Significant effects were only found for step 1 model (without interaction). Moreover, personality traits only show a few significant effects in both office workers and students. Neuroticism shows a negative coefficient in both subjective norm (β = -0.21) and attitude toward purchase of mobile apps (β = -0.29). Openness to experience indicates significant on subjective norms (β = 0.24). There are no significant in any interaction term between attitude toward purchase of mobile apps and personality traits or subjective norms and personality traits. The standardized coefficients of attitude toward purchase of mobile apps are different between office workers and students. The office workers (β = 0.81) has higher beta values more than students (β = 0.66) that mean the attitude toward purchase of mobile apps of office worker has more impact on the intention to purchase mobile apps.

Table 3. Hierarchical regression result of Intention To Purchase as predictor to Actual Purchase

		Office Worker		Student	
		ACT		ACT	
		ΔR^2	β	ΔR^2	β
Intention To Purchase					
Step 1:	INT	0.73*	0.86*	0.55*	0.73*
	EXT		0.06		0.08
Step 2:	INT X EXT	0	0.11	0.01	-0.61
Step 1:	INT	0.73*	0.85*	0.55*	0.73*
	AGR		-0.03		0.067
Step 2:	INT X AGR	0	0.36	0.01	-0.478
Step 1:	INT	0.73*	0.85*	0.55*	0.75*
	OPEN		0.02		-0.34
Step 2:	INT X OPEN	0	0.03	0.01	0.711
Step 1:	INT	0.73*	0.85*	0.55*	0.73*
	CON		0.01		0.05
Step 2:	INT X CON	0	0.1	0	-0.86
Step 1:	INT	0.73*	0.86*	0.55*	0.75*
	NEU		0.06		0.1
Step 2:	INT X NEU	0	0.11	0.01	0.56

*Note: * = p<0.05*

In the Table 3, Actual purchase were used as dependent variable. It was predicted by intention to purchase. Personality traits were served as moderator for their relationship. The finding supports previous research into this brain area which the relationship between intention and actual perform of behavior which have high level of coefficient standardized value for both office worker (β = 0.86) and student (β = 0.73). The adjusted R square of those 2 groups also can explain 71% (adjusted R square = 0.71) of variance of office worker and 53% of student (adjusted R square = 0.53). However, there are no significant of coefficient standardized value of the interaction, Moreover, the R Square change are very low. Figure 3 and 4 shows the statistical summarize from our research model.

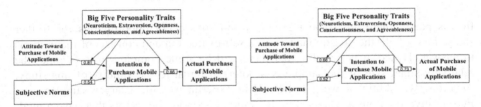

Fig. 3. Results from office workers   **Fig. 4.** Results from students

5   Discussion and Interpretation of Results

The findings are rather disappointing in that the moderating role of personality traits did not show a significant effect. The interaction terms were found to be non-significant in predicting the overall variance of the model. Thus, the Question 1-3 has been answered. The personality traits did not have any moderating effects in any relationship of TRA. This may be lead to conclusion that the ability to buy mobile apps has an overriding influence such as financial status, occupation, major of study, etc.

Nevertheless, this study produced results that corroborate the findings of a great deal of the original TRA. It indicates that intention to purchase mobile apps is highly determined by the joint of attitude toward purchase of mobile apps and subjective norms. Furthermore, the higher level of intention to purchase mobile apps will lead to higher possibility of actual purchase of mobile apps. Office workers show higher significant relationship between attitudes toward purchase of mobile apps and intention to purchase mobile apps, which can describe that the office worker will buy mobile apps more than IT students. Subjective norms indicate nearly the same level of relationship for both office workers and students. Hence, the perceptions of most important people around them toward the intention to purchase mobile apps have the same effect for both office workers and students. However, office workers show a significant increase in the relationship between intention to purchase and actual purchase. This led to the conclusion that office workers purchase more applications based on their attitudes than students.

In conclusion, this study was designed to determine the moderating effect of personality traits in a mobile applications purchasing context. Hierarchical multiple regression analysis revealed that the personality traits did not have a significant effect on the intention to purchase mobile applications. However, the finding of graphical interaction indicates that an interaction coefficient exists in the students meaning that the moderating effects exist but were overridden by the homogeneity of the sample. Therefore, this research has raised some questions that need further investigation. For example, does any moderator exist in this context? Will be overridden by the homogeneity of the samples such as age, sex, occupation, major of education, etc.

6   Limitations of the Study and Future Research

In this paper, there are some limitations and subsequent opportunities for further study. First of all, the questionnaire was a self-evaluation and consists of many items to answer. Hence, it is possible that there will be some common bias. Second, the relatively small size of the sample is a potential threat to the validity of this study. Accordingly, additional work is needed to experiment with a larger samples size. Further investigations are needed in the future to explore the factors that have a moderating effect in the intention to purchase mobile apps context. As the initial data was only 147 respondents, a more extensive study will have to follow up our preliminary results. Relationships between factors not addressed in this paper will be the subject of future works.

Acknowledgements. The authors would like to express their appreciation of the financial support provided by Austrian Federal Ministry for Science and Research (Ernst Mach-ASEA UNINET scholarship) and the infrastructure support of the Faculty of Computer Science at the University of Vienna. Also, the authors would like to thank the reviewers for their valuable suggestions, which have either been incorporated in this paper or will be the subject of current or future research.

References

1. Research, A.B.I.: The Mobile App Market will be Worth $27 Billion in 2013 as Tablet Revenue Grows (2013),
   https://www.abiresearch.com/press/
   the-mobile-app-market-will-be-worth-27-billion-in-
2. Gartner: Worldwide PC, Tablet and Mobile Phone Shipments to Grow 4.5 Percent in 2013 as Lower-Priced Devices Drive Growth (2013),
   http://www.gartner.com/newsroom/id/2610015
3. Apple Press: Apple - Press Info - Apple Reports Fourth Quarter Results,
   http://www.apple.com/pr/library/2013/10/
   28Apple-Reports-Fourth-Quarter-Results.html
4. De Oliveira, R., Cherubini, M., Oliver, N.: Influence of personality on satisfaction with mobile phone services. ACM Trans. Comput. Interact. 20, 1–23 (2013)
5. Chittaranjan, G., Blom, J., Gatica-Perez, D.: Who's Who with Big-Five: Analyzing and Classifying Personality Traits with Smartphones. In: 2011 15th Annu. Int. Symp. Wearable Comput., pp. 29–36 (2011)
6. Lane, W., Manner, C.: The Influence of Personality Traits on Mobile Phone Application Preferences. J. Econ. Behav. Stud. 4, 252–260 (2012)
7. Fishbein, M., Ajzen, I.: Belief, Attitude, Intention, and Behavior: An Introduction to Theory and Research. Addison-Wesley, Reading (1975)
8. Valentine, C.W.: Personality—A Psychological Interpretation (by Gordon W. Allport. London: Constable, pp. xiv + 588, price 16s.). Br. J. Educ. Psychol. 13, 48–50 (1943)
9. McCrae, R.R., John, O.P.: An introduction to the five-factor model and its applications. J. Pers. 60, 175–215 (1992)

10. Donnellan, M.B., Oswald, F.L., Baird, B.M., Lucas, R.E.: The mini-IPIP scales: tiny-yet-effective measures of the Big Five factors of personality. Psychol. Assess. 18, 192–203 (2006)
11. Bauer, H.H., Reichardt, T., Barnes, S.J., Neumann, M.M.: Driving Consumer Acceptance of Mobile Marketing: A Theoretical Framework and Empirical Study 6, 181–192 (2005)
12. Srisawatsakul, C., Papasratorn, B.: Factors Affecting Consumer Acceptance Mobile Broadband Services with Add-on Advertising: Thailand Case Study. Wirel. Pers. Commun. 69, 1055–1065 (2013)
13. Goldberg, L.R., Johnson, J.A., Eber, H.W., Hogan, R., Ashton, M.C., Cloninger, C.R., Gough, H.G.: The international personality item pool and the future of public-domain personality measures. J. Res. Pers. 40, 84–96 (2006)
14. Costa, P.T., MacCrae, R.R.: Psychological Assessment Resources, I.: Revised NEO Personality Inventory (NEO PI-R) and NEO Five-Factor Inventory (NEO FFI): Professional Manual. Psychological Assessment Resources (1992)
15. Saucier, G.: Mini-Markers: A Brief Version of Goldberg's Unipolar Big-Five Markers. J. Pers. Assess. 63, 506–516 (1994)
16. John, O.P., Srivastava, S.: The Big Five trait taxonomy: History, measurement, and theoretical perspectives. In: Pervin, L.A., John, O.P. (eds.) Handbook of Personality: Theory and Research, pp. 102–138. Guilford Press, New York (1999)
17. Tsaousis, I., Kerpelis, P.: The Traits Personality Questionnaire 5 (TPQue5). Eur. J. Psychol. Assess. 20, 180–191 (2004)
18. Cooper, A.J., Smillie, L.D., Corr, P.J.: A confirmatory factor analysis of the Mini-IPIP five-factor model personality scale. Pers. Individ. Dif. 48, 688–691 (2010)
19. Bernard, L., Walsh, R., Mills, M.: Ask once, tell: Comparative validity of single and multiple item measurement of the Big-Five personality factors. Couns. Clin. Psychol. J. 2, 40–57 (2005)
20. Aronson, Z.H., Reilly, R.R., Lynn, G.S.: The impact of leader personality on new product development teamwork and performance: The moderating role of uncertainty. J. Eng. Technol. Manag. 23, 221–247 (2006)
21. Woods, S., Hampson, S.: Measuring the Big Five with single items using a bipolar response scale. Eur. J. Pers. 390, 373–390 (2005)
22. Gosling, S.D., Rentfrow, P.J., Swann, W.B.: A very brief measure of the Big-Five personality domains. J. Res. Pers. 37, 504–528 (2003)
23. Credé, M., Harms, P., Niehorster, S., Gaye-Valentine, A.: An evaluation of the consequences of using short measures of the Big Five personality traits. J. Pers. Soc. Psychol. 102, 874–888 (2012)
24. Baldasaro, R.E., Shanahan, M.J., Bauer, D.J.: Psychometric properties of the mini-IPIP in a large, nationally representative sample of young adults. J. Pers. Assess. 95, 74–84 (2013)
25. Shafer, A.B.: Brief Bipolar Markers for the Five Factor Model of Personality. Psychol. Rep. 84, 1173–1179 (1999)
26. Cortimiglia, M., Ghezzi, A., Renga, F.: Mobile Applications and Their Delivery Platforms. IT Prof. 13, 51–56 (2011)

Intelligent Method for Dipstick Urinalysis Using Smartphone Camera

R.V. Hari Ginardi, Ahmad Saikhu, Riyanarto Sarno, Dwi Sunaryono,
Ali Sofyan Kholimi, and Ratna Nur Tiara Shanty

Department of Informatics, Institut Teknologi Sepuluh Nopember (ITS) Surabaya
hari@its.ac.id

Abstract. This paper introduces an intelligent method for helping people to maintain their healthy by doing a self urinalysis utilising a smartphone camera. A color sensing method using a smartphone camera is designed to determine the value of a reagent strip in a urinalysis dipstick. In the dipstick urinalysis, a color change in each reagent strip is examined. This color change is a result of the reaction of dipstick to the chemical contents of urine including pH, Protein, Glucose, Ketones, Leucocyte, Nitrite, Bilirubine, and Urobilinogen. Performing disptick urinalysis can be done in almost any places even on the very remote area where medical laboratory cannot be found, and it is much easier and cheaper than medical lab visit.

The proposed intelligent method includes a framework for color acquisition using a smartphone camera which covers the color management system, color correction, color matching, and quantification. The usage of RGB and CIELAB color space is discussed in the color management part. An automated color constancy approach is introduced to provide a better color correction, and a step-wise linear interpolation is introduced to better estimate the urinalysis value.

To implement this proposed method, a closed acquisition box does not required. Disptick capturing can be done directly with a smartphone camera in almost any normal lighting condition.

Keywords: color sensing, dipstick urinalysis, color constancy.

1   Introduction

Many methods have been applied to reduce or control the blood sugar for diabetes mellitus (DM) patients. A periodic postprandial glucose test and fasting plasma glucose test are among the most commonly practiced. Those require the patient to visit a medical laboratory. The test itself requires a blood sample from patient which is taken using a needle. Besides these blood glucose tests, an examination of the concentration of glucose in patient urine is performed through a method called urinalysis.

Urinalysis has been largely used as a method to determine the presence of chemical composition in urine. Currently, urinalysis can be performed using urine dipstick reagents. It can be done by placing the dipstick into a collected sample of urine and

Linawati et al. (Eds.): ICT-EurAsia 2014, LNCS 8407, pp. 66–77, 2014.

visually comparing the reactive color of each reagent with the dipstick color chart based on their color similarities. This manual interpretation has its limitation, including differences in a perception of color, differences in the lighting condition [1] and limitation on categorical or semi-quantitative assessment only [2].

Dipstick reader is a device used by most laboratories to interpret the dipstick results automatically. This device can minimize errors caused by lighting condition and differences in color perception, significantly [3]. However, its price is expensive for individual treatment. Considering the possibility of most smartphones to capture color image using its digital camera, a smartphone could be an alternative device to interpret urine dipstick results.

Automatic dipstick interpretation using a smartphone camera requires a method for color acquisition and a method of color similarity measurement to determine the corresponding chemical content concentration. Incosistencies may occur in lighting condition, focus, and angle of view [4]. A color constancy technique is used to approximate the original color of the captured image [5],[6]. It enables consistent color acquisition.

In this research, a framework for intelligent dipstick color acquisition using a smartphone is proposed. We analyse the color constancy measurement for image acquisition using a smartphone camera in a daily lighting condition without a closed box, and choose the optimal color constancy method to provide the color correction. An approach for smoother color quantification is done by introducing a stepwise linear interpolation [7]. It gives a better approximation to determine the reagent score of urine substances with quantitative assessment such as glucose.

2   Related Works

2.1   Color Space

A color space is a mathematical model to specify and visualize colors. Several color spaces have been defined namely RGB, CIEXYZ, CIELAB, HSV, and CMYK.

Color perception by human visual is defined by three basic attributes. Those are hue, saturation, and brightness [8]. Hue defines the differences in specific tone of color; such as red, green blue, or yellow; brightness defines the level of lightness or darkness of a color, while saturation describes the purity of a color.

RGB is a standard color space used by electronic imaging devices such as monitor, camera, and scanner [9]. It consists of red, green, and blue components which are represented in a three-dimensional cube. Each component has a value ranged from 0 to 255 [10]. RGB does not represent how the human visual interprets colors [11].

CIELAB is a color space defined by CIE (*Comission Internationale de l'Eclairage/International Commission on Illumination*) in 1976. It is used in most of digital image processing, because it describes the representation of human visual interprets the color.

2.2   Color Constancy

Digital color images which are taken by using a digital camera, is highly dependent on three things, they are illuminants, sensor sensitivity, and reflectance. It is represented by the following Equation 1.

$$fc(x) = m(x) \int_{\omega} I(\lambda)\rho_c(\lambda)S(x,\lambda)d\lambda, \qquad (1)$$

where fc is the captured color, I is illuminant, λ is wavelength, ρ_c is camera sensitivity, and S is the ability for reflecting lightness from the object,

Assuming the sensitivity ρ_c and the wavelength λ in different types of camera are constant, those variables can be neglected, therefore the differences in color acquisition will be highly dependent on the varieties of illumination.

Color constancy is a process to restore an image into a certain illumination value even if it is captured in different illumination conditions [6]. Color constancy plays significant roles when color recognition or quantification is required in an image acquisition with varieties of illumination such as colorimetric analysis[12][13][14], and it is also applied in *dipstick urine analysis.*

In general, color constancy process is begun with an evaluation of lighting source color and its intensity to determine the required color correction. The result is an image in which its color is corrected as it was captured with a white source color.

White Patch Retinex is one of the color constancy method based on the amount of illumination. It is done by using white color as a ground truth. This color is used to adjust the level of illumination [6]. It ignores the differences on reflectance value of the object. Other methods are uniform, non-uniform, and learning method. Uniform method is capable for image enhancement purpose.

Based on its complexity, Gijsenij[6] divided color constancy algorithms into three methods, namely stastistical method, gamut method, and machine learning. Statistical method has a lower computing complexity, but it is less accurate in correcting image with high variance such as real photos.

Another method, Grey-World, is a uniform [11] and statistical method. This method failed to correct an image with one dominant color such as leaf color image [11]. Gerson [15] improves the Grey-World by applying a segmentation first. An illumination correction is performed differently for each segment.

Grey World and White Patch uses low level of RGB values of an image. Van de Weijer, et all [16] proposed the usage of high level RGB which is derived from low level RGB Worlds, which is then named Grey Edge algorithm. However, Grey Edge is not optimal for images with one dominant color.

2.3   Color Distance Measurement

Color similarity can be done by measuring the distance between points on a geometry space. Several techniques to calculate distances on a geometry space are Euclidean distance, angle vector distance, Canberra distance, and Minkowski. However, Canberra distance and Minkowski distance perform poorly in color similarity for an image retrieval research [17].

Vector angle distance and Euclidean distance are mostly used for measuring color distance. Hue and saturation differences can be quantified well using Vector angle distance. While Euclidean distance quantifies well illumination intensity. Since Euclidean distance has the lower computational complexity, we prefer this technique as a first step to determine the color similarity.

3   Methodology

3.1   Proposed System

Our proposed system is shown in Fig.1. A test dipstick is captured by using a smartphone camera. Due to the lighting condition and the characteristic of the camera sensor, the color in the produced digital image might be different with the original color of tested dipstick. Therefore, color constancy measurement is needed to approximate its original color and perform an automated color correction. For each image capture, the whole dipstick is captured, containing a series of ten or more reagent color. To separate each reagent color into an individual image file, a cropping process is required. Those reagent color can be organized in a RGB color space or CIELAB color space.

Quantification is done by matching the tested color with its corresponding color chart based on their color similarity and retrieve the related chemical value. For qualitative or semi-quantitative urine analysis, a color similarity approach is adequate, however a further analysis is required for an absolute value determination. Concerning the stepped value in the color chart, a stepwise linear interpolation method is proposed. This interpolation method can estimate a more precise measurement value.

The result from above color quantification is used by the health monitoring system application. A prototype of this application has been built in an Android platform.

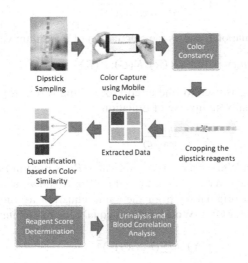

Fig. 1. Process Flow of the Proposed System

3.2   Color Constancy

The proper color constancy method is obtained by evaluating the existing methods. Evaluation is done by measuring the distribution of colors on each reagent in a specific color space.

A statistical range of color distribution in a reagent image is chosen to evaluate how the result is spread or fold-up. Range is used rather than variance since it provides a wider result [18] and it is more sensitive to outlier.

White Patch Color Constancy method is done by getting the maximum value of color from each color component (R, G, and B) as described in Equation 2.

$$Kmax = \max(max(R), max(G), max(B)) \tag{2}$$

After obtaining the maximum value, the ratio of each color component is calculated, as described in Equation 3.

$$Rc = \frac{\max(C)}{Kmax}, \tag{3}$$

where C is color of R,G,B color space.

After getting the ratio, the value range of each color component will be widened according to the ratio as described by Equation 4, in order to get the original color.

$$I(X) = R_c \times F_c(X) \tag{4}$$

As an improvement method from White-Patch, Grey-World [19] has a similar approach. Firstly it calculates statistical mean of each color element. An inversion is required as shown in Equation 5, where C is a color from RGB color space.

$$K(C) = \frac{1}{avg(avg(C))} \tag{5}$$

The following Equation 6 shows the calculation of maximum value K from K(C).

$$Kmax = \max(K(R), K(G), K(B)) \tag{6}$$

The result of $Kmax$ is used to find a ratio for scaling factor as given in Equation 7. This Equation is actually an inverse of Equation 3.

$$Rc = \frac{Kmax}{\max(C)} \tag{7}$$

Furthermore, as in White-Patch, this ratio value Rc is used in Equation 4. The pattern similarity between White-Patch and Grey-World shows that both methods are equivalent. They are originating from the same equation as shown in Equation 8, where p is equal to 1 for Grey-World and p is equal to ∞ for White-Patch.

$$I(X) = \sum (Fc(X))^p)^{\frac{1}{p}} \tag{8}$$

3.3   Quantitative Assessment

By its nature, reagents in dipstick urinalysis provides result in a stepped values. Glucose reagent for example, has a specific color for value 0, 2.8, 5.5, 14, 28 and >= 55.

Comparing the color in the tested dipstick to the series of color in the dipstick color chart and finding its similarity will select one of the closest color as the quantification result. This method is used in most dipstick reader device.

To improve the accuracy of dipstick color interpretation, a curve fitting approach is considered. This curve is used to estimate the value if the tested color lies between two reference colors in the color chart as shown in the following Fig. 2.

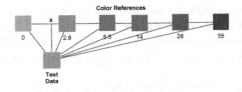

Fig. 2. Dipstick Color Interpretation

3.4   Stepwise Linear Interpolation

A stepwise linear interpolation is used to estimate the value between two given values. This interpolation is applied for each pair of neighboring color in the color chart. The distance between two colors in the color chart and the distance between a tested color and a color chart is evaluated in a cartesian coordinate system with three-elements of color space are used as the coordinate system. From the previous research[7], a CIELAB color space is chosen, therefore its color component L, a, b are mapped into a cartesian coordinate system. X, Y axis defines the level of a reagent, and the value of color component, respectively. Assessing the score of the tested reagent is described as follows:

1. Using euclidean distance, calculate the distance between two adjacent reference data, and the distance between a test data and each reference data using Equation 9, as shown in Fig. 3.

$$d = \sqrt{(\Delta L)^2 + (\Delta a)^2 + (\Delta b)^2} \, , \qquad (9)$$

where $\Delta L = L_{test} - L_{ref}$, $\Delta a = a_{test} - a_{ref}$, $\Delta b = b_{test} - b_{ref}$

2. Find a node n in reference data that has the shortest distance to test data. The value of n represents the location of the selected data.
    a. If n 1 is equal to 0, then the node is located on the first level. Assign the node number n as node "B" and the node number $n+1$ as node "C". Go to step 3.
    b. If $n+1$ is more than the numbers of reference data, then the node located is on the last level. Assign the node number n as node "C" and the node number n 1 as node "B". Go to step 3.
    c. Otherwise, this node is between two nodes. Continue to step 4.

3. Check if the distance between test data to node "B" is longer than the distance between node "B" and node "C", OR the distance between test data and node "C" is longer than the distance between node "B" and node "C", this test data is beyond the color chart range. Skip the next step and mark the test data as an error.

4. Calculate the distance of test data to node n 1 and the distance of test data to $n+1$. Find the shortest one and note the node.

5. If the resulted node is n 1, check whether the distance between test data and node n 1 is smaller than the distance between node n 1 and n. If it is true, denote n 1 as "B" and denote n as "C".

6. If the resulted node is $n+1$ check whether the distance between test data and node $n+1$ is smaller than the distance between node $n+1$ and n. If it is true, denote $n+1$ as "C" and denote n as "B".

7. If both of two conditions on step 5 and 6 above are not fulfilled, this test data is beyond the color chart range. Skip the next step and mark the test data as an error.

8. As shown in Fig. 4, the relationship between test data, B, and C is evaluated using trigonometry model to project the current test node position into its relative position between node B and C. Equation 6 is used for this evaluation model.

9. The tested reagent score can be assessed using Equation 11.

$$Cx = \frac{AB^2 - BC^2 - AC^2}{-2BC} \qquad (10)$$

$$\left(\frac{Bx}{Bc} \times (ScoreofC - ScoreofB) \right) + ScoreofB \qquad (11)$$

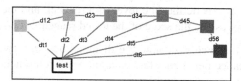

Fig. 3. Test Data and Reference Data Distances Calculation

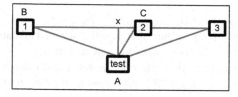

Fig. 4. The Relationship between Test Data, B, and C

4   Results and Analysis

4.1   Color Constancy

As shown in Table 2, White Patch technique able to reduce the range of inconsistency up to 63% of red component, 88% of green component, and 59% of blue component.

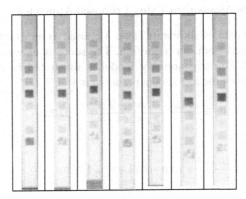

Fig. 5. Color Constancy using White Patch

Table 1. Color Constancy Result Using White Patch

	R	G	B
Original	**51**	**51**	**49**
Grey World	50	52	53
White Patch*	19*	6*	20*
Shades of Grey	51	52	50
Grey Edge	98	99	39
Gamut Mapping X-Derivation	93	105	46
Gamut Mapping Y-Derivation	86	113	45
Gamut Mapping 1st Order	104	111	40

4.2   Color Quantification Result for Glucose Reagent

A glucose estimation is chosen for color interpretation using our approach. A series of test data and reference data considered as the real color from reagent is prepared in Table 3. The reagent score assessment in ten samples is shown in Table 4. We provide quantitative assessment resulted from our approach, assessment by dipstick reader, and interpretation by human visual. The interpretation results produced by dipstick reader and human visual are in categorical values only, therefore the results of quantitative assessment cannot be compared exactly. Furthermore, we provide qualitative assessment to be evaluated.

Outlier data might occur from wrongly captured reagent or out-of-range colors as shown in Table 5, and it should be detected. We evaluate the assessment using our approach by comparing with the assessment using Euclidean distance and human visual. The system is able to determine the score of glucose for the first type of real data and recognise the rest as unwanted or outlier colors.

4.3   Reagent Score Assessment Using Proposed Approach

In this section, a test data as shown in Table 3 is used as an example to be measured by the formula resulted from our algorithm. The score is assessed and described by Equation 12 and 13. The trigonometry model is illustrated in Fig. 6. Proportional position determination of the tested data is shown in Fig. 7.

$$Cx = \frac{21.35^2 - 42.94^2 - 22.83^2}{-2 \times 42.94} = 22.23 \tag{12}$$

Score of Glucose =

$$\left(\frac{20.704}{42.94} \times (2.8 - 0)\right) + 0 = 1.3502 \tag{13}$$

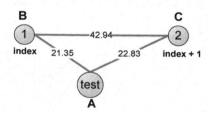

Fig. 6. The Relationship between Test Data, Reference Data 1, and 2

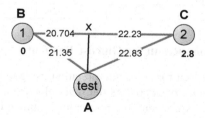

Fig. 7. Proportional position determination of the tested data

Table 2. Interpretation Result of Glucose Reagent

Level (mmol/L)	Reference Data
(0)	
± **(2.8)**	
+ **(5.5)**	
++ **(14)**	
+++ **(28)**	
++++ **(≥ 55)**	
Test Data	
Visual	– (0)
Dipstick Reader	– (0)
Quantitative	1.35

Table 3. Score Assessment Comparison in Several Samples

Sample	Quantitative	Qualitative	Dipstick Reader	Visual
1	1.35	– (0)	– (0)	– (0)
2	1.16	– (0)	– (0)	– (0)
3	1.24	– (0)	– (0)	– (0)
4	1.20	– (0)	– (0)	– (0)
5	1.32	– (0)	– (0)	– (0)
6	26.73	+++ (28)	+++ (28)	+++ (28)
7	42.12	++++ (≥ 55)	++++ (≥ 55)	++++ (≥ 55)
8	36.39	++++ (≥ 55)	++++ (≥ 55)	++++ (≥ 55)
9	2.23	± (2.8)	± (2.8)	± (2.8)
10	1.52	– (0)	– (0)	– (0)

Table 4. Interpretation Comparison Result of Outlier Data

Level (mmol/L)	Reference Data
1	
2	
3	
4	
5	
6	
Test Data	
Stepwise Linear Interpolation	Outlier
Visual	Outlier
Euclidean Distance	1

5   Conclusion

Using the proposed intelligent method for dipstick urinaysis, a self monitoring of blood sugar of diabetes mellitus patient can be done without examining the patient blood. This approach helps people in remote areas which have limited access to the hospital or medical labratory to maintain their health. Evenmore, this approach does not require any physical intervention compare to blood test, makes it painless alternative for blood sugar control. With the highly availability and cheaper dipstick reagent strips, the operational cost of this method is considered cheaper than bood test.

The accuracy of the color quantification using this digital approach is very high makes the automatic color acquisition using smartphone is possible, even in the various lighting conditions.

The further improvement is a challenge to improve the color constancy performance with an automatic color calibration or using a relative calibration technique.

Acknowledgment. This research is supported by Japan Indonesia Corporation Agency (JICA)-Predicts phase-2, group B2-6 and a research grant from the Ministry of Education and Culture, The Republic of Indonesia

References

1. Peele, J.D.: Evaluation of Ames Clini-Tek. Clinical Chemistry 23(12), 2238–2241 (1997)
2. Penders, J., Fiers, T., Delanghe, J.R.: Quantitative Evaluation of Urinalysis Test Strips. Clinical Chemistry 48(12), 2236–2241 (2002)
3. Tighe, P.: Laboratory-based quality assurance programme for near-patient urine dipstick testing. 1990–1997: development, management and results. Br. J. Biomed. Sci. 56, 6–15 (1999)
4. Capurso, J.: Mobile Document Capture: Scanner vs. Phone Camera. Xerox White Paper (2012)
5. Bianco, S., Ciocca, G., Cusano, C., Schettini, R.: Automatic color constancy algorithm selection and combination. Journal of Pattern Recognition 43 (2010)
6. Gijsenij, A., Gevers, T., Van De Weijer, J.: Computational color constancy: Survey and experiments. IEEE Transactions on Image Processing 20(9) (2011)
7. Shanty, R.N.T., Hari Ginardi, R.V., Sarno, R.: Interpretation of Urine Dipstick Results Based On Color Similarity Using Linear Interpolation Curve Fitting. In: IEEE International Conference on Computational Intelligence and Cybernetics, pp. 36–39 (2013)
8. Burns, B., Shepp, B.E.: Dimensional interactions and the structure of psychological space: The representation of hue, saturation, and brightness. Perception & Psychophysics 43(5), 494–507 (1988)
9. Süsstrunk, S., Buckley, R., Swen, S.: Standard RGB Color Spaces. In: The Seventh Color Imaging Conference: Color Science, Systems, and Applications, pp. 127–134 (1999)
10. Pascale, D.: A Review of RGB Color Spaces. The BabelColor Company, 5700 Hector Desloges, Montreal (Quebec), Canada H1T 3Z6 (2003)
11. CIE (Commission Internationale de l'Eclairage) (1978); Recommendations on Uniform Color Spaces. Color Difference Equations, Psychometric Color Terms (suppl. 2). CIE Publication, Paris Cedex 16, Paris, France, 68 (1791)
12. Iqbal, Z., Bjorklund, R.B.: Colorimetric analysis of water and sand samples performed on a mobile phone. Talanta 84(4), 1118–1123 (2011)
13. García, A., et al.: Mobile phone platform as portable chemical analyzer. Sensors and Actuators B: Chemical 156(1), 350–359 (2011)
14. Bianco, S., Schettini, R.: Color constancy using faces. In: 2012 IEEE Conference on Computer Vision and Pattern Recognition (CVPR). IEEE (2012)
15. Gershon, R., Jepson, A.D., Tsotsos, J.K.: From [R, G, B] to Surface Reflectance: Computing Color Constant Descriptors in Images. IJCAI (1987)
16. Van De Weijer, J., Gevers, T., Gijsenij, A.: Edge-based color constancy. IEEE Transactions on Image Processing 16(9), 2207–2214 (2007)
17. Androutsos, D., Plataniotis, K.N., Venetsanopoulos, A.N.: Distance measures for color image retrieval. In: IEEE Intrnational Conference on Image Processing, Chicago (1998)
18. Ebner, M.: Color constancy, vol. 6 (2007), http://Wiley.com
19. Buchsbaum, G.: A spatial processor model for object colour perception. Journal of the Franklin Institute 310(1), 1–26 (1980)

Empirical and Computational Issues
of Microclimate Simulation

Aida Maleki, Kristina Kiesel, Milena Vuckovic, and Ardeshir Mahdavi

Department of Building Physics and Building Ecology,
Vienna University of Technology, Vienna, Austria
{aida.gavgani,kristina.kiesel,milena.vuckovic,bpi}@tuwien.ac.at

Abstract. The dynamic variability of weather conditions and complex geometry and semantics of urban domain impose significant constraints on the empirical study of urban microclimate. Thus, numerical modeling is being increasingly deployed to capture the very dynamics of urban microclimate. In this context, the present paper illustrates the basic processes of calibrating and preparing a numerical model for the simulation of the urban microclimate.

Keywords: Urban climate, Modeling, Evaluation, CFD.

1   Introduction

Urban microclimate displays a considerable variance due to the differences in morphology and density of urban spaces and the thermal and radiative properties of surfaces [1,2]. Microclimate conditions are affected by two main parameters: the local weather conditions and the urban fabric at the very location [3,4]. Random weather patterns and the wide variances of the urban geometry impose significant limitations regarding purely empirical microclimatic studies such as simple on-site collection of weather data [5]. Hence, detailed numerical models are being increasingly deployed as they can provide additional information toward urban microclimate analyses. The numerical simulation thoroughly deals with the complexities and nonlinearities of the urban climate systems [2,6].

In this context, the present study addresses the use of numerical tools for the simulation of urban microclimates. As such, an increasing number of differing tools are becoming available for microclimatic modeling of urban areas [7]. Some tools are rather limited in terms of the range of pertinent variables they can consider. Other, more detailed tools display limitations in terms of domain size and resolution. Nonetheless, numerical models still present a valuable resource for the assessment of complex thermal processes in the urban field. For the purposes of the present contribution, we focus on a state of art CFD-based numeric simulation environment (ENVI-met [8]). We describe the general structure of ENVI-met, its features and limitations, and the model calibration process (including the application of sensitivity analysis).

Linawati et al. (Eds.): ICT-EurAsia 2014, LNCS 8407, pp. 78–85, 2014.
© IFIP International Federation for Information Processing 2014

2   Methodology

2.1   Overview of the Deployed Modeling Tool

The tool ENVI-met was selected as it has the capability to simulate the urban micro-climate while considering a relatively comprehensive range of factors (complex building shapes, vegetation and different types of pavements, etc.). The high-resolution output generated by this tool includes air, soil and surface temperature, air and soil humidity, wind speed and direction, short wave and long wave radiation fluxes, gas particles and many other important metrological factors.

ENVI-met 3.1 was deployed at the early stage of our inquiry. Additional simulations were run in version 4.0 and the results were compared.

General Structure. ENVI-met is a 3-dimensional non-hydrostatic model fit for the simulation of surface-plant-air interactions within urban environments. It is a micro-scale model with a time step between 1 to 10 seconds and resolution that ranges from 0.5 to 10 m, for the grid length (x) and the width (y). Height of the grids (z) can be more than 10 m. ENVI-met calculates the dynamics of microclimate during a diurnal cycle (24 to 48 hours) using the fundamental laws of fluid dynamics and thermodynamics [9]. An overview of the data flow within the ENVI-met is given in Figure 1.

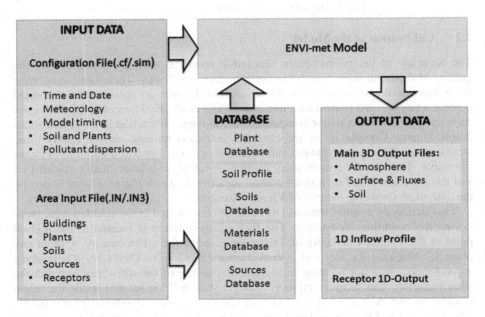

Fig. 1. The overview over the data flow within the ENVI-met

Model Layout. The ENVI-met model consists of three main components: 1D boundary model, 3D atmospheric model, and 1D soil model. The one dimensional boundary model expands from ground level to the height of 2500 m and defines the values of the model boundary. The Three-Dimensional atmospheric model incorporates rectangular grids with the dimension of x, y, and z. Δx and Δy are constant throughout the model, although Δz can be set to increase with the height of model. Every grid can be completely filled by a building volume or just by the air. The grid size of the one dimensional boundary model is the same as of the 3D model, but in the case of the 1D soil model, the vertical size of the grid is defined by the model. The 1D soil model consists of 19 grid units and is extended down 4.5 m below the ground surface. A schematic overview of the model layout is shown in Figure 2.

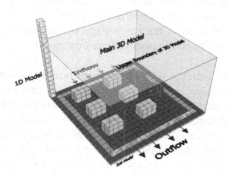

Fig. 2. The schematic overview of the model layout

2.2   Calibration of the Model

The accuracy of the microclimate simulation results is strongly dependent on the quality of the input data, and the initial/boundary conditions. Therefore, appropriate input data should be prepared for the simulation. Ideally, an optimization-supported approach can be used toward an automated model calibration process [10]. However, such an approach faces major computational challenges if applied in the urban simulation domain: Complexity of the climatic simulation models and the highly time-intensive simulation runs make comprehensive optimization-based calibration rather infeasible. Thus, in the present case, calibration relied on a heuristically guided trial and error process based on a small control area (as shown in Figure 3, area bound by the dashed rectangle) in the city of Vienna, Austria.

Two stationary weather stations (BPI and C*) are located in the selected area, monitoring the conditions constantly. The BPI weather station is located at the highest point of the Vienna University of Technology, above the urban canopy, without any obstacles blocking the sky –Sky View Factor (SVF) = 1. Therefore, it represents a good model receptor location to evaluate the ability of the software to predict the solar radiation. The second stationary weather station C* is located inside the urban canopy, at the height of 7 m, and records the weather condition continuously. The data obtained from this station was used to evaluate the accuracy of the simulation outputs for the urban canopy.

As it is shown in Figure 3, the input data of the simulation model is composed of two types of data, the weather data and geometry/materials of the area. Since the geometry of the area is not subjected to calibration, the geometrical model was

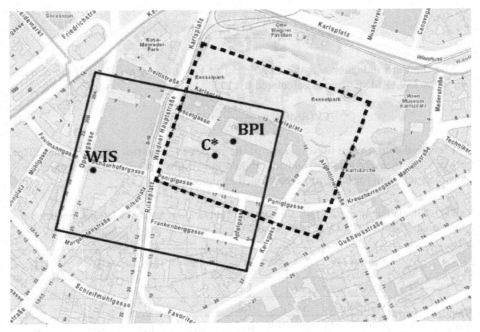

Fig. 3. The plan of the selected areas for model calibration and application

generated with relatively low resolution (the grid size equal to 5×5×2) to accelerate the calibration process.

In order to determine the optimal settings for the initial/boundary conditions, a number of trial runs were conducted. Several combinations of input variable options were probed until an acceptable convergence of the simulated and measured results was achieved.

To evaluate the offset between the modelling results and the values obtained through measurements, three different indicators were defined. First indicator was the *index of agreement* (d) suggested by (Willmott 1982). *Index of agreement* is a descriptive measure and can be applied to make Cross-Comparison between models as a relative and bounded measure. *Index of agreement* (d) is calculated as follows:

$$d = 1 - \frac{\sum_{i}^{n}(s_i - m_i)^2}{\sum_{i}^{n}(|s_i'| - |m_i'|)^2} \qquad 0 \le d \le 1 \qquad (1)$$

where $s_i' = s_i - \bar{m}$ and $m_i' = m_i - \bar{m}$, $\bar{m}$ is the mean value of measured variables, m_i is the measured variable, and s_i the simulated one.

The second used indicator was the *Root Mean Square Deviation* (RMSD) or *Root-Mean Square Error* (RMSE), a measure of the differences between outcomes of a model and the associated observed values. RMSE is a good measure to show the accuracy by comparing different prediction errors within a dataset, lower values indicate less error in prediction. It is calculated using the following formula:

$$RMSE = \sqrt{\frac{\sum_{i=1}^{n}(m_i - s_i)^2}{n}} \qquad (2)$$

And the third indicator was the *Coefficient of Variation of the Root Mean Square Deviation* CV (RMSE), and is calculated by:

$$CV(RMSE) = \left(\frac{RMSE}{\bar{m}}\right) \times 100 \qquad (3)$$

These indicators were used in each of the modelled scenarios to obtain the offset between the measured values and the simulation results concerning air temperature and solar radiation for both, aforementioned receptors.

Table 1. Simulation input data for various model calibration stages (simulations conducted for a location in Vienna, 22nd of July 2010, wind direction = 163°, relative humidity = 57%)

	Scenarios	0	Ia	Ib	II	III
Basic Input data	ENVI-met Version	3.1	3.1	4	4	4
	Wind Speed [m.s^{-1}]	0.2	2	2	2	2
	Initial Temperature [K]	301	303	303	303	303
	Solar Adjustment	1	0.82	0.82	0.82	0.82
	Specific Humidity [g/kg air^{-1}]	7	8	8	8	8
Buildings	Albedo Walls	0.2	0.4	0.4	0.4	0.4
	Albedo Roofs	0.2	0.4	0.4	0.4	0.4
Simple Forcing	Max temperature [K]	---	---	---	306.85	306.85
	Time of Max temperature	---	---	---	16:00	16:00
	Min temperature [K]	---	---	---	295.15	295.15
	Time of Min temperature	---	---	---	04:00	04:00
	Max relative humidity [K]	---	---	---	76	76
	Time of Max relative humidity	---	---	---	04:00	04:00
	Min relative humidity [%]	---	---	---	39	39
	Time of Min relative humidity	---	---	---	17:00	17:00
	Forcing	---	---	---	hourly	Min / Max

The calibration process proceeded as follows. Slight modifications to the starting model input assumptions for trial runs (Scenario 0 in Table 1) using ENVI-met 3.1 ("none-forcing" mode) resulted in the input data set of Scenario Ia and a better predictive performance. Subsequently, the use of the same input information (Scenario Ib) with the updated ENVI-met 4.0 further improved the results, albeit slightly. Since ENVI-met 4.0 introduced the possibility of user defined diurnal variations of atmospheric boundary conditions (forcing), allowing the creation of user specific weather scenarios, this new feature was tested within the Scenario II (hourly forcing). Again, an improvement was achieved. However, the forcing option with minimum and maximum air temperature values (Scenario III) did not result in improvements.

The respective statistics pertaining to the comparison of modelled and measured results are given in tables 2 to 4.

Table 2. d, RMSE, and CV (RMSE) for comparison of simulated temperatures with weather station measurements (BPI)

Scenarios	0	Ia	Ib	II	III
d	0.50	0.88	0.92	0.95	0.92
CV(RMSE) [%]	11.04	7.84	6.32	4.51	11.04
RMSE [K]	3.15	2.24	1.80	1.29	3.15

Table 3. d, RMSE and CV (RMSE) for comparison of simulated global solar irradiance values with measurements (BPI)

Scenarios	0	Ia	Ib	II – III
d	0.98	1.00	0.99	1.00
CV(RMSE) [%]	13.82	5.05	10.44	6.45
RMSE [W.m^{-2}]	73.81	27.00	55.79	34.45

Table 4. d, RMSE, and CV (RMSE) for comparison of simulated temperatures with measurements (C*)

Scenarios	0	Ia	Ib	II	III
d	0.67	0.91	0.94	0.97	0.95
CV(RMSE) [%]	9.25	6.89	5.30	3.36	10.04
RMSE [K]	2.64	1.97	1.51	0.96	2.87

Given these results, the input value set of scenario II was selected as the most appropriate one for the intended simulation studies.

2.3   Illustrative Use of the Calibrated Simulation Model

The Model. To illustrate the application of the calibrated model, a slightly larger urban domain was selected (see Figure 3, rectangle with continuous boundary).

The size of the modelled area was 296 by 296 m, which allowed for the complex building structure to be modelled in higher detail. Two stationary weather stations are located within the boundaries of the study area. First one is BPI and the second one WIS ("Wien, Innere Stadt"), operated by the Central institute for meteorology and geodynamic (ZAMG).

Sensitivity Analysis of the Grid Size. In order to examine the sensitivity of the simulation results with respect to the grid size, three identical models with different grid sizes (3x3x2), (4x4x2), and (5x5x2), were generated. The weather data collected by WIS was used for forcing the diurnal variations of atmospheric boundary conditions. The 3x3x2 model produced erroneous results, thus it was ignored. The models with 4 m and 5 m grid sizes, named 4m-w and 5m-w respectively, were used for further analysis. These models were used to compute temperatures for a day in summer 2011 at two locations corresponding to BPI and WIS weather station locations. Table 5 shows the summary of the statistics pertaining to the comparison of the simulation results with the corresponding measurement results. The difference between the two is not significant, but due to a higher resolution and potential of having more detailed outputs, model with 4 m grid size was selected as the most appropriate for subsequent inquiries.

Table 5. Predictive performance of the calibrated urban microclimate model

Model	grid size	Forced by	at BPI			at WIS		
			RMSE	CV	d	RMSE	CV	d
4m-w	4m	WIS-data	1.54	5.54	0.95	0.88	3.10	0.99
5m-w	5m	WIS-data	1.59	5.74	0.95	0.78	2.75	0.99

Future Applications. A process was demonstrated to calibrate a comprehensive urban microclimate simulation tool with the aid of limited measurement data. The calibrated tool displays improved predictive performance and can be used to evaluate the effect of different urban intervention scenarios (e.g. mitigation measures pertaining to the Urban Heat Island phenomena) on the respective temporal and spatial variance of urban microclimate. Such interventions imply certain changes to specific urban features such as areas of vegetation, bodies of water, surface properties of constituent materials in the urban canyon, etc. The outcome of such parametric simulation-based analyses of urban intervention scenarios can provide valuable feedback to the decision makers toward more sustainable urban environment design and maintenance practices.

References

1. Oke, T.R.: The energetic basis of the urban heat island. Quarterly Journal of the Royal Meteorological Society 108(455), 1–24 (1982)
2. Arnfeld, A.J.: Two decades of urban climate research: a review of turbulence, exchanges of energy and water, and the urban heat island. International Journal of Climatology 23(1), 1–26 (2003)
3. Katzschner, L., Thorsson, S.: Microclimatic Investigations as Tool for Urban Design. In: 7th International Conference on Urban Climate, Yokohama, Japan, 29 June-3 July (2009)
4. Kurbjuhn, C., Goldberg, V., Westbeld, A., Bernhofer, C.: Impact of different urban structures on the microclimate in the city of Dresden, Germany, EGU General Assembly 2010, Vienna, Austria, May 2-7 (2010)
5. Bourikas, L., Shen, P., James, A.B., Chow, D.H.C., Jentsch, M.F., Darkwa, J., Bahaj, A.S.: Addressing the Challenge of Interpreting Microclimatic Weather Data Collected from Urban Sites. Journal of Power and Energy Engineering 1, 7–15 (2013)
6. Yao, R., Luo, Q., Gao, Y.: Simulation of urban microclimates. In: CIBSE ASHRAE Technical Symposium, Imperial College, London, UK, April 18-19 (2012)
7. Mirzaei, P.A., Haghighat, F.: Approaches to study Urban Heat Island – Abilities and limitations. Building and Environment 45, 2192–2201 (2010)
8. Huttner, S., Bruse, M.: Numerical modelling of the urban climate – A preview on ENVI-met 4.0. In: 7th International Conference on Urban Climate ICUC-7, Yokohama, Japan, 29 June-3 July (2009)
9. Elnabawi, M.H., Hamza, N., Dudek, S.: Use and evaluation of the ENVI-met model for two different urban forms in Cairo, Egypt: measurements and model simulations. In: 13th Conference of International Building Performance Simulation Association, Chambéry, France, August 26-28 (2013)
10. Taheri, M., Tahmasebi, F., Mahdavi, A.: A case study of optimization-aided thermal building performance simulation calibration. In: 13th Conference of International Building Performance Simulation Association, Chambéry, France, August 26-28 (2013)

A Distributed Generic Data Structure for Urban Level Building Data Monitoring

Stefan Glawischnig, Harald Hofstätter, and Ardeshir Mahdavi

Vienna University of Technology
Department for Building Physics and Building Ecology
Karlsplatz 13, 1040 Vienna, Austria
{stefan.glawischnig,harald.e259.hofstaetter,
ardeshir.mahdavi}@tuwien.ac.at

Abstract. Building a generic data structure that handles building re-alated data at an urban scale offers certain challenges. Real world entities must be captured in an environment that allows for the communication of relevent data. The associated software components must be maintainable and reliable. The present contribution describes efforts to enhance a well tested building monitoring framework to handle building data at an urban scale. This requires the development of a distributed, generic and enhancable data store, as well as the conceptualization of a modular and scalable application architecture. The scalable data store is introduced, as well as the modularization process of the application logic, including data handling and communication routines. Furthermore, the concept of Virtual Datapoints and Virtual Datapoint Collections enables urban entities (for instance buildings) to communicate their status to the system in an effective way.

Keywords: Urban Monitoring, Generic Data Structure, Distributed Systems.

1 Introduction

Urbanization and sustainability strategies (e.g. Europe 2020) raise the need to address ecologic and economic issues on an urban level. A building is not to be recognized as a discrete entity but as part of a dynamic system, that interacts with it's surroundings [1]. The urban environment produces massive amounts of data, not all of them related to buildings, but nevertheless influential. For instance, it is common practice to integrate weather forecasts and historical weather data into a building's Energy Management and Control System (EMCS) as well as to utilize it as base data for light and thermal simulation [2][3]. Pang et al. introduced a framework to compare the building performance with predictive values of an EnergyPlus simulation in real time [4]. The EMCS transmits data to the simulation via a BACnet interface. The presented approach offers a promising solution for accessing EnergyPlus models in real time, but the resulting data collection is very specific and task oriented.

Linawati et al. (Eds.): ICT-EurAsia 2014, LNCS 8407, pp. 86–95, 2014.

Previous research by the authors concentrated on the development of a vendor and platform independent building monitoring system [5][6]. The motivation was to develop a storage concept that handles building related data in an unified way, regardless of the initial data format or producer. Nevertheless, a majority of research projects focused on various stages of a building's life cycle and considered buildings as singular entities. For instance, the SEMERGY project developed a concept to help remove data-related disincentives and to facilitate the integration of building performance evaluation in building design and retrofit [7]. On a lower application level, monitoring related projects elaborated a generic data structure that is used in a number of simulation applications and building data representations.

1.1 Monitoring System Toolkit

The Monitoring System Toolkit (MOST) was designed to offer platform and vendor independent access to building data and follows a distributed and service oriented approach [9]. It offers the possibility to integrate third party data (EMCS, BMS, etc.) by implementing a connector interface [8]. The toolkit consists of various decoupled services (Fig. 1).

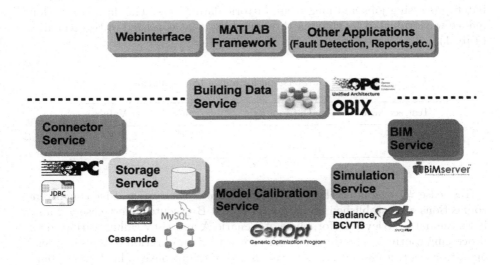

Fig. 1. Monitoring system service structure

A building data service establishes connections between client applications and the system backend. To handle input data sources generically, all data is organized by datapoints and zones. A datapoint is mapped to any data producing entity, for instance a physical sensor, an entire building's accumulated energy demand or a person. Zones define administrative entities that establish location contexts for datapoints. Data might be added to the data store via three methods: a connector implementation, the service layer or a virtual datapoint [10]. The connector service introduces a vendor independent communication process with common building management systems and building automation technologies. Furthermore, connector implementations enable the integration of historical datasets, for instance weather data that was generated by a CSV export. Beside connectors, the framework's functionality is exposed via two standard industry protocols, OPC Unified Architecture, and Open Building Information Xchange (oBIX). Additionally, a custom REST and RPC implementation offer data access. Entities that access the service layer always read or write one specific datapoint value at a time. The initial data store consists of a relational database (MySQL) that defines entities for datapoints and zones with the respective configurations, as well as an data entity that stores the imported or recorded values. A data tuple has the following form: $< tuple\_id, timestamp, value, datapoint\_ref >$.

Data access (read, write) as well as data processing routines (calculating periodic values) are encapsulated in database procedures. To minimize the security risk of SQL injections, database access is restricted to these procedures. To fit different use cases data replication was introduced. The partitions on the master machine were optimized to provide live data access. Two slave machines handeled batch processing jobs and long term, historic data access. The database performance was evaluated by running three testcases that consisted of two scenarios (Tab. 1).

Table 1. Database performance test scenarios

Test scenario	#Datapoints	#Zones	#Values
A	$10*10^3$	$2.5*10^3$	$2.5*10^6$
B	$10*10^4$	$2.5*10^4$	$>2.5*10^6$

Test case #1 evaluated the write performance of the system. Five concurrent connections are established and scenario A and B executed. Test case #2 analyzes the data retrieval performance of scenario A and B by calling various data processing routines. The third test case consists of an iteration of the same read operations as test case #2, as new values are simultaneously added every 50ms. The benchmarking results showed no significant performance bottlenecks. For instance, test case #1 performed a maximum write throughput of 1000 values per second. A thorough documentation of the performance tests can be found at [11].

To test the suitability of the application and data store architecture at an urban scale five buildings were concurrently administrated by one framework instance. Physical sensor's recording intervals are specified in seconds and can theoretically be defined as $r = [1, 1844674407e + 19]$ for r $\in \mathbb{N}$ sec.

Practically sensor recording intervals $r = [3600, 86000]$ sec. This corresponds to a range between one hour and an entire day. Currently, the database handles $8.0*10^4$ transactional commits, $1.3*10^5$ inserts, $7.0*10^5$ selects and $5.3*10^5$ updates per day. Managing multiple buildings simultaneously revealed performance problems that were not identified by the performance tests. Adding and retrieving data, especially functions that conduct calculations, resulted in severe performance incursions and eventually even crashed the system. Aside the given technical limitations the lack of framework modularization appeared as an conceptual limitation.

1.2   Approach

The initial framework implementations were intended for single building use and did not support several buildings or even entire cities. Although it followed a web-based approach with well defined layers, the framework was only deployable as one compound application, entailing problems both in scalability and reliability. To provide an environment that operates at an urban scale and thus allows simultaneous handling of buildings, as well as the establishment of relationships between buildings and building data required the solution the following conceptual problems:

- Optimize and generalize the data store
- Modularize the application into standalone components
- Establish a data communication process between components

2   Data Storage

The database was designed to offer a generic data store for one building. Sensor measurements as well as other building related data (for instance user data, sensor configurations, datapoint definitions, etc.) are stored in one central database. Experience showed that up to 90% of the database-induced network traffic was caused by read and write operations on the measurement data table. Resolving this issue was established by these steps:

- Seperating the highly dynamic data entities from the configuration data
- Move data processing routines to a higher application layer to allow parallelization at software level

As can be seen in Fig. 2 four objects show a highly dynamic behaviour: datapoint, data, zone and warning. A datapoint maps a physical entity, be it a sensor, a person or a calculated aggregation object (e.g. accumulated temperature of a room). A zone administrates datapoints and handles access right management. A zone might refer to a room or a floor. The data table holds all imported and recorded data tuples. If an error occurs (for instance a broken batch process, or a broken sensor) it is written into the warning table.

To store these data generically, multiple relational and non-relational data stores were analyzed regarding their performance, scalability and data model. Following requirements were elaborated to ensure scalability:

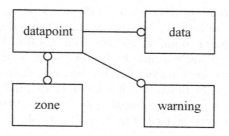

Fig. 2. High-traffic producing database entities. Excerpt from the ER diagram.

- Ensure transaction security for sensitive master data (for instance configurations, user information)
- Flexible and extensible data model
- High read and write performance for the datapoint value data
- High read performance for the master data store

Due to potential security risks [12] of non-relational stores and the fact that relational databases are well established in productive environments the master data should be kept in a relational environment. Transaction security is not a crucial condition for storing datapoint values. In practice, sensors send a vlaue every minute or even second. In case a measurement gets lost, the effect on an entire day's data is negligible. As to the reduction of transactional checks, NoSQL stores provide better access speeds than relational databases. Bogdan et al. compared various databases and found that NoSQL databases provided better read and write latencies in a write intensive environment than relational databases [13]. Specifically Cassandra [14] is well established in high load environments [15] and was therefore chosen to be integrated in the framework. Another benefit of NoSQL data stores is the schemaless data model that allows the extension of the database schema at runtime. As mentioned before, collecting building related data at an urban level must be generic, easily extensible and flexible. To store generic data of various data sources, the need to refer to a datapoint was removed from the tuple definition. A generic data tuple is thus defined as $< tuple\_id, timestamp, value >$. The context of the measurment is established via a partition or node id and is not stored in the tuple itself. To develop a sustainable scaling strategy, the data store requirements were calculated as followed: To allow real-time data analysis a short recording interval is chosen. It is assumed that one entity contacts the database every second. This results in $3.15*10^7$ operations per year. The tuple size is calculated by considering the data type (64-bit IEEE-754 floating point) and the Cassandra specific overhead of 39 bytes per tuple. This results in 1.18 GB data per year for one sensor. Considering the Cassandra specific maximum file size (5 TB) specifies that one file can hold 4237 years of data per sensor. NoSQL stores distribute data randomly accross nodes. To increase read performance, 30-day shards are introduced. One monthly shard can hold $2.6*10^6$ measurements.

3 Application Architecture

3.1 Highly Reliable and Scalable Design

A scalable architecture is realized by a distributed system that is based on loosely coupled modules for

- data processing
- data retrieval
- data persistence
- data access
- data presentation

To reduce the database load that is induced by processing routines [9] the responsible logic was extracted from the database and moved to an indepedent module in a higher application layer. To realize modularity, scalability and to increase reliability on the application level, modules can be deployed redundantly and on different machines. Stateless core components allow new instances to be added during runtime, for instance to serve load peaks (i.e. monitoring occupancy during the morning rush hour) and to be removed in the cooling-down period.

Such a concept implementation requires a central distribution mechanism that routes requests between modules, respective physical machines that are distributed via a city's buildings. As the proposed framework is written in Java, all components are bundled by a Message Oriented Middleware (MOM) that is accessed via a Java Message Service (JMS) API.

The communication process is established by dynamically created queues (point-to-point) and topics (publish-subscribe). On binary protocol level, the Advanced Message Queuing Protocol (AMQP) was chosen, as it is secure, reliable, high performant and vendor-neutral [16].

Every single instance of redundantly deployed components listens to the same queue. The transferred request messages are always handled by exactly one instance (the one who initially took the message from the queue). Changes in datapoint values can be observed by subscribing to a datapoint's topic. That specific topic is identified via the owning datapoint's unique name and the prefix "*OBSRV_*": *OBSRV_<dp-name>*. For instance, the activity observation of the specific sensor "con1" (contact sensor) would be realized via the topic id *OBSRV_con1*.

3.2 Virtual Datapoint Collections

Datapoints always represent physical entities (for instance sensors). As has already been mentioned, the concept of virtual datapoints realizes data representations that are not bound to a physical sensor. For instance, this might be the on demand calculation of an entire building's accumulated energy consumption, average temperature or requesting values from a weather forecast. As VDPs work at a very low application level and behave like native datapoints, other application parts can use them transparently. VDPs can be seen as plug-in components and are extensively used to support data simulation, model calibration and data prediction. The implementation of a virtual datapoint is deployed as a distinctive component and is accessed through a dynamically created queue which's name is derived from the VDP's type by prefixing "*DATA_*": *DATA_<type>*. For instance, a VDP that provides Radiance [17] simulations could use the queue *DATA_RADIANCE*. VDPs that implement the same type share the same queue which realizes support for multiple instances and hence increases reliability and availability.

VDPs offer a way to establish communication between buildings and components within one application context which is an essential step towards a distributed urban monitoring and simulation structure. However, VDPs can only return a primitive value, for instance the aforementioned overall energy consumption. To decrease configuration effort for buildings we introduce Virtual Datapoint Collections (VDC) that combine a set of VDPs to a bundle. This bundle is configured once and applies standardized calculations on the respective building's data. A VDC uses the same communication process and protocols as described in the VDP concept.

3.3   Security

Application access is only granted to registered users. By default, communication between components is entirely encrypted via SSL to prevent eavesdropping of sensitive data. Data access is handled at zonal level but will not be introduced in the scope of this paper.

4   Results

The application is divided into four layers. As Fig. 3 shows, these are a persistance, service and presentation layer, as well as a service adapter that offers access to the data collection via standardized protocol implementations (OPC Unified Architecture, oBIX, REST). The presentation layer consists of two client applications, a web client and a mobile client. The service layer implements the BMS business logic (data processing) and the VDCs. The persistence layer manages the relational master data store and the NoSQL datapoint value store. To allow a distributed module deployment, all components communicate via the MOM.

Fig. 4 illustrates the specific module implementations of the persistence layer after the revising process. Configuration and security sensitive data is stored in a MySQL database. Sensor configurations are partly kept in BIM models that are managed by a BiMserver instance. The metadata-module handles configuration requests and accesses the two databases. Datapoint values are either stored in the well tested initial MySQL environment, in a Cassandra cluster or a neo4j graph database. Neo4j support was partly introduced to monitor relationships between urban entities, partly to store sensor measurements. The configuration data and datapoint data is merged and connected in the persistence-module.

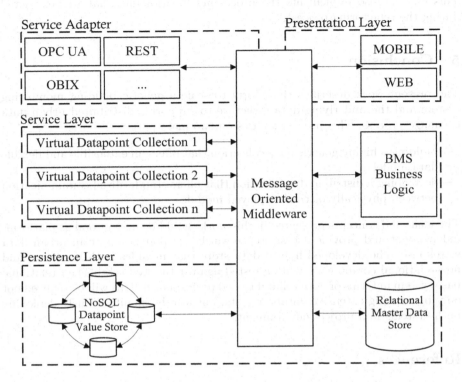

Fig. 3. The proposed urban monitoring framework's system architecture

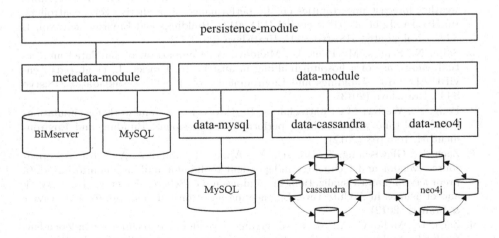

Fig. 4. Persistence layer: specific module implementation

This module also implements the processing functionality that was extracted during the refactoring process.

5   Conclusion

The present work describes the efforts to scale a generic building monitoring system and the underlying data structure to support a distributed urban data exchange process. This process focuses on two main parts:

- building a highly generic data collection that offers an extensible and flexible data model
- developing a distributed application that offers standardized communication between physically distinct deployed modules

The ideas and concepts presented in this work should be understood as platform-independent and provide a first step towards the realization of an urban data warehouse. The developed hybrid data store that includes both relational and non-relational components will be tested against the well established relational base system in terms of both reliability and performance. This will be realized not only by running extensive database tests, but also by simultaneously deploying both systems in a project environment.

References

1. Mahdavi, A.: From Building Physics to Urban Physics. In: Stadt: Gestalten, ch. 34, pp. 181–186. Springer Vienna (2012)
2. Schuss, M., Tahmasebi, F., Vazifeh, E., Mahdavi, A.: The influence of online weather forecast uncertainties on the performance of predictive zone controllers. In: Hraska, J., et al. (eds.) enviBUILD 2013 - Buildings and Environment, vol. 1. STU - Nakladate#318;stvo STU, Bratislava (2013)
3. Saipi, N., Schuss, M., Pont, U., Mahdavi, A.: Comparison of simulated and actual energy use of a hospital building in austria. In: Hraska, J., et al. (eds.) enviBUILD 2013 - Buildings and Environment, vol. 1. STU - Nakladate#318;stvo STU, Bratislava (2013)
4. Pang, X., Wetter, M., Bhattacharya, P., Haves, P.: A framework for simulation-based real-time whole building performance assessment. Building and Environment 54, 100–108 (2012)
5. Zach, R., Glawischnig, S., Hönisch, M., Appel, R., Mahdavi, A.: Most: An open-source, vendor and technology independent toolkit for building monitoring, data preprocessing, and visualization. In: Gudnason, G., Scherer, R., et al. (eds.) eWork and eBusiness in Architecture, Engineering and Construction, pp. 97–103. Taylor & Francis (2012)
6. Zach, R., Mahdavi, A.: Most - designing a vendor and technology independent toolkit for building monitoring, data preprocessing, and visualization. In: Proceedings - First International Conference on Architecture and Urban Design - 1-ICAUD, EPOKA Univ.; Dep. of Arch., vol. 1, Epoka University Press (2012)

7. Wolosiuk, D., Ghiassi, G., Pont, U., Shayeganfar, F., Mahdavi, A., Fenz, S., Heurix, J., Anjomshoaa, A., Min Tjoa, A.: Semergy: Performance-guided building design and refurbishment within a semantically augmented optimization environment. In: Hraska, J., et al. (eds.) enviBUILD 2013 - Buildings and Environment, vol. 1, STU - Nakladate#318;stvo STU, Bratislava (2013)

8. Zach, R.: An open-source, vendor and technology independent toolkit for building monitoring, data preprocessing, and visualization. PhD thesis, Abteilung Bauphysik und Bauökologie, Institut für Architekturwissenschaften (2012)

9. Zach, R., Hofstätter, H., Glawischnig, S., Mahdavi, A.: Incorporation of run-time simulation-powered virtual sensors in building monitoring systems. In: Building Simulation 2013 - 13th International Conference of the International Building Performance Simulation Association, IBPSA, pp. 2083–2089. IBPSA (2013)

10. Zach, R., Tahmasebi, F., Mahdavi, A.: Simulation-powered virtual sensors in building monitoring systems. In: Mahdavi, A., Martens, B. (eds.) Proceedings of the 2nd Central European Symposium on Building Physics, Vienna, Austria, September 9-11, vol. 1, pp. 657–664 (2013)

11. Zach, R., Schuss, M., Bräuer, R., Mahdavi, A.: Improving building monitoring using a data preprocessing storage engine based on mysql. In: Gudnason, G., Scherer, R., et al. (eds.) eWork and eBusiness in Architecture, Engineering and Construction, pp. 151–157. Taylor & Francis (2012)

12. Okman, L., Gal-Oz, N., Gonen, Y., Gudes, E., Abramov, J.: Security Issues in NoSQL Databases. In: 2011 IEEE 10th International Conference on Trust, Security and Privacy in Computing and Communications (TrustCom), pp. 541–547 (2011)

13. Tudorica, B.G., Bucur, C.: A comparison between several NoSQL databases with comments and notes. In: 2011 10th Roedunet International Conference (RoEduNet), pp. 1–5 (2011)

14. Cassandra. The apache cassandra project (January 2014)

15. an, J., Haihong, E., Le, G., Du, J.: Survey on NoSQL database. In: 2011 6th International Conference on Pervasive Computing and Applications (ICPCA), pp. 363–366 (2011)

16. Vinoski, S.: Advanced message queuing protocol. IEEE Internet Computing 10(6), 87–89 (2006)

17. Radiance. A validated lighting simulation tool (January 2014)

Toward a Data-Driven Performance-Guided Urban Decision-Support Environment

Neda Ghiassi, Stefan Glawischnig, Ulrich Pont, and Ardeshir Mahdavi

Vienna University of Technology,
Department of Building Physics and Human Ecology Vienna, Austria
{neda.ghiassi,stefan.glawischnig,ulrich.pont,
amahdavi}@tuwien.ac.at

Abstract. The present contribution briefly represents the structure and main features of SEMERGY, a performance-guided multi-objective building optimization environment, supported by Semantic Web technologies. It establishes the importance of urban-scale performance considerations, discusses particular features of urban data, and suggests a framework to upscale the SEMERGY approach towards development of a data-driven performance-guided urban decision support environment. The suggested task-based ontology framework can facilitate data and knowledge sharing within the domain of urban performance inquiries.

Keywords: GIS. Semantic Web Technologies. Ontologies. Data-Driven. Building Performance. Urban Performance. Urban planning. Sustainability. Information Systems.

1   Introduction

Building Performance Evaluation (BPE), defined as "the process of obtaining knowledge about building performance and using the feedback to improve buildings" originated in the 1960's [1]. Ever since, efforts have been directed towards development and refinement of tools and methods to assess and/or predict the performance of buildings in terms of use of natural resources, contribution to undesired environmental phenomena, and user comfort.

Despite the advances in the development of Building Performance Evaluation (BPE) tools over the past decades, the adoption of such tools to support and guide design decisions has been relatively slow and their implementation mostly limited to certification purposes [2, 3]. Among stated reasons for the insufficient adoption of such tools for sustainable planning and informed decision making were non-technical, socio-cultural barriers such as lack of financial justification, lack of motivation, or professional skepticism and prejudices [3, 4]. Stated technical barriers include the discordance of the available tools with the capabilities and expectations of the design community [5] and complexities related to data availability and accessibility, which render the process of data provision for BPE applications cumbersome, error prone and time consuming [6].

Linawati et al. (Eds.): ICT-EurAsia 2014, LNCS 8407, pp. 96–107, 2014.

The SEMERGY project [7, 8], was a recent (2011-2013) research and development effort, intended to address the data-related technical barriers to the integration of performance assessment tools in the building design process. SEMERGY aimed to explore the potential of semantic web technologies to facilitate the process of data accumulation and entry for building performance evaluation and optimization.

Although integration of performance evaluation in the design of new buildings and retrofit projects supports informed decisions and sustainable design, an approach focused on individual buildings may not be singularly sufficient to insure energy efficiency and sustainability of the built environment. Certain performance aspects of the built environment, such as microclimatic conditions (air flows, incident solar radiation) or energy flows are only properly grasped, when buildings are regarded as active agents within a network of interconnected and inter-influential elements, as opposed to independent entities isolated from the context. Such a perspective reveals opportunities and issues, which may have been overlooked, when considering a single building.

On the other hand, the decision to improve the performance of a building depends mainly on the owner, who may be affected by the previously-stated barriers such as lack of motivation or financial means for such an undertaking. As such performance guided decision making has to be endorsed also at a higher level by local/national authorities to support conception of sustainability strategies, efficient allocation of resources and identification of opportunities. Intended as a comprehensive software environment to facilitate performance-guided decision making at various scales, this top-down perspective was also included in the initial description of the SEMERGY project as a future use-case. As such, a second phase of the SEMERGY project has been planned to support performance-enhancing decisions transcending the scale of a single building, through utilization of Semantic Web technologies to harness the potential of the immense pool of web-based urban data.

The present contribution briefly represents the structure and main features of the SEMERGY environment, discusses the particularities of urban scale performance considerations, offers an overview of related previous research, and suggests a framework to upscale the SEMERGY approach towards development of a data-driven performance-guided urban decision support environment.

2   SEMERGY Structure and Features

As mentioned earlier, the primary objective of the SEMERGY project was to help remove data-related disincentives to integration of BPE in building design process. SEMERGY intended to explore developmental opportunities toward effective evaluation environments for comparative assessment of alternative design and retrofit options [7], focusing in particular (as proof of concept) on the scattered pool of web-based building product and material data.

The overall structure of SEMERGY is depicted by Figure 1. SEMERGY consists of three main components: The User Interface, which is reponsible for the communication of user intents and initial design to the program, the Reasoning Interface, which includes the relevant performance computation methods and the optimization algorithms, and most importantly, the Semantic Interface which provides links between SEMERGY and web-based data sources to facilitate semi-automatic extraction of appropriate data.

Efficient generation of BPE-compliant models is hampered in part by the missing link between users' simplified component representations (e.g., "external wall", "window") versus the complexity of specifications of real world products. In other words, users are obliged to map such simple notions of building components to appropriate real world products that meet calculation procedures' informational requirements [8]. In optimization tasks, the model iteratively assumes alternative sets of properties and is subjected to the evaluation procedures, which lead to the identification of the optimal set of solutions according to the estimated values of functional, ecological, and economical performance indicators.

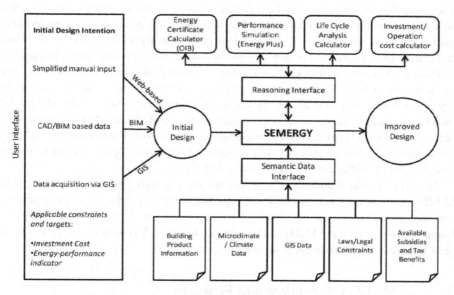

Fig. 1. SEMERGY structure

The SEMERGY project's approach to bridge the gap between required and available AEC data sets was based on two main pillars: First, creation of a compact and versatile ontology of building products compliant with a shared perception of AEC concepts; Second, mapping of the scattered building product information resources on the web to this ontology [8].

To achieve an acceptable building data representation, compatible with the requirements of BPE methods of various resolutions and precisions, and in accordance with the notion of the design community, various building data models were studied and several BPE applications were reversed analyzed. These efforts led to the development of a coherent and sufficient view of building data, known as the SEMERGY Building Model (SBM) [9]. Further on, an ontology of building products and construction materials was created, which structurally complied with the developed model. This ontology was linked to data sources, which represent building products by their various physical attributes, production data and cost information. The property inheritance structure of the ontology allowed the systematic enrichment of the extracted data with additional properties, which are obvious to human observer (such as stability of shape), yet essential for rule based queries that support the semi-automatic identification of design alternatives, in accordance with user-specified preferences and constraints [10, 11, 12, 13]. The same method can theoretically be applied to other relevant types of web-based data such as building codes, financial subsidies, microclimatic data, building systems, etc. Since these domain ontologies are developed based on a unique perception of a building (SBM) or mapped to it, they can be combined to cater for various types of inter-domain inquiries. For instance, building systems data and building product data can be used in combination to identify the optimal retrofit strategies for a historical building, according to budget limitations expressed by the user.

This approach is expected to encourage the utilization of BPE methods to guide design and retrofit of individual buildings by overcoming certain structural barriers to data accumulation and entry. However, data availability and accuracy issues still hamper the systematic implementation of such a method due to the wide distribution of data sources and lack of standard data formats acknowledged by various data providers.

3   Particularities of Urban Data

3.1   Data size

Decision making and development of policies and strategies at an urban scale require dependable, robust, and up-to-date information. A large amount of potentially useful data exists on-line. Much of this data is either partially available or is intended to be made available to the public as part of open data initiatives (e.g., demographics, detailed representations of buildings and their various properties, transportation patterns, energy flows, natural resources, etc.). Analyzing this large source of rather unstructured data with conventional methods may not lead to the discovery of opportunities, detection of systemic problems or leakages of resources.

3.2   Data Diversity

City is an ecosystem composed of intertwined and interacting sub-systems, which may be physical or virtual, static or dynamic, predictable or complex, alive or inanimate. Buildings, climate and natural context, transport systems, media, energy production and distribution networks, financial and legal structures, inhabitants, etc. are all various subsystems forming this ecosystem. The entire system's performance is a product of the various chains of events within different sub-systems and the interactions between them. Data pertaining to these various sub-systems is collected and organized by domain specialists from different sectors. The availability of data on various aspects of the city presents an immense potential for conception of inter-domain sustainability strategies. Nonetheless, due to this diversity, navigation through the available data – to identify data sources relevant to a certain inquiry – may not be trivial.

3.3   Multiple Perceptions, Multiple Representations

Urban data is produced and accumulated by various stakeholders, each perceiving the city from a domain-specific point of view. These varied perceptions are also observed at the scale of single buildings, where involved disciplines are much less divergent than at the urban scale. The fundamental differences in common and standard building representation schemas such as IFC [14] and gbXML [15] are rooted in these multiple viewpoints. However, the scale and scope of building related data makes a mapping between these perceptions possible (See, for example, [16]).

At the urban scale, though, the wide range of disciplines and authorities involved in the production and storage of the urban data, results in a large number of parallel perceptions of the urban environment. The available data sources may capture certain aspects of the urban environment and ignore others, view the same physical phenomena from different perspectives, or use different terminologies to express the same concept. A building for instance may be viewed as an active agent from the urban performance point of view, as a mere physical obstruction from the mobility point of view or ignored completely by a botanist.

Analyzing this data to find strategies to overcome various types of problems respond to different inquiries or identify hidden opportunities is hampered not only by the overwhelming size and diversity of the available data, but also by the multiplicity of perceptions and representations, according to which the data is produced.

In order to effectively utilize urban data, it needs to be properly structured and presented in a coherent and interoperable form. The effectiveness and efficiency of Semantic Web technologies to organize and structure web-based building related data has been tested and approved through the SEMERGY experience. However, to up-scale this method to the urban level, the above-mentioned particularities of urban data have to be considered.

3.4   Data Availability and Currentness

A data-driven approach to decision making, requires substantial data to support implemented analytical methods. Despite the existence of various types of urban data, certain computational methods or optimization tasks may have informational requirements not met by the existing data sources. Furthermore, time is a significant aspect of a large portion of data pertaining to the built environment. Collection of such data occurs in different intervals, resulting in various temporal resolutions.

Certain computational methods may require resolutions of data unsupported by the existing data collection structures. Facilitation of collection and storage of urban data in required temporal resolutions is fundamental to any data-driven endeavor.

4   Related Work

Use of ontologies to capture and structure urban data was discussed in the field of Geographical Information Systems (GIS) by Fonseca and Egenhofer [17] in the late 1990's, leading to the suggestion of Ontology-Driven Geographical Information Systems (ODGIS) as means to share urban knowledge and data [18]. Fonseca and Egenhofer identified "the lack of formal methods to reuse knowledge and data" as a major obstacle hampering the utilization of existing data and knowledge. They support an object-oriented view of the world to represent geographic entities and propose a system-architecture with four main components. These components are data ontologies, the container (domain model), data warehouses and the User Interface. The user selects the desired type of data by browsing the ontologies through the User Interface. The ontology server provides pointers to relevant data warehouses. The container communicates with the data warehouses commanding the extraction of the desired information while maintaining the ontological hierarchies and structure, serving the data to the end user [17]. In a similar attempt, Pundt and Bishr [19] demonstrate the effectiveness of ontologies in enhancement of interoperability is a specific information community in the field of GIS.

Wiegand and Garcia [20], explore the potential of a task-based Semantic Web model to help automate the discovery of web-based data sources, thereby, facilitating the rapid generation of task-appropriate models. They argue that certain tasks such as crisis management activities require the same types of data, regardless of the location of the event. Establishing formal relationships between a type of task and the types of data sources needed for its completion, adds a level of organization to the data, allowing for the rapid retrieval of the desired data, given the intended task and location. In other words, they extend the work of Fonseca and Egenhofer by establishing links between various GIS-related tasks and the types of data stored in different databases, reducing user effort in the development of the model.

Sharing the same perception or committing to the same conceptualization of the object under study is a pre-condition of data sharing and integration. In order to overcome the predicament of parallel perceptions and expressions, in this case of the urban environment concepts, different solutions have been extensively discussed, which are beyond the scope of this paper [21, 22, 23].

Ongoing research conducted by the authors, concerns communication processes of urban entities (for instance buildings, people, and smart infrastructure). Integrating diverse and distributed data sources establishes the need for a modular and extensible data store design. Experiences in building related data handling [24] shows that these requirements are hardly met by common building data collections. To ease the rigid structure of these static data models, other data storage mechanisms are considered (for instance non-relational). By modifying common databases, a generic and scalable data store is developed that can hold any kind of data. Relational concepts cannot provide a solution for this issue.

5   Proposed Framework

Based on the experience of the SEMERGY project and the above mentioned research activities, the present contribution would suggest a twofold approach to bridge the informational gap between building scale and urban scale performance evaluation requirements. The proposed strategy, on one hand, utilizes ontologies to structure the available urban data repositories with a task-based approach; and on the other hand, addresses the low-level issues of data collection and storage, where the requirements of the task are not met by available data sources.

A globally acknowledged ontology of the urban environment data shared by all involved disciplines and data providers may be an ideal solution to the data accessibility and heterogeneity issues. However, such a solution, given the diversity of the urban data and the variety of domain representations is non-trivial, to say the least. Even if such a comprehensive urban model (encompassing informational requirements and vocabularies of all involved disciplines and sectors) was possible to develop, the complexity of the schema would render its navigation a daunting task.

Definition of a domain, in our case the domain of energy performance of the urban building stock, reduces the scope of the data substantially, however not enough to warrant a manageable degree of complexity. Specifying defined tasks within this domain helps provide a manageable framework for the development of task-based data ontologies, which facilitate automatic creation of task-based models of the desired geographic location or boundary.

Given the multi-disciplinary nature of nearly any urban performance inquiry, such task-based ontologies must not only acquire data pertaining to various fields, but also define a common basis to associate these various data structures with one another to provide data interoperability. The resulting ontology presents a network of Linked Data relevant to the specified task. Different task-ontologies defined in a certain domain include in all likelihood shared data-sources. Given the inter-connected nature of each ontology, such data overlaps establish links between various task-ontologies resulting in the gradual formation of a network of Linked domain Data.

On the other hand, the existing pool of data can be augmented with virtual (calculated) data and/or qualitative information through inclusion of the intermediate or final results of the performance-operation within the task-ontology. This provides a base for exchange of field knowledge through previously formed interoperable (mapable) task-ontologies .

Figure 2 illustrates the proposed ontology structure for two tasks within the same domain. Each task involves two sub-tasks, for accomplishment of which certain data types are required. Each data type is referenced to one (or multiple) datasets belonging to various databases. Based on the geographic location or boundary of the intervention case, the appropriate portion of data from the referenced dataset can be extracted. Different subtasks within a certain task or sub-tasks of different tasks may share data requirements (e.g., sub-task 1.2 and 2.1 both utilize dataset B1). If the compatibility issue of the shared dataset with the general schema of one task ontology is solved (for instance through use of a mediator to translate data to the right format), the interoperability of the translated dataset with the second ontology is simultaneously achieved. This diminishes the need for redevelopment of translation methods and mapping schemas for various applications, which share some informational requirements. If various tasks include similar sub-tasks, the results of that specific sub-task linked to one task-ontology can be directly used in the second task (knowledge sharing), provided that the geographic perimeter of the first task includes that of the second.

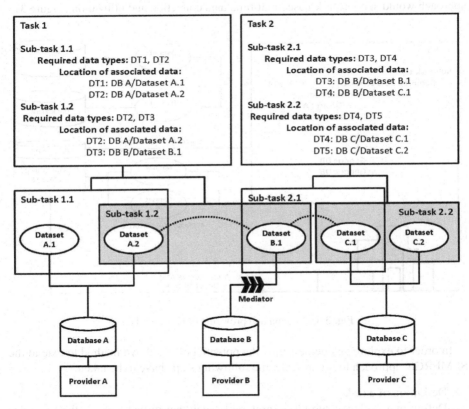

Fig. 2. Proposed task ontology structure

The above schema would help reorganize the existing data to surmount the challenge of web-based data navigation for a specific task. However, data availability issues (within the limits of the task at hand) must be solved before the computational procedures can utilize the data. Each building typically maintains its own data store. These stores handle similar data, however it is not possible to integrate the data in a generic structure. In the majority of cases this is not caused by differences in the data typology but simply by differences in the data storage concepts. Generalizing data stores facilitates automated enhancement of data models at runtime, suitable to solve a certain task. In case certain types of data required by the task are not available, the ontology assumes the generic database as the source of data, thereby issuing a request for the collection of the missing data. Collection and storage of unknown urban Big Data can be supported by generic storage concepts. Custom data might be stored in generic databases regardless of the data model. Such databases do not have a fix structure. Rather, the data model is extended at runtime to fit the incoming information. Regarding the importance and size of imports, new nodes might be added on demand.

Requested data types are collected via automated search routines (i.e. web crawl) and made available to the computational procedure through the ontology. Such an approach would support task-based real-time data collection and utilization (Figure 3).

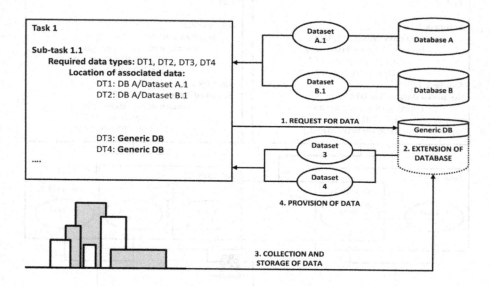

Fig. 3. Collection and provision of required data

In order to explore and demonstrate the potential of the above method to extend the SEMERGY approach to urban scale, the following steps have to be taken.

1. Definition of a task
2. Definition of relative sub-tasks (preferably such that further tasks in the same domain may be supported by the outcomes of these sub-tasks)
3. Identification of required data types
4. Identification of associated existing data-bases and missing data
5. Identification of an ontological representation compliant with the involved datasets and the task in hand (where such a unique structure does not exist, a convenient representation is to be selected in accordance with the data composition and the task nature)

6. Development of methods or mediators to help represent data from non-compatible sources in the above-mentioned vocabulary and structure
7. Integration of the extensible database as a generic container of the missing data in the developed ontology
8. Automatic readjustment of the generic data structure to the required data
9. Collection and storage of the required yet missing data
10. Integration of computational and visual analytics methods to accomplish the desired sub-tasks (and ultimately task), using the developed task ontology
11. Organization of the intermediate and final results under new ontology classes linked to the original data
12. Development of an appropriate interface to support user interaction

6 Conclusion

Sustainable design and retrofit of the built environment requires software solutions to facilitate integration of performance assessment and optimization in the design process. Such software solutions should cater for interventions at building scale, as well as at larger (neighborhood and urban) scales. SEMERGY is a recent research and development effort, aimed at addressing the data-related barriers to performance-based design by exploring the potential of Semantic Web technologies towards utilization of the abundant, yet ill-structured web-based data. Ongoing work intends to extend and augment SEMERGY so as to transcend building scale performance optimization towards urban scale.

Various characteristics of urban data including the overwhelming size, diversity, and multiplicity of perceptions and representations hamper the efficient use of such data in urban performance analysis and optimization tasks. Based on the SEMERGY experience at building scale and previous research on implementation of ontologies (Linked Data concept) for semi-automatic generation of domain models in the field of GIS, a twofold approach was proposed to overcome the data navigation challenge. A task-based approach to creating domain ontologies reduces the scope of the data to a manageable size. Moreover, such an approach provides a strong basis for exchange of previously structured data and knowledge derived from related tasks, within a shared geographical boundary.

Despite the importance of organizing the available yet unstructured data, such a top-down approach is not sufficient. The process of data collection and storage should be supported by generic, efficient, and sizable data structures to tackle the low-level urban data issues. Integration of such databases in the task-based ontology facilitates the task-based automatic retrieval of the missing data for computational purposes.

Once such a data structure is in place, various intervention scenarios can be simulated and optimization techniques may be employed to identify the best course of action in response to objectives pertaining to energy efficiency, environmental performance, and spatial quality of urban domains. Such a data-driven approach could alter conventional problem-solving trends, actively engage stakeholders, accelerate change, and support realization of long term goals.

Acknowledgements. The SEMERGY project (first phase) was funded under the FFG Research Studio Austrian Program (grant No. 832012) by the Austrian Federal Ministry of Economy, Family and Youth (BMWFJ). In addition to the authors, the SEMERGY team includes: A. M. Tjoa, F. Shayeganfar, A. Anjomshoaa, S. Fenz, J. Heurix, T. Neubauer, C. Sustr, M. Taheri, D. Wolosiuk, K. Hammerberg, and A. Wurm.

References

1. BSRIA Topic Guides- Building Performance Evaluation. BSRIA Limited, Berkshire (2011)
2. Hensen, J., Djunaedy, E., Radosevic, M., Yahiaoui, A.: Building Performance Simulation for Better Design: Some Issues and Solutions. In: de Wit, M.H. (ed.) Proceedings of the 21th Conference on Passive and Low Energy Architecture, vol. 2, pp. 1185–1190. Eindhoven University of Technology, Eindhoven (2004)
3. Pang, X., Hong, T., Piette, M.A.: Improving Building Performance at Urban Scale with a Framework for Real-Time Data Sharing. Report. Ernest Orlando Lawrence Berkeley National Laboratory, San Diego (2013)
4. Alsaadani, S., Bleil De Souza, C.: The Social Component of Building Performance Simulation- Understanding Architects. In: Wright, J., Cook, M. (eds.) Proceedings of the 2012 Building Simulation and Optimization Conference, Loughborough, pp. 332–339 (2012)
5. Attia, S.: State of the Art of Existing Early Design Simulation Tools for Net Zero Energy Buildings: a Comparison of Ten Tools. Université catholique de Louvain, Louvain La Neuve (2011)
6. Mahdavi, A., El-Bellahy, S.: Efforts and Effectiveness Considerations in Computational Design Evaluation: a Case Study. Building and Environment 40(12), 1651–1664 (2005)
7. Mahdavi, A., Pont, U., Shayeganfar, F., Ghiassi, N., Anjomshoaa, A., Fenz, S., Heurix, J., Neubauer, T., Tjoa, A.: SEMERGY: Semantic Web Technology Support for Comprehensive Building Design Assessment. In: Gudnason, G., Scherer, R. (eds.) eWork and eBusiness in Architecture, Engineering and Construction, pp. 363–370. Taylor&Francis, Reykjaví (2012)
8. Mahdavi, A., Pont, U., Shayeganfar, F., Ghiassi, N., Anjomshoaa, A., Fenz, S., Heurix, J., Neubauer, T., Tjoa, A.M.: Exploring the Utility of Semantic Web Technology in Building Performance Simulation. In: Proceedings of BauSIM 2012, pp. 58–64. Universität der Künste Berlin, Berlin (2012)
9. Ghiassi, N., Shayeganfar, F., Pont, U., Mahdavi, A., Heurix, J., Fenz, S., Anjomshoaa, A., Tjoa, A.M.: A Comprehensive Building Model for Performance-Guided Decision Support. In: Mahdavi, A., Martens, B. (eds.) Proceedings of the 2nd Central European Symposium on Building Physics, pp. 35–42. Vienna University of Technology, Vienna (2013)
10. Ghiassi, N., Shayeganfar, F., Pont, U., Mahdavi, A., Fenz, A., Heurix, A., Anjomshoaa, A., Neubauer, T., Tjoa, A.M.: Improving the Usability of Energy Simulation Applications in Processing Common Building Performance Inquiries. In: Sikula, O., Hirs, J. (eds.) Simulace Budov a Techniky Prostredi. Ceska Technika - nakladatelstvi, Brno (2012)
11. Shayeganfar, F., Anjomshoaa, A., Heurix, J., Sustr, C., Ghiassi, N., Pont, U., Fenz, S., Neubauer, T., Tjoa, A.M., Mahdavi, A.: An Ontology-Aided Optimization Approach to Eco-Efficient Building Design. In: Proceedings of the 13th Conference of International Building Performance Simulation Association, Chambery, pp. 2194–2200 (2013)

12. Pont, U., Shayeganfar, F., Ghiassi, N., Taheri, M., Sustr, C., Mahdavi, A., Heurix, J., Fenz, S., Anjomshoaa, A., Neubauer, T., Tjoa, A.M.: Recent Advances in SEMERGY: a Semantically Enriched Optimization Environment for Performance-Guided Building Design and Refurbishment. In: Mahdavi, A., Martens, B. (eds.) Proceedings of the 2nd Central European Symposium on Building Physics, pp. 35–42. Vienna University of Technology, Vienna (2013)

13. Heurix, J., Taheri, M., Shayeganfar, F., Fenz, S., Pont, U., Ghiassi, N., Anjomshoaa, A., Sustr, C., Neubauer, T., Mahdavi, A., Tjoa, A.M.: Multi-Objective Optimization in the SEMERGY Environment for Sustainable Building Design and Retrofit. In: Mahdavi, A., Martens, B. (eds.) Proceedings of the 2nd Central European Symposium on Building Physics, pp. 35–42. Vienna University of Technology, Vienna (2013)

14. Building Smart, http://www.buildingsmart-tech.org

15. gbXML, http://www.gbxml.org/aboutgbxml.php

16. Bazjanac, V.: IFC BIM-Based Methodology for Semi-Automated Building Energy Performance Simulation. In: Rischmoller, L. (ed.) Proceedings of the 25th CIB W78 Conference: Improving the Management of Construction Projects Through IT Adoption. Universidad de Talca, Santiago (2008)

17. Fonseca, F.T., Egenhofer, M.J.: Ontology-Driven Geographic Information Systems. In: Bauzer Medeiros, C. (ed.) zth ACM Symposium in Geographic Information Systems, Kansas (1999)

18. Fonseca, F.T., Egenhofer, M.J., Davis Jr., C.A., Borges, K.A.V.: Ontologies and Knowledge Sharing in Urban GIS. Computer, Environment and Urban Systems 24(3), 232–251 (2000)

19. Pundt, H., Bishr, Y.: Domain Ontologies for Data Sharing- an Example from Environmental Monitoring Using Field GIS. In: Computers and Geosciences, vol. 28, pp. 95–102. Elsevier (2002)

20. Wiegand, N., Garcia, C.: A Task-Based Ontology Approach to Automate Geospatial Data Retrieval. Transactions in GIS 11(3), 335–376 (2007)

21. Bergamaschi, S., Castano, S., De Capitani di Vimercati, S., Montanari, S., Vincini, M.: An Intelligent Approach to Information Integration. In: Guarino, N. (ed.) Formal Ontology in Information Systems. IOS Press, Amsterdam (1998)

22. Rodríguez, M.A., Egenhofer, M., Rugg, R.D.: Assessing Semantic Similarities among Geospatial Feature Class Definitions. In: Včkovski, A., Brassel, K.E., Schek, H.-J. (eds.) INTEROP 1999. LNCS, vol. 1580, pp. 189–202. Springer, Heidelberg (1999)

23. Bishr, Y.: Overcoming the Semantic and other Barriers to GIS Interoperability. International Journal of Geographic Information Science 12(4), 299–314 (1998)

24. Zach, R., Schuss, M., Braeuer, R., Mahdavi, A.: Improving Building Monitoring Using a Data Preprocessing Storage Engine Based on Mysql. In: Gudnason, G., Scherer, R., et al. (eds.) eWork and eBusiness in Architecture, Engineering and Construction, pp. 151–157. Taylor & Francis (2012)

Knowledge Management: Organization Culture in Healthcare Indonesia

Dana Indra Sensuse[1], Yudho Giri Sucahyo[1], Siti Rohajawati[2], Haya Rizqi[1], and Pinkie Anggia[1]

[1] Computer Science Faculty,
University of Indonesia, Depok, Indonesia
{dana,yudho}@cs.ui.ac.id, {pinkie.anggia.id,cold.ryz}@gmail.com
[2] Dept. of Information System,
Bakrie University, Jakarta, Indonesia
siti.rohajawati@bakrie.ac.id

Abstract. Nowadays organizations realize that knowledge is an important asset to achieve a competitive advantage. In the favor of that, it is necessary for organizations to manage and utilize the knowledge as much as possible through knowledge management (KM). KM concept is not only used in large companies, but also has begun to be adopted by healthcare organization in an effort to improve the quality of services. Managing knowledge is not easy, a lot of factors to consider, one of which is the culture of the organization. Organizational culture is defined as a set of practices, values, and assumptions held by members of the organization and are able to influence the behavior of the organization [12, 13]. According to Kim Cameron and Robert Quinn (2006), organizational culture can be examined using 'Organizational Culture Assessment Instrument' (OCAI) which has a framework, called the competing value framework (CVF). This framework consists of four culture types i.e. clan, adhocracy, market, and hierarchy. In this research, we found that healthcare organization in Indonesia have developed a dominant culture-style. It is a mix of the market and hierarchy. In addition, we also discuss the relationship of four culture types with KM, and six dimensions of organizational culture.

Keywords: Organizational Culture, Knowledge Management, Healthcare Organization.

1 Introduction

Today, organizations are competing to be more creative, innovative, and competitive in order to survive in the competitive business world [1]. In achieving a competitive advantage, knowledge becomes the most important asset in the organization as compared to other assets [2]. Knowledge can be trusted to make the action taken and the individual organizations more effectively and efficiently so as to stimulate the emergence of innovations to improve the quality of the products and services of the organization [3]. Therefore, organizations need to manage, identify, deploy, and exploit their knowledge assets to take advantage of such knowledge as much as possible [4].

Linawati et al. (Eds.): ICT-EurAsia 2014, LNCS 8407, pp. 108–118, 2014.

Knowledge management (KM) defines the process of doing what needs to be done to manage knowledge resources [5]. KM can also be defined as a process to manage, store, distribute, and use knowledge [3]. KM can improve availability and access to valuable knowledge, provide it at the right time and at the right people, and be able to make the organization to adapt to new market conditions rapidly [4]. Managing knowledge is not easy. This is because many factors need to be considered outside of the knowledge itself that affect the success or failure of KM, one such factor is the organizational culture. Organizational culture is considered as a foundation in KM and serves to understand how an organization behaves and gains competitive advantage [9]. However, organizational culture can act not only as an advocate but also inhibiting the activity of KM [6, 9]. Therefore, organizations need to understand the organizational culture that is embedded in the organization to be able to create an effective KM [9]. It is very important to do so, because the organizational culture can affect the way individuals in learn and share knowledge [6, 9].

Application of KM is not only used in large companies or manufacturing industry, but also has begun to be adopted in the hospital industry in an effort to improve the quality of services [3]. Hospital industry is an industry that is rich in knowledge, but unfortunately this knowledge is not utilized properly [7]. According to Gray and Densten successful organization is not caused by the amount of knowledge possessed by an organization, but rather due to the dynamic social processes that affect the application and development of knowledge within the organization [6]. According Hemmelgarn, et al. in Saame et al., in industries engaged in services such as hospitals, organizational culture affects the nature and quality of services provided, where the quality of these services is one indicator of the success of the organization [8]. Based on these two concepts, it can be concluded that the organization needs to develop a culture that encourages the sharing of knowledge. It should be triggered in order to achieve organizational success [6, 8].

Based on the above, it is known that the concept of KM cannot be separated from the culture of the organization. This is the foundation of this research. In this study, we discuss the relationship or influence of organizational culture on KM, especially in the hospital industry. The concept of organizational culture was adopted from the concept of Competing Value Framework (CVF) proposed by Cameron and Quinn (2006). This concept divides organizational culture into four types i.e. clan, adhocracy, market, and hierarchy. The purpose of this study was to identify the culture type or culture-style of healthcare organization in Indonesia. We also needed to find out the Dominant Characteristics, Organizational Leadership, Management of Employee, Organization Glue, Strategic Emphases, and Criteria of Success.

2   Knowledge Management in the Hospital Industry

Knowledge has been considered as an important asset in the organization as the primary source of gaining competitive advantage [2, 10]. KM includes the management of knowledge from the knowledge discovered, created, codified, transferred or shared and used [5,10]. Since 1990, many organizations define and develop a knowledge management focus to align individual-individual, processes and technology, so that the organization can successfully create, capture, share, and use traditional knowledge required [11].

Hospital industry is an industry that is rich in knowledge. However, it has the lack of attention and awareness of members in the field of making maximum use of the knowledge yet [7]. In this industry, KM is defined as the alignment of individuals, processes, and technology to optimize information, collaboration, expertise, and experience necessary to drive growth and performance of the organization [11]. KM in the industry can also be defined as the formation, modeling, division, operation, and translation of knowledge in the hospital industry to improve the quality of services to patients [7]. The goal of knowledge management is to provide knowledge optimally, timely, and effective for all stakeholders in wherever and whenever they need to assist them in taking the right decision and quality [3, 7]. The application of KM principles is believed to improve performance in terms of both medical and hospital operations [11].

3   Organizational Culture

Organizational culture is defined as a set of norms, beliefs, values, and assumptions held by members of the organization and influence the behavior of the organization [12, 13]. According to Schein in Wiewiora, et al., organizational culture comprises several levels: artifacts, values and basic assumptions [9]. Artifacts are things that can be seen in his form as the physical layout, attitude or manner of a person talking to another person, and other physical objects such as archives, products, and annual reports. Values are norms, ideologies, and philosophies that exist in the organization. The basic assumption is made up of events that have occurred in the organization that determines the perceptions, thoughts, feelings, and behaviors. Of the three levels, the value is the most easily and frequently studied to understand the cultural context of the organization as it provides a deep understanding of the social norms that define the rules of social interaction [9]. In organizations, in order to act and make decisions, assessment is mostly influenced by the behavior of the members of the organization [12].

Several studies have shown that organizational culture can establish a pattern of interaction in the context of social interaction and establish a norm within the organization. Therefore, culture can affect the way people communicate and share knowledge [9]. Thus, organizational culture influences the behavior of members of the organization, learning and development, creativity and innovation, and KM [1]. According to Yun, the type of organizational culture can affect one's attitude in using or adopting KM system [4]. But in practice, it is rare to find an organization that only has a culture [6]. Hence, it is necessary to more in-depth analysis to determine the effect of each type of organizational culture on KM.

4   Relationship Organizational Culture with KM

KM provides a way to capture the existing knowledge in the organization with the advanced principle of sharing knowledge. However, the desire to share knowledge or not is in the hands of individuals. The desire of individuals to share knowledge depends on the culture in the organization, whether that culture encourages knowledge sharing or not [5]. Organizational culture plays an important role in the organization, because it can be a barrier or an advocate of knowledge generation and knowledge sharing [5, 6, 9]. Culture in the hospital industry tends to focus on the internal environment and emphasis on stability, as well as having clear rules [8]. However, this culture may be different depending on the ownership of the hospital. According Seren and Baykal in Saame et al., private hospitals more emphasize on cooperative culture, while government hospitals more emphasize on cultural hierarchy [8]. To better understand the types of organizational culture, there are many models that can be used for example Schein models, Schwartz, Hofstede, O'Reilly, and the Competing Values Framework (CVF) [13]. CVF in the hospital industry is the most commonly used model to investigate the influence of organizational culture on the performance of the hospital.

This framework was developed by Cameron and Quinn where in the framework of organizational culture distinguished into two dimensions, namely the structure and focus [12, 13]. Dimensional structure is divided into the stability and flexibility. This dimension describes the difference between organizations that seek to maintain a consistent pattern of behavior and organizations that tries to provide the freedom for members to develop their own behavior [12]. The focus dimension is divided into internal focus and external focus. Internal focus has its emphasis on internal factors within the organization such as member satisfaction, while the external focus emphasizes the organization's ability to run well on the environment [12]. Furthermore, Cameron and Quinn states "to the left-side describes the internally focused of organization (what is important for the organization, how do the organization wants to work) and to the right-side, the organization describes the externally focused of the organization (what is important for the outside world, the clients, the market)" [15]. Based on these dimensions, CVF resulted in a cultural profile that includes four basic types/domains of organizational culture [12, 13, 14]. Type of organizational culture is clan, adhocracy, market, and hierarchy. The four type of culture is illustrated in Figure 1.

Fig. 1. Competing Value Framework [13]

Based on the four types of culture (clan, adhocracy, market, and hierarchy) and litera-ture study on the effect of organizational culture on KM, we described the relation of each of them with the concept of KM.

4.1   Clan Culture and KM

This culture emphasizes the high degree of flexibility and a focus on internal organi-zation [12, 14]. Organization is seen as a convenient place to work together and have higher family properties [1, 13]. In this culture, leaders act as mentors or facilitators for subordinates [13]. The characteristic of this culture is the emphasis on participa-tion teamwork, loyalty, cohesion and morale. The types are also often referred to as human relations or relationship-based [9, 14].

According to Lopez et al., Saeed et al. in a culture that is collaborative as clan cul-ture helps shape knowledge to improve the exchange of knowledge among members of the organization [16]. This is in line with the concept proposed by Gray and Dens-ten, which states that the clan culture is related to the socialization process of know-ledge sharing [6]. Clan culture has a positive relationship with knowledge creation and has a considerable influence on knowledge sharing [2, 16].

The main objective of KM is to gain a competitive edge so that the organization can compete with other organizations. One of the indicators to measure the success of KM is to measure the performance of the organization. According to Safran et al. in Saame et al., this type of culture can improve the quality of hospital services and the performance of the organization as a whole [8]. Another study also showed that this culture is positively related to the satisfaction of patients and is associated with the least complaints received by the organization [8]. Moreover, in the context of the adoption of KM systems in hospitals, this culture also has a positive relation [4]. This means that organizations that have a high clan culture will more easily adapt to the new KM system.

4.2   Adhocracy Culture and KM

This culture emphasizes a high level of flexibility and focus on external environment [12, 14]. This type of organization is a dynamic workplace, innovative, and creative which provides an opportunity for individuals to develop themselves over the line with the objectives of the organization [1, 13, 15]. In this culture is the leader's role as an entrepreneur or innovator who inspired the formation of creativities in subordinates and encourages innovation, and the search for new ideas [12, 13]. The focus of this type of organization is the opportunity to get as much as possible from the external environment with emphasis on the development of new products and services, adap-tability, growth, change, productivity, efficiency [1, 13].

According to the Yun Shu -Mei, an organization that has a high degree of external orientation will make it easy to spread the knowledge to the individual, group, or other organization levels [4]. Based on this it can be concluded that the adhocracy culture that focuses on the external also has a positive influence on knowledge sharing. This statement is also supported by other concepts presented by Gray and

Densten. They mention that the adhocracy culture congruent with externalization process that involves the conversion of knowledge from tacit to explicit form [6]. Given the explicit knowledge in the form of access to such knowledge would be increased because it no longer depends on the individual. Therefore, the dissemination of knowledge will become easier. Moreover, culture is also positively related to the behavior of individuals that exist in the organization in the context of the adoption of KM systems in hospitals [4]. Hospitals that embrace this culture has a high degree of success in implementing KM systems, and can be easier to use and adapt the KM system [4].

4.3   Market Culture and KM

This culture emphasizes and focuses on the degree of external stability [12, 14]. This type of organization tends to be oriented on the outcome (result-oriented) [1, 15]. This culture is very concerned about the reputation and success so there is much emphasis on effectiveness in achieving goals [13, 15]. The achievement of goals is an important value in this culture, because the purposes of the control action represent a form of organizational members and direct the behavior of the external environment [12].

According to the Saame Voon, this culture is needed to produce good quality care [8]. However, in the context of KM, according to Hendriks in Nicolas and Cerdan, this culture inhibits the process of KM in the organization [17]. This statement is also supported by the KM concept in the context of the adoption of a system which states that this culture negatively correlated with the ease of an organization in implementing and using the KM system. This is due to the tendency of members of the organization who see the possibility that the implementation of KM in the organization will lose the benefit or profit of the organization [4]. Hence, they become more resistant to the implementation of the system.

4.4   Hierarchy Culture and KM

This culture emphasizes and focuses on the level of internal stability [12, 14]. Organization is seen as a place to work in a structured and formal, as well as having a clear organizational structure. The rules and procedures are standardized, with strict control, moreover the responsibility are clearly defined [13, 15]. This type of culture is sometimes also referred to as internal type process due emphasis on stability and continuity [14].

Having a hierarchal culture for KM implementation in the organization has negative correlation [2]. According to Hendriks in Nicolas and Cerdan, the existence of this culture can inhibit knowledge sharing within the organization [17]. This is because the formalities of culture inhibit the formation of creativity and innovation, and KM [6]. According to Gray and Densten, culture correlates with internalization process model of knowledge creation. This process occurs in the conversion of knowledge into tacit and explicit which are formed by defining responsibilities, assessment systems, and documentation [6].

5   Research Methods

The research conducted to gauge the type of culture in healthcare organization using OCAI. It was claimed that the instrument is validate to examine organizational culture. OCAI questionnaire consists of six questions to assess the dominant characteristics, forms of leadership, management style, organization glue, strategic emphasis, and criteria of success of the organization.   According to Cameron and Quinn (2006), the four alternatives of each dimension are described on detail in questionnaire (see on appendix).

The test-taker was 150 respondents includes structural management (top, medium, and low level), and medical personnel (doctors, nurses, pharmacists, radiologists, etc.) in hospital institution. From the total, respondents valid are 132, and 18 respondents are ignored because they do not fully charge. From the cumulative answers, we counted a number of choices as follow: A (clan) = 172, B (adhocracy) = 109, C (market) = 260, and D (hierarchy) = 245 for column 'Now'. Meanwhile, the preferred column are A = 345, B = 140, C = 68, and D = 132.

The cumulative answers (similarly) will be divided to 6, then the totally of culture should represent 100 points over four alternatives.   The choice column is correspond to the four culture types according to the present and preferred organization. The outcome measures the mix of or extent to which one of the four culture types dominates the present and preferred organizational culture [15].

6   Result and Discussion

The diagram is depicted in Figure 2. The solid lines represent the current culture and the dash lines represent the preferred culture. From this graphic, we can deduct the dominant culture is market culture (33.08 points) which concentrates results-oriented, production, goals and targets and competition. It is followed by hierarchy culture (31.17 points) which concentrates structure, procedures, efficiency and predictability. The third is clan culture (21.88 points) which is a very pleasant place to work where people share a lot of themselves and commitment is high. The adhocracy culture is present as well (13.87 points) which has a dynamic, entrepreneurial, and creative place to work. For more details about OCAI calculation results can be seen in Table 1. The points represent the cumulative answers (similarly) divided the 100 points into four alternatives.

The organizational culture of hospitals in Indonesia is more likely to be a market culture and hierarchy culture rather than clan culture and adhocracy culture. Based on literature, it appears that the market culture and hierarchy culture negatively correlated with KM in the organization. Even the hierarchy tends to inhibit the culture of knowledge sharing in the organization. In addition, the market culture that tends to be result-oriented KM will make it difficult to apply due to the results of KM cannot be quickly or easily visible. Therefore, hospitals need to make changes to its organizational culture in order to encourage knowledge creation or knowledge sharing. It is

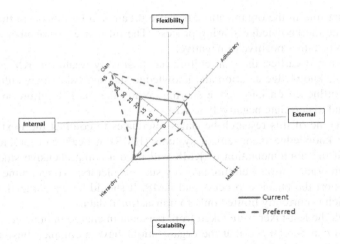

Fig. 2. A diagram OCAI of hospitals institution at CVF

Table 1. Results of OCAI Measurement of hospitals institution

Types of Organizational Culture	Current	Preferred
Clan	21.88	43.95
Adhocracy	13.87	17.83
Market	33.08	8.66
Hierarchy	31.17	29.55
Total	100	100

the basis of the existing KM in the organization. Moreover, it is also supported by the results of OCAI measurement on preferred culture indicator. The majority of respondents preferred clan culture as the dominant culture (43.95 points). It was claimed that clan culture is positively related to KM. Thus, it is believed to help the formation of knowledge by enhancing the exchange of knowledge among members of the organization.

Therefore, based on the results of the analysis can be concluded that hospitals in Indonesia have not been noticed KM as a process to manage the existing knowledge within the organization. However, it is not directly that members of the organization have the awareness that knowledge is an important asset in the organization. This is evidenced by the high expectations of members of the organization. The organizational culture is more towards the clan culture with emphasize of the relationship or collaboration among members of the organization.

7 Conclusion

KM provides a way to capture the existing knowledge in the organization with the advanced principle of sharing knowledge. In this case, the organizational culture has an important role in the organization, because it can be a barrier or, in the other side, can advocate the knowledge sharing process. The influence of organizational culture on KM can be either positive or negative.

As mentioned earlier, the clan culture has positively related to KM as an encouragement for knowledge creation and knowledge sharing. Adhocracy culture also has a positive influence on knowledge sharing. While the market culture and hierarchy cultures tend to correlate negatively to KM.

The outcome of this research becomes references to conduct the next research of developing knowledge management systems (KMS) at healthcare organization. We believe that the implementation of KMS will need a comprehensive study, such the barrier from organizational culture and key success factors. We recommend for using ICT to support the business process and KMS. It should be encouraged to be empowered, which is currently limited only to transactional data.

Although the test-taker were taken from personal in charge in big five and referral hospitals, it can be claimed that the organizations have a complex business process. We assumed that they can represent as healthcare organization in Indonesia. Even the results of this study may still not represent a pattern or profile of organizational culture within the hospitals in general.

References

1. Yesil, S., dan Kaya, A.: The Effect of Organizational Culture on firm Financial Performance: Evidence from A Developing Country. Procedia Social and Behavioral Sciences 81, 428–437 (2013)
2. Moradi, E., Saba, A., Azimi, S., dan Emami, R.: The Relationship between Organizational Culture and Knowledge Management. International Journal of Innovative Ideas (IJII) 12(3), 30–46 (2012)
3. Rocha, E.S.B., Nagliate, P., Furlan, C.E.B., Rocha, K., Trevizan, M.A., dan Mendes, I.A.C.: Knowledge management in health: a systematic literature review. Rev. Latino-Am. Enfermagem 20, 392–400 (2012)
4. Yun, E.K.: Predictors of attitude and intention to use knowledge management system among Korean nurses. Nurse Education Today 33, 1477–1481 (2013)
5. Ahmed, S.: Organisation Culture and its Influence on Knowledge Sharing: Relevance of a framework in virtual group
6. Gray, J.H., dan Densten, I.L.: Towards An Integrative Model Of Organizational Culture And Knowledge Management. International Journal of Organisational Behaviour 9, 594–603
7. Abidi, S.S.R.: Healthcare Knowledge Management: The Art of the Possible. In: Riaño, D. (ed.) K4CARE 2007. LNCS (LNAI), vol. 4924, pp. 1–20. Springer, Heidelberg (2008)
8. Saame, I., Reino, A., dan Vadi, M.: Organizational culture based on the example of an Estonian hospital. Journal of Health Organization and Management 25(5), 526-548 (2011)
9. Wiewiora, A., Trigunarsyah, B., Murphy, G., dan Coffey, V.: Organizational culture and willingness to share knowledge: A competing values perspective in Australian context. International Journal of Project Management 31, 1163–1174 (2013)
10. Chena, C.J., dan Huang, W.J.: How organizational climate and structure affect knowledge management—The social interaction perspective. International Journal of Information Management 27, 104–118 (2007)

11. Guptill, J.: Knowledge Management in Health Care. Journal of Health Care Finance, 10–14 (Spring 2005)
12. Gregory, B.T., Harris, S.G., Amenakis, A.A.: Organizational culture and effectiveness: A study of values, attitudes, and organizational outcomes. Journal of Business Research 62, 673–679 (2009)
13. Aktas, E., Cicek, I., dan Kiyak, M.: The Effect of Organizational Culture On Organizational Efficiency: The Moderating Role of Organizational Environment and CEO Values. Procedia Social and Behavioral Sciences 24, 1560–1573 (2011)
14. Mallak, L.A., Lyth, D.M., Olson, S.D., Ulshafer, S.M., dan Sardone, F.J.: Culture, the built environment and healthcare organizational performance. Managing Service Quality 13(1), 27–38 (2003)
15. Organizational Culture Assessment Instrument (May 31, 2010), http://www.uiowa.edu/~nrcfcp/dmcrc/documents/OCAIProExampleReport.pdf
16. Saeed, T., Tayyab, B., Haque, M.A.U., Ahmad, H.M., dan Chaudhry, A.: Knowledge Management Practices: Role of Organizational Culture. Proceedings of ASBBS 17(1), 1027–1036 (2010)
17. Nicolas, C.L., dan Cerdan, A.L.M.: The Impact of organizational culture on the use of ICT for knowledge management. Electron Markets 19, 211–219 (2009)

Appendix (is noted fully from Cameron and Quinn [15]):

Dominant Characteristics

A. The organization is a very personal place. It is like an extended family. People seem to share a lot of personal information and features.

B. The organization is a very dynamic entrepreneurial place. People are willing to stick out their necks and take risks.

C. The organization is very results-oriented. A major concern is getting the job done. People are very competitive and achievement-oriented.

D. The organization is a very controlled and structured place. Formal procedures generally govern what people do.

Organizational Leadership

A. The leadership in the organization is generally considered to exemplify mentoring, facilitating, or nurturing.

B. The leadership in the organization is generally considered to exemplify entrepreneurship, innovation, or risk taking.

C. The leadership in the organization is generally considered to exemplify a nononsense, aggressive, results-oriented focus.

D. The leadership in the organization is generally considered to exemplify coordinating, organizing, or smooth-running efficiency.

Management of Employees

A. The management style in the organization is characterized by teamwork, consensus, and participation.

B. The management style in the organization is characterized by individual risk taking, innovation, freedom, and uniqueness.

C. The management style in the organization is characterized by hard-driving competitiveness, high demands, and achievement.
D. The management style in the organization is characterized by security of employment, conformity, predictability, and stability in relationships.

Organization Glue
A. The glue that holds the organization together is loyalty and mutual trust. Commitment to this organization runs high.
B. The glue that holds the organization together is commitment to innovation and development. Here is an emphasis on being on the cutting edge.
C. The glue that holds the organization together is an emphasis on achievement and goal accomplishment.
D. The glue that holds the organization together is formal rules and policies. Maintaining a smooth-running organization is important.

Strategic Emphases
A. The organization emphasizes human development. High trust, openness, and participation persist.
B. The organization emphasizes acquiring new resources and creating new challenges. Trying new things and prospecting for opportunities are valued.
C. The organization emphasizes competitive actions and achievement. Hitting stretch targets and winning in the marketplace are dominant.
D. The organization emphasizes permanence and stability. Efficiency, control and smooth operations are important.

Criteria of Success
A. The organization defines success on the basis of development of human resources, teamwork, employee commitment, and concern for people.
B. The organization defines success on the basis of having the most unique or newest products. It is a product leader and innovator.
C. The organization defines success on the basis of winning in the marketplace and outpacing the competition. Competitive market leadership is key.
D. The organization defines success on the basis of efficiency. Dependable delivery, smooth scheduling and low-cost production are critical.

Semantic Versioning of In-Process *Scientific Document*

Imran Asif and M. Shuaib Karim

Department of Computer Sciences, Quaid-i-Azam University, Islamabad, Pakistan
`imranasifquaidian@gmail.com,`
`skarim@qau.edu.pk`

Abstract. The development of scientific documents is an iterative process. Scientific documents go through a continuous informal review phase during writing process and as a result keep changing. The informal review changes are casually recorded. The key issue for maintaining the changes in scientific document is to maintain the review history of individual components within source file at component level. Scientific document is meaningfully organized and it can be easily transformed into an ontology. For this purpose, we use Document Ontology to map each component of the scientific document and manage changes in this ontology by enhancing an already existing technique of semantic repository versioning. In this paper, we explore document change process using semantic versioning and provide the review comments history along each change. In addition, we define a usage scenario to present the viability and benefit of our approach. To achieve this, we developed a prototype system which represents the meaningful track of change in individual components of a scientific document, provides the review comments history along each change and at the end of document writing the author can see the progress report.

Keywords: Scientific Document, Ontology, Semantic Versioning.

1   Introduction

Suzanne Briet [1] describes *Document* as an entity that is used to organize the physical evidence and to record the textual representation. It is also defined as a piece of written, printed, or electronic matter that provides information or evidence, or that serves as an official record [2]. For the purpose of our study, a document which represents a scientific discourse is a *Scientific Document*. It has a meaningful structure. There are several types of scientific documents which are used to explain work and preserve information for technical writing. The most common types of scientific documents are research thesis, research papers, articles, manuals, software reports, software requirements specification reports, books, research magazines, journals, and many others. Mostly, these scientific documents follow the same document structure, i.e., having keywords, sentences, paragraphs, sections, headings, subheadings, references, tables and

Linawati et al. (Eds.): ICT-EurAsia 2014, LNCS 8407, pp. 119–128, 2014.
© IFIP International Federation for Information Processing 2014

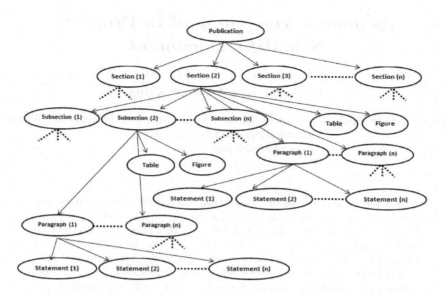

Fig. 1. Structure of *Scientific Document*

figures (see Figure 1). Due to meaningful structure of scientific document, we can easily map document components to ontological concepts. The term ontology means a specification of the shared conceptualization of a domain [3]. Ontology represents an extensive collection of formal representation, including taxonomies, hierarchical terminology, vocabularies, or describes logical theories of a domain [4]. It is also described as a collection of concepts and describes relationships between concepts that represent the meaning of the domain [5].

Due to iterative development process of *Scientific Document*, handling the change in document and maintaining the review comments history along each change is a difficult issue to handle. There is a need to maintain and keep track of each change in a meaningful way. Semantic versioning is used to maintain the ontology evolution and ontological differences and make each version of ontology compatible with each other [6]. Semantic versioning is exploited in real world application such as for e-Government [7]. Similarly, it can be used in case of research documents.

1.1 Scenario: Tracking Changes and Maintaining Review Comments in *Scientific Documents*

"An author is writing a *Scientific Document*. He needs to consult his supervisor to complete this work. He is refining the document using the review comments that are given by the supervisor. He manages the reviewing comments for further use and also manages the document change history manually. He makes use of different folders to save the modified document or rename the modified document and makes several copies. The supervisor gives the comments. Those are managed by student through writing different notes using some software (Notepad, Word files, html editors) or in hard form (diaries, registers). In subsequent meetings supervisor may look for modifications of his previous remarks too. Student often forget to take into account all the remarks or sometimes supervisor modifies his previous remarks. As a result document is not finalized in-time."

In this paper, we propose a meaningful change process of the *Scientific Document* with review comments history. Collectively all this information helps the author to complete document authoring within time while bearing minimum overhead of offline tracking and storage of review comments.

2 Background and Literature Review

In the past few years, useful models have been proposed for scientific document representation which aim to express the rhetoric and argumentation within publications [8]. Harmsze's model [9] is one of the first inclusive models for providing the rhetorical structure of scientific information in electronic articles. The ABCDE Format [10] categorizes papers by five types of rhetorical blocks: Annotation, Background, Contribution, Discussion, and Entities. SALT (Semantically Annotated LaTeX) [11] is created by three ontologies (Document Ontology, Rhetorical Ontology, and Annotation Ontology). The Scientific Knowledge Object (SKO) [12] proposed patterns for scientific document representation model particularly for knowledge management in the evolving social web and semantic web. It has strong capabilities of semantic annotations, semantic search and strategic authoring grounded on logical reasoning (i.e. deduction, induction, and abduction) and focused on section level representation of the scientific document. Traditionally version control systems (VCS) are used to keep track of changes in a document. There are two types of version control systems, Centralized Version Control Systems (CVCS) and Distributed/Decentralized Version Control Systems (DVCS) [13]. The CVCS contains CVS and SVN[1], and DVCS contains Git[2], Bazar[3] and Mercurial[4] software tools.

While Writing the scientific document, some authors use versioning system like SVN or Microsoft word to manage versions. But these versioning systems do not keep track of component level changes along with review comments history. Microsoft Word enables for writing the comments, perform operations like addition/deletion with each change. But it does not identify the complex operations, such as, displacement of text or block of text within a document. For example

---

[1] http://subversion.apache.org/
[2] http://git-scm.com/
[3] http://bazaar.canonical.com/en/
[4] http://mercurial-scm.org/

the paragraph in the section of a scientific document was moved to a new section. There are several techniques of semantic versioning such as PROMPTDIFF [14], SEMVERSION [15] and RDF(S) Repository Technique [16].

The RDF(S) Repository Versioning Technique works on RDF triple format of the OWL [17] ontology. It has two variables i.e., Update Counter (UC) and Update Identifier (UI). The UC is an integer variable and its value increases when the repository is updated. Each value of UC is identified by Update Identifier. UI represents the state of the repository. This technique performs two basic operations that are add and remove, which together represents the lifetime of the statement. The complete history of the repository is presented via add/remove operations. Versioning information is stored in ontology. Each version transaction has the format: UID:nn add—remove ⟨subj, pred, obj⟩ [16].

3   Initial Survey Based Upon Usage Scenario

We conducted an initial survey to assess the viability of the identified problem. The survey consists of questions that are asked from the research students. This questionnaire represents the personal and versioning information, how they manage their documents during write-up and also asked about the benefit of review comments history, separation of document's components and component level versioning within document. Our target audience for this survey is academic researchers who know about versioning process and in-process *Research Thesis* written in LATEX and MS-Word. We selected 40 researchers (Faculty, doctorate student and post doctorate students) out of 50 from different departments of a University[5], and conducted the survey. The actual population statistics are shown in Table 1.

Figure 2 shows that, 100% faculty *mostly demanded* the previous review comments. 25% of the doctorate students gave response that their supervisors *mostly demanded* the previous review comments, while 12% said supervisors *always demanded* previous comments. The remaining doctorate students gave response

Table 1. Qualifying Candidates for our study

Characteristic	Value	Number
Academic Position	Faculty	2
	Doctorate student	8
	Post Graduate Student	30
Department	Computer Sciences	6
	Mathematics	19
	Economics	15
Versioning Information	Use Versioning System	10
	Know about versioning	30

---

[5] Quaid-i-Azam University, Islamabad, Pakistan.

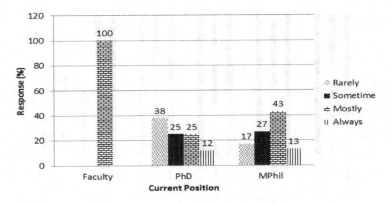

Fig. 2. Supervisor Demand previous Review Comments

that supervisor *sometimes or rarely demanded* previous review comments. 43% of MPhil students gave response that *mostly* supervisor demanded the previous review comments and 13% shows that they *always demanded* the review comments. Collectively all this information represents that review comments history is very important to save.

Figure 3 shows the graph which represents that the review comments are beneficial for the research students. In this Graph, 100% faculty *agreed* to give response that review comments are beneficial in write-up process. 25% and 75% doctorate students *strongly agreed* and *agree* respectively, that they have interest about review comments. Similarly 30% and 63% post-doctorate students *strongly agree* and *agree* about review comments and remaining 3% each *disagree* and *strongly disagree* about review comments usefulness.

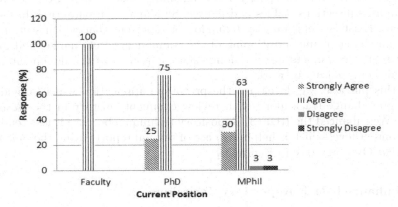

Fig. 3. Qualifying Candidates Response about benefit of Review Comments

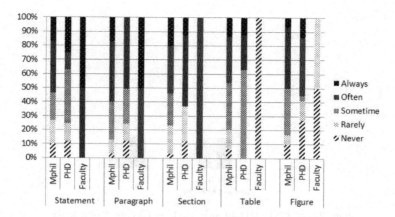

Fig. 4. Qualifying Candidates Response about Separate display of document Components

Figure 4 shows the usefulness of different components of the document if displayed separately. Mostly, response from the MPhil students, doctorate students and faculty members is that the sections, paragraphs and sentences are *always* to be displayed separately. Some of them gave response that figures and tables are *rarely* needed to be displayed separately. Collectively all this information represents that specific components of the document are necessary to be displayed separately. Based upon the finding in literature review and survey in local context a technique is proposed.

4   Proposed Work

Our technique is able to specify more meanings like each section has some paragraphs, subsections, tables and figures. Similarly each paragraph has some sentences. Existing versioning systems do not represent that which section has maximum change count, positioning of the component after change, and maintaining review comments history along each component of the document. This gap is also covered in our work.

For this purpose, we developed the prototype application which provides a meaningful change track along with review comments history in the *Research Thesis*. We enhanced the RDF(S) Repository technique, because it is extendable up-to content level which is helpful in case of textual reports using the *Scientific Document* Ontology (see in Figure 5).

4.1   Enhanced RDF Repository Technique

In existing technique there is no way to store the review comments history along each change. So we enhanced the existing RDF Repository technique according

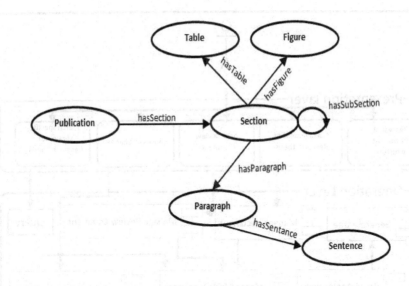

Fig. 5. *Scientific Document* Ontology

to our research problem. Along with each update counter and update identifier we used RCID that represents Review Comment Identifier. The RCID is used for storing additional information along with each component of the document. So versioning history of the research thesis in RDF Repository can be represented as UID: nn, RCID: mm add — delete ⟨subject, predicate, object⟩.

During first time population of RDF(S) repository, only addition operation is performed and RCID is set to 0 for all the statements. e.g.,

- UID: 1, RCID:0 add ⟨A, r1, B⟩.
- UID: 2, RCID:0 add ⟨E, r1, D⟩.
- UID: 3, RCID:0 add ⟨E, r3, B⟩.
- UID: n, RCID:0 add ⟨D, rn, A⟩.

If the contents change in the document then repository is also changed to new state. If document is modified then two operations are performed (add, remove) along with updated RCID value. The RDF(S) Repository contains all operations from start, so we can easily find that which statements are added, removed or updated.

In our prototype system, author provides the LaTeX source file as input. Then it is automatically converted to document ontology and system shows the tree structure of the *Scientific Document*. It helps author to navigate to different components within the document. For each change, author can easily add, delete or update section, subsection, paragraph, statement. Our prototype system consists of three component i.e., tree structure of the scientific document, contents of the document and review comment history along each component of the scientific

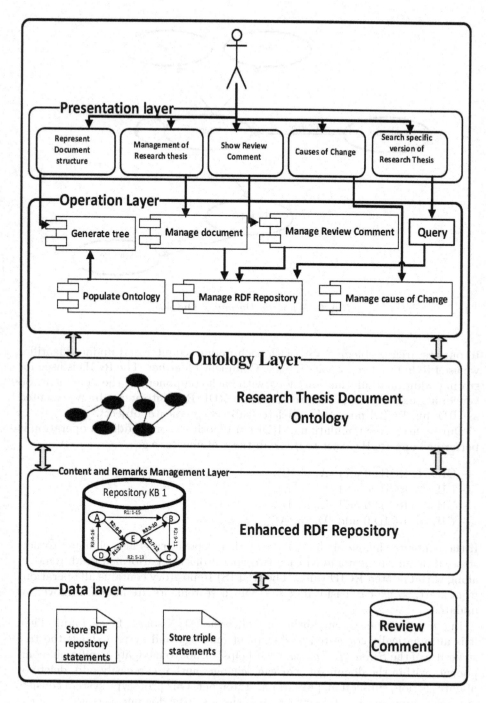

Fig. 6. Architectural Design for Proposed Framework

document. Our system also provides the weekly or monthly progress report. It helps the author that at which stage he could not work properly.

Prototype system is used to help the author to maintain each change and view the previous changes in a meaningful way and also reduces the communication gap between the supervisor and the author. One of the aims of this study is to reduce the authors' effort which causes a lot of their energy to cope with review comments of each change in the scientific document.

4.2   Implementation

We have developed a prototype (see System Architecture in Figure 6) for experimentation and testing. We used java language to develop the system. Jena API[6] is used to create the ontology of the *Scientific Document*. RDF Repository Technique is used to maintain each change in the document along with review comments. The source code of our prototype can be downloaded from SourceForge[7].

5   Conclusion and Future work

In this paper, we have highlighted the need for tracking the changes along review comments in a document. Our survey shows that author has to face a lot of difficulties to save review comments along each change and there is no usable way of displaying a meaningful track of each change in the document. So our proposed work is used to help the author to maintain each change and view the previous change in a meaningful way and thus reduces the communication gap between the supervisor and the author. Our proposed prototype also shows document components in tree format to provide ease to the author.

Our in-process work, is to integrate proposed work with the LaTeX software. This will help authors to manage their changes and keep track of review comments of each change in a meaningful way. Behind each change there is a cause. The cause represents why the document is changed. So we will also explore the *Change Causality Model* for *Scientific Documents*.

Acknowledgements. The authors would like to give special thanks to Higher Education Commission (HEC), Pakistan, for providing travel support for presenting this work in a conference.

References

1. Briet, S., Martinet, L., Day, R.E., Anghelescu, H.G.B.: What is documentation?: English translation of the classic French text. Scarecrow Press (2006)
2. Buckland, M.K.: What is a "document"? JASIS 48(9), 804–809 (1997)

---

[6] http://jena.apache.org/
[7] http://sourceforge.net/projects/nbiaak/

3. Gruber, T.R., et al.: A translation approach to portable ontology specifications. Knowledge Acquisition 5(2), 199–220 (1993)
4. Noy, N.F., Klein, M.: Ontology evolution: Not the same as schema evolution. Knowledge and Information Systems 6(4), 428–440 (2004)
5. Liang, Y., Alani, H., Shadbolt, N.: Ontology versioning and evolution for semantic web-based applications. 9-month progress report (2005)
6. Liang, Y., Alani, H., Shadbolt, N.: Change management: The core task of ontology versioning and evolution (2005)
7. Santoso, H.A., Abdul-Mehdi, Z.T., Haw, S.-C.: Semantic enhancement framework for e-government using ontology versioning approach. In: Proceeding of the 6'th Conference on Information Technology and Application (ICITA 2009), Hanoi, pp. 296–301 (2009)
8. Groza, T., Handschuh, S., Clark, T., Buckingham Shum, S., de Waard, A.: A short survey of discourse representation models (2009)
9. Harmsze, F.-A.P.: A modular structure for scientific articles in an electronic environment (2000)
10. Waard, A.d., Tel, G.: The abcde format enabling semantic conference proceedings. In: SemWiki (2006)
11. Groza, T., Handschuh, S., Möller, K., Decker, S.: Salt-semantically annotated LaTeX for scientific publications. In: The Semantic Web: Research and Applications, pp. 518–532. Springer (2007)
12. Giunchiglia, F., Xu, H., Birukou, A., Chenu, R.: Scientific knowledge object patterns. In: Proceedings of the 15th European Conference on Pattern Languages of Programs, p. 15. ACM (2010)
13. Sink, E.: Version control by example. Pyrenean Gold Press (2011)
14. Noy, N.F., Musen, M.A.: Promptdiff: A fixed-point algorithm for comparing ontology versions. In: AAAI/IAAI, pp. 744–750 (2002)
15. Völkel, M., Groza, T.: Semversion: An rdf-based ontology versioning system. In: Proceedings of the Iadis International Conference WWW/Internet, vol. 2006, p. 44 (2006)
16. Ognyanov, D., Kiryakov, A.: Tracking changes in rdf (s) repositories. In: Gómez-Pérez, A., Benjamins, V.R. (eds.) EKAW 2002. LNCS (LNAI), vol. 2473, pp. 373–378. Springer, Heidelberg (2002)
17. McGuinness, D.L., Van Harmelen, F., et al.: Owl web ontology language overview. W3C Recommendation 10(2004-03), 10 (2004)

Towards Semantic Mashup Tools
for Big Data Analysis

Hendrik[1], Amin Anjomshoaa[2], and A Min Tjoa[2]

[1] Department of Informatics, Faculty of Industrial Technology
Islamic University of Indonesia
hendrik@uii.ac.id
[2] Institute of Software Technology and Interactive Systems
Vienna University of Technology, Austria
{anjomshoaa,amin}@ifs.tuwien.ac.at

Abstract. Big Data is generally characterized by three V's: *volume, velocity,* and *variety.* For the Semantic Web community, the *variety* dimension could be the most appropriate and interesting aspect to contribute in. Since the real-world use of Big Data is for data analytics purposes of knowledge workers in different domains, we can consider mashup approach as an effective tool to create user-generated solution based on available private/public resources. This paper gives brief overview and comparison of some semantic mashup tools which can be employed to mash up various data sources in heterogenous data format.

Keywords: Mashup, Linked Data, Big Data, Semantic Web.

1   Introduction

According to [16], Big Data is a common concept to define datasets whose size exceeds the processing capacity of traditional database systems. While this is not the commonly agreed definition, Big Data is generally characterized by three V's: *volume, velocity,* and *variety*[16,9,5,7]. **Volume** dimension relates to the size of data from one or more data resources in tera-, peta-, or exabytes. The **velocity** dimension focuses on the data streams and how to store near real-time data as well as handling the increasing rate of the data amount. The latter, **variety** dimension associates with the heterogeneity of data both at the schema-level and the instance-level.

For the Semantic Web community, the *variety* dimension could be the most appropriate and interesting aspect to contribute in. Here, Linked Data can be considered as an alternative solution for addressing the issues of *variety* dimension. Since its introduction by Tim Berners-Lee in 2006, Linked Data (LD) has emerged as a recent trend in the current era of the Web. Linked Data refers to an approach to publish and interlink structured data on the web using some principles forming a global database, called Web of Data [4]. The effort for adopting LD in real life was initiated by Linking Open Data Project[1]. Starting from 2007,

---

[1] http://www.w3.org/wiki/SweoIG/TaskForces/CommunityProjects/
LinkingOpenData

Linawati et al. (Eds.): ICT-EurAsia 2014, LNCS 8407, pp. 129–138, 2014.

a significant number of datasets are published and interlinked into Linked Open Data Cloud (LOD Cloud) by both individuals and private/public organisations. The LOD Cloud covers various domains such as government, life science, entertainment, etc. Moreover, today not less than 928 active datasets, comprise around 62 billion RDF triples are available as Linked Data[2].

The typical target group of Big Data solutions is knowledge workers in different domains who are not familiar with technical details of Big Data and data integration. As a result, there is a growing need to provide a solution with less learning curve for such users. We can consider mashup as an effective tool to support users in creating user-generated solutions based on available private/public resources and integrate several data sources with different formats easily. As a result both skilled programmers and non-skilled users are able to benefit from the large amount of data and solve their problems.

The aim of this paper is to compare the existing semantic mashup tools to help the readers in choosing the suitable tool to mash up data from various sources for data analytics purposes. Using such tools can help the end users to design a prototype or even visualize the data analysis results for their use cases.

The remainder of this paper is organized as follows. In section 2 the definitions and detailed description of semantic mashups will be introduced. Then, we give the overview of each existing semantic mashup tool in section 3. Finally, we conclude this study in section 4.

2   Traditional Mashups versus Semantic Mashups

Mashup approach allows users to build ad-hoc applications by combining several different data sources and services from across the web. The foundation of the approach consists of sharing, reusing, and combining applications, code, components and APIs which is not an innovation in computer science area. However, the approach is innovative by the fact that this approach is widely used to speed up the process of realizing creative ideas.

There are three approaches for development of mashup solutions [2]. First, **manual** approach, which requires programming or scripting skills of users to integrate the data sources, generate visualizations, and create new functionalities. Second, **semi-automatic**, which assists the users to build a mashup application using provided tools. Third, **automatic** approach which allows creation of mashups without user's involvement, as the resources (data, visualization, as well as functionality) are chosen and invoked automatically by the tool.

The semi-automatic approach is further categorized as follows:

1. spreadsheet-based tools, in which the users provide the data directly into a spreadsheet; The examples of this category are AMICO:CALC [3] and MashSheet[6].

---

[2] http://stats.lod2.eu
[3] http://amico.sourceforge.net/amico-calc.html

2. widget-oriented tools, allow users to create the mashup through a visual editor. Yahoo Pipes[4] and Intel Mash Maker[5] are examples of this category of mashups.
3. demonstration-based tools, allow users to mash up their data by providing examples and completing the data integration task via a visual step-by-step process. The instances of this category are Dapper[6] and Karma[18].

Semantic mashups can be seen as a complementary extension of the traditional mashup approaches. The Semantic Web and mashups can provide a solid basis for many interesting applications and boost each other. The Semantic Web and ontologies may facilitate the creation of mashup solutions for novice users. This application of Semantic Web has its roots in Semantic Web Service concept that is aiming to automate service discovery and composition without human intervention. The basic difference between Semantic Web Services and Semantic Mashups approaches is derived from different target users. The Semantic Web Services are mainly managed and used by IT experts who are aware of underlying data structures and corresponding services; however, the Semantic Mashups target group is novice users who need to combine the Mashup Widgets for their specific purposes [1,8]. Semantic web can be used to annotate combination of several APIs especially to automate the selection and composition of these APIs [14]. It also benefits the data integration process by adding semantic to the data using ontologies and semantic web languages (RDF), which enable the machine to automate data exchange. Combining mashups with Linked Data opens a lot of possibilities for data integration and more efficient use of distributed data.

3   The Existing Semantic Mashup Tools

As defined by [10], ideally there are three requirements that should be fulfilled by mashup tools: first it should be *generic* and able to address various application domains, secondly it should be *powerful* to manage complex logics of the problems, and thirdly it should be *simple* to be used by novice users. Based on these essentials, we classify the existing mashup tools into two different groups: data analytics tools and generic tools. The data analytics tools are targeting the analysis of large amount of specific data and derive required information. While the generic tools can be used for different kind of purposes. In the rest of this section, some examples of these two groups will be presented.

3.1   Data Analytics Tools

As mentioned before, this group of tools is targeting the analysis of large amount of data. The data is usually taken from a specific domain and using the mashup tools this data will be processed to derive the required results.

---

[4] http://pipes.yahoo.com/pipes/
[5] http://software.intel.com/en-us/articles/
   intel-mash-maker-mashups-for-the-masses
[6] http://open.dapper.net

3.1.1   Black Swan Events [7]

This mashup tool was inspired by the **Black Swan Theory** which represents a black swan as an unpredictable event that has massive effects [17]. The aim of this tool is to help domain experts to find important (*black swan*) events based on historical or statistical data [13]. The tool integrates statistical data and events data into a single repository, which come in various data formats including structured (e.g., CSV, RDF, or XML) and unstructured (e.g., plain text) data. Currently, it manages more than 400 statistical time series datasets which cover annual data of 200 countries for the past 200 years. The statistical data is gathered from international organisations such as World Bank or International Monetary Fund (IMF), as well as some projects such as Gapminder[8] and Correlates of War[9]. Furthermore the events data are collected from available sources such as DBpedia, Freebase, and BBC historical timeline.

The collected data is then analyzed using several methods such as regression techniques and rule mining to discover the interesting events and patterns in statistical data. In order to help users to investigate the correlation between an event and statistical data easily, the tool comes with interactive visualisation feature which depicts an 'annotated time line' using a graph chart. There are two methods to explore the data by using the visualization, i.e statistic-based method and rule-based method. The first method enables users to select any statistic indicators such as Economy, Health, Energy, etc., for a target country. This will help the users to find the events that match to country's statistical outliers and the rules that generate event-outlier pairs. For instance, Fig. 1 shows the Black Swan visualization for the effect of the German reunification and income growth in Germany. The second method aims to be used by the advanced users. It allows the users to select a rule and find the matching pairs of statistical outliers and historical events[10].

3.1.2   Super Stream Collider [11]

Super Stream Collider (SSC)[15] is a web-based mashup tool to aggregate live stream data (e.g., sensor stream data from Linked Sensor Middleware[12] for data streams such as weather, traffic, flight, etc., and social stream data such as twitter streams) and Linked Data resources such as DBpedia and Sindice. While the input data comes in various data formats, the output is only available as RDF.

This tool provides an easy to use interface for either novice users, who do not have any technical knowledge about Semantic Web, as well as advanced users, who have knowledge of Semantic Web standards and technologies. By using widget-based paradigm, the users can drag-n-drop any data source widget into

---

[7] http://blackswanevents.org
[8] http://www.gapminder.org/
[9] http://www.correlatesofwar.org/
[10] http://blackswanevents.org/?page_id=179
[11] http://http://superstreamcollider.org/
[12] http://lsm.deri.ie

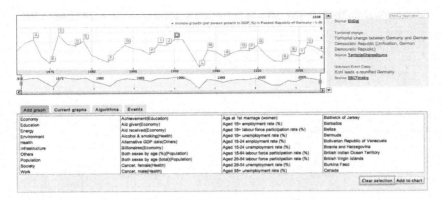

Fig. 1. The blackswan visualization to show the effect of the German reunification and income growth in Germany

the visual editor and connect them via several operator widgets such as merge, location and timer widgets. For the advanced users, SSC provides additional operators such as SPARQL/CQELS[13] editor. These can be used either by writing the query directly in the query text area or by using the visual editor which helps the users to learn writing SPARQL/CQELS interactively. SSC's user interface is depicted in Fig. 2.

The mashup process can be monitored by inspecting the flow of data from the sources to the final output via SSC's debugging component. Using this tool, the users may receive the result data as raw data, RDF data or even data visualisation in several types of charts. The final output, then can be queried, visualised, and published using supported stream protocols (i.e., PubSubHubbub, XMPP and WebSockets). For example, using WebSockets, the HTML and Android developers can embed the output widget in their application without extra efforts and knowledge about RDF or SPARQL query.

3.2   Generic Tools

Unlike the data analytics tools which are focusing on specific domain and data processing pattern, the generic tools are equipped with generic functions which can be used for different kind of solutions.

3.2.1   DERI Pipes [14]

DERI Pipes which is also known as Semantic Web Pipes (SWP) is a Semantic Web tool which was inspired by Yahoo pipes. While the Yahoo pipes is mainly aimed to work with RSS feeds as data source, DERI pipes focuses on graph based data model [12], i.e, RDF data.

---

[13] https://code.google.com/p/cqels/
[14] http://pipes.deri.org/

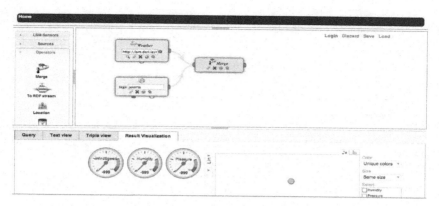

Fig. 2. The Super Stream Collider User Interface

The tool has an easy to use web based GUI called pipe editor to compose workflow of connected operators which form the data pipes. These operators are visualised as widgets and have input and output ports (Fig. 3). There are two kinds of supported operators, namely general operators and base operators. The general base operators only support merge and split operations. The latter operators comprise of getRDF and getXML operator for fetching data from web URL and converting it to RDF or XML formats, XSLT operator to execute XSL transformation of XML input, RDFS and OWL operator to materialize RDFS or OWL inference rule for a specific input, and SPARQL and CONSTRUCT operator to query and align RDF data.

By adopting the concept of UNIX pipeline, the output of the pipeline workflow can be fed directly as an input for other pipeline workflows. The pipeline output is in RDF or JSON format and for visualizing the results, SWP uses SIMILE exhibit[15]. It also provides RSS feeds output thus can be used as an input for other mashup tools such as Yahoo Pipes which only accept RSS as input. Finally, the users can store and publish their pipes to be reused by the other users.

3.2.2   MashQL [16]

This tool enables users to exploit the benefits of Web of Data without prior knowledge of semantic web technologies such as RDF and SPARQL. By using the query-by-diagram paradigm, it allows users to query and mash up a massive amount of structured data on the web intuitively [11].

The core element of MashQL system is a visual editor that processes the input data and generate the required output. Here, the users merely choose the attributes of input concepts that should appear in the widgets output. It also enables the users to filter data with some arithmetic and relational operators for string and numeric attributes. The widget output can be then piped as a

---

[15] http://www.simile-widgets.org/exhibit/
[16] http://sina.birzeit.edu/mashql/

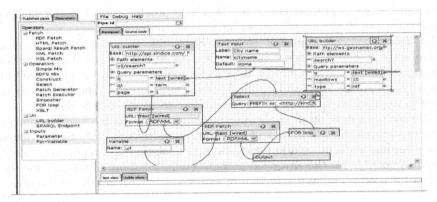

Fig. 3. DERI Pipes User Interface

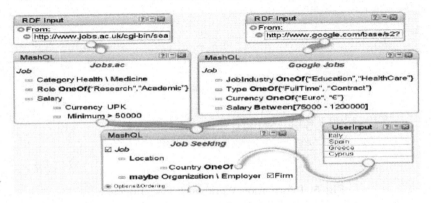

Fig. 4. MashQL User Interface

new input for other MashQL widgets and mashed up with other data inputs as shown in Fig. 4. The system then translates this process into a SPARQL query which is transparent to the users.

3.2.3 Information Workbench [17]

Among the other semantic web tools explained before, Information Workbench (IWB) has more comprehensive features as a mashup tool. It supports collaborative knowledge management among the end users and integrates both structured and unstructured data coming from internal or external resources. The IWB provides a framework to develop, maintain and deploy applications and supports Big Data analysis scenarios by providing a comprehensive SDK (Solution

---

[17] http://www.fluidops.com/information-workbench/

Development Kit). Furthermore, the IWB also provides solutions for business intelligence and data analytics in an integrated environment.

Its *data provider* component collects, integrates, and maintains data from several data resources into a central triple data repository based on dataware-housing techniques. Alternatively, it provides a federation layer called FedX, to virtually integrates local and public Linked Data sources. The benefit of the latter is to provide capability of on-demand access to up-to-date data [3].

The users can develop an application by composing available common purpose widgets such as visualisation and exploration widgets, social media widgets, authoring and content creation widgets, and analytics and reporting widgets. It is also possible for the advanced users to create customized widgets for their special purposes. The user interface of Information Workbench can be seen in Fig. 5.

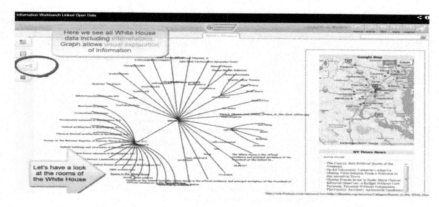

Fig. 5. Information Workbench User Interface

4   Conclusion

This paper provides a survey of existing semantic mashup tools. Using such tools the knowledge workers will be able to create ad-hoc data integration solutions based on the available structured and unstructured data resources such as Linked Open Data (LOD), Open Government Data (OGD), and private datasets. The results of this survey is provided in Table 1 which demonstrate the features of these Semantic Mashup tools including supported input data formats, data source registration, mashup approach, and visualization form.

The data gathering, processing, and integration tasks in Big Data domain are the main challenging issues for the knowledge workers and solution providers. Lowering such entrance barriers is, therefore, essential for the evolution and development of Big Data solutions. In our belief the mashup solutions have the potential to address these requirements and to empower the solution providers and novice users to create and adapt individual Big Data applications based on

Table 1. Comparison of Existing Semantic Mashup Tools

	Input Data Format	Data Source Registration	Mashup Approach	Visualization Form
BlackSwan Events	CSV, RDF, XML, Linked Data, Plain Text	manual	manual	line chart
Super Stream Collider	Stream Data,Linked Data, Social Stream Data, RDF	input widgets	semi automatic (Widget-based)	various chart
Semantic Web Pipe	RDF, XML, HTML, Linked Data	input widgets	semi automatic (Widget-based)	faceted browser
MashQL	RDF, XML, HTML	input widgets	semi automatic (Widget-based)	table data
Information Workbench	Linked Data, RDF, HTML, CSV, XML, Relational	data provider, federation layer	semi automatic (Widget-based)	various chart

elaborated and domain-specific widgets in a user-friendly environment without worrying about technical challenges of data integration.

Acknowledgments. This research has received support from *Ernst-Mach-Stipendien granted by the OeAD* - Austrian Agency for International Cooperation in Education & Research, financed by BMWF.

References

1. Anjomshoaa, A., Tjoa, A.M., Hubmer, A.: Combining and integrating advanced it-concepts with semantic web technology mashups architecture case study. In: Nguyen, N.T., Le, M.T., Świątek, J. (eds.) ACIIDS 2010. LNCS, vol. 5990, pp. 13–22. Springer, Heidelberg (2010)
2. Fischer, T., Bakalov, F., Nauerz, A.: An overview of current approaches to mashup generation. In: Proceedings of the International Workshop on Knowledge Services and Mashups (2009)
3. Haase, P., Schmidt, M., Schwarte, A.: The information workbench as a self-service platform for linked data applications. In: COLD (2011)

4. Heath, T., Bizer, C.: Linked Data: Evolving the Web into a Global Data Space. Morgan & Claypool Publishers (2011)
5. Hendler, J.: Broad Data: Exploring the Emerging Web of Data. Big Data 1(1), 18–20 (2013), http://online.liebertpub.com/doi/abs/10.1089/big.2013.1506
6. Hoang, D., Paik, H.Y., Ngu, A.: Spreadsheet as a generic purpose mashup development environment. In: Maglio, P.P., Weske, M., Yang, J., Fantinato, M. (eds.) ICSOC 2010. LNCS, vol. 6470, pp. 273–287. Springer, Heidelberg (2010), http://dx.doi.org/10.1007/978-3-642-17358-5_19
7. Hopkins, B., Evelson, B., Hopkins, B., Evelson, B., Leaver, S., Moore, C., Cullen, A., Gilpin, M., Cahill, M.: Expand Your Digital Horizon With Big Data. Tech. rep. (2011)
8. Hoyer, V., Stanoevska-Slabeva, K.: The changing role of it departments in enterprise mashup environments. In: Feuerlicht, G., Lamersdorf, W. (eds.) ICSOC 2008. LNCS, vol. 5472, pp. 148–154. Springer, Heidelberg (2009)
9. Analytics, I.B.M.: The real-world use of big data. Tech. rep. (2012)
10. Imran, M., Kling, F., Soi, S., Daniel, F., Casati, F., Marchese, M.: ResEval Mash: A Mashup Tool for Advanced Research Evaluation. In: World Wide Web Conference, pp. 361–364 (2012)
11. Jarrar, M., Dikaiakos, M.D.: Mashql: A query-by-diagram topping sparql. In: Proceedings of the 2nd International Workshop on Ontologies and Information Systems for the Semantic Web, ONISW 2008, pp. 89–96. ACM, New York (2008), http://doi.acm.org/10.1145/1458484.1458499
12. Le-Phuoc, D., Polleres, A., Hauswirth, M., Tummarello, G., Morbidoni, C.: Rapid prototyping of semantic mash-ups through semantic web pipes. In: The 18th International Conference on World Wide Web, WWW 2009, p. 581. ACM Press, New York (2009), http://portal.acm.org/citation.cfm?doid=1526709.1526788
13. Lorey, J., Mascher, A., Naumann, F., Retzlaff, P., Forchhammer, B., Zamanifarahani, A.: Black Swan: Augmenting Statistics with Event Data. In: 20th ACM Conference on Information and Knowledge Management (2011)
14. Malki, A., Benslimane, S.M.: Building semantic mashup. In: ICWIT, pp. 40–49 (2012)
15. Nguyen, H., Quoc, M., Serrano, M., Le-phuoc, D., Hauswirth, M.: Super Stream Collider Linked Stream Mashups for Everyone. In: Proceedings of the Semantic Web Challenge co-located with ISWC 2012, vol. 1380 (2012)
16. Oracle: Information Management and Big Data A Reference Architecture. Tech. Rep. (February 2013), http://www.oracle.com/technetwork/topics/entarch/articles/info-mgmt-big-data-ref-arch-1902853.pdf
17. Taleb, N.N.: The Black Swan:: The Impact of the Highly Improbable Fragility. Random House LLC (2010)
18. Tuchinda, R., Szekely, P., Knoblock, C.A.: Building mashups by example. In: Proceedings of the 13th International Conference on Intelligent User Interfaces, pp. 139–148. ACM (2008)

Acceptance and Use of Information System: E-Learning Based on Cloud Computing in Vietnam

Thanh D. Nguyen[1], Dung T. Nguyen[1], and Thi H. Cao[2]

[1] HCMC University of Technology, Vietnam
{thanh.nguyenduy,dung.nguyentien090}@gmail.com
[2] Saigon Technology University, Vietnam
thi.caohao@stu.edu.vn

Abstract. E-learning is an inevitable trend of education in the future. Although there are several researches about E-learning based on cloud computing, not many researches on the cloud computing adoption model, on the other hand, there are not many studies on the adoption of cloud-based E-learning in Vietnam and in the World. This study adapts the extended of Unified Theory of Acceptance and Use of Technology (UTAUT2) [48] to research the acceptance and use of E-learning based on cloud computing in Vietnam. These elements, namely facilitating condition, performance expectancy, effort expectancy, social influence, hedonic motivation, price value and habit influence on the intention and use of cloud-based E-Learning, the results show that seven out of eleven hypotheses are supported. The results will help implementing E-learning based on cloud and learning strategies to be more successful.

Keywords: Adoption, cloud computing, E-learning, factors, UTAUT.

1   Introduction

In contemporary society, the learning process is becoming a vital factor in business and socioeconomic growth [22]. The first E-learning (E-L) courses were launched in 1998. Since then E-L business has gone global and the competition is fierce. Now, 70% of E-L takes place in the United State and Europe, but Asia Pacific is catching up fast, with Vietnam and Malaysia grow the fastest [9]. According to Ambient Insight [6], Vietnam is ranked (1st) within the top ten countries in the world in terms of high-growth in E-L revenues over the next few years (2011-2016), the VN projected growth rate in E-L of 44.3%. Vietnam Government and Ministry of Education and Training effort to introduce content digitalisation in school systems[*], a large expansion of online higher education possibilities and a growing demand for E-L in the corporate sector will drive the educational growth. Recently, cloud computing (CC) has changed the nature of internet from the static environment to a highly dynamic environment, which allows users to run software applications collaborate, share

---

[*] Vietnam Ministry of Education and Training had guided the deployment of information technology task for the academic year of 2011-2012, dispatch no. 4960/BGDĐT-CNTT.

The original version of this chapter was revised: The affiliation of Thanh D. Nguyen and Dung T. Ngyuen was corrected. An erratum to this chapter can be found at https://doi.org/10.1007/978-3-642-55032-4_72

information, create application virtual, learn online... According to Venkatraman [49], moving its E-L to CC platform, Marconi University (Italy) has achieved cost savings and financial flexibility. It is 23% cheaper to run in a year than the previous solution.

Although there are several researches about cloud-based E-learning (CBE-L), not many researches on the CC adoption model. On the other hand, there are not many studies on the adoption of CBE-L in Vietnam and also in the World. Based on the review of the literature, Unified Theory of Acceptance and Use of Technology (UTAUT) [47], and UTAUT2 [48], the model of Acceptance and Use of E-Learning based on cloud computing in Vietnam is proposed.

1.1   Background

E-L is one of the most famous technologies discovered to make the traditional way of education, learning easier, with the help of software applications and virtual learning environment. According to Tavangarian and et al. [41], E-L includes numerous types of media that deliver text, audio, images, animation, streaming video. It includes technology applications and processes such as audio, video, satellite TV, and computer-based learning as well as local intranet or extranet, and web-based learning. Information and communication systems, whether freestanding, based on either local networks or the Internet in networked learning, underlies many E-L processes.

CC is one of the popular buzzword used all over the information technology world. The CC term is actually derived from the way the Internet is often signified in network diagrams [34, 35]. Based on the different virtual levels, CC is typically divided into 3 types according to the packaging of computing resources in different abstraction layers, these are Infrastructure as a Service (IaaS), Platform as a Service (PaaS) and Software as a Service (SaaS) [39]. According to Zheng and Jingxia [55], CBE-L services can be divided into 4 types as described in Table 1.

Table 1. Types of content and cloud computing services

	Content	Cloud
1	Standard data, audio, video, data, images, text...	*IaaS*
2	Data can be converted into standard data content	*SaaS*
3	Web-based proprietary data, player embedded in web pages...	*SaaS*
4	Private defined data, player needs to download manually...	*PaaS*

Source: Zheng and Jingxia. [55]

2   Research Model

2.1   Literature Review

Technology acceptance has been examined extensively in the research of information system. Most of the studies associated in the analysis of behavioral intention that is conscious of user decision to accept technology. Several theories were developed to explain the phenomena from different research. Theory of Reasoned Action (TRA) was researched in psychosocial perspective in order to identify elements of the trend-conscious behavior [5, 17]. Theory of Planned Behavior (TPB) was constructed by Ajzen [1, 2, 3] from the original TRA theory and added perceived behavioral control element. Technology Acceptance Model (TAM) based on the theoretical foundation of the TRA to establish relationships between variables to explain human behavior regarding acceptance of information systems [12, 13]. Innovation Diffusion Theory (IDT) explained the process of technological innovation that is accepted by users [36].

Unified Theory of Acceptance and Use of Technology (UTAUT) had been built by Venkatesh et al. [47] to explain intention and use behavior of information system users. UTAUT model was developed through theoretical models as TRA [5, 17], TPB [1, 2, 3]; TAM [12, 13], integrated mode of TPB and TAM [42], IDT [31], Motivation Model (MM) [14], Model of PC Utilization (MPCU) [43] and Social Cognitive Theory (SCT) [11, 21]. UTAUT was formulated with 4 core elements of intention and use as performance expectancy, effort expectancy, social influence and facilitating condition. Venkatesh et al. [48] adopted an approach that complements the original constructs in UTAUT, called UTAUT2, which had been integrated hedonic motivation, price value and habit factors into UTAUT. Also, demographic variables such as age, gender and experience - drop voluntariness, which is part of the original UTAUT.

Although there are many researches about E-L based on CC platform which were researched by Zaharescu [53]; Manop [29]; Deepanshu et al. [15]; Bhruthari et al. [7]; Masud and Huang [30]; Viswanath et al. [51]; Zheng and Jingxia [55]; Utpal and Majidul [44]... there are not many researches on the CC adoption model such as Leonardo et al. [25]; Muhambe and Daniel [32]; the studies of E-L acceptance and usage had been researched by Sun et al. [40]; Will and Allan [52]; Soud and Fisal [38]; Lin et al. [28]... On the other hand, there are not many researches on the acceptance and use of CBE-L in Vietnam and also in the world.

2.2   Theoretical Framework

Based on the review of the literature, Unified Theory of Acceptance and Use of Technology (UTAUT) [47], and UTAUT2 [48], the model of Acceptance and Use of E-Learning based on cloud computing in Vietnam is built in Fig. 1. The following are theoretically supported and resulting hypotheses that elicit relationships in the model.

Facilitating Condition (FC) is the degree to which an individual believes that an organizational and technical infrastructure exists to support the use of the system. This definition captures concepts embodied by 3 different constructs on perceived behavioral control in TPB [1, 2, 3]; TAM [12, 13], facilitating condition in MPCU [43], and compatibility in IDT [31, 36]. Venkatesh [45] found support for full mediation of the effect of facilitating condition on intention and usage by effort expectancy. According to Will and Allan [52], there are all sorts of problems involved in using an E-L system because of hardware, software and support. Thus, under CBE-L in Vietnam, it hypothesizes that:

Hypothesis $H1_a$: FC has a positive effect on CBE-L intention (CEI).
Hypothesis $H2_a$: FC has a positive effect on CBE-L usage (CEU).

Performance Expectancy (PE) means that an individual believes that using the system will help them to attain gains in job performance. The five constructs from the different models that pertain to performance expectancy are perceived usefulness in TAM [12, 13]; TAM 2 [46], extrinsic motivation in MM [14], job-fit in MPCU [43], relative advantage in IDT [31, 36], and outcome expectations in SCT [11, 21]. The learner believed that the E-L system was helpful to their performance and the individual learner would be more satisfied with the E-L [52]. Thus, under CBE-L in Vietnam, it hypothesizes that:

Hypothesis H1$_b$: PE has a positive effect on CEI.

Effort Expectancy (EE) indicates that the degree of ease associated with the use of the system. Three constructs from the existing models capture the concept of effort expectancy as perceived ease of use in TAM [12, 13]; TAM 2 [46], complexity in MPCU [43], and ease of use in IDT [31, 36]. The effort expectancy of an E-L system would influence users in their deciding whether or not to use the system [52]. Thus, it hypothesizes that:

Hypothesis H1$_c$: EE has a positive effect on CEI.

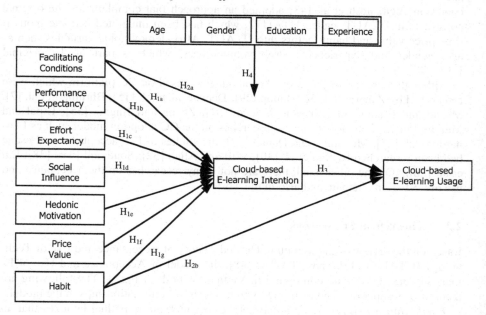

Fig. 1. Research Model: Acceptance and Use of E-learning based on Cloud Computing (Source: Adapted from UTAUT2 [48])

Social Influence (SI) is defined as the degree to which an individual perceives that important others believe people should use the new system. Social influence as a direct determinant of behavioral intention is represented as subjective norm in TRA [5, 17]; TAM [12, 13]; TAM 2 [46], social elements in MPCU [43], and image in IDT [31], [36]. According Venkatesh et al. [47], the role of social influence in technology acceptance decisions is complex and subject to a wide range of contingent influences. Will and Allan [52] noted that individual learners also recognized the fact that there might be a lot of problems in the E-L process. Thus, it hypothesizes that:

Hypothesis H1d: SI has a positive effect on CEI.

Hedonic Motivation (HM) has been the fun or pleasure derived from using a technology, and it has been shown to play an important role in determining technology acceptance and use [8]. In information system research, such hedonic motivation has been found to influence the technology acceptance and use directly [20]. According to Childers et al. [10]; Brown and Venkatesh [8], in the consumer context, hedonic motivation has also been found to be an important determinant of technology acceptance and use. Thus, it hypothesizes that:

Hypothesis H1e: HM has a positive effect on CEI.

Price Value (PV) means the cost and pricing structure may have a significant impact on the consumer technology user. The monetary cost and price is usually conceptualized together with the quality of products or services to determine the perceived value of products or services [54]. Dodds et al. [16] defined the price value as a consumer cognitive tradeoff between the perceived benefits of the applications and the monetary cost for using them. According to Venkatesh et al. [48], the price value is positive when the benefits of using a technology are perceived to be greater than the monetary cost, and such price value has a positive impact on intention. Thus, it hypothesizes that:

Hypothesis H1f: PV has a positive effect on CEI.

Habit (HA) has been defined as the extent to which people tend to perform behaviors automatically because of learning and equate habit with automaticity [23, 27]. Ajzen and Fishbein [4] noted that feedback from previous experiences influence various beliefs and consequently, future behavioral performance. According to Venkatesh et al. [48], the role of habit in technology use has delineated different underlying processes by which habit influences technology use. Thus, it hypothesizes that:

Hypothesis H1g: Habit has a positive effect on CEI.

Hypothesis H2b: Habit has a positive effect on use CEU.

CBE-L Intention (CEI), consistent with the underlying theory for all of the intention models are reviewed in studies such as Sheppard et al. [37]; Venkatesh et al. [47]; Venkatesh et al. [48] for literature review of the intention-behavior relationship, so that behavioral intention has a significant positive influence on technology usage. Thus, under CBE-L in Vietnam, it hypothesizes that:

Hypothesis H3: CEI has a positive effect on CEU.

Demographic (DE), including age, gender, experience and voluntariness were suggested as part of UTAUT [47], and were included in the analysis. They were analyzed to find out how they influenced the acceptance elements, including performance expectancy, effort expectancy, social influence and facilitating condition towards intention and use. According to Venkatesh et al. [48], in UTAUT2 model, voluntariness has been dropped in part of the original UTAUT. Thus, under CBE-L in Vietnam, it hypothesizes that:

Hypothesis H4: Independent and dependent elements are influenced by DE.

3   Research Results

3.1   Data

Data collection was undertaken by a survey using convenient sampling. The questionnaires were sent to respondents on google docs, via email, E-L forums, and sent hard copy questionnaires to respondents who have used or intend to use CBE-L in Vietnam. A total of 320 respondents was obtained, of which 282 were usable (38 invalid respondents). All scales were in the form of five-point Likert [26] scale with 29 observed variables. The data were analyzed by Structural Equation Modeling (SEM) techniques with the application of SPSS and AMOS.

Table 2. All variables of the research model in factor analysis

			Factor loading	
			EFA	CFA
		α = 0.685; AVE = 0.549		
FC	FC$_1$	The resources necessary to use CBE-L	0.913	.890
	FC$_3$	Knowledge necessary to use CBE-L	0.724	0.615
		α = 0.830; AVE = 0.520		
	PE$_3$	CBE-L useful in job	0.839	0.771
PE	PE$_2$	Using CBE-L enables to accomplish tasks quickly	0.820	0.758
	PE$_1$	Using CBE-L increases productivity	0.789	0.684
	PE$_4$	Increase chances of getting a raise	0.786	0.675
		α = 0.784; AVE = 0.589		
	EE$_3$	Learning how to use CBE-L is easy	0.840	.868
EE	EE$_2$	Interaction with CBE-L is clear and understandable	0.786	.754
	EE$_4$	Finding CBE-L easy to use	0.775	.716
	EE$_1$	It is easy to become skillful at using CBE-L	0.772	.666
		α = 0.740; AVE = 0.535		
SI	SI$_1$	People are important to think that should use EL	0.797	0.792
	SI$_2$	People influence behavior think that should use EL	0.783	0.760
	SI$_3$	People whose opinions that value prefer use EL	0.650	0.637
		α = 0.807; AVE = 0.584		
HM	HM$_1$	Using CBE-L is fun	0.813	0.792
	HM$_3$	Using CBE-L is enjoyable	0.754	0.778
	HM$_2$	Using CBE-L is entertaining	0.728	0.718
		α = 0.784; AVE = 0.520		
PV	PV$_3$	CBE-L is a good value for the money	0.857	.641
	PV$_2$	At the current price, CBE-L provides a good value	0.849	0.628
		α = 0.804; AVE = 0.607		
HA	HA$_2$	Using CBE-L has become a habit	0.892	0.871
	HA$_3$	Addicted to use CBE-L	0.804	0.791
	HA$_1$	Must use CBE-L	0.660	0.647
		α = 0.822; AVE = 0.523		
CEI	CEI$_2$	Intend to use CBE-L in the future	0.862	0.779
	CEI$_3$	Will try to use CBE-L in daily life	0.858	0.713
	CEI$_1$	Will plan to use CBE-L frequently	0.857	0.642
		α = 0.805; AVE = 0.612		
CEU	CEU$_1$	Intend to use CBE-L in the next 1 months	0.919	0.787
	CEU$_2$	Plan to use CBE-L in the next 3 months	0.902	0.778

α: Cronbach alpha; AVE: Average Variance Extracted.

A descriptive statistic is conducted for indicators related to the users who have used cloud-based E-learning. *Gender*: there are approximately 64% male and 36% female, it is uneven. *Age*: as regards the 19 - 23 age group, 24 - 30 group, and older-30 group, the former is by far the highest at nearly 50%, followed by the latter at 27% and 21% respectively. *Education:* there are nearly 70% of E-learners in university degree, about 24% of E-learners in post-graduated degree and percentage of the other is low. *Experience:* although about 60% of the people who are good at computing, only about 1% people are bad at computing, 39% average experience in computer using. Therefore, most of people have experienced in computing. *Cloud computing*: similarities exist between google drive, and modify where roughly 32% respondents use CC, 20% use dropbox, 13% use sky drive...

3.2   Exploratory and Confirmatory Factor Analysis

After eliminating 1 item that is FC_4 of facilitating condition element in reliability analysis (Cronbach alpha) due to the correlation-item of FC factor < 0.60 [33]. The composite reliability of constructs ranges from 0.685 to 0.830. Eliminating 2 items these are PV_1 and FC_3 of price value and facilitating condition elements in the 1st Exploratory Factor Analysis (EFA) due to the factor loading < 0.50 [19]. The 2nd EFA and then Confirmatory Factor Analysis (CFA) are conducted to assess and refine the measurement scales. The CFA on the overall measurement model yields the following measures: Chi-square (χ^2)/dF = 1.928; p = 0.000; TLI = 0.901; CFI = 0.917; RMSEA = 0.054. The CFA loading of all items ranges from 0.602 to 0.879. The Average Variance Extracted (AVA) of constructs ranges from 0.520 to 0.612 (> 0.50) which are good scales [18]. Therefore, the measurement scales for all constructs are satisfactory. The results of factor analysis are shown in Table 2.

Table 3. Analysis of hypothesized relationships (H1$_x$, H2$_y$ and H3)

	H	Relationships			Estimate	S. E.	p-value	Result
1	H1$_a$	FC	→	CEI	0.113	0.091	0.076	*Rejected*
2	H1$_b$	PE	→	CEI	0.137	0.057	0.027	*Supported*
3	H1$_c$	EE	→	CEI	0.071	0.050	0.220	*Rejected*
4	H1$_d$	SI	→	CEI	0.348	0.065	***	*Supported*
5	H1$_e$	HM	→	CEI	0.568	0.059	***	*Supported*
6	H1$_f$	PV	→	CEI	0.154	0.438	0.689	*Rejected*
7	H1$_g$	HA	→	CEI	0.201	0.038	***	*Supported*
8	H2$_a$	FC	→	CEU	0.071	0.088	0.220	*Rejected*
9	H2$_b$	HA	→	CEU	0.129	0.047	0.048	*Supported*
10	H3	CEI	→	CEU	0.841	0.093	***	*Supported*

x: a, b, c, d, e, d, e, f, g; y: a, b, c; *** $p < 0.001$.

3.3   Structural Model

The estimation of structural model was then conducted using ML estimation. The indexes for the model showed adequate fit with $\chi^2/dF = 1.768$; p = 0.000; TLI=0.918; CFI=0.931; RMSEA=0.048. The standardized path coefficients presented in Table 3: Support the positive effect of *PE* on *CEI* with $\gamma = 0.137$ (p = 0.027), that supports $H1_b$. *SI* and *HM* have strongly positive effect on *CEI* with $\gamma = 0.348$ (p < 0.001) and 0.568 (p < 0.001), which in turn $H1_d$ and $H1_e$ are supported. Support the positive effect of *HA* on *CEI* and *CEU* with $\gamma = 0.201$ (p < 0.001) and 0.129 (p = 0.040), which support $H1_g$ and $H2_b$. However, the path from *FC, EE* and *PV* to *CEI* and from *FC* to *CEU* are non-significant at p = 0.05. Therefore, $H1_a$, $H1_c$, $H1_f$ and $H2_a$ are rejected. Moreover, the results support H3 by showing a strong impact of *CEI* on *CEU* with $\gamma = 0.841$ (p < 0.001).

Table 4. ANOVA analysis follow age, gender, education and experience (H4)

Demographic	FC	PE	EE	SI	HM	PV	HA	CEI	CEU	Note
Age	x**	x**	–	x*	x*	–	x*	–	–	5 elements
Gender	x*	x**	x***	x*	–	–	x*	x*	–	6 elements
Education	–	x*	x*	x**	x**	–	x*	–	–	5 elements
Experience	x***	–	x*	–	x*	–	–	–	–	3 elements

x: individual differences; * p < 0.05; ** p < 0.01; *** p < 0.001.

ANOVA test is carried out to analyze if there are any differences in the relationship between *FC, PE, EE, SI, HM, PV, HA, CEI* and *CEU* can be attributed to the demographic variables namely age, gender, education and experience. The results show that the relationship between independent and dependent variables differ by age (5 elements: *FC, PE, SI, HM* and *HA*), gender (6 elements: *FC, PE, EE, SI, HA* and *CEI*), education (5 elements: *PE, EE, SI, HM* and *HA*) and experience (3 elements: *FC, EE* and *HM*) are significant with p < 0.05. The results of ANOVA analysis are shown in Table 4. Although there are no differences in *PV* and *CEU* with demographic variables, but most of the variables are differences. Thus, H4 is supported. Generally, 7 out of 11 hypotheses are supported in this study.

The results show that facilitating condition, performance expectancy, effort expectancy, social influence, hedonic motivation, price value and habit are able to explain in both cloud-based E-learning intention nearly 60% ($R^2 = 0.598$) and cloud-based E-learning usage about 78% ($R^2 = 0.781$) are substantial. The results are also compared to the baseline UTAUT [47]; UTAUT2 [48] which explained roughly 56% and 40% (UTAUT); 74% and 52% (UTAUT2) of the variance in behavioral intention and technology use respectively. Research results can contribute to the theory of information system, it is not only in Vietnam but also in the globe, here user acceptance and use of cloud-based E-learning.

4   Conclusions

The study illustrates that all scales of independent variables, intention of cloud-based E-learning and use of cloud-based E-learning ensure reliability. Exploratory and confirmatory factor analysis indicates that measurement scales for all constructs are satisfactory. The results also provide that are relationships between the performance expectancy, social influence, hedonic motivation, habit, and cloud-based E-learning intention, and cloud-based E-learning usage. The facilitating condition, effort expectancy, price value and habit are non-significant with cloud-based E-learning intention, and facilitating condition is non-significant with cloud-based E-learning usage. In addition, the study provides the differences in variables are attributed to the demographic. There are seven out of eleven hypotheses are supported in this research. The research model explains the behavioral intention and technology usage is better than the UTAUT [47] and UTAUT2 [48]. Which is harmonized to the context of user acceptance and use of information system.

References

1. Ajzen, I.: Behavioral Control, Self-Efficacy, Locus of Control and the Theory of Planned Behavior. Journal of Applied Social Psychology 32, 665–683 (2002)
2. Ajzen, I.: From Intentions to Action: A theory of Planned Pehavior, pp. 11–39. Springer (1985)
3. Ajzen, I.: The Theory of Planned Behavior. Organization Behavior and Human Decision Process 50, 179–211 (1991)
4. Ajzen, I., Fishbein, M.: The Influence of Attitudes on Behavior. In: Albarracin, D., Johnson, B.T., Zanna, M.P. (eds.) The Handbook of Attitudes, pp. 173–221. Erlbaum, Mahwah (2005)
5. Ajzen, I., Fishbein, M.: Understanding attitudes and predicting social behavior. Prentice Hall, Englewood Cliffs (1980)
6. Ambient Insight: Worldwide Market for Self-paced eLearning Products and Services: 2011-2016 Forecast and Analysis. Ambient Insight Report (2013),
   http://www.ambientinsight.com
7. Bhruthari, G.P., Sanil, S.N., Prajakta, P.D.: Appliance of Cloud Computing on E-Learning. International Journal of Computer Science and Management Research, 276–281 (2012)
8. Brown, S.A., Venkatesh, V.: Model of Adoption of Technology in the Household: A Baseline Model Test and Ext. Incorporating Household Life Cycle. MIS Quarterly 29(4), 399–426 (2005)
9. Certifyme: Announces E-learning Statistics for 2013 (2013),
   http://www.certifyme.net
10. Childers, T.L., Carr, C.L., Peck, J., Carson, S.: Hedonic and Utilitarian Motivations for Online Retail Shopping Behavior. Journal of Retailing 77(4), 511–535 (2001)
11. Compeau, D.R., Higgins, C.A.: Computer self-efficacy: Development of a measure and initial test. MIS Quarterly 19(2), 189–211 (1995)
12. Davis, F.D.: Perceived usefulness, perceived ease of use and user acceptance of Information Technology. MIS Quaterly 13(3), 319–340 (1989)

13. Davis, F.D.: User acceptance of information technology: System characteristics, user perceptions and behavioral impacts. International Journal of Man-Machine 38, 475–487 (1993)
14. Davis, F.D., Bagozzi, R.P., Warshaw, P.R.: Extrinsic and Intrinsic Motivation to Use Computers in the Workplace. Journal of Applied Social Psychology 22(14), 1111–1132 (1992)
15. Deepanshu, M., Ashish, P., Suneet, K., Arjun, A.: E-learning based on Cloud Computing. International Journal of Advanced Research in Computer Science and Software 2(2), 1–6 (2012)
16. Dodds, W.B., Monroe, K.B., Grewal, D.: Effects of Price, Brand and Store Information for Buyers. Journal of Marketing Research 28(3), 307–319 (1991)
17. Fishbein, M., Ajzen, I.: Belief, attitude, intention and behavior: An introduction to theory and research. Addision-Wesley (1975)
18. Fornell, C., Larcker, D.F.: Evaluating Structural Equation Models with unobservable variables and measurement error. Journal of Marketing Research 18(1), 39–50 (1981)
19. Hair, J.F., Black, W.C., Babin, B.J., Anderson, R.E.: Multivariate data analysis: A global perspective. Pearson, London (2010)
20. Heijden, V.D.: User Acceptance of Hedonic Information Systems. MIS Quarterly 28(4), 695–704 (2004)
21. Hill, T., Smith, N.D., Mann, M.F.: Role of efficacy expectations in predicting the decision to use advanced technologies: The case of computers. Journal of Applied Psychology 72(2), 307–313 (1987)
22. Kamel, S.: The role of virtual organizations in post-graduate education in Egypt: The case of the regional IT institute. In: Tan, F.B. (ed.) Courses on Global IT Applications and Management: Success and Pitfalls, pp. 203–224. Idea Group Publishing, Hershey (2002)
23. Kim, S.S., Malhotra, N.K., Narasimhan, S.: Two competing perspectives on automatic use: A Theoretical and Empirical Comparison. Information Systems Research 16(4), 418–432 (2005)
24. Laisheng, X., Zhengxia, W.: Cloud Computing a New Business Paradigm for E-learning. In: International Conference on Measuring Technology and Mechatronics Automation, pp. 716–719 (2011)
25. Leonardo, R.O., Adriano, J.M., Gabriela, V.P., Rafael, V.: Adoption analysis of cloud computing services. African Journal of Business Management 7(24), 2362–2374 (2013)
26. Likert: A Technique for the Measurement of Attitude. Archive Psychology 140 (1932)
27. Limayem, M., Hirt, S.G., Cheung, C.M.K.: How Habit Limits the Predictive Power of Intentions: The Case of IS Continuance. MIS Quarterly 31(4), 705–737 (2007)
28. Lin, P.C., Lu, S.C., Liu, S.K.: Towards an Education Behavioral Intention Model for E-Learning Systems: an Extension of UTAUT. Journal of Theoretical and Applied Information Technology 47(3), 1120–1127 (2013)
29. Phankokkruad, M.: Implement of Cloud Computing for e-Leaming System. In: International Conference on Computer & Information Science. IEEE (2012)
30. Masud, A.H., Huang, X.: An E-learning System Architecture based on Cloud Computing. World Academy of Science, Engineering and Technology 62, 71–76 (2012)
31. Moore, G.C., Benbasat, I.: Development of an instrument to measure the perception of adopting an information technology innovation. Information Systems Research 2(3), 192–222 (1991)
32. Muhambe, T.M., Daniel, O.O.: Post adoption evaluation model for cloud computing services utilization in universities in Kenya. International Journal of Management & Information Technology 5(3), 615–628 (2013)
33. Nunnally, J.C., Bernstein, I.H.: Psychometric theory. McGraw Hill, New York (1994)

34. Pocatilu, P., Alecu, F., Vetrici, M.: Using Cloud Computing for E-learning Systems. In: Recent Advances on Data Networks, Communications, Computers, pp. 54–59 (2009)
35. Pocatilu, P., Alecu, F., Vetrici, M.: Cloud Computing Benefits for E-learning Solutions. Economics of Knowledge 2(1), 9–14 (2010)
36. Rogers, E.M.: Diffusion of innovations. Free Press, New York (1995)
37. Sheppard, B.H., Hartwick, J., Warshaw, P.R.: The Theory of Reasoned Action: A Meta-Analysis of Past Research with Recommendations for Modifications and Future Research. Journal of Consumer Research 15(3), 325–343 (1988)
38. Soud, A., Fisal, A.R.: Factors that determine continuance intention to use e-learning system: an empirical investigation. In: International Conference on Telecommunication Technology and Applications, vol. 5, pp. 241–246. IACSIT Press, Singapore (2011)
39. Sun Microsystem: Cloud Computing Guide. Sun Microsystems Inc. (2009)
40. Sun, P., Tsai, R., Finger, G., Chen, Y., Yeh, D.: What drives a successful e-Learning? An empirical investigation of the critical factors influencing learner satisfaction. Computers & Education 50, 1183–1202 (2008)
41. Tavangarian, D., Leypold, M.E., Nolting, K., Roser, M., Voigt, D.: Is e-Learning the solution for individual learning? Electronic Journal of e-Learning 2(2), 273–280 (2004)
42. Taylor, S., Todd, P.: Understanding Information Technology Usage: A Test of Competing Models. Information Systems Research 6(2), 144–176 (1995)
43. Thompson, R., Higgins, R., Howell, L.: Personal computing: Toward a conceptual model of utilization. MIS Quarterly 15(1), 125–143 (1991)
44. Utpal, J.B., Majidul, A.: E-Learning using Cloud Computing. International Journal of Science and Modern Engineering, 9–13 (2013)
45. Venkatesh, V.: Determinants of Perceived Ease of Use: Integrating Perceived Behavioral Control, Computer Anxiety and Enjoyment into the Technology Acceptance Model. Information Systems Research 11(4), 342–365 (2000)
46. Venkatesh, V., Davis, F.D.: A Theoretical Extension of the Technology Acceptance Model: Four Longitudinal Field Studies. Management Science 46(2), 186–204 (2000)
47. Venkatesh, V., Morris, M.G., Davis, G.B., Davis, F.D.: User acceptance of information technology: Toward a unified view. MIS Quarterly 27(3), 425–478 (2003)
48. Venkatesh, V., Thong, Y.L.J., Xin, X.: Consumer Acceptance and Use of Information Technology: Extending the Unified Theory of Acceptance and Use of Technology. MIS Quarterly 36(1), 157–178 (2012)
49. Venkatraman Archana: Italian university reduces costs by 23% with cloud platform (2013), http://www.computerweekly.com
50. Vietnam Ministry of Education and Training: The guide about deployment task for the academic year of 2011-2012. Dispatch no. 4960/GDĐT-CNTT (2011)
51. Viswanath, K., Kusuma, S., Gupta, S.K.: Cloud Computing Issues and Benefits Modern Education. Global Journal of Computer Science and Technology Cloud & Distributed 12(10), 1–7 (2012)
52. Will, M., Allan, Y.: E-learning system Acceptance and usage pattern. In: Technology Acceptance in Education: Research and Issue, pp. 201-216 (2011)
53. Zaharescu, E.: Enhanced Virtual E-Learning Environments Using Cloud Computing Architectures. International Journal of Computer Science Research and Application 2(1), 31–41 (2012)
54. Zeithaml, V.A.: Consumer Perceptions of Price, Quality, and Value: A Means-End Model and Synthesis of Evidence. Journal of Marketing 52(3), 2–22 (1988)
55. Zheng, H., Jingxia, V.: Integrating E-Learning System Based on Cloud Computing. In: International Conference on Granular Computing. IEEE (2012)

Requirements Identification for Migrating eGovernment Applications to the Cloud

Evangelos Gongolidis, Christos Kalloniatis, and Evangelia Kavakli

Cultural Informatics Laboratory, Department of Cultural Technology and Communication
University of the Aegean, University Hill, GR 81100 Mytilene, Greece
{vgogol,chkallon@aegean.gr}, kavakli@ct.aegean.gr

Abstract. Increasing citizens' participation in the use of eGovernment services is one of the main goals that governments all around the world are aiming to satisfy. While the number of Internet users is increasing rapidly and the percentage of the use of ICT services follows the same increment it is obvious that governments are seeking to take advantage of the modern alternative technological solutions in order to design the next generation of eGovernment systems and services. Without any doubt one of the most advanced solution that offers many advantages both in hardware and software levels is cloud computing. This paper aims on identifying the major functional and non-functional requirements that a traditional eGovenrment system should realise for its safe migration into a cloud environment.

Keywords: eGovernment, Cloud Computing, functional requirements, non-functional requirements, cloud migration.

1   Introduction

According to United Nations, eGovernment is defined as the employment of the Internet and the World Wide Web to deliver government services [1]. Cloud computing according to NIST [2], is based on a new model for the delivery of information and service through the Internet, which is based on the concept that involves a large number of computers who are inter-connected and act as one to each request. In cloud computing, software, hardware and network play the main role [3]. The type of request can vary and is based to the user himself but the most important gain in cloud computing is that it is very economic as it is based on large scale architecture concept (the more you build/use/take, the better) and the cloud client can at any time define the amount of sources that wants to use. As a result, eGovernment in all over the world has significantly changed the idea of delivery specific services through a single server and perform all required maintenance on it [4] by moving to the cloud.

However, there are several differences and aspects that needs to be examined and reinstated before moving from traditional server systems to the cloud. Also, during the last years a discussion has started over whether cloud computing is able to host and handle information and requests provided from different types of users

Linawati et al. (Eds.): ICT-EurAsia 2014, LNCS 8407, pp. 150–158, 2014.

(government, companies etc) [5]. The scope of this paper, is to focus on traditional eGovernment systems and present the requirements a porta/system must fulfil in order to be characterized as a functional eGovernment system. Specifically, in section 2 the main functional and non-functional requirements that an eGovernment platform should satisfy in traditional environments are presented and described. All characteristics are treated of equal importance and significance when designing respective services into the cloud. In section 3 a brief description of cloud service and deployment models is presented. In section 4 an analysis of the identified requirements and their role in the cloud-based eGovernment systems is presented along with a matching of every requirement with the respective cloud service models that has an applicability on.

2   eGovernment

From the establishment of ICT technologies, governments all over the world tried to insert ICT into the daily procedures. However, that act was not easy as there were several requirements that should be adopted for each government system and there were also several legislation requirements. As a result almost 80% of the projects in the early 20s were in the failure category [6]. The requirements that are presented below were extracted from reports provided by the European Union for i2010 initiatives [7], United Nations reports for eGovernment Systems characteristics and the Greek Interoperability Framework [8].

2.1   Interoperability

Interoperability is one of the most important characteristics of eGovernment systems. Interoperability can be described as a chain that allows information and computer systems to be joined up both within organizations and then across organization boundaries with other organizations, administrations, enterprises or citizens [9].

Interoperability is defined in 3 layers: technical, semantic and organization.

- o   Technical is concerned with the technical aspects of connecting computer systems, the definition of open interfaces, data formats and protocols including telecommunication.
- o   Semantic, is the ability for an external system to be able to realize that the stored or provided information has a specific meaning and is not treated as raw data. Semantic interoperability is obtained by the common use of predefined standards and prototypes.
- o   Organizational interoperability is concerned with modelling business processes, aligning information architectures with organizational goals and helping business process to cooperate. The most important part of organization interoperability refers to the ability of different implemented services that take part in a specific government process to be able to cooperate automatically and generate a specific result.

2.2   eInclusion

eInclusion is the characteristic that requires the eGovernment services to be able to be delivered to all people, breaking any technological barrier that could arise. eInclusion has the power to close the gap between developed and less developed countries, can also promote democracy, participation and mutual understanding between different countries or different social parties. It can also empower disadvantaged individuals, such as the poor, the disabled, and the unemployed.

2.3   eAccesibility

eAccesibility refers to the ease of use of information and communication technologies (ICTs), such as the Internet or services provided by the Internet, by people with disabilities. For eGovernment services each service or each portal that provides the government service needs to be developed so that disabled users can access the information. For example:

- for people who are blind, web sites need to be able to be interpreted by programs which can recognize and read text aloud and also describe any visual images.
- for people who have low vision, web pages need adjustable sized fonts with an easy way to increase or decrease the size of the fonts. Also the use of sharply contrasting colors is greatly encouraged.
- for people who are deaf or hard of hearing, audio content should be accompanied by text versions of the dialogue. Sign language video can also help make audio content more accessible.

2.4   User Registration

User registration is the procedure that a user needs to follow in order to register to a specific eGovernment system. The procedure must be clearly defined, must not violate any legislation related to personal data and must also give the user the ability to cancel his account or retrieve a lost password.

2.5   Single Sign On – One Stop Service

This characteristic requires that all implemented systems that are related to eGovernment will use the same account credentials for each government entity that provides eGovernment services. As a result, implemented systems from different government entities of the same country will require the same credentials. Also, it is of great importance for each country to provide their services from a one stop shop which will be declared as the national eGovernment service portal.

2.6   eTransparency

Transparency is related to the act of make open and searchable by all the act of decision and actions related to a government policy. As a result, eTransparency is the use of ICT for handling or providing information or tools for those steps related to transparency flow. eTransparency can also be categorized in the following levels:

- Publication: providing basic information about a particular area of government.
- Transaction: automating some public sector process and generate automated reporting on that process.
- Reporting: providing specific details of public sector decisions/spending/actions (e.g. via performance indicators or via list of spending).
- Openness: allowing users to compare public servant performance against pre-set benchmarks.
- Accountability: allowing users some mechanism of control (e.g. reward or punishment) over public servants.

An interesting aspect of eTransparency is project Diavgeia [10] which was established in Greece since 2009. Diavgeia, aims to solve the publication and reporting level of eTransparency by providing information about public spending made from the greek government sector.

2.7   Adaptivity

Every implemented system or service must be easily adapted, without any great financial cost, to new requirements that are provided by the government entity. Adaptivity is of great importance for matters related to legislation and technology evolution.

2.8   Use of Standards/Prototypes

Each implemented service or procedure should be based on a trusted prototype. The use of open source standards is also greatly encouraged. Several countries in their eGovernment frameworks also provide the standard that they require to be used for specific services so apart from using a trusted standard the developer must also verify that the developed service is compliant with the country defined standard.

2.9   Scaling

The ability for the systems to easily decrease or extend the current use of hardware so it can easily provide better quality of service to a different number of interested users for with the least financial cost.

2.10   System/Service Availability

All implemented systems or services must be available to the users without any interaction of service. In case of a system or service failure the user must be informed immediately about the reason of failure.

2.11   Fault Tolerance/Auditing/Logging

All implemented systems must provide an automate procedure to recover from failure states and also the system must be able to move to the last good state automatically. Internally, the system must have auditing and logging mechanisms that would keep track on any change or request that is done through the system/service.

2.12   Maintenance/Update

The implemented system or service should be easily maintained and updated when required. Each act must not be related or based on a specific constructor and must be able to be accomplished by anyone related to the government entity.

2.13   Trust of Citizen for Proper Use of Data

EGovernment is based on the use of confidential data for the provision of each service. As a result, each government entity that use data for a citizen must be able to process only confidential data that is related to the service/system state and not all data that is stored.

3   Cloud Computing

Cloud computing was a revolutionary change in the state-of-the-art for the provision of both software and hardware services. Cloud computing can be briefly described as a collection of scalable and virtualized resources and is capable of providing specific services on demand [11]. The main goal of cloud computing is to provide ICT services with the use of shared infrastructure and the collection of many systems. For government the value that is gained from moving to the cloud is especially appealing, given both changing demands for IT and challenging economic conditions [12].

3.1   Cloud Service Models

In order to correlate the above mentioned characteristics of eGovernment with cloud computing we must distinguish the service models of cloud computing. Cloud computing mainly consists of three service models:

- Infrastructure as a Service(IaaS)
- Platform as a Service (PaaS)
- Software as a Service (SaaS)

Infrastructure as a Service can be briefly described as buying or scaling recently bought infrastructure resources using a predefined service model. IaaS can also be classified in two categories: Computation as a Service (CaaS) and Data as a Service (DaaS). CaaS refers to the ability to buy or rent specific resources for a period of time in order to perform difficult computation calculations and is related to processor, RAM or deployed software. DaaS refers to the ability to buy or rent storage space which can either be used instantly or can be delegated to third-party users.

Platform as a Service refers to ability of buy of enhance a predefined platform, which results in providing a set of software and services that can be used to provide a better working environment or a better quality of service. The concept of using PaaS relies on the ability to use a platform which provides specific capabilities (ie the ability to build a website) without already know how to do it. PaaS also lies on the ability to support all required procedures or intermediate steps to get the expected outcome.

Software as a Service (SaaS) is based on the use of software of application, which are hosted in the cloud environment of the provider and are provided on demand to the end-user. As a result, the user does not have to worry about licensing or maintaining costs as the provided software is licensed and upgraded by the provider.

3.2 Deployment Models

Apart from the above described service delivery models, cloud computing is also characterized by how it is deployed and specifically who has access in the cloud environment. The delegation of the above mentioned responsibilities forms up the following cloud deployment models [13]:

Private Cloud: Private cloud refers to those organizations which solely operate the cloud environment, whether it is managed by the same operation or it is managed by a third party. Private cloud is the most closest to the traditional use of ICT as every operation performed in the cloud model must be funded by the organization.

Community Cloud: Community cloud refers to a model where the cloud is operated by organizations which share similar interests and can also be managed internally of externally. As a result, the required costs are spread between the different organizations.

Public Cloud: Public cloud is deployed and operated for the public and can be maintained by one or several organizations. Access to this type of cloud is allowed to everyone.

Hybrid Cloud: Hybrid cloud is a composition of different models which retain their independence but cooperate with a specific manner. The manner that they cooperate must be clearly defined by the cloud provider to all interested parties.

4   Categorization of eGovernment Requirements to Cloud Service Models

As a result, eGovernment entities who are willing to move to cloud must first decide how they will handle the above mentioned requirements that are related to traditional eGovernment systems. Moving to the cloud for eGovernment systems is not only a matter of breaking technical obstacles but also finding a methodology that would be compliant with all provided government requirements. The first step of providing a compliant methodology for the cloud migration would be to distinguish in which Service Level each requirements would be delegated.

Interoperability is mainly a matter of data and the way that these data could be used or passed to another system using the cloud. As a result, interoperability could be handled with a SaaS approach that will provide specific data for a simple call or as a PaaS approach where interoperability would be handled inside of a model with specific preconditions and post conditions.

eInclusion and eAccesibility are both requirements that are strongly related and act complementary. EGovernment systems should promote the inclusion of all parties' regardless of current financial state/ education/ hardware, while eAccesibility cares mostly about the sensitive parts of modern societies. As a result, both could be handled with a three cloud level approach. IaaS would be responsible for providing the required hardware on demand for each request, while PaaS and SaaS would be able to tackle accessibility problems in a platform or service oriented approach.

User Registration / Single Sign on are also similar problems which should be tackled in the same way. Moving to the cloud should be accompanied by a mechanism for authentication which should also be used by other systems simultaneously. As a result, this matter could be solved with a PaaS approach where the platform would xbe dedicated to authorization and rights delegation or a SaaS approach where each required action would be provided as a Service (i.e. logging, access rights).

Transparency is a very important characteristic for eGovernment systems and is decomposed in five levels as described above. As a result, eTransparency could be achieved by a SaaS approach where each step would be treated as a service of a PaaS approach where the concept and the requirements of transparency would be handled in a provided platform.

Scaling is a clear matter of an IaaS approach as it refers to the ability to scale up or down provided infrastructure either automatically or on demand.

Adaptivity is a more complex problem and it refers to several matters in different levels of service provision. All provided services to the end users must be easily adapted to new requirements that are provided. As a result, a service oriented approach could formalize the way the adaptions could be done.

Use of standards / prototypes could be handled as a SaaS or PaaS approach. The SaaS approach would handle and store the prototype that is used by each provided service, while PaaS can also move further and provide the capability of online uploading, validating and use of prototypes that are already stored in the platform.

System Service / Availability and Fault Tolerance are inextricably linked. The system must be online 100% using specific cloud features and also there must be services that would enable the tracking of availability, the use of precaution actions (i.e. reboot) or the ability to roll back system data. The provided solution can be software oriented regarding each subject like logging and auditing or Platform oriented regarding the main subject.

Maintenance /Update is clear a matter of SaaS as the update actions should be provided by a software which would be able to handle and perform update requests on its own.

Security - Privacy/Trust of Citizen is a matter of all service levels. Security and privacy issues are identified specifically for every cloud service model separately [14]. In order for an eGovernment system or individual service to be trusted and protected respective security measures should be implemented in all service models.

An outline of the service level where each concept could be handled is provided in table 1.

Table 1. Matching eGov Requirements with Cloud Service Models

Requirement	IaaS	PaaS	SaaS
Interoperability		X	X
eInclusion/ eAccessibility	X	X	X
User Registration / Single Sign on		X	X
Transparency		X	X
Scaling	X		
Adaptivity			X
Use of prototypes		X	X
System Service Availability and Fault Tolerance		X	X
Maintenance /Update			X
Security-Privacy / Trust of Citizen	X	X	X

5   Conclusions

The transformation from the use and maintenance of traditional services to the cloud can be a long and difficult procedure. For government applications it is even more complex because the transformation should not break or violate the relationship or the legislation that was already adopted by the traditional approach.

In this paper we presented the known requirements that an eGovernment system should satisfy and the way that these requirements could be satisfied from respective service models when migrating into the cloud. It is of major importance to mention here that the government entity could act both as the cloud provider or the end user.

Regarding the concept of migrating eGovernment application to the cloud we must also take into serious consideration that the stakeholder is not only the cloud provider but also the legislation and the political will of the government entity. Finally, it is important to mention that the government entities among countries can be of various levels (ministries, municipalities etc.) and the move from the traditional ICT services to the cloud should also try to bridge the gaps that already exist in communication or in data exchange.

Future work includes the identification of respective technical solutions that can realise these requirements into the cloud and especially for every service model and deployment model correspondingly. The definition of protocols in each level will also act as a comparison factor on finding which methodology could be better in terms of implementation and performance. Finally, we will try to provide a specific cloud framework which could act as a PaaS and provide auxiliary steps to eGovernment entities that are willing to migrate their systems to the cloud.

References

[1] D. o. E. a. S. Affairs, E-Government Survey, United Nations, New York (2012)
[2] Mell, P., Glance, T.:The NIST Definition of Cloud, NIST (2011)
[3] Y.L. e. al: Towards a unified ontology of cloud computing. In: Computing Environments Workshop (2008)
[4] M. e. al: Above the Clouds: A Berkeley view of Cloud Computing, University of California, Berkeley (2009)
[5] L. N: Is cloud computing really ready for the prime time. J. of ACM 42(1), 15–20 (2009)
[6] H. R: Implemenation and Managing of eGovernment. Vistaar Publication (2006)
[7] Millard, J., et al.: E. Commision. European Commision (2009)
[8] Information Society, Greek Interoperability Framework (2008)
[9] Commision of the European Communities, Linking up Europe: the Importance of Interoperability for eGovernment Services (2003)
[10] T. e. al: Open data for e-government, the greek case, Information, Intelligence, Systems and Applications (IISA), Piraeus (2013)
[11] F. B. a. Escalante: Handbook of Cloud Computing. Springer Science(2010)
[12] Wyld, D.: Moving to the cloud: An introduction to cloud computing in Government (2009)
[13] Zwattendorfer, B., Stranacher, K., Tauber, A., Reichstädter, P.: Cloud Computing in E-government across Europe: A Comparison. In: Kő, A., Leitner, C., Leitold, H., Prosser, A. (eds.) EDEM 2013 and EGOVIS 2013. LNCS, vol. 8061, pp. 181–195. Springer, Heidelberg (2013)
[14] Kalloniatis, C., Mouratidis, H., Manousakis, V., Islam, S., Gritzalis, S., Kavakli, E.: Towards the design of secure and privacy-oriented Information Systems in the Cloud: Identifying the major concepts. Computer, Standards and Interfaces 36(4), 759–775 (2014)

A GPU-Based Enhanced Genetic Algorithm
for Power-Aware Task Scheduling Problem in HPC Cloud

Nguyen Quang-Hung, Le Thanh Tan, Chiem Thach Phat, and Nam Thoai

Faculty of Computer Science & Engineering, HCMC University of Technology, VNUHCM
268 Ly Thuong Kiet Street, Ho Chi Minh City, Vietnam
{hungnq2,nam}@cse.hcmut.edu.vn,
{50902369,50901901}@stu.hcmut.edu.vn

Abstract. In this paper, we consider power-aware task scheduling (PATS) in
HPC clouds. Users request virtual machines (VMs) to execute their tasks. Each
task is executed on one single VM, and requires a fixed number of cores (i.e.,
processors), computing power (million instructions per second - MIPS) of each
core, a fixed start time and non-preemption in a duration. Each physical machine
has maximum capacity resources on processors (cores); each core has limited
computing power. The energy consumption of each placement is measured for
cost calculating purposes. The power consumption of a physical machine is in a
linear relationship with its CPU utilization. We want to minimize the total energy
consumption of the placements of tasks. We propose here a genetic algorithm
(GA) to solve the PATS problem. The GA is developed with two versions: (1)
BKGPUGA, which is an adaptively implemented using NVIDIA's Compute
Unified Device Architecture (CUDA) framework; and (2) SGA, which is a serial
GA version on CPU. The experimental results show the BKGPUGA program
that executed on a single NVIDIA® TESLA™ M2090 GPU (512 cores) card obtains significant speedups in comparing to the SGA program executing on Intel®
Xeon™ E5-2630 (2.3 GHz) on same input problem size. Both versions share the
same GA's parameters (e.g. number of generations, crossover and mutation
probability, etc.) and a relative small (10^{-11}) on difference of two finesses between BKGPUGA and SGA. Moreover, the proposed BKGPUGA program can
handle large-scale task scheduling problems with scalable speedup under limitations of GPU device (e.g. GPU's device memory, number of GPU cores, etc.).

1 Introduction

Cloud platforms have become more popular in provision of computing resources under virtual machine (VM) abstraction for high performance computing (HPC) users to
run their applications. An HPC cloud is such a cloud platform. Keqin Li [1] presented
a task scheduling problems and power-aware scheduling algorithms on multiprocessor
computers. We consider here the power-aware task scheduling (PATS) problem in the
HPC cloud. The challenge of the PATS problem is the trade-off between minimizing
of energy consumption and satisfying Quality of Service (QoS) (e.g. performance or
on-time resource availability for reservation requests). Genetic algorithm (GA) has
proposed to solve task scheduling problems [2]. Moreover, GA is one of evolutionary

Linawati et al. (Eds.): ICT-EurAsia 2014, LNCS 8407, pp. 159–169, 2014.

inspired algorithms that are used in green computing [3]. The PATS problem with N tasks (each task requires a VM) and M physical machines can generate M^N possible placements. Therefore, whenever the PATS problem increases its problem size, the computation time of these algorithms to find out an optimal solution or a satisfactory solution is unacceptable.

GPU computing has become a popular programming model to get high performance on data-parallel applications. NVIDIA introduces CUDA parallel computing framework where a CUDA program can run on GeForce®, Quadro®, and Tesla® products. Latest Tesla® architecture is designed for parallel computing and high performance computing. In the newest Tesla architecture, each GPU card has hundreds of CUDA cores and gets multiple Teraflops that target to high performance computing. For example, a Tesla K10 GPU Accelerator with dual GPUs gets 4.58 teraflops peak single precision [4]. Therefore, study of genetic algorithm on GPU has become an active research topic. Many previous works proposed genetic algorithm on GPU [5][6][7][8]. However, none of these works has studied the PATS. In this paper, we propose BKGPUGA, a GA implemented in CUDA framework and compatible with the NVIDIA Tesla architecture, to solve the PATS problems. The BKGPUGA proposes applying same genetic operation (e.g. crossover, mutation, and selection) and evaluation fitness of chromosomes on whole population in each generation that uses data-parallel model on hundreds of CUDA threads concurrently.

2   Problem Formulation

We describe notations used in this paper as following:

T_i Task i

M_j Machine j

$r_j(t)$ Set of indexes of tasks that is allocated on the M_j at time t

$mips_{i,c}$ Allocated MIPS of the c-th processing element (PE) to the T_i by M_j

$MIPS_{j,c}$ Total MIPS of the c-th processing element (PE) on the M_j

We assume that total power consumption of a single physical machine $(P(.))$ has a linear relationship with CPU utilization (U_{cpu}) as mentioned in [9]. We calculate CPU utilization of a host is sum of total CPU utilization on PE_j cores:

$$U_{cpu}(t) = \sum_{c=1}^{PE_j} \sum_{i \in r_j(t)} \frac{mips_{i,c}}{MIPS_{j,c}} \tag{1}$$

Total power consumption of a single host $(P(.))$ at time t is calculated:

$$P\left(U_{cpu}(t)\right) = P_{idle} + (P_{max} - P_{idle}).U_{cpu}(t) \tag{2}$$

Energy consumption of a host (E_i) in period time $[t_i, t_{i+1}]$ is defined by:

$$E_i(t) = \int_{t_i}^{t_{i+1}} [P_{idle} + (P_{max} - P_{idle}).U_{cpu}(t)]dt \tag{3}$$

In this paper, we assume that $\forall t \in [t_i, t_{i+1}]$: $U_{cpu}(t)$ is constant (u_i), then:

$$E_i = [P_{idle} + (P_{max} - P_{idle}).u_i].(t_{i+1} - t_i) \tag{4}$$

Therefore, we obtain the total energy consumption (E) of a host during operation time: $\bigcup_{i=0,1,2,...} [t_i, t_{i+1}]$: $E = \sum E_i$

We consider the power-aware task scheduling (PATS) in high performance computing (HPC) Cloud. We formulate the PATS problem as following:

Given a set of n independent tasks to be placed on a set of m physical machines. Each task is executed on a single VM.

The set of n tasks is denoted as: $V = \{T_i(pe_i, mips_i, ram_i, bw_i, ts_i, d_i) | i = 1,...,n\}$

The set of m physical machines is denoted as: $M = \{M_j(PE_j, MIPS_j, RAM_i, BW_j) | j = 1,...,m\}$

Each i-th task is executed on a single virtual machine (VM_i) requires pe_i processing elements (cores), $mips_i$ MIPS, ram_i MBytes of physical memory, bw_i Kbits/s of network bandwidth, and the VM_i will be started at time (ts_i) and finished at time ($ts_i + d_i$) with neither preemption nor migration in its duration (d_i). We concern three types of computing resources such as processors, physical memory, and network bandwidth. We assume that every M_j can run any VM and the power consumption model ($P_j(t)$) of the M_j has a linear relationship with its CPU utilization as described in formula (2). The objective of scheduling is minimizing total energy consumption in fulfillment of maximum requirements of n tasks (and VMs) and following constraints:

Constraint 1: Each task is executed on a VM that is run by a physical machine (host).

Constraint 2: No task requests any resource larger than total capacity of the host's resource.

Constraint 3: Let $r_j(t)$ be the set of indexes of tasks that are allocated to a host M_j. The sum of total demand resource of these allocated tasks is less than or equal to total capacity of the resource of the M_j. For each c-th processing element of a physical machine M_j ($j=1,..,m$):

$$\forall c = 1 \dots PE_j, \forall i \in r_j(t): \sum_{i \in r_j(t)} mips_{i,c} \leq MIPS_{j,c} \tag{5}$$

For other resources of the M_j such as physical memory (RAM) and network bandwidth (BW):

$$\forall i \in r_j(t): \sum_{i \in r_j(t)} ram_i \leq RAM_j, \forall i \in r_j(t): \sum_{i \in r_j(t)} bw_i \leq BW_j \tag{6}$$

HPC applications have various sizes and require multiple cores and submit to system at dynamic arrival rate [10]. An HPC application can request some VMs.

3   Genetic Algorithm for Power-Aware Task Scheduling

3.1   Data Structures

CUDA framework only supports array data-structures. Therefore, arrays are an easy ways to transfer data from/to host memory to/from GPU. Each chromosome is a mapping of tasks to physical machines where each task requires a single VM. Fig. 1 presents a part of a sample chromosome with six tasks (each task is executed on a single VM), the task ID=0 is allocated to machine 5, the task ID=1 is allocated to machine 7, etc.

Task ID	0	1	2	3	4	5
Machine ID	5	7	8	4	5	9

Fig. 1. A part of chromosome

Finesses of chromosomes are evaluated and stored in an array similar to that in Fig. 2. Chromosome 0 has fitness of 1.892; chromosome 1 has fitness of 1.542, etc.

Chromosome	0	1	2	3	4	5
Fitness	1.892	1.542	1.457	1.358	1.355	1.289

Fig. 2. A part of a sample array of finesses of chromosomes

3.2   Implementing Genetic Algorithm on CUDA

We show the BKGPUGA's execution model that executes genetic operations on both CPU and GPU as shown in the Fig. 3 below.

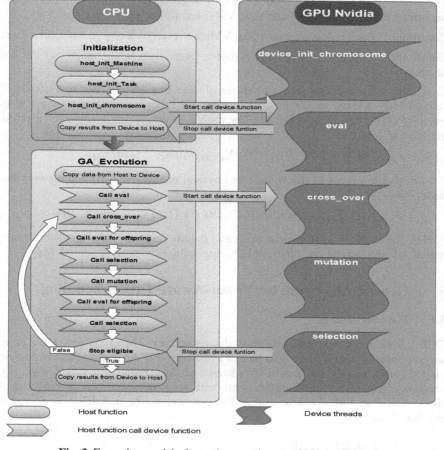

Fig. 3. Execution model of genetic operations on CPU and GPU

Initialize population: Initial population using CUDA's cuRAND library.
GA_Evolution method: This is the main loop of the GA on CPU-GPU. The Algorithm 1 illustrates the GA_Evolution method.

Algorithm 1: GA_Evolution

```
Input: num_generations, Chromosomes[], Fitness[], TaskInfo[], MachineInfo[]
Output: The best chromosome with highest fitness

size_arr_chrom = A=sizeof(int)*length(chromosome)*pop_size ;
d_NST[], d_tem[]; /* Array of parent and offspring chromosomes on GPU */
size_arr_fitness = B = sizeof(float) * pop_size
d_fitness[], d_tem_fitness[];/* Parent fitness and Offspring fitness on GPU */
cudaMalloc ( d_NST, d_tem , A);
cudaMalloc ( d_fitness, d_tem_fitness, pop_size);
cudaMemcpy ( d_NST, host_NST, A, HostToDevice) ;
cudaMemcpy ( d_tem, host_NST, A, HostToDevice) ; /* Cloning */
Load tasks and machines information to GPU;
eval_fitness <<< n_chromosomes >>>(d_NST, d_fitness) ;
for c = 1 to num_generations do
    crossover<<<n_chromosomes>>>(d_NST, d_tem, cu_seeds);
    eval_fitness<<<n_chromosomes>>>(d_tem,d_tem_fitness);
    selection<<<n_chromosomes>>>(d_NST,d_tem,d_fitness, d_tem_fitness);
    mutation<<< n_chromosomes x length(chromosome)>>>( d_tem, pop_size, cu_seeds);
    eval_fitness<<<n_chromosomes>>>(d_tem,d_tem_fitness);
    selection<<<num_chromosomes>>>(d_NST,d_tem,d_fitness,d_tem_fitness, cu_seeds);
cudaMemcpy( host_NST, d_NST, DeviceToHost);
cudaMemcpy( host_fitness, d_fitness, DeviceToHost);
cudafree(d_NST, d_tem, d_fitness, d_tem_fitness);
```

Fitness Evaluation

The Fig. 5 shows the flowchart of the fitness evaluation. The placement of each task/VM on a physical machine has to calculate the power consumption increase as the VM is allocated to a physical machine and reduce power consumption when the task/VM is finished its execution.

Selection Method

The BKGPUGA does not use random selection method, the BKGPUGA's selection method is rearrangement of chromosomes according to the fitness from high to low, then it pick up the chromosomes have high fitness until reach the limit number of populations. The selection method is illustrated in Fig. 6. After selection or mutation, chromosomes in Parents and Offspring population will have different fitness, size of new population that included both Parents' and Offspring's is double size. Next, the chromosomes are rearranged according to the fitness value, the selection method simply retains high fitness of chromosome in the region, and the population is named after F1, whose magnitude is equal to the original population. To prepare for the next step of the algorithm GA (selection or mutation), F1 will be given a copy of Clones. The next calculation is done on Clones, Clones turn into F1's offspring. After each operation, the arrangement and selection is repeatedly.

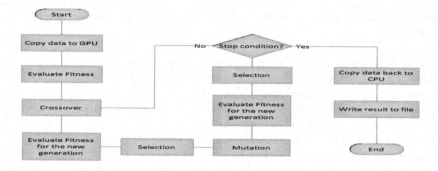

Fig. 4. GA_Evolution method

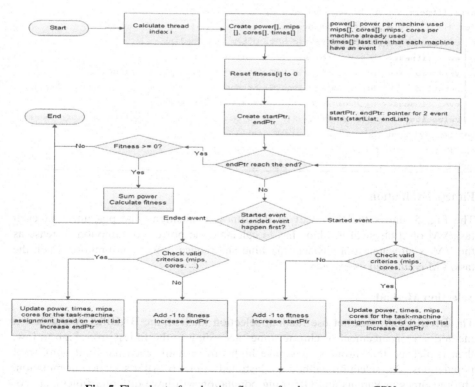

Fig. 5. Flowchart of evaluation fitness of a chromosome on GPU

In order to simplify and speedup the sorting operation, the program has used the CUDA Thrust Library provided by NVIDIA. The selection method keeps the better individuals. This is not only improves the speed of evolution, but also increases the speedup of overall program because of the parallel steps.

Mutation Method

Each thread will execute decisions on each cell mutagenic or not based on a given probability. If the decision is *yes*, then the cell will be changed randomly to different values. Fig. 7 shows mutation with 12.5% probability. Call n is the total number of cell populations, p is the probability change of each cell, q=(1 - p). The probability to have k cells modified Bernoulli calculated by the formula: $P(k) = C_n^k \times p^k \times q^{n-k}$

The cells that are likely to be modified: $(n \times p - q)$ or $(n \times p - q + 1)$

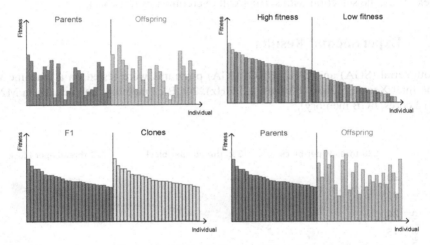

Fig. 6. Fitness of Parents and Offspring populations in Selection method

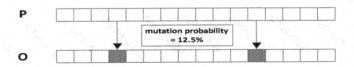

Fig. 7. Mutation process with 12.5% probability

Crossover Method

Crossover is the process of choosing two random chromosomes to form two new ones. To ensure that after crossover it allowed sufficient number of individuals to form Offspring population, the probability of it is 100%, which mean all will be crossover.

Fig. 8. Selection process between two chromosomes

Crossover process is using one-point crossover and the cross point is randomly chosen. Fig. 8 shows an example of section process between two chromosomes. The result is two new chromosomes. This implementation is simple, ease of illustrating. It creates the children chromosomes randomly but it does not guarantee the quality of these chromosomes. To improve the quality of the result, we can choose the parents chromosomes with some criteria but this makes the algorithm becoming more complex. Thus, the selection with sorting will overcome this drawback.

4 Experimental Results

Both serial (SGA) and GPU (BKGPUGA) programs were tested on a machine with one Intel Xeon E5-2630 (6 cores, 2.3 GHz), 24GB of memory, and one Tesla M2090 (512 cores, 6GB memory).

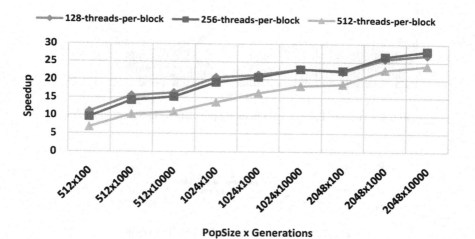

Fig. 9. Speedup of BKGPUGA that executes on NVIDIA Tesla M2090 and computational time SGA that executes on CPU. The X-axis is the size of population and the number of generations. The green/blue/yellow line is the speedup of BKGPUGA with 128/256/512 CUDA threads-per-block.

Table 1. Experimental result of SGA and BKGPUGA: Problem size is 500x500

Pop. size	Generations	#Threads-per-block	SGA Comp. time (sec.)	BKGPUGA Comp. time (sec.)	Speedup
512	100	128	22.501	2.028	11.10
512	100	256	22.501	2.340	9.61
512	100	512	22.501	3.316	6.79
512	1000	128	255.123	16.390	15.57
512	1000	256	255.123	17.967	14.20
512	1000	512	255.123	24.764	10.30
512	10000	128	2,564.250	157.058	16.33
512	10000	256	2,564.250	168.187	15.25
512	10000	512	2,564.250	231.165	11.09
1024	100	128	60.077	2.918	20.59
1024	100	256	60.077	3.121	19.25
1024	100	512	60.077	4.373	13.74
1024	1000	128	516.906	24.228	21.34
1024	1000	256	516.906	24.971	20.70
1024	1000	512	516.906	31.743	16.28
1024	10000	128	5,351.200	232.682	23.00
1024	10000	256	5,351.200	233.576	22.91
1024	10000	512	5,351.200	293.717	18.22
2048	100	128	114.827	5.156	22.27
2048	100	256	114.827	5.098	22.52
2048	100	512	114.827	6.152	18.66
2048	1000	128	1,035.470	39.912	25.94
2048	1000	256	1,035.470	38.958	26.58
2048	1000	512	1,035.470	45.428	22.79
2048	10000	128	10,124.880	374.850	27.01
2048	10000	256	10,124.880	359.827	28.14
2048	10000	512	10,124.880	421.728	24.01

We generated an instance of the PATS with the number of physical machines and the number of tasks is 500 x 500. On each experiments, mutation probability is 0.005, the number of chromosomes (*popsize* - size of population) is {512, 1024, 2048}, the number of generations is {100, 1000, 10000}, the number of CUDA threads-per-block is {128, 256, 512}. Table 1 shows experimental results of the computation time of the serial GA (SGA) and the computational time of the BKGPUGA. Fig. 9 shows the speedup chart of the BKGPUGA program on configurations of 128, 256 and 512 CUDA threads-per-block (green, blue and yellow lines respectively). The maximum speedup of BKGPUGA is 28.14 when using 256 CUDA threads-per-block to run the GPU GA with 2048 chromosomes and 10,000 generations. The number of generations is the main factor that affects the execution time, when number of generations increases from 100 to 1000 and 10,000 generations the BKGPUGA's average execution time increases approximately ×7.66 and ×71.67 and the SGA's average execution time increases approximately ×9.16 and ×91.39 respectively. The fitness comparison between BKGPUGA and CPU version shows that the difference is relative small (10^{-11}). The fitness values on 1,000 and 10,000 generations are almost equal; that they figure out if it nearly reaches the best solution, the increase of generations makes the fitness is better but not much and a tradeoff is the increased execution time on the BKGPUGA.

5   Conclusions and Future Work

Compared to previous studies, this paper presents a parallel GA using GPU computation to solve the power-aware task scheduling (PATS) problem in HPC Cloud. Both BKGPUGA and the corresponding SGA programs are implemented carefully for performance comparison. Experimental results show the BKGPUGA (CUDA program) executed on NVIDIA Tesla M2090 obtains significant speedup than SGA (serial GA) executed on Intel Xeon E5-2630. The execution time of BKGPUGA depends on the number of generations, size of the task scheduling problems (number of tasks/VMs, number of physical machines). To maximize speedup, when the number of generations is less than or equal to 1,000 we prefer to use 128 CUDA threads per block, and when the number of generations is greater than or equal to 10,000 we prefer to use 256 CUDA threads per block. The limitation on the number of tasks and number of physical machines is the size of local memory on each CUDA thread in internal GPU card.

In the future work, we will concern on some real constraints (as in [11]) on the PATS and we will investigate on improving quality of chromosomes (solutions) by applying EPOBF heuristic in [12] and Memetic methodology in each genetic operation.

Acknowledgments. This research is funded by Vietnam National University Ho Chi Minh (VNU-HCM) under grant number B2012-20-03TĐ.

References

1. Li, K.: Performance Analysis of Power-Aware Task Scheduling Algorithms on Multiprocessor Computers with Dynamic Voltage and Speed. IEEE Trans. Parallel Distrib. Syst. 19, 1484–1497 (2008)

2. Braun, T.D., Siegel, H.J., Beck, N., Bölöni, L.L., Maheswaran, M., Reuther, A.I., Robertson, J.P., Theys, M.D., Yao, B., Hensgen, D., Freund, R.F.: A Comparison of Eleven Static Heuristics for Mapping a Class of Independent Tasks onto Heterogeneous Distributed Computing Systems. J. Parallel Distrib. Comput. 61, 810–837 (2001)

3. Kołodziej, J., Khan, S., Zomaya, A.: A Taxonomy of Evolutionary Inspired Solutions for Energy Management in Green Computing: Problems and Resolution Methods. Adv. Intell. Model. Simul. 422, 215–233 (2012)

4. Tesla Kepler GPU Accelerators (2013)

5. Chen, S., Davis, S., Jiang, H., Novobilski, A.: CUDA-based genetic algorithm on traveling salesman problem. In: Lee, R. (ed.) Computer and Information Science 2011. SCI, vol. 364, pp. 241–252. Springer, Heidelberg (2011)

6. Luong, T., Van, M.N., Talbi, E.-G.: GPU-based island model for evolutionary algorithms. In: Proceedings of the 12th Annual Conference on Genetic and Evolutionary Computation - GECCO 2010, p. 1089. ACM Press, New York (2010)

7. Arenas, M.G., Mora, A.M., Romero, G., Castillo, P.A.: GPU computation in bioinspired algorithms: A review. In: Cabestany, J., Rojas, I., Joya, G. (eds.) IWANN 2011, Part I. LNCS, vol. 6691, pp. 433–440. Springer, Heidelberg (2011)

8. Zhang, S., He, Z.: Implementation of Parallel Genetic Algorithm Based on CUDA. In: Cai, Z., Li, Z., Kang, Z., Liu, Y. (eds.) ISICA 2009. LNCS, vol. 5821, pp. 24–30. Springer, Heidelberg (2009)

9. Fan, X., Weber, W.-D., Barroso, L.A.: Power provisioning for a warehouse-sized computer. ACM SIGARCH Comput. Archit. News. 35, 13 (2007)

10. Garg, S.K., Yeo, C.S., Anandasivam, A., Buyya, R.: Energy-Efficient Scheduling of HPC Applications in Cloud Computing Environments. arXiv Prepr. arXiv0909.1146 (2009)

11. Quang-Hung, N., Nien, P.D., Nam, N.H., Huynh Tuong, N., Thoai, N.: A Genetic Algorithm for Power-Aware Virtual Machine Allocation in Private Cloud. In: Mustofa, K., Neuhold, E.J., Tjoa, A.M., Weippl, E., You, I. (eds.) ICT-EurAsia 2013. LNCS, vol. 7804, pp. 183–191. Springer, Heidelberg (2013)

12. Quang-Hung, N., Thoai, N., Son, N.T.: EPOBF: Energy Efficient Allocation of Virtual Machines in High Performance Computing Cloud. J. Sci. Technol. Vietnamese Acad. Sci. Technol. 51(4B), 173–182 (2013)

Ball Distance Estimation and Tracking System of Humanoid Soccer Robot

Widodo Budiharto, Bayu Kanigoro, and Viska Noviantri

School of Computer Science, Bina Nusantara University, Jakarta, Indonesia
{wbudiharto,bkanigoro}@binus.edu, viskanoviantri@yahoo.com

Abstract. Modern Humanoid Soccer Robots in uncontrolled environments need to be based on vision and versatile. This paper propose a method for object measurement and ball tracking method using Kalman Filter for Humanoid Soccer, because the ability to accurately track a ball is one of the important features for processing high-definition image. A color-based object detection is used for detecting a ball while PID controller is used for controlling pan tilt camera system. We also modify the robots controller CM-510 in order able to communicate efficiently using main controller. The proposed method is able to determine and estimate the position of a ball and kick the ball correctly with the success percentage greater than 90%. We evaluate and present the performance of the system.

1 Introduction

The humanoid soccer robots are popular nowadays for the entertainment or contests such as RoboCup Humanoid League. The important features of humanoid soccer, such as accuracy, robustness, efficient determination and tracking of ball size and location; has proven to be a challenging subset of this task and the focus of much research. With the evolution of robotics hardware and subsequent advances in processor performance in recent years, the temporal and spatial complexity of feature extraction algorithms to solve this task has grown[1].

In the case of Humanoid soccer, vision systems are one of the main sources for environment interpretation. Many problems have to be solved before having a fully featured soccer player. First of all, the robot has to get information from the environment, mainly using the camera. It must detect the ball, goals, lines and the other robots. Having this information, the robot has to self-localize and decide the next action: move, kick, search another object, etc. The robot must perform all these tasks very fast in order to be reactive enough to be competitive in a soccer match. It makes no sense within this environment to have a good localization method if that takes several seconds to compute the robot position or to decide the next movement in few seconds based on the old perceptions[2]. At the same time many other topics like human-machine interaction, robot cooperation and mission and behavior control give humanoid robot soccer a higher level of complexity like no any other robots[3]. So the high speed processor with efficient algorithms is needed for this issue.

Linawati et al. (Eds.): ICT-EurAsia 2014, LNCS 8407, pp. 170–178, 2014.

One of the performance factors of a humanoid soccer is that it is highly dependent on its tracking ball and motion ability. The vision module collects information that will be the input for the reasoning module that involves the development of behaviour control. Complexity of humanoid soccer makes necessary playing with the development of complex behaviours, for example situations of coordination or differ rent role assignment during the match. There are many types of behaviour control, each with advantages and disadvantages: reactive control is the simplest way to make the robot play, but do not permit more elaborated strategies as explained for example in [4]. On the other side, behaviour-based control are more complex but more difficult to implement, and enables in general the possibility high-level behaviour control, useful for showing very good performances. Intelligent tracking algorithm for state estimation using Kalman filter has been successfully developed [5], and we want to implement that method for ball tracking for humanoid soccer robot.

In this paper we propose architecture of low cost humanoid soccer robot compared with the well known humanoid robots for education such as DarwIn-OP[1] and NAO humanoid robot[6] and test its ability for image processing to measure distance of the ball and track a ball using color-based object detection method, the robot will kick the ball after getting the nearest position between the robot and the ball. The Kalman filter is used here to estimate state variable of a ball that is excited by random disturbances and measurement noise. It has good results in practice due to optimality and structure and convenient form for online real time processing.

2   Proposed System

Humanoid soccer robots design based on the vision involves the need to obtain a mechanical structure with a human appearance, in order to operate into a human real world. Another important feature for modern humanoid robot is the ability to process tasks especially for computer vision. We propose an embedded system that able to handle high speed image processing, so we use main controller based on the ARM7 Processor. Webcam and servo controller are used to track a ball, and the output of the main controller will communicate with the CM510 controller to control the actuators and sensors of the robot as shown in Fig 2.

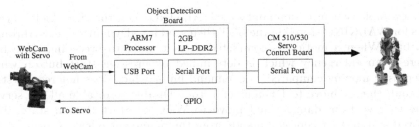

Fig. 1. The architecture of Object Avoiding system

The main controller uses Odroid X2[7] that consist of Cortext-A9 1.7 GHz and sufficient memory and ports to be connected with other devices. The specification of the Odroid X2 is shown in table 1,

Table 1. Odroid X2 Specification

Type	Description
Processor	Exynos4412 Quad-core ARM Cortex-A9 1.7GHz
Memory Capacity	2 GBytes
I/O	6× High Speed USB2.0 Host Port
Network	10/100Mbps Ethernet with RJ-45 LAN Jack

The Firmware of the robot to control the servos is modified from the original one named Robotis Firmware due to the limitation for sending a motion command by serial interface based on Peter Lanius works published in google code[8]. This firmware instead using RoboPlus Task[9] to program the robot controlling its movement but it directly program the AVR Microcontroller inside the CM-510[10] controller using C language. Using this alternative can reduce the size of the program from originally 170KB to 70KB in the memory. By this firmware, the robot can be connected directly to Ball Tracking System using USB Serial Interface to command its motion. Based on this framework, it opens an opportunity to built Real Time Operating System for the robot. The robots control starts with initialization routines of CM-510 controller then move to Wait for Start Button state. In this state, it waits the button to be pressed to change the start_button_pressed variable from FALSE to TRUE then move to Dynamixel servos[11] and Gyro Initialization which send broadcast ping to every Dynamixel servos connected to CM-510. When one or more servos do not respond of the ping then CM-510 will send a message mentioning the failure of a servo to serial terminal. Gyro Initialization does gyro calibration in the robot to get center reference and sends the value to serial terminal. Next state is Waiting Motion Command that waits the command through serial interface, from terminal or tracking module, then check if the command is valid or not. If it does not valid then the state will repeat to Wait Motion Command or continue to next Execute Motion Command state when the command is valid. Execute Motion Command executes a motion command to move a servos based on defined Look-Up-Table (LUT).

For example, when a command says WALKING then the state looks servos values for WALKING stored in the LUT then send it to Dynamixel servo through serial bus. When a motion is completed then it move to preceding state but if there is an emergency which is determined by pressing start button when the servos is moving compared to command input which does not receive stop command, then it move to Dynamixel Torque Disable to disable all the servos torque to save from damage and move to Wait for Start Button state. The improved system to accept commands from the main controller is shown as the state machine in fig. 2.

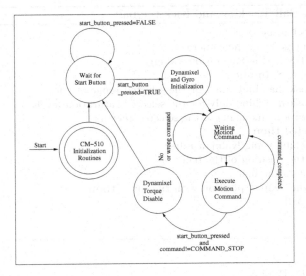

Fig. 2. State machine of the robot's controller

Computer vision is one of the most challenging applications in sensor systems since the signal is complex from spatial and logical point of view. An active camera tracking system for humanoid robot soccer tracks an object of interest (ball) automatically with a pan-tilt camera. We use OpenCV for converting to HSV (Hue Saturation-Value), extract Hue and Saturation and create a mask matching only the selected range of hue value.

To have a good estimation, the object must be in the centre of the image, i.e. it must be tracked. Once there, the distance and orientation are calculated, according to the necks origin position, the current neck's servomotors position and the position of the camera in respect to the origin resulting of the design [12]. We considered method for distance estimation of the ball by centering the ball on the camera image, using the head tilt angle to estimate the distance to the ball.

Region growing algorithms are also used to locate the ball color blobs that have been identified by region growing and are useful and robust source for further image processing, as demonstrated by [13]. The ball will be tracked based on the color and webcam will track to adjust the position of the ball to the center of the screen based on the Algorithm 1.

The Kalman Filter is a state estimator which produces an optimal estimate in the sense that the mean value of the sum (actually of any linear combination) of the estimation errors gets a minimal value. In other words, The Kalman Filter gives the following sum of squared errors:

$$E[e_x^T(k)e_x(k)] = E[e_{x_1}^2(k) + \ldots e_{x_n}^2(k)] \tag{1}$$

Algorithm 1. Ball Tracking and Kick the ball

Require: Object to be tracked
1: Get input image from the camera.
2: Convert to HSV (Hue-Saturation-Value)
3: Extract Hue & Saturation
4: Create a mask matching only for the selected range of hue
5: Create a mask matching only for the selected saturation levels
6: Find the position (moment) of the selected regions
7: **if** ball detected **then**
8:    Object tracking using Kalman Filter
9:    Centering the position of the ball
10:    Move robot to the ball
11:    **if** ball at the nearest position with the robot **then**
12:       Kick the ball
13:    **end if**
14: **end if**

---

a minimal value. Here

$$e_x(k) = e_{est}(x) - x(k) \tag{2}$$

is the estimation error vector.

By assuming discrete-time state space model as system model of Kalman Filter then,

$$x(k+1) = f[x(k), u(k)] + Gw(k) \tag{3}$$

where x is the state vector of n state variables, u is the input vector of m input variables, f is the system vector function, w is random noise vector, G is the process noise gain matrix relating the process noise to the state variables. It is common to assume that $q = n$, making G square. In addition it is common to set the elements of G equal to one. Assuming that non-linear then the measurement model is,

$$y(k) = g[x(k), u(k)] + Hw(k) + v(k) \tag{4}$$

where y is the measurement vector of r measurement variables, g is the measurement vector function, H is a gain matrix relating the disturbances directly to the measurements. It is however common to assume that H is a zero matrix of dimension $(r \times q)$,

$$H = \begin{bmatrix} 0 & 0 & 0 & 0 \\ 0 & 0 & \ddots & \vdots \\ 0 & 0 & \cdots & H_{rq} \end{bmatrix} \tag{5}$$

and v is a random (white) measurement noise vector.

The calculation of Kalman Filter is to be done by following these steps:

1. Calculate the initial state estimation x_p,

$$x_p(0) = x_{init} \tag{6}$$

where x_{init} is the initial guess of the state.

2. Calculate the predicted measurement estimate y_p from the predicted state estimation:

$$y_p(k) = g[x_p(k)] \tag{7}$$

3. Calculate innovation variable as the difference between the measurement $y(k)$ and the predicted measurement $y_p(k)$:

$$e(k) = y(k) - y_p(k) \tag{8}$$

4. Calculate corrected state estimate x_c:

$$x_c(k) = x_p(k) + Ke(k) \tag{9}$$

where K is the Kalman Filter gain

5. Calculate the predicted state estimate for the next time step, $x_p(k+1)$:

$$x_p(k+1) = f[x_c(k), u(k)] \tag{10}$$

The estimated position (x, y) from Kalman Filter is used as an input to PID controller. PID controller calculates an error value as the difference between a measured (input) and a desired set point to control high speed HS-85[14] servos. The controller attempts to minimize the error by adjusting (an Output). The generic model of PID Controller shown in figure 3.

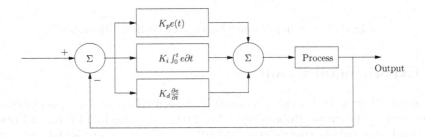

Fig. 3. A Generic PID Controller

The output of a PID controller, equal to the control input to the system, in the time-domain is as follows:

$$u_c(t) = K_p e(t) + K_i \int_0^t e\partial t + K_d \frac{\partial e}{\partial t} \tag{11}$$

Measuring distance between the robot and the ball can be accomplished by using trigonometric function. Assume h_{robot} is a height of the robot, then d_{ball} which is a distance between the robot and the ball can be approximately measured by,

$$\tan \alpha = \frac{d_{ball}}{h_{robot}} \tag{12}$$

$$d_{ball} = \tan \alpha \times h_{robot} \tag{13}$$

The angle α shown in equation 12 and 13 is the angle between robot's body and camera which is placed on the robot. The best angle of the camera is around $15° - 20°$ when the robot will kick the ball.

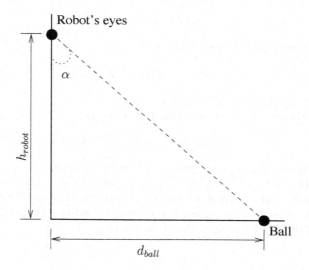

Fig. 4. Measuring distance between the ball and the robot

3   Experimental Result

The approach proposed in this paper was implemented and tested on a humanoid Robot named Humanoid Robot Soccer Ver 2.0 based on Bioloid Premium Robot. By modify the robots controller (CM-510) in order to accept serial command from the main controller, this system able to communicate efficiently. Detecting several colors means creating several binary image maps, as shown in figure 5. The tracking system is able to track a ball with the maximum speed of 6 cm/s. The ball will be kicked by the robot when it be detected, tracked, and determined if nearest to the robot by using equation 12 and 13.

The result of estimation of position of ball using Kalman filter is shown in figure 6, it shows that the estimated point able to follow and estimate the position of the ball.

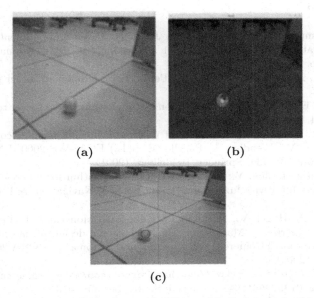

(a)   (b)

(c)

Fig. 5. The original image (5a), the mask (5b) and ball detected and tracked using Kalman Filters in the green circle (5c)

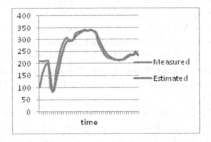

Fig. 6. True measurement versus estimation using Kalman Filter

4 Conclusion

In this paper, we introduced the hardware architecture implemented on our humanoid robot soccer. They are based on Odroid X2 that has powerful ability for high speed image processing. We propose the simple way to estimate distance and track a ball based on the color, and kick the ball after getting the nearest position of the robot from the ball. The Kalman filter is a robust method to track a ball in the real situation. For future work, we want to use Extended Kalman Filter and shape-based object tracking and defining intelligent behavior for the humanoid robot soccer.

References

1. Ha, I., Tamura, Y., Asama, H., Han, J., Hong, D.W.: Development of open humanoid platform darwin-op. In: 2011 Proceedings of SICE Annual Conference (SICE), pp. 2178–2181. IEEE (2011)
2. Martín, F., Aguero, C., Cañas, J.M., Perdices, E.: Humanoid soccer player design (2010)
3. Blanes, F.: Embedded distributed vision system for humanoid soccer robot. Journal of Physical Agents 5(1), 55–62 (2011)
4. Behnke, S., Rojas, R.: A hierarchy of reactive behaviors handles complexity. In: Hannebauer, M., Wendler, J., Pagello, E. (eds.) ECAI-WS 2000. LNCS (LNAI), vol. 2103, pp. 125–136. Springer, Heidelberg (2001)
5. Noh, S., Park, J., Joo, Y.: Intelligent tracking algorithm for manoeuvering target using kalman filter with fuzzy gain. Radar, Sonar & Navigation, IET 1(3), 241–247 (2007)
6. Gouaillier, D., Hugel, V., Blazevic, P., Kilner, C., Monceaux, J., Lafourcade, P., Marnier, B., Serre, J., Maisonnier, B.: Mechatronic design of nao humanoid. In: IEEE International Conference on Robotics and Automation, ICRA 2009, pp. 769–774. IEEE (2009)
7. Hardkernel: Odroid X2, http://www.hardkernel.com/main/products/prdt_info.php?g_code=G135235611947 (accessed: September 30, 2013)
8. Lanius, P.: Bioloidcontrol, http://code.google.com/p/bioloidcontrol/ (accessed: September 30, 2013)
9. Robotis: RoboPlus, http://support.robotis.com/en/ (accessed: September 30, 2013)
10. Robotis: CM-510 controller, http://support.robotis.com/en/ (accessed: September 30, 2013)
11. Robotis: Dynamixel AX-12A robot actuator, http://www.robotis.com/xe/dynamixel_en (accessed: September 30, 2013)
12. Maggi, A., Guseo, T., Wegher, F., Pagello, E., Menegatti, E.: A light software architecture for a humanoid soccer robot. In: Workshop on Humanoid Soccer Robots of the IEEE-RAS International Conference on Humanoid Robots (Humanoids 2006), Genoa, Italy (2006)
13. Ghanai, M., Chafaa, K.: Kalman filter in control and modeling (2010)
14. Hitec: HS-85BB Premium Micro Servo, http://hitecrcd.com/products/servos/micro-and-mini-servos/analog-micro-and-mini-servos/hs-85bb-premium-micro-servo/product (accessed: September 30, 2013)

Image Clustering Using Multi-visual Features

Bilih Priyogi[1], Nungki Selviandro[1], Zainal A. Hasibuan[1], and Mubarik Ahmad[2]

[1] Faculty of Computer Science, University of Indonesia, Indonesia
[2] Faculty of Information Technology, YARSI University, Indonesia
(bilih.priyogi31,nungki.selviandro21)@ui.ac.id,
zhasibua@cs.ui.ac.id, mubarik.ahmad@yarsi.ac.id

Abstract. This paper presents a research on clustering an image collection using multi-visual features. The proposed method extracted a set of visual features from each image and performed multi-dimensional K-Means clustering on the whole collection. Furthermore, this work experiments on different number of visual features combination for clustering. 2, 3, 5 and 7 pair of visual features chosen from a total of 8 visual features used, to measure the impact of using more visual features towards clustering performance. The result show that the accuracy of multi-visual features clustering is promising, but using too many visual features might set a drawback.

Keywords: Image Clustering, Visual Feature, K-Means Clustering.

1   Introduction

There is an enormous growth in image collection all around the world, especially in the past few years with the emerging trend of social media. Many social media such as Facebook, Twittter, Path, and Instagram allow people to publish their own generated image, out to the world. Not to mention images produced from other areas such as from commerce, government, scientific and medical field. It is believed that the collections of data in the form of image contain precious information, as well as textual data does.

However, it is hard to obtain precious information from all of those image collections without an effective and efficient technique for image retrieval. Content-Based Image Retrieval (CBIR) address this issue by using visual contents of an image such as color, shape and texture, to decides the similarity and differences between images. Thus, we can explore and analyze images in collection based on its visual feature.

Furthermore, retrieving, exploring and analyzing from a huge amount of images will be a challenging problem. Thus, we need such method to organize the image in a way that enables efficient image retrieval. One of the proposed technique is clustering [1] [2] [3], which is useful to discover the patterns and characteristics stored in image collection by dividing them into set of clusters. Images in each cluster share similar patterns, but very dissimilar to images in other clusters. In addition, [1] also suggest that clustering could be used for faster image retrieval by minimizing the search area only in cluster which the image belong to, rather than exhaustively searching an entire image collection.

Linawati et al. (Eds.): ICT-EurAsia 2014, LNCS 8407, pp. 179–189, 2014.

Another motivation of this research is the possibility of image-language semantic, which based on the idea of finding semantically related text in visually-similar images. This idea offers alternative way of exploring relationship among term's meaning across languages that could be used to build thesaurus, dictionaries, question answering modules etc. The argument is that similar images might contain text caption that is possibly related. For instance if we can recognize the similarity among images in Figure 1, then we might draw inferences that word 'beach' is related with 'pantai' and 'sanur'. Moreover, with some work on the reasoning part, we also can infer that 'sanur' is a 'beach' and 'pantai' is translation of 'beach' in Indonesian language.

Fig. 1. Image-Language Semantic

Furthermore, this research also wants to address the phenomenon called "curse of dimensionality", in which using more than one visual feature when clustering might improve the performance. This performance improvement will occur until certain number of features, or threshold, when the peak performance of multi-dimensional clustering will be obtained. Any features addition or increase in dimensionality beyond the threshold will suffer the clustering accuracy.

2   Proposed Method

Figure 2 illustrates the overview of proposed method in this research. For the sake of simplicity, the illustration only shows the clustering performed on image collection

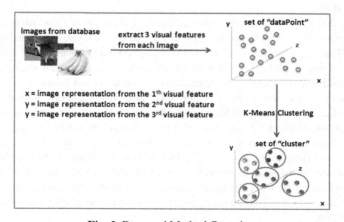

Fig. 2. Proposed Method Overview

based on 3 visual features. This research also performed clustering based on 1, 2, 5 and 7 visual features to measure the impact of using more visual features, which follows similar process.

Visual feature extraction of each image yields a value to represent an image in the visual feature's context and distinguish one image from another. Then based on visual information, image clustered to organize visually-similar image in the same cluster. K-Means clustering algorithm is used to cluster images based on value from the extraction process of different visual features combination. In other words, the clustering done in high dimensional space (2, 3, 5 and 7) in which each image considered as a point with coordinate of the n-axis (n = {2, 3, 5, 7}). These are the K-Means algorithm used in this research :

1. Choose number of cluster output desired, k.
2. Randomly make k clusters and calculate center point of each cluster, or randomly choose k points as initial center point.
3. Assign each point to cluster with nearest center point.
4. Re-calculate the center point of each cluster.
5. Repeat step number 3 and 4 until the convergence criterion achieved (there is no membership change in each cluster or until some number of iteration)

There are 8 descriptors used to extract visual features in this research, this choice based on the all available and usable descriptors in tools used. The tools used for visual extraction is LIRE (Lucene Image Retrieval) java-based API. Here are some overviews of descriptors used:

1. Auto Color Correlogram
   This descriptor extracts the color spatial correlation information in image [5]. It is known for its simple computation and small extraction result size. This descriptor is not affected regardless of changes in background or point of view.
2. CEDD (Color and Edge Directivity Descriptor)
   This descriptor extracts a combination of color and texture from an image into one histogram [6]. The color information extracted based on HSV (Hue, Saturation, Values) color space, whereas texture information extracted by classifying each pixel into one or more texture category. CEDD uses relative modest amount of computing resource in extraction process comparer to MPEG-7 descriptors (Scalable Color, Color Layout, Edge Histogram etc.).
3. Color Layout
   This descriptor extracts information of color spatial-distribution in an image [7]. It divides an image to a 8x8 matrix and applies Discrete Cosine Transform based on YCbCr color space (Yellow, Chromatic blue, Chromatic red). This descriptor is not affected with image dilatation and able to distinguish a sketch image from one another.
4. Edge Histogram
   This descriptor extracts local edge distribution in an image to a histogram [8]. Edge represents frequency and directionality of color changes on image. It divides an image into number of blocks, apply digital filtering and classify each block into one out of five edge categories. This descriptor is not affected with image rotation or translation.

5. FCTH (Fuzzy Color and Texture Histogram)

This descriptor extracts same information as CEDD does [9], but the difference is the extraction result size of FCTH 30% bigger than CEDD and the texture extraction process. FCTH extracts texture information by applying Haar transform to each of image blocks and classifying them with a fuzzy texture linking system. This descriptor also persists regardless of images distortion.

6. Gabor

This descriptor explores texture feature from an image by applying a series of linear filter in edge detection process. An image is processed through a set of Gabor filter which have different scale and orientation, then the average and standard deviation compared to original image is calculated. Gabor descriptor has many similarities with human visual system and proven to be capable of distinguishing image based on texture information [10].

7. Scalable Color

This descriptor extracts statistical color information of an image in HSV color space into a histogram. Each bin in histogram represents number of pixels containing certain color. The extraction process also involving a Haar transform and a set of low-pass and high-pass filter [7].

8. Tamura

This descriptor exploits texture feature in an image, such as coarseness, contrast, directionality, line-likeness, regularity and roughness [11]. Now, only the first three characteristics implemented because considered to be the most important part in human vision. Coarseness related to size of texture element, contrast related to image quality and directionality related to orientation of texture.

3   Experiments

For the experiments, an image dataset was obtained from the website wang.ist.psu.edu/iwang/test1.tar. In this scheme, 50 images from 5 categories (each

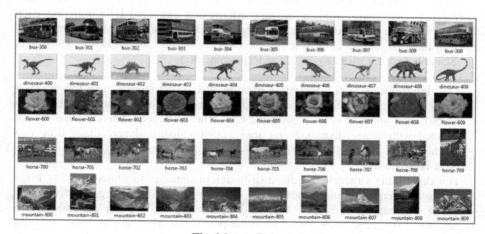

Fig. 3. Image Dataset

category contain 10 images) are tested against the proposed method. The 5 categories are bus, dinosaur, flower, horse, and mountain. Each image named with its correspondence categories in order to ease the process of accuracy measurement.

The accuracy measurement based on the number of images that is properly clustered. An image said to be in proper cluster if its category is the dominant category belong to the cluster. For example, cluster 1 occupied by 10 images that is 8 bus images, 1 flower image and 1 horse image, then it can be said that the cluster is a bus' cluster and there is 8 images properly clustered into this cluster.

If somehow there are two dominant categories, only one of them will be regarded as dominant category in a cluster by alphabetical order. For example in cluster 2 occupied by 5 horse images, 5 flower images and 1 mountain image, then flower will be picked as dominant category by alphabetical order. It should also be noted that either if we chose horse as dominant category, there still be a total of 5 images properly clustered.

Each experiment's run tested a combination of visual feature for clustering purpose. To simplify the scope of research and as there is prior information of the number of categories existed in dataset, the k parameter in K –Means clustering is set to 5. So, each run will always resulting 5 clusters and the accuracy of it can be calculated as:

$$accuracy = \frac{total\ of\ properly\ clustered\ images}{total\ of\ all\ images\ clustered}$$

The total of all images clustered is the size of dataset, which are 50.

4   Results

Table 1 shows the overall results of experiments per clustering type, which this research used combination of 2, 3, 5 and 7 pair out of 8 visual features. In addition, clustering with only 1 feature also performed to have a thorough comparison of the advantage of high dimensionality clustering. The experiments take on all possible combination of visual features in each clustering type, which are 8 for 1D clustering, 28 for 2D clustering, 56 for 3D clustering, 56 for 5D clustering and 8 for 7D clustering.

The highest accuracy obtained by 3D clustering type, which uses CEDD-EdgeHistogram-ColorLayout as the visual feature combination. These three visual features evidently the best combination to distinguish visually similar images from another images. The lowest accuracy occurred in 3D clustering that uses visual feature combination of CEDD-EdgeHistogram-ScalableColor (see appendix).

Based on Table 1, the average accuracy of all runs in each clustering dimension generally decreasing when the number of visual feature used for clustering is increasing, except for 2D clustering. This fact shows the "curse of dimensionality" existence, which the threshold or number of features combination to get the best average accuracy would be 2.

If we look at other perspective, highest accuracy obtained, it would be fair to say that the "curse of dimensionality" also exist with the threshold would be 3. This means that using multi visual features would improve clustering performance until certain number of dimension. Nevertheless, employing too many visual features beyond the dimension's threshold might raise some confusion instead of clarity when distinguishing and classifying an image.

Table 1. Experiment Results per Clustering Type

Type	Total Combination	Highest Accuracy	Lowest Accuracy	Average Accuracy
1D	8	0.88	0.54	0.688
2D	28	0.94	0.52	0.691
3D	56	0.98	0.5	0.670
5D	56	0.96	0.52	0.610
7D	8	0.66	0.52	0.570

There are 18 runs with accuracy equal or more than 0.9 as shown in Table 2. Most of them obtained with 3D clustering (9 out of 18), 5 of them used 2D clustering and 4 used 5D clustering. This shows that 3D clustering give most of the best clustering performance in this research.

Table 2. Run Result with Accuracy >= 0.9

Type	Features	Accuracy
3D	CEDD-EdgeHistogram-ColorLayout	0.98
5D	AutoColorCorrelogram-CEDD-Gabor-EdgeHistogram-ColorLayout	0.96
5D	CEDD-FCTH-Gabor-EdgeHistogram-ColorLayout	0.96
3D	FCTH-EdgeHistogram-ColorLayout	0.96
3D	AutoColorCorrelogram-EdgeHistogram-ColorLayout	0.94
5D	AutoColorCorrelogram-FCTH-Gabor-EdgeHistogram-ColorLayout	0.94
3D	AutoColorCorrelogram-Gabor-ColorLayout	0.94
2D	EdgeHistogram-ColorLayout	0.94
2D	Gabor-ColorLayout	0.94
3D	Gabor-EdgeHistogram-ColorLayout	0.94
3D	AutoColorCorrelogram-CEDD-EdgeHistogram	0.92
2D	CEDD-EdgeHistogram	0.92
3D	CEDD-FCTH-ColorLayout	0.92
2D	FCTH-EdgeHistogram	0.92
5D	AutoColorCorrelogram-CEDD-FCTH-Gabor-ColorLayout	0.9
2D	AutoColorCorrelogram-FCTH	0.9
3D	CEDD-Gabor-ColorLayout	0.9
3D	FCTH-Gabor-ColorLayout	0.9

Moreover, by taking a close look into images in each cluster result, it was found that the dinosaur category is the easiest category to cluster. Table 3 shows result of the proposed method which able to cluster the dinosaur images perfectly in 20 runs out of 56 - 3D clustering runs done. Another category that ever been clustered perfectly in the experiments are horse and mountain category.

Table 3. Perfectly Clustered Categories per Clustering Type

Type	Perfectly Clustered
1D	dinosaur (2x), horse (1x)
2D	dinosaur (12x), horse(2x)
3D	dinosaur (20x), horse(7x), mountain (1x)
5D	dinosaur (15x), horse(5x)
7D	dinosaur (1x)

5   Conclusions and Future Possibilities

Based on the experiment results, clustering with multi visual features could improve clustering performance compared to using only one visual feature. Nevertheless, using too many visual features in combination might lower the accuracy of the result. In this research scope, combination of CEDD, Edge Histogram and Color Layout proven to be the most promising set of visual feature to cluster the image collection.

Different visual extraction tools and another type of visual features might be worth to try in the future. Finding the right combination of type and number of visual feature for clustering might increase the chance to distinguish one image from another in more precise manner. Furthermore, finding the right number of clusters for K-Means clustering initialization is also a problem when dealing with real-world image collection which prior knowledge of clusters existed is unknown.

References

1. Chary, Sunitha, Lakshmi: Similar Image Searching from Image Database using Cluster Mean: Sorting and Performance Estimation (2012)
2. Maheshwari, Silakari, Motwani: Image Clustering using Color and Texture. In: First International Conference on Computational Intelligence, Communication Systems and Networks (2009)
3. Yildizier, Balci, Jarada, Alhajj: Integrating Wavelets with Clustering and Indexing for Effective Content-Based Image Retrieval (2011)
4. Lux, M., Chatzichristofis, S.A.: Lire: Lucene Image Retrieval – An Extensible Java CBIR Library. In: Proceedings of the 16th ACM International Conference on Multimedia, Vancouver, Canada, pp. 1085–1088 (2008)
5. Huang, J., Zabih, R.: Combining Color and Spatial Information for Content-based Image Retrieval. Cornell University, New York (1998)

6. Chatzichristofis, S.A., Boutalis, Y.S.: CEDD: Color and Edge Directivity Descriptor, a Compact Descriptor for Image Indexing and Retrieval. Democritus University of Thrace, Xanthi (2008)
7. Ohm, Cieplinski, Kim, Krishnamachari, Manjunath, Messing, Yamada: The MPEG-7 Color Descriptors (2001)
8. Won, C.S., et al.: Efficient Use of MPEG-7 Edge Histogram Descriptor. ETRI Journal 24(1), 23–30 (2002)
9. Chatzichristofis, S.A., Boutalis, Y.S.: FCTH: Fuzzy Color and Texture Histogram, a Low Level Feature for Accurate Image Retrieval. Democritus University of Thrace, Xanthi (2008b)
10. Yang, Y., Newsam, S.: Comparing SIFT Descriptors and Gabor Texture Features for Classification of Remote Sense Imagery. In: Proceedings of ICIP (2008)
11. Tamura, H., Mori, S., Yamawaki, T.: Textual Features Corresponding to Visual Perception. IEEE Transactions on Systems, Man, and Cybernetics, 460–473 (1978)

Appendix

Type	Features	Accuracy	Perfectly Clustered Category
1D	-AutoColorCorrelogram-	0.64	horse;
1D	-CEDD-	0.84	
1D	-ColorLayout-	0.88	horse; dinosaur;
1D	-EdgeHistogram-	0.76	
1D	-FCTH-	0.68	dinosaur;
1D	-Gabor-	0.54	dinosaur;
1D	-ScalableColor-	0.62	
1D	-Tamura-	0.54	
2D	-AutoColorCorrelogram-CEDD-	0.64	
2D	-AutoColorCorrelogram-ColorLayout-	0.8	dinosaur;
2D	-AutoColorCorrelogram-EdgeHistogram-	0.82	
2D	-AutoColorCorrelogram-FCTH-	0.9	dinosaur;
2D	-AutoColorCorrelogram-Gabor-	0.56	dinosaur;
2D	-AutoColorCorrelogram-ScalableColor-	0.62	
2D	-AutoColorCorrelogram-Tamura-	0.54	
2D	-CEDD-ColorLayout-	0.84	horse; dinosaur;
2D	-CEDD-EdgeHistogram-	0.92	
2D	-CEDD-FCTH-	0.78	dinosaur;
2D	-CEDD-Gabor-	0.66	dinosaur;
2D	-CEDD-ScalableColor-	0.56	
2D	-CEDD-Tamura-	0.54	
2D	-EdgeHistogram-ColorLayout-	0.94	dinosaur;
2D	-EdgeHistogram-ScalableColor-	0.7	
2D	-FCTH-ColorLayout-	0.78	dinosaur;
2D	-FCTH-EdgeHistogram-	0.92	
2D	-FCTH-Gabor-	0.62	dinosaur;
2D	-FCTH-ScalableColor-	0.6	
2D	-FCTH-Tamura-	0.54	
2D	-Gabor-ColorLayout-	0.94	horse; dinosaur;
2D	-Gabor-EdgeHistogram-	0.68	dinosaur;
2D	-Gabor-ScalableColor-	0.6	
2D	-Gabor-Tamura-	0.54	
2D	-ScalableColor-ColorLayout-	0.72	
2D	-Tamura-ColorLayout-	0.52	
2D	-Tamura-EdgeHistogram-	0.54	

2D	-Tamura-ScalableColor-	0.54	
3D	-AutoColorCorrelogram-CEDD-ColorLayout-	0.84	horse; dinosaur;
3D	-AutoColorCorrelogram-CEDD-EdgeHistogram-	0.92	
3D	-AutoColorCorrelogram-CEDD-FCTH-	0.78	dinosaur; horse;
3D	-AutoColorCorrelogram-CEDD-Gabor-	0.66	dinosaur;
3D	-AutoColorCorrelogram-CEDD-ScalableColor-	0.58	
3D	-AutoColorCorrelogram-CEDD-Tamura-	0.54	
3D	-AutoColorCorrelogram-EdgeHistogram-ColorLayout-	0.94	dinosaur;
3D	-AutoColorCorrelogram-EdgeHistogram-ScalableColor-	0.7	
3D	-AutoColorCorrelogram-FCTH-ColorLayout-	0.78	dinosaur;
3D	-AutoColorCorrelogram-FCTH-EdgeHistogram-	0.74	dinosaur;
3D	-AutoColorCorrelogram-FCTH-Gabor-	0.62	dinosaur;
3D	-AutoColorCorrelogram-FCTH-ScalableColor-	0.6	
3D	-AutoColorCorrelogram-FCTH-Tamura-	0.54	
3D	-AutoColorCorrelogram-Gabor-ColorLayout-	0.94	horse; dinosaur;
3D	-AutoColorCorrelogram-Gabor-EdgeHistogram-	0.64	dinosaur;
3D	-AutoColorCorrelogram-Gabor-ScalableColor-	0.64	
3D	-AutoColorCorrelogram-Gabor-Tamura-	0.54	
3D	-AutoColorCorrelogram-ScalableColor-ColorLayout-	0.72	
3D	-AutoColorCorrelogram-Tamura-ColorLayout-	0.52	
3D	-AutoColorCorrelogram-Tamura-EdgeHistogram-	0.54	
3D	-AutoColorCorrelogram-Tamura-ScalableColor-	0.54	
3D	-CEDD-EdgeHistogram-ColorLayout-	0.98	horse; mountain; dinosaur;
3D	-CEDD-EdgeHistogram-ScalableColor-	0.5	
3D	-CEDD-FCTH-ColorLayout-	0.92	horse; dinosaur;
3D	-CEDD-FCTH-EdgeHistogram-	0.88	dinosaur;
3D	-CEDD-FCTH-Gabor-	0.7	dinosaur;
3D	-CEDD-FCTH-ScalableColor-	0.6	
3D	-CEDD-FCTH-Tamura-	0.54	
3D	-CEDD-Gabor-ColorLayout-	0.9	horse; dinosaur;
3D	-CEDD-Gabor-EdgeHistogram-	0.74	dinosaur;
3D	-CEDD-Gabor-ScalableColor-	0.6	
3D	-CEDD-Gabor-Tamura-	0.54	
3D	-CEDD-ScalableColor-ColorLayout-	0.74	
3D	-CEDD-Tamura-ColorLayout-	0.52	
3D	-CEDD-Tamura-EdgeHistogram-	0.54	
3D	-CEDD-Tamura-ScalableColor-	0.54	
3D	-EdgeHistogram-ScalableColor-ColorLayout-	0.68	
3D	-FCTH-EdgeHistogram-ColorLayout-	0.96	dinosaur;
3D	-FCTH-EdgeHistogram-ScalableColor-	0.74	
3D	-FCTH-Gabor-ColorLayout-	0.9	horse; dinosaur;
3D	-FCTH-Gabor-EdgeHistogram-	0.8	dinosaur;
3D	-FCTH-Gabor-ScalableColor-	0.64	
3D	-FCTH-Gabor-Tamura-	0.54	
3D	-FCTH-ScalableColor-ColorLayout-	0.74	
3D	-FCTH-Tamura-ColorLayout-	0.52	
3D	-FCTH-Tamura-EdgeHistogram-	0.54	
3D	-FCTH-Tamura-ScalableColor-	0.54	
3D	-Gabor-EdgeHistogram-ColorLayout-	0.94	dinosaur;
3D	-Gabor-EdgeHistogram-ScalableColor-	0.62	dinosaur;
3D	-Gabor-ScalableColor-ColorLayout-	0.6	
3D	-Gabor-Tamura-ColorLayout-	0.52	
3D	-Gabor-Tamura-EdgeHistogram-	0.54	
3D	-Gabor-Tamura-ScalableColor-	0.52	
3D	-Tamura-EdgeHistogram-ColorLayout-	0.52	
3D	-Tamura-EdgeHistogram-ScalableColor-	0.54	
3D	-Tamura-ScalableColor-ColorLayout-	0.56	
5D	-AutoColorCorrelogram-CEDD-EdgeHistogram-ScalableColor-ColorLayout-	0.68	dinosaur;
5D	-AutoColorCorrelogram-CEDD-FCTH-EdgeHistogram-ColorLayout-	0.8	horse; dinosaur;

5D	-AutoColorCorrelogram-CEDD-FCTH-EdgeHistogram-ScalableColor-	0.7	
5D	-AutoColorCorrelogram-CEDD-FCTH-Gabor-ColorLayout-	0.9	horse; dinosaur;
5D	-AutoColorCorrelogram-CEDD-FCTH-Gabor-EdgeHistogram-	0.74	dinosaur;
5D	-AutoColorCorrelogram-CEDD-FCTH-Gabor-ScalableColor-	0.66	dinosaur;
5D	-AutoColorCorrelogram-CEDD-FCTH-Gabor-Tamura-	0.54	
5D	-AutoColorCorrelogram-CEDD-FCTH-ScalableColor-ColorLayout-	0.78	
5D	-AutoColorCorrelogram-CEDD-FCTH-Tamura-ColorLayout-	0.52	
5D	-AutoColorCorrelogram-CEDD-FCTH-Tamura-EdgeHistogram-	0.54	
5D	-AutoColorCorrelogram-CEDD-FCTH-Tamura-ScalableColor-	0.54	
5D	-AutoColorCorrelogram-CEDD-Gabor-EdgeHistogram-ColorLayout-	0.96	horse; dinosaur;
5D	-AutoColorCorrelogram-CEDD-Gabor-EdgeHistogram-ScalableColor-	0.64	dinosaur;
5D	-AutoColorCorrelogram-CEDD-Gabor-ScalableColor-ColorLayout-	0.6	
5D	-AutoColorCorrelogram-CEDD-Gabor-Tamura-ColorLayout-	0.52	
5D	-AutoColorCorrelogram-CEDD-Gabor-Tamura-EdgeHistogram-	0.54	
5D	-AutoColorCorrelogram-CEDD-Gabor-Tamura-ScalableColor-	0.52	
5D	-AutoColorCorrelogram-CEDD-Tamura-EdgeHistogram-ColorLayout-	0.52	
5D	-AutoColorCorrelogram-CEDD-Tamura-EdgeHistogram-ScalableColor-	0.54	
5D	-AutoColorCorrelogram-CEDD-Tamura-ScalableColor-ColorLayout-	0.56	
5D	-AutoColorCorrelogram-FCTH-EdgeHistogram-ScalableColor-ColorLayout-	0.76	
5D	-AutoColorCorrelogram-FCTH-Gabor-EdgeHistogram-ColorLayout-	0.94	horse; dinosaur;
5D	-AutoColorCorrelogram-FCTH-Gabor-EdgeHistogram-ScalableColor-	0.6	dinosaur;
5D	-AutoColorCorrelogram-FCTH-Gabor-ScalableColor-ColorLayout-	0.6	
5D	-AutoColorCorrelogram-FCTH-Gabor-Tamura-ColorLayout-	0.52	
5D	-AutoColorCorrelogram-FCTH-Gabor-Tamura-EdgeHistogram-	0.54	
5D	-AutoColorCorrelogram-FCTH-Gabor-Tamura-ScalableColor-	0.52	
5D	-AutoColorCorrelogram-FCTH-Tamura-EdgeHistogram-ColorLayout-	0.52	
5D	-AutoColorCorrelogram-FCTH-Tamura-EdgeHistogram-ScalableColor-	0.54	
5D	-AutoColorCorrelogram-FCTH-Tamura-ScalableColor-ColorLayout-	0.56	
5D	-AutoColorCorrelogram-Gabor-EdgeHistogram-ScalableColor-ColorLayout-	0.7	dinosaur;
5D	-AutoColorCorrelogram-Gabor-Tamura-EdgeHistogram-ColorLayout-	0.56	
5D	-AutoColorCorrelogram-Gabor-Tamura-EdgeHistogram-ScalableColor-	0.52	
5D	-AutoColorCorrelogram-Gabor-Tamura-ScalableColor-ColorLayout-	0.56	
5D	-AutoColorCorrelogram-Tamura-EdgeHistogram-ScalableColor-ColorLayout-	0.56	
5D	-CEDD-FCTH-EdgeHistogram-ScalableColor-ColorLayout-	0.68	dinosaur;
5D	-CEDD-FCTH-Gabor-EdgeHistogram-ColorLayout-	0.96	horse; dinosaur;
5D	-CEDD-FCTH-Gabor-EdgeHistogram-ScalableColor-	0.7	dinosaur;
5D	-CEDD-FCTH-Gabor-ScalableColor-ColorLayout-	0.6	
5D	-CEDD-FCTH-Gabor-Tamura-ColorLayout-	0.56	
5D	-CEDD-FCTH-Gabor-Tamura-EdgeHistogram-	0.54	
5D	-CEDD-FCTH-Gabor-Tamura-ScalableColor-	0.52	
5D	-CEDD-FCTH-Tamura-EdgeHistogram-ColorLayout-	0.52	
5D	-CEDD-FCTH-Tamura-EdgeHistogram-ScalableColor-	0.54	
5D	-CEDD-FCTH-Tamura-ScalableColor-ColorLayout-	0.56	
5D	-CEDD-Gabor-EdgeHistogram-ScalableColor-ColorLayout-	0.72	dinosaur;
5D	-CEDD-Gabor-Tamura-EdgeHistogram-ColorLayout-	0.56	
5D	-CEDD-Gabor-Tamura-EdgeHistogram-ScalableColor-	0.52	
5D	-CEDD-Gabor-Tamura-ScalableColor-ColorLayout-	0.56	

5D	-CEDD-Tamura-EdgeHistogram-ScalableColor-ColorLayout-	0.56	
5D	-FCTH-Gabor-EdgeHistogram-ScalableColor-ColorLayout-	0.7	dinosaur;
5D	-FCTH-Gabor-Tamura-EdgeHistogram-ColorLayout-	0.56	
5D	-FCTH-Gabor-Tamura-EdgeHistogram-ScalableColor-	0.52	
5D	-FCTH-Gabor-Tamura-ScalableColor-ColorLayout-	0.56	
5D	-FCTH-Tamura-EdgeHistogram-ScalableColor-ColorLayout-	0.56	
5D	-Gabor-Tamura-EdgeHistogram-ScalableColor-ColorLayout-	0.56	
7D	-AutoColorCorrelogram-CEDD-FCTH-Gabor-EdgeHistogram-ScalableColor-ColorLayout-	0.66	dinosaur;
7D	-AutoColorCorrelogram-CEDD-FCTH-Gabor-Tamura-EdgeHistogram-ColorLayout-	0.56	
7D	-AutoColorCorrelogram-CEDD-FCTH-Gabor-Tamura-EdgeHistogram-ScalableColor-	0.52	
7D	-AutoColorCorrelogram-CEDD-FCTH-Gabor-Tamura-ScalableColor-ColorLayout-	0.56	
7D	-AutoColorCorrelogram-CEDD-FCTH-Tamura-EdgeHistogram-ScalableColor-ColorLayout-	0.56	
7D	-AutoColorCorrelogram-CEDD-Gabor-Tamura-EdgeHistogram-ScalableColor-ColorLayout-	0.56	
7D	-AutoColorCorrelogram-FCTH-Gabor-Tamura-EdgeHistogram-ScalableColor-ColorLayout-	0.56	
7D	-CEDD-FCTH-Gabor-Tamura-EdgeHistogram-ScalableColor-ColorLayout-	0.56	

A Robust Visual Object Tracking Approach on a Mobile Device

Abdulmalik Danlami Mohammed and Tim Morris

School of Computer Science, University of Manchester,
Oxford Road, Manchester, UK
Abdulmalik.mohammed@postgrad.manchester.ac.uk,
tim.morris@manchester.ac.uk

Abstract. In this paper, we present an approach for tracking an object in video captured on a mobile device. We use a colour-based approach. The performance of many of these approaches degrades due to lighting changes and occlusion. To address the issue of lightning changes, our approach makes use of colour histogram that is generated by accumulating histograms derived from target objects imaged under different conditions. A CAMShift tracking algorithm is applied to the back-projected image to track the target object.

We have tested our approach by tracking an Emergency Exit sign and the results obtained show that the tracking is robust against lightning changes.

Keywords: CAMShift Algorithm, Histogram Backprojection, Colour Space.

1 Introduction

Object tracking is an important task that is required in many high-level computer vision applications. It is concerned with estimating the trajectory of an object in a given scene [1]. Recent advances in mobile phones technology, in particular, the low-cost, high-resolution camera, has opened a new research direction in object tracking technique.

Object Tracking algorithm have been use in applications such as face and head tracking, video surveillance system, human-computer-interaction, traffic monitoring system, document retrieval system[1].

Many tracking approaches utilise features such as colours, edges and textures to model the object to track. The choice of feature to use for tracking depends largely on how robust it is against challenges such as lighting changes, blurring due to camera motion and occlusion; they are robust to different challenges. Many implementations will therefore use a combination of features that collectively address most, or all of these issues. However, this will involve additional computation to the tracking system which may prevent real-time tracking from being achieved in devices with low processing power.

Most Visual objects contain colour combinations that make them distinct from the surrounding environment. For example, a standard exit sign in the UK is a green

Linawati et al. (Eds.): ICT-EurAsia 2014, LNCS 8407, pp. 190–198, 2014.

rectangular object with some or all of a schematic running man, an open door, an arrow and possibly the word "EXIT". The arrow and running man give an indication of the direction to be taken in the event of emergency. Hence, colour information should be helpful to detect and track sign.

In this paper, we utilise the colour information and the CAMShift tracking algorithm to detect and track sign using a camera phone. We aimed to implement a robust, light weight tracking algorithm on devices with low processing capability.

The contribution of this paper is in the application of CAMShift tracking algorithm based on robust histogram back projection on a mobile device.

The remainder of this paper is organised as follows: In Section 2 we discuss in detail works related to tracking of objects and their suitability for mobile devices. Section 3 provides an overview of a CAMShift tracking algorithm and its limitation in a controlled environment. In Section 4 we present an introduction to histogram backprojection, which is one of the useful steps required in CAMShift tracking algorithm. Section 5 discusses in detail our proposed approach utilising colour, we emphasise the methods we adopted to mitigate the effect of lighting changes. The experimental result of implementing our proposed tracking approach on mobile device is presented in Section 6. Finally, Section 7 concludes.

2   Related Work

In this section, we will discuss in details some of the several tracking approaches that have been proposed in the literature and their suitability for implementing on mobile devices.

Li and Zhi-Chun [3] enhance the CAMShift tracking algorithm by utilising skin-colour and contour information to respectively detect and track human ear. The proposed approach is divided into two stages. The first stage used CAMShift based on skin-color to track a face in the video frame, the second stage used contour information to track and locate the ear.

Tsen Min Chen et al [12] proposed an object tracking method that is based on probability distribution. To deal with issues of lighting changes, the method adjusts the model parameter during run-time.

Alper et al. [4] combine colour and texture features to track object and a shape feature to improve object tracking with CAMShift, especially in occlusion. The fused features (colour and textures) enable tracking in different appearances, even partial.

Yingyin et al [7] proposed a frame-differencing approach for moving object detection and further utilised the hue and edge orientation histogram of the target object to improve the CAMShift tracking algorithm.

Lixin Fan et al [13] proposed a tracking approach on mobile device using a haar-like feature matching to track target objects. They made use of an online update schema to improve tracking.

Jianwei Gong et al [14] present colour-based segmentation method with CAMShift tracking algorithm for detection and tracking of traffic lights using a camera that is mounted on a moving vehicle.

Donghe and Jinson [5] integrate a filtering prediction with a CAMShift tracking algorithm to improve object tracking against occlusion. The algorithm works by locating the face in the first three frames of the video sequence and using the position to initialise the parameters of the filter prediction for finding the location of the face in the following frame.

Gary Bradski [2] presents a face tracking approach in perceptual user interface using hue in the HSV colour system for tracking face and head.

In contrast to [2], David et al [6] make use of accumulated histograms to model same object in different appearances and for monitoring the object identities during tracking. The reference histogram is computed offline. However, the large memory requirement of [3,4,5], [7] makes those approaches unsuitable to be implemented on devices with limited processing capability.

Our approach is motivated by [2],[6] because of their low computational demand. A comprehensive review of object tracking approaches based on different object representation and features selection can be found in [1].

3   CAMShift Tracking Algorithm

In this Section, we provide an overview of the CAMShift tracking algorithm and its shortcomings, in particular when object's appearance changes and when an object is occluded.

Continuously Adaptive Mean Shift (CAMShift) is a tracking algorithm that uses colour features for tracking an object in a scene. This algorithm is an extension of the mean shift algorithm. It finds the mode of a probability distribution using the mean shift algorithm and then iteratively adjusts the parameter of the distribution until convergence. The basic principle of CAMShift is well documented in [2],[8]. Figure 1 shows the object tracking workflow.

The following steps describe the CAMShift algorithm:

(1) Set the initial location and size of the search window.
(2) Calculate the colour probability distribution within the search window.
(3) Find the new location and size of the search window using the mean shift algorithm.
(4) Compute the orientation and scale of the target.
(5) Capture the next frame and repeat from step 3.

The zeroth, first and second order image moments as shown below are used to find the mean location of the target object.

$$M_{00} = \sum_x \sum_y I(x, y). \tag{1}$$

$$M_{10} = \sum_x \sum_y x I(x, y); \quad M_{01} = \sum_x \sum_y y I(x, y); \tag{2}$$

$$M_{20} = \sum_x \sum_y x^2 I(x,y); \quad M_{02} = \sum_x \sum_y y^2 I(x,y); \quad (3)$$

Where $I(x,y)$ is the pixel (probability) value at position (x,y) in the image, and x and y range over the search window. Then the mean location (centroid) in the search window is computed as:

$$x_c = \frac{M_{10}}{M_{00}}; \quad y_c = \frac{M_{01}}{M_{00}}; \quad (4)$$

To update the search window, the target object aspect ratio given below:

$$ratio = \frac{\frac{M_{20}}{x_c^2}}{\frac{M_{02}}{y_c^2}} \quad (5)$$

is used with:

$$width = 2M_{00} \cdot ratio; \quad height = \frac{2M_{00}}{ratio} \quad (6)$$

CAMShift performs better given a simple background where lighting changes and object occlusion are absent. However, the algorithm can perform poorly in cases of occlusion by other objects or the presence of objects of similar colouration.

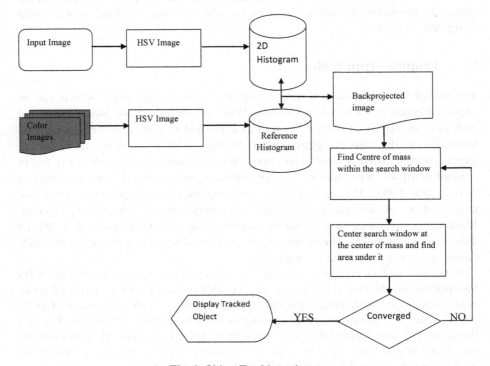

Fig. 1. Object Tracking schema

4   Histogram Backprojection

Histogram back projection is a simple technique proposed by [10] to find object correspondence in a colour image. The technique utilises the colour histogram of the captured image and histogram of the target object as a look-up table to generate a probability distribution image. Initially, a histogram M_j of the target object in some colour space is pre-computed followed by the histogram I_j of the scene where the search for the object is to take place. At this point, a ratio histogram R_j is computed by dividing the M_j and I_j and the backprojected image $B_{x,y}$ is generated according to equation (8).

$$R_j = min[M_j/I_j, 1]$$ (7)

Where j represents the index of a bin

$$B_{x,y} = R_{h(C_{x,y})}$$ (8)

Where $C_{x,y}$ is the colour value at location (x, y) of the searched image and $h(C_{x,y})$ is the bin corresponding to $C_{x,y}$ [11].

At this point, a blurring mask is applied to the back projected image and the location of the peak value in the image corresponds to the location of the object in the image. In particular, the technique is useful where a large database of the model histogram is required.

5   Propose Approach

We utilised the colour content of an object for tracking since many objects can be identified based on their colour contents. However, to address the issues associated with most colour-based tracking system as explained in section 3, we accumulated histograms of the objects captured under different lighting conditions to model the target object in different views. Our approach is motivated by the work of [6], but in contrast to [6], we implement the tracking algorithm on a mobile device rather than on device with GPU. The approach has low computational requirement since the accumulation of histograms is offline and thus suitable for mobile devices. Illumination invariance is achieved by retaining only the chrominance data. Whilst there are many ways to achieve this, we have selected to capture images in the HSV colour space and discard the V component.

In the case an Exit sign, its background is a standard green hence, we prebuilt a 2D histogram using the Hue and Saturation in the HSV colour space for individual green colour image captured under different lighting conditions. The advantage of HSV colour space for colour image processing is well researched and reported in the literatures [9]. The required data was manually cropped, to exclude white elements of the sign. Whilst this type of sign is extremely simple, having a one-colour background, the method is clearly applicable to any coloured sign.

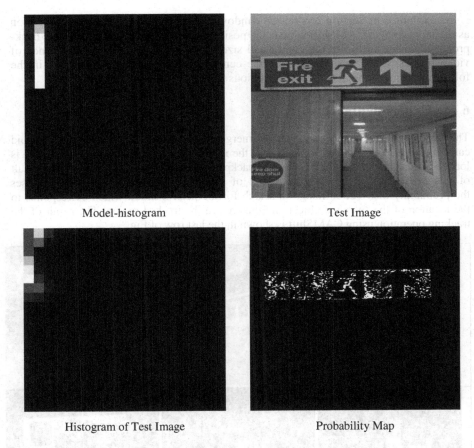

Model-histogram   Test Image

Histogram of Test Image   Probability Map

Fig. 2. (L-R) Model histogram, Input image, Histogram of input image, Backprojected image

In our experiment, we use a data set of 100 images to model the signs' colour distribution. The large number of images is to compensate for changes in the object appearance occasioned by camera motion, and, more importantly, lighting changes. The histogram's bin count is reduced to a manageable number to improve the histogram's accuracy and to reduce the computational requirement [8]. We tested our model histogram using different numbers of bins for the hue and saturation channels respectively and observed that a dense rather than a sparse histogram produced a better detection and tracking result. We performed all the steps prior to the back projection of the input image and saved the model histogram offline. This is to enhance tracking during run-time.

As explained in section 3, the model histogram served as a look-up table to generate a probability distribution image from the captured image. The result of histogram backprojection of the input image using the model histogram is shown in Figure 2.

As explained in Section 2, a search window is initialized with its size and position as the input image. CAMShift adjusts the position and size of the window in the back-projected image to locate the centre and size of the target object. In a sequence of video frames, CAMShift can predict the centre and size of the target object in the following frame using data from the previous frame.

6   Experimental Result

The first row of Fig. 3 shows images of emergency exit signs captured with an Android camera phone. As explained in Section 4, the model histogram that was saved offline is loaded at run-time to perform histogram backprojection on the input images. The result of this operation can be seen in row 2 of Fig. 3. Following this, CAMShift uses the probability distribution image to search for the peak location which corresponds to the location of the searched object and thus return the tracked region. The result of the tracking operation using CAMShift is shown in the last row of Fig. 3.

Fig. 3. Row 1: Original Exit sign Image; Row 2: Backprojected Image; Row 3: Tracked region of the exit image

7   Conclusion

In this paper, we have presented an approach to tracking an object on a mobile device. It makes use of reference colour histograms generated by accumulating and normalising histograms of target objects captured under various conditions that replicate the expected illuminations when the system is live. The reference histogram is saved offline to reduce computational time. This is a useful step towards tracking using CAMShift.

Our approach is simple and robust against lighting changes as shown in the results obtained, but fails to track the whole region of one of the signs because of the extreme camera viewpoint. This is evident in the tracked image shown in the second column of Fig. 3. This can be solved by integrating a shape feature to the detector. Furthermore, shape features can help improve tracking due to occlusion by object of similar colour.

References

1. Yilmaz, A., Javed, O., Shah, M.: Object Tracking: A Survey. ACM Computing Survey 38, 1–45 (2006)
2. Bradski, G.R.: Computer Vision Face Tracking for Use in a Perceptual User Interface. Intel Technology Journal (1998)
3. Yuan, L., Mu, Z.-C.: Ear Detection Based on Skin-Color and Contour Information. In: 6th International Conference on Machine Learning and Cybernetics, vol. 4, pp. 2213–2217. IEEE, Hong Kong (2007)
4. Yilmaz, A., Li, X., Shah, M.: Contour-Based Object Tracking with Occlusion Handling in Video Acquired Using Mobile Cameras. In: IEEE Transaction on Pattern Analysis and Machine Intelligence, vol. 26, pp. 1531–1536. IEEE Computer Society (2004)
5. Yang, D., Xia, J.: Face Tracking Based on Camshift Algorithm and Motion Prediction. In: International Workshop on Intelligent Systems and Applications, pp. 1–4. IEEE, Wuhan (2009)
6. Exner, D., Bruns, E., Kurz, D., Grundhofer, A., Bimber, O.: Fast and Robust CAMShift Tracking. In: Computer Society Conference on Computer Vision and Pattern Recognition Workshops, pp. 9–16. IEEE, San Francisco (2010)
7. Yue, Y., Gao, Y., Zhang, X.: An Improved Camshift Algorithm Based on Dynamic Background. In: 1st International Conference on Information Science and Engineering, pp. 1141–1144. IEEE, Nanjing (2009)
8. Allen, J.G., Xu, R.Y.D., Jin, J.S.: Object Tracking Using Camshift Algorithm and Multiple Quantized Feature Spaces. In: 5th Pan-Sydney Area Workshop on Visual Information Processing, pp. 3–7. ACM, Australia (2004)
9. Sural, S., Qian, G., Pramanik, S.: Segmentation and Histogram Generation Using the HSV Color Space for Image Retrieval. In: International Conference on Image Processing, vol. 2, pp. 589–592. IEEE (2002)
10. Swain, M.J., Ballard, D.H.: Indexing via Colour Histogram. In: Active Perception and Robotic Vision, vol. 83, pp. 261–273. Springer (1992)
11. Yoo, T.-W., Oh, I.-S.: A Fast Algorithm for Tracking Human Faces Based on Chromatic Histograms. In: Patter Recognition Letters, vol. 20, pp. 967–968. Elsevier (1999)

12. Chen, T.M., Luo, R.C., Hsiaso, T.H., Chia-Yi: Visual Tracking Using Adaptive Colour Histogram Model. In: 25th Annual Conference of IEEE, vol. 3, pp. 1336–1341. IEEE, San Jose (1999)
13. Fan, L., Riihimaki, M.: A Feature-Based Object Tracking Approach for Real Time Image Processing on Mobile Devices. In: 17th International Conference on Image Processing. IEEE, Hong Kong (2010)
14. Gong, J., Jiang, Y., Xiong, G., Guan, C., Tao, G., Chen, H.: The Recognition and Tracking of Traffic Lights Based on Colour Segmentation and CAMShift for Intelligent Vehicles. In: Intelligent Vehicles Symposium (IV), pp. 431–435. IEEE, San Diego (2010)

Self-generating Programs – Cascade
of the Blocks

Josef Kufner and Radek Mařík

Department of Cybernetics, Faculty of Electrical Engineering,
Czech Technical University in Prague, Czech Republic
kufnejos@fel.cvut.cz, marikr@k333.felk.cvut.cz

Abstract When building complex applications the only way not to get
lost is to split the application into simpler components. Current programming languages, including object oriented ones, offer very good utilities
to create such components. However, when the components are created,
they need to be connected together. Unluckily, these languages are not a
very suitable tool for that. To help with composition of the components
we introduce *cascade* – a dynamic acyclic structure built from blocks,
inspired by the Function Block approach. The cascade generates itself
on-the-fly during its evaluation to match requirements specified by input
data and automatically orders an execution of the individual blocks. Thus
the structure of a given cascade does not need to be predefined entirely
during its composing/implementation and fixed during its execution as
it is usually assumed by the most approaches. It also provides a real-time
and fully automatic visualization of all blocks and their connections to
ease debugging and an inspection of the application.

1 Introduction

In last 30 years object oriented languages have developed to state, where they
are a pretty good tool for creating components, but when it comes to composing
these components together, the situation is far from perfect.

There are not many successful and widely used tools or design patterns to
compose applications. Probably the most known approach, which is well established in the field of programmable logic controllers, is *Function Blocks* [1], and
its simplified variant, used by unix shells, known as *Pipes and Filters*. Despite
these approaches are decades old [2], they are used in only few specific areas,
and there is very low development activity in this direction.

A basic idea of both Function Blocks and Pipes and Filters is to split a complex
application to simpler blocks, and then connect them together using well defined
and simple interfaces. This adds one level of abstraction into the application and
simplifies significantly all involved components. Simpler components are easier
to develop. Well defined interfaces improve reusability of the components. In
total, it means faster and more effective development.

From other point of view the connections between blocks can be easily visualized in a very intuitive way and conversely these connections can be specified

Linawati et al. (Eds.): ICT-EurAsia 2014, LNCS 8407, pp. 199–212, 2014.

using a graphical editor. This significantly lowers programming skill requirements and allows non-programmers to build or modify applications if a suitable
GUI tool is provided.

A main limitation of Function Blocks is that blocks are often connected together in advance by a programmer and this structure remains static for the
rest of its life time. Therefore, an application cannot easily adapt itself to changing requirements and environment, it can usually change only few parameters.
The next few sections will present how to introduce dynamics into these static
structures and what possibilities it brings.

In this paper we introduce *cascade*, a dynamic acyclic structure built of blocks.
The next two sections (2, 3) describe the blocks and how they are composed into
a cascade, including a description of their important properties. Then, we explain
the most interesting features of the cascade in Section 4. Finally, in the last two
sections (6, 5) a practical use of cascade is described and it is also compared to
existing tools and approaches.

2   Creating the Blocks

As mentioned above, object oriented languages are very good tools to create
components. So it is convenient to use them to create blocks.

In cascade a block is atomic entity of a given type (class), which has named
inputs and outputs, each block instance is identified by unique ID, and can be
executed. During execution the block typically reads its inputs, performs an
action on received data, and puts results to its outputs.

The symbol used in this paper to represent a block is in Figure 1a. There are
an ID and a block type in the header, named inputs on the left side and outputs
on the right. A color of the header represents the current state of the block. At
the bottom a short note may be added, for example a reason of failure.

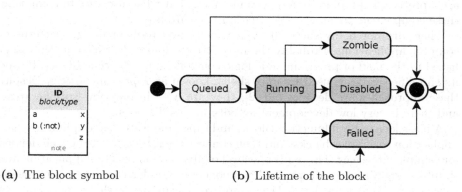

(a) The block symbol   (b) Lifetime of the block

Fig. 1. The block

The block is implemented as a class, which inherits from the abstract block class. This abstract class implements a required infrastructure to manage inputs, outputs and execution of the block. Execution itself consists of calling `main` method of the block class.

Each block instance is executed only once. During its lifetime block goes through a few states as presented in Fig. 1b. It starts in the state *queued*, where waits for execution. Then it enters state *running*, and when execution is completed, one of the final states *zombie* (success), *disabled*, or *failed* is entered. In the final state the block exists only to maintain its outputs for other blocks[1]. This means that the block can process only one set of input data. To process another data set, a new block instance must be created. But because the lifetime of the block ends before another input data arrive, it causes no trouble (this will be explained later).

3 Connecting the Blocks

To create something interesting out of the blocks, we need to connect them together. These connections are established by attaching an input of the second block to the output of the first block – the connections are always specified at inputs, never at outputs. So the input knows where its value came from, but the output does not know whether it is connected somewhere at all. Transfers of values over the earlier established connections are also initiated by the inputs. That means the outputs are passive publishers only. By connecting blocks together a *cascade* is being built.

The cascade is a directed acyclic graph composed of blocks, where edges are connections between outputs and inputs of the blocks.

When a block is inserted into cascade, its inputs are already entirely defined. It means, that a connection to another block or a constant is assigned to each of its inputs. At this moment, connections are specified using block ID and output name. Later, when block is being executed, actual block instances assigned to these block IDs are resolved, so the specified connections can be established and values transferred from outputs to inputs. Thanks to that, it does not matter in which order blocks are inserted into cascade, as long as there are all required blocks present before they need to be executed.

3.1 Evaluation

Evaluation of the cascade is a process, in which the blocks are executed in a correct order, and data from the outputs of executed blocks are passed to the inputs of the blocks waiting for execution.

By creating a connection between two blocks, a dependency (precedence constraint) is defined, and these dependencies define the partial order, in which

---

[1] Therefore the successful state is called *zombie*, like terminated unix process whose return value has not been picked up by parent process.

blocks need to be executed. For single threaded evaluation, a simple depth-first-search algorithm with cycle detection can be used to calculate topological order compatible with given partial order [3].

Since DFS algorithm requires a starting point to be defined, selected blocks (typically output generators[2]) are enqueued to a *queue*, when inserted into cascade. Then the DFS is executed for each block in the queue. If a block is not enqueued, it will not be executed, unless some other block is connected to its outputs. This allows preparing set of often, but not always, used blocks and let them execute only when required. Evaluation of the cascade ends, when execution of the last block is finished and the queue is empty.

These features relieve the programmer from an explicit specification of execution order, which is required in traditional procedural languages.

3.2 Visualization

It is very easy to automatically visualize connections between blocks. Once cascade evaluation is finished, its content can be exported as a code for Graphviz[3], which will automatically arrange given graph into a nice image, and this generated image can be displayed next to results of the program with no effort. It is a very useful debugging tool.

Note that there is no need for a step-by-step tracing of cascade evaluation, since the generated image represents the entire process, including errors and presence of values on connections.

For example, Figure 2 shows a cascade used for editing an article on a simple web site. An article is loaded by the block `load`, then is passed to the block `form`, which is displayed to user by the block `show_form`. Because form has not been submitted yet, the block `update`, which will store changes in the article, is disabled (a grey arrow represents `false` or `null` value). This figure was rendered by Graphviz and similar figures are generated automatically when creating web sites with a framework based on the cascade (see section 6).

3.3 Basic Definitions

It is necessary to define few basic concepts and a used notation, before a behavior of cascade can be described in detail.

A block name in the text is written using monospaced font, for example `A`. An execution of the block `A` starts with an event A (i.e. begin of the execution) and ends with an event $\bar{A}$ (i.e. end of the execution).

During the event A the `main` method of the block is called. Within the `main` method block reads its inputs, performs an operation on received data, and sets its outputs.

---

[2] Output generator is a block which prepares data for a future HTTP response as a side-effect. The prepared data are passed to template engine when cascade evaluation is finished.

[3] Graphviz: `http://www.graphviz.org/`

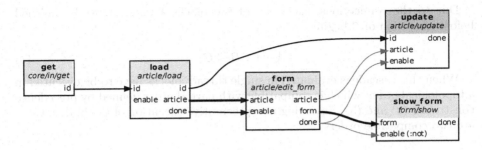

Fig. 2. Cascade example

During the event $\bar{A}$ cascade performs all requested output forwarding (see section 4.4) and the block execution is finished. The block itself performs nothing at this point.

Because any execution of a block must begin before it ends, a trivial precedence constraint is required for each block:

$$A \prec \bar{A} \tag{1}$$

3.4   Automatic Parallelization

One of the first questions usually asked after a short look at the cascade is whether the blocks can be executed in parallel. A short answer is "yes, of course" and in this section we try to explain how straightforward it is.

Let there are blocks A, B and C, where C is connected to some outputs of blocks A and B, as displayed in Figure 3.

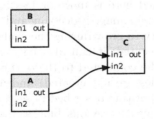

Fig. 3. Automatic parallelization example

Because the begin of block execution precedes its end, trivial precedence constraints are defined:

$$A \prec \bar{A},\, B \prec \bar{B},\, C \prec \bar{C} \tag{2}$$

Due to the connections, execution of the blocks A and B must be finished before execution of C begins:

$$\bar{A} \prec C, \ \bar{B} \prec C \tag{3}$$

When this cascade is evaluated in single thread, blocks have to be executed in a topological order, which is compatible with partial order defined by precedence constraints (2) and (3). Assuming non-preemptive execution of the blocks, there are two compatible orders:

$$A \prec \bar{A} \prec B \prec \bar{B} \prec C \prec \bar{C} \tag{4}$$
$$B \prec \bar{B} \prec A \prec \bar{A} \prec C \prec \bar{C} \tag{5}$$

Both (4) and (5) will give exactly the same results, because blocks A and B are completely independent. Therefore these two blocks can be executed in parallel with no trouble:

$$\left((A \prec \bar{A}) \parallel (B \prec \bar{B}) \right) \prec C \prec \bar{C} \tag{6}$$

A naive implementation of a parallel execution can be done by spawning a new thread for each block, and using a simple locking mechanism to postpone execution of blocks with unsolved dependencies. More efficient implementations may involve a thread pool and per-thread block queues for solving dependencies. Since cascade is being used to generate web pages, the block-level parallelization was not investigated any further, because all web servers implement parallelization on per-request basics.

4   Growing Cascade

So far, everything mentioned here is more or less in practical use by various tools, especially in data mining, image processing and similar areas. What makes cascade unique, is the ability to grow during the evaluation.

When block is being executed, it can also insert new blocks into cascade. Inputs of these blocks can be connected to the outputs of any other blocks (as long as circular dependencies are not created) and it can be enqueued to the queue for execution. The algorithm described in section 3 will handle these new blocks exactly the same way as previous blocks, because it iterates over the queue and the new blocks will be enqueued there before the enqueuing block is finished.

4.1   Namespaces

To avoid collisions between block IDs, each block inserts new blocks into its own namespace only. These namespaces are visualized using a dashed rectangle with an owner block ID under the top edge of the namespace rectangle.

In traditional languages like C namespaces are used to manage visibility (scope) of local variables, where code located outside of a namespace cannot access a variable defined inside this namespace, but the inner code can reach global variables. However the global variables can be hidden by local variables.

The same approach is used in the cascade with a small difference – it is possible to *explicitly* access content of a namespace from outside, so connections across the namespaces can be made with no limitation.

To identify block in other namespace, a dot notation is used. For example block B in the namespace of block A in the root namespace is referred as .A.B (see Figure 4b). If there is no leading dot, the first block is searched in the namespace of current block and all its parent namespaces up to the root. By specifying additional blocks it is possible to enter namespaces of other and completely unrelated blocks.

Since the primary purpose of namespaces is to avoid collisions in IDs, there is no reason to deny connections from the blocks outside of the namespace (see block D in Figure 4b). This allows to extend existing applications by attaching additional blocks without need to change the application.

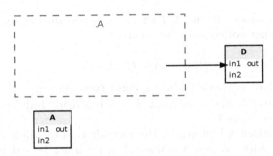

(a) Cascade *before* execution of the block A

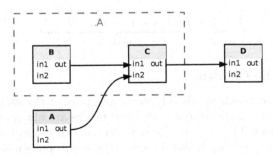

(b) Cascade *after* execution of the block A

Fig. 4. Growing cascade

4.2   Dependencies during the Growth

The secondary purpose of the namespaces is to help handling dependencies on blocks that are not yet present in the cascade.

Take a look at Figure 4a. The block D is connected to a so far nonexistent block C inside the namespace of the block A, and block A has not been executed yet. In this moment, the only known precedence constraint is $\bar{C} \prec D$ and because there is no connection between A and D, block D could be executed before A. But that would end up with a "block C not found" error.

Since the only block, which can insert blocks into namespace of the block A, is the block A, additional precedence constraint can be introduced: Each block depends on its parent (creator). Therefore cascade in Figure 4a contains following precedence constraints:

$$\bar{A} \prec C, \bar{C} \prec D \tag{7}$$

And because block C is not present yet, the only compatible topological order is:

$$A \prec \bar{A} \prec D \prec \bar{D} \tag{8}$$

Block A inserts blocks B and C into the cascade during its execution and additional precedence constraints are created:

$$\bar{B} \prec C, \bar{A} \prec C, \bar{A} \prec B \tag{9}$$

Note that $\bar{A} \prec C$ is there for the second time, because of the connection between blocks A and C. And constraint $\bar{A} \prec B$ is already fulfilled, because block A has been executed already.

Now, after the block A is finished, the cascade contains new blocks and new precedence constraints, so new topological order must be calculated before a next block is executed. The only topological order compatible with (7) and (9) is:

$$\underbrace{A \prec \bar{A}}_{\text{executed}} \prec \underbrace{B \prec \bar{B} \prec C \prec \bar{C} \prec D \prec \bar{D}}_{\text{queued}} \tag{10}$$

4.3   Safety of the Growth

It is not possible to break an already evaluated part of the cascade by adding new blocks. Reason is fairly simple – the new blocks are always appended after the evaluated blocks. That means the new precedence constraints are never in conflict with already existing constraints, and the new topological order is always compatible with the old one.

Each block is executed only after execution of all blocks it depends on. And because connections are specified only when a block is inserted into the cascade, the already executed part of the cascade cannot be modified. It also means that all precedence constraints in the executed part of the cascade have been fulfilled.

When inserting a new block, there are two kinds of connections which can be created: a connection to an already executed block, and connection to enqueued or missing block. When connected to the already executed block, any new precedence constraint is already fulfilled. When connected to the enqueued or missing block, the order of these blocks can be easily arranged to match the new constraints – the situation is same as before execution of the first block.

For example, the only difference between topological orders (8) and (10) is in added blocks B and C, thus the relative order of all actions occurring in (8) is same as in (10).

4.4   Nesting of the Blocks and Output Forwarding

The basic idea of solving complex problems is to hierarchically decompose them into simpler problems. Function call and return statement are the primary tool for this decomposition in λ-calculus and all derived languages (syntactical details are not important at this point). The function call is used to breakdown a problem and the return statement to collect partial results, so they can be put together to the final result.

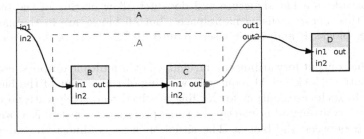

Fig. 5. Idea of nested blocks

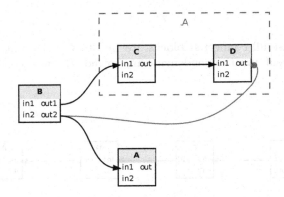

Fig. 6. "Nested" blocks in real cascade

But the cascade evaluation is one-way process. The entire concept of return value makes no sense here. Everything in the cascade goes forward and never looks back. Also there is no stack in the cascade where return address could be stored, so even if something would want to return a result, it has no chance of knowing where to.

To allow a hierarchical problem decomposition in the cascade, a slightly different tool was created – *output forwarding*. When block solves some problem, it presents results on its outputs. When block delegates solving to some other blocks, the results are on their outputs. To achieve the same final state as before, the results must be transferred to the original outputs of the delegating block. This schema exhibits similar behavior as the return statement.

From other point of view, there is no need to transfer result values back, if all connections are redirected to the forwarded outputs. Both approaches are equivalent and they both preserve all properties of the cascade mentioned earlier.

For example, let block A perform a complex task and block D display result of this task – see Figure 5. Block A inserts blocks B and C into the cascade, and passes a parameter from its input to the input of the block B and then collects a result from block C, which received a partial result from the block B. The final result is then published on an output of the block A. Figure 5 presents this solution as it is usual in λ-calculus based languages.

The cascade is a flat structure and does not allow nesting of the blocks. It emulates this hierarchy using namespaces, but all blocks are in the flat space. Therefore, blocks B and C are inserted next to the block A, as presented in Figure 6.

Note that output forwarding can be chained over multiple outputs. For example some other blocks could request forwarding of the output of the block A in Figure 6. In such cases output forwarding is solved recursively with no trouble.

Output forwarding adds exactly the same precedence constraint as any other connection between the blocks. The situation here is almost the same as on Figure 4b. When the value copying approach is used, the output forwarding adds the following constraint:

$$\bar{C} \prec \bar{A} \tag{11}$$

This is because all connected blocks are tied to the $\bar{A}$ event, so it is easier to delay this event until dependencies are solved. If the second (redirecting)

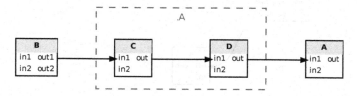

Fig. 7. Equivalent cascade without output forwarding

approach is used, the situation would be exactly the same as presented in Figure 7, but an implementation of this transformation may be too complicated.

All constraints in the example cascade in Figure 6 are:

$$\bar{A} \prec B, \bar{A} \prec C, \bar{B} \prec C, \bar{A} \prec D, \bar{C} \prec \bar{A}$$

And the compatible topological order is:

$$A \prec B \prec \bar{B} \prec C \prec \bar{C} \prec \bar{A} \prec D \prec \bar{D} \tag{12}$$

4.5 Semantics of the Output Forwarding

Using the output forwarding a block says to the cascade: "When I'm done, set my output to a value which is on that output of that block." From a block's point of view the output forwarding is exactly the same process as setting a value to an output. Only difference is in specifying what value will be set – output forwarding uses a reference instead of a value.

The namespaces and the output forwarding were both designed to allow a hierarchical decomposition of a problem, but they are completely independent tools in contrast to a function call and a return statement in λ-calculus based languages. And since the output forwarding is not limited to any particular namespace, it allows creation of a very unusual use cases, where the "return values" can be picked up anywhere in the cascade.

5   Comparison with Other Approaches

Probably the most similar approach to the cascade is Function Block programming [1], which has a very long history in industrial automation to program PLCs[4]. The main difference from the cascade is that blocks and connections between them are static. The connections are left unchanged as long as the programmer does not upload a new version of software into PLC. The second difference is in data transmitted via inputs and outputs. In the cascade once output is set, it stays constant forever. But in Function Blocks it is a stream of values.

Various data processing tools like Orange [4], Khoros Cantata [5], and Rapid Miner [6] adopted the function blocks approach with some modifications. But the basic difference still stands – all these tools use a static structure built from blocks by the programmer.

λ-calculus differs from the cascade in the semantics of a return statement and in a heavy use of a stack. Because there is no stack in the cascade, the return statement is thrown away and replaced by the output forwarding mechanism, which has a slightly different semantics, but it can be used to achieve the same goals.

---

[4] PLC: Programmable Logic Controller.

Cascade exhibits a number of shared features with Hierarchical Task Networks (HTN) planning [7]. HTN planning provides a much more sophisticated approach including backtracking and different constraint mechanisms, such as constraint refinement, constraint satisfaction, constraint propagation, etc. Cascade trades these advanced methods with an execution speed. The fast execution is achieved by the elimination of decomposition alternatives.

The preference calculus based on properties of partial order relations forms a foundation of dependency trees heavily used in scheduling theory [8].

A dependency injection is a software design pattern used to ease dependencies in the code [9]. A basic idea is in a separation of tool users (code) from creators (factory) of the tool (object), so the creators can be easily replaced. In the cascade, this approach is very natural to use, since it is easy to wrap the creator into a common block and let users connect to this block and retrieve the tool. Thanks to the embedded visualization of the cascade it is very easy to track these dependencies in an application.

6 Real World Application

6.1 Web Framework

The cascade serves as a core of a push-style web framework written in PHP, where cascade takes a place of a controller (as in MVP pattern). Since a cascade does not have any own inputs and outputs, specialized blocks are used as a connectors to receive input data from a HTTP request and to pass response data into a template engine (view). Processing of any HTTP request is split into two stages. During the first stage the cascade is evaluated and response data are prepared as a result. In the second stage the template engine generates a final web page using the prepared data.

When a development mode is enabled, each web page contains automatically generated visualization of a cascade used to create that page (see Section 3.2), so the debugging tool is always at hand.

Also a simple profiler is embedded into the framework. An average time needed to evaluate a cascade in real applications (ca. 20–40 blocks per page) is approximately 30 ms and an overhead of the cascade is less than 3 ms of that time, which is as good as widely used web frameworks.

6.2 Modular Applications

Extensible applications typically declare places, where they can be extended, which is usually done using hooks or virtual methods. The cascade uses different approach. It offers user a set of blocks and it is up to him what he will build. And when there is some special need, which cannot be satisfied using available blocks, an additional set of blocks shall be created.

The cascade introduces an unified mechanism allowing various blocks from foreign sets to be connected into one structure, but it does not specify, how this structure should look like. It is a job for the framework built above the cascade to specify common fragments of these structures and define configuration style, so the solid base for application is created.

6.3   Rebuild Rather Than Modify

The cascade tries to make maximal use of block reusability. When a new part of an application is to be created, a many of required blocks are already available for use, so the new part of the application can be built in a little time. Thanks to this, a need for adjusting existing structures to suit current needs is significantly reduced, because they can be thrown away and easily replaced.

6.4   Generating the Application

To avoid repetition while composing blocks, it is possible to algorithmically generate these structures. A block which inserts additional blocks into the cascade is not limited on how it should get a list of these blocks. It may be from a static configuration file or a database, but the block can interpret these data and use them as templates or as parameters of a predefined template.

The cascade is designed to support this behavior. The dynamic insertion of blocks into the cascade is its key feature. The way, how the cascade is built (see Section 3), makes very easy to attach new blocks to existing sources of data. Because the order of blocks is not significant while inserting them into the cascade, the generating blocks can be much simpler than traditional code generators. Also, it is easy to use multiple blocks to generate a single structure, since connections can be made across namespaces (see Section 4.1).

When this approach is combined with sufficient metadata about entities in the application, the results may be very interesting.

7   Conclusion

In practice the cascade made development more effective, because it supports a better code reusability while creating a new application, and it helps the developer to analyse an old code when modifying or extending an existing application. The graphical representation of the code is very helpful when tracking from where broken data arrived and what happen to them on their way. It reduces significantly time required to locate a source of problems.

A dynamic nature of the cascade allows the programmer to cover a large number of options while using a fairly simple structure to describe them. And since the execution order is driven by the cascade, the programmer does not have to care about it. That means less code and less space for errors.

A main contribution of the cascade is extending the time-proven function blocks approach with new features making it suitable for many new use cases and preparing base ground for further research.

Acknowledgments. This work was supported by the Grant Agency of the Czech Technical University in Prague, grant No. SGS14/193/OHK3/3T/13.

References

1. John, K., Tiegelkamp, M.: IEC 61131-3: Programming Industrial Automation Systems: Concepts and Programming Languages, Requirements for Programming Systems, Decision-Making AIDS. Springer (2001), http://books.google.cz/books?id=XzlYGLulBdIC
2. Ritchie, D.M.: The evolution of the unix time-sharing system. Communications of the ACM 17, 365–375 (1984)
3. Cormen, T.H., Leiserson, C.E., Rivest, R.L., Stein, C.: Introduction to Algorithms, 3rd edn. The MIT Press (2009)
4. Curk, T., Demsar, J., Xu, Q., Leban, G., Petrovic, U., Bratko, I., Shaulsky, G., Zupan, B.: Microarray data mining with visual programming. Bioinformatics 21, 396–398 (2005), http://bioinformatics.oxfordjournals.org/content/21/3/396.full.pdf
5. Konstantinides, K., Rasure, J.: The Khoros software development environment for image and signal processing. IEEE Transactions on Image Processing 3(3), 243–252 (1994)
6. Mierswa, I., Wurst, M., Klinkenberg, R., Scholz, M., Euler, T.: Yale: Rapid prototyping for complex data mining tasks. In: Ungar, L., Craven, M., Gunopulos, D., Eliassi-Rad, T. (eds.) KDD 2006: Proceedings of the 12th ACM SIGKDD International Conference on Knowledge Discovery and Data Mining, pp. 935–940. ACM, New York (2006), http://rapid-i.com/component/option,com_docman/task,doc_download/gid,25/Itemid,62/
7. Sohrabi, S., Baier, J.A., McIlraith, S.A.: Htn planning with preferences. In: Proceedings of the 21st International Jont Conference on Artifical Intelligence, IJCAI 2009, pp. 1790–1797. Morgan Kaufmann Publishers Inc., San Francisco (2009), http://dl.acm.org/citation.cfm?id=1661445.1661733
8. Rasconi, R., Policella, N., Cesta, A.: *SEaM:* analyzing schedule executability through simulation. In: Ali, M., Dapoigny, R. (eds.) IEA/AIE 2006. LNCS (LNAI), vol. 4031, pp. 410–420. Springer, Heidelberg (2006)
9. Schwarz, N., Lungu, M., Nierstrasz, O.: Seuss: Decoupling responsibilities from static methods for fine-grained configurability. Journal of Object Technology 11(1), 3:1–3:23 (2012), http://www.jot.fm/contents/issue_2012_04/article3.html

State Machine Abstraction Layer

Josef Kufner and Radek Mařík

Department of Cybernetics, Faculty of Electrical Engineering,
Czech Technical University in Prague, Czech Republic
{mailto:kufnejos,kufnejos,mailto:marikr}@fel.cvut.cz

Abstract. Smalldb uses a non-deterministic parametric finite automaton combined with Kripke structures to describe lifetime of an entity, usually stored in a traditional SQL database. It allows to formally prove some interesting properties of resulting application, like access control of users, and provides primary source of metadata for various parts of the application, for example automatically generated user interface and documentation.

1 Introduction

The most common task for a web application is to present some entities to an user, and sometimes the user is allowed to modify these entities or to create a new one. Algorithms behind these actions are usually very simple, typically implemented using few SQL queries. The tricky part of web development is keeping track of the behavior and lifetime of all entities in application. As number and complexity of the entities are growing, it is getting harder for a programmer to orientate in the application, and situation is even worse when it comes to testing.

Smalldb brings a bit forgotten art of state machines into the web development, unifying specifications of all entities in an application, creating a single source of all important metadata about many aspects of each entity, and allowing to build formal proofs of application behavior.

The basic idea of Smalldb is to describe lifetime of each entity using state machine, and map all significant user actions to state transitions. To make the best of this approach, the state machine definition is extended with additional metadata, which are not essential for the state machine itself, but can be used by user interface, documentation generator, or any other part of the application related to the given entity.

Smalldb operates at two levels of abstraction within the application. At the lower level it handles database access, it acts as the model in MVC pattern. At higher level of abstraction it can describe API, URIs and behavior of large parts of the application, however, it does not directly implement these parts.

In the next two sections an example of typical entity in web application is presented. In section 4 Smalldb state machine is formally defined. And section 5 describes relation between state machine instances and underlaying database. A basic implementation with some interesting implications is roughly described in

Linawati et al. (Eds.): ICT-EurAsia 2014, LNCS 8407, pp. 213–227, 2014.

section 6. Section 7 introduces Smalldb as a primary metadata source. Remaining sections are dedicated to application correctness.

2   REST Resource as a State Machine

Let's start with simple example of generic resource (entity) in RESTful application [1]. RESTful applications typically use HTTP API to manipulate resources. Since REST does not specify a structure of a resource nor exact form of the API (simply because it is out of REST's scope), it is impossible to use this API without additional understanding of application behind this API. However, HTTP defines only a limited set of usable methods, so a general example can be provided.

Figure 1 presents a generic state machine equivalent to a REST resource. The resource is created by HTTP POST request on a collection, where the resource is to be stored. Then it can be modified using HTTP PUT (or similar HTTP methods), and finally it can be removed using HTTP DELETE method.

Without further investigation of the resource an influence of the "modify" transition cannot be determined, but we can safely assume the resource is more complex than Figure 1 presents, otherwise the "modify" transition would make no sense.

Transitions from the initial state and to the final state represents creation and destruction of the resource and the machine itself. These two states are denoted as a separate features, but they both represent the same thing – resource does not exist. This semantics is one of the key ideas behind Smalldb.

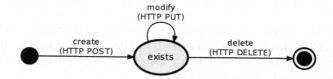

Fig. 1. REST resource state machine

3   Real-World Example

When building real web application, situation is rarely as simple as example in previous section. Typically there is more actions to perform on an entity, and the entity passes through a few states during its lifetime.

A very common application on the Web is a blog. Typical blog is based on publication of posts. Each post is edited for some time after its creation, and then it is published. Some posts are deleted, but they can also be undeleted (at least in this example).

A state machine representing lifetime of the post is in Figure 2. As we can see, there are three states and a few transitions between them. Note that there is no final state in this state machine. That is because the blog post is never completely destroyed.

There is one interesting feature in this state machine – the undelete action. In both HTTP specification and REST there is nothing like it. It is possible to implement it using an additional attribute of the blog post, but it does not fit well into RESTful API, for example there is no counterpart to HTTP DELETE method. Similar troubles occur when controlling nontrivial long-running asynchronous processes, since it is unnatural to express events and commands in REST.

There is also one big problem with both this and previous examples. If these state machines are interpreted as usual finite automata, the edit action has no effect. Invoking the edit action makes no difference, because it starts and ends in the same state. To justify this behavior, the state machine must use a concept very similar to Kripke structures. Each state represents a possibly infinite group of sub-states, which have common behavior described by the encapsulating state. Therefore, the edit transition is in fact a transition between different sub-states within the same state, i.e. sub-states belong to the same equivalency class. Omitting these sub-states from the state diagram is very practical since it allows easy comprehension. The sub-states are implemented using "properties" of the state machine instance, for example title, author and text of the blog post (this concept will be described in Section 4.4).

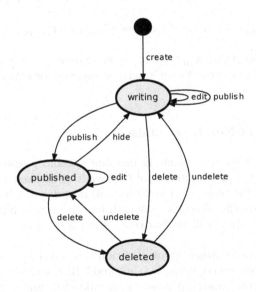

Fig. 2. State diagram of blog post

4 State Machine

As previous examples showed, it is necessary to modify and extend definition of finite automaton [2], to make any use of it. In this section a Smalldb state machine is formally defined and its features are explained. The definition is designed to follow an actual implementation as close as possible, so it can be used to formally infer properties of final applications.

4.1 Smalldb State Machine Definition

Smalldb state machine is modified non-deterministic parametric finite automaton, defined as a tuple $(Q, P, s, P_0, \Sigma, \Lambda, M, \alpha, \delta)$, where:

- Q is finite set of states.
- P is set of named properties. P^* is (possibly infinite) set of all possible values of P. P_t is state of these properties in time t. $P_t \in P^*$.
- s is state function $s(P_t) \mapsto q$, where $q \in Q$, $P_t \in P^*$.
- P_0 is set of initial values of properties P, $P_0 \in P^*$.
- Σ is set of parametrized input events.
- Λ is set of parametrized output events (optional).
- M is finite set of methods: $m(P_t, e_{in}) \mapsto (P_{t+1}, e_{out})$, where $P_t, P_{t+1} \in P^*$, $m \in M$, $e_{in} \in \Sigma$, $e_{out} \in \Lambda$.
- α is assertion function: $\alpha(q_t, m) \mapsto Q_{t+1}$, where $q_t \in Q$, $Q_{t+1} \subset Q$, $e_{in} \in \Sigma$.

$$\forall m \in M : s(P_{t+1}) \in \alpha(s(P_t), m) \Leftrightarrow (\exists e_{in} : m(P_t, e_{in}) \mapsto (P_{t+1}, e_{out}))$$

- δ is transition function: $\delta(q_t, e_{in}, u) \mapsto m$, where $q_t \in Q$, $e_{in} \in \Sigma$, $m \in M$, and u represents current user's permissions and/or other session-related attributes.

4.2 Explanation of Non-determinism

Non-determinism in the state machine has one specific purpose. It expresses possibility of a failure and uncertainty of the result of invoked action.

For example when the blog post (see Section 3) is undeleted, it is not known in advance in which state the blog post will end, because if user has no permission to publish, the result state will be "writing", even if the blog post was already published.

Similar situations occur when invoked action can fail. For example when the blog post cannot be published, because requested URI is already used by another post, or if some external material must be downloaded during publication and remote server is inaccessible.

In all these cases, a requested action is invoked, but which transition of state machine is used, is determined by result of invoked action.

4.3   Simplified Deterministic Definition

Because the complete definition described in section 4.1 is a bit too complex, here is a simplified deterministic definition with most of unimportant features thrown away. These features are present in the implementation, but they are not important for a basic understanding. This definition may also be useful for some formal proofs, where these two definition can be considered equivalent, if thrown away features are not significant for the proof.

Please keep in mind, that the rest of this paper always refers to the full definition in the section 4.1.

The simplified definition is: Smalldb state machine is defined as a tuple $(Q, q_0, \Sigma, \Lambda, \delta', m')$, where:

- Q is finite set of states.
- q_0 is starting state, $q_0 \in Q$.
- Σ is set of input events.
- Λ is set of output events (optional).
- δ' is transition function: $\delta'(q_t, e_{in}, w) \mapsto q_{t+1}$, where $q_t, q_{t+1} \in Q$, $e_{in} \in \Sigma$, and w is unpredictable influence of external entities.
- m' is output function: $m'(q_t, e_{in}, w) \mapsto e_{out}$, where $e_{in} \in \Sigma$, $e_{out} \in \Lambda$, $q_t \in Q$, and w is the same external influence as in δ'.

This is basically Mealy (or Moore[1]) machine [3,4], only difference is in introducing additional constraint w to handle possibility of failure. However, the w is not known in advance when transition is triggered (see Section 4.2).

Main simplification is made by chaining transition function δ and assertion function α into one transition function δ':

$$\forall q_t \forall e_{in} \forall w \; : \; \big(\delta'(q_t, e_{in}, w) \; = \; Q_{t+1}\big) \; \Leftrightarrow \; \big(\alpha(q_t, \delta(q_t, e_{in}, w)) \; = \; Q_{t+1}\big)$$

This simplification assumes, that the implementation of the transitions is flawless, which is way too optimistic for real applications.

4.4   Properties and State Function

As came out in the blog post example (see Section 3), finite state automaton is not powerful enough to store all arbitrary data of an entity. To overcome this limitation, Smalldb state machine has properties. Each property is identified by name, and rest is up to the application. Properties can be implemented as a simple key–value store, columns in SQL table, member variables in OOP class, or anything like that.

Since properties are not explicitly limited in size, they can store very big, theoretically infinite, amount of data, data of high precision, or very complex

---

[1] Slight differences between Mealy and Moore machines are not important here, and e_{in} may or may not be used in m'.

structures. To handle these data effectively, the state function is used to determine state of the machine. The state function converts properties to single value, the state, which is easy to handle and understand.

Because applying the state function on different sets of properties can (and often will) result in the same state, the state represents entire equivalence class, rather than single value. This approach is very similar to Kripke structures [5].

The state function must be defined for every possible set of properties:

$$\forall P \in P^* : s(P) \in S$$

On the other side, an inverse function to s usually does not exist, so it is not possible to reconstruct properties from state. The only exception is a null state q_0, in which entity represented by state machine does not exist and properties are set to P_0, in short, $q_0 = s(P_0)$.

Typically the state function is very simple. In trivial case (like the first example in section 2) it only detects existence of a state machine. In more common cases (like the blog post example in section 3) it is equal to one of properties, or checks whether a property fits in a predefined range (for example, if date of publication is in future). Since the state function is key piece of the machine definition and it is used very often, it should be kept as simple and fast as possible.

The state is not explicitly stored and it is calculated every time it is requested. If both the state function and a property storage allow, the state may be cached to increase performance, but it is not possible to allow it in general. However, it is usually possible to store some precalculated data within properties to make state function calculations very fast.

4.5   Input Events

The input events Σ can be understood as *actions* requested by user. The action is usually composed of method name $m \in M$ and its arguments. Input events are implementation specific and their whole purpose is to invoke one of expected transitions in a state machine.

4.6   Output Events

The output events Λ are simply side effects of methods M, other than modifications of state machine's properties. These events usually include feedback to user and/or sending notification to an event bus interface, so other parts of application can be informed about change.

4.7   Methods

The methods M implement each transition of the state machine. They modify properties and perform all necessary tasks to complete the transition. These methods are ordinary machine-specific protected methods as known from object oriented languages, invoked by universal implementation of the state machine. Since the methods cannot be invoked directly, access to them is controlled by state machine, and it is possible to implement advanced and universal access control mechanism to secure an entire application.

There is a few methods with special meaning in object oriented languages. If $\forall e_{in} \forall u : m_c = \delta\left(s(P_0), e_{in}, u\right)$, then m_c is known as constructor or factory method. If $\forall q \in Q : \alpha(q, m_d) = s(P_0)$, then m_d is known as destructor. However, in Smalldb both these methods are ordinary methods with no special meaning, and both can occur multiple times in single state machine.

4.8   Transitions and Transition Function

Main difference from classic non-deterministic finite automaton is in division of each transition into two steps. The transition function δ covers only the first step. The second step is performed by method $m \in M$, which was selected by the transition function δ. Point of this separation is to localize the source of non-determinism (see Section 4.2) and accurately describe a real implementation.

The complete transition process looks like this (explanation will follow):

$$(P_t, e_{in}) \xrightarrow{\delta(s(P_t), e_{in}, u)} (P_t, e_{in}, m) \xrightarrow{m(P_t, e_{in})} P_{t+1}$$
$$\xrightarrow{\alpha(s(P_t), m)} s(P_{t+1})$$

Before a transition is invoked, only the properties P_t and the input event e_{in} are known. First, the transition function δ is evaluated, which results in the method m being identified. Then the m is invoked and the properties get updated. Finally, the assertion function is evaluated to check, whether the state machine ended in correct state.

The transition function δ also checks, if an user is authorized to invoke the requested transition. User's permissions are represented by u. This check can be used alone (without transition invocation) to determine, which parts of user interface should be presented to user.

4.9   Assertion Function

A simple condition must be always valid:

$$s(m(P_t, e_{in})) \in \alpha(s(P_t), m)$$

Otherwise there is an error in the function m.

Purpose of the assertion function α is to describe expected behavior of m and validate its real behavior at run-time. Since m is piece of code written by humans, it is very likely to be wrong.

5   Space of State Machines

Everything said so far was only about definition of a state machine. This definition is like a class in an object oriented language – it is useless until instances are created. In contrast with the class instances, the state machine instances are persistent. Definition is implemented in source code or written in configuration files, and properties of all state machine instances are stored in database.

But there is one more conceptual difference: The state machine instances are not created. All machines come to existence by defining a structure of a machine ID, which identifies machine instance in the space of all machines.

At the beginning, all machines are in null state q_0, which means "machine does not exist" (yes, it is slightly misleading). Since it is known, that properties of a machine in q_0 state are equal to P_0, there is no need to allocate storage for all these machines.

Machine ID is unique across entire application. There is no specification how such ID should look like, but pair of machine type and serial number is a good start. A string representation of the ID is URI, a world wide unique identifier. Conversion between string URI and application-specific ID should be simple and fast operation which does not require determining a state of given machine.

Once machine instance is identified, a transition can be invoked. Once machine enters state different than q_0, its properties are stored in database. This corresponds with calling a constructor in an object oriented language. When machine enters the q_0 state again, its properties are removed from database, like when destructor is called. But keep in mind that machine still exists, it only does not use any memory.

5.1   Smalldb and SQL Database

An SQL database can be used to store machine properties. In that case, each row of the database table represents one state machine instance, and each column one property. The table name and primary key are used as the machine ID. Machines in q_0 state do not have their row in the table.

It is useful to implement the state function using an SQL statement, so it can be used as regular part of SQL query. That way it is easy and effective to obtain list of machines in given state.

Machine methods M typically call few SQL queries to perform state transitions. It is not very practical to implement the methods in SQL completely, since it is usually necessary to interact with other non-SQL components of the application.

5.2   RESTful HTTP API

URI as a string representation of the machine ID was chosen to introduce Smalldb HTTP API. This API respects the REST approach [1], and mapping to Smalldb state machine is very straightforward: HTTP GET request can be used to read state machine status and properties, HTTP POST request to invoke a transition.

This may remind RPC[2] a little, where procedures on remote machine were invoked. Smalldb tries to pick the best of both REST and RPC, since these approaches are not in direct conflict. Entities are identified using URI, just like REST requires. Transitions are identified in RPC fashion, but structure of the machine behind this API is unified and data are retrieved in standard way, so close coupling does not happen, in contrast with RPC.

Question is, how to specify the transition to invoke. Probably the best approach is to append transition name to URI using query part (for example `http://example.org/post/123?action=edit`). This may not be as elegant as somebody could wish, but it is compatible with old plain HTML forms, because HTTP GET on such URI with the transition name can result in obtaining a form, which will be used to create HTTP POST request later. This makes it possible to use Smalldb without need to create a complex JavaScript frontend.

But if more interactive frontend is required, a HTTP header `Accept` can be used to specify other format than HTML page, and retrieve data in JSON or XML, just like any modern RESTful API offers. Also a HTTP GET on URI with a transition name specified can return transition definition, like HTTP OPTIONS does in REST API.

This approach was chosen pragmatically for the best compatibility with current stable (old) and widely available technologies.

6   Smalldb Implementation

6.1   Prototype

A basic implementation is composed of two base abstract classes, `Backend` and `StateMachine`, and two helper classes, `Reference` and `Router`.

The `Backend` class manages `StateMachine` instances and takes care of stuff like shared database connection. It acts as both factory and container class. The `Backend` must be able to determine a type of requested machine from its ID, to prepare correct instance of `StateMachine` class, and delegate almost all requests to it. This way the `Backend` is responsible for entire state machine space without even touching it. Classes derived from the Backend class implement application specific way to access list of known state machines (descendants of `StateMachine` class).

The abstract `StateMachine` class and classes derived from it contain definition of the state machine and implementation of methods M (see Section 4.1). There is only one instance of `StateMachine` class per `Backend` and state machine type, which handles all state machines instances of given type. So the `StateMachine` instances are responsible for disjunctive subspaces of state machine space. When transition is to be invoked, machine ID and input event is passed to a `StateMachine::invokeTransition` method, which validates request

---

[2] RPC: Remote Procedure Call.

using machine definition and executes appropriate protected method implementing the transition.

The Reference class is mostly only syntactic sugar to make application code prettier. It is created by Backend's factory method, which takes state machine ID as an argument. It contains the ID and a reference to both the Backend and the corresponding StateMachine (obtained from the Backend). The Reference is used as proxy object to invoke state machine transitions and retrieve its state and properties. Its implementation is very specific to used language. Usage of Reference object is similar to Active Record pattern, however, the semantics is different.

Finally, the Router class is a little helper used to translate URI to state machine ID and back. Each application may require specific mapping of URIs, so the instance of Router class is injected into Backend during its initialization.

6.2 Metaprogramming

Since the StateMachine class is responsible for loading of a state machine configuration, it is possible to generate the configuration dynamically in StateMachine constructor. This allows to create more general state machines for similar entities using one StateMachine class initialized with different configuration.

It is also possible to determine state machine properties from structure of SQL tables, and load rest of the definition from the SQL database too. This way it is possible to define new state machines and entities without need to write a single line of code, using only an administration interface of the application.

6.3 Spontaneous Transitions

When state function includes time or some third party data source, it may happen that state machine will change from one state to another without executing any code. Since this changes happen completely on their own and without any influence of Smalldb, it is not possible to perform any reaction when they happen.

There are two ways of dealing with this problem. The first way is to live with them and simply avoid any need of reaction. This approach can be useful in simple cases where an entity should be visible only after specified date. For example the blog post (see Section 3) can have "time of publication" property and state function defined like "if time of publication is in the future, post is in state writing, otherwise post is published".

Other way is to not include these variables into the state function and schedule transitions using cron or similar tool. This, however, usually require introduction of "enqueued" state. For example the blog post will have additional "is published" boolean property and there will be regular task executed every ten minutes, which will look for "enqueued" posts with "time of publication" in the past and will invoke their "publish" transition.

The spontaneous transitions can be useful tool, it is only necessary to be aware of their presence and handle them carefully. They also should be marked in state diagram in generated documentation.

7 State Machine Metadata

Role of the Smalldb state machine in an application is wider than it is typical for a model layer (as M in MVC), because Smalldb provides many useful metadata for the rest of the application. The state machine definition can be extended to cover the most of entity behavior, which allows Smalldb to be the primary and only source of metadata in the application.

Having this one central source makes the application simpler and more secure. Simpler because metadata are separated from application logic, so they do not have to be repeated everywhere, which also makes maintainability easier and development faster. More secure because metadata located at one place are easier to validate and manage.

Other important benefit of centralized metadata source is generated documentation. Since the metadata are used all over the application, it is practically guaranteed that they will be kept up to date, otherwise the application will get broken. And in addition, the metadata in the state machine definition are already collected and prepared for a further processing. All this makes it very valuable source for documentation generator.

For example, the Figures 1 and 2 used in examples (sections 2 and 3) were rendered automatically from a state machine definition in JSON using Graphviz [6] and a simple, 120 lines long, convertor script.

Additional use for these metadata is in generating user interface, determining which parts of it user can see and use, user input validation, access control, or API generating. And if metadata are stored in static configuration files or database, they can be modified using administration interface embedded in the application, which allows to easily alter many aspects of the application itself. Dynamically generated metadata then allows building of large and adaptive applications with very little effort.

8 Application Correctness

A lot of research was done in model checking and finite automata, resulting in tools, like Uppaal [7], which allows to formally verify statements about given automaton. Since Smalldb is built on top of such automata, it is very convenient to use these tools to verify Smalldb state machines. And thanks to existence of formal definition of Smalldb state machine, it is possible to export state machine definition to these tools correctly.

8.1   Access Control Verification

Verification of basic properties, like state reachability[3], safety[4] and liveness[5], is nice to have in basic set of tests, however, these properties are not very useful on their own. Situation gets much more interesting, when user permissions are introduced.

User access is verified just before transition is invoked. Therefore, an user with limited access is allowed to use only subset of transitions in state diagram, and some states may become unreachable. If expected reachability of a state by given user is stated in the state machine definition, it is easy to use the earlier mentioned tools to verify it. And in the most cases, any allowed transition originating from unreachable state means security problem.

Similar situation is with liveness property, where unintentional dead ends, created by insufficient permissions, can be detected.

Because access control is enforced by general implementation of state machine (in abstract `StateMachine` class, see Section 6), which can be well tested and it is not modified often, probability of creating security issue is significantly reduced.

8.2   Optimizations vs. Understandability

In the era of discrete logical circuits, a state reduction was very important task, because circuits were expensive and less states means less circuits.

In Smalldb, a state machine is used in very different fashion. The state machine is expected to express real behavior of a represented entity in a way, which can be understood and validated by non-technical user (customer). A connection between understandability of state diagram and automated generation of this diagram from the single source of truth (see Section 7) is important feature, since it eliminates an area, where errors and misunderstandings can occur – a gap between expectations and software specification.

From this point of view, any state diagram optimizations are undesirable.

8.3   Computational Power of Smalldb Machine

Classical finite state automaton is not Turing complete, because it has limited amount of memory, so it cannot be used, for example, to count sheeps before sleeping. But in Smalldb state machine this limitation was overcome by introducing properties and methods implemented in Turing-complete language (see Section 4.1), so the sheep counting can be done using one state, increment loop-back transition and sheep counter property.

Smalldb state machine is a hybrid of two worlds. On one side, there is nice non-deterministic finite automaton, which allows all the nice stuff described in

---

[3] State reachability: "Is there path to every state?"
[4] Safety property: "Something bad will never happen."
[5] Liveness property: "Machine will not get stuck."

this paper. On the other side, there are Turing-complete methods M, the barely controllable mighty beasts, which do the hard work. As long as these two parts are together, the computational power is the same as of the language used to implement the methods M.

By introducing properties and state function, the used automaton cannot be easily considered finite, since single state represents an equivalence class of property sets, which is not required to be finite. It is also possible to let methods M to modify state machine definition on the fly. And since both state function and transition function are also implemented using Turing-complete language, it is possible to define them in the way where the amount of the states is not finite at all. However, rest of this paper does not consider these possibilities and, for sake of clarity, expects reasonable definitions of all mentioned functions.

A practical example of self-modifying Smalldb state machine is a graphical editor of state machine definition which uses Smalldb to store modified configuration.

8.4   Troubles with Methods M

Because methods M (see Section 4.7) are Turing complete, it is not possible to deduce their behavior automatically. This means it is not possible to predict, whether all transitions of the same name will be used by machine, and therefore some of the states considered reachable, when methods M were not took into account, may not be ever reached. This problem can be partially solved by careful testing and reviewing of the methods M.

Another problem is, when some of the methods are flawed and machine ends up in other state than transition allowed. This is detected by assertion function and it must be reported as a fatal error to a programmer.

Smalldb cannot solve these troubles completely, but it is designed to locate these kinds of errors as accurate as possible.

9   Workflow Correctness

9.1   State Machine Cooperation

The workflow can be understood as cooperation of multiple entities with compatible goals. When these entities are specified as Smalldb state machines, it is relatively straightforward to involve tool like Uppaal (see Section 8), and let it calculate, what will happen, when these entities are put together.

Once state machine instances are required to cooperate, there is a danger that state machines will got stuck in deadlock. As Smalldb state machines represent entity lifetime, the cooperation troubles may mean there is something wrong with processes outside an application.

But the Smalldb state machine does not have to represent the entity within an application only. It also can be used to describe behavior of external entities, however, such entity should not be included in the application.

9.2 BPMN and BPEL

Entity lifetime is closely related to users' workflow and related processes. BPMN[6] and BPEL[7] were developed to describe them in some formal way. It should be possible to extract a formal model of each entity included in the process from BPMN and/or BPEL description, and convert them to Smalldb state machines. Then the state machine representing an application entity can be used as starting point of its implementation. And the other state machines, which represents humans and external applications, can be used to execute a simulation of complete process.

This approach should eliminate need for software specification when there is model of the entire process. Another benefit could be possibility of testing and formal proving of the application not against its specification, but rather against other entities in the process, removing the gap between what is expected and what is specified.

This area will require a lot of research and it is mostly out of the scope of Smalldb and this paper, however, it might be inspirational to put a bit wider context here.

10   Conclusion

Smalldb represents valuable source of metadata in an application, and allows to formally verify various aspects of the application, while maintaining practical usability and development effectivity.

From certain points of view it is similar to object oriented programming, where invoking of a transition is similar to method call in OOP, but with benefits of additional validation and better documentation of entity lifetime, which helps to manage complex and long-term behavior of the entities.

Smalldb also allows definition of simple RESTful HTTP API, which includes some aspects of RPC, to make the API more universal and easier to use. This API is also compatible with standard HTML forms, so it can be used on web sites without creating complex JavaScript clients.

Smalldb is meant as both as production-ready solution and as a building block for further research of software synthesis. However, there are areas left unexplored in integration of Smalldb with business process modeling (see section 9) and various aspects of verification.

Acknowledgments. This work was supported by the Grant Agency of the Czech Technical University in Prague, grant No. SGS14/193/OHK3/3T/13.

References

1. Fielding, R.T.: Architectural styles and the design of network-based software architectures. Ph.D. dissertation, aAI9980887 (2000)

---

[6] BPMN: Business Process Model and Notation.
[7] BPEL: Business Process Execution Language.

2. Gill, A.: Introduction to the theory of finite-state machines. McGraw-Hill electronic sciences series. McGraw-Hill (1962)
3. Moore, E.F.: Gedanken Experiments on Sequential Machines. In: Automata Studies, pp. 129–153. Princeton U. (1956)
4. Mealy, G.H.: A Method for Synthesizing Sequential Circuits. Bell System Technical Journal 34(5), 1045–1079 (1955)
5. Schneider, K.: Verification of Reactive Systems: Formal Methods and Algorithms. Texts in Theoretical Computer Science. An EATCS Series. Springer, Heidelberg (2004)
6. Ellson, J., Gansner, E.R., Koutsofios, E., North, S.C., Woodhull, G.: Graphviz and dynagraph – static and dynamic graph drawing tools. In: Graph Drawing Software, pp. 127–148. Springer (2003)
7. Behrmann, G., David, A., Larsen, K.G.: A tutorial on UPPAAL. In: Bernardo, M., Corradini, F. (eds.) SFM-RT 2004. LNCS, vol. 3185, pp. 200–236. Springer, Heidelberg (2004)

Concern Based SaaS Application Architectural Design

Aldo Suwandi, Inggriani Liem, and Saiful Akbar

School of Electrical Engineering and Informatics,
Institut Teknologi Bandung, West Java, Indonesia
aldosuwandi@gmail.com, {inge,saiful}@informatika.org

Abstract. With SaaS application, tenant can focus on application utilization while Independent Software Vendor (ISV) is responsible for application deployment, installation, operation and maintenance. Using Aspect Oriented Software Development (AOSD), we propose eight concerns, i.e. configurability, discriminator, measurement, monitoring, tenant management, billing management, performance management, and application management. Those concerns are integrated into a SaaS system architectural design, to enhance SaaS operational flexibility and maintainability. As a proof of concept, we developed a SaaS operational environment using Spring and AOP. Two Java applications have been integrated to this environment after tailoring. We have tested the modules, classes and services and then the applications, to demonstrate that the platform is able to run a set of web applications as a SaaS. Using this system, ISV can modify an existing Java application easily to be a part of SaaS and measure resource usage and monitor SaaS operation by a dashboard.

Keywords: SaaS, Software as a Service, Concern, Aspect Oriented Software Development.

1 Introduction

Traditional software users are typically overburdened with operational work such as maintenance and software deployment. SaaS model is raised to overcome these problems. Many software companies start adopting this model. Instead of buying, more and more individual users and companies rent software. Software maintenance and deployment that were previously handled by users now is handled by ISV.

Based on [1], [2], [3], [4], [5], [6], SaaS is a hosted software and delivered over a network on a subscription basis. SaaS operational systems could be categorized into platform centric or service provider centric [7]. ISV and tenant are two main factors of SaaS operational systems. The maturity of SaaS application is determined by tenancy, configurability, and scalability [8].

Seven pricing models for SaaS application has been studied by Kalisa [9]. Billing should be built as part of SaaS application [14]. However, this functionality must be flexible because each tenant may have a preference of its his own billing scheme.

Enhancement of SaaS application design is required. Aspect oriented software development is one of the application development model to improve the structuring, reusability, and reduce the complexity of the model compared with object oriented model [10].

Linawati et al. (Eds.): ICT-EurAsia 2014, LNCS 8407, pp. 228–237, 2014.

Our research has studied "concerns" that should be considered to develop SaaS application based on AOSD. Separation of concern is a fundamental principle to facilitate software deployment [11]. Concern is interest which pertains to the system's development, its operation or any other aspects that are critical or otherwise important to one or more stakeholders [12]. Core concern represents functional requirement. Cross-cutting concern represents non-functional requirement. Object oriented model is appropriate for core concern development, whereas AOSD is better for developing cross-cutting concern. Cross-cutting concern could be implemented with aspect oriented programming (AOP). Implementation of AOP is based on four design elements, namely aspect, join point, point cut and advice [4]. Aspect is a class consisting of one or a number of advices. Join point is a point on program that will be intercepted by the aspect class. Point cut is a boolean expression that determines join point. Advice is a method containing a logical process to be executed when the class aspect intercepts.

In this paper, we describe our approach in using AOSD for identifying general SaaS requirements, proposing a SaaS system architecture that contains all of the proposed concerns, and the proof of concept for the proposed architecture.

2   Related Work

Chate [13] proposed a way to build multi-tenant SaaS application either from scratch or from existing application. Corrent's SaaS-Factory is used to convert legacy database into a new multi-tenant database. Tang, et al [14] proposed SaaS Platform Management Framework as modules that can be considered to manage SaaS application platform. The platform of this framework consists of two levels, namely business and operations. Business contains related modules with billing management, whilst operation contains related modules with operational system such as metering, configuration, monitoring, etc. Those modules should be considered when implementing SaaS management platform.

Different from Chate[13] and from Tang et all[14], in this paper we focused on applying AOSD as fundamental technique to build a SaaS framework for the benefit of ISV and tenant. We also provided dashboard in the environment that we consider important for monitoring the operation of SaaS. We believe that aspect oriented software development (AOSD) can contribute as a fundamental approach for operating applications in a SaaS environment.

3   Separation of Concern

In AOSD, separation of concern is the first phase of design. Concern affecting SaaS application could be identified from SaaS application requirement.

Before adopting AOSD, we tried to describe the different characteristics of SaaS and non SaaS applications using McCall's Software Quality Factor. However, our observation proved that McCall Software Quality factors don't relate closely to software operational factor that is tightly coupled to SaaS operational characteristics.

Most of the quality factors which are used to assess non SaaS application also can be used for SaaS application. The only difference is on maintainability factor. A non SaaS application is maintained by user, while a SaaS application is maintained by ISV. Thus, we decide using another approach to define general requirement of SaaS application. We chose to make further study based on AOSD and AOP.

Aspect-oriented software development (AOSD) is software development technology that seeks for new modularizations of software systems in order to isolate secondary or supporting functions from the main program's business logic. AOSD allows multiple concerns to be expressed separately and automatically unified into working systems. AOSD is supported by AOPL (Aspect-oriented programming languages). By combining AOSD and AOPL, designer can modularize concerns that cannot be modularized using traditional procedural or object-oriented (OO) methods. Examples of crosscutting concerns include tracing, logging, transaction, caching and resource pooling. These examples are relevant to SaaS application.

Two main actors of SaaS application are tenant and ISV. Tenant's main purpose is to use application functionalities as a service. Multi-tenant SaaS application should be configurable to fulfill tenant's requirement varieties. Furthermore tenant should have an isolated data, that can only be accessed or modified by authorized users.

To make it easier for the tenant, ISV manages application deployment and maintenance for them. ISV could have one or many applications to be operated with SaaS model. ISV requires design enhancement on SaaS application to reduce maintenance and development cost to operate multiple SaaS application. It is also important for ISV to know the performance of each SaaS operated application. Furthermore ISV also needs information of resources usage and transaction by each tenant. In order for an application to be considered as having high level maturity, not only it has to have billing functionality, but it also has to be configurable and scalable, and have multitenant [9].

In this research we focused on the design of configurable multi-tenant SaaS application. We specify six main generic-requirements of SaaS application:

1. Tenant should have appropriate functional requirement needed.
2. Tenant should have their own copy of data.
3. ISV should be provided with a centralized application management enabling it to operate many SaaS applications.
4. ISV should be informed of each application's performance status.
5. ISV should be informed of resources which are used by tenant in each application.
6. ISV should be provided with transaction management in order to manage billing transaction of each application.

These six main user requirements are shown in the diagram below (see Figure 1). User requirements derive one or more concerns. We proposed eight concerns depicted on Figure 1. Those concerns are configurability, discriminator, measurement monitoring, tenant management, billing management, performance management, and application management. We derived those concerns from ISV and tenant requirement, and crosscutting elements of SaaS application. Concerns are grouped into core concern and cross-cutting concern, referring to AOSD terminology.

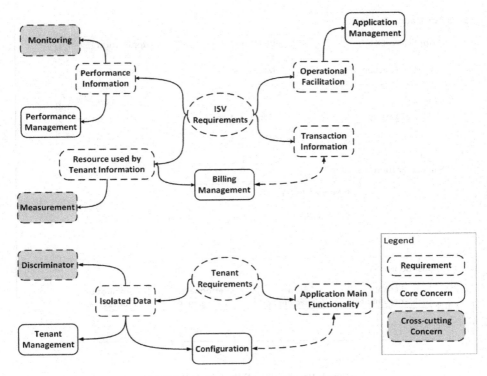

Fig. 1. Concern Derivation Process and Result

4   Proposed SaaS System Architecture

By applying AOSD, the architectural design of a SaaS system contains eight modules. Each module is the implementation of corresponding proposed concern. The architecture is shown on Figure 2.

Concerns are implemented into module, service, or library. Those concerns are integrated into SaaS system architecture that consists of SaaS operational system and set of applications.

Core concerns are implemented as modules. Concern configuration is attached into application main functionality, to support variation of configuration as proposed by W.-T.Tsai [15] i.e. GUI, service, workflow, data, and QoS. Other core concerns such as tenant management, billing management, performance management, and application management will be implemented as modules on SaaS operational system's dashboard. This dashboard provides centralized SaaS operational system information from set of applications (application x1, x2, ..., xn). It will facilitate ISV to monitor and to control its SaaS operated applications.

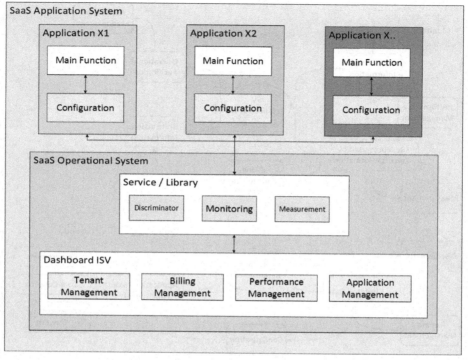

Fig. 2. Proposed SaaS System Architecture

Discriminator, monitoring, and measurement are considered as cross-cutting concern, used by all SaaS applications. These concerns are implemented into web service or library. The Service helps application to communicate with SaaS operational system. The Library contains of aspect classes, representing the interoperability of application with SaaS operational system. These classes reduces the complexity of application operational model of SaaS application. Aspect classes in the library will be implemented with AOP.

5   Implementation

To test our proposed SaaS system architecture, a case study has been conducted as a proof of concept. A SaaS system called **Olympus** shown on Figure 3. has been developed as SaaS system implementation of the designed architecture in Figure 2.

We have developed and implemented SaaS application (**Vulcan**) and ISV dashboard (**Plutus**). To prove that it is easy to integrate an existing application to our proposed SaaS application, we use **Affablebean**, an e-commerce application [16]. We have implemented **Vulcan** and **Affablebean** in different mode of SaaS operation and billing.

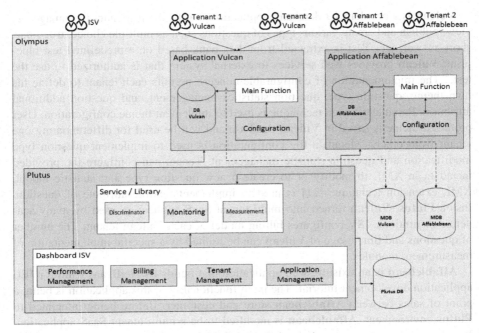

Fig. 3. Example of Implementation

Vulcan and **Plutus** have been developed using **Spring Framework** [17], **Spring AOP** [17], **Jerseyclient** [18] and **Jamon library** [19]. **Spring Framework** and **Spring AOP** are chosen as the application framework because of their support to AOP. **Jersey client library** is used as a client for REST web service. **Jamon** is used as a library application monitoring.

ISV configures SaaS operational system such as billing model and application info through **Plutus** dashboard. AOP facilitates billing model on SaaS operated application without modification of existing code. AOP also increases reusability. For example if an application has a number of resources to be measured, programmer's task is to implement annotation with boolean expression as join point where the resource is used.

ISV is provided with performance information such as application's method response time and error report on performance management. This information will help ISV tracing error on application and to decide maintenance activity. Performance management works by monitoring service and monitoring aspect. Techniques that have been implemented for billing can be used to monitor SaaS application.

We also integrate applications one by one, to simulate how applications in the architecture grow. Those applications are integrated with **Plutus** via combination of provided service and library to be operated as SaaS model. ISV configures SaaS operational system such as billing model and application info through **Plutus** dashboard.

Vulcan is a problem set databank application that facilitates tenant to manage, review, publish and create various types of questions such as multiple choice, true/false, short answer, etc. Test is extracted from data bank based on a predefined test blueprint. **Vulcan** provides web services to external system that is authorized to use the test. The implementation of configurable concern permits each tenant to define his own theme, question type, question statistics management, and question additional attributes. Parameterization technique is used to implement theme configuration. User preferred theme is saved in **Vulcan** database and will be used for differentiating one tenant from others. Metadata file configuration is used to implement question type modification and question statistic management. Tenant can configure the provided metadata in XML to modify or to create a new question type and statistic model. XML extension technique [21] is used to implement flexible attribute of question. Inside **Plutus**, **Vulcan** turned into multi-tenant SaaS application used by many academic institutions. ISV configures billing model of each **Vulcan** tenant. The number of questions and time usage of **Vulcan** can be limited by a specific implementation of measurement modules.

Affablebean is an existing web application that builds by NetBeans team for JEE application development tutorial. The main functionality of this application is being a point of sales between **Affablebean** store and customer. Before being integrated to **Plutus** environment, **Affablebean** is modified to be a multi-tenant SaaS application. It is assumed that there are a number of **Affablebean** stores, where each store has different kinds of product and customer. Instead of usage limitation, the resource model in **Affablebean** is implemented by a period of time.

Before integrating a new application to the environment, we have to configure and to tailor it to a multitenant SaaS application, then to register the application to the environment. The following steps illustrate the process:

a. Change the old database connection to new multi-tenant database. This connection will be provided when ISV registers their application to **Plutus**. We adopted shared database separated schema model for supporting multi-tenant database architecture. ISV should save the application database schema. The saved database schema will be used to automatically generate new parameterized schema (schema with all table name extended with tenant identifier) for each tenant when ISV registers new tenant

b. Extend the **Plutus** library to support the new database. All supporting libraries needed by new application should also be included.

c. Include service identifier method, provided by **Plutus** library on SaaS application login method. It permits application to be recognized by the system. This method is used to identify tenant and billing method when they login to SaaS application.

d. Define annotation in measurement and monitoring class using **Plutus** library, to specify which method or class needed to be metered or monitored.

6   Testing

Our SaaS system has been tested in two folds: testing the environment and dashboard, and then testing the integration of a new operated SaaS Application as shown in Figure 4. Each fold consists of unit testing, functional and integration testing. Both of the testing process (adding new application and SaaS environment) can be done separately until interoperability testing is done.

The flow of unit testing, functional testing, interoperability testing for the environment and dashboard is shown in Figure 4. **JUnit** is used to test each class containing services and module of Dashboard. All **Plutus Dashboard** functional requirement [22] has also been tested.

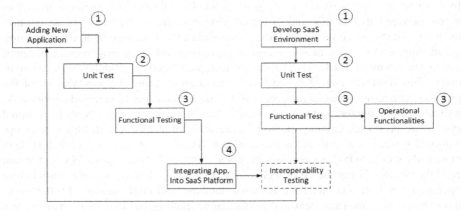

Fig. 4. The Whole Testing Proces

Some of the functionalities are related to SaaS operational issues such as measurement, transaction, and performance information. **Plutus** provides operation related functionalities that are needed by ISV such as registering SaaS application and creating new multi-tenant database, new database schema for new tenant, and new billing model. The other functionalities have been performed in interoperability testing.

Once the environment is ready, we can add SaaS application to the environment by doing the configuration steps that have been explained in section 5. This process can be easily done without modifying the existing application code, as we take benefit from AOP technology.

JUnit is also used for testing each application (**Vulcan, Affablebean**) before integration. The purpose of functional testing is to assure that each application will meet the requirement. This functional testing was performed on each functional requirement of **Vulcan** and **Plutus**. **Vulcan** has 18 functional requirements [22] and has been tested with test scenarios in Figure 4. Once an application passed Unit and functional test, it is ready to be deployed in **Olympus**.

Interoperability testing is used to show how easy is to start an existing application to operate. For this test, **Vulcan** and **Affablebean** are integrated into **Plutus**. These tests are conducted after functional testing is done. We register **Vulcan** and **Affablebean** in **Plutus** application management and configure billing management. We also include **Plutus** library in those application projects, and configure aspect class in **Plutus** library according to their needs. All of these integration processes do not require modification from the existing code. However, the three testing processes must be done, each time ISV needs to add a new application to the environment.

7   Conclusion

In this research we have identified general SaaS application requirement from two points of views that of ISV and of tenant. Concerns are derived from those requirements. Eight (8) concerns are identified, including tenant management, discriminator, monitoring, performance management, measurement, billing management, and application management. Each concern has been implemented as modules, service, or library. This research also proposed SaaS system architecture that contains all of the proposed concerns. Those eight concerns are implemented as library and services. As a result, an architecture consists of sets of SaaS applications and a SaaS operational system are proposed. Each application in the set of applications will utilize SaaS operational system as a centralized management system, so it can be operated as SaaS model. By using AOSD approaches on this architectural design, both ISV and tenant can take benefit. Using the AOP technology, ISV easily deploy an application before operation where tenant can have his own database and configuration. Furthermore, through resource measurement and performance monitoring, ISV and tenant have a transparent and accountable billing. ISV can separate its concern to tenant requirement, and reuse **Plutus**. Integration of **Affablebean** showed that the architecture permits a non aspect oriented application to be integrated and operated as SaaS after small effort of tailoring.

References

1. Turner, M., Budgen, D., Brereton, P.: Turning Software into a Service, pp. 38–44. IEEE Computer Society (2003)
2. What is Software as a Service, http://www.salesforce.com/saas/
3. Carraro, G., Chong, F.: Software as a Service (SaaS): An Enterprise Perspective (October 2006), http://msdn.microsoft.com/en-us/library/aa905332.aspx
4. Sommerville, I.: Software Engineering. Pearson (2009)
5. Laplante, P.A., Zhang, J., Vias, J.: Distinguishing Between SaaS and SOA, pp. 46–50. IEEE Computer Society (2008)
6. Chou, D.C., Chou, A.Y.: Software as a Service (SaaS) as an outsourcing model: an economic model analysis, pp. 386–391 (2011)
7. Tao, C., Liao, H.: An Anatomy to SaaS Business Mode Based on Internet. In: International Conference on Management of e-Commerce and e-Government, pp. 215–220 (2008)
8. Chong, F., Carraro, G.: SaaS Simple Maturity Model (2006), http://

`blogs.msdn.com/b/gianpaolo/archive/2006/03/06/544354.aspx`

9. Kalisa, A.: Kajian Software as a Service denganStudiKasusRumahSakit di Daerah Rural danTerpencil, Bandung (2012)
10. Brichau, J., Hondt, D.T.: Aspect-Oriented Software Development - An Introduction, pp. 1–20
11. Sutton Jr., S.M., Rouvellou, I.: Concern Modeling for Aspect-Oriented Software Development. In: Aspect Oriented Software Development, pp. 479–505 (2004)
12. IEEE, IEEE recommended practice for architectural description of software-intensive-system. IEEE Std (2000)
13. Chate, S.: Convert your web application to a multi-tenant SaaS solution (December 14, 2010), `http://www.ibm.com/developerworks/cloud/library/cl-multitenantsaas/`
14. Tang, K., Zhang, J.M., Jiang, Z.B.: Framework for SaaS Management Platform. In: IEEE International Conference on E-Business Engineering, pp. 345–350 (2010)
15. Tsai, W.-T., Sun, X.: SaaS Multi-Tenant Application Customization. In: IEEE Seventh International Symposium on Service-Oriented System Engineering, pp. 1–12 (2013)
16. The NetBeans E-commerce Tutorial - Designing the Application (September 11, 2013), `https://netbeans.org/kb/docs/javaee/ecommerce/design.html`
17. Spring Framework, GoPivotal (2013), `http://projects.spring.io/spring-framework/` (accessed September 26, 2013)
18. Jersey - RESTful Web Services in Java. Oracle (2013), `https://jersey.java.net/` (accessed September 26, 2013)
19. Souza, S.: JAMon (Java Application Monitor) (2013), `http://jamonapi.sourceforge.net/` (accessed September 26, 2013)
20. Chong, F., Carraro, G., Wolter, R.: Multi-Tenant Data Architecture (June 2009), `http://msdn.microsoft.com/en-us/library/aa479086.aspx`
21. Aulbach, S., Grust, T., Jacobs, D., Kemper, A., Seibold, M.: A Comparison of Flexible Schema for Software as a Service. In: SIGMOD, pp. 881–888 (2009)
22. Suwandi, A.: Kajian Aspek pada Aplikasi SaaS. ITB, Bandung (2013)

Hybridization of Haar Wavelet Decomposition and Computational Intelligent Algorithms for the Estimation of Climate Change Behavior

Haruna Chiroma[1], Sameem Abdulkareem[1], Adamu I. Abubakar[2],
Eka Novita Sari[3], Tutut Herawan[4], and Abdulsalam Ya'u Gital[5]

[1] Department of Artificial Intelligence, University of Malaya
50603 Pantai Valley, Kuala Lumpur, Malaysia
[2] Department of Information System
International Islamic University
Gombak, Kuala Lumpur, Malaysia
[3] AMCS Research Center, Yogyakarta, Indonesia
[4] Department of Information Systems, University of Malaya
50603 Pantai Valley, Kuala Lumpur, Malaysia
[5] Department of Computer Science
University of Technology Malaysia
Kampus Skudai, Johor Baru, Malaysia
{Freedonchi,asgital}@yahoo.com, 100adamu@gmail.com,
{sameem,tutut}@um.edu.my, eka@amcs.co

Abstract. We propose a hybrid of haar wavelet decomposition, relevance vector machine, and adaptive linear neural network (HWD-RVMALNN) for the estimation of climate change behavior. The HWD-RVMALNN is able to improve estimation accuracy of climate change more than the approaches already discussed in the literature. Comparative simulation results show that the HWD-RVMALNN outperforms cyclical weight/bias rule, Levenberg-Marquardt, resilient back-propagation, support vector machine, and learning vector quantization neural networks in both estimation accuracy and computational efficiency. The model proposes in this study can provide future knowledge of climate change behavior. The future climate change behavior can be used by policy makers in formulating policies that can drastically reduce the negative impact of climate change, and be alert on possible consequences expected to occur in the future.

Keywords: Haar Wavelet Decomposition, Relevance Vector Machine, Adaptive Linear Neural Network, Climate Change.

1 Introduction

In the last ten (10) to fifteen (15) years, the greater portion of the world experiences an unprecedented change in the temperature of sea water. For instance, the ice covering the Arctic is dramatically vanishing; the glaciers and green ice cap are

Linawati et al. (Eds.): ICT-EurAsia 2014, LNCS 8407, pp. 238–247, 2014.

observed to be significantly melting; reduction in the volume of Antarctic ice sheets; unusual increase of sea level, and the seas are getting stormier; upsurge in the intensity, and frequency of rainfall due to precipitation variability; earlier occurrence of springtime, and high intensity of hurricane [1]. In addition, the world is experiencing an extraordinary warming. These changes experience throughout the globe are consequences of the climate change [2]. There is a growing report of numerous natural disasters triggered by climate change [3]. Therefore, the future knowledge of climate change is required for proper planning in order avoid the negative impact of natural disasters expect to be caused by the behavior of climate change. In the literature, several studies have been conducted using neural networks to predict climate change. For example, [4] proposed a neural network to build a model for predicting weather in Jordan. Goyal *et al.* [5] uses neural network to develop a downscaled model for predicting maximum and minimum temperature across 14 stations in Upper Thames River Basin Ontario, Canada. Holmberg *et al.* [6] proposed neural network to model the concentration of organic carbon, Nitrogen and phosphorus in a runoff stream water collected from Finland. The model is then used to predict future fluxes under climatic change. Tripathi [7] applied support vector machine (SVM) for statistical downscaling of precipitation. Subsequently, the SVM model is used to predict future climate changes in India. The results obtained from the SVM model was compared to the neural network and it was found that the SVM model performs better than the neural network. However, the studies are limited to the region where the research data were conducted.

The studies in the literature for predicting climate change using computational intelligent techniques, mainly focus on individual intelligent technique (IITs) whereas it is well known that hybrid intelligent technique is superior to the IITs when properly design. Hybrid techniques capitalized on their strengths to eliminate their weaknesses to build a synergistic model for effective prediction. Haar wavelet decomposition (HWD) has the ability to project data into time scale domain, and perform multi scale analysis to unveil useful hidden patterns in the historical data [8]. The sensitivity of the relevance vector machine (RVM) to parameters is less compared to the SVM, and RVM is faster than SVM [9]. We propose to apply RVM to different scales coefficients produce by HWD to predict global climate change in order to reduce estimation bias that might be introduced by the HWD. Adaptive linear neural network (ALNN) will be used to ensemble the results produce by each RVMs to produce more accurate ensemble result than the results produce by individual RVMs. We intend to investigate whether the propose hybrid of HWD, RVM and ALNN can yield superior novel results than the approaches in the literature.

2 Essential Rudiments

2.1 Haar Wavelet Decomposition

The HWD can be considered on the basis of the real line (IR) [10]: Let consider $L_2(IR)$ to be the space of complex value function (f) on IR in such a way that

$$\|f\| = \left(\sqrt{\int_{-\infty}^{\infty} |f(x)|^2 \, dx}\right) < \infty. \tag{1}$$

Eq. (1) is donated with scalar product, as such we have

$$f(f,g) = \int_{-\infty}^{\infty} f(x)g\overline{(x)}dx. \tag{2}$$

where the complex conjugate of $g(x)$ is given by $\overline{g(x)}$. If $(f,g) = 0$ then $f, g \in L_2(IR)$ can be definedl to each other, the functions can be define as

$$\{\varphi_k, k \in Z\}, \varphi_k \in L_2(IR). \tag{3}$$

Eq. (3) is referred to as an orthonormal system if Eq. (4) is satisfied

$$\int \varphi_k(x)\overline{\varphi_j(x)}dx = \delta_{jk}. \tag{4}$$

where δ_{jk} and $\{\varphi_k, k \in Z\}$ are Kronecker delta, and orthonormal basis in a subspace V of $L_2(IR)$ if any function $f \in V$ has a depiction

$$f(x) = \sum_k C_k \varphi_k(x). \tag{5}$$

The coefficient satisfy $\sum_k |C_k|^2 < \infty$

$$Z = \{...,-1,0,1...\}, \sum_k = \sum_{k=-\infty}^{\infty}, \int = \int_{-\infty}^{\infty}. \tag{6}$$

The subspace V_o of $L_2(IR)$ is define as $V_o = \{f, \in L_2(IR) : f$ which is constant on $(k, k+1], k \in Z\}$, therefore

$$f \in V_0 \Leftrightarrow f(x) = \sum C_{k\varphi}(x-k), \tag{7}$$

where $\sum_k |C_k|^2 < \infty$, the series converges in Eqs. (8) and (9)

$$L_2(IR), \tag{8}$$

$$\varphi(x) = I\{x \in (0,1]\} = \begin{cases} 1, x \in (0,1] \\ 0, x \in (0,1] \end{cases}, \tag{9}$$

where $\varphi_{ok}(x) = \varphi(x - k), k \in \mathbb{Z}$ in which $\{\varphi_{ok}\}$ is the orthonormal basis in V_o, as such a new linear subspace of $L_2(IR)$ is defined as

$$V_1 = \{h(x) = f(2x) : f \in V_o\},\tag{10}$$

comprises of all functions in $L_2(IR)$ that are constant within the intervals of $\left(\dfrac{k}{2}, \dfrac{k+1}{2}\right], k \in \mathbb{Z}$. The $V_o \subset V_1$, orthonormal basis in V_1 is given by $\{\varphi_{1k}\}$ where $\varphi_{1k}(x) = \sqrt{2}\varphi(2x - k), k \in \mathbb{Z}$. This process continues and the space is generally defined as

$$V_j = \{h(x) = f(2^j x) : f \in V_o\}\tag{11}$$

The V_j is a linear subspace of $L_2(IR)$ with the orthonormal basis in Eqs. (12) and (13)

$$\varphi_{jk}(x) = 2^{\frac{j}{2}}\varphi(2^j x - k), k \in \mathbb{Z}.\tag{12}$$

$$V_o \subset V_1 \subset ... \subset V_j \subset ...\tag{13}$$

In a similar manner we define V_j for $j < 0, j \in \mathbb{Z}$ to get the inclusions

$$... \subset V_{-1} \subset V_o \subset V_1 \subset ...\tag{14}$$

The process is infinitely continued until the entire space $L_2(IR)$ is approximated. The orthogonal sum decomposition of V_j is expressed as

$$L_2(IR) = V_o \bigoplus_{j=0}^{\infty} w_j\tag{15}$$

where $w_j = V_{j+1} \Theta V_j$ which is the orthogonal complement of V_j in V_{j+1}. Eq. (15) indicates that each $f \in L_2(IR)$ can be represented as series in the form

$$f(x) = \sum \alpha_{ok}\varphi_{ok}(x) + \sum_{j=0}^{\infty}\sum_{k}\beta_{jk}\Psi_{jk}(x)\tag{16}$$

where α_{ok}, β_{jk}, and Ψ_{jk} are representation of coefficients of the expansion.

2.2   Adaptive Linear Neural Network

The ALNN can mathematically be defined as [11]:

$$f(x) = \varphi\left(\sum\nolimits_{i=1}^{m} w_i x_i + b\right). \tag{17}$$

where $x_i (i = 1,2,3...,n), f(x), b, w_i (i = 1,2,3,...,n), m,$ and $\varphi(\cdot)$ are the input variables, output, bias, weights, number of input neurons, and activation function for computation in the ALNN neurons. The architecture of the ALNN comprised of only one layer. The activation function and learning algorithm are pure linear and Widrow-Hoff, respectively. The learning algorithm minimizes mean square error (MSE) to optimized weights and bias as defined in Eq. (18)

$$MSE = \frac{1}{N}\sum\nolimits_{j=1}^{N}\left[e_j(x)\right]^2 = \frac{1}{2}\sum\nolimits_{j=1}^{N}\left[T_j(x) - p_j(x)\right]^2, \tag{18}$$

where $N, e_j(x), T_j(x),$ and $p_j(x)$ are the number of data points in the samples, error, target output, and network output. An adaptation of the weights and bias for multiple neurons can be defined as

$$w(x+1) = w(x) + 2\eta e(x)T^T(x). \tag{19}$$

$$b(x+1) = b(x) + 2\eta e(x), \tag{20}$$

where η is the learning rate.

2.3   Relevance Vector Machine

The RVM is typically used for solving classification and regression problems. In this study, we present regression relevance vector machine algorithm for our problem is a regression. Let $\{X_i, t_i\}_{i=1}^{N}$ be input-dethe datasetutput pairs of dataset. Each desired output t_i assumed a normal distribution with mean $y(x_i)$ and uniform variance δ^2 of the noise $\in$ define as

$$p(t/x) = N(t/y(x), \delta^2) \tag{21}$$

The desired output is also assumed joint normal distribution expressed as $N(\mu, \Sigma)$, where μ and Σ are unknown variables which can be determined by the RVM [13].

3 Experiments

3.1 Dataset

The global annual land-ocean temperature (GLOT) is chosen as the indicator of the climate change behavior because it significantly determines climate change more than other indicators such as atmospheric temperature, heat emanating from the sun, among others [14]. The GLOT data are provided in degrees Celsius (degree C) extracted from the National Aeronautic and Space Administration (NASA) website (www.nasa.gov), Goddard Institute for Space, for a period from 1880 to 2012 on a yearly basis. The GLOT data is a global data that is not restricted to a particular region, and were not normalized as the data are already provided in approximately equal proportion within -1 to 1.

3.2 The Propose Ensemble HWD-RVMALNN Framework

The propose ensemble HWD-RVMALNN paradigm is represented in the flowchart illustrated in Fig. 1. The major components of the entire process composed of the following stages: The original GLOT time series data are decomposed using HWD into five scale coefficient. For each of the scale coefficient, the RVM is employed as an estimation technique to model the decomposed scale coefficient and estimate for each of the five scale coefficient. The estimation results produce by each of the RVMs (HWD-RVM1, HWD-RVM2, HWD-RVM3, HWD-RVM4, and HWD-RVM5) is integrated by ALNN to generate an ensemble estimate of the GLOT which can be viewed as the estimation result of the original GLOT time series data. The optimal parameters of RVM were obtained through initial experimentation. The methodology can be summarized as a hybrid ensemble approach comprising of HWD (Decomposition) -RVM (estimate) -ALNN (ensemble) referred to HWD-RVMALNN. To verify the effectiveness of the our approach, we compared the

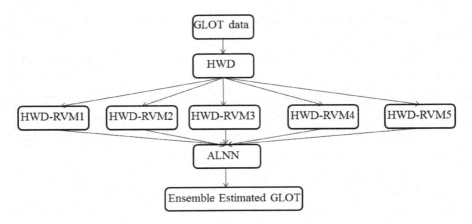

Fig. 1. The propose ensemble HWD-RVMALNN framework

proposed HWD-RVMALNN with the popular approaches of prediction such as Levenberg-Marquardt (LMQ), resilient backpropagation (RBP), Cyclical weight/bias rule (CWB), learning vector quantization (LVQ), and SVM. These algorithms are used as the benchmarks since they are the popular approaches in the literature for the estimation of climate change, readers can refer to [4-6] for details. The algorithms are also applied to estimate the GLOT for the purpose of comparing with the results generated by our proposal.

4   Results and Discussion

In this section, the simulated results are presented and discussed. The original GLOT signal is depicted in Figure 2. Decomposition of the GLOT time series data that significantly influence the fluctuation of climate is shown in Figure 3 displaying the multi resolution analysis that includes fifth approximation and five (d_1, d_2, d_3, d_4, and d_5) levels of details. The five levels of detail coefficients including amplitude of the scaling

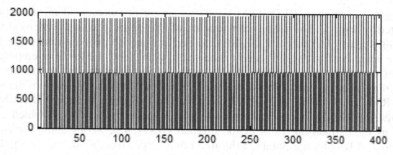

Fig. 2. The original signal of the GLOT

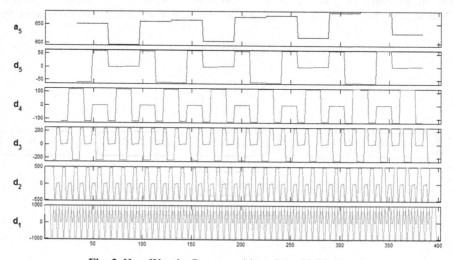

Fig. 3. Haar Wavelet Decomposition of the GLOT Signal

coefficient are shown in Figure 4. The decomposition contributed to an understanding of the time varying patterns in the GLOT data. Some useful information is revealed from the analysis, and interpretation of the GLOT data. The original GLOT data (Figure 2) and the extracted portion (Figure 3) is in degree Celsius.

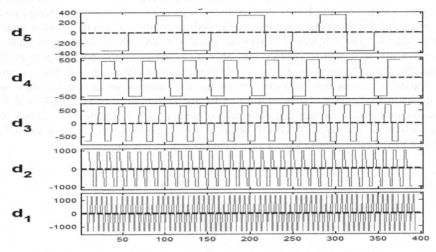

Fig. 4. Original details coefficients of the GLOT signal

The optimal parameters of RVM obtained after the initial experimentation were kernel function = radial basis, relevance vectors = 241, γ = 1.7, kernel length = 4.6, minimum delta scale = 0.0002, and maximum was 1×10^4.

Table 1. Performance metrics of the algorithms compared with the propose ensemble HWD-RVMALNN

Algorithm	MSE	MAE	SSE	R^2	RT(sec.)
LMQ	0.00413	0.0071	0.422	0.7047	2
CBW	0.00828	0.01923	0.51193	0.87268	932
RBP	0.015	0.0788	1.14	0.7932	3
SVM	0.002911	0.019884	0.195	0.88626	5
LVQ	0.091	0.234	8.07	0	2
HWD-RVMALNN	**0.00081**	**0.00721**	**0.00916**	**0.93087**	**0**

Mean absolute error (MAE), Sum of square error (SSE), Runtime (RT)

It is clear shown in Table 1 that the algorithms compared with our approach estimated GLOT with a good degree of accuracy as suggested by the simulated results. The SVM performs better than the LM, CBW, RBF, and LVQ in terms of R^2, MSE and MAE. The results corroborate with the study conducted by [7]. The possible reason for this performance exhibited by SVM could be attributed to the use of support vectors by the

SVM due to its ability to improve performance. The worst performance exhibited by LVQ in terms of R^2 which is merely random could likely be caused by the non-zero differentiability of the LVQ. The runtime of LM and LVQ outperform SVM, CBW, and RBP in terms of computational speed. The poorest convergence speed is observed to be exhibited by the CBW. The likely cause of this poor convergence can best be attributed to the cyclical nature of the CBW to present inputs to the network which might have caused the delay. An algorithm that converges to the optimal solution within the shortest time is considered the most efficient. The propose HWD-RVMALNN as reported in Table 1 based on the performance metrics was able to improve on the performance of the approaches typically use in the estimation of climate change in the literature. They propose an approach performs better than the commonly used approaches in both accuracy and computational efficiency. The likely reason for the performance of HWD-RVMALNN could be attributed to the fact that the results of several experts are ensemble to produce superior output. Estimates of GLOT obtained from simulating the propose ensemble HWD-RVMALNN on the independent test dataset is plotted in Figure 5.

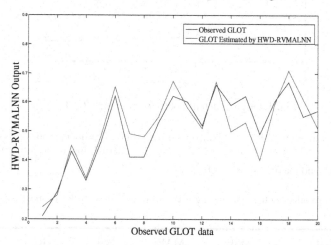

Fig. 5. Performance of the propose HWD-RVMALNN on the test dataset

5   Conclusion

In this research, a hybrid of wavelet transform and computational intelligent algorithms has been proposed for the estimation of climate change behavior. Specifically HWD, RVM, and ALNN were hybridized to propose ensemble HWD-RVMALNN. A series of comparative simulations were performed and it was found that the propose HWD-RVMALNN performs better in both accuracy and computational speed. The propose HWD-RVMALNN can provide better understanding of the future knowledge of climate change behavior than the methods already proposed in the literature. The model can assist policy makers in formulating global response policy in tackling the negative impact expected to be cause by the behavior of climate change. We intend to further this research by developing the real life application of the propose HWD-RVMALNN model to help climate change experts and policy makers in the decision making process.

Acknowledgments. This work is supported by University of Malaya High Impact Research Grant no vote UM.C/625/HIR/MOHE/SC/13/2 from Ministry of Higher Education Malaysia.

References

1. Hoegh-Guldberg, O., Bruno, J.F.: The impact of climate change on the world's marine ecosystems. Sci. 328, 1523–1528 (2010)
2. Belkin, I.M.: Rapid warming of Large Marine Ecosystems. Progr. Oceanogr. 81, 207–213 (2009)
3. Marvin, H.J.P., Kleter, G.A., et al.: Proactive systems for early warning of potential impacts of natural disasters on food safety: Climate-change-induced extreme events as case in point. Food Control 34(2), 444–456 (2013)
4. Matouqa, M., El-Hasan, T., Al-Bilbisi, H.: The climate change implication on Jordan: A case study using GIS and Artificial Neural Networks for weather forecasting. J. Taibah University Sci. 7, 44–55 (2013)
5. Goyal, M.K., Burn, D.H., Ojha, C.S.P.: Statistical downscaling of temperatures under climate change scenarios for Thames river basin, Canada. Int. J. Global Warm. 4(1), 13–30 (2012)
6. Holmberg, M., Forsius, M., Starr, M., Huttunen, M.: An application of artificial neural networks to carbon, nitrogen and phosphorus concentrations in three boreal streams and impacts of climate change. Ecol. Model. 195(1-2), 51–60 (2006)
7. Tripathi, S., Srinivas, V.V., Nanjundiah, R.S.: Downscaling of precipitation for climate change scenarios: A support vector machine approach. J. Hydrol. 330, 621–640 (2006)
8. Jammazi, R., Aloui, C.: Crude oil forecasting: experimental evidence from wavelet decomposition and neural network modeling. Energ. Econ. 34, 828–841 (2012)
9. Demir, B., Ertürk, S.: Hyperspectral image classification using relevance vector machines. IEEE. Geosci. Remote S. 4(4), 586–590 (2007)
10. Hardle, W., Kerkyacharian, G., Pikard, D., Tsybakov, A.: Wavelets, Approximation, and Statistical Applications. Lec. Notes Stat., vol. 129. Springer, New York (1998)
11. Hagan, M.T., Demuth, H.B., Beale, M.H.: Neural Network Design. PWS Publishing Company, Boston (2006)
12. Wipf, D., Palmer, J., Rao, B.: Perspective on spares Bayesian learning. In: Adv. Neural Inf. Processing Syst. 16. MIT Press, Cambridge (2004)
13. Tipping, M.E.: Sparse Bayesian learning and the relevance vector machine. J. Mach. Learn. Res. 1, 211–244 (2001)
14. Richardson, K., Steffen, W., Joachim, H.S., et al.: Climate change: Global Risk, Challenges & decisions. The United Nations Framework on Climate Change Synthesis Report. University of Copenhagen, Denmark (2009)

An Improved Ant Colony Matching
by Using Discrete Curve Evolution

Younes Saadi[1], Eka Novita Sari[2], and Tutut Herawan[1]

[1]Department of Information System
University of Malaya
50603 Pantai Valley, Kuala Lumpur, Malaysia
[2]AMCS Research Center
Yogyakarta, Indonesia
younessaadi@gmail.com, eka@amcs.co, tutut@um.edu.my

Abstract. In this paper we present an improved Ant Colony Optimization (ACO) for contour matching, which can be used to match 2D shapes. Discrete Curve Evolution (DCE) technique is used to simplify the extracted contour. In order to find the best correspondence between shapes, the match process is formulated as a Quadratic Assignment Problem (QAP) and resolved by using Ant Colony Optimization (ACO). The experimental results justify that Discrete Curve Evolution (DCE) performs better than the previous Constant Sampling (CS) technique which has been selected for the ACO matching.

Keywords: Ant Colony Optimization, Quadratic assignment problem, Discrete curve evolution, Contour matching.

1   Introduction

Nowadays, shape analysis has become an important topic in computer vision. It has been widely adopted in many applications of computer graphics. In particular, shape matching one of the fundamental techniques of shape analysis. It plays a primordial role in shape retrieval, recognition and classification, and medical registration [1]. Shape matching has reached a state of maturity in which many real products based on shape matching are commercialized in different areas [2]. In the commercial domain, shape matching methods are being used to retrieve and classify images, for personal and institutional needs like security and military. In the medical domain, shape matching is used in radiology to diagnose and to assess medical images to determine the progress and the suitable treatment options.

Shape matching is application dependent. Different applications may have different requirements on invariance and tolerance to noise, distortion, blur, transformation, scale and orientation. Thus, it is difficult to design a universal method which is suitable for all applications. Nowadays, many techniques have been proposed but most of them only focus on the applications where shape is invariant to transformation.

Linawati et al. (Eds.): ICT-EurAsia 2014, LNCS 8407, pp. 248–256, 2014.

Based on the representation techniques, shape matching techniques can be classified into two categories: contour based matching and region based matching [3]. This research is focusing on contour based matching techniques, in which only the information located on the shape contour is explored. Majority of the past researches have concentrated on how to achieve a meaningful correspondence. On the other hand, some researches focused on improving representation methods of a contour in such a way that the resulted contour could be used to extract meaningful information. This is called simplification, evolution or smoothing in some sources [3] [4] [5] [6] [7].

However, challenges still remain. The first challenge is the invariance [8] [9]. Since shape in many applications is often discussed based on the property of invariance, shape matching is expected to be invariant to transformations such as example translation, scale and orientation. The second challenge is tolerance as noise, blur, crack and deformation are usually introduced when the shape of an object is extracted from an image [10]. In this case, a shape matching is required to be robust to these imperfections.

Moreover, in contour based matching, the points along the contours as a bipartite graph can be figured out and formulated as a QA. This is considered as an NP-hard problem [11]. In order to find an acceptable solution, heuristic1s techniques are often used. The main idea is to compute the mapping between two contours by minimizing the global dissimilarity. Many research studies have been proposed. For example, Hungarian method uses the simple greedy matching [12], and COPAP [13] takes into account the order preserving. However, the main drawback of these techniques is the omission of proximity information measurement between feature points on the same shape contour. For this reason, Kaick [14] proposed an Ant Colony Optimization (ACO) approach based on incorporating proximity into an optimization framework. However, the huge number of points incorporated in the correspondence makes the matching more complex and less accurate [11]. A modified ACO matching approach has been proposed by Ruberto and Morgera [11] based on genetic algorithm; only dominant points are used instead of the sampling distribution of contour points, which improves the correspondence accuracy and reduces the complexity.

Generally, speaking a heuristic is a method that achieves good (but not necessarily optimal) results at low expense. However, which results are to be considered good heavily depends on the application at hand. Analysing contour matching we can figure out the points along the contour as a bipartite graph, which can be formulated as a Quadratic Assignment (QA). This is one of the NP-hard problems [15]. Finding an optimal solution for such problem seems difficult by using conventional methods. Heuristics methods are used to find an acceptable solution for such cases.

It is important to mention the Hungarian method as one of the well-studied methods in this context. In fact it is based on solving the complexity which is a part of the combinatorial optimization solved by using Iterative Closest Point (ICP) scheme [16]. Following the requirements of the applications, many versions of heuristics approaches have been proposed. A review about correspondence introduced in [17] shows clearly the importance of heuristic methods to solve complexity related to shape matching issues.

In this paper, an improved ACO matching approach based on Discrete Curve Evolution (DCE) was proposed. In order to reduce the number of contour points incorporated in the correspondence, a polygonal approximation proposed previously by

Latecki and Lakamper [18] was selected to simplify the extracted contour. Mainly, it simplifies the contour by neglecting distortions while at the same time preserving the perceptual appearance at a level sufficient for object recognition. To test the effectiveness of our approach, an MPEG-7 subset described by Ruberto and Morgera [11] was used to test shape retrieval considering noise and distortions effect. The results were also compared with the previous work of ACO matching by Ruberto and Morgera [11].

2   Proposed Method

The structure of the proposed method is shown in (Fig. 1). It operates into four stages. In the first stage the contour is traced by using a basic Matlab function. In the second stage the extracted contours are approximated by using Discrete Curve Evolution (DCE) which is proposed previously by Latecki and Lakamper [18]. After that, Ant Colony Optimization proposed previously [14] is used to compute the correspondence in the third stage. Finally in the fourth stage, the Euclidean distance has been selected to compute the dissimilarity between shapes according to the resulted matrix of correspondence.

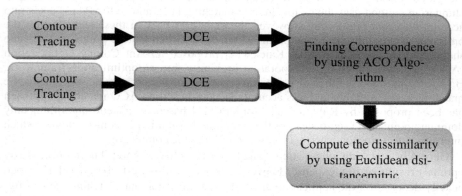

Fig. 1. Method structure

After analyzed the shortcoming of polygonal evolution methods, discrete curve evolution [18] has been selected to be used in our approach (See Figures 2, 3, and 4). The main reason is that this method allows the user to control the degree of evolution according to the human judgment. In every iteration, a pair of consecutive line segments s1, s2 is replaced with a single line related to the endpoints of $s_1 \cup s_2$. The substitution is calculated according to the relevance value K given by the following equation:

$$K(s_1, s_2) = \frac{\beta(s_1,s_2)l(s_1)l(s_2)}{l(s_1)+l(s_2)}. \tag{1}$$

$\beta(s_1, s_2)$ is the turn angle at the common vertex between s_1 and s_2. l is the length function normalized with respect to the total length of a polygonal curve C.

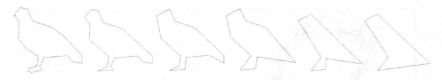

Fig. 2. A series of polygonal evolution

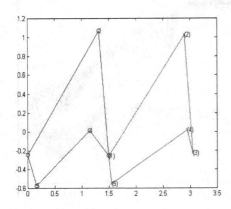

Fig. 3. Two simplified contours

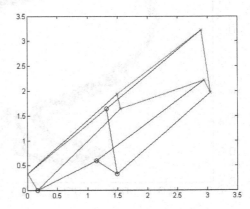

Fig. 4. ACO matching after DCE

A new matching algorithm based on ant colony optimization is described previously [14]. It consists of taking in consideration the proximity measured between feature points on the same shape (Fig. 5). The matching is formulated as a two sets of points I and J where the ants cross these two sets doing a complete tour. All the movements produce a collection of possible paths between the two sets. During building of these paths Ants release the pheromone with different amounts for each possible path. A bigger amount of pheromone on a path means that it is more eligible in term of cost of correspondence. The traversing from a vertex $i \in I$ to a vertex $j \in J$ is given by the equation below [11].

2.1 Edge Probability

$$p_{ij}^{k} = \frac{\alpha\tau_{ij}+(1-\alpha)\eta_{ij}}{\sum_{l\in N_i}[\alpha\tau_{il}+(1-\alpha)\eta_{il}]}. \tag{2}$$

The pheromone accumulated on the edge (i,j) is quantified by τ_{ij}, η_{ij} indicates the desirability (or probability) of traversing (i,j) based on heuristic information, $N_i = \{l \in J : (i,l) \in E\}$ is the immediate neighbourhood of vertex i. The parameter $0 \leq \alpha \leq 1$ regulates the influence of pheromones over heuristic information. After a complete tour of the ants, an ACO iteration, the cost of solutions is computed as defined in second.

Pheromones are updated at the end of ACO iteration. First, pheromones are evaporated at n constant pheromone rate [11] $\rho, 0 \leq \rho \leq 1$.

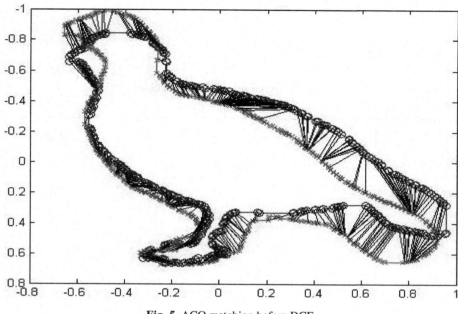

Fig. 5. ACO matching before DCE

2.2   Pheromone Evaporation

$$\tau_{ij} \leftarrow (1 - \rho)\tau_{ij}\,, \tag{3}$$

where ρ is the pheromone evaporation rate and the new pheromone deposition on the edges that were traversed by the ants is regulated by pheromone deposition:

$$\tau_{ij} \leftarrow \tau_{ij} + \sum_{k=1}^{m} \Delta\tau_{ij}^{k}\,, \tag{4}$$

where $\Delta\tau_{ij}^{k}$ is the amount of pheromone that an ant ^{k} has deposited on the edge (i, j).

2.3   Cost Function

The formulation of the problem is done by a QAP. When augmenting the shape descriptor R with proximity information. The general objective function is in the form:

$$QAP(\pi, R, I, J) = (1 - \nu)S(\pi, R, I, J) + \nu\chi(\pi, I, J), \tag{5}$$

where $0 \le \nu \le 1$ is used to control parameter between S and the proximity χ and the arguments I, J represents the two points sets, πa mapping such that to a pint of I correspondents a point in J and R the set of shape descriptors. The form S and χ is detailed in [11].

```
Input data:
Query shape and stored shapes: An ordered set of shape contours.
Output data:
Matrix of dissimilarity between the query shapes and all the stored
shapes
1. for i= 1 to M do {M number of query shapes}
2. Read a query shape S_i
3.      Contour tracing of shape S_i
4.      Apply DCE
5. end for
6. for j = 1 to N do {N number of stored shapes}
7.      Read a stored shape S_j
8.      Contour tracing of shape S_j
9.      Apply DCE
10. End for
11. for i= 1 to M do
12.      for j = 1 to N do
13.   Compute the best correspondence bc between S_i and S_j contours
14. Compute the degree of dissimilarity
14. end for
15. for each class sort the dissimilarity degree of each pairwise
    (query-stored) ascending where the first retrieved is the one with a
    min value.
```

3   Experimental Results

In order to test the effectiveness of our approach, which is based on DCE and ACO matching, an MPEG-7 subset (Fig. 6) is used to test shape retrieval and contour matching issues [11]. The database constitutes of 18 classes, each class contains 11 items plus 18 query shapes selected from each class. Basically this database assesses universal measures that are translation rotation and scaling invariant. However, in our scope we are not interested in rotation since we are using the classic shape context as a shape descriptor. For this reason we are using a set of parameters consist of 1 as number of ants and 100 as number of iterations each ants make in optimization process. The experiment is executed on a Matlab environment (Windows 32 OS) running on Intel Pentium 2.2 GHz.

As stated in section 2, DCE reduce the number of points located on the contour. After the evolution, ACO is convoked to establish best possible correspondence between the approximated contours.

We compared our approach to retrieval similar objects by using Constant Sampling points (CS) [11]. It is important to mention that comparison is not possible with Dominant Points (DP) approach proposed by Ruberto and Morgera since it is based on rotational descriptor, which is not the case of our research. Table 1 shows the accuracy rate for each class of our method compared to the CS approach. In Table 1 we show the experiments made to MPEG-7 subset with CS and the proposed method. Table 1 also introduces a comparison with 18 classes for both CS and the proposed method.

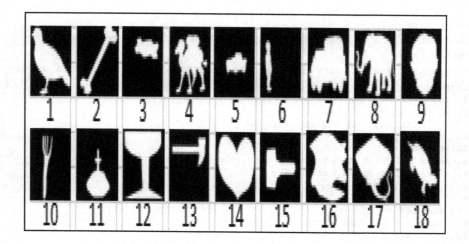

Fig. 6. MPEG-7 dataset [4]

Table 1. Retrieval rates of different MPEG-7 CE-Shape-1 Part B data set [11]

	Class	Proposed Method	CS
	1	0.9166	0.6909
	2	1.0000	0.9273
	3	0.9166	0.8818
	4	0.8333	0.7273
	5	0.9166	0.9909
	6	1.0000	1.0000
	7	0.9266	0.9909
	8	0.9100	0.8818
	9	1.0000	0.9727
Average accuracy for each class	10	1.0000	0.9455
	11	0.9166	1.0000
	12	1.0000	1.0000
	13	0.5000	0.6818
	14	1.0000	1.0000
	15	0.9166	0.8545
	16	1.0000	1.0000
	17	0.5833	0.7545
	18	0.6666	0.5636
Global Average		**0.8890**	0.8854

It is important to notice the highly performance affected by DCE compared to CS as a result of the lower number of points incorporated in the matching. There is dependence between lower accuracy and the smoothing of the contour. However th distribution of dominant points along the contour plays an important role to preserve the original frame of the shape and thus increasing the matching accuracy. The results obtained with classes 5 and 7 as shown in Table 1 by constant points CS is due to the nature of CS simplification.

Although the descriptor used in our approach is not invariant to rotation, the global average shows that our method performs better than CS. Thus the advantage of incorporating DCE and proximity using ACO is demonstrated.

4   Conclusion

In this study, an improved ACO matching algorithm based on curve evolution has been introduced. The main challenge to the contour matching was to find the best correspondence between the huge numbers of points along the contours incorporated in the matching. Whenever the number of points participated in the matching increased, the complexity of matching also increased which directly affected the performance of the matching process. A solution based on dominant points has been proposed by Ruberto and Morgera [11]. The obtained results showed the efficiency of our approach.

This research produced an improved ACO matching based on curve evolution. Before starting matching, a proposed DCE was applied in order to simplify the shape contour. This reduced the contour points incorporated along the contour. The DCE algorithmcan be personalized according to the number of iterations required. The iterations can be predefined to approximate the shape contour. Instead of the original ACO, the improved ACO matching as shown to be more accurate although the used descriptor is not invariant to rotation.

This does not mean, that heuristics methods might be useful for all matching applications, but the applicability of such methods is only related to: firstly, the domain of application for example sometimes in image registration it is enough to get an approximated matching to obtain the abnormalities. Secondly the applicability depends the requirements of the matching for example in some cases considering proximity between the points along the contour is compulsory which allow the usage of heuristic methods as a key for the solution.

Acknowledgments. This work is supported by University of Malaya High Impact Research Grant no vote UM.C/625/HIR/MOHE/SC/13/2 from Ministry of Higher Education Malaysia.

References

1. Tsapanos, N., Tefas, A., Nikolaidis, N., Pitas, I.: Shape matching using a binary search tree structure of weak classifiers. Pattern Recognition 45(6), 2363–2376 (2012)
2. Aaron, S.K., Christopher, R.I., Sharon, C.G.: Characterizing complex particle morphologies through shape matching: descriptors, applications, and algorithms. Journal of Computational Physics 230(17), 20 (2011)

3. Luciano, D.F.C., Roberto, M.C.J.: Shape Classification and Analysis: Theory and Practice, 2nd edn. CRC Press (2009)
4. Kolesnikov, A.: ISE-bounded polygonal approximation of digital curves. Pattern Recognition Letters 33(10, 15), 1329–1337 (2012)
5. Parvez, M.T., Sabri, A.M.: Polygonal approximation of digital planar curves through adaptive optimizations. Pattern Recognition 31(13), 1997–2005 (2010)
6. Poyato, A.C., Cuevas, F.J.M., Carnicer, R.M., Salinas, R.M.: Polygonal approximation of digital planar curves through break point suppression. Pattern Recognition 43(1), 14–25 (2010)
7. Parvez, M.T., Sabri, A.M.: Polygonal Approximation of Planar Curves Using Triangular Suppression. In: Proceeding of International Conference on Information Science, Signal Processing and their Applications (2010)
8. Aaron, S.K., Christopher, R.I., Sharon, C.G.: Characterizing complex particle morphologies through shape matching: descriptors, applications, and algorithms. Journal of Computational Physics 230(17), 6438–6463 (2011)
9. de Sousa, S., Artner, N.M., Kropatsch, W.G.: On the Evaluation of Graph Centrality for Shape Matching. In: Kropatsch, W.G., Artner, N.M., Haxhimusa, Y., Jiang, X. (eds.) GbRPR 2013. LNCS, vol. 7877, pp. 204–213. Springer, Heidelberg (2013)
10. Li, G., Kim, H., Tan, J.K., Ishikawa, S.: 3D Organic Shape Correspondence Using Spherical Conformal Mapping. In: World Congress on Medical Physics and Biomedical Engineering, Beijing, China, May 26-31. IFMBE Proceedings, vol. 39, pp. 943–946 (2013)
11. Ruberto, C.D., Morgera, A.: ACO contour matching: a dominant point approach. In: 4th International Congress on Image and Signal Processing, vol. 03, pp. 1391–1395 (2012)
12. Papadimitriou, C., Stieglitz, K.: Combinatorial Optimization: Algorithms and Complexity. Prentice Hall (1982) ISBN:0-13-152462-3
13. Scott, C., Nowak, R.D.: Robust contour matching via the order-preserving assignment problem. IEEE Trans. on Image Processing 15(7), 1831–1838 (2006)
14. Kaick, O.V., Hammarneh, G., Zhang, H., Wighton, P.: Contour Correspondence Via Ant Colony Optimization. In: Proc. 15th Pacific Graphic 2007, United States, pp. 271–280 (2007)
15. Zhu, X.: Shape Matching Based on Ant Colony Optimization. In: Huang, D.-S., Wunsch II, D.C., Levine, D.S., Jo, K.-H. (eds.) ICIC 2008. CCIS, vol. 15, pp. 101–108. Springer, Heidelberg (2008)
16. Rusinkiewicz, S., Levoy, M.: Efficient Variants of the ICP Algorithm. In: Third International Conference on 3-D Digital Imaging and Modeling, pp. 145–152. IEEE (2001)
17. Kaick, O.V., Zhang, H., Hamarneh, G., Cohen-Or, D.: A survey on shape correspondence. Computer Graphics Forum 30(6), 1681–1707 (2011)
18. Latecki, L.J., Lakämper, R.: Shape Similarity Measure Based on correspondence of visual parts. IEEE Transactions on Pattern Analysis and Machine Intelligence 22(10), 1185–1190 (2000)

A Novel Approach to Gasoline Price Forecasting Based on Karhunen-Loève Transform and Network for Vector Quantization with Voronoid Polyhedral

Haruna Chiroma[1], Sameem Abdulkareem[1], Adamu I. Abubakar[2],
Eka Novita Sari[3], and Tutut Herawan[4]

[1] Department of Artificial Intelligence
University of Malaya
50603 Pantai Valley, Kuala Lumpur, Malaysia
[2] Department of Information System
International Islamic University
Gombak, Kuala Lumpur, Malaysia
[3] AMCS Research Center
Yogyakarta, Indonesia
[4] Department of Information Systems
University of Malaya
50603 Pantai Valley, Kuala Lumpur, Malaysia
freedonchi@yahoo.com, 100adamu@gmail.com ,
{sameem,tutut}@um.edu.my, eka@amcs.co

Abstract. We propose an intelligent approach to gasoline price forecasting as an alternative to the statistical and econometric approaches typically applied in the literature. The linear nature of the statistics and Econometrics models assume normal distribution for input data which makes it unsuitable for forecasting nonlinear, and volatile gasoline price. Karhunen-Loève Transform and Network for Vector Quantization (KLNVQ) is proposed to build a model for the forecasting of gasoline prices. Experimental findings indicated that the proposed KLNVQ outperforms Autoregressive Integrated Moving Average, multiple linear regression, and vector autoregression model. The KLNVQ model constitutes an alternative to the forecasting of gasoline prices and the method has added to methods propose in the literature. Accurate forecasting of gasoline price has implication for the formulation of policies that can help deviate from the hardship of gasoline shortage.

Keywords: Vector quantization, Gasoline price, Karhunen-Loève Transform.

1 Introduction

Gasoline is obtained from the refining of crude oil through a process called fractional distillation. The gasoline is highly utilized by the general public for daily activities. Shortage of gasoline can inflict pain on communities, especially in US where long queues of vehicles were typically experienced when the gasoline is scarce. Similarly, the shortage of gasoline causes cuts in motoring, reduction of work weeks, and threats

Linawati et al. (Eds.): ICT-EurAsia 2014, LNCS 8407, pp. 257–266, 2014.

of job cuts in automobile industries [1]. Forecasting that is of low quality contributes to poor or inadequate investment which in turn might result in losses in welfare. When forecasting is bias, it makes investors not to make a cost effective investment in the energy efficiency [2].

There are studies in the literature that forecast gasoline price in order to provide advance knowledge of the price so that its negative impact can be reduced successfully. For example, asymmetric and symmetric models were applied to build a model for the forecasting of the gasoline price. It was found that the regression results emanated from the study suggested asymmetric model performs better than the symmetric in out of sample forecast accuracy [3]. The linear trend correlation error was used to build a model for the forecasting of gasoline price [4]. Similarly, Autoregressive Integrated Moving Average (ARIMA) was used for the forecasting of gasoline price by [5]. Anderson *et al.* [2] used the Michigan Consumers Survey data to forecast the price of Gasoline. The results indicated that the forecast accuracy outperform the Econometrics Auto Regressive Moving Average (ARMA). The studies in the literature mainly focus on statistics and econometric models for the forecasting of the gasoline price. However, those models assume linear distribution for input data, whereas gasoline price is nonlinear and volatile. Therefore, those models cannot provide effective solution to the problem of gasoline price forecasting. In addition, experimental evidence documented in the literature shows that artificial intelligence techniques such as neural network, fuzzy logic, expert systems, Genetic algorithms provide better solution for forecasting than statistical and econometric models. Though, there are very few instances in which statistical tools perform better the artificial intelligence methodologies [6]. Despite the significance of gasoline price, we have not found a reference in the literature that investigates the forecast of gasoline prices using artificial intelligence techniques.

In this paper, we propose to forecast the price of gasoline based on the network for vector quantization with Voronoid Polyhedral, and Karhunen-Loève Transform (KL) to select the most relevant inputs and eliminate the irrelevant attributes to improve forecast accuracy.

The rest of this paper is organized as follows. Section 2 describes the theoretical background of the study. Section 3 describes the experimentations. Section 4 describes results and discussion. Finally the conclusion of this work is described in Section 5.

2   Theoretical Background of the Study

2.1   Karhunen-Loève Transform

Suppose that the vector Y is for random variables V and the point of interest is covariance or correlation of V. The approach here is to find the most valuable subset of V (<< V) that have the most relevant information given by these variances and co-variances or correlations. The KLT mainly concentrates on variants, although correlations and co-variances are not totally ignored. Let x_1, x_2, and x_3 be variables as given by equation (1)

$$(X = x_1, x_2, x_3, \cdots, x_V).$$ (1)

$$\alpha_1' X. \tag{2}$$

The linear function of X is given by Equation (2) in which α_1 is a vector of V constants as given in Equation (3)

$$\alpha_{11}, \alpha_{12}, \alpha_{13}, \cdots, \alpha_{1V}, \tag{3}$$

where α_1' is the transpose of α_1 therefore,

$$\alpha_1' X = \alpha_{11} x_1 + \alpha_{12} x_2 + \alpha_{13} x_3 + \cdots + \alpha_{1V} x_V = \sum_{i=1}^{V} \alpha_{1j} x_j. \tag{4}$$

$$\alpha_2' X = \alpha_{21} x_1 + \alpha_{22} x_2 + \alpha_{23} x_3 + \cdots + \alpha_{2V} x_V = \sum_{i=1}^{V} \alpha_{2j} x_j. \tag{5}$$

$$\alpha_3' X = \alpha_{31} x_1 + \alpha_{32} x_2 + \alpha_{33} x_3 + \cdots + \alpha_{3V} x_V = \sum_{i=1}^{V} \alpha_{3j} x_j. \tag{6}$$

Eqs. (1), (2) and (3) are uncorrelated having maximum variance up to Equation (7) so that in step kth a linear function given in Equation (8) with maximum variance subject to being uncorrelated with Equation (9)

$$\alpha_V' X. \tag{7}$$
$$\alpha_k' X. \tag{8}$$
$$\alpha_1' X, \alpha_2' X, \alpha_3', \cdots, \alpha_{k-1}' X. \tag{9}$$

The principal component kth is the Equation (8), as such the principal component can be found up to V principal components. In this way it is expected that the highest number of variations in X will account for m principal components, where $m \ll V$ [7-8].

2.2   Network for Vector Quantization

Vector quantization (VQ) methods encode a manifold such that sub manifold $V \subseteq \Re^D$, use a finite set $w = (w_1, w_2, \cdots, w_n)$ of reference (codebook) or cluster centers. $w_i \in \Re^D$, $i = 1, \cdots, N$ vector of a data $v \in V$ can best be defined as the optimal matched or wining reference vector $w_{i(v)}$ of w for $d(v, w_{i(v)})$ which is a distortion error, for instance, square error $\|v - w_{i(v)}\|^2$ is minimum as possible. The procedure further divides the V into smaller units of regions

$$V_i = \left\{ v \in V \Big\| \|v - w_i\| \leq \|v - w_j\| \forall_j \right\} \tag{10}$$

Equation (10) is referred to as voronoid polyhedral through which every data vector v corresponds to reference vector w_i if probability of the data vectors over V is defined by $p(v)$, then Equation (11) is the average of reconstruction error (distortion error)

$$E = \int d^D v p(v)(v - w_i)^2. \tag{11}$$

Equation (11) is optimized to the minimal by the optimum selection of the w_i (reference vector).

Theorem 1. *For a set of reference vectors* $w = (w_1, ... w_N)$, $w_i \in \Re^D$, *and a density distribution* $p(v)$ *of data points* $v \in \Re^D$ *over the input space* $V \subseteq \Re^D$, *then*

$$\int_v d^D v p(v) h\lambda(k_i(v,w))(v - w_i) = -\frac{\partial E}{\partial w_i}, \tag{12}$$

$$E = \frac{1}{2} \sum_{j=1}^{N} d^D v p(v) h\lambda(k_j(v,w))(v - w_j)^2, \tag{13}$$

where $k_j(v,w)$ *represent the number of reference vectors* w_i *with* $\|v - w_i\| < \|v - w_j\|$.

By substituting $d_i(v) = v - w_i$ for ease we obtain

$$-\frac{\partial E}{\partial w_i} = R_i + \int_v d^D v p(v) h\lambda(k_i(v,w))(v - w_i). \tag{14}$$

$$R_i = -\frac{1}{2} \sum_{j=1}^{N} \int d^D v p(v) h'\lambda(k_j(v,w)) d_j^2 \frac{\partial k_j(v,w)}{\partial w_i}. \tag{15}$$

The derivative of $h'\lambda(\bullet)$ is $h\lambda(\bullet)$ $\forall_i = 1,...,N$ R_i vanishes for $k_j(v,w)$ then

$$k_j(v,w) = \sum_{i=1}^{N} \theta(d_j^2 - d_i^2). \tag{16}$$

Equation (16) is valid with the heavy-side step function $\theta(\bullet)$

$$\theta(x) = \begin{cases} 1, & for \ x > 0 \\ 0, & for \ x \le 0 \end{cases}. \tag{17}$$

$$\theta(x) = 0 \quad for \quad x \neq 0. \tag{18}$$

$$R_i = \int_v d^D v p(x) h' \lambda(k_i(v, w)) d_i^2 d_i \sum_{l=1}^{N} \partial(d_j^2 - d_l^2). \tag{19}$$

$$- \sum_{j=1}^{N} \int_v d^D v p(x) h' \lambda(k_j(v, w)) d_j^2 d_i \partial(d_j^2 - d_i^2). \tag{20}$$

The integral of the N integrands in the 2nd term of Equation (20) is non-vanishing only for those in which $d_j^2 \approx d_i^2$. Those $v's$ can be defined as

$$k_j(v, w) = \sum_{l=1}^{N} \theta(d_j^2 - d_l^2) = \sum_{l=1}^{N} \theta(d_i^2 - d_l^2) = k_i(v, w). \tag{21}$$

Hence, $R_i = \int_v d^D v p(v) h' \lambda(k_i(v, w)) d_i^2 d_i \sum_{l=1}^{N} \partial(d_i^2 - d_l^2).$ \hfill (22)

$$- \int_v d^D v p(v) h' \lambda(k_i(v, w)) d_i^2 d_i \sum_{j=1}^{N} \partial(d_j^2 - d_i^2). \tag{23}$$

R_i vanishes $\forall i = 1, \cdots, N$ because $\partial(x) = \partial(-x)$. If the priori of the data point distribution $(p(v))$ is not given whereas stochastic sequence of input data points $v(t = 1)$, $v(t = 2)$, ... govern by $P(x)$ drives the adaptation procedure, adjusting steps for the reference vectors or cluster centers w_i is defined by

$$\Delta w_i = \epsilon . \partial_{ii}(v(t)).(v(t) - w_i). \tag{24}$$

where ϵ and ∂_{ij} are the step size and Kronecker delta, respectively.

Due to Equation (11) having many local minima, soft max is introduced into the learning process to adjust the winning reference vector $i(x)$ as shown in Equation (25) to prevent the network for vector quantization from being trapped in local minima.

$$\Delta w_i = \epsilon . \frac{\ell^{-\beta(v - w_i)}}{\sum_{j=1}^{N} \ell^{-\beta(v - w_j)^2}} .(v - w_i). \tag{25}$$

$$E_{min} = -\frac{1}{\beta} \int d^D v p(v) \ln \sum_{i=1}^{N} \ell^{-\beta(v - w_i)^2}. \tag{26}$$

Equation (25) corresponds to stochastic gradient decent on the cost function. The cost function (E_{min}) as given in Equation (26) is equivalent to E of Equation (11) [9].

3   Experiments

3.1   Dataset

The data of New York Harbor Conventional Gasoline Regular Sport Price FOB ($/Gallon) were collected from the Energy Information Administration of the US Department of Energy. The data are freely available through the official website of the organization. The data were collected on a daily frequency from 2 of Jun, 1986 to October 15, 12012. Fig. 1 depicted the window of the original gasoline price data clearly showing its nonlinearity and volatile nature. The dataset consist of 6639 observations within the period under study, weekends and other public holidays created empty spaces of which we have used imputation to fill in the empty spaces. The value of 0 was used to fill the empty spaces since the dataset were normalized within the range of -1 to 1. Therefore, adding zero to empty spaces cannot affect the results because they are approximately equal proportion. Future contract prices (price of gasoline agreed between two parties today, but payment to be made on a specific future date) determine the gasoline price as pointed out in [5]. Therefore, fifteen futures contract prices were collected as the independent attributes, whereas gasoline price is the dependent variable. Descriptive statistics of the time series are reported in Table 1 showing the minimum and maximum gasoline price for the period under study. The standard deviation suggests that the gasoline price data are in good agreement with the observations.

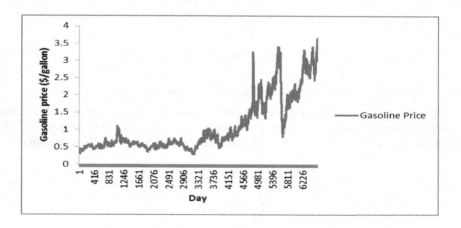

Fig. 1. Window of the gasoline price

Table 1. Descriptive statistics of the gasoline price

	Observations	Min	Max	Mean		SD
				Statistics	Standard error	Statistics
Gasoline price	6637	0.29	3.67	1.0901	0.00959	0.7811

3.2 The Proposed Application of the Network for Vector Quantization

The KLT is applied to reduce the number of input attributes in order to eliminate irrelevant inputs and used only minimum and relevant attributes. Including irrelevant attributes in the modeling process could affect the model performance, accuracy and increase the complexity of the network. The data of the gasoline price are partitioned into training, validation and testing dataset in the ration of 80%: 10%: 10% after several trials, since there is no ideal way for determining the exact percentage ratio. In building an NVQ model, initial parameter selection is critical to the performance of the model. For our study, we conducted several initial experimentation for choosing the optimal values that can yield global or near global solution. Number of adaptation steps, w_i, minimal distribution error E_0, performance measure were all set at the beginning of our experimentations.

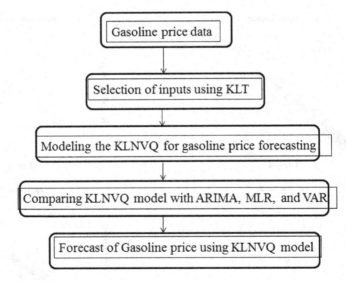

Fig. 2. The propose conceptual framework for the KLNVQ model

The KLNVQ model builds in this study was used to forecast the prices of gasoline. For the purpose of comparison, ARIMA, Multiple Linear Regression (MLR) and Vector Auto-regression (VAR) models were also used to forecast the gasoline price.

The entire process of building the KLNVQ model is presented in Fig. 2 and it was implemented in MATLAB (2013a) neural network ToolBox and SPSS version 16 on a machine (HP L1750 model, 4Gb RAM, 232.4 GB HDD, 32- bit OS, Intel (R) Core (TM)2 Duo CPU @ 3.00 GHz).

4   Results and Discussion

4.1   Analysis of the Results

We use KLT for the selection of input attributes in order to reduce its dimension. The attributes selected for the study are future contract 1 = 21.7, future contract 2 = 16.31, future contract 3 = 11.61, futures contract 4 = 9.4, future contract 5 = 8.7, future contract 6 = 7.2, future contract 7 = 6.5, future contract 8 = 6.1, and future contract 8 = 5.55 accounts for 93.07% cumulative variance. Others were rejected for inclusion in the model, therefore, six attributes were not included. The KLNVQ model has nine (9) inputs neurons, four hidden layer neurons, one (1) output neuron, soft max is used during adaptation. Number of adaptation steps = 0.2, w_i = 0.04, minimal distribution error E_0 = 0.0012. These are the optimal parameters for the KLNVQ model. The performance of the model for training, validation, test and complete datasets is presented in Fig. 3. The Mean Square Error (MSE) for training, validation and out of sample test are 0.006241, 0.006134, and 0.001284 respectively.

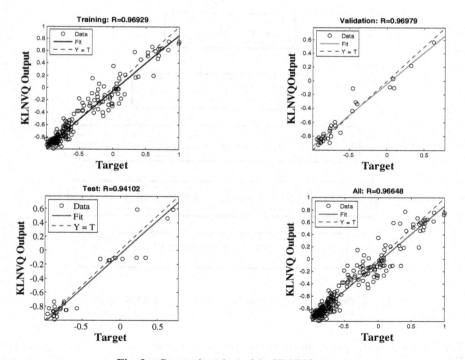

Fig. 3.   Regression plots of the KLNVQ model

For comparison purpose as earlier mentioned we also forecast the gasoline price using statistics and econometric models such as ARIMA, MLR, and VAR. The ARIMA model was first identified several models were tried in order to identify the best fit model. The models that were built and tested are ARIMA (1,0,0), ARIMA (2,1,0), ARIMA (2,2,2), ARIMA (1,0,3), ARIMA (1,3,4), ARIMA (3,0,0) and ARIMA (1,1,1). The model ARIMA (1,0.0) was identified as the best among other comparable models. Ljung-Box was used to validate the ARIMA (1,0,0) model and the results obtained are: $R^2 = 0.74$, statistics = 9.822, Sig. 0.341 and predictors = 5. The MSE of the gasoline price predicted by the ARIMA (1,0,0) and observed prices was completed and it was found to be 0.471101. MLR model was used for the forecasting of gasoline prices. The R^2 measurement of variability generated by the independent variables is 0.61522 and MSE is 0.83522. The R^2 adjusted value of 0.61522 was identical with the original R^2 showing how well the MLR models were able to generalize. This is because shrinkage was not found from the adjusted values. VAR model is also applied for the forecasting of gasoline price and the adjusted R^2 value obtained is 0.79137. The MSE measured for the forecasted and observed gasoline price values is 0.339014.

4.2   Comparing Performances of the Propose KLNVQ Model with ARIMA, MLR, and VAR

From the simulation results of the models presented in section 4.1, it can be summarized that the forecast accuracy of KLNVQ is better than the ARIMA, MLR and VAR in terms of MSE and R^2 (see Fig. 3). Evidence from this research has suggested that the propose KLNVQ can be a substitute for the statistical and econometric models commonly use in the literature for forecasting gasoline price. This performance demonstrated by the propose KLNVQ model can best be attributed to the capability of the model to approximate any nonlinear function with acceptable accuracy as well as the use of Voronoid Polyhedral which likely makes it easier for the model to detect patterns in the historical data. The research will be extended to compare the accuracy of several attribute selection methods such as genetic algorithm, particle swarm optimization, and hybridization of genetic algorithms and wavelet transform.

5   Conclusion

In this paper, we have presented a novel approach for the forecasting of the gasoline price. The approach is modeled based on KLT and NVQ with Voronoid Polyhedral. The experimental data were collected from the Energy Information Administration of the US Department of the Energy. Our approach is effective, robust, and efficient more than the statistical and econometric models propose in the literature. Comparative analysis suggested that the propose KLNVQ model performs better than the ARIMA, MLR, and VAR. Accurate forecasting of gasoline price has implication for the formulation of policies related to sustainable economic development which might improve the economic standard. In addition, having future knowledge of gasoline price can significantly assist policy makers in taking decisions that might successfully deviate from hardship typically cause by shortage of gasoline.

Acknowledgments. This work is supported by University of Malaya High Impact Research Grant no vote UM.C/625/HIR/MOHE/SC/13/2 from Ministry of Higher Education Malaysia.

References

1. Hamilton, J.D.: Historical oil shocks. In: Handbook of Major Events in Economic History (2011) (forthcoming)
2. Anderson, S.R., Kellogg, R., Sallee, J.M., Curtin, R.T.: Forecasting Gasoline Prices Using Consumer Surveys. Am. Econ. Rev. 101(3), 110–114 (2011)
3. Deltas, G.: Retail gasoline price dynamics and local market power. J. Ind. Econ. 56(3), 613–628 (2008)
4. Borenstein, S., Cameron, C.A., Gilbert, R.: Do gasoline prices respond asymmetrically to crude oil price change? Q. J. Econ. 102, 305–339 (1997)
5. Chinn, M., LeBlanc, M., Coibion, O.: The predictive of energy futures: An update on petroleum, natural gas, heating oil and gasoline. National Bureau of Economics research, Massachusetts, Cambridge, working paper 11033 (2005)
6. Bahrammirzaee, A.A.: comparative survey of artificial intelligence applications in finance: artificial neural networks, expert system and hybrid intelligent systems. Neural Comput. Appl. 19, 1165–1195 (2010)
7. Jolliffe, I.T.: Principal component analysis, 2nd edn. Springer, New York (2002)
8. Karhunen, J.: Robust PCA methods for complete and missing data. Neural Netw. World 5, 357–392 (2011)
9. Martinetz, T.M., Berkovich, S.G., Klaus, J., Schulten, K.J.: "Neural-Gas" Network for Vector Quantization and its Application to Time-Series Prediction. IEEE T. Neural Networ. 4(4), 558–569 (1993)

Enhancing the Use of Digital Model with Team-Based Learning Approach in Science Teaching

Bens Pardamean[1], Teddy Suparyanto[1], Suyanta[2], Eryadi Masli[3], Jerome Donovan[3]

[1] Graduate Program of Information Technology, Bina Nusantara University, Jakarta, Indonesia
[2] SMP Negeri 142, Jakarta, Indonesia
[3] Faculty of Business and Enterprise, Swinburne University of Technology, Hawthorn, Australia
bpardamean@binus.edu

Abstract. This study describes the introduction of digital models and team-based learning (TBL) for teaching science; in this case, the teaching of the magnetic induction portion of a physics class. This new approach required students' active construction of knowledge as both an individual and team. Students were asked to begin their studies through the viewing of digital models in videos through an online learning portal. *Camtasia Studio* was utilized in creating video contains class material and experiments along with the teacher's audio explanation. The TBL approach was implemented as the instructional strategy during in-class sessions. A portion of the classroom time was spent ensuring that students master the class material and a vast majority of class time was used for team assignments that focused on problem-based learning and simulating complex questions that the student would face as the course developed. The utilization of digital models and TBL improved the students' ability to learn independently and to present their ideas coherently, transforming them into more engaged, independent learners, not just in science learning but also in their overall academic experience.

Keywords: Team-Based Learning, TBL, digital model, science teaching.

1 Introduction

The latest data indicates that the development of secondary education, especially in the science and mathematics, in Indonesia experienced a declining trend, in comparison with other countries. The TIMSS (Trends International in Mathematics and Science Study) report showed that in 2007, Indonesian was ranked 35 (out of 49 countries) in eighth grade science. However, four years later, its rank went down to 40 (from 42 countries). Realizing that science (and technology) plays significant role in shaping the future of the country, the Indonesian government is putting efforts to improve the quality of education through National Education Standard (NES). One of the issues that impede the government's endeavor is the practice of learning and teaching, especially in science.

Currently, the teaching of science-related courses at primary as well as secondary school level in Indonesia is based on a relatively traditional teaching method; the

Linawati et al. (Eds.): ICT-EurAsia 2014, LNCS 8407, pp. 267–276, 2014.

instructor imparts knowledge to students in the classroom, explaining various concepts, facts, and other learning contents [1]. As teaching time is limited, the students listens to, absorbs, and memorizes what the teacher has said while activities, such as homework and material review would then complement the teaching activities. This renders the students to be more of a group of passive participants in the learning process. Furthermore, students rely on textbooks as a primary information source; they are urged to read the text but in reality, many do not do so. As a result, the teacher spends more time organizing and clarifying the text's information for the students. In this more traditional method of teaching, students are not maximally engaged in the learning process and do not reach their maximum potential in mastering the content material. (The Content Standard of the NES is the minimum criteria in the Indonesian educational system; thus, mastering the material is essential). Furthermore, in the traditional teaching method, there is a lack of opportunity for students to develop the attitudes necessary for scientific inquiry [2]. In the traditional curriculum, the science is taught as proven facts and absolute truth, which is treated as a static body of knowledge [3]. Thus, we believe that an effective teaching method should involve the students' active participation in the learning process. The focus of instruction would be learning how to apply the concepts and ideas substantially instead of merely learning about them theoretically. Marx et al. (2004) argue that learning science should be active and constructive [4]. In this student-centered teaching method, a different kind of instructional strategies to teach science is employed. It includes using digital models as well as putting students in groups for them to collaborate as an effective team.

The use of models and analogies in the pedagogy of science teaching was directed to assist students to gain understanding of the subject [5]. However, the advances in Information and Communication Technology (ICT) within the past three decades which positively impact on the teaching and learning in science [6] have provided the opportunities for some educators to employ the digital models in the teaching and learning activities, especially for science-related subjects. Many digital models and applications have been developed to address students' difficulties in understanding the concept. However, the students' grasping of a concept does not depend solely on the model; there should be a learning process that ensures the model can help students optimally in their learning activities. This problem is often exacerbated by the fact that the students are not accustomed to working in groups. Coll, France and Taylor (2005) suggest that the collaborative work and peer discussion are important factors to enhance students' cognitive thinking skills, which are crucial in the understanding of science-related subjects [5]. Thus, the aim of the paper is to present a method of science teaching with digital models that requires students to actively construct knowledge in both an independent and group setting.

This method is currently employed in the Grade 9 in one of public junior high schools in Jakarta, Indonesia. The students learnt about magnetic induction in their physics class in. Students were asked to examine digital models in the form of instructional videos through an online learning portal. The video content consisted of class materials and experiments, along with the teacher's narration, which was created using *Camtasia Studio*.

In learning science-related subjects, it is not enough just to study the concepts; the Indonesian Ministry of National Education in its science curriculum policy expect that students to develop their domain knowledge as well as cognitive process [7].

As students learn from cognitive processes of their peers [8], during classroom activities, the Team-Based Learning (TBL) would be employed as the instructional strategy. In this method, the students would learn about magnetic induction concepts and its applications through individual and group activities.

1.1   Models in Science Teaching and Learning

Learning is defined as any relatively permanent change in behavior that occurs as a result of practice or experience [9]. This definition consists of two important concepts, "change in behavior" and "a result of practice or experience". Thus, a teaching method should aim to achieve these two ideas in learning. For science, models can be one of the tools for shaping the students' learning experience.

Models are defined as intended physical, computational, or mental representations of a more concrete entity, set of concepts, or phenomena [10]. There are three different types of model in science education [11]: conceptual, mental, and physical models.

Conceptual models are external representations. They are precise, complete, and consistent with the shared scientific knowledge specifically created to facilitate the comprehension or the teaching of systems in the world [12]. Mental models are internal and cognitive representations of familiar objects and concepts [10, 13]. They are psychological representations of real or imaginary situations [11]. Lastly, physical models are considered by the science-education community as a simplified and/or idealized version of a more complex physical system or phenomenon [11].

The conceptual models consists of mathematical, computer, and physical models. Ornek (2008) states that the definitions of each conceptual model are as follows [11]:

- A mathematical model is the use of mathematical language to describe the behavior of a system.
- A computer model has a program that attempts to simulate the behavior of a particular system. The program was created through the use of a mathematical model to find analytical solutions to problems, enabling the prediction of a complex system's behavior via a set of parameters and initial conditions.
- Physical models in the science-education community are considered to be tangible representations that can be carried, touched, or held.

1.2   ICT for Science Teaching and Learning

With computer technology's rapid advancement as well as widespread use of the Internet, teaching and learning with communication/information processing technologies have become a current, popular interest among researchers and educators [14]. The implementation of Information and Communication Technology (ICT) influenced the teaching methodology and teaching material. For the science teaching and learning, ICT could provide digital contents and a deliver mechanism to the students. Due to difference with a traditional class, the students must "adjust" their concept cognition to reap the benefits of conceptual change learning [14].

1.3   Digital Model

A digital model is created and delivered via ICT, with the ability to incorporate not only a computer model, but also a mathematical or physical model. The resulting digital data can range from videos to interactive games to virtual simulation.

This research addressed the use of digital video presentations. The instructor/teacher created the video with *Camtasia*, a computer software that captures both the computer's screen and teacher's voice. With this software, the teacher recorded his power point presentation then added with his own explanation in synch with the presentation's progress.

1.4   Webblog

A web blog (blog) was used to deliver the digital model. From an educational point of view, weblogs are the development of traditional learning logs for students and teachers, whether as a complement to traditional lectures or as an e-learning tool [15].

1.5   Team-Based Learning (TBL)

The primary learning objective in TBL is to go beyond simply covering content, shifting more focus to ensuring that students have the opportunity to practice course concepts via problem solving. Thus, TBL is designed to provide students with both conceptual and procedural knowledge [16]. Although a portion of the classroom time is still spent ensuring that students master the course content, the vast majority of class time is used for team assignments that focus on problem-based learning, simulating complex questions that the student will face as the course develops.

Figure 1 outlines a general scheme of how a TBL course is organized. Students are strategically organized into permanent groups for the term, and the course content is organized into major units— typically five to seven. Before any in-class content work, students must study assigned materials since each unit begins with the readiness assurance process (RAP), which consists of a short test on the key ideas from the readings that students complete as individuals. Subsequently, the students would work on the test as a team, coming to consensus on team answers. Immediate feedback is given on the team test, allowing the opportunity to write evidence-based appeals and valid arguments for incorrect responses. The final step in the RAP is short and specific lecture to clarify any common misunderstandings found within the team test and appeals. Upon the completion of the RAP, the majority remainder of learning unit is spent on in-class activities and assignments that require students to practice using the course content.

1.6   TBL Structure

Shifting from simply familiarizing students with course concepts to requiring that students use those concepts to solve problems is no small task [16]. The realization of this shift requires changes in the roles of both instructor and students. The instructor's primary role shifts from dispensing information to designing and managing the overall instructional process. On the other hand, the students' role shifts from being passive recipients of information to actively responding to initial exposure to the course content during the process of preparing for in-class teamwork. Changes of this magnitude do not happen automatically and may even seem improbable. They are, however, achievable when the four essential elements of TBL are implemented successfully [16]:

- Teams: groups of students must be properly formed and managed
- Accountability: students must be accountable for the quality of their individual and group work
- Feedback: instructors must provide frequent and timely feedback to students
- Assignment design: group questions must promote both learning and team development

When these four elements are implemented in a course, the stage is set for student groups to evolve into cohesive learning teams [16].

1.7   Advantages of TBL

Forming student teams for group work, even in a casual manner, produces benefits that cannot be achieved with students's being in a strictly passive learning role. While even the casual use of teams is beneficial, it must be stressed that team-based learning allows the achievement and maintenance of important outcomes only through consistent utilization of the method. Some of these benefits include [16]: 1) developing students' higher level cognitive skills in large classes, 2) providing social support for "at-risk" students, 3) promoting the development of interpersonal and team skills, and 4) building and maintaining faculty members' enthusiasm for their teaching role.

2   Methods

This study was conducted to implement digital models and Team Based Learning (TBL) approach in the magnetic induction portion of a   physics class. This research was done in a group consisting of 36 Grade 9 students at a public junior high school in Jakarta, Indonesia.

Magnetic induction is a part of Indonesia's physics curriculum for the junior high school level. This material is chosen because of students' difficulty in grasping the concept of induction with prior utilization of direct classroom demonstration. Some animations or digital models had been created but garnered no significant result, presumably because of the passive role that the students still assumed. Thus, TBL was applied as an attempt to make students construct knowledge actively.

This research conducted a blended learning model; that is, the course taught magnetic induction with part traditional (in-person) lectures and part modern ICT over internet [17]. This course consisted of three stages: online learning, first in-person, and second in-person sessions. Fig. 1 shows the research design's stages.

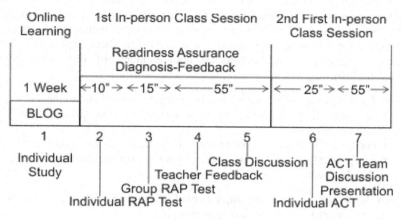

Fig. 1. Research Design [16]

During the online learning stage, students learned the material by watching digital models that were uploaded onto the teacher's blog. The 'video presentation' materials consisted of presentation slides on Magnetic Induction along with the teacher's audio explanation, generated with *Camtasia Studio*. Every student could to study this video's contents independently, one week prior to the implementation of the next learning stage. They could access video presentation multiple times until they achieved good understanding on the topic.

At in-person stages, students completed a test and collaborated in a small group. The first in-person meeting had the students perform an RAP (Readiness Assurance Process) test individually for 10 minutes. The RAP gauged a student's comprehension of the concept through 10 multiple-choice questions, each of which had four answer choices. Students must distribute a total of 4 points to each question. This way, the students could receive partial credit based on their point distributions on the questions. An RAP test has a maximum possible score of 40. After the individual RAP testing, students split into nine groups (four students per group) with systematic grouping to ensure uniform distribution of genders and comprehension levels. Teachers checked the individual students' RAP tests while the students discussed the questions within their groups. The groups RAP's worksheet was a scratched paper. The students could scratch their group answer for every question. If they got a star in the first scratch, they would get 4 point for one question. For the second scratch, they got 2 point and 1 point for third scratch. From the individual and group RAP answers, the teacher compiled the wrong answers as basis for reviewing the RAP worksheet. At the end of the review, students could ask for a more in-depth explanation if confusion still remained. This first in-person meeting would last for approximately 80 minutes.

In the second in-person meeting, the students completed the Application Concept Test (ACT), which consisted of two essay questions. The student wrote out explanations to their answers individually then discussed those explanations with their team. This session also lasted for 80 minutes. The discourse among the team members is the key characteristic feature of students' engagement in their learning.

3   Discussions

The most important preparation for this research was to the creation of the video presentation and their subsequent uploading to the teacher's blog. The magnetic induction presentation consisted of fifteen power point slides. The details of each slide's content are shown in Table 1. All slides were synched with the recorded explanations with *Camtasia Recorder* version 3.0. The video's duration was 12:38.

The video presentation was saved in mpeg format with 720-pixel frame width and 576-pixel frame height. This screen resolution size produced a video that was difficult to see. However, higher resolutions led to data size that was too large. The total data size of the final video was 300 MB, which was too large for internet uploads in Indonesia. Thus, the file was split into three parts for easier uploads and downloads. Fig. 2 shows a screen capture of video presentation.

Table 1. Power Point Presentation's Description

Slide Number	Description
Slide 1	Introduction and definition of magnetic induction
Slide 2	Animation about galvanometer when a wire was moved between magnetic poles
Slide 3-5	Animation about how to create electromagnetic induction in AC and DC powers
Slide 6-8	Animation about the direction of Induced Electromotive Force (EMF)
Slide 9-11	Animation about factors affecting EMF
Slide 12-15	Animation about tools that uses the working principle of electromagnetic induction

The RAP test consisted of ten conceptual questions, all of which were based on the video presentation. The questions covered definitions, examples, and tools for creating magnetic induction. This test also covered how magnetic induction could be created as well as factors that influenced EMF.

The entire study was completed within two weeks; the first week was spent on Stage 1 while the second week was split between Stages 2 and 3. The following details the results from each step:

Stage 1: Online Learning
Students had the opportunity to learn independently during in Stage 1 at their own convenience since virtually, the blog can be accessed anytime after school for the number of times the students needed until adequate comprehension was achieved. Half of the research participants repeated the video more than three times. By doing this repetition, students have well understanding about the topics.

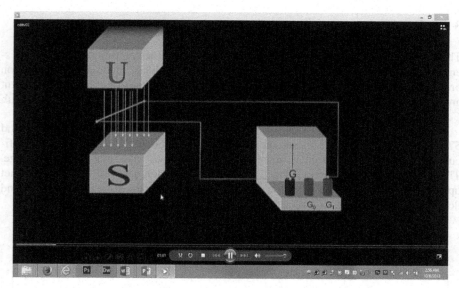

Fig. 2. Screen Capture of Video Presentation

Stage 2: First In-person Class Session
For the first ten minutes of class, students took the RAP test individually. Students can earn partial credit through point allocations for each question. For example, if a student is confident that the correct choice is "A", all 4 points would be assigned to "A". However, if a student is fairly certain of the answer "A", but is hesitant to rule out "C", they could allot 3 points to "A" and 1 to "C". After students had completed the RAP test individually, the teacher collected the worksheets and had the students discuss and decide on their group answers. They seemed happy to work in groups. They can evaluate their own answers. If they do not find "star" in the first scratch, they discuss their answers again to find the correct answer.

Based on the individual and group RAP worksheets, most of mistakes came from the question on factors that influenced EMF. After the individual and group RAP test were completed, the teacher gave explanations on common mistakes. The teacher also replayed parts of the video presentation that covered concepts that most of the students missed. This session concluded with a question and answer session.

Stage 3: Second In-person Class Session
This session begins with individual ACT that lasted for twenty minutes. After this test, the students returned to their groups to discuss and prepare a presentation on their ACT answers. Students were allowed to present with a flip chart or power point. During the presentation, the class was allowed to ask questions to the presenters.

4   Conclusion

TBL can be a solution to improve the use of digital media in teaching and learning processes. TBL helps students to self-evaluate their learning outcomes through small groups. The use of digital models without strict control can lead to misconceptions about student comprehension of course materials. Additionally, TBL can help teachers provide a quick feedback mechanism to student learning outcomes. Moreover, TBL improves students' ability to learn independently and to present their ideas coherently. This ability is important to transform students into independent learners, one of key features for engaging students in not just science learning but in their overall academic experience.

References

1. Hasil, P. K. D. P. Pembelajaran IPA dan Matematika di Sekolah Dasar, Oleh: Rigiarti, Hendra K. 2, Puput Eriska W. 3, Dedi, PN 4, Uswatun Khasanah 5 PGSD FKIP Universitas Sebelas Maret. Jl. Slamet Riyadi No. 449, Surakarta 57126, http://jurnal.fkip.uns.ac.id/index.php/pgsdkebumen/.../208 (viewed October 20, 2013)
2. Taraban, R., Box, C., Myers, R., Polard, R., Bowen, C.W.: Effects of Active-Learning Experiences on Achievement, Attitudes, and Behaviors in High School Biology. Journal of Research in Science Teaching 44, 960–979 (2007)
3. Roth, W., Roychoudhury, A.: Physics Students' Epistemologies and Views about Knowing and Learning. Journal of Research in Science Teaching 40(suppl), S114–S139 (2003), http://www.ristek.go.id/file/upload/File/profil/jakstra2010/193MKpIV2010JAKSTRANAS.pdf
4. Marx, R.W., Blumenfeld, P.C., Krajcik, J.S., Fishman, B., Soloway, E., Geier, R., Tal, R.T.: Inquiry-Based Science in the Middle Grades: Assessment of Learning in Urban Systemic Reform. Journal of Research in Science Teaching 41, 1063–1080 (2004)
5. Coll, R.K., France, B., Taylor, I.: The Role of Models and Analogies in Science Education: Implications from Research. International Journal of Science Education 27(2), 183–198 (2005)
6. Linn, M.: Technology and Science Education: Starting Points, Research Programs, and Trends. International Journal of Science Education 25(6) (2003)
7. PKBPDPDPN (Pusat Kurikulum Badan Penelitian dan Pengembangan Departemen Pendidikan Nasional). Naskah Akademik Kajian Kebijakan Kurikulum Mata Pelajaran IPA (2007), http://puskurbuk.net/web/download/prod2007/51_Kajian%20Kebijakan%20Kurikulum%20IPA.pdf
8. Brindley, C., Scoffield, S.: Peer Assessment in Undergraduate Programmes. Teaching in Higher Education 3(1), 79–90 (1998)
9. Morgan, C.T., King, R.A., Weisz, J.R., Schopler, J.: Introduction to Psychology. McGraw-Hill International Edition, Singapore (1986)
10. Rapp, D.N., Sengupta, P.: Models and Modeling in Science Learning. In: Encyclopedia of the Sciences of Learning, pp. 2320–2322 (2012)
11. Ornek, F.: Models in Science Education: Applications of Models in Learning and Teaching Science. International Journal of Environmental & Science Education 3(2), 35–45 (2008)
12. Greca, I.M., Moreire, M.A.: Mental models, conceptual models, and modeling. International Journal of Science Education 1, 1–11 (2000)

13. Buckley, B.C., Gobert, J.D., Kindfield, A.C.H., Horwitz, P., Tinker, R.F., Gerlits, B., Wilensky, U., et al.: Model-based teaching and learning with BioLogica: What do they learn? How do they learn? How do we know? Journal of Science Education and Technology 13, 23–41 (2004)
14. Hsien, T.C., Lin, T.H., Chin, C.C., Chi, C.J.: Students' Concept Learning in Digital Learning Context–Atom and Molecule. In: Proceeding of the 2nd NICE Symposium, Taipei, Taiwan (2007)
15. Luján-Mora, S., de Juana-Espinosa, S.: The Use of Weblogs in Higher Education: Benefits and Barriers. In: Proceedings of the International Technology, Education and Development Conference (INTED 2007), March 7-9, pp. 1–7. IATED, Valencia (2006) ISBN: 978-84-611-4517-1
16. Michaelsen, L.K., Sweet, M.: The Essential Elements of Team-Based Learning. New Directions for Teaching and Learning 116, 7–21 (2008)
17. Nedelko, Z.: Participant Characteristics for E-learning. In: Leadership Conferences. E-Leader, Krakow (2008)

Improving Reusability of OER

Educational Patterns for Content Sharing

Peter Baumgartner

Donau-Universität Krems (Danube University Krems)
peter.baumgartner@donau-uni.ac.at

Abstract. The effect of Open Educational Resources (OER) on Higher Education is still disappointing. (Re)use of materials, which can be accessed and employed freely, has not developed in such a way that it has changed the attitudes and behavior of teachers. After analyzing several aspects of the problem the article will focus on educational reasons to improve this situation. It is argued that to strive for context free learning objects is heading in the wrong direction. The author proposes to link OER not only with an educational taxonomy of learning outcomes but also with typical patterns of educational scenarios.

1 Barriers to Overcome for Using OER

The work for reusable learning objects (RLO's) started almost 15 years ago [1–3]. In combination with the idea of open educational resources (OER) – material, which can be accessed and used freely – it was assumed that the typical provision of learning material would change radically: from printed material protected by copyright to OER delivered electronically by the internet.

There is growing critique about the missing impact of RLO & OER in Higher Education. In February 2013 Gerd Kortemayer summed up the situation in educause.edu: "OERs have not noticeably disrupted the traditional business model of higher education or affected daily teaching approaches at most institutions" [4]. He is only one member of the increasing camp of skeptics and there are many different assumptions why there is so little success and acceptance of OER. The following paragraphs summarize some of the hurdles to overcome.

1.1 Difficulty to Find the Appropriate Learning Material

It is still not easy to find quickly the appropriate material for the intended learning/teaching purpose. There exist different dimensions of this problem:

— *Economy of scale*: Even with objects in the magnitude order of billions we face the problem of dragnet investigation. We are not looking for educational material as such but for an object with many detailed characteristics. This desired list of qualities are linked with the "and" operator and are therefore limiting the search result with every additional property. It is very doubtful if teachers trying to find these kinds of specified objects might succeed. Imagine for instance a teacher searching

Linawati et al. (Eds.): ICT-EurAsia 2014, LNCS 8407, pp. 277–285, 2014.

- for a course in a specified subject (e.g. mathematics)
- for a specified very detailed teaching/learning area (e.g. factorizing quadratic trinomials)
- for a specified pedagogical strategy (e.g. to explain, to practice, to demonstrate, to visualize)
- for a specified language (e.g. German)
- for a specified target group (e.g. adults with rudimental mathematic knowledge/experience)
- for a specified number of learners
- for a certain learning time (in hours)
- for a specified learning environment or learning platform (e.g. lecture hall, moodle, etc.)
- for a specified license model (e.g. creative common: by name, commercial and share alike)
- ...

— *Educational metadata*: In spite of sophisticated federated search engines and well known huge content portals we are still missing a formal educational taxonomy where important sectors of the educational community can agree. The LOM-standard is for the above specified educational purposes ridiculous weak. What does it mean for instance that some educational elements like level of interactivity, semantic density, and difficulty vary in five categories (very easy, easy, medium, difficult, very difficult)? And what is the yardstick for these properties and who judges them? – But even though there are agreed application profiles: Who will undertake the tedious task of filling in all the many necessary details? Experiences show that most of the material collected in portals or found with sophisticated search engines lack educational metadata at all.

— *Educational culture*: There is the well know problem to overcome the barrier that objects created for a limited personal usage have to undergo still a long and cumbersome enterprise to make it fool proof for every possible standard situations. Who will get the payoff for this work? In order to promote the development and improvement of OER educational systems would have to cherish exchange or gift cultures in contrast to traditionally predominant business models.

— *Educational quality assurance*: Evaluating the quality of OER for learning/teaching purposes has to overcome different hurdles:

- Who has the necessary qualification and authority? This is not only a question of competence but in a participatory community model also a question of regulatory procedure and power relations.
- What kind of agreed and fast procedure is to follow? The blind peer review as the traditional model of quality assurance in science is not only far too slow but also seems inadequate in an open community model of fine grained different needs and diverse interest/target groups committed to a variety of educational models and approaches.

As one can see I have focused my list of difficulties to the organizational and pedagogical sphere and not elaborated on technical problems related to RLO's and

OER. This concentration on organizational and educational issues is not only governed by my own competences in pedagogy but is also a result of my conviction that we have to enforce the pedagogical point of view in order to move forward OER practices considerably.

1.2   For a Conceptual Turn – Context (not Content) Is King

During the last 15 years I have argued from an educational point of view that content is just another element of the complex learning situation (also known as "context"). I have stressed the relationship of educational theory such as behaviorism, cognitivism and constructivism to the dynamics of content provision [5]. I described the different learning attitudes as Learning I, II and III and demonstrated the different perspective to the role of content in these three models. Only in "Learning I" is the transfer of "correct" or "true" knowledge the predominant strategy. In constructivist environments ("Learning III") even "bad" content can be used to the best advantage of learning processes (e.g. when students have to find mistakes and wrong assumptions in order to improve or elaborate the material).

I believe that there are two key features essential for a paradigmatic turn:

From Sender/Receiver Model to the Self-determined Learner. The idea that high reusable content has to be context free as much as possible is still following the – at least in education – long ago outdated communication model where the teacher (sender) is just transmitting neutral information to the learner (receiver). The congenial categorical teaching model of this approach is the so-called "educational triangle" (cf. Fig. 1), which has only a unidirectional sequence from teacher to learner transferring the content [6, 7].

Nowadays categorical teaching models are not only more complex but are centered on the learner and not on the teacher. In addition to simply transfer content there is also the contextual/situational learning challenge learner have to meet. (Cf. as an example of an advanced categorical educational model Fig. 2. The numbers in the diagramm shows all the different bilateral connections as a subset of a dynamic network of the huge variety of possible relationships between the different educational categories.)

Additionally we know that various types of motivations shape learning experiences essentially. This qualification refers not only to the somewhat crude and well known distinction of external and internal motivation but also – as Deci/Ryan have shown empirically and convincingly – to different degrees between these opposites [8–10].

From Thinking in Separated Modules to a Holistic Network Approach. The second new important change in the conceptual orientation to overcome problems in using OER is abandoning the so-called Lego approach of learning objects. According to this now criticized view we have to build small content units with standardized interfaces [12–14, 1, 3]. Similar like Lego's building blocks we can assemble complex structures by putting these different components via their interfaces together. A consequence of using the Lego metaphor is the discussion on granularity: How small grained should the standardized building block be? [15–17].

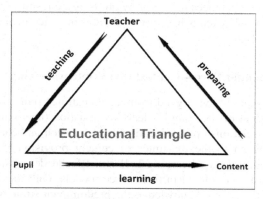

Fig. 1. Educational Triangle

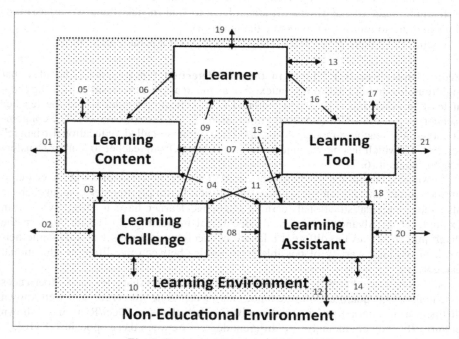

Fig. 2. Categorical Educational Model [11]

But this approach does not even work with Lego as the ingenious enterprise knows. Lego is providing quite a different range of building blocks to support a variety of usage and construction ideas (cf. Fig. 3). And as one can see the heuristic rule "build content block as small as possible in order to be maximized for reuse" does not work even in the basic metaphor: The Lego "atom" cannot provide even for the simple constructions in the right hand upper blue arc sitting on a red bridge.

Fig. 3. Lego: Uniform buildings block do not match the variety of user wants

But what is wrong with a module approach in pedagogy? Aren't we using this conception of building blocks, so-called "modules", for the development of our course curricula as well? No, there is one big difference: Planning a curriculum is a holistic enterprise, starting top-down, not bottom-up: The first question is: "What are the learning outcomes (necessarily acquired competences) for a specific curriculum?" Only after answering this primal question we are concerned with modularization. Knowing all the time that a good curriculum should not only have modules which build on each other but also have as many relations between modules as possible. The Lego approach in learning objects goes the reverse direction: "What are feasible small learning units which could be used many times in different situation/curricula so that there is a high return of investments (ROI) for the development costs?".

From the educational point of view there is also a ROI schema, which is very different: I call it the Reusability of Instruction paradox (ROI paradox): Instead of a standardized learning environment which covers all possible situations the art of instructional design has to reflect and integrate all the different contextual conditions of the learning environment in order to be a learning process of high efficiency. Some of the questions to be answered and to be accounted for are:

- What is the specific purpose of the intended learning process?
- What is the previous knowledge/experience of the learners?
- How much time is available (for learner as well as for teacher)?
- What group size is expected?
- What kind of (virtual) educational environment can be accounted for?
- What kind of intervention for the intended learning outcome is most appropriate?
- …

In the rest of the article I will outline an alternative approach of building blocks for dynamic and interrelated learning processes.

2   Reestablish the Wholeness of the Learning Situation

2.1   The Reconceptualization of the Learning Object

The main problem of the Lego approach for learning object is the destruction of the wholeness of the learning situation. One part of a complex learning arrangement – the learning content – is taken as the representative for the interrelated connection of all parts. The consequence is a certain overemphasis of content ("Content is king") and a fallback to the education triangle model. To distinguish this extended conception I will change the name "learning object" of this building block with regard to content to information object (IO). To reestablish the wholeness of the learning experience we would need to focus our attention of all the relevant elements of the educational situation. I call the collection of these interrelated parts the educational scenario (ES).

But how are these two essential parts of every learning situation linked together? The glue that brings them together and attaches them to each other is the learning target (LT). Nowadays educational specialists distinguish between learning goals and learning outcomes. As far as this paper is concerned I will use both terms equivalent. Therefore we have saved the abbreviation "LO" (learning object) for the whole new construction (cf. Fig. 4).

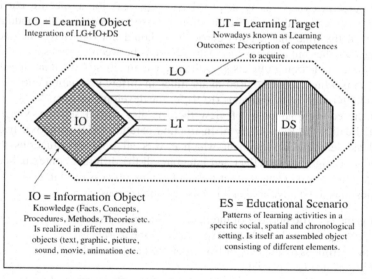

Fig. 4. The parts of the new learning object

2.2 Educational Repositories Instead of Just Content Repositories

Instead of content portals where one can find just information objects the new educational repository consists of three different collections:

— *Information Objects (IO):* This repository has a similar structure like the content repositories we already know. The only differences are shown in the classification part of the LOM metadata. Especially the "Purpose" element has to be reconceptionalized in a much more formal way. It has to be based on a sophisticated taxonomy of learning objectives. Either the enhanced taxonomy of Bloom [18–21] or the approach of Marzano/Kendall [22, 23] could be used.

It is important to understand that the same information object could be used for different learning targets. For instance, using the vocabulary of the revised taxonomy by Anderson and colleagues one information object could be targeted at different cognitive process dimensions: remember, understand, apply, analyze, evaluate, create. In that case the information object would need alternative classification elements.

— *Learning Target (LT):* These days the description of learning outcomes for modules or courses is obligatory. Therefore it should be easy to collect and provide this essential information and to pack it into a searchable object. But there is still some homework to be done: The used vocabulary has to be restricted to a chosen taxonomy of learning objectives. This chosen taxonomy has to be made explicit and their vocabulary has to be used throughout the whole system, e.g. the collection of learning targets, information objects and educational scenarios have to apply the same taxonomy.

— *Educational Scenario (ES):* Here is the real challenge: We do not have an agreed taxonomy of educational scenarios and we are also lacking a formal system of descriptions in order to specify the dynamic and complexity of these elements of the learning situation. In some educational communities the pattern language approach of the architect Christopher Alexander [24–26] is discussed as a possible candidate for this kind of description [27–31]. This discussion is grounded on the conception of teaching as a design science and community endeavor [32]. There is also starting a lively debate about philosophical underpinnings of this approach after Alexander has published his four volume magnum opus "The Nature of Order" [33].

3 Summary and Outlook

Especially on the educational side of the learning object equation much work has still to be done. We need a huge collection of educational scenarios based on a (somewhat) formalized description system, which could be derived from the Alexandrian pattern language approach.

The result would be a new kind of educational repository as demonstrated in figure 5. At edu-sharing.net, an interdisciplinary community of computer scientists, psychologists, educational specialists, teachers and administrators are currently constructing and exploring the viability of the conceptual approach described in this paper.

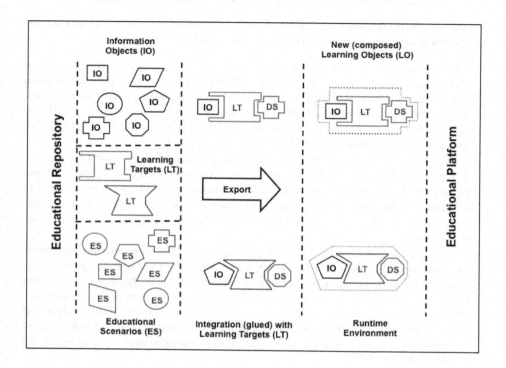

References

1. Hodgins, H.W.: The future of learning objects. Educ. Technol. 46, 49 (2006)
2. Longmire, W.: A primer on learning objects. Learn. Circuits 1 (2000)
3. McGreal, R.: Learning objects: A practical definition. Int. J. Instr. Technol. Distance Learn. 1, 21–32 (2004)
4. Kortemeyer, G.: Ten Years Later: Why Open Educational Resources Have Not Noticeably Affected Higher Education, and Why We Should Care,
   http://www.educause.edu/ero/article/ten-years-later-why-open-educational-resources-have-not-noticeably-affected-higher-education-and-why-we-should-ca
5. Baumgartner, P.: The Zen Art of Teaching - Communication and Interactions in eEducation. In: Auer, M.E., Auer, U. (eds.) ICL 2003. Kassel University Press, Villach (2004)
6. Fricke, R.: Methoden der Evaluation von E-Learning-Szenarien im Hochschulbereich. In: Meister, D.M. (ed.) Evaluation von E-Learning: Zielrichtungen, Methodologische Aspekte, Zukunftsperspektiven, pp. 91–107. Waxmann (2004)
7. Schulmeister, R.: Didaktisches Design aus hochschuldidaktischer Sicht: ein Plädoyer für offene Lernsituationen. In: Meister, D.M., Rinn, U. (eds.) Didaktik und neue Medien: Konzepte und Anwendungen in der Hochschule. Waxmann (2004)
8. Deci, E.L., Ryan, R.M.: Handbook of self-determination research. University of Rochester Press, Rochester (2002)

9. Ryan, R.M., Deci, E.L.: Intrinsic and extrinsic motivations: Classic definitions and new directions. Contemp. Educ. Psychol. 25, 54–67 (2000)
10. Ryan, R.M., Deci, E.L.: Self-determination theory and the facilitation of intrinsic motivation, social development, and well-being. Am. Psychol. 55, 68 (2000)
11. Baumgartner, P.: Taxonomie von Unterrichtsmethoden: Ein Plädoyer für didaktische Vielfalt. Waxmann, Münster (2011)
12. Baumgartner, P.: Didaktische Arrangements und Lerninhalte - Zum Verhältnis von Inhalt und Didaktik im E-Learning. In: Baumgartner, P., Reinmann, G. (eds.) Überwindung von Schranken durch E-Learning, pp. 149–176. Studienverlag, Innsbruck (2007)
13. Wiley, D.A.: The post-LEGO learning object (1999)
14. Parrish, P.E.: The trouble with learning objects. Educ. Technol. Res. Dev. 52, 49–67 (2004)
15. Ip, A., Morrison, I., Currie, M.: What is a learning object, technically? In: WebNet, pp. 580–586 (2001)
16. McGreal, R.: Online education using learning objects. Routledge (2004)
17. Polsani, P.R.: Use and abuse of reusable learning objects. J. Digit. Inf. 3 (2006)
18. Bloom, B.S.: Taxonomy of educational objectives; the classification of educational goals. Longmans, Green (1956)
19. Anderson, L.W.: Revising Bloom's taxonomy. Ohio State University, Columbus (2002)
20. Anderson, L.W., Krathwohl, D.R.: A taxonomy for learning, teaching, and assessing: a revision of Bloom's taxonomy of educational objectives. Longman, New York (2001)
21. Anderson, L.W., Sosniak, L.A., Bloom, B.S.: National Society for the Study of Education: Bloom's taxonomy: a forty-year retrospective. NSSE: Distributed by the University of Chicago Press, Chicago (1994)
22. Marzano, R.J., Kendall, J.S.: The new taxonomy of educational objectives. Corwin Press, Thousand Oaks (2007)
23. Marzano, R.J., Kendall, J.S.: American Association of School Administrators. National Association of Elementary School Principals (U.S.), N.A. of S.S.P. (U. S.), Designing & assessing educational objectives: applying the new taxonomy. Corwin Press, Thousand Oaks (2008)
24. Alexander, C.: Notes on the synthesis of form. Harvard University Press, Cambridge (1964)
25. Alexander, C.: The timeless way of building. Oxford University Press, New York (1979)
26. Alexander, C., Ishikawa, S., Silverstein, M.: A pattern language: towns, buildings, construction. Oxford University Press, New York (1977)
27. Bagert, D., Bergin, J.: Pedagogical patterns: advice for educators. Joseph Bergin Software Tools, Pleasantville, NY (2012)
28. Köppe, C.: A Pattern Language for Teaching Design Patterns (Part 1). In: Proceedings of the 16th European Conference on Pattern Languages of Programs, pp. 2:1–2:21. ACM, New York (2012)
29. Kohls, C.: A Pattern Language for Online Trainings. In: EuroPLoP (2009)
30. Bauer, R., Baumgartner, P.: Showcase of learning: towards a pattern language for working with electronic portfolios in higher education. Presented at the EuoPLopP 2011, New York, NY, USA (2011)
31. Kohls, C., Wedekind, J.: Investigations of E-learning Patterns: Context Factors, Problems, and Solutions. Information Science Publishing (2011)
32. Laurillard, D.: Teaching as a design science: building pedagogical patterns for learning and technology. Routledge, New York (2012)
33. Alexander, C.: The nature of order: an essay on the art of building and the nature of the universe, 4. vols. Center for Environmental Structure, Berkeley (2002)

Online Learning for Two Novel Latent Topic Models

Ali Shojaee Bakhtiari[1] and Nizar Bouguila[2]

[1] Department of Electrical and Computer Engineering
Concordia University, Montreal, QC, Canada
al_sho@encs.concordia.ca
[2] Concordia Institute for Information Systems Engineering
Concordia University, Montreal, QC, Canada
nizar.bouguila@concordia.ca

Abstract. Latent topic models have proven to be an efficient tool for modeling multitopic count data. One of the most well-known models is the latent Dirichlet allocation (LDA). In this paper we propose two improvements for LDA using generalized Dirichlet and Beta-Liouville prior assumptions. Moreover, we apply an online learning approach for both introduced approaches. We choose a challenging application namely natural scene classification for comparison and evaluation purposes.

Keywords: Generalized Dirichlet, Beta-Liouville, online learning, Latent model, variational learning, count data.

1 Introduction

In order to extract the hidden information within count data various models have been proposed in the past. The first widely used model for count data modeling was the naive Bayes model combined with multinomial distribution [14,6,1]. However several researchers proceeded with mentioning the oversimplifications and the subsequent drawbacks of the Naive Bayes assumption [13,5,8]. The foremost solution offered to compensate for the deficiencies of the naive assumption was considering the Dirichlet distribution [13,5] as the prior assumption for the multinomial distribution. Based on the Dirichlet assumption, several models have been developed for proper count data modeling. One model that has gained much acceptance among the research community is the latent Dirichlet allocation (LDA) model firstly proposed in [2]. LDA model uses a Bayesian model for data generation using a variational Bayes (VB) approach for parameter inference. The majority of the models developed thus far have been based on the Dirichlet prior assumption. However, researchers began questioning the merit of Dirichlet assumption [7]. The main drawback of the Dirichlet assumption is the fact that it has a strictly negative covariance matrix and therefore it inherently fails to properly model the data in which topics have positive correlation in between. The other main drawback of the Dirichlet distribution is the fact that the elements with similar mean need to have similar variance, which clearly is an

Linawati et al. (Eds.): ICT-EurAsia 2014, LNCS 8407, pp. 286–295, 2014.

oversimplification. To overcome these shortcomings research has recently been shifted towards finding models with better modeling accuracy.

Recently it has been shown that the generalized Dirichlet distribution is a good replacement for the Dirichlet distribution when using finite mixture models [3]. One important factor of the generalized Dirichlet is that like Dirichlet distribution it is a conjugate prior to the multinomial distribution. Generalized Dirichlet distribution also does not carry the restrictions of the Dirichlet distribution and allows more relaxed modeling capabilities. Another modeling prior that has recently attracted notice is the Beta-Liouville distribution [7]. The advantage point of the Beta-Liouville distribution in comparison to generalized Dirichlet is that it requires only two more parameters to be estimated compared to Dirichlet distribution compared with the twice the parameters the generalized Dirichlet distribution requires. Based on the above facts we proceed with proposing two different latent topic models based on the LDA model but with the generalized Dirichlet and the Beta-Liouville assumptions. The former model is called latent generalized Dirichlet allocation (LGDA) and the latter is called latent Beta-Liouville allocation (LBLA). The learning of both models is performed online using the approach proposed in [10].

The structure of the paper is as follows. In section 2, we introduce the LGDA and LBLA models. In section 3 we shall describe the adaption of the online learning model on the two models. In section 4 we shall bring the experimental results and we will finalize the paper with conclusion.

2   Proposed Latent Topic Models

In this section we briefly describe the two proposed latent topic models. Both models essentially have the same generative model as the LDA:

1. Choose $N \propto Poisson(\zeta)$.
2. Choose $(\theta_1, \ldots, \theta_d) \propto Dir(\boldsymbol{\xi})$.
3. For each of the N words w_n:
   (a) choose a topic $z_n \propto Multinomial(\boldsymbol{\theta})$.
   (b) Choose a word w_n from $p(w_n|z_n, \beta_w)$.

In above z_n is a d dimensional binary vector of topics defined so that $z_n^i = 1$ if the $i - th$ topic is chosen and zero, otherwise. We define, $\boldsymbol{\theta} = (\theta_1, \ldots, \theta_d)$. A chosen topic is attributed to a multinomial prior β_w over the vocabulary of words so that $\beta_{w(ij)} = p(w^j = 1|z^i = 1)$, from which every word is randomly drawn. $p(w_n|z_n, \beta_w)$ is a multinomial probability conditioned on z_n and $Dir(\boldsymbol{\xi})$ is a d-variate Dirichlet distribution with parameters $\boldsymbol{\xi} = (\alpha_1, \ldots, \alpha_d)$. The main inference problem of LGDA is estimating the posterior of the hidden variables, $\boldsymbol{\theta}$ and $\boldsymbol{z}$:

$$p(\boldsymbol{\theta}, \boldsymbol{z}|\boldsymbol{w}, \boldsymbol{\xi}, \beta_w) = \frac{p(\boldsymbol{\theta}, \boldsymbol{z}, \boldsymbol{w}|\boldsymbol{\xi}, \beta_w)}{p(\boldsymbol{w}|\boldsymbol{\xi}, \beta_w)} \tag{1}$$

The above equation is known to be intractable. As proposed in [2], an efficient way to estimate the parameters of this intractable posterior is to use the vibrational Bayes (VB) inference. VB inference offers a solution to the intractability problem by determining a lower bound on the log likelihood of the observed data which is mainly based on considering a set of vibrational distributions on the hidden variables [11]:

$$q(\boldsymbol{\theta}, \boldsymbol{z} | \boldsymbol{w}, \boldsymbol{\xi_q}, \boldsymbol{\Phi_w}) = q(\boldsymbol{\theta} | \boldsymbol{\xi_q}) \prod_{n=1}^{N} q(z_n | \phi_n) \qquad (2)$$

The details of the parameter estimation algorithm can de found in [2]. In this section we proceed with introducing LGDA and LBLA subsequently.

2.1 Latent Generalized Dirichlet Allocation

The major difference between the LGDA and the LDA model is the consideration of the generalized Dirichlet assumption:

1. Choose $N \propto Poisson(\zeta)$.
2. Choose $(\theta_1, \ldots, \theta_d) \propto GenDir(\boldsymbol{\xi})$.
3. For each of the N words w_n:
   (a) choose a topic $z_n \propto Multinomial(\boldsymbol{\theta})$.
   (b) Choose a word w_n from $p(w_n | z_n, \beta_w)$.

In above z_n is a $d+1$ dimensional binary vector of topics defined so that $z_n^i = 1$ if the $i - th$ topic is chosen and zero, otherwise. We define, $\boldsymbol{\theta} = (\theta_1, \ldots, \theta_{d+1})$, where $\theta_{d+1} = 1 - \sum_{i=1}^{d} \theta_i$. A chosen topic is attributed to a multinomial prior β_w over the vocabulary of words so that $\beta_{w_{(ij)}} = p(w^j = 1 | z^i = 1)$, from which every word is randomly drawn. $p(w_n | z_n, \beta_w)$ is a multinomial probability conditioned on z_n and $GenDir(\boldsymbol{\xi})$ is a d-variate generalized Dirichlet distribution with parameters $\boldsymbol{\xi} = (\alpha_1, \beta_1, \ldots, \alpha_d, \beta_d)$ and probability distribution function given by:

$$p(\theta_1, \ldots, \theta_d | \boldsymbol{\xi}) = \prod_{i=1}^{d} \frac{\Gamma(\alpha_i + \beta_i)}{\Gamma(\alpha_i)\Gamma(\beta_i)} \theta_i^{\alpha_i - 1} (1 - \sum_{j=1}^{i} \theta_j)^{\gamma_i} \qquad (3)$$

where $\gamma_i = \beta_i - \alpha_{i+1} - \beta_{i+1}$. It is straightforward to show that when $\beta_i = \alpha_{(i+1)} + \beta_{(i+1)}$, the generalized Dirichlet distribution is reduced to Dirichlet distribution [4]. Therefore it is understood that under certain conditions LGDA will also behave like LDA and subsequently LDA is a special case of the LGDA model. To estimate the posterior of the hidden variables of the LGDA model we use a similar VB approach as the one proposed for LDA, where $q(\boldsymbol{\theta} | \boldsymbol{\xi_q})$ can be viewed as a variational generalized Dirichlet distribution, calculated once per document, $q(z_n | \phi_n)$ is a multinomial distribution with parameter ϕ_n extracted once for every single word inside the document, and $\boldsymbol{\Phi_w} = \{\phi_1, \phi_2, \ldots, \phi_N\}$. Using Jensen's inequality [11] one can derive the following:

$$\log p(\boldsymbol{w} | \boldsymbol{\xi}, \beta_w) \geq E_q[\log p(\boldsymbol{\theta}, \boldsymbol{z}, \boldsymbol{w} | \boldsymbol{\xi}, \beta_w)] - E_q[\log q(\boldsymbol{\theta}, \boldsymbol{z})] \qquad (4)$$

Assigning $L(\boldsymbol{\xi_q}, \boldsymbol{\Phi_w}; \boldsymbol{\xi}, \beta_w)$ to the right-hand side of the above equation it can be shown that the difference between the left-hand side and the right-hand side of the equation is the KL divergence between the variational posterior probability and the actual posterior probability, thus we have:

$$\log p(\boldsymbol{w}|\boldsymbol{\xi}, \beta_w) = L(\boldsymbol{\xi_q}, \boldsymbol{\Phi_w}; \boldsymbol{\xi}, \beta_w) + KL\big(q(\boldsymbol{\theta}, \boldsymbol{z}|\boldsymbol{\xi_q}, \boldsymbol{\Phi_w}||p(\boldsymbol{\theta}, \boldsymbol{z})|\boldsymbol{w}, \boldsymbol{\xi}, \beta_w)\big) \quad (5)$$

The left hand side of the above equation is constant in relation to variational parameters, therefore to minimize the KL divergence on the right-hand side one can proceed with maximizing $L(\boldsymbol{\xi_q}, \boldsymbol{\Phi_w}; \boldsymbol{\xi}, \beta_w)$. Up to here the formulation basically follows the LDA model. The divergence of the models begins when we proceed with assigning the generalized Dirichlet distribution as the parameter generator instead of the LDA Dirichlet assumption. The breakdown of $L(\boldsymbol{\xi_q}, \boldsymbol{\Phi_w}; \boldsymbol{\xi}, \beta_w)$ to maximize the lower bound $L(\boldsymbol{\xi_q}, \boldsymbol{\Phi_w}; \boldsymbol{\xi}, \beta_w)$ with respect to ϕ_{nl}, leads to the following updating equations for the variational multinomial:

$$\phi_{nl} = \beta_{lv}e^{(\lambda_n - 1)}e^{(\Psi(\gamma_l) - \Psi(\gamma_l + \delta_l))} \quad \phi_{n(d+1)} = \beta_{(d+1)v}e^{(\lambda_n - 1)}e^{(\Psi(\delta_d) - \Psi(\gamma_d + \delta_d))}(6)$$

where Ψ is the digamma function, $\beta_{lv} = p(w^v = 1|z^l = 1)$ and the weighing constant $e^{\lambda_n - 1}$ is given by:

$$e^{\lambda_n - 1} = \frac{1}{\sum_{l=1}^{d} \beta_{lv}e^{(\Psi(\gamma_l) - \Psi(\gamma_l + \delta_l))} + \beta_{(d+1)v}e^{(\Psi(\delta_d) - \Psi(\gamma_d + \delta_d))}} \quad (7)$$

Maximizing the lower bound L with respect to the variational generalized Dirichlet parameter gives the following updating equations:

$$\gamma_l = \alpha_l + \sum_{n=1}^{N} \phi_{nl} \quad \delta_l = \beta_l + \sum_{n=1}^{N} \sum_{ll=l+1}^{d+1} \phi_{n(ll)} \quad (8)$$

The above equations show that the variational generalized Dirichlet for each document acts as a posterior in the presence of the variational multinomial parameters. The same conclusion was observed in [2] for the LDA case. This is a direct result of the conjugacy between the generalized Dirichlet and the multinomial distribution. The LGDA parameters are corpus parameters and therefore they are estimated by considering all M documents inside the corpus. In the following, we denote $L = \sum_{m=1}^{M} L_m$ as the lower bound corresponding to all the corpus, where L_m is the lower bound corresponding to each document m. Maximizing the corpus lower bound L with respect to $\beta_{w(lj)}$ delivers the following updating equation:

$$\beta_{w(lj)} \propto \sum_{d=1}^{M} \sum_{n=1}^{N_d} \phi_{dnl} w_{dn}^{j} \quad (9)$$

The model's parameters are derived using a Newton-Raphson method.

2.2   Latent Beta-Liouville Allocation

The model that we briefly discuss in this subsection, latent Beta-Liouville allocation (LBLA), is another model developed based on the LDA model. The model
assumes a Beta-Liouville as its topic generating prior. The model proceeds with
generating every single word (or visual word) of the document (or the image)
through the following steps:

1. Choose $N \propto Poisson(\zeta)$.
2. Choose $(\theta_1, \ldots, \theta_D) \propto BL(\boldsymbol{\xi})$.
3. For each of the N words w_n:
   (a) choose a topic $z_n \propto Multinomial(\boldsymbol{\theta})$.
   (b) Choose a word w_n from $p(w_n|z_n, \beta_w)$.

In above z_n is a $D+1$ dimensional binary vector of topics defined so that $z_n^i = 1$
if the $i - th$ topic is chosen and zero, otherwise. We define, $\boldsymbol{\theta} = (\theta_1, \ldots, \theta_{D+1})$,
where $\theta_{D+1} = 1 - \sum_{i=1}^{D} \theta_i$. A chosen topic is attributed to a multinomial prior β_w
over the vocabulary of words so that $\beta_{w(ij)} = p(w^j = 1|z^i = 1)$, from which every
word is randomly drawn. $p(w_n|z_n, \beta_w)$ is a multinomial probability conditioned
on z_n and $BL(\boldsymbol{\xi})$ is a d-variate Beta-Liouville distribution with parameters $\boldsymbol{\xi} =
(\alpha_1, \beta_1, \ldots, \alpha_d, \beta_d)$ and probability distribution function given by:

$$P(\theta_1, \ldots, \theta_D|\boldsymbol{\xi}) = \frac{\Gamma(\sum_{d=1}^{D} \alpha_d)\Gamma(\alpha+\beta)}{\Gamma(\alpha)\Gamma(\beta)} \prod_{d=1}^{D} \frac{\theta_d^{\alpha_d-1}}{\Gamma(\alpha_d)} (\sum_{d=1}^{D} \theta_d)^{\alpha-\sum_{l=1}^{D} \alpha_l} (1 - \sum_{l=1}^{D} \theta_l)^{\beta-1}$$

(10)

where $\gamma_i = \beta_i - \alpha_{i+1} - \beta_{i+1}$. It is straightforward to show that when $\beta_i =
\alpha_{(i+1)} + \beta_{(i+1)}$, the Beta-Liouville distribution is reduced to Dirichlet distribution
[4]. We define, $\boldsymbol{\theta} = (\theta_1, \ldots, \theta_{D+1})$, where $\theta_{D+1} = 1 - \sum_{i=1}^{D} \theta_i$. The maximization
of the lower bound $L(\boldsymbol{\xi_q}, \boldsymbol{\Phi_w}; \boldsymbol{\xi}, \beta_w)$ with respect to ϕ_{nl}, leads to the following
updating equations:

$$\phi_{nl} = \beta_{lv} e^{(\lambda_n-1)} e^{(\Psi(\gamma_i)-\Psi(\sum_{ii=1}^{D} \gamma_{ii}))}$$

(11)

$$\phi_{n(D+1)} = \beta_{(D+1)v} e^{(\lambda_n-1)} e^{(\Psi(\beta_\gamma)-\Psi(\alpha_\gamma+\beta_\gamma))}$$

(12)

where Ψ is the digamma function, $\beta_{lv} = p(w^v = 1|z^l = 1)$ and the weighing
constant e^{λ_n-1} is given by:

$$e^{\lambda_n-1} = \frac{1}{\beta_{(D+1)v} e^{(\Psi(\beta_\gamma)-\Psi(\alpha_\gamma+\beta_\gamma))} + \sum_{i=1}^{D} \beta_{iv} e^{(\Psi(\gamma_d)-\Psi(\sum_{ii=1}^{D} \gamma_{II}))}}$$

(13)

$$\gamma_i = \alpha + \sum_{n=1}^{N} \phi_{ni} \quad \alpha_\gamma = \alpha + \sum_{n=1}^{N} \sum_{d=1}^{D} \phi_{nd} \quad \beta_\gamma = \beta + \sum_{n=1}^{N} \phi_{n(D+1)}$$

(14)

The above equations show that the variational Beta-Liouville for each document acts as a posterior in the presence of the variational multinomial parameters. The same conclusion was observed in [2] for the LDA case. This is a

direct result of the conjugacy between the Beta-Liouville and the multinomial distribution.

One needs to consider that the LBLA parameters are corpus parameters and therefore they are estimated by considering all M documents inside the corpus. In the following, we denote $L = \sum_{m=1}^{M} L_m$ as the lower bound corresponding to all the corpus, where L_m is the lower bound corresponding to each document m. Maximizing the corpus lower bound L with respect to $\beta_{w(lj)}$ delivers the following updating equation:

$$\beta_{w(lj)} \propto \sum_{d=1}^{M} \sum_{n=1}^{N_d} \phi_{dnl} w_{dn}^{j} \tag{15}$$

The model's parameters are the last ones to be derived using a Newton-Raphson algorithm, also.

3   Online Latent Topic Models

The variational Bayes model of the LDA model and the subsequent adaption for the LGDA and LBLA are shown to coverage to a local likelihood of the actual posterior of the hidden parameters of the models. However, the main problem with the original VB approach is that it needs to consider the entire corpus beforehand for parameter estimation. This in return emerges two serious problems. Firstly, the need for the collection of the entire training corpus and secondly the computational requirements of dealing with a huge corpus. To overcome this problem the authors in [10] offered an online learning model that fixes the mentioned issues. The solution is based on a time dependent (time defined as the index of the part of the data given to the model in each iteration) weight:

$$\rho_t \triangleq (\tau_0 + t)^{-\kappa}, \kappa \in (0.5, 1] \tag{16}$$

The parameter τ_0 slows down the effect of early parameter estimations. The online learning algorithm can easily be extended to cover LGDA and LBLA models as well. The steps of the algorithm are as follows.

1. In each learning interval the model performs a batch VB over the patch of the training set attributed to that interval and assigns a weight value to the patch according to 16.
2. Prior parameter estimation: Perform the Newton-Raphson algorithm over the entire corpus for $t = 0$ to ∞ as: $\xi \leftarrow \xi - \rho_t \widetilde{\alpha}(\xi_t)$ where $\widetilde{\alpha}(\xi_t)$ is the inverse of the Hessian times the gradient in respect to α of the posterior lower bound.
3. Word dictionary update: $\widetilde{\beta_w}(t+1) = normalize((1-\rho_t)\widetilde{\beta_{wt}} + \rho_t\beta_w(t))$ where $\widetilde{\beta_w}(t)$ is the available estimation of the word dictionary at t-th step.

It was shown in [10] that the condition $\kappa \in (0.5, 1]$ is necessary for keeping the online learning model stable.

4   Experimental Results

In this section we shall proceed with applying our proposed two models, online LBLA and LGDA, on the challenging task of natural scene classification and make a comparison between the classification success rates offered by the two models versus that of the online LDA. The main idea that we use here is based on the description of scenes using visual words [9]. This approach has emerged over the past few years and received strong interest that is mainly motivated by the fact that many of the techniques previously proposed for text classification can be adopted for images categorization [9,17,16].

For the construction of the visual words vocabulary, we need first to extract local descriptors from a set of training images. Many descriptors have been proposed in the past, but scale invariant feature transform (SIFT) descriptor [12], that we consider here, has dominated the literature. The extracted features are then quantized through clustering (the K-Means algorithm in our case) and the obtained d clusters centroids are considered as our visual words. Having the visual vocabulary in hand, each image can be represented as a d-dimensional vector containing the frequency of each visual word in that image. In our experiment we take 7 classes from the natural scenes dataset introduced in [15]. The 7 classes chosen from the data set described in [15] are coast, forest, highway, inside of cities, open country, street, and tall building, which contain 361, 329, 261, 309, 411, 293, and 356 images, respectively. Examples of images from the different considered classes are shown in figure 1.

Fig. 1. Sample images from each group. (a) Highway, (b) Inside of cities, (c) Tall building, (d) Streets, (e) Forest, (f) Coast, (g) Open country, (h) Bedroom.

4.1   Comparison between the Performance of LBLA and LGDA Models against LDA

At first the models were given 5 chunks of training images each containing 20 images. In this set of experiments the effect of the online learning was

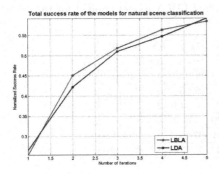
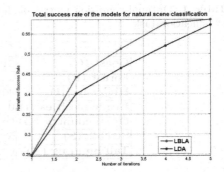

Fig. 2. Comparison of the success rates of the online LBLA model against online LDA model for the natural scene classification application for a training size that equals 20 for two different extracted number of topics

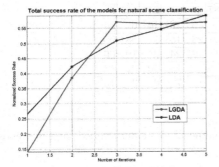
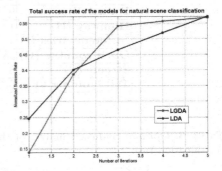

Fig. 3. Comparison of the success rate of the online LGDA model against online LDA model for the natural scene classification application over a training size that equals 20 for two different extracted number of topics

reduced since the small number of iterations plus the big chunks of test data quite resembled the Batch LDA and LGDA models. The results of applying the online LDA and LBLA models are brought in Fig. 2. Under the same experimental conditions we proceed with delivering the results for the LGDA model as well in Fig. 3. The optimal confusion matrix of the online LBLA model is brought in table 1. The optimal confusion matrix of the online LBLA model is brought in table 2 and the optimal confusion matrix of the online LDA model is brought in table 3.

Table 1. Optimal confusion matrix of the online LBLA model applied for the scenes classification task

	C	F	H	I	O	S	T
Coast (C)	216	1	86	3	50	3	2
Forest (F)	3	242	15	53	4	51	0
Highway (H)	40	1	69	5	6	3	15
Inside of cities (I)	0	2	4	146	2	12	6
Open country (O)	90	39	23	22	331	14	50
Streets (S)	5	41	60	57	9	203	2
Tall building (T)	6	2	3	22	8	6	281

Table 2. Optimal confusion matrix of the online LGDA model applied for the scenes classification task

	C	F	H	I	O	S	T
Coast (C)	282	4	130	5	98	7	14
Forest (F)	9	287	24	84	24	167	3
Highway (H)	19	2	55	13	16	6	94
Inside of cities (I)	4	19	23	157	1	58	9
Open country (O)	38	7	19	24	241	19	66
Streets (S)	8	7	8	18	30	32	13
Tall building (T)	0	2	1	7	0	3	157

Table 3. Optimal confusion matrix of the online LDA model applied for the scenes classification task

	C	F	H	I	O	S	T
Coast (C)	316	25	133	40	296	45	175
Forest (F)	1	213	9	25	0	61	0
Highway (H)	1	0	15	0	0	0	0
Inside of cities (I)	2	35	18	187	1	62	14
Open country (O)	31	36	46	27	113	45	14
Streets (S)	0	11	28	3	0	69	0
Tall building (T)	9	8	11	26	0	10	153

5   Conclusion

In this work we proposed two new online learning multitopic models. We performed a series of experiments over a challenging application, natural scene classification, and we showed and compared the merits of our proposed models in comparison with online LDA. The two models show promising results when adapted for the online learning scheme and tend to surpass the online LDA model in the scope of the experiments performed.

Acknowledgments. The completion of this research was made possible thanks to the Natural Sciences and Engineering Research Council of Canada (NSERC).

References

1. Shojaee Bakhtiari, A., Bouguila, N.: A novel hierarchical statistical model for count data modeling and its application in image classification. In: Huang, T., Zeng, Z., Li, C., Leung, C.S. (eds.) ICONIP 2012, Part II. LNCS, vol. 7664, pp. 332–340. Springer, Heidelberg (2012)
2. Blei, D.M., Ng, A.Y., Jordan, M.I.: Latent Dirichlet allocation. Journal of Machine Learning Research 3, 993–1022 (2003)
3. Bouguila, N.: Clustering of count data using generalized dirichlet multinomial distributions. IEEE Trans. Knowl. Data Eng. 20(4), 462–474 (2008)
4. Bouguila, N., Ziou, D.: High-dimensional unsupervised selection and estimation of a finite generalized Dirichlet mixture model based on minimum message length. IEEE Trans. on Pattern Analysis and Machine Intelligence 29(10), 1716–1731 (2007)
5. Bouguila, N., Ziou, D.: Unsupervised learning of a finite discrete mixture: Applications to texture modeling and image databases summarization. Journal of Visual Communication and Image Representation 18(4), 295–309 (2007)
6. Bouguila, N.: A model-based approach for discrete data clustering and feature weighting using map and stochastic complexity. IEEE Trans. Knowl. Data Eng. 21(12), 1649–1664 (2009)
7. Bouguila, N.: Count data modeling and classification using finite mixtures of distributions. IEEE Trans. on Neural Networks 22(2), 186–198 (2011)
8. Bouguila, N., ElGuebaly, W.: A generative model for spatial color image databases categorization. In: Proc. of the IEEE International Conference on Acoustics, Speech, and Signal Processing (ICASSP), pp. 821–824 (2008)
9. Csurka, G., Dance, C.R., Fan, L., Willamowski, J., Bray, C.: Visual categorization with bags of keypoints. In: Workshop on Statistical Learning in Computer Vision, 8th European Conference on Computer Vision (ECCV), pp. 1–12. Springer (2004)
10. Hoffman, M.D., Blei, D.M., Bach, F.R.: Online learning for latent dirichlet allocation. In: NIPS, pp. 856–864 (2010)
11. Jordan, M.I., Ghahramani, Z., Jaakkola, T., Saul, L.K.: An introduction to variational methods for graphical models. Machine Learning 37(2), 183–233 (1999)
12. Lowe, D.G.: Distinctive image features from scale-invariant keypoints. International Journal of Computer Vision 60(2), 91–110 (2004)
13. Madsen, R.E., Kauchak, D., Elkan, C.: Modeling word burstiness using the Dirichlet distribution. In: Proc. of the 22nd International Conference on Machine Learning (ICML), pp. 545–552. ACM Press, Bonn (2005)
14. Nigam, K., McCallum, A., Thrun, S., Mitchell, T.: Text classification from labeled and unlabeled documents using EM. Machine Learning 39(2), 103–134 (2000)
15. Oliva, A., Torralba, A.: Modeling the shape of the scene: A holistic representation of the spatial envelope. International Journal of Computer Vision 42(3), 145–175 (2001)
16. Scalzo, F., Piater, J.: Adaptive patch features for object class recognition with learned hierarchical models. In: Proc. of the IEEE Computer Society Conference on Computer Vision and Pattern Recognition (CVPR), pp. 1–8. IEEE (2007)
17. Weston, J., Bengio, S., Usunier, N.: Large scale image annotation: learning to rank with joint word-image embeddings. Machine Learning 81(1), 21–35 (2010)

An Infinite Mixture Model of Generalized Inverted Dirichlet Distributions for High-Dimensional Positive Data Modeling

Nizar Bouguila[1] and Mohamed Al Mashrgy[2]

[1] Concordia Institute for Information Systems Engineering
Concordia University, Montreal, QC, Canada
nizar.bouguila@concordia.ca
[2] Department of Electrical Engineering
Concordia University, Montreal, QC, Canada
m_almash@encs.concordia.ca

Abstract. We propose an infinite mixture model for the clustering of positive data. The proposed model is based on the generalized inverted Dirichlet distribution which has a more general covariance structure than the inverted Dirichlet that has been widely used recently in several machine learning and data mining applications. The proposed mixture is developed in an elegant way that allows simultaneous clustering and feature selection, and is learned using a fully Bayesian approach via Gibbs sampling. The merits of the proposed approach are demonstrated using a challenging application namely images categorization.

Keywords: Clustering, feature selection, generalized inverted Dirichlet, mixture models, Bayesian inference, image databases.

1 Introduction

The important proliferation of digital content requires the development of powerful approaches for knowledge extraction, analysis, and organization. Clustering, in particular, has been widely adopted for knowledge discovery and data engineering. The main goal of any clustering algorithm is to partition a given data set into groups so that objects within a cluster are more similar than those in different clusters [26]. Many clustering techniques have been developed in the past and have been applied successfully on different data types (e.g. binary, discrete, continuous) extracted within various applications [6,11,15]. Among these techniques, mixture models have played important roles in many areas including (but not confined to) image processing, computer vision, data mining, and pattern recognition, thanks to their flexibility and strong statistical foundations which offer a formal principled way to clustering. In particular, Gaussian mixture model has drawn considerable attention in the machine learning community and has achieved good results [21]. However, recent concentrated research efforts have shown that this mixture model may fail to provide good generalization capabilities when the per-cluster data distributions are clearly non-Gaussian, which is the case of positive data as deeply discussed in [3,2,1].

Linawati et al. (Eds.): ICT-EurAsia 2014, LNCS 8407, pp. 296–305, 2014.

The main contribution of [3,2] was the introduction of the finite inverted Dirichlet mixture model for the clustering of positive data which are naturally generated by many real-world applications. The authors have proposed a detailed approach for the learning of the parameters of this finite mixture, also. In order to handle huge number of classes and avoid over- or under-fitting problems (a.k.a. controlling variance, model selection), which is a central issue in learning-based techniques, the finite inverted Dirichlet mixture was extended to the infinite case in [2]. This extension was based on the consideration of Dirichlet processes which have been widely used in the case of nonparametric Bayesian approaches [9,8]. Despite its advantages and flexibility, the inverted Dirichlet has a very restrictive covariance structure that is generally violated by data generated from real-life applications. Thus, we propose an alternative to the inverted Dirichlet namely the generalized inverted Dirichlet (GID) that has a more general covariance structure. Our work can be viewed as a principled and natural extension to the framework developed in [2], since we consider the GID within an infinite mixture model by taking feature selection into account. The feature selection process is formalized by introducing a background distribution, common to all mixture components, into the infinite model to represent irrelevant features. Moreover, we develop an algorithm for the learning of the resulting model using Markov chain Monte Carlo (MCMC) sampling techniques namely Gibbs sampling and Metropolis-Hastings [20].

The paper is organized as follows: Section 2 presents our infinite mixture model. Section 3 provides empirical evaluation based on the challenging problem of images categorization. Finally, Section 4 concludes the paper.

2 The Model

In this section, we start by presenting the finite GID mixture model, then its infinite counterpart is developed. A feature selection approach is proposed, also.

2.1 Finite Model

Let us consider a data set $\mathcal{Y} = (\boldsymbol{Y}_1, \boldsymbol{Y}_2, \ldots, \boldsymbol{Y}_N)$ of N D-dimensional positive vectors, where $\boldsymbol{Y}_i = (Y_{i1}, \ldots, Y_{iD}), i = 1, \ldots, N$. We assume that $\boldsymbol{Y}_i$ follows a mixture of M GID distributions:

$$p(\boldsymbol{Y}_i|\Theta) = \sum_{j=1}^{M} \pi_j p(\boldsymbol{Y}_i|\Theta_j) \qquad (1)$$

where $p(\boldsymbol{Y}_i|\Theta_j)$ is a GID distribution [18]:

$$p(\boldsymbol{Y}_i|\Theta_j) = \prod_{l=1}^{D} \frac{\Gamma(\alpha_{jl} + \beta_{jl})}{\Gamma(\alpha_{jl})\Gamma(\beta_{jl})} \frac{Y_{il}^{\alpha_{jl}-1}}{T_{il}^{\eta_{jl}}} \qquad (2)$$

where $T_{il} = 1 + \sum_{k=1}^{l} Y_{ik}$ and $\eta_{jl} = \beta_{jl} + \alpha_{jl} - \beta_{j(l+1)}$ with $\beta_{j(D+1)} = 0$. Each $\Theta_j = (\alpha_{j1}, \beta_{j1}, \alpha_{j2}, \beta_{j2}, \ldots, \alpha_{jD}, \beta_{jD})$ is the set of parameters defining the jth component, and π_j is the mixing weight of the jth cluster. Of course, being probabilities, the π_j must satisfy: $\pi_j > 0, j = 1, \ldots, M$, and $\sum_{j=1}^{M} \pi_j = 1$.

In mixture-based clustering [21], each vector $\boldsymbol{Y}_i$ is assigned to all classes with different posterior probabilities $p(j|\boldsymbol{Y}_i) \propto \pi_j p(\boldsymbol{Y}_i|\boldsymbol{\Theta}_j)$. It is possible to show that the properties of the GID distribution allows the factorization of the posterior probabilities as: $p(j|\boldsymbol{Y}_i) \propto \pi_j \prod_{l=1}^{D} p_{ib}(X_{il}|\theta_{jl})$, where $X_{i1} = Y_{i1}$ and $X_{il} = \frac{Y_{il}}{1+\sum_{l=1}^{D} Y_{il}}$ for $l > 1$, $p_{ib}(X_{il}|\theta_{jl})$ is an inverted Beta distribution with $\theta_{jl} = (\alpha_{jl}, \beta_{jl}), l = 1, \ldots, D$:

$$p_{ib}(X_{il}|\alpha_{jl}, \beta_{jl}) = \frac{\Gamma(\alpha_{jl} + \beta_{jl})}{\Gamma(\alpha_{jl})\Gamma(\beta_{jl})} X_{il}^{\alpha_{jl}-1} (1 + X_{il})^{-\alpha_{jl}-\beta_{jl}}$$

Thus, the clustering structure underlying $\mathcal{Y}$ is the same as that underlying $\mathcal{X} = (\boldsymbol{X}_1, \ldots, \boldsymbol{X}_N)$ described by the following mixture model with conditionally independent features:

$$p(\boldsymbol{X}_i|\Theta) = \sum_{j=1}^{M} \pi_j \prod_{l=1}^{D} p_{ib}(X_{il}|\theta_{jl}) \tag{3}$$

This means that GID mixture model has the ability to reduce complex multidimensional clustering problems to a sequence of one-dimensional ones.

2.2 Infinite Model

Let Z_i be a variable indicating from which cluster each vectors $\boldsymbol{X}_i$ arose (i.e $Z_i = j$ means that $\boldsymbol{X}_i$ comes from component j), thus $\pi_j = p(Z_i = j), j = 1, \ldots, M$ and

$$p(Z|P) = \prod_{j=1}^{M} \pi_j^{n_j} \tag{4}$$

where $P = (\pi_1, \ldots, \pi_M)$, $Z = (Z_1, \ldots, Z_N)$, $n_j = \sum_{i=1}^{N} \mathbb{I}_{Z_i=j}$ is the number of vector in cluster j. It is common to consider a Dirichlet distribution as a prior for P which is justified by the fact that the Dirichlet is conjugate to the multinomial [7]:

$$p(P|\eta_1, \ldots, \eta_M) = \frac{\Gamma(\sum_{j=1}^{M} \eta_j)}{\prod_{j=1}^{M} \Gamma(\eta_j)} \prod_{j=1}^{M} p_j^{\eta_j-1} \tag{5}$$

where $(\eta_1, \ldots, \eta_M) \in \mathbb{R}^{+M}$ are the parameters of the Dirichlet. By taking $\eta_j = \frac{\eta}{M}, j = 1, \ldots, M$, where $\eta \in \mathbb{R}^+$, we obtain

$$p(P|\eta) = \frac{\Gamma(\eta)}{\Gamma(\frac{\eta}{M})^M} \prod_{j=1}^{M} p_j^{\eta-1} \tag{6}$$

Because the Dirichlet is a conjugate prior to the multinomial, we can marginalize out P:

$$p(Z|\eta) = \int_P p(Z|P)p(P|\eta)dP = \frac{\Gamma(\eta)}{\Gamma(\eta+N)} \prod_{j=1}^{M} \frac{\Gamma(\frac{\eta}{M}+n_j)}{\Gamma(\frac{\eta}{M})}$$

which can be considered as a prior on Z. We have also

$$p(P|Z,\eta) = \frac{p(Z|P)p(P|\eta)}{p(Z|\eta)} = \frac{\Gamma(\eta+N)}{\prod_{j=1}^{M} \Gamma(\frac{\eta}{M}+n_j)} \prod_{j=1}^{M} p_j^{n_j+\frac{\eta}{M}-1} \tag{7}$$

which is a Dirichlet distribution with parameters $(n_1 + \frac{\eta}{M}, \ldots, n_M + \frac{\eta}{M})$ from which we can show that:

$$p(Z_i = j|\eta, Z_{-i}) = \frac{n_{-i,j} + \frac{\eta}{M}}{N - 1 + \eta} \tag{8}$$

where $Z_{-i} = \{Z_1, \ldots, Z_{i-1}, Z_{i+1}, \ldots, Z_N\}$, $n_{-i,j}$ is the number of vectors, excluding Y_i, in cluster j. Letting $M \to \infty$ in Eq. 8, the conditional prior gives the following limits [23]

$$p(Z_i = j|\eta, Z_{-i}) = \begin{cases} \frac{n_{-i,j}}{N-1+\eta} & \text{if } n_{-i,j} > 0 \text{ (cluster } j \in \mathcal{R}) \\ \frac{\eta}{N-1+\eta} & \text{if } n_{-i,j} = 0 \text{ (cluster } j \in \mathcal{U}) \end{cases} \tag{9}$$

where $\mathcal{R}$ and $\mathcal{U}$ are the sets of represented and unrepresented clusters, respectively. The previous equation describes actually a Dirichlet process of mixtures which learning is generally based on the MCMC technique of Gibbs sampling [1] by generating the assignments of vectors according to the posterior distribution

$$p(Z_i = j|Z_{-i}, \mathcal{X}) \propto p(Z_i = j|Z_{-i}) \int p(X_i|Z_i = j, \Theta_j)p(\Theta_j|Z_{-i}, \mathcal{X}_{-i})d\Theta_j \tag{10}$$

where Z_{-i} represents all the vectors assignments except Z_i and $\mathcal{X}_{-i}$ represents all the vectors except X_i.

In order to obtain the conditional posterior distributions of our infinite model's parameters given the data that we would like to cluster, we need to choose appropriate priors. Here, we consider the same priors previously proposed in [1] for the inverted Dirichlet which is actually the multivariate case of the inverted Beta in Eq. 3. Thus, we need to parametrize the inverted Beta as following:

$$p_{ib}(X_{il}||\alpha_{jl}|, \mu_{jl}) = \frac{\Gamma(|\alpha_{jl}|)}{\Gamma(\mu_{jl}|\alpha_{jl}|)\Gamma((1-\mu_{jl})|\alpha_{jl}|)} X_{il}^{\mu_{jl}|\alpha_{jl}|-1}(1+X_{il})^{-|\alpha_{jl}|} \tag{11}$$

where $|\alpha_{jl}| = \alpha_{jl} + \beta_{jl}$, $\mu_{jl} = \frac{\alpha_{jl}}{|\alpha_{jl}|}$, and for which we impose independent uniform and inverse Gamma priors, respectively:

$$p(\mu_{jl}) \sim \mathcal{U}_{[0,1]}^{jl} \qquad p(|\alpha_{jl}||\sigma, \varpi) \sim \frac{\varpi^\sigma \exp(-\varpi/|\alpha_{jl}|)}{\Gamma(\sigma)|\alpha_{jl}|^{\sigma+1}} \tag{12}$$

where σ and ϖ are hyperparameters, common to all components, representing shape and scale of the distribution, respectively, and for which we consider the following priors to add more flexibility to the model:

$$p(\sigma|\lambda,\delta) \sim \frac{\delta^\lambda \exp(-\delta/\sigma)}{\Gamma(\lambda)\sigma^{\lambda+1}} \qquad p(\varpi|\phi) \sim \phi\exp(-\phi\varpi) \qquad (13)$$

Having all our priors in hand, the calculation of the parameters posteriors given the rest of the variables becomes straightforward:

$$p(|\alpha_{jl}||\ldots) \propto \frac{\varpi^\sigma \exp(-\varpi/|\alpha_{jl}|)}{\Gamma(\sigma)|\alpha_{jl}|^{\sigma+1}} \prod_{Z_i=j} p(\boldsymbol{X}_i|\Theta) \qquad (14)$$

$$p(\boldsymbol{\mu}_j|\ldots) \propto \prod_{Z_i=j} p(\boldsymbol{X}_i|\Theta) \qquad (15)$$

$$p(\sigma|\ldots) \propto \frac{\varpi^{M\sigma}\delta^\lambda \exp(-\delta/\sigma)}{\Gamma(\sigma)^M \Gamma(\lambda)\sigma^{\lambda+1}} \prod_{j=1}^M \frac{\exp(-\varpi/|\alpha_{jl}|)}{|\alpha_{jl}|^{\sigma+1}} \qquad (16)$$

$$p(\varpi|\ldots) \propto \frac{\varpi^{M\sigma}\phi\exp(-\phi\varpi)}{\Gamma(\sigma)^M} \prod_{j=1}^M \frac{\exp(-\varpi/|\alpha_{jl}|)}{|\alpha_{jl}|^{\sigma+1}} \qquad (17)$$

With these posteriors, the learning algorithm can be summarized as follows:

– Initialization.
– Generate $\boldsymbol{Z}_i$ from Eq. 10, $i = 1,\ldots,N$ using the algorithm in [22].
– Update the number of represented components M.
– Update n_j and $\pi_j = \frac{n_j}{N+\eta}$, $j = 1,\ldots,M$.
– Update the mixing parameters of unrepresented components $\pi_U = \frac{\eta}{\eta+N}$.
– Generate $|\mu_{jl}|$ from Eq. 15 and $|\alpha_{jl}|$ from Eq. 14, $j = 1,\ldots,M$ using Metropolis-Hastings [20].
– Update the hyperparameters: Generate σ from Eq. 16 and ϖ from Eq. 17 using adaptive rejection sampling as proposed in [13].

Note that in the initialization step, the algorithm starts by assuming that all the vectors are in the same cluster and the initial parameters are generated as random samples from their prior distributions.

2.3   Feature Selection

It is noteworthy that the model proposed in the previous section does not take into account the fact that different features may have different weights in the clustering structure, and that some features may be noise and then compromise the generalization capabilities of the model [12]. In order to introduce feature selection in our model, it is possible to use the following formulation:

$$p(\boldsymbol{X}_i|\Xi) = \sum_{j=1}^M \pi_j \prod_{l=1}^D \left[\rho_l p_{ib}(X_{il}||\alpha_{jl}|,\mu_{jl}) + (1-\rho_l)p_{ib}(X_{il}||\alpha_{jl}^{irr}|,\mu_{jl}^{irr})\right] \qquad (18)$$

where $\Xi = \{\Theta, \rho, \Theta^{irr}\}$ is the set of all the model parameters, $\rho = (\rho_1, \ldots, \rho_D)$, $\Theta^{irr} = \{|\alpha_{jl}^{irr}|, \mu_{jl}^{irr}\}$, and $p_{ib}(X_{il}||\alpha_{jl}^{irr}|, \mu_{jl}^{irr})$ is a background distribution, common to all mixture components, to represent irrelevant features. $\rho_l = p(z_{il} = 1)$ represents the probability that the lth feature is relevant for clustering where z_{il} is a hidden variable equal to 1 if the lth feature of $\boldsymbol{X}_i$ is relevant and 0, otherwise. By introducing feature selection, the learning algorithm proposed in the previous section has to be slightly modified by adding simulations from the posteriors of $|\alpha_{jl}^{irr}|$, μ_{jl}^{irr}, for which we choose the same priors considered for $|\alpha_{jl}|$, μ_{jl}, and ρ for which we consider a Beta prior with location δ_1 and scale δ_2 common to all dimensions:

$$p(\rho|\delta_1, \delta_2) = \left[\frac{\Gamma(\delta_2)}{\Gamma(\delta_1\delta_2)\Gamma(\delta_2(1-\delta_1))} \right]^D \prod_{d=1}^{D} \rho_d^{\delta_1\delta_2-1}(1-\rho_d)^{\delta_2(1-\delta_1)-1} \quad (19)$$

Moreover, the z_i are generated from a D-variate Bernoulli distribution with parameters $(\hat{z}_{i1}, \ldots, \hat{z}_{iD})$, where $\hat{z}_{il} = \frac{\rho_l p_{ib}(X_{il}||\alpha_{jl}|, \mu_{jl})}{\rho_l p_{ib}(X_{il}||\alpha_{jl}|, \mu_{jl}) + (1-\rho_l)p_{ib}(X_{il}||\alpha_{jl}^{irr}|, \mu_{jl}^{irr})}$ denotes the expectation for z_{il}:

$$p(z|\rho) = \prod_{i=1}^{N}\prod_{d=1}^{D} \rho_d^{z_{id}}(1-\rho_d)^{1-z_{id}} = \prod_{d=1}^{D} \rho_d^{f_d}(1-\rho_d)^{N-f_d} \quad (20)$$

where $f_d = \sum_{i=1}^{N} \mathbb{I}_{z_{id}=1}$. Then, the posterior for ρ is

$$p(\rho|\ldots) \propto p(\rho|\delta_1, \delta_2)p(z|\rho) \propto \prod_{d=1}^{D} \rho_d^{\delta_1\delta_2+f_d-1}(1-\rho_d)^{\delta_2(1-\delta_1)+N-f_d-1} \quad (21)$$

Note that the feature selection process starts by assuming that all features have a probability of 0.5 to be relevant, then this relevancy value is updated during the learning iterations.

3   Experimental Results: Images Categorization

In this section we demonstrate the utility of our model by applying it on a challenging application namely visual scenes categorization. Moreover, we compare the proposed approach with the infinite inverted Dirichlet proposed in [2]. Comparing our results with many other generative and discriminative techniques is clearly out of the scope of this paper. In this application, the values of the hyperparameters have been set experimentally to one. This choice has been found reasonable according to our simulations.

The wealth of images generated everyday has spurred a tremendous interest in developing approaches to understand the visual content of these images. In this section, we shall focus on the challenging problem of images categorization, to validate our GID infinite mixture model, which is a crucial step in several applications such as annotation [5,10], retrieval [14,27], and object recognition

[25]. A common recent approach widely used for images categorization, that we follow in this application, is the consideration of the so-called bag of visual words generated via quantization of local image descriptors such as SIFT [19].

We considered two challenging datasets in our experiments namely the 15 class scene recognition data set [16] and the 8 class sport events data set [17]. The 15 class scene recognition data set contains the following categories: coasts (360 images), forest (328 images), mountain (374 images), open country (410 images), highway (260 images), inside of cities (308 images), tall buildings (356 images), and streets (292 images), suburb residence (241 images), bedroom (174 images), kitchen (151 images), livingroom (289 images), and office (216 images), store (315 images), and industrial (311 images). Figure 1 displays examples of images from this data set. The 8 class sports event dataset contains the following categories: rowing (250 images), badminton (200 images), polo (182 images), bocce (137 images), snowboarding (190 images), croquet (236 images), sailing (190 images), and rock climbing (194 images). Figure 2 displays examples of images from this data set. We construct our visual vocabulary for each data set, from half of the available images in each data set, by detecting interest points from these images using the difference-of-Gaussians point detector, since it has shown excellent performance [19]. Then, we used SIFT descriptor [19], computed on detected keypoints of all images and giving 128-dimensional vector for each keypoint. Moreover, extracted vectors were clustered using the K-Means

Fig. 1. Sample images from each group in the 15 class scene recognition data set. (a) Highway, (b) Inside of cities, (c) Tall buildings, (d) Streets, (e) Suburb residence, (f) Forest, (g) Coast, (h) Mountain, (i) Open country, (j) Bedroom, (k) Kitchen, (l) Livingroom, (m) Office, (n) Store, (O) Industrial.

Fig. 2. Sample images from each group in the 8 class sports event dataset. (a) rowing, (b) badminton, (c) polo, (d) bocce, (e) snowboarding, (f) croquet, (g) sailing, (h) rock climbing.

algorithm providing 250 visual-words. Each image in the data sets was then represented by a 250-dimensional positive vector describing the frequencies of visual words, provided from the constructed visual vocabulary. These vectors are separated into a test set of vectors and a training set of vectors. Then, we apply our learning algorithm to the training vectors in each class. After this stage, each class in the database is represented by a statistical model. Finally, in the classification stage each unknown image is assigned to the class increasing more its loglikelihood. A summary of the classification results, measured by the average values of the diagonal entries of the confusion matrices obtained for the different classification tasks, is shown in table 1. This table clearly shows that the GID infinite mixture outperforms the infinite inverted Dirichlet mixture. The results can be explained by the fact that the GID is more flexible than the inverted Dirichlet. We can clearly notice, also, that introducing feature selection improves further the results.

Table 1. Classification performance (%) obtained for the two tested data sets using three different approaches

	GID	GID + feature selection	Inverted Dirichlet
Data set 1 (15 categories)	74.52	75.31	70.11
Data set 2 (8 events)	73.25	74.03	70.72

4   Conclusion

Clustering plays a crucial role in various data mining and knowledge discovery applications. The majority of existing clustering algorithms, however, either assume that clusters follow Gaussian distributions; or are very sensitive to the presence of irrelevant features. In this paper we have proposed a new clustering algorithm devoted to positive data that is robust to irrelevant features, and identifies automatically clusters having non-Gaussian distributions. Our approach achieves this by representing the data using an infinite mixture model of GID distributions in which a feature weighting component is introduced. Feature selection is introduced in order to remove irrelevant features that may compromise the clustering process. Our simulations based on the challenging problem of images categorization have shown the efficiency of the proposed model. A potential future work could be the development of a variational approach, like the one proposed in [12], to improve the learning of our model from a computational point of view. Several other directions present themselves for future efforts. Indeed, the developed approach could be applied to many real-world problems such as 3D object recognition [24] or to the generation of SVM kernels using the methodology recently proposed in [4].

References

1. Bdiri, T., Bouguila, N.: An infinite mixture of inverted dirichlet distributions. In: Lu, B.-L., Zhang, L., Kwok, J. (eds.) ICONIP 2011, Part II. LNCS, vol. 7063, pp. 71–78. Springer, Heidelberg (2011)
2. Bdiri, T., Bouguila, N.: Learning inverted dirichlet mixtures for positive data clustering. In: Kuznetsov, S.O., Ślęzak, D., Hepting, D.H., Mirkin, B.G. (eds.) RSFD-GrC 2011. LNCS, vol. 6743, pp. 265–272. Springer, Heidelberg (2011)
3. Bdiri, T., Bouguila, N.: Positive vectors clustering using inverted dirichlet finite mixture models. Expert Systems with Applications 39(2), 1869–1882 (2012)
4. Bdiri, T., Bouguila, N.: Bayesian learning of inverted dirichlet mixtures for svm kernels generation. Neural Computing and Applications 23(5), 1443–1458 (2013)
5. Benitez, A., Chang, S.F.: Semantic knowledge construction from annotated image collections. In: Proc. of the IEEE International Conference on Multimedia and Expo (ICME), vol. 2, pp. 205–208 (2002)
6. Bezdek, J.C., Hathaway, R.J., Huband, J.M., Leckie, C., Ramamohanarao, K.: Approximate clustering in very large relational data. International Journal of Intelligent Systems 21(8), 817–841 (2006)
7. Bouguila, N., ElGuebaly, W.: On discrete data clustering. In: Washio, T., Suzuki, E., Ting, K.M., Inokuchi, A. (eds.) PAKDD 2008. LNCS (LNAI), vol. 5012, pp. 503–510. Springer, Heidelberg (2008)
8. Bouguila, N., Ziou, D.: A nonparametric bayesian learning model: Application to text and image categorization. In: Theeramunkong, T., Kijsirikul, B., Cercone, N., Ho, T.-B. (eds.) PAKDD 2009. LNCS, vol. 5476, pp. 463–474. Springer, Heidelberg (2009)
9. Bouguila, N., Ziou, D.: A dirichlet process mixture of generalized dirichlet distributions for proportional data modeling. IEEE Transactions on Neural Networks 21(1), 107–122 (2010)
10. Chang, E.Y., Goh, K., Sychay, G., Wu, G.: Cbsa: content-based soft annotation for multimodal image retrieval using bayes point machines. IEEE Transactions on Circuits Systems and Video Technology 13(1), 26–38 (2003)
11. Chen, W., Feng, G.: Spectral clustering with discriminant cuts. Knowledge-Based Systems 28, 27–37 (2012)

12. Fan, W., Bouguila, N., Ziou, D.: Unsupervised hybrid feature extraction selection for high-dimensional non-gaussian data clustering with variational inference. IEEE Transactions on Knowledge and Data Engineering 25(7), 1670–1685 (2013)
13. Gilks, W.R., Wild, P.: Algorithm as 287: Adaptive rejection sampling from log-concave density functions. Applied Statistics 42(4), 701–709 (1993)
14. He, J., Li, M., Zhang, H.J., Tong, H., Zhang, C.: Manifold-ranking based image retrieval. In: Proc. of the 12th Annual ACM International Conference on Multimedia (MM), pp. 9–16 (2004)
15. Huang, K.Y.: A hybrid particle swarm optimization approach for clustering and classification of datasets. Knowledge Based Systems 24(3), 420–426 (2011)
16. Lazebnik, S., Schmid, C., Ponce, J.: Beyond bags of features: Spatial pyramid matching for recognizing natural scene categories. In: Proc. of the IEEE Computer Society Conference on Computer Vision and Pattern Recognition (CVPR), vol. 2, pp. 2169–2178 (2006)
17. Li, L.J., Fei-Fei, L.: What, where and who? Classifying events by scene and object recognition. In: Proc. of the IEEE 11th International Conference on Computer Vision (ICCV), pp. 1–8 (2007)
18. Lingappaiah, G.S.: On the generalised inverted dirichlet distribution. Demostratio Mathematica 9(3), 423–433 (1976)
19. Lowe, D.G.: Distinctive image features from scale-invariant keypoints. International Journal of Computer Vision 60(2), 91–110 (2004)
20. Marin, J.M., Robert, C.P.: Bayesian Core: A Practical Approach to Computational Bayesian Statistics. Springer (2007)
21. McLachlan, G., Peel, D.: Finite Mixture Models. Wiley-Interscience (2000)
22. Neal, R.M.: Markov chain sampling methods for dirichlet process mixture models. Journal of Computational and Graphical Statistics 9, 249–265 (2000)
23. Rasmussen, C.E.: The infinite gaussian mixture model. In: Advances in Neural Information Processing Systems (NIPS), pp. 554–560 (2000)
24. Selinger, A., Nelson, R.C.: A perceptual grouping hierarchy for appearance-based 3d object recognition. Computer Vision and Image Understanding 76(1), 83–92 (1999)
25. Spirkovska, L., Reid, M.B.: Higher-order neural networks applied to 2d and 3d object recognition. Machine Learning 15(2), 169–199 (1994)
26. Topchy, A., Law, M., Jain, A., Fred, A.: Analysis of consensus partition in cluster ensemble. In: Proc. of the IEEE International Conference on Data Mining (ICDM), pp. 225–232 (2004)
27. Wang, X.J., Ma, W.Y., Xue, G.R., Li, X.: Multi-model similarity propagation and its application for web image retrieval. In: Proc. of the 12th Annual ACM International Conference on Multimedia (MM), pp. 944–951 (2004)

On If-Then Multi Soft Sets-Based Decision Making

R.B. Fajriya Hakim[1], Eka Novita Sari[2], and Tutut Herawan[3]

[1] Department of Statistics
Universitas Islam Indonesia
Jalan Kaliurang KM 14, Yogyakarta Indonesia
[2] AMCS Research Center
Yogyakarta, Indonesia
[3] Department of Information System
University of Malaya
50603 Pantai Valley, Kuala Lumpur, Malaysia
hakimf@fmipa.uii.ac.id, eka@amcs.co, tutut@um.edu.my

Abstract. Soft set theory as a new mathematical tool for dealing with uncertainties was first introduced by Molodtsov has experienced rapid growth. Various applications of soft set for the purpose of decision-making have been shown by several researchers. From various studies presented mostly shows the role of soft sets as a tool in the collection of the various attributes needed by a person to determine which decisions will be taken. In this paper, we show how soft set can play a role in the decision made by a person based on a history of decisions that have been made earlier and used as a reference for the next decision. Therefore, we introduce an (*if-then*) multi soft sets as a developments of application of soft set which is stated in the form *if* (antecedent) and *then* (consequence). The antecedent and consequence are derived from previously several decisions that have been made by people when using a soft set as a tool to help them for making a decision.

Keywords: Soft Set, Multi Soft Set, If-then, Decision making.

1   Introduction

Choosing one product to be purchased could be started by describing the product they want using some simple characteristics, attributes, information or knowledge they have about those product. Any parameters which had been regarded as an important characteristic that might be owned by the product to be bought could be collected in the structure of mathematical notion. Collection of those parameters can be laid on the form of soft set theory. Soft set theory first introduced by Molodtsov [1] in 1999 and has been applied in many fields by researchers. Hakim *et al.* [2] had proposed a recommendation analysis as a buyer tool to assist their decision in purchasing a product. Many researchers including Chen *et al.* [3], Feng *et al.* [4,5], Herawan and Mat Deris [6], Jiang *et al.* [7], Kong *et al.* [8], Maji *et al.* [9,10], Roy and Maji [11] mostly show the role of soft sets as a tool in the collection of various attributes or parameters of objects needed by a person and then determine using some calculations which decisions will be taken. The development of the use of soft set may actually be

Linawati et al. (Eds.): ICT-EurAsia 2014, LNCS 8407, pp. 306–315, 2014.

more than that, this paper will show how soft set can play a role in the decision made by a person based on a history of decisions that have been made by some people earlier and used as a reference for the next decision.

Deciding a product to be purchased is a difficult matter for a buyer. Hakim *et al.* [2] has introduced a recommendation system based on soft set theory to purchase a product from buyer side. This recommendation analysis is an advantage for buyers in helping them to determine the product they need. This paper also trying to use a soft set theory from a view of store team to observe the personality of buyer by means of the ability of the store owner and store assistant to evaluate their buyer when purchase goods. As a continuation of previous work, in this paper we develop an alternative application of soft set in the form *if* (antecedent) *then* (consequence) with antecedent as a condition attribute and consequence as a decision attribute that are derived from previously several decisions which had been made by other buyers. Because it involves a condition and decision attribute, we need a language of 'decision rules'. A decision rule is an implication in the form *if* A *then* B, where A is called the 'condition' and B the 'decision' of the rule. Decision rules state relationship between conditions and decisions. In this paper, we are trying to combine the decision rules and dual soft sets that will produce a new application of soft set which can be known as *if-then* multi soft-set. This application not only helping buyer in deciding the product to be chosen, but also help the store to map their buyer when determining the product needed.

The rest of this paper is organized as follow. Section 2 describes rudimentary of soft set theory and soft solution for soft set. Section 3 describes the proposed application of if-then multi soft sets. Finally, the conclusion of this work is described in Section 4.

2   Soft Set Theory and Soft Solution

2.1   Soft Set Theory

Molodtsov [1] first defined a soft set which is a family of objects whose definitions depend on a set of parameter. Let U be an initial universe of objects, E be the set of adequate parameters in relation to objects in U. Adequate parameterization is desired to avoid some difficulties when using probability theory, fuzzy sets theory and interval mathematics which are in common used as mathematical tool for dealing with uncertainties. The definition of soft set is given as follows.

Definition 1. (See [1]). *A pair (F, E) is called a soft set over U if and only if F is a mapping of E into the set of all subsets of the set U.*

From definition 1, a soft set (F, E) over the universe U is a parameterized family that gives an approximate description of the objects in U. Let e any parameter in E, $e \in E$, the subset $F(e) \subseteq U$ may be considered as the set of e-approximate elements in the soft set (F, E).

Example 1. Let us consider a soft set (F, E) which describes the "attractiveness of houses" that Mr. X is considering to purchase.

U – is the set of houses under Mr. X consideration

E – is the set of parameters. Each parameter is a word or a sentence

E = {expensive, beautiful, wooden, cheap, in the green surroundings, modern, in good repair, in bad repair}

In this example, to define a soft set means to point out expensive houses, that shows which houses are expensive due to the dominating parameter is 'expensive' compared to other parameters that are possessed by the house, in the green surrounding houses, which shows houses that their surrounding are greener than other, and so on.

2.2   Soft Solution of Soft Set Theory

Many researches on soft set in decision making could be grouped into two groups. First, researchers that treat the soft set as an attribute of information system including the works of Herawan and Mat Deris [6], Zou and Xiao [12]) then using Rough Set to handle the vagueness for making a decision [5]. Second, researchers that use fuzzy theory to soft set including the works of Jun *et al.* [13], Feng *et al.* [4] and Jiang *et al.* [7]. Both of them gave techniques which produce best decision based on binary or fuzzy number rather than recommendation that may be little bit more satisfying Molodtsov's soft set philosophy. From the entire study could be seen that the whole objects under consideration was assessed through the parameters by the decision makers and will get the solution in the form of a subset of the objects itself that each of them has a dominating parameters. According to this understanding we will give the definition for soft solution of soft sets.

From that Definition 1, a soft set (F, E) over the universe U is a parameterized family that gives an approximate description of the objects in U. Let e any parameter in E, $e \in E$, the subset $F(e) \subseteq U$ may be considered as the set of e-approximate elements in the soft set (F, E). It is worth noting that the sets $F(e)$ may be arbitrary. Some of them may be empty, some may have nonempty intersection. That is, the solution of the soft set is a set which are a subset of object and a subset of parameters that shows the objects and its parameters.

Definition 2. (soft solution). *A pair (F', E') over U' is said to be a soft solution of soft set (F, E) over U if and only if*

i) $U' \subseteq U$

ii) $\{e_{/U'} \mid e \in E\} = E'$ *where $e_{/U'}$ is the restriction parameter of e to U'*

iii) F' *is a mapping of E' into the set of all subsets of the set U'*

We shall use the notion of restriction parameter of $e \in E'$ to U' in order to obtain the parameters which dominate an object compared to other parameters that may be possessed by those objects.

A soft set (F, E) over U might be considered as an information system (U, AT) (Demri and Orlowska [14]) such that $AT = \{F\}$ and value of a mapping function of $F = e \in E$ make available the same information about objects from U. It is a common thing to identify a wide range of matters (parameters) relating to the object and then create a collection of objects that possess this parameters. To compose this intuition, for a given soft set $S = (F, E)$ over U, we define a soft set formal context $S = (U, E, F)$

where U and E are non-empty sets whose elements are interpreted as objects and parameters (features), respectively, and $F \subseteq U \times E$ is a binary relation. If $x \in U$ and $e \in E$ and $(x, e) \in F$, then the object x is said to have the feature e. In this concept, the soft set formal context provides the following mappings $ext: \mathbf{P}(E) \to \mathbf{P}(U)$, that shows extensional information for objects under consideration. This means an object parameters may be able to be expanded on someone views as the set of those objects that possess the parameters.

Definition 3. *For all $X \subseteq U$ and $e \subseteq E$ we define $ext(E) \overset{def}{\Rightarrow} \{x \in U \mid (x,e) \in F, for\ every\ e \in E\}$; $ext(E)$ is referred to as the extent of E.*

A soft set formal context $S = (U, E, F)$ is an urn for a collection of soft sets. Not necessarily soft set formal context will only give one soft set. $S = (U. E, F)$ could be viewed as multi soft set, say dual soft set S_1 and S_2 where $S_1, S_2 \subseteq S$ and S_1 is soft set (F_1, E_1) over U_1, S_2 soft set (F_2, E_2) over U_2, and $U_1, U_2 \subseteq U$ and $E_1, E_2 \subseteq E$ and $E_1 \cap E_2 = \emptyset$

Lemma 1. *For Soft set formal context $S = (U. E, F)$, $S_1, S_2 \subseteq S$ and S_1 is soft set (F_1, E_1) over U_1, S_2 soft set (F_2, E_2) over U_2, for all $U_1, U_2 \subseteq U$ and $E_1, E_2 \subseteq E$ if $E_1 \cap E_2 = \emptyset$, then $ext\ (E_1) \cap ext\ (E_2) = \emptyset$*

Lemma above shows that a soft formal context can be divided into a number of soft sets (multi soft sets) with each object and its parameters are different but still in the same context. It is different from the multi soft sets proposed by Herawan and Mat Deris [15] who break the soft set but with the same object and parameters.

3   The Proposed Application of If-Then Multi Soft Sets

In this paper we will develop again the examples given by Hakim *et al.* [2] which illustrate a user interface of soft set recommendation analysis for purchasing furniture products in some furniture store. System (See Figure 1) displays three columns, first columns consists of customer identification and buyers are offered to get assistant from furniture expert for choosing and question of some specific purpose in intending buying the furniture. All collections of furniture items are shown in second column and buyer was asked to choose one of collections. In this example, buyers choose dining chairs then the third column display all collection of dining chairs. Four selected chairs as depicted in Figure 2 are chosen by customer and buyers could determine their own requirements for their dining chairs. Buyer has several things that he thought as a dining chairs precondition, he could type any perspective inside the form, for example, 'match with my dining room decoration', 'fit the space of my dining room', 'cheap', 'comfort', 'classic' and 'wood color'. This could be expressed in the form of soft set. A soft set (F_1, E_1) of this example could be described as the preconditions of the chairs which buyer is going to buy.

U_1 – is the set of chairs under consideration {Ch1, Ch2, Ch3, Ch4}
E_1 – is the set of parameters. Each parameter is a word or a sentence.
E_1 = {match with my dining room decoration, fit the space of my dining room, cheap, comfort, classic and wood color}

Those preconditions could be regarded as parameters of each chair. He thought that, those information/ knowledge/parameters are necessary parameters for him to choose a chair that he need for inviting a special guest for dinner. Soft set has applied here, that someone could use any parameterization he wants for purchasing chairs. It might he only knows what he need and conditions that he must consider putting the chairs then. Meanwhile, in this cases we offer a judgment from expert based on buyer's precondition which is available in the form below the 'customer request', this form shows what Expert Says with the valuation of each chair below of its pictures. In the second column, it also displays the form of customer evaluation that he could determine his own judgment for each chair. The simple act to evaluate the selected items is to compare them in a fairly flexible way by giving a mark to the chairs that meet his requirements. More asterisks more meet parameters. After giving an assessment of the selected chairs, the last column gives the soft solution. The soft solution of soft set for this problem is

Soft solution (F_1', E_1') = {(Match the dining room decoration) = Ch1, (Wood color, Comfort, Classic) = Ch2, (Fit the space of dining room, Cheap, Match the dining room decoration) = Ch3, (Cheap) = Ch4}

This set of soft solution is used as a recommendation for buyer to purchase the chairs. This soft solution is a result of soft set using hierarchical clustering and multidimensional scaling techniques. Outcome of this solution is a recommendation based on buyer's evaluation, for example, the first picture show that the chair tends to match with the dining room decoration while second picture meet a lot of customer requests, i.e., wood color, comfort and classic style. The final decision is verified by customer to buy that chair. The last row could be utilized as an offer to buyer for buying another product which is usually bought by others while buying that chair.

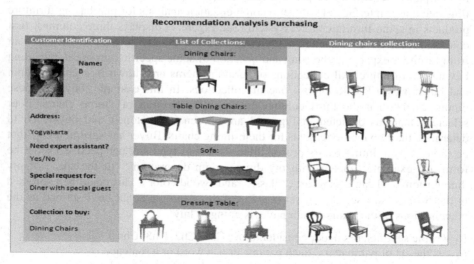

Fig. 1. Soft set recommendation analysis on first page

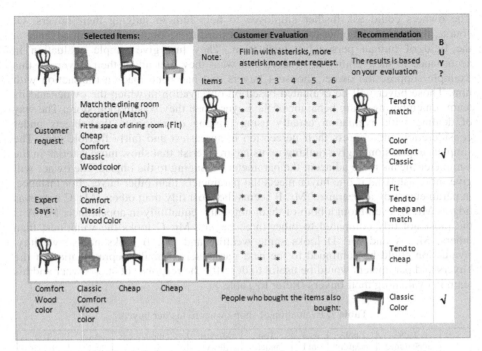

Fig. 2. Soft set recommendation analysis on second page

Nowadays buyers are miserly to give personal information due to security reason and get annoyed when shop assistant started asking personal things. Shop assistant also cannot force the buyers ask for personal information, but much better if observing the behavior of buyers when selecting products and make their choice. Simple research will be carried out if the shop owner does not assume the arrival of buyer to their shop only as a destiny. Buyer that has already coming to their shops should be noticed use any kind of characteristics or parameters which the owner or shop assistant could do. Some simple parameters that might could be used to differentiating one person to another such as, appearance of buyers, style of buyers when asking something, gesture of buyers, speaking style of buyer and so on.

In this example, the furniture store owner and their team trying to observe their buyer using several parameter which could be put in the form of set {tidy appearance, looks wealthy, age-old, too much questions, modern lifestyle, complicated requests, busy and in hurry, too much bargain} that they think sufficient to evaluate their buyer. Other owners could add or reduce the parameter used in this set, depend on the observation to their own buyers. A soft set (F_2, E_2) of this example could be described as the behavior of buyers as the result of observation of the owner

U_2 – is the set of buyers under consideration {A, B, C, D}

E_2 – is the set of parameters. Each parameter is a word or a sentence.

E_2 = {{tidy appearance, looks wealthy, age-old, too much questions, modern lifestyle, complicated requests, busy and in hurry, too much bargain}.

The owners could ask his/her employee to help him in judging their buyers. Of course, the owner and other employee do not need to become an expert in advance at the field of human personality evaluation. They just give simple evaluation in accordance to their ability to observe and what they feel about their buyer. In this example suppose the owner choose 4 buyers that had been made a transaction with him. Those buyer will be evaluated based on observation in which the owner and its team remembering again behavior of the buyer when they was in their store. The way of dealing with evaluation usually using ranking or rating to the objects under consideration and express their perception in an easiest and fairly flexible way. The simplest expression is give ranking by using an asterisk that show more asterisk in the parameter means more adjacent the parameter belonging to the object. The owner will give more asterisks if one buyer meets the parameters than other buyer. For instance, in parameter 'tidy appearance' Mr. B seems the most tidy than others. Mr. C seems as tidy as Mr. D, even though both of them not really equal tidy in appearance. Mr. A is the most not tidy compared to other three buyers. Mr. C looks the wealthiest than others, Mr. A and Mr. D looks same wealthy and Mr. B looks not so wealthy. Evaluation could be continued to the next parameters. Tabular representation of the buyers and parameters would be useful to describe the response of shop owner and his team in evaluating their buyers (Refer to Table 1).

Table 1. Evaluation of shop owner to his/her buyers

	Tidy appearance	Looks wealthy	Age-old	Too much question	Modern lifestyle	Complicated requests	Busy and in hurry	Too much bargain
A	*	**	***	**	*	**	*	**
B	***	*	***	***	*	***	*	***
C	**	***	**	*	***	*	***	**
D	**	**	*	***	***	*	**	*

To better utilizing information from the tables and providing added value for the shop owner, the multidimensional scaling techniques will be used. Non-metrix multidimensional scaling techniques are common techniques which based on ordinal or qualitative rankings of similarities data [16]. Therefore, Table 1 needs to be transformed via the numbers into an ordinal table (Refer to Table 2).

Table 2. Ordinal numbers of Table 1

	Tidy appearance	Looks wealthy	Age-old	Too much question	Modern lifestyle	Complicated requests	Busy and in hurry	Too much bargain
A	1	2	3	2	1	2	1	2
B	3	1	3	3	1	3	1	3
C	2	3	2	1	3	1	3	2
D	2	2	1	3	3	1	2	1

Using the software R (R Development Core Team [17]) with *vegan* package and *meta*MDS procedure (Dixon and Palmer [18]), we get the mapping of buyers and its parameters as depicted in Figure 3.

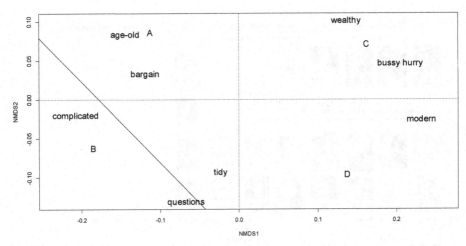

Fig. 3. Multidimensional scaling plot of buyers and its parameters

And the soft solution of soft set for the behavior of buyers is

Soft solution (F_2', E_2') = {(Age-old, Too much bargain) = A,
(Tidy appearance, Too much questions, Complicated requests) = B,
(Wealthy, Busy and hurry) = C,
(Modern lifestyle) = D}

From this two soft set (F_1, E_1) and (F_2, E_2) give a result of two soft solution which are (F_1', E_1') and (F_2', E_2') and due to high relationship between two soft set, the owner could get the decision rules of two soft solution which are

If (F_1', E_1') then (F_2', E_2') or   if (F_2', E_2') then (F_1', E_1')

Say, the owner would like to take one of those buyer to see the decision rules of multi soft set, say Mr. B, then he will get the rules,

| if | Mr. B bought chair {Classic, Comfort, Wood color} = (Ch2) | then | Mr. B is {Tidy appearance, Too much questions, Complicated requests} |

or

| If | Mr. B is {Tidy appearance, Too much questions, Complicated requests} | then | Mr. B bought chair {Classic, Comfort, Wood color} = (Ch2) |

Second rule seems reasonable for recommendation which will be used by the owner and his sales person to a buyer who have behavior looks like Mr. B. Of course this rule will not be disclosed to the buyer, because the rules are based on the assessment of shopkeeper to their buyers quietly. Even though this recommendation is

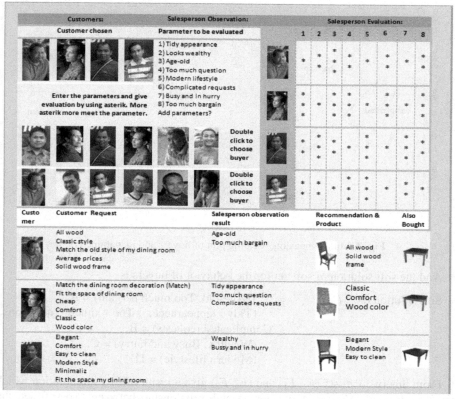

Fig. 4. Interface of application *if-then* multi soft set

not exact decision but this rules could help the owner and the sales person to assist the buyers while they are determining to choose one chair from several chairs of dining room. Figure 4 shows the interface of recommendation analysis of the owner to their buyers. This work has already shown the applied of soft set when it is implemented in the rules *if-then*. The usage of multi soft set, could help not only buyer when he/she need to choose the object he wants but also help the shop owner to give recommendation to his/her buyer based on buyer behavior.

4   Conclusion

Soft set theory which is a new mathematical tool in decision making already gave lack of restrictions to one whom using them in achieving the final decision. Anyone could use any parameters in deciding which objects will be chosen. From many previous studies mostly shows the role of soft sets as a tool in the collection of the various parameters needed by a person to determine which decisions will be taken, however in this paper we have already shown the development of the use of soft set to multi soft sets and its lemma. We have shown how *if-then* multi soft set can play a role in the decision made by a person based on a history of decisions that have been made by some people earlier and used as a reference for the next decision.

Acknowledgments. This work is supported by University of Malaya High Impact Research Grant no vote UM.C/625/HIR/MOHE/SC/13/2 from Ministry of Higher Education Malaysia.

References

1. Molodtsov, D.: Soft Set Theory – First Results. Computers and Mathematics with Applications 37, 19–31 (1999)
2. Hakim, R.B.F., Subanar, Winarko, E.: Recommendation Analysis Based on Soft Set for Purchasing Products. In: Proceedings of the 6th Southeast Asian Mathematical Society (SEAMS) International Conference of Mathematics and Its Application, pp. 831–848 (2011)
3. Chen, D., Tsang, E.C.C., Yeung, D.S., Wang, X.: The Parameterization Reduction of Soft Sets and its Applications. Computers and Mathematics with Applications 49, 757–763 (2005)
4. Feng, F., Jun, Y.B., Liu, X., Li, L.: An adjustable approach to fuzzy soft set based decision making. Journal of Computational and Applied Mathematics 234, 10–20 (2010)
5. Feng, F., Liu, X., Leoreanu-Fotea, V., Jun, Y.B.: Soft set and soft rough sets. Information Sciences 181, 1125–1137 (2011)
6. Herawan, T., Mat Deris, M.: A soft set approach for association rules mining. Knowledge Based System 24, 186–195 (2011)
7. Jiang, Y., Tang, Y., Chen, Q.: An adjustable approach to intuitionistic fuzzy soft sets based decision making. Applied Mathematical Modeling 35, 824–836 (2011)
8. Kong, Z., Gao, L., Wang, L., Li, S.: The normal parameter reduction of soft sets and its algorithm. Comput. Math. Appl. 56, 3029–3037 (2008)
9. Maji, P.K., Roy, A.R., Biswas, R.: An Application of Soft Sets in A Decision Making Problem. Computers and Mathematics with Applications 44, 1077–1083 (2002)
10. Maji, P.K., Roy, A.R., Biswas, R.: Soft Sets Theory. Computers and Mathematics with Applications 45, 555–562 (2003)
11. Roy, A.R., Maji, P.K.: A Fuzzy Soft Set Theoretic Approach to Decision Making Problems. Computational and Applied Mathematics 203, 412–418 (2007)
12. Zou, Y., Xiao, Z.: Data Analysis Approaches of Soft Sets under Incomplete Information. Knowledge Based System 21, 941–945 (2008)
13. Jun, Y.B., Lee, K.J., Park, C.H.: Fuzzy soft sets theory applied to BCK/BCI-algebras. Computers and Mathematics with Applications 59, 3180–3192 (2010)
14. Demri, S.P., Orlowska, E.S.: Incomplete Information: Structure, Inference, Complexity. Springer, Heidelberg (2002)
15. Herawan, T., Mat Deris, M.: On multi soft sets construction in information systems. In: Huang, D.-S., Jo, K.-H., Lee, H.-H., Kang, H.-J., Bevilacqua, V. (eds.) ICIC 2009. LNCS (LNAI), vol. 5755, pp. 101–110. Springer, Heidelberg (2009)
16. Kruskal, J.B.: Nonmetric multidimensional scaling: A numerical method. Psychometrika 29, 115–129 (1964)
17. R Development Core Team: R: A language and environment for statistical computing, R Foundation for Statistical Computing, Vienna, Austria (2006)
18. Dixon, P., Palmer, M.W.: Vegan, a package of R function for community ecology. Journal of Vegetation Science 14, 927–930 (2003)

Predicting Size of Forest Fire
Using Hybrid Model

Guruh Fajar Shidik and Khabib Mustofa

Universitas Dian Nuswantoro Indonesia,
Universitas Gadjah Mada, Indonesia
guruh.fajar@research.dinus.ac.id,
khabib@ugm.ac.id

Abstract. This paper outlines a hybrid approach in data mining to predict the size of forest fire using meteorological and forest weather index
(FWI) variables such as Fine Fuel Moisture Code (FFMC), Duff Moisture Code (DMC), Drought Code (DC), Initial Spread Index (ISI), temperature, Relative Humidity (RH), wind and rain. The hybrid model is
developed with clustering and classification approaches. Fuzzy C-Means
(FCM) is used to cluster the historical variables. The clustered data are
then used as inputs to Back-Propagation Neural Network classification.
The label dataset having value greater than zero in fire area size are clustered using FCM to produce two categorical clusters,i.e.: *Light Burn*, and
Heavy Burn for its label. On the other hand, fire area label with value
zero is clustered as *No Burn Area*. A Back-Propagation Neural Network
(BPNN) is trained based on these data to classify the output (burn area)
in three categories, *No Burn Area, Light Burn* and *Heavy Burn*. The experiment shows promising results depicting classification size of forest
fire with the accuracy of confusion matrix around 97, 50 % and Cohens
Kappa 0.954. This research also compares the performance of proposed
model with other classification method such as SVM, Naive Bayes, DCT
Tree, and K-NN that showed BPNN have best performance.

Keywords: Forest fire Prediction, FCM, Back-Propagation Neural
Network, Data Mining.

1 Introduction

Forest fire is a common natural world phenomenon. Every year millions of
hectares of forests in the world are destroyed [1], between 1980 - 2007 at least 2.7
million hectares were burnt in Portugal [2]. This caused severe damages to the
natural environment and resulted in loss of precious human lives. Forest fire is
one of the major environmental concern that affects the preservation of forests,
resulting in economical and ecological damage that causes human suffering.

Referring to Elmas [3], quick fire detection and response are effective ways in
reducing the damages caused by forest fires. Various studies have been made in
order to improve early fire prediction and detection systems that helps to develop
response strategies during the fire. It means, one of the key successes of putting

Linawati et al. (Eds.): ICT-EurAsia 2014, LNCS 8407, pp. 316–327, 2014.

out forest fire is by providing an early warning detection. Early warning detection is related to accurate prediction of results based on determined parameters. There are three trending techniques that could be used in predicting forest fire such as the use of satellite data, infra red or smoke scanners and local sensors, for example, using the meteorological ones [2].

Safi et al [4] tried to overcome forest fire impacts by making prediction using data mining technique. A future event has always been considered a mysterious activity scientists trying to treat into scientific activities based on theories and models. Predictions in data mining can be used in identifying many real world problems such as financial forecasting and prediction of environmental applications or to test scientific understanding of the behaviour of complex systems or phenomena. The predictions are also used as a guide or basis for decision making [2].

In [5], based on the perspectives of forest fire, it is mentioned that several scientists around the world had utilized statistical approaches such as regression analysis, probabilistic analysis and artificial intelligence. Some data mining techniques have been applied in the domain of fire detection, for example by adopting meteorological data to predict forest fire [2]. Back propagation neural network and the rule generation approach [6], fuzzy c-means clustering application in the case of forest fire [5], artificial neural network to the real word problem of predicting forest fire [4], Neural Network (NN) and Support Vector Machines to predict forest fire occurrence based on weather data [7], decision tree algorithm namely C4.5 to extract a forest fire data and classifying hotspot occurrences [8].

This research aims at proposing an approach for predicting the size of forest fire occurs based on meteorological and forest weather index dataset consisting of eight variables: FFMC, DMC, DC, ISI, temperature, RH, wind and rain. The size of forest fire will be classified using Back-Propagation Neural Network into three categories,i.e: *No Burn Area, Light Burn* and *Heavy Burn*. As the label (area) in datasets of size of forest fire is numerical, before classification process, the data should be clustered into three classes. We split the dataset into two part: *the data with zero value* and *data having value greater than zero*. The process of clustering two categories dataset (light and heavy burn) is done with unsupervised method FCM in label data (area) that have value greater than zero, while for No Burn Area, it is done by selecting label (area) that have value zero. We used ten fold cross validations in separating training dataset and testing dataset with shuffled and stratified sampling. Confusion matrix and Kappa is used in evaluating the performance of the model.

The remaining of this paper will be organised as follows: chapter two talks about related works, chapter three talks about fundamentals of the approach, chapter four describe the research method used to predict the size of forest fire. The rest of the papers are discussion on the results and, the last chapter is conclusion and future work of this research.

2   Related Works

Satoh et al [9] developed a system for predicting the dangers of a forest fire. A simulation of dangers related to forest fire was developed not only using the previous weather condition, but also coupled with data on population density and some other factors.

Cortez and Morais [2] used five different data mining techniques to predict the burnt area of forest fire using Support Vector Machines (SVM) and Random Forests. With four distinct features likes spatial, temporal, Fire Weather Index components and weather variables (such as temperature, relative humidity, rain and wind), it was found that the best configuration was reached using Support Vector Machine, which is capable of predicting the frequent burnt areas due to small fire.

A study to increase the Fuzzy C-means model intelligently using a flexible termination criteria for the clustering of forest fire was conducted by Illadis et al[5]. This approach enables the algorithm to be more flexible and human-like in an intelligent way. It also avoids possible infinite loops and unnecessary iterations.

Decision tree C4.5 algorithm is implemented to predict the location of the incident hotspots in Rokan Hilir district, Riau province, Indonesia [8]. The dataset consists of hotspot locations, human activity factors, and land cover types. The human activity factors include city center locations, road network and river network.

Safi et al [4] applied artificial neural networks to the real world problem of predicting forest fire, using back propagation learning algorithm. Yu et al [6] conducted a research investigating the nonlinear relationship between the size of a forest fire and meteorological variables (temperature, relative humidity, wind speed and rainfall) using two hybrid approaches. At first phase Self Organizing Map is used to cluster the data. Than, in second phase the clustered data were used as inputs for two different approaches, the back-propagation neural network and the rule generation approaches.

Sakr et al [10] applied a description and analysis of forest fire prediction methods based on Support Vector Machines to predict the fire hazard level of a day, where the algorithm depended on previous weather conditions. Moreover, in [7], Sakr et al try to reduced a set of weather parameters utilizing relative humidity and cumulative precipitation to estimate the risk of the output, to predict the occurrence of forest fire by comparing two artificial intelligence-based methods: Artificial Neural Networks (ANN) and Support Vector Machines (SVM).

Based on the above existing researches, this paper proposes an approach to predict the size of forest fire using hybrid model, between Fuzzy C-Means (FCM) clustering technique and Back-Propagation Neural Network (BPNN) classification technique in processing meteorological and forest weather index data as input.

3   Fundamentals

3.1   Forest Fire

Forest fire as a kind of common natural disaster possibly makes a great danger to people living in the burnt forest as well as to wildlife. Such disaster may be caused by lightning, human negligence or arson that can burn thousands of square kilometers. According to Brown and Davis [11], there are three types of forest fire namely: *ground fire, surface fire* and *crown fire.*

3.2   Data Mining

Data mining can be seen as a process of discovering patterns in large volume of data having meaningful information [11]. The process must be automatic or (more usually) semi-automatic. Among several existing methods commonly applied in data mining, in this research, clustering and classification are chosen to be implemented. Clustering technique is used to cluster the size of forest burning size area having value greater than zero into four clusters, while classification technique is to determine which type of burning size that will probably occur based on meteorological data.

Fuzzy C-Means (FCM). is one of popular fuzzy clustering techniques that used for finding similarities in data and putting similar data into several groups, has been proposed by Dunn [12] in 1973 and then later modified by Bezdek [13] in 1981. It is an approach where the data points have their membership values with cluster center, to be updated iteratively. The detail explanation of FCM algorithm, could be seen at [14].

Back-Propagation Neural Network (BPNN). is classification technique highly dependent on the network structure and training process that has better learning rate [15]. The number of input layer nodes, hidden layer and output layer in BPNN will determine the structure of the network.

Back-propagation learning process requires a pair of input vectors and the target vectors. The output vector of each input vector will be compared with the target vector. This measurement is necessary in order to minimize the difference between the output vector and the target vector.

In BPNN it begins with the initialization of weights and thresholds at random. The weights are updated in each iteration to minimize the Mean Square Error (MSE) between the output vector and the target vector, where the detail information of BPNN was explain in [16].

3.3   Preprocessing

There are several steps in data mining preprocessing [17], such as data cleansing, data integration, data reduction and data transformation. In this research, data transformation is used to normalize the data. Data normalization is useful for classification involving neural networks or distance measurements such as nearest neighbour classification and clustering. Beside that, it can affect to speed up the learning rate of BPNN for classification. In this research Min-max normalization is applied to perform a linear transformation on the original data [11], where the formula could be seen at (1). The data of eight variables or attribute used in this research will be transform in new range with min value is 0 and max value is 1.

$$v_i' = \frac{v_i - min_A}{max_A - min_A}(New\_max_A - New\_min_A) + New\_min_A \qquad (1)$$

Where min_A is existing minimum value and $maxA$ is existing maximum values of an attribute A. vi is existing data value in attribute A that will be mapped to current data value v_i' in the new range [0 , 1] [New_min_A, New_max_A].

4   Research Method

Fig.1 depicts the overall process in this research, describing the position the proposed hybrid model in predicting size of forest fire.

4.1   Data Collection

Data on forest fire are collected from the study by Cortez and Morais, available in the UCI machine learning repository [2] . The dataset contains 12 variable with their respective labels, forest fire weather index (FWI) components in Montesano Natural Park, a northeast region of Portugal. Weather observations are collected by Braganza Polytechnic Institute and integrated to the forest fire dataset. The park was divided into 81 distinct locations by placing a 9×9 grid onto the map of the park. The dataset has a total of 517 samples, from year 2000 until 2007. This research only select 8 variables to be considered: FFMC, DMC, DC, ISI, Temperature, RH, Wind and Rain.

4.2   Splitting the Dataset

In this steps, the dataset is split into two categories. The process of splitting data is conducted by selecting label dataset(Area). The label (Area) that have value zero, it means have not any total burn area size will be separate from label (Area) that have value more than zero as showed in Fig. 2. After that, all data with zero value will be categorized as data "No Burn Area". Otherwise, the label (Area) data with value more than zero will be cluster by FCM to categorized as data Light Burn or Heavy Burn.

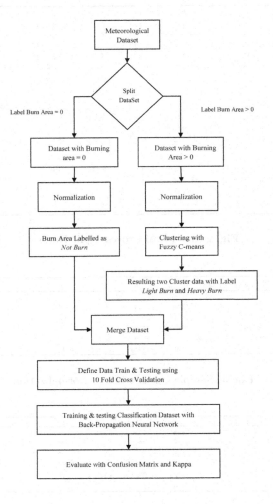

Fig. 1. Research Method Outline

4.3 Normalization

After splitting dataset into two categories between dataset that have value zero or more than zero in attribute label, we continue with the process of normalization. Normalization process in this research uses equation (1) with min max normalization. The normalization process, only transform 8 variables that will be used in clustering and classification process such as FFMC, DMC, DC, ISI, temperature, RH, wind, and rain. This process results in minimum and maximum values between $[0, 1]$ in dataset. The sample of process before and after normalization could be seen in Fig.3 and Fig.4.

FFMC	DMC	DC	ISI	temp	RH	wind	rain	area
93.500	139.400	594.200	20.300	17.600	52	5.800	0	0
92.400	124.100	680.700	8.500	17.200	58	1.300	0	0
90.900	126.500	686.500	7	15.600	66	3.100	0	0
85.800	48.300	313.400	3.900	18	42	2.700	0	0.360
91	129.500	692.600	7	21.700	38	2.200	0	0.430
90.900	126.500	686.500	7	21.900	39	1.800	0	0.470

FFMC	DMC	DC	ISI	temp	RH	wind	rain	area
93.500	139.400	594.200	20.300	17.600	52	5.800	0	0
92.400	124.100	680.700	8.500	17.200	58	1.300	0	0
90.900	126.500	686.500	7	15.600	66	3.100	0	0

FFMC	DMC	DC	ISI	temp	RH	wind	rain	area
85.800	48.300	313.400	3.900	18	42	2.700	0	0.360
91	129.500	692.600	7	21.700	38	2.200	0	0.430
90.900	126.500	686.500	7	21.900	39	1.800	0	0.470

Fig. 2. Sample of Process Split Dataset

FFMC	DMC	DC	ISI	temp	RH	wind	rain	area
93.100	157.300	666.700	13.500	21.700	40	0.400	0	2.470
93.100	157.300	666.700	13.500	26.800	25	3.100	0	0.680
93.100	157.300	666.700	13.500	24	36	3.100	0	0.240
93.100	157.300	666.700	13.500	22.100	37	3.600	0	0.210
91.900	109.200	565.500	8	21.400	38	2.700	0	1.520
91.600	138.100	621.700	6.300	18.900	41	3.100	0	10.340

Fig. 3. Sample Dataset before Normalization

FFMC	DMC	DC	ISI	temp	RH	wind	rain	area
0.960	0.538	0.771	0.595	0.627	0.259	0	0	2.470
0.960	0.538	0.771	0.595	0.791	0.074	0.300	0	0.680
0.960	0.538	0.771	0.595	0.701	0.210	0.300	0	0.240
0.960	0.538	0.771	0.595	0.640	0.222	0.356	0	0.210
0.945	0.373	0.651	0.352	0.617	0.235	0.256	0	1.520
0.941	0.472	0.717	0.278	0.537	0.272	0.300	0	10.340

Fig. 4. Sample Dataset after Normalization

4.4   Fuzzy C-Means Clustering Dataset

The process of categorizing dataset into two categorise of size of fire is done in this phase. Fuzzy C-Means here will cluster the data based on eight Meteorological variables. Since FCM is unsupervised method, it will automatically categorise the dataset into two categorise by default: cluster_0 (as Light Burn) and custer_1 (as Heavy Burn).

We observed several distance similarity measurements algorithm in FCM such as Correlation Similarity, Cosine Similarity, Dice Similarity, Inner Product Similarity, Jaccard Similarity, Overlap Similarity, Kernel Euclidian Distance,

Manhattan Distance, Chebychev Distance, Euclidean Distance, Canberra Distance, Dynamic Time Warping Distance to achieve the best performance of classification BPNN .

4.5   Merge Dataset

After clustering process has been done, the data that has been categorize as No Burn Area will be merged with the data that has been cluster by FCM. Therefore, after this process we will have the dataset that contain label No Burn Area, Light Burn, and Heavy Burn. As you can see in Fig.5.

FFMC	DMC	DC	ISI	temp	RH	wind	rain	area
0.965	0.479	0.692	0.362	0.475	0.435	0.645	0	no_burn_area
0.933	0.047	0.021	0.219	0.475	0.141	0.645	0	no_burn_area
0.862	0.113	0.077	0.320	0.476	0.148	0.500	0	light_burn
0.862	0.113	0.077	0.320	0.476	0.148	0.500	0	light_burn
0.722	1	1	0.146	0.476	0.642	0.500	0	heavy_burn
0.942	0.258	0.838	0.139	0.479	0.282	0.355	0	no_burn_area

Fig. 5. Sample of Merge Dataset

4.6   Back-Propagation Neural Network Architecture

The architecture of Back-Propagation Neural Network in this research uses only one hidden layer, where the learning rate has been fixed at $\beta = 0.3$ and the maximum number of iteration is $\alpha = 500$. The detail steps of BPNN could be seen at [16]. Fig.6 is showed the architecture of BPNN.

5   Result Evaluation and Discussion

5.1   Performance Measurement

After classification process, to assess the performance results of our proposed hybrid method for predicting forest burning size, we used confusion matrix [11] to measures accuracy of classifier can be calculated by equation (2) and Cohen's Kappa statistic measurement [18] to assess inter-rater reliability when observing categorical variables can be calculate by equation (3).

$$Accuracy = \frac{TP + TN}{TP + TN + FP + FN} \tag{2}$$

$$Kappa = \frac{Observed\ Agreement - Expected\ Agreement}{1 - Expected\ Agreement} \tag{3}$$

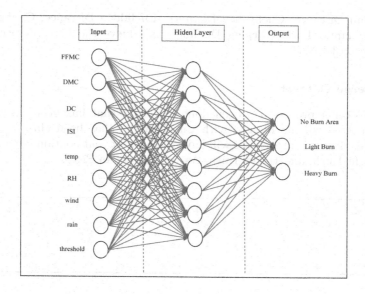

Fig. 6. Back-Propagation Neural Network Architecture

5.2   Experiment Result

This research used RapidMinner tools to conduct the experiment. All the process from normalization phase, clustering, classification until Validation and Evaluation were conducted in RapidMiner. Based on the results displayed in Table 1 and Table 2, it is shown performance of Back-Propagation neural network could achieve best results with accuracy around 97.50% and index of Cohens Kappa 0.961. The best performance of proposed model are gathered with combination

Table 1. Performance of Hybrid Model in Stratified Sampling

Type of Distance Similarity in FCM	Accuracy	Kappa
Correlation Similarity	95.74%	0.933
Cosine Similarity	**97.10%**	**0.954**
Dice Similarity	96.91%	0.945
Inner Product Similarity	96.71%	0.936
Jaccard Similarity	96.91%	0.945
Overlap Similarity	91.30%	0.861
Kernel Euclidian Distance	96.14%	0.938
Manhatan Distance	96.13%	0.935
Chebychev Distance	95.74%	0.930
Euclidean Distance	96.33%	0.941
Canberra Distance	93.42%	0.897
Dynamic Time Warping Distance	86.26%	0.780

Table 2. Performance of Hybrid Model in Shufled Sampling

Type of Distance Similarity in FCM	Accuracy	Kappa
Correlation Similarity	95.75%	0.932
Cosine Similarity	**97.50%**	**0.961**
Dice Similarity	97.30%	0.952
Inner Product Similarity	96.34%	0.927
Jaccard Similarity	97.30%	0.952
Overlap Similarity	89.56%	0.833
Kernel Euclidian Distance	96.92%	0.951
Manhatan Distance	96.90%	0.947
Chebychev Distance	96.91%	0.949
Euclidean Distance	96.92%	0.951
Canberra Distance	92.65%	0.884
Dynamic Time Warping Distance	84.56%	0.754

of BPNN with FCM that used Cosine Similarity. Besides that, to show the performance of BPNN, we also compare the performance of another classification method such as SVM, KNN, DCT, and Naive Bayes, that include with same clustering technique FCM in categorizing the dataset. The results comparison could be seen at Fig 7 and Fig.8.

The proposed Hybrid model for predicting the size of forest fire indicates a promising result. Compared with other methods such as SVM, K-NN and DCT Tree, the proposed method is still showing better performance, more over Naive Bayes and Random Forest have lowest performance classification with accuracy less than 74% and Cohens Kappa 0.54.

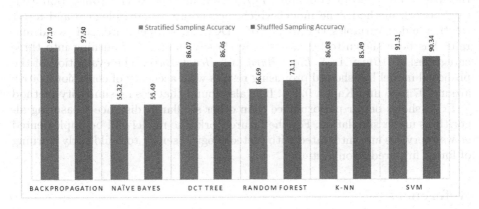

Fig. 7. Results of Accuracy Confusion Matrix Performance

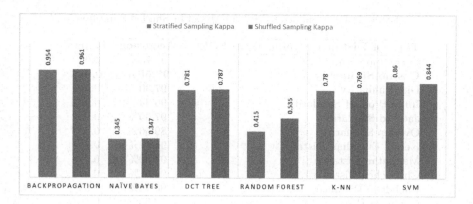

Fig. 8. Results of Cohen's Kappa Performance

The overall approach of experiment in this study is different to the existing work done by Cortez and Morais [2] that also used same dataset. However, in their study used twelve variables which our approach used eight variables. Besides that, they only evaluate pure prediction methods such as Neural Network, SVM, Naive Bayes, Multiple Regression and Decision Trees without combining cluster methods that provide burn area prediction in numerical results without categorizing the type of result forest burning size.

6   Conclusion

This research has proposed an alternative hybrid model capable of predicting the size of forest fire by combining Fuzzy C-Means and Back-Propagation Neural Network method. The model which incorporates meteorological and forest weather index variables (FFMC, DMC, DC, ISI, temperature, RH, wind and rain) has been shown to be successfully classify the level of burning into three categories: *No Burn Area, Light Burn* and *Heavy Burn*. The evaluation of the proposed model has showed promising results with accuracy of confusion matrix around 97.50% and Kappa 0.961. It is also found that cosine similarity method in FCM shows better performance than other similarity distance measuring algorithms under simulation. For the future work, the model will be implemented as web services and integrated with meteorological sensor to build early warning of forest fire prediction system.

References

1. Alonso-Betanzos, A., Fontenla-Romero, O., Guijarro-Berdinas, B., Hernndez-Pereira, E., Paz-Andrade, M.I., Jimenez, E., Legido, J.L., Carballas, T.: An intelligent system for forest fire risk prediction and fire fighting management in galicia. Expert Syst. Appl. 25(4), 545–554 (2003)

2. Cortez, P., Morais, A.: A data mining approach to predict forest fires using meteorological data. In: Neves, J., Santos, M.F., Machado, J. (eds.) EPIA 2007, pp. 512–523 (2007)
3. Elmas, C., Sonmez, Y.: A data fusion framework with novel hybrid algorithm for multi-agent decision support system for forest fire. Expert Syst. Appl. 38(8), 9225–9236 (2011)
4. Safi, Y., Bouroumi, A.: A neural network approach for predicting forest fires. In: 2011 International Conference on Multimedia Computing and Systems (ICMCS), pp. 1–5 (2011)
5. Iliadis, L., Vangeloudh, M., Spartalis, S.: An intelligent system employing an enhanced fuzzy c-means clustering model: Application in the case of forest fires. Computers and Electronics in Agriculture 70(2), 276–284 (2010); Special issue on Information and Communication Technologies in Bio and Earth Sciences
6. Yu, Y.P., Omar, R., Harrison, R.D., Sammathuria, M.K., Nik, A.R.: Pattern clustering of forest fires based on meteorological variables and its classification using hybrid data mining methods. Journal of Computational Biology and Bioinformatics Research 3, 47–52 (2011)
7. Sakr, G.E., Elhajj, I.H., Mitri, G.: Efficient forest fire occurrence prediction for developing countries using two weather parameters. Engineering Applications of Artificial Intelligence 24(5), 888–894 (2011)
8. Sitanggang, I., Ismail, M.: Hotspot occurrences classification using decision tree method: Case study in the rokan hilir, riau province, indonesia. In: 2010 8th International Conference on ICT and Knowledge Engineering, pp. 46–50 (2010)
9. Satoh, K., Weiguo, S., Yang, K.T.: A study of forest fire danger prediction system in japan. In: Proceedings of the 15th International Workshop on Database and Expert Systems Applications, pp. 598–602 (2004)
10. Sakr, G., Elhajj, I., Mitri, G., Wejinya, U.: Artificial intelligence for forest fire prediction. In: 2010 IEEE/ASME International Conference on Advanced Intelligent Mechatronics (AIM), pp. 1311–1316 (2010)
11. Witten, I.H., Frank, E.: Data Mining: Practical Machine Learning Tools and Techniques with Java Implementations. Morgan Kaufmann, San Francisco (2005)
12. Dunn, J.C.: A fuzzy relative of the isodata process and its use in detecting compact well-separated clusters (1973)
13. Bezdek, J.C.: Pattern recognition with fuzzy objective function algorithms. Kluwer Academic Publishers (1981)
14. Chattopadhyay, S., Pratihar, D.K., Sarkar, S.C.D.: A comparative study of fuzzy c-means algorithm and entropy-based fuzzy clustering algorithms. Computing and Informatics 30(4), 701–720 (2011)
15. Singh, D., Dutta, M., Singh, S.H.: Neural network based handwritten hindi character recognition system. In: Shyamasundar, R.K. (ed.) Bangalore Compute Conf., p. 15. ACM (2009)
16. Eleyan, A., Demirel, H.: PCA and LDA based Neural Networks for Human Face Recognition, Number June, Viena, Austria (2007)
17. Han, J., Kamber, M.: Data mining: concepts and techniques. Kaufmann, San Francisco (2005)
18. Byrt, T., Bishop, J., Carlin, J.B.: Bias, prevalence and kappa. Journal of Clinical Epidemiology 46(5), 423–429 (1993)

Understanding eParticipation Services in Indonesian Local Government

Fathul Wahid[1,2] and Øystein Sæbø[2]

[1] Department of Informatics, Universitas Islam Indonesia, Yogyakarta, Indonesia
[2] Department of Information Systems, University of Agder, Kristiansand, Norway

Abstract. This study aims at understanding how local government from a developing country, in this case Indonesia, implement and manage eParticipation services. In doing so, we combine institutional theory and stakeholder theory to build a sharper analytical lens. From an interpretive case study in the city of Yogyakarta, we reveal the institutionalization process of the services since their inception and identify major stakeholders and their salience. Based on our findings, we propose implications for practice and suggest implications for further research. Future work, based on a multiple case strategy including several eParticipation cases from other parts of Indonesia, will further explore the findings reported here.

Keywords: eParticipation, eGovernment, Stakeholder Theory, Institutional Theory, Institutionalization, Developing Country, Indonesia.

1 Introduction

In recent years, eParticipation services have proliferated in local governments, influencing on the communication between governments, politicians and citizens. As society becomes ever more digitized, governments are attempting to boost democratic interests through various eParticipation services [1, 2]. Triggering the interests of stakeholders is vital in eParticipation efforts. Through such services, citizen can communicate easily with local government through various channels to increase citizens' participation [3-5]. In general, eParticipation includes technology-mediated interaction between the civil society, politicians and administration [6].

While the initiatives are promising in promoting citizen participation, there is lack of research aiming at understanding the phenomenon and eventually accessing its impact in decision-making quality in the context of developing countries. Moreover, citizen participation in developing countries are very low compared to developed countries [7]. Hence, this research seeks to answer an explorative question: *how does Indonesian local government implement and manage eParticipation services?*

In Indonesia, during the 'new order' of Suharto regime (1965-1998), government decisions were entirely limited to government officers, especially high-level bureaucrats. Citizen participation was restricted, if not discouraged, as the central government neglected local demands and problems [8, 9]. After the fall of the Suharto

Linawati et al. (Eds.): ICT-EurAsia 2014, LNCS 8407, pp. 328–337, 2014.

regime, citizens could freely articulate their opinions. Citizen participation in the Indonesian context becomes even more important after decentralization in 2001 when some of the national government authorities were delegated to the local government [9], encouraging the development of local and contextualized policies.

In order to answer our research questions, we conducted a case study that traces back the implementation of eParticipation services in the city of Yogyakarta since its inception in 2003. Yogyakarta is among the pioneers in the provision of eParticipation services. The study is framed within the concepts of institutional theory and stakeholder theory. Both theories have been used in information system (IS) studies for various purposes [10-12]. Institutional theory helps to understand the institutionalization process of eParticipation services and identifying institutional actors. Stakeholder theory (ST) further expands our understanding of the actors, by identifying their salience and connections between them. By combining the two, we develop a sharper theoretical lens to better understand the phenomenon under study.

The remainder of the paper is organized as follows. Next, we introduce theoretical premises for the study before we describe the research setting and method. Then we present findings followed by the discussion, before reflecting on limitations and contributions.

2   Theoretical Premises

2.1   Institutional Theory

Institutional theory sees institutions as "multifaceted, durable social structures made up of symbolic elements, social activities, and material resources" [13]. It offers rich concepts to study institutional effects of IS (e.g. eParticipation services in this study), institutionalization, and interactions between IS and institutions [10]. The concepts include institutional isomorphism [14], institutional logics [15], institutionalization [16], and institutional entrepreneurship [17, 18].

Institutional theory is relevant to our study for two reasons. First, eParticipation services can be seen as institutions, provided they have been widely accepted and have become an integral part of day-to-day practices. Second, institutional theory can be used to explain the history of IS implementation [19], which in this proposed study is the institutionalization of an eParticipation services. The theory is useful to understand how institutional transformation takes place [20]. In Selznick's [21] words, "institutional theory traces the emergence of distinctive forms, processes, strategies, outlooks, and competencies as they emerge from patterns of organizational interaction and adaptation". Previous studies [22-24] in eGovernment have successfully used institutional theory to understand various phenomena.

2.2   Stakeholder Theory

The *theory of stakeholder* salience [25] offers sound theoretical arguments to explain why some stakeholders are salient, whereas others are not, depending on the relationship between power, legitimacy and urgency (Figure 1). The sum of the attributes determines the salience of a stakeholder, where definitive stakeholders possess all three attributes and are more salient than those who possess only one or two of the attributes. Mitchell et al. [25] argued for a numeric understanding of these attributes to identify whether stakeholders have, or have not, power, legitimacy and urgency. Recent work within the eGovernment area has successfully applied the salience perspective with a more narrative approach [11, 12, 26], more in line with the approach applied in our study.

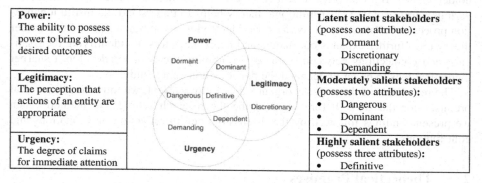

Power: The ability to possess power to bring about desired outcomes		Latent salient stakeholders (possess one attribute): • Dormant • Discretionary • Demanding
Legitimacy: The perception that actions of an entity are appropriate		Moderately salient stakeholders (possess two attributes): • Dangerous • Dominant • Dependent
Urgency: The degree of claims for immediate attention		Highly salient stakeholders (possess three attributes): • Definitive

Fig. 1. Attributes determining a stakeholder's salience
Source: Adapted from Mitchell et al. [25]

Stakeholder salience analyses have been introduced to explain stakeholder actions in eParticipation efforts [27]. Stakeholder analysis is introduced here for two reasons. First, it helps to identify actors being involved or influencing on the initiative. Second, it sheds lights on stakeholders´ salience. Thus, stakeholder analysis may help to identify whom to include, whom to pay attention to, and whom who may have the possibility to influence, negatively or positively on the initiative.

3   Research Setting and Method

3.1   The Case

The eParticipation service under study was initiated in the city of Yogyakarta in 2003. At that time, the mayor intended to improve public services by providing a hotline service enabling the public to send messages directly to the local government, by phone calls or SMS messages. Yogyakarta collaborated with a national telecommunication company to provide a special easy-to-remember number (2740) for receiving SMS messages. Incoming messages were tabulated and responded manually. The service was under the responsibility of a One-roof Service Unit (*Unit Pelayanan Terpadu Satu Atap* [UPTSA]) which in 2006 became the Department of License (*Dinas Perijinan*).

The system remained the same until 2013, due to the fact that UPIK did not have access to the source code, making it difficult to maintain and further develop the system. A new web-based version (http://upik.jogjakota.go.id), implemented late 2013, allows automated management of incoming messages. In implementing the system, Yogyakarta gained support from Swisscontact, an international development agency, which collaborated with PKPEK, a local NGO. Now, messages posted through a website or SMS are automatically registered. A Unit for Information and Complaint Services (*Unit Pelayanan Informasi dan Keluhan* [UPIK]) was then established to manage the system.

3.2   The Method

Our study is exploratory in nature, aiming to define questions, proposing new constructs and eventually construct new theoretical propositions, additional constructs and the relationships between constructs [28] that may complement the original framework [29]. Exploratory case studies typically address how and why questions concerning the dynamics present within a contextual setting [30].

In this paper, reporting from research in progress, we have interviewed seven informants: two administrators at UPIK, head of the Subsection for Application Development, head of UPIK, head of the Section for Information Technology, vice head of the Department of License, and the Mayor. Interviews at UPIK, conducted in November 2013, focused on the implementation and management of the services. Interviews with other informants, conducted in July and August 2011, covered a broader area of the use of information technology in Yogyakarta. Findings from the interviews were further enriched by consulting and analysing documents and information such as internal reports, presentation slides and news in the media.

Data were analysed based on concepts from institutional and stakeholder theory, such as institutional pressure, institutional logic, institutionalization, resource mobilization, power, urgency, and legitimacy.

4   Findings

The flow of incoming messages is illustrated in Figure 2. Citizens may send messages through various channels: SMS, website, e-mail, phone, fax, regular letter, or by visiting UPIK. Only messages retrieved through SMS and the website are automatically registered. The administrators at UPIK filter and forward messages to the appropriate technical department within 24 hours. The forwarded messages will be accessible online, as long as they are not considered sensitive (e.g. discussing corruption). The technical departments have two days to respond to ordinary messages, six days for more complicated issues. Some specific messages, such as those demanding for written public information, will be handled separately by the Managing Officer of Information and Documents (PPID).

Although an online web-based service has been in place for around ten years, SMS is still the most preferred channel (see Table 1). In 2004, 85% of the incoming messages came through SMS, whereas only 1% through the website. Interestingly, 11% came through face-to-face meetings at the UPIK office. The picture changed slightly in 2006, when 16% were sent through the websites, only to decrease down to 6% in 2010. Now, SMS messages accounted for 94% of the total messages.

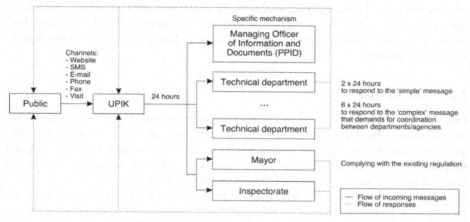

Fig. 2. Flow of incoming messages and responses

Table 1. Statistics of the incoming messages through various channels

Channel	Number of messages										
	2004	2005	2006	2007	2008	2009	2010	2011	2012	2013*	All
SMS	1,862	2,950	2,166	1,928	2,873	2,510	3,220	3,272	3,092	3,502	27,375
Website	23	0	402	455	426	255	190	138	132	74	2,095
Phone	34	4	0	0	1	0	4	5	1	4	53
Fax	2	0	0	0	0	0	0	0	0	0	2
Email	15	8	0	0	0	1	0	0	0	10	34
Visit	236	291	0	0	0	0	0	0	1	3	531
Other	13	0	1	2	1	0	0	3	1	5	26
Total	2,172	3,253	2,568	2,383	3,300	2,766	3,414	3,415	3,226	3,598	30,095

Notes: *Until November 2013.

Regardless of the channels used, the number of messages sent through the services indicates good acceptance among citizens, with a total of 30,000 messages received since 2004 until November 2013. The incoming messages are categorized (by UPIK) into four groups: complaints (28.5%), questions (25.6%), information (31.7%), and suggestions (14.3%). Around 90% of the messages have been responded.

4.1 Institutionalization

Institutional Pressure. The services, when initiated in 2003, were among the pioneers in Indonesia. External pressure came from the demand from the public for more transparent government, as asserted by the head of UPIK:

"We are fully aware that the public of Yogyakarta are intelligent. This was one of the reasons [behind the establishment of the eParticipation services]. If we did not improve our transparency, we might easily become a target of the public criticism."

Institutional Logic. The intention was to provide communication channels enabling citizens to convey messages to local government, as a part of affirmative actions taken by the local government to improve public participation. The logic behind the services was to provide better services to the public. Such services were not only beneficial to the public, but also to local government. Expected benefits include: (1) increase citizens´ role in controlling local government, (2) allowing government to collect public aspirations, and (3) as a result, enabling local government to design programs that accommodate the public aspirations. In general, the services enable local government to gain trust from the public. Lack of trust to government is among the chronic problem in the Indonesian context.

Institutionalization. A main challenge in the initiation phase of the implementation of the eParticipation services was to change the department heads mind-set. From the beginning, the mayor realized this challenge, and coped it with instilling values that would be important to guide the implementation of the services. The mayor lead by example, by spending substantial time to visit and discuss with citizens, and by sending messages and answers through the system. The mayor argued that the local government should have willingness to be controlled and corrected by the public. According to him:

"We have to make our position less sacred. It is only division of job. When we are talking about eGovernment, we do not pay attention to the social status. ... I am talking about how to work in more effective, efficient, transparent, and accountable ways. All are inseparable in good governance practices. eGovernment initiatives are taken for that purpose."

An administrative staff at UPIK confirmed the mayor's statement. He explained:

"The mayor would like to change the mind-set of government officers, from acting as 'pangreh praja' [those with power to command] to becoming 'pamong praja' [those who serve the people]. ... At that time, we were not ready to change ourselves."

Resource Mobilization. The mayor gained support from external and internal actors to improve the services. External actors include Swisscontact (an international development agency), PKPEK (a local NGO), a national telecommunication company, and more importantly, the public. Several initiatives were taken to make the public aware of the eParticipation service and to attract their support. Initiatives include the arrangement of public meetings at the village level, advertising in local newspapers and radio stations, distributing stickers, and placing banners in all the village and sub-district offices.

Some internal resistance from the technical departments could be identified, primarily in the initiation phase. For instance, some incoming messages to the technical department were not answered. Then the mayor usually called the head of the respective technical department to solve the problem. The head of sub-section metaphorically described: "[The phone call from the mayor] is enough to make them sweating that morning." For the same purpose, every month, District Secretary (*Sekretaris Daerah*) sends a warning letter to the unresponsive technical departments. Close oversight is among of the strategies to mobilize support from internal stakeholders.

4.2   Stakeholders and Their Salience

Stakeholders. Table 3 summarizes our initial assessment of the involved stakeholders along with the level of salience related to their power, urgency, and legitimacy. The *mayor* is a driving force, as he insisted to implement the services and supervised the actions to make sure that the services run as expected. *UPIK* is established to manage the services and serves as a 'hub' or intermediary between the public and local government. *Technical departments* (including sub-district offices) are the 'busiest' stakeholders as they are responsive to the incoming messages. *Section for Information Technology* is the stakeholder responsible for procuring and maintaining the supporting system. *Operators* in each technical department are responsible for replying, routing incoming messages to the respective head of department and collecting responses from the targeted agencies.

Table 2. Stakeholders and their salience

Stakeholder	Power	Urgency	Legitimacy	Salience
Mayor	High	High	High	High
UPIK	Medium	Medium	Medium	Medium
Technical Department	Medium	Low/Medium	High	Medium
Section for IT	Medium	Medium	Medium	Medium
Operator	Low	Low	Medium	Low
Public	Low	High	High	Medium/High

Stakeholder Salience. The mayor is a *definitive* stakeholder with high level of power, urgency, and legitimacy. UPIK and Section for Information Technology are *definitive* stakeholders though with a lower level of salience compared to the mayor. Public is *dependent* stakeholder as although they have high urgency and legitimacy, they lack (formal) power. So are the operators at the technical departments. Technical departments are *dominant* stakeholders since most of the incoming messages are addressed to them.

5   Discussion

Discussion is made in light of the research question stated in the outset: *how does Indonesian local government implement and manage eParticipation services?* In doing so, we focus on two intertwined aspects: the institutionalization process and the relationship between the stakeholders.

The eParticipation services are certainly collective initiatives and involve political decision-making. However, it is obvious that the role of the mayor was very influential, considering that, especially at the beginning, some stakeholders implicitly indicated reluctance to take part in the services. Here, we may consider that the mayor acted as institutional entrepreneur, who directed and led the organizational changes in implementing the services. In doing so, at the beginning, he cultivated values to the services beyond the instrumental utility of the services [31]. In addition, the mayors and his backers, mobilized resources and supports from other stakeholders (cf. [22]). A set of institutional logics was introduced to legitimate the services, to mobilize supports, and to guide the implementation.

Afterwards, the institutionalization was strengthened by typification process [13], where certain forms of responsibilities were associated with certain stakeholders who, in this case, have different level of salience. The only definitive stakeholder is the mayor. As a definitive stakeholder, he would be given attention not only because he represents a legitimate claim, but also since he is likely to exercise power because of a sense of urgency. A mayor will always possess *legitimacy* and *power*. Interestingly, the mayor of Yogyakarta also possessed *urgency,* based on his personal interest in the initiative. After implementation, a new mayor was elected possessing the same *legitimacy* and *power,* but less (personal) *urgency* to champion the initiative. Recent research [26] argues that salience, especially urgency, needs to be high for one or another key stakeholder at each phase of a project. Future analysis is needed to explore consequences of decreasing *urgency* from the definitive stakeholder.

The salient analyses further unveil the low salience of those being responsible for handling the request from the public, the operators. They have low urgency and power, and were not directly involved in development of the services. Without concerning "doers" interests, by involving them in the processes to increase their awareness and, consequently, their salience, the initiatives run the risks of operators giving less priority to providing answers. Moreover, the operators are highly dependent on the heads of technical department. Some of them also have low urgency. Hence, increasing the level of urgency of both the heads of technical department and the operators is important to improve and sustain the eParticipation services.

Although the public has low formal power, they are successful in giving institutional pressure to the local government due to strong support from the definitive stakeholder, the mayor. It is important to include the notion of informal power in this context, which will be part of future analyses. Furthermore, our study indicates the need for a more thoroughly analysis of the public, to further expand our understanding of differences between various groups and the level of salience; such as activist citizens, consumer citizens, local businesses, NGOs and so on. For example, it will be important to understand why the number of incoming messages only changed slightly from 2004 to 2013 (see Table 1).

6   Conclusion

We revealed that the eParticipation services are collective initiatives that need resource or support mobilization from various stakeholders. The salience level of the involved stakeholders to some extent has impact on how they perceive the services and take a part in the implementation process. To act as institutional entrepreneur, a stakeholder needs to have a certain level of salience in three aspects (power, urgency, and legitimacy). With all the three qualities, combined by a set of strategies to mobilize resources, the mayor acted as the institutional entrepreneur who drove the organisational changes.

The main contributions of this paper are twofold. First, it reports the implementation of eParticipation services from the context of a developing country, which so far, is under-researched and less articulated in the extant literature. We expect to fill this void. Second, it makes a first attempt to combine two theories to build a sharper analytical lens, but with recognizing their distinct contributions, which complement to each other. For example, Clegg [32] suggests to bring back the discussion of power into institutional theory.

However, as a research in progress, we cannot provide a complete picture, and hence, we need to delve further to better understand the situated practices of each stakeholder. We will collect additional data from Yogyakarta by involving more stakeholders, and include cases from other parts of Indonesia. By doing so, we expect to provide a fuller picture on how eParticipation services are implemented in different contexts of developing countries and how to harvest such services to improve the quality of public participation.

References

1. Macintosh, A., McKay-Hubbard, A., Shell, D.: Using weblogs to support local democracy. In: Böhlen, M.H., Gamper, J., Polasek, W., Wimmer, M.A. (eds.) TCGOV 2005. LNCS (LNAI), vol. 3416, pp. 1–12. Springer, Heidelberg (2005)
2. Tambouris, E., Liotas, N., Tarabanis, K.: A framework for assessing eParticipation projects and tools. In: Proceedings of the 2007 Hawaii International Conference on System Sciences (2007)
3. Effing, R., van Hillegersberg, J., Huibers, T.: Social media and political participation: Are Facebook, Twitter and YouTube democratizing our political systems? In: Tambouris, E., Macintosh, A., de Bruijn, H. (eds.) ePart 2011. LNCS, vol. 6847, pp. 25–35. Springer, Heidelberg (2011)
4. Jackson, N.A., Lilleker, D.G.: Building an architecture of participation? Political parties and Web 2.0 in Britain. Journal of Information Technology & Politics 6, 232–250 (2009)
5. Kalnes, Ø.: Norwegian parties and Web 2.0. Journal of Information Technology & Politics 6, 251–266 (2009)
6. Sæbø, Ø., Rose, J., Skiftenes Flak, L.: The shape of eParticipation: Characterizing an emerging research area. Government Information Quarterly 25, 400–428 (2008)
7. United Nations: E-Government Survey 2012: E-Government for the People, United Nations, New York (2012)
8. Jackson, K.D.: Bureaucratic polity: A theoretical framework for the analysis of power and communications in Indonesia. In: Jackson, K.D., Pye, L.W. (eds.) Political Power and Communications in Indonesia, pp. 3–22. University of California Press, Berkeley (1978)
9. Widianingsih, I., Morrell, E.: Participatory planning in Indonesia: Seeking a new path to democracy. Policy Studies 28, 1–15 (2007)
10. Mignerat, M., Rivard, S.: Positioning the institutional perspective in information systems research. Journal of Information Technology 24, 369–391 (2009)
11. Scholl, H.J.: Involving salient stakeholders Beyond the technocratic view on change. Action Research 2, 277–304 (2004)
12. Flak, L.S., Rose, J.: Stakeholder governance: Adapting stakeholder theory to e-government. Communications of the Association for Information Systems 16, 642–664 (2005)

13. Scott, W.R.: Institutions and Organizations: Ideas and Interest. Sage, Thousand Oaks (2008)
14. DiMaggio, P.J., Powell, W.W.: The iron cage revisited: Institutional isomorphism and collective rationality in organizational fields. American Sociological Review 48, 147–160 (1983)
15. Thornton, P.H., Ocasio, W.: Institutional Logics. In: Greenwood, R., Oliver, C., Suddaby, R., Sahlin-Andersson, K. (eds.) The SAGE Handbook of Organizational Institutionalism, pp. 99–129. Sage, London (2008)
16. Scott, W.R.: The adolescence of Institutional Theory. Administrative Science Quarterly 32, 493–511 (1987)
17. DiMaggio, P.J.: Interest and agency in institutional theory. In: Zucker, L.G. (ed.) Institutional Patterns and Organizations: Culture and Environment, Ballinger, Cambridge, MA, pp. 3–21 (1988)
18. Battilana, J., Leca, B., Boxenbaum, E.: How actors change institutions: Towards a theory of institutional entrepreneurship. The Academy of Management Annals 3, 65–107 (2009)
19. Avgerou, C.: IT and organizational change: an institutionalist perspective. Information Technology & People 13, 234–262 (2000)
20. Dacin, M.T., Goodstein, J., Scott, W.R.: Institutional theory and institutional change: Introduction to the special research forum. Academy of Management Journal 45, 45–56 (2002)
21. Selznick, P.: Institutionalism "old" and "new". Administrative Science Quarterly 41, 270–277 (1996)
22. Wahid, F., Sein, M.K.: Institutional entrepreneurs: The driving force in institutionalization of public systems in developing countries. Transforming Government: People, Process and Policy 7 (2013)
23. Gil-Garcia, J.R., Martinez-Moyano, I.J.: Understanding the evolution of e-government: The influence of systems of rules on public sector dynamics. Government Information Quarterly 24, 266–290 (2007)
24. Kim, S., Kim, H.J., Lee, H.: An institutional analysis of an e-government system for anti-corruption: The case of OPEN. Government Information Quarterly 26, 42–50 (2009)
25. Mitchell, R.K., Agle, B.R., Wood, D.J.: Toward a theory of stakeholder identification and salience: Defining the principle of who and what really counts. Academy of Management Review 22, 853–886 (1997)
26. Sæbø, Ø., Flak, L.S., Sein, M.K.: Understanding the dynamics in e-Participation initiatives: Looking through the genre and stakeholder lenses. Government Information Quarterly 28, 416–425 (2011)
27. Axelsson, K., Melin, U., Lindgren, I.: Public e-services for agency efficiency and citizen benefit—Findings from a stakeholder centered analysis. Government Information Quarterly 30, 10–22 (2012)
28. Cavaye, A.L.M.: Case study research: A multi - faceted research approach for IS. Information Systems Journal 6, 227–242 (1996)
29. Dibbern, J., Winkler, J., Heinzl, A.: Explaining variations in client extra costs between software projects offshored to India. MIS Quarterly 32, 333 (2008)
30. Eisenhardt, K.M.: Building theories from case study research. Academy of Management Review 14, 532–550 (1989)
31. Selznick, P.: Leadership in Administration. Harper and Row, New York (1957)
32. Clegg, S.: The state, power, and agency: Missing in action in institutional theory? Journal of Management Inquiry 19, 4–13 (2010)

Document Tracking Technology to Support Indonesian Local E-Governments

Wikan Sunindyo, Bayu Hendradjaya, G.A. Putri Saptawati, and Tricya E. Widagdo

Data and Software Engineering Research Group
School of Electrical Engineering and Informatics, Bandung Institute of Technology
Labtek V 2nd floor, Ganesha Street 10 Bandung 40132 Indonesia
{wikan,bayu,putri,cia}@informatika.org

Abstract. Currently, many information and communication technologies have been used to support electronic government systems (e-gov) to become more effective and efficient. However, in the practical level, some specific issues are still needed to be handled, for example how to manage, handle and track electronic documents in the government institutions, which also can support frequent business process modification. In this paper, we propose to integrate document tracking technology into e-government business process to improve efficiency and effectiveness of e-government application in Indonesia. We offers three integrated generic models of a document tracking system. The models has been applied at a pilot project in an administration office and a city that is enthusiastic to apply a complete e-gov system. We expect that the solution approach can be applied in other local e-governments in Indonesia. Initial results show that the document tracking prototype application can enhance the productivity, clear and simplify the business process, and support process measurement, such that it can be used to improve the quality of local e-government services.

Keywords: Document Tracking, E-Government, Business Process, Information and Communication Technology.

1   Introduction

To accelerate and expand economic development in Indonesia, the Indonesian government has launched many research and development programs and used many technologies including Information and communication technologies (ICT) to achieve the goal, especially in bureaucratic reformation. The Indonesian bureaucratic reformation should follow these principles, namely (1) to create effective bureaucracy that can organize people and support business sector requirements, (2) to create a strong and effective bureaucracy institution, by making clean administration, responsible legislation, and independent judicial institution, (3) to create a good governance application commitment, and (4) to create feedback channel for the future planning [3].

Linawati et al. (Eds.): ICT-EurAsia 2014, LNCS 8407, pp. 338–347, 2014.

To support these bureaucratic reformation programs, a document tracking system is proposed to facilitate the government work process in different sectors and layers. Currently there are some challenges in processing documents in the governmental institutions, such as:

(1) It is not easy to track the status of some documents/requests. Currently in the location of our case study, there is no document tracking system, thus document finding and tracking is done manually.

(2) Bottlenecks in the system are undetected. The work process is not measured properly, therefore the bottlenecks cannot be spotted and the process may take longer than expected.

(3) Delayed requests cannot be resolved immediately. Unclear workflow [8], manual process and undocumented delegation cause the requests frequently postponed and cannot be resolved immediately. This is due the fact that there are unclear regulations and slow decision making process in the bureaucracy.

In this paper, we propose to integrate document tracking technology into the e-government business process. By using document tracking systems, it is expected that the e-government implementation can be achieved more efficiently and effectively. The document tracking system supports faster delivery of the documents and easier handling of documents.

We have developed a prototype of document tracking system and use Payakumbuh city government as our pilot project of document tracking system implementation. Payakumbuh was chosen because the mayor is keen to have an E-Government implementation.

The initial results show that the prototype can help the bureaucracy in finding and tracking the documents, thus it can enhance the productivity, clear and simplify the business process, and support process measurement, such that it can be used to improve the quality of local e-government services.

The remainder of this paper is structured as follows. Section 2 presents related work. Section 3 identifies the research questions. Section 4 describes the solution approach. Finally, section 5 concludes and identifies the future work.

2   Related Work

This section discusses definition of information and communication technology and related works on e-government and document tracking.

2.1   Information and Communication Technology

Information and communication technology (ICT) is a big umbrella of terminology used for covering all technical devices to process and convey information.

ICT includes two different aspects, namely information technology and communication technology. Information technology covers all about how to process information, the utility of information as a tool, and how to manipulate and manage information, while communication technology involves all about how to use tools to process and transfer data from one device to others. That's why we can't separate those two concepts [4].

2.2   ICT Development Principles

Development and implementation of ICT in the government are based on these principles [1].

a. Human Resources Quality Improvement Principle
The development and implementation of information technology should be able to strengthen and improve human resources quality, internally and externally.

b. Synergy Principle
The development and implementation of information technology should be able to integrate all available information in the government effectively to support decision making process. The standardization of data and information between institutions is required to support this synergy principle.

c. Utility Principle
The development and implementation of information technology should become more efficient, economical, and effective. The system should be able to deliver information faster, more accurate and on time so it can be used for decision making.

d. Flexibility Principle
The development and implementation of information technology should be done in modular and incremental way to guarantee the flexibility of the systems to adapt internal and external changes.

e. Security and Reliability Principle
The reliability of information technology development and implementation should be guaranteed, such that it can be used anytime. The security and confidentiality of the data should follow the rules and regulations.

f. Legality Principle
The development and implementation of information technology should obey the law, i.e. respect the intellectual property right, including copyrights and other rights that are protected by the laws.

g. Equality of Access Rights Principle
The development and implementation of information technology should guarantee and provide the equality of access rights to governmental information which is open to the public. This principle is intended to avoid digital gaps in certain regions or society.

h. Open Systems, Open Source and Legal Software Principle
The development and implementation of information technology is using open system standard, such that it can integrate different technologies efficiently. The government is expected to use open source application to increase efficiency, economic value to investment, and avoid absolute dependency to certain companies and support IGOS (Indonesia, Go Open Source) movement. If the government uses proprietary applications, it should consider legality aspects [7].

2.3   E-Government

E-Government (electronic government, digital government, online government, or connected government) consists of the digital interactions between a government and citizens (G2C), government and businesses/Commerce (G2B), government and employees (G2E), and also between government and governments /agencies (G2G). Essentially, the e-Government delivery models can be briefly summed up as [2]

(1) G2C (Government to Citizens)
(2) G2B (Government to Businesses)
(3) G2E (Government to Employees)
(4) G2G (Government to Governments)

This digital interaction consists of governance, information and communication technology (ICT), business process re-engineering (BPR), and e-citizen at all levels of government (city, state/province, national, and international) [9].

2.4   Document Tracking

In products distribution and logistics, the product tracing and tracking should consider the process of tracking the location of certain item or property (including other information), for example documents.

Some researchers have been developing document tracking systems as follows.

(1) Schick and Ruland [5] proposed a new security services that provides reliable technologies for traitor tracing
(2) Solic et al [6] proposed an RFID-based location tracking system as the next generation communication services in business processes for distributed offices

3   Research Issues

The research issues are defined as follows.

(1) How to integrate document tracking system into the e-government business process, including the governmental organization, its environmental interaction, the workflow and rules.
(2) How to model the document tracking system and implement it.

4   Proposed Solution

This section presents answer to the research issues mentioned in Section 3. We design the document tracking system first and then implement the prototype of it.

4.1   Document Tracking System Modeling

We found that there are at least two categories of document that should be tracked in a organization.

(1) A document approval tracking: A document that is sent by a user to an organization and this document need to get back to this user after a specific process is performed.

(2) A letter or document delivery: An incoming letter or document need to be enrouted to the right person or unit. The letter or document may be originated from internal or external sources.

A document approval tracking is needed when somebody requests an approval from a department body. A person can submit an application document for approval, and a department or unit should examine this document finally give an approval or disapproval. While waiting for the approval process, this person should be able to track his application. This model gives the benefits that the applicant can always check the progress of his/her online application. In addition to that, at the same time people from the department could be encouraged to process the application faster.

An incoming documents or letters are sorted, and sent to the person in charge to handle the documents. The incoming documents sometimes are in the form of a mail letter. The documents sometimes are routed from high level of management hierarchy to lower level. We classify the routing process into two types:

(1) A document or letter that needs a response from a destination unit back to the origin unit or other specific unit

(2) A document or letter that does not need a response.

In both cases, the origin unit usually needs to know that the letter or document is actually reached its destination.   The system need to show that the document or letter is actually received. The sender of the documents or letters may come from external parties or from internal unit. The sender unit may need to be able to track down the documents.

Therefore each document should be marked with a unique identification. By using this identification, we can always trace the location of documents. A visualization of this tracking is preferred method to help trace these documents. A notification system can also be used to inform the source if needed.

A visual interaction is a benefit, and we propose that it is a must to have a visual interaction for both parties. A screen can display the units involved and also the current location of the documents.

A user who submits a document can visually track the document through his browser, or by accessing company's special application. The management of an organization can make sure that each documents or letters are being taken care of by a unit.

Fig 1. and Fig. 2 show an interaction's model between the document tracking system and its environment. The sources of documents can be from different units (unit 1, unit 2, unit 3, and so on). This model is designed to be generic so that both types of documents uses the same model. Basically the system interacts with units and also the person who is actually part of a unit. The users of the systems are actually can be just a person for Document Approval Tracking or may also be more than one unit for Document/Letter Delivery System.

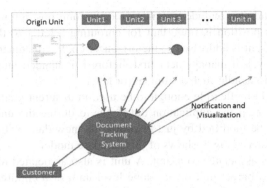

Fig. 1. Context Diagram of The Document Tracking System for Approval Tracking

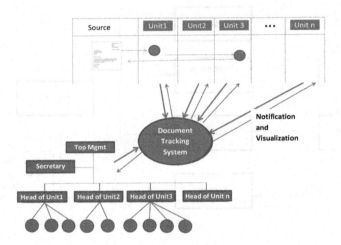

Fig. 2. Context Diagram of The Document Tracking System for Delivery of Documents or Letters

4.2   Database Requirement Model

The documents need to be recorded in a good database structure. The record needs two kinds of media data, namely as a binary image and as metadata of the document. As a binary image, the scan image of the actual documents (or letters) will be provided. A high speed scanner may need to be presented to scan such documents. The metadata of the document is needed for unique identification and also storing other important information (the incoming date, the sender information, and the receiver information or also the current unit).

The model should also include information of the unit position in the organization structure. The unit position is important for enrouting a letter to the right unit. For example if a document is addressed to the organization, the document may have to be enroute the high level of management first, before it is handed into lower level unit that is responsible to handle such document (or letter).

The model should be flexible enough to be used in different kind of organizations. The model should help the application developer to define the unit structures. The unit structures can be modified by just recording the new data, without changing the structure of the database. Fig 3. shows of this database model.

The document is associated to a unit. A unit is also associated to other units. The other units can be a parent unit or the same level unit, or a children unit. A parent unit has higher hierarchical structure, and the child is a lower unit.

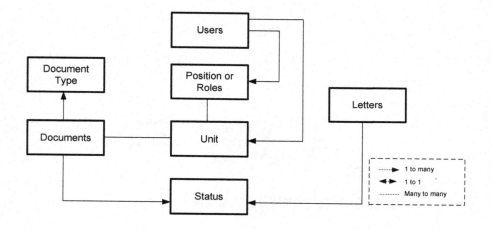

Fig. 3. Database Model

For this document tracking model, we propose a simple and generic model that is flexible to be used in different environment. However a further exploration still be needed to enhance this model.

4.3   Implementation Model

The system can be implemented in three platforms (Fig 4)

   (1) Desktop based platform
   (2) Web application (this application can be accessed by using an internet browser)
   (3) Mobile application (this application can be accessed in certain platform, like Android, IOS, Blackberry or Windows-Phone)

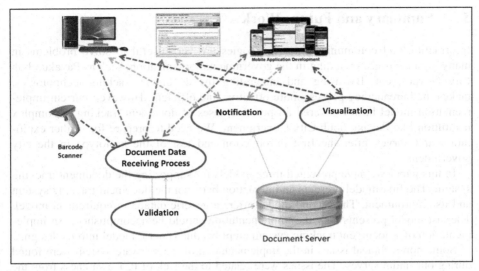

Fig. 4. Implementation Model Diagram

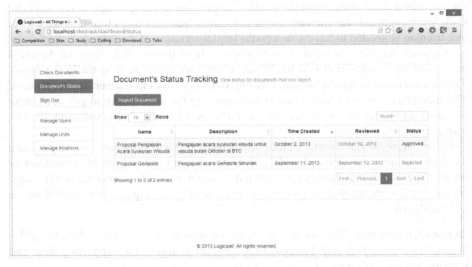

Fig. 5. Document Status Tracking Page

Currently, the prototype of the system is already implemented as a web based application and has been introduced and partially tested in Payakumbuh.

Figure 5 shows a one page example of document status tracking screen. After logging into the document tracking system, a user (e.g. a government officer) can check related documents assigned to this user. They can check and review the name, description, time created, creator, status, and notes of the documents. They can also check the detail of the document. Checking into the document's detail produces the status of the documents which can be changed during the document processing (e.g., the document has been approved or rejected).

5   Summary and Future Work

Information and communication technologies are very useful to solve problems in many organizations, including in the governmental organization, such as Payakumbuh City Government. By using and integrating the document tracking technologies, makes the bureaucracy process more effective and efficient. However, current implementation model hasn't covered all possible cases of document tracking in complex institution like Payakumbuh City Government. We need to prepare for further exploration and survey after the first introduction and test of the prototype in the city government.

In this paper we have presented three models for supporting the document tracking system. The first model presents an interaction between the document tracking system and its environment. The second model offers a generic database requirement model. The last model presents how the implementation should be accomplished. An implementation of a document tracking system employs this generic model into its design.

Some non-technical issues in the implementation of the software system were found during our initial survey. The issues were related to the lack of ICT awareness from the local office people who run the department. Many of them knows how to run computer for a standard office need, however to run a customized software system needs a special skill. We recognized that running a system requires qualified users too, thus we expect that training is needed to have a successful implementation of the system.

We also need to invent new indicators to help demonstrate that the business process of an organization is actually improved after applying new tracking system. Thus another works should include defining indicators to help measuring this process. The indicators can be executed first before applying the new system to get an existing process baseline. A second execution should be performed to help evaluating the improvement from the first.

Other future works should include assessment of local governmental rules. Each local government may have slightly different rules on the handling of documents or letters. The model may have to be updated to adopt new rules; however at this stage we believe that the adoption of the model to some specific requirements should not be a difficult task.

Acknowledgements. This work has been supported by Penprinas MP3EI 2013. Thanks to Dirdik ITB and Payakumbuh City Government for supporting data and information for this paper.

References

1. BPPT: IT Master Plan Pemerintah Kota Banda Aceh 2010 - 2014 (Banda Aceh City Government IT Master Plan 2010 - 2014) (2009)
2. Hai, J.C.: Fundamental of Development Administration. Scholar Press, Selangor (2007)
3. Kementerian Koordinator Bidang Perekonomian: Masterplan Percepatan dan Perluasan Pembangunan Ekonomi Indonesia (Masterplan for Acceleration and Expansion of Indonesia Economic Development) (2011)

4. KPDE-Kampar: Laporan Akhir Penyusunan Master Plan E-Government Kabupaten Kampar (Final Report of E-Government Master Plan Building for Kampar Regency) (2009)
5. Schick, R., Ruland, C.: Document Tracking - On the Way to a New Security Service. In: Conference on Network and Information Systems Security (SAR-SSI 2011), pp. 1–5 (2011)
6. Solic, P., et al.: ROADS: RFID Office Application for Document tracking over SIP. In: 17th International Conference on Software, Telecommunications & Computer Networks (SoftCOM 2009), pp. 95–100 (2009)
7. Sunindyo, W.D., Akbar, S., Iqbal, M.: Towards a smart world class city - Case: Building Bandung ICT master plan. In: International Conference on ICT for Smart Society 2013 (ICISS 2013), pp. 1–5. IEEE Computer Society (2013)
8. Sunindyo, W.D., Moser, T., Winkler, D., Mordinyi, R., Biffl, S.: Workflow Validation Framework in Distributed Engineering Environments. In: Proceedings of 3rd International Workshop on Information Systems in Distributed Environment (ISDE 2011), pp. 1–10 (2011)
9. United Nations Department of Economic and Social Affairs: United Nations E-Government Survey 2012 (2012)

Modern Framework for Distributed Healthcare Data Analytics Based on Hadoop

P. Vignesh Raja and E. Sivasankar

Dept. of Computer Science and Engineering, National Institute of Technology, Trichy, India
vigneshrp@cdac.in, sivasankar@nitt.edu

Abstract. Evolution in the field of IT, electronics and networking resulted in enhancements in connectivity and in computation capabilities. Proliferation of miniaturized devices paved way for Body Area Network. Healthcare systems have been going through cycles of modernization as the advent of IT system in the field of medical sciences. Body Area Network is a network of lightweight wearable sensor nodes that sense human body functions. Modern healthcare informatics systems produce lots of data that emerge from sensors. Even though many healthcare informatics systems exist and produce volume of data, such solutions exist in silos. Existing Healthcare IT systems intend to gather multivariate medical data about the patients by the means of electronic format. They capture multi variant types of data, process and store them in a RDBMS. Inferring knowledge from such systems is tedious. This paper aims at proposing a framework for modernizing the healthcare informatics systems. Proposed framework is based on Apache Hadoop platform which is open source and its implementation is distributed in nature as it is deployable at various healthcare centers in different geographic locations.

Keywords: E-Health, Medical Informatics, Hadoop, Map Reduce, Hive, Massive Multivariate Data sets, BigData Analytics.

1 Preliminaries

1.1 Health Informatics Systems

Health informatics is a multidisciplinary field that deals with computer science, information science, biology, medicine and analytics. Evolution in the electronics, IT field fostered various health informatics solutions. Almost all of the healthcare centers are equipped with health informatics solutions [1] [13]. Such solutions generally consists of modules like hospital information management system, telemedicine solutions and others. These systems basically collect data about the patients and medication in text format, also they store x-rays, scan reports in image format. Such implementations eventually result in "data silo". Data captured by each of the system is local to that environment and they became less reusable. The more the number of health informatics solutions the more is the data they produce. Appropriate mechanism is needed in order to store, process and extract knowledge from the massive amount of

Linawati et al. (Eds.): ICT-EurAsia 2014, LNCS 8407, pp. 348–355, 2014.

data. Exchange of vital medical practices and medication assistances through the present healthcare informatics systems have the following concerns

- Ability to exchange the data externally
- Issues related to data integration standards
- Veracity of the healthcare data.

As a health informatics solution, system should provide mechanism for better understanding of medication compliance. Huge amount of money is spent wastefully in healthcare across worldwide is attributed due to excess hospitalization which is triggered by non-compliance of medication procedures. Such incidents are also caused by situations where it lacks of clinically proven medication solutions.

1.2   Body Sensor Networks

As the miniaturized sensors emerge as the promising method of self-care medication, establishment of Body Area Network or Body Sensor Network is feasible [14][2]. The purpose of "Body Sensor Networks for Healthcare" is to bring the expertise of doctors in the urban areas closer to the patients in the rural areas. It would bridge geographical distances and provide healthcare to those who do not have access to quality healthcare. More than 70 % of the land area is covered with GSM/GPRS for Internet access [2]. Integration of existing healthcare IT system with wearable health monitoring system is niche in the healthcare IT solutions [3]. One of the major limitations for wider acceptance of such system was non-existent support for massive data collection and knowledge discovery.

Implementation of BSN for healthcare is carried out through infrastructure like medical Kiosk that can enable any person to walk into the kiosk and check the vital parameters like ECG, Blood Pressure, and Pulse Rate etc. The data measured at these kiosks is stored in the distributed datastore and is made available to the doctors / Paramedics. The data could range from text (health records, reports) to image (x-ray, ECG images). Data gathered at each of the healthcare centers are stored in the relational database management system. With such system we have variety and volume of data.

RDBMS lacks of fault tolerance, linear scalability, processing of unstructured data and it cannot effectively handle high concurrent reading and writing of database [4]. Also true decentralized approach is required whereby valuable medication information can be shared. Present health informatics systems do not allow exchange of data or when there is need for "healthcare related knowledge" within from the existing data. Along with the massive multivariate data, a mechanism for inferring knowledge from such data is highly required.

2   Proposed Framework

Implementation of new architecture is needed because of the following reasons, the storage required to store healthcare records for large number of patients may results in terabytes (TB) to petabytes (PB) in a typical distributed environment. Also the new architecture is expected to provide storage of massive structured and unstructured data, parallelism in data processing and high availability with fault tolerance. Performing analytics on the historical data to infer knowledge is also a feature of this framework. Proposed model envisages to infer knowledge from such distributed, multivariate data. This framework enables provisions for "Knowledge on Demand". This framework also have a mechanism to seamlessly interface with the legacy system where from the data is imported to perform analytics. As this framework is built using open source tools, extension of functionalities to suit custom requirements is made possible.

Variety of choices including RDBMS (Postgresql 9.x) with high availability, Pandas the open source Python language based analytics library were considered for performing analytics on the data. Even though the recent versions of Postgresql offer ability to handle large volume of data (up to TBs) [15], a hardware infrastructure of higher configuration is required to support such a high volume of data. Further such RDBMS are prone to mid query faults, whereas the proposed Hadoop based framework offers mid query fault tolerance. Pandas – Python based data analytics library [16] offers many features such as high performance merging and joining, integrated indexing on the given dataset. But most of the data sets using which the analytics is performed, is distributed in nature. Proposed framework provides mechanism to interface with the data sources and it performs analytics using the commodity hardware. So setting up of such a framework does not require the hardware with higher configuration.

Multi variant types of data generated by the existing BSN framework is stored in RDBMS, which is distributed at many locations. This RDBMS based framework cannot be relied on, when the nature of application is with volume, variety of health care data. It is also very cumbersome to manage such data and to perform analytics on such data to infer knowledge [4]. By using Hadoop, Hive existing framework can still be exploited to perform analytics on the data it generates. Hadoop based tool sets are introduced in order to alleviate such limitations.

Following are the few usecases that can be executed using this modern framework. Finding out the age group and demography where a particular disease is spreading. Such information will help the Government in planning and implementing suitable health schemes. When the doctors are dealing with critical medical cases, where immediate medical assistance is required, knowledge inferred using the proposed framework can be used in a near real time (Near real-time does not mean the on-demand data by monitoring the patients, but the provision to assist the users by performing analytics on the existing voluminous multivariate datasets). Another usecase is the analytics of structured and unstructured data to provide knowledge when doctors search for specific issues. Any kind of data (medical records, CT scans, emails) can processed through this framework and doctors can then extract the information that they need based on specific symptoms. Below is the components of the framework.

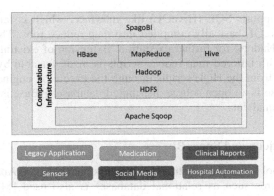

Fig. 1. Proposed Framework

2.1   Apache Hadoop

Apache Hadoop is a software framework and it processes large data sets across clusters. Such clusters could be on commodity hardware. With MapReduce (the default programming model), the application is divided into many small fragments of work (Jobs), each of which can execute or re-execute on any node in the cluster [5]. Jobs submitted to the Hadoop cluster is managed by Job Tracker and Task Tracker. Hadoop is designed to scale up from single servers to thousands of machines, each offering local computation and storage. It also provides a distributed file system, HDFS [6]. Overall functioning of inferring knowledge (analytics) is shown below,

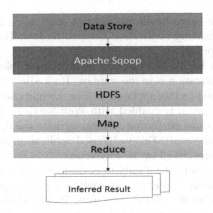

Fig. 2. Map Reduce Process

2.2   Apache Hive and HBase

Hive is a data warehouse infrastructure built on top of Hadoop and it facilitates querying and managing large datasets residing in distributed storage [7]. Proposed framework supports analysis of data from legacy systems, where the data is available in the

RDBMS. Hive supports SQL (HiveQL) like interface, which is familiar to the data professionals. HiveQL basically compiled into map reduce jobs. These jobs are then submitted to the Hadoop for further execution. Extension of existing queries in order to be equipped with tailored map reduce scripts is made feasible by HiveQL. Query plan is generated from the HQL scripts through the execution engine that is available in the Hive. HBase is an open source distributed database. HBase is highly suited for storing non-relational data.

2.3   Apache Sqoop and SpagoBI

Apache Sqoop, tool for efficiently transferring bulk data between Apache Hadoop and structured datastores such as relational databases is also used [8] [9] [12]. Sqoop transfers data from data stores like MySQL, Postgresql and Oracle to Hive and HBase. Proposed framework will also contain SpagoBI to offer BI solutions. SpagoBI is an open source business intelligence suite. Apart from performing query and analytics on large volume of heterogeneous, structured and unstructured data, SpagoBI provides mechanism to extract useful information. SpagoBI can extract information from various platforms such as Hadoop, Hive, HBase and Cassandra. SpagoBI analytical engine can produce charts, reports, thematic maps and cockpits from the information retrieved from such platforms [10] [11].

3   Related Work

3.1   Web Based Health Informatics Application

Existing traditional web based health informatics application is used in order to evaluate this framework. Existing application is based on Java Technologies (J2EE, JSP, and Hibernate). This application is capable interfacing with various sensors that are meant to sense various health factors such as heart beat, blood pressure etc. In its aboriginal form this application is in the state of "Data Silo". All the data captured by this application is internal to this application. For the purpose of interfacing with external application this system is enabled with Web Services. But as the size of total data increases there happens performance lagging since the data is maintained in the traditional database (Postgresql). This web based application also captures medication for various symptoms, prescribed by the Physicians.

Currently this system lacks the ability to perform analytics (RDBMS systems analytics performance depends on the factors such as types of queries, number of joins and hardware capacity) on the massive datasets. Proposed framework is applied for this scenario with various options and the results are recorded. Performance evaluation on healthcare data analysis using MapReduce and Hive is carried out against the traditional RDBMS system. Experiment results proves the limitations of the RDBMS when it comes to voluminous data to be dealt and eventually RDBMS based solutions fail to perform data analytics. But MapReduce and Hive continue to work for voluminous data whereas Hive has an edge over MapReduce in terms of performance.

As the SpagoBI is highly configurable Business Intelligence suite is made available as the main interface to the underlying computation infrastructure, various health related information (medication, lab reports etc.) can be easily obtained. SpagoBI is highly customizable to display the rate of change in the health information inferred from the data store via dashboards.

3.2   Test Environment

The following environment is setup to evaluate this framework, whereas the data for experiment is taken from web based health informatics application. The data is obtained using Sqoop and stored in the HBase datastore. Data from the application is about heart beat rate, blood pressure level. Total size of the data is approximately 200 GB. Even though 200 GB is not a really the large one, sample dataset was generated based on this dataset of size 200 GB to result in more GBs. The existing database based system's performance has come down and the mid query faults brought havoc to the execution of analytics jobs.

We have used four machines with Intel i7 processors (up to 3.70GHz) and each machine is equipped with 8GB of main memory, 750 GB of storage. We have purposely used commodity hardware to exploit the features of Hadoop. Out of these four machines one machine is configured as Name Node, two machines for data storage and on the fourth machine the application is configured. This system is set with default replication factor (3 replicas) that is configured in the Hadoop environment. We have experimented this setup with operations like uploading of data and querying of data. Data on the aforementioned health parameters for about 75 patients is uploaded to the system. The system is simulated (based on the sample data) to produce as many records as it requires for conducting the comparison. Heart beat rate of a patient for a day is initially queried, also we queried the number of days when the heart beat rate exceeds certain threshold value. We ended up this experiment analyzing the age group of patients who are likely to get higher heart beat rates. The results of this experiments is tabulated below.

Table 1. Hadoop vs RDBMS

Data Size (No of Patient Records)	Time taken by proposed framework (sec)	Time taken be RDBMS (sec)	Operation
5000	0.823	4.213	Upload
5 Million	1.145	8.987	Upload
50 Million	3.652	47.598	Upload
5000	12.467	75.912	Query
5 Million	22.445	140.876	Query
50 Million	35.098	270.045	Query

From the table above it is evident that the performance of proposed framework is stable even when the number of record increased drastically whereas the performance of the RDBMS based system is lagging as the data size increases. The sample dataset used for this application consists of data such as blood pressure level, heart beat rate, age and the disease along with other information. In order to infer knowledge from such datasets, queries are constructed and these queries are execued both on the RDBMS also on the proposed framework. Hadoop based framework converts the the given task into Map-Reduce tasks and executes these tasks on the nodes. We have inferred knowledge (finding out the age group and variation in the heart beat rate due to a disease) in the form of a triplet, {*Age Group,Heart Beat Rate,Disease*}. The more is the details of the inferrence so is the complexity of queries to be constructed. For inferring such knowledge we have used the Select, Aggregation and Join queries.

It is observed that the RDBMS based system failed as we increase the size of datasets also the execution involved in in may sub queris and joins. The   next experiment that we performed is to evaluate the performance of MapReduce and that of Hive. Basically this involves quering the massive database thereby to arrive at knowledge from the datastore. Aforementioned health data is again used for this purpose. One intersting phenomenon observed out of this experiment is that the performance of Hive proved to be better than that of the MapReduce. When the same experiment is repeated on the archived data of various intervals, and as the data size increases Hive had offered better performance than that of MapReduce jobs. RDBMS cannot be applied in situations like analyzing the archived data of massive data size. Such analysis is required to infer knowledge as we have indicated few usecases in section 2.

4   Conclusion

In this paper capabilities of exisitng healthcare informatics systems is addressed. Also the need for decentralized parallel architecture for processing and extracting knowledge out of the datasets is highlighted. For this purpose a modern framework for processing and inferring of voluminous multivariate data is proposed. The proposed framework is fully based on open source tools which provides options for customization and really suits the existing distributed architecture. Also we highlighted the performance evaluation of this framework against RDBMS based data storage. This framework can be configureable on any commodity hardware because of the inherent fault tolerance mechanisms provided by the Hadoop environment.

References

1. PWC on Clinical Informatics,
   http://www.pwc.com/us/en/press-releases/2012/clinical-informatics-full-report-press-releases.jhtml
2. TRAI, http://www.trai.gov.in/WriteReadData/PressRealease/Document/PR-TSD-03JULY2013.pdf
3. Darwish, A., Hassanien, A.E.: Wearable and Implantable Wireless Sensor Network Solutions for Healthcare Monitoring. Sensors 11(6), 5561–5595 (2011)

4. Bao., Y., Ren., L., Zhang., L., Zhang., X., Luo, Y.: Massive sensor data management framework in Cloud manufacturing based on Hadoop. In: 10th IEEE International Conference on Industrial Informatics (INDIN), pp. 397–401 (2012)
5. Apache Hadoop, http://hadoop.apache.org/
6. White, T.: Hadoop: The Definitive Guide, pp. 9–72. O'Reilly Media Inc., CA (2012)
7. Apache Hive, http://hive.apache.org/
8. Apache Sqoop, http://sqoop.apache.org/
9. Ting, K., Cecho, J.J.: Apache Sqoop Cookbook, pp. 1–23. O'Reilly Media Inc., CA (2013)
10. SpagoBI, http://en.wikipedia.org/wiki/SpagoBI
11. Spago BigData,
    http://www.spagoworld.org/xwiki/bin/view/SpagoBI/BigData
12. Dobre., C., Xhafa, F.: Parallel Programming Paradigms and Frameworks in Big Data Era. International Journal of Parallel Programming (2013)
13. McKinsey healthcare Report, http://www.mckinsey.com/insights/
    health_systems_and_services/
    the_big-data_revolution_in_us_health_care
14. Ullah, S., Higgins, H., Braem, B., Latre, B., Blondia, C., Moerman, I., Saleem, S., Rahman, Z., Kwak, K.S.: A Comprehensive Survey of Wireless Body Area Networks. Journal of Medical Systems 36(3), 1065–1094 (2012)
15. Postgresql Wiki, http://wiki.postgresql.org/wiki/FAQ
16. Python data analytics library, http://pandas.pydata.org/

A Bioinformatics Workflow for Genetic Association Studies of Traits in Indonesian Rice

James W. Baurley[1], Bens Pardamean[1] Anzaludin S. Perbangsa[1],
Dwinita Utami[2], Habib Rijzaani[2], and Dani Satyawan[2]

[1] Bioinformatics Research Group, Bina Nusantara University, Jakarta, Indonesia
bpardamean@binus.edu
http://www.binus.edu
[2] Indonesian Center for Agricultural Biotechnology and Genetic Resources Research
and Development, Bogor, Indonesia

Abstract. Asian rice is a staple food in Indonesia and worldwide, and its production is essential to food security. Cataloging and linking genetic variation in Asian rice to important traits, such as quality and yield, is needed in developing superior varieties of rice. We develop a bioinformatics workflow for quality control and data analysis of genetic and trait data for a diversity panel of 467 rice varieties found in Indonesia. The bioinformatics workflow operates using a back-end relational database for data storage and retrieval. Quality control and data analysis procedures are implemented and automated using the whole genome data analysis toolset, PLINK, and the [R] statistical computing language. The 467 rice varieties were genotyped using a custom array (717,312 genotypes total) and phenotyped for 12 traits in four locations in Indonesia across multiple seasons. We applied our bioinformatics workflow to these data and present prototype genome-wide association results for a continuous trait - days to flowering. Two genetic variants, located on chromosome 4 and 12 of the rice genome, showed evidence for association in these data. We conclude by outlining extensions to the workflow and plans for more sophisticated statistical analyses.

Keywords: data analysis, workflow, agriculture genetics, genome-wide association study, bioinformatics, statistical genetics.

1 Introduction

Indonesia is located in one of the most biodiverse regions in the world. Studying the biodiversity unique to this region for agriculturally important species can lead to crop and animal improvements. *Oryza saliva* or Asian rice is a staple food in Indonesia and worldwide, and its production is essential to food security. Cataloging and linking genetic variation in Asian rice to important traits, such as quality and yield, is needed to develop new varieties of rice with superior properties.

The 389 Megabase (Mb) Asian rice genome consist of 12 chromosomes [1]. Throughout the genome, sequence variations called single-nucleotide polymorphism (SNP) are common. At these locations (or loci), the alternative nucleotides

Linawati et al. (Eds.): ICT-EurAsia 2014, LNCS 8407, pp. 356–364, 2014.
© IFIP International Federation for Information Processing 2014

are called alleles, and the two alleles from the paired chromosomes are called SNP genotypes. High-throughput genotyping and sequencing technologies have revolutionized agriculture genetics, allowing for genome-wide interrogation of thousands of SNPs. Recent research using these technologies, have focused on genome-wide genotyping of a rice diversity panel consisting of 413 varieties from 82 countries [2]. While this research has identified genetic regions associated with many complex traits, there is still much to learn about the genetics of rice varieties specific to Indonesia.

The Indonesian Center for Agricultural Biotechnology and Genetic Research and Development (ICABIOGRAD) has developed an unique rice diversity panel of 467 rice varieties found in Indonesia. The panel was planted in a greenhouse (BG) with controlled environment and three fields at different elevations, located in the cities of Citayam, Subang, and Kuningan. The rice was planted in multiple seasons. The diversity panel was genotyped with two panels of 384 and 1,536 SNPs on the GoldenGate platform (Illumina, Inc). The rice was also extensively phenotyped at each location (see Table 1). Given the complexity and volume of the data collected, center researchers needed an efficient and easy system to manage these data and perform numerous genetic association analyses by traits and location.

We designed and implemented a custom bioinformatics workflow for the genetic association study of these traits in Indonesian rice. In the next sections, we present the workflow design, the specifics of the implementation, and prototype results.

Table 1. Rice complex traits measured on 467 rice varieties in 4 locations

Trait	Units	Description
Days to flowering		days after planting when 50% of the plants have flowers
Days to harvest		days after planting until physiological maturity
Total tiller		number of tillers per hill
Productive tiller		number of tillers that produce panicles
Plant height	cm	measured from the ground to the base of the panicle, at the time of flowering
Total panicle		panicles in a square meter
Panicle length	cm	main stem panicle length, measured from the base to the tip of the panicle, 7 days after anthesis.
Filled grain		average number of filled grain clumps per panicle
Unfilled grain		average number of empty grain clumps per panicle
Grain per panicle		total number of grain per panicle
1000 grain weight	gr	weight of 1000 full grain
Yield	t/ha	tons of rice per hectare

2   Methods

2.1   Bioinformatics Workflow

We constructed a workflow that captures the bioinformatics needed for data quality control and analysis for both genotypes and phenotypes (trait) (Figure 1). Quality control procedures were designed to process the panel of 467 rice varieties captured across the four locations and the genetic data generated from the 384 and 1,536 genotyping arrays. The output of the quality control steps were cleaned data ready for downstream statistical modeling. These datasets were inputs to multi-step analyses pipelines. The output were summary tables and figures of statistical association (Figure 1). The workflow was implemented using a combination of software tools and custom programming that included a relational database, the whole genome association analysis toolset PLINK [3], and the [R] statistical language [4].

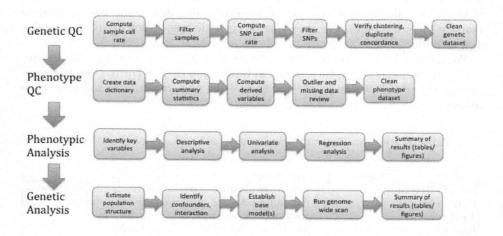

Fig. 1. Bioinformatics workflow of rice genetic and phenotypic data

2.2   Rice Relational Database

The bioinformatics workflow operates on a backend relational database for data storage and retrieval. We selected PostgreSQL as a database management system (DBMS) because it is open source and well known for its security, scalability, and active developer community. The entity-relationship diagram for the rice database is presented in Figure 2.2.

The database consists of three schemas containing the plant genotypes and trait characteristics. This included genotypes from the 1,536 and 384 SNP arrays from ICABIOGRAD and comparative data from the International Rice Research

Institute (IRRI). The snp_map table describe the SNPs contained on the array, such as where (chromosome and position); the polymorphic nucleotides - adenine (A), cytosine (C), thymine (T), and guanine (G); and attributes of the array design. The sample_map table contains data on the DNA samples and links to the trait data. The final_report contains the genotypes for all the samples as well as information on the quality of the genotype calling. Trait data is stored in the phenotype table and linked to the sample_map by a one-to-many relationship.

The primary key for final_report is the combination of sample_index and snp_index and dramatically improves the speed of sample based data retrieval (i.e., queries by sample). A second index for final_report with the order of the columns reversed allows for quick retrieval of SNP-based queries (e.g., genotypes for particular SNPs). Once the genotype data is imported into the database, the data can be extracted (in whole or by subsets) using Structured Query Language (SQL). This allows for sophisticated filtering and quality control.

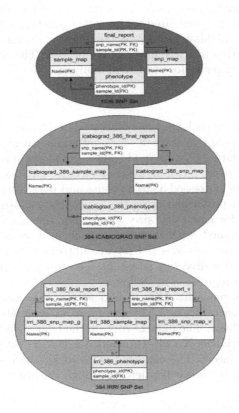

Fig. 2. Rice genetic and phenotypic database

2.3   Quality Control

For phenotypes, the database is queried using the RPostgreSQL package in [R]. Various [R] scripts and functions are then called to summarize the distribution of each trait by location. Histograms and box plots are used to visually compare the distributions and assess normality. Summaries of each variable are created (i.e., minimum, quartiles, maximum) and outliers are reported for verification.

For the array data, the genotypes are exported from the database into PLINK and converted to binary format for improved performance. The genotype call rate (i.e., the rate of non-missing genotypes) for SNPs and samples are computed and removed if less than 75%. The minor allele frequency (MAF), the frequency of the least common allele, are computed and SNPs with a MAF < 0.05 are flagged as rare variants. When samples were duplicated, genotype concordance is computed to identify SNPs that were not consistently called by clustering algorithms.

Plots are created to evaluate if the clustering algorithm was correctly assigning genotypes. A database query retrieves the r, theta, allele1 ab, and allele2 ab columns from the final_report table for particular SNPs. The polar intensities (r, theta) are plotted and compared to the called genotypes AA, AB, BB. When there are genotype misclassifications or missingness, further investigation into the clustering algorithm and assumptions are needed. The quality control steps yield cleaned datasets ready for statistical analyses.

2.4   Data Analysis

Descriptive statistics for each trait are generated in [R] and stratified by location and season/year. Descriptive statistics for continuous variables are expressed as mean, median, standard deviation, and ranges. Analyses of continuous variables are performed using t-test or an analysis of variance (ANOVA), as appropriate. Discrete variables are expressed as frequencies and percentages. The analyses of discrete variables are performed using the appropriate chi-squared test. Fishers exact test are used for small cell sizes (< 5). For the phenotypes, all tests of significance are two-tailed, with statistical significance set at $p < 0.05$.

Principal components analysis (PCA) was implemented in [R] to correct for stratification in the rice diversity panel [5]. The top principal components are used as covariates in regression modeling.

The workflow uses generalized linear models (GLM) to model the relationship between traits and each of the 1,536 genotypes. This analysis is stratified by location and season/year. The data $\mathbf{D}$ contain the trait variable Y and a matrix of P explanatory variables $\mathbf{X}$ (which included each SNP and the top principal components as covariates). The expected value of Y_i, the trait variable for rice variant i, depends on the linear predictors through the link function g such that,

$$g(\mu_i) = \beta_0 + \sum_p^P \beta_p X_{ip} I_p \tag{1}$$

where $\mu_i = \mathsf{E}(Y_i)$, β_p is the regression coefficient of variable p, and I_p is a variable indicating if X_p is included in the model M. The genotypes are coded additively

0, 1, or 2 for the number of minor alleles. For continuous traits, the identity link function (i.e., linear regression) is used. For binary traits, the logit link function is used, $g(\pi_i) = \log\left(\frac{\pi_i}{1-\pi_i}\right)$ (i.e., logistic regression).

The workflow concludes with summarizes of the results obtained from previous steps. Quantile-quantile (QQ) plots are generated for each trait to compare the observed p-value distribution to the expected uniform distribution. Additionally, Manhatten plots are generated to show the p-value results of each association scan by rice chromosome, with p-values less than the user-defined genome-wide threshold for statistical significance highlighted.

3   Prototype Results

The rice database consists of 17 tables in three schemas, the 1,536 and 384 SNP arrays from ICABIOGRAD and the IRRI 384 SNP array as an standard for assessment. The size of database is 280 Megabytes (Mb). The bioinformatics workflow (Figure 1) was run on the largest genotyping array (1,536 SNPs). With the entire diversity panel genotyped, there were 717,312 genotypes in the final_report.

A PLINK file was generated and quality control was performed. 16 rice samples and 139 SNPs were removed with poor call rates ($< 75\%$). 451 samples and 1397 SNPs were available for statistical analysis. Principle components (PC) analysis was performed using all SNPs, and the first four PCs were included in model 1 as covariates.

The days to flowering trait was used for prototyping. A summary of the distribution for this trait by location is presented in Figure 3. The box plot shows that there is variation in this trait by location.

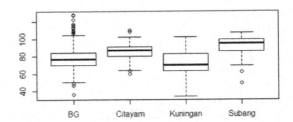

Fig. 3. Boxplot for days to flowering by location (n=467)

A genome-wide association analysis was performed on days to flowering for the rice planted in the greenhouse (BG). The resulting Manhattan plot for the association scan is presented in Figure 4. The $-log_{10}p$ are presented along the y-axis and the position of the SNP along the 12 rice chromosomes are presented

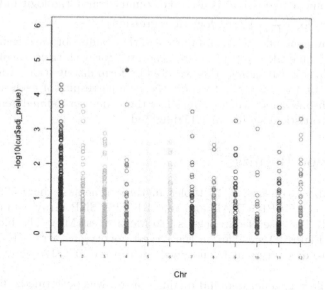

Fig. 4. Genome-wide association results for days to flowering, greenhouse

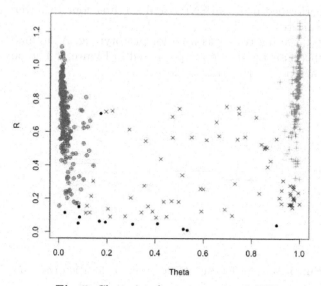

Fig. 5. Clustering for top associated SNP

on the x-axis. Two SNPs showed evidence for association with days to flowering in the greenhouse rice (colored red). These SNPs were located on chromosome 4 and 12 of the rice genome (Figure 4).

For the top associated SNP, the polar intensities were plotted versus the called genotypes. Intensities with the homozygous genotypes AA and BB were colored in red and green respectively. Heterozygous genotypes AB were plotted in blue. Uncalled genotypes were plotted in black. The graphic illustrates that for this SNP there was a distinct cluster for homozygous genotypes (AA and BB) and a large cluster for heterozygous genotypes (AB). There were 12 samples with no genotype for this SNP.

4   Conclusions

We developed a custom bioinformatics workflow for a genome-wide association study of traits in Indonesian rice. The workflow consisted of a relational database and multi-step quality control and data analysis procedures automated in PLINK and [R]. The prototype results demonstrated that the workflow is useful for summarizing and visualizing the complex data from this study.

Future work includes configuring the workflow to run for all traits, locations, and seasons. Additionally, improvements to the clustering algorithm and statistical modeling framework may be made. Given the small sample sizes in this study and that rice is highly homozygous, an alternative algorithm such as ALCHEMY may improve genotype calling [6]. Model 1 may be extended to account for the relatedness among the rice varieties using a mixed model [7]. Environmental factors include the habitat, location, season, and year are possible modifiers of the relationship between genetics and traits. The statistical framework can be modified to consider gene-environment interactions (GxE).

This bioinformatics workflow gives researchers the tools needed to easily and consistently quality control and analyze complex data. This research will help locate genes that are important for developing new rice varieties that ensure future food security in Indonesia.

Acknowledgements. This research is funded by the Indonesian Center for Agricultural Biotechnology and Genetic Resources Research and Development, Indonesian Agency for Agricultural Research and Development, Ministry of Agriculture, Indonesia. Computing support by AWS in Education Grant award.

References

1. International Rice Genome Sequencing Project: The map-based sequence of the rice genome. Nature 436(7052), 793–800 (2005)
2. Zhao, K., Tung, C.W., Eizenga, G.C., Wright, M.H., Ali, M.L., Price, A.H., Norton, G.J., Islam, M.R., Reynolds, A., Mezey, J., McClung, A.M., Bustamante, C.D., McCouch, S.: Genome-wide association mapping reveals a rich genetic architecture of complex traits in Oryza sativa. Nat. Commun. 2, 467 (2011)
3. Purcell, S., Neale, B., Todd-Brown, K., Thomas, L., Ferreira, M.A., Bender, D., Maller, J., Sklar, P., de Bakker, P.I., Daly, M.J., Sham, P.: PLINK: a tool set for whole-genome association and population-based linkage analyses. Am. J. Hum. Genet. 81(3), 559–575 (2007)

4. R Development Core Team.: R: A Language and Environment for Statistical Computing. R Foundation for Statistical Computing, Vienna, Austria, http://www.R-project.org/, ISBN 3-900051-07-0
5. Price, A.L., Patterson, N.J., Plenge, R.M., Weinblatt, M.E., Shadick, N.A., Reich, D.: Principal components analysis corrects for stratification in genome-wide association studies. Nat. Genet. 38(8), 904–909 (2006)
6. Wright, M.H., Tung, C.W., Zhao, K., Reynolds, A., McCouch, S.R., Bustamante, C.: ALCHEMY: a reliable method for automated SNP genotype calling for small batch sizes and highly homozygous populations. Bioinformatics 26(23), 2952–2960 (2010)
7. Yu, J., Pressoir, G., Briggs, W.H., Vroh Bi, I., Yamasaki, M., Doebley, J.F., McMullen, M.D., Gaut, B.S., Nielsen, D.M., Holland, J.B., Kresovich, S., Buckler, E.S.: A unified mixed-model method for association mapping that accounts for multiple levels of relatedness. Nat. Genet. 38(2), 203–208 (2006)

Fuzzy Logic Weight Estimation in Biometric-Enabled Co-authentication Systems

Van Nhan Nguyen, Vuong Quoc Nguyen,
Minh Ngoc Binh Nguyen, and Tran Khanh Dang

Faculty of Computer Science and Engineering, HCMC University of Technology,
VNUHCM, Ho Chi Minh City, Vietnam
khanh@cse.hcmut.edu.vn

Abstract. In this paper, we introduce a co-authentication system that combines password, biometric features (face, voice) in order to improve the false reject rate (FRR) and false accept rate (FAR) in Android smartphone authentication system. Since the system performance is often affected by external conditions and variabilities, we also propose a fuzzy logic weight estimation method which takes three inputs: password complexity, face image illuminance and audio signal-to-noise-ratio to automatically adjust the weights of each factor for the security improvement. The proposed method is evaluated using Yale [5] and Voxforge [1] Databases. The experimental results are very promising, the FAR is 0.4 % and FRR almost equal 0% when the user remembers his password.

Keywords: Co-authentication, fuzzy logic weight estimation, biometric features, privacy.

1 Introduction

Nowadays, private information (bank accounts, email passwords, credit card numbers, etc.) is usually stored in personal mobile devices storage. This leads to the urgent need of secured authentication mechanism. However, current authentication systems still witness weaknesses, which allow attackers to access sensitive information illegally. For example, most classical user authentication relies on tokens and passwords which may be easily lost. Password-based authentication is not highly secured, but it is still used widely because of simplicity. In order to support users with other authentication methods and take advantage of mobile device sensors, some research of biometric-based authentication have been conducted which bring potential results.

Regarding biometric-based co-authentication [3], [8], the use of "Fuzzy logic control system" as a method to estimate weight of biometric factors has been presented in many papers, such as [7] and [2]. In detail, the two systems proposed in [7] and [2] include membership functions and fuzzy logic rule sets for only three biometric traits (face, voice and fingerprint). In this paper, we present one construction that offers multi-feature verification system involving biometrics

Linawati et al. (Eds.): ICT-EurAsia 2014, LNCS 8407, pp. 365–374, 2014.

(face, voice) and non-biometric feature (password) to make the authentication system adaptive to mobile devices.

The rest of the paper is structured as follow: in section 2 , we introduce the general concepts and co-authentication system structure; in section 3, we describe all components of Fuzzy Logic Weight Estimation System ; in section 4, the experimental results for system performance evaluation is shown; finally, in section 5, we conclude the paper with findings and directions for future research.

2   Co-authentication System

The system proposed in this paper consists of *Fuzzy Logic Weight Estimation System* and other five main supporting components: *Face Authenticator, Voice Authenticator, Password Authenticator, Score & Decision Fusion* and *Co-Authentication*. System structure is described in Fig. 1.

Firstly, user's biometric features are extracted and transformed into suitable forms through *Face Authenticator* and *Voice Authenticator*. These two components are in charge of extracting necessary information of biometric for authentication process in the system. Besides, *Password Authenticator* takes user's password and then, sends out password information.

Secondly, along with the information extracted by three authenticators, the weights of three features (face, voice and password) measured by *Fuzzy Logic Weight Estimation System* are put into the *Score & Decision Fusion* component. *Score & Decision Fusion* produces a number after calculating a specified formula using the previous weights as inputs.

Finally, based on that number, *Co-Authentication* can make the decision whether user access is accepted or rejected.

2.1   Biometric Authenticator

Enrollment. First of all, two pre-processed vectors: P_{e1} and P_{e2} are generated from real-valued representation of the biometric samples: R_{e1} and R_{e2} by the *Pre-Processing* module. In this stage, we perform histogram equalization for face feature and pre-processing steps (normalization, silence removal, pre-emphasising, framing, windowing) for voice feature. Then, feature vectors F_{e1}, F_{e2} ($F_{ei} \in R^{N_F}$, i=1,2) are extracted by *Biometric Feature Extractor*. In this step, we use Eigenface method proposed by Turk and Pentland in [11], and Mel-Frequency Cepstral Coefficients (MFCCs) algorithm in [10] for face and voice feature extraction respectively. Finally, in order to protect biometric templates, we transform feature vectors to different forms, called distance vectors: d_{e1} and d_{e2} by *Biometric Vector Transformator*. The detail of this technique is shown in [12].

Authentication. Like enrollment phase, a new biometric sample is taken and transformed into distance vectors: d_{a1} and d_{a2}. Euclidean distance between new distance vectors and stored distance vectors is then computed using following equation:

$$D_i = \sqrt{\sum_{k=0}^{M} (d_{ei_k} - d_{ai_k})^2} \tag{1}$$

where M is the length of the distance vector and $i = 1, 2$. Distance D is calculated by the average of all distances D_i. Next, score s and validating variable d are obtained using Equation 2:

$$\begin{cases} s = 0, d = false, & \text{if } D > D_{thres} \\ s = S_{thres} + (S_{Range} - S_{thres})\frac{D_{thres}-D}{D_{thres}}, d = true, & \text{if } D \leq D_{thres} \end{cases}, \tag{2}$$

where D_{thres} is pre-set distance threshold, S_{thres} is pre-set score threshold and S_{Range} is the range of score value.

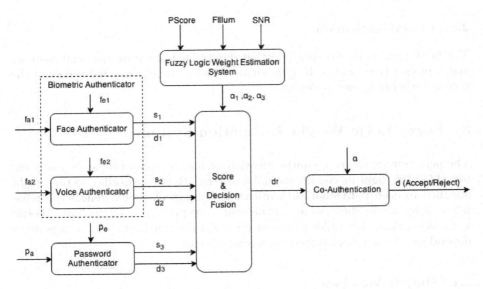

Fig. 1. Co-Authentication system architecture

2.2   Password Authenticator

In *Password Authenticator*, we use salted hashing algorithm to protect user's password. During the enrollment phase, P_e is hashed into hash value H_e using *SHA-256* algorithm. This value is then stored in database for later phase. In the authentication phase, the hash value of P_a is compared with H_e to generate d and s (see Equation 3):

$$\begin{cases} d = false, s = 0, & \text{if } H_e \neq H_a \\ d = true, s = S_{default}, & \text{if } H_e = H_a \end{cases}, \tag{3}$$

where $S_{default}$ is pre-set score value.

2.3   Score and Decision Fusion

The final value d_f is computed from the triad of score (s_1, s_2, s_3), validating value (d_1, d_2, d_3) and weight value $(\alpha_1, \alpha_2, \alpha_3)$ which are the output values of face, voice and password authenticator. We use two methods for obtaining weight value $(\alpha_1, \alpha_2, \alpha_3)$: (i) average score fusion (each α_i equals to $\frac{1}{3}$) , (ii) fuzzy logic fusion. The experimental results of each method are shown in Section 4.

$$
d_f = \begin{cases} s_1\alpha_1 + s_2\alpha_2 + s_3\alpha_3, & \text{if } d_1 = d_2 = d_3 = true \\ 0, & \text{if } d_1 = false \text{ or } d_2 = false \text{ or } d_3 = false \end{cases} \tag{4}
$$

where $\alpha_1 + \alpha_2 + \alpha_3 = 1$. Noted that, (s_1, s_2, s_3) is normalized to range of $[0, 100]$.

2.4   Co-authentication

The final decision d (Accept/Reject) is determined based on the final score d_f and a pre-set threshold α. If d_f is greater than α, user is granted access to the system, otherwise, user is denied.

3   Fuzzy Logic Weight Estimation System

The performance of one co-authentication system is often affected by many external factors (lighting conditions, noise or strength of passwords), so the weight assigned to each individual authentication component should reflect the reliability of its use in the system. In this work, we propose a *Fuzzy Logic Weight Estimation System* in order to adjust the weight for authentication components depending on the external factors mentioned above.

3.1   Output Variables

Output of the system are three fuzzy variables W_{face}, W_{voice} and W_{Pass} which correspond to three weights for face-based authentication, voice-based authentication and password-based authentication respectively. These values range from 0 to 1 (higher values implying higher confidence). The fuzzy sets of these output variables are triangular membership functions that define three levels of output weight (high/medium/low) for each variable. Before these weights are used in score fusion, they need to be normalized (see Equation 5):

$$
W^j_{normalized} = \frac{W_j}{\sum\limits_{i=1}^{n} W_i}, \tag{5}
$$

where W_j is j^{th} weight and n is the total number of weights.

3.2   Input Variables

There are three input variables, FIllumi, PScore and SNR corresponding to illuminance of face images, strength of passwords the signal-to-noise-ratio of audios. The fuzzy sets of these variables are trapezoidal membership functions (see Equation 6) that define three levels of input variables (high/medium/low).

$$f(x) = \begin{cases} 0, & , (x < a) \text{ or } (x > d) \\ \frac{x-a}{b-a}, & , a \leq x \leq b \\ 1, & , b \leq x \leq c \\ \frac{d-x}{d-c}, & , c \leq x \leq d \end{cases} \tag{6}$$

FIllum. FIllum is illuminance of face images, this value ranges from 0 to 255 and it is estimated using two following steps:

1. Convert the input face image to grayscale (see Equation 7):

$$P_{Bi} = 0.299R_i + 0.587G_i + 0.114B_i, \tag{7}$$

where R_i, G_i and B_i are Red, Green and Blue values of ith pixel.
2. Calculate the average brightness of the grayscale image (see Equation 8):

$$FIllum = \frac{\sum_{i=1}^{n} P_{Bi}}{n}, \tag{8}$$

where P_{Bi} is the grayscale value of ith pixel and n is the total number of pixels.

Illuminance is divided into five groups: very low [0-40], low [40-109], medium [110-146], high [147-214] and very high [215-255], their Equal error rate (ERR) are shown in Table 1. Based on the ERRs of the illuminance groups, parameters used by FIllum membership functions are selected and detailed in Table 2:

SNR. SNR is defined as the power ratio between a signal (meaningful information) and the background noise (unwanted signal):

$$SNR = 10 \log_{10} \frac{P_{signal}}{P_{noise}}, \tag{9}$$

where SNR is measured in decibel (dB), P_{signal} is the peak speech power and P_{noise} is the mean noise power. The SNR values are obtained by using the WADA algorithm [9]. SNR is divided into five groups of intervals: very low [10-16], low [17-22], medium [23-43], high [44-50] and very high [51-60] (their ERR

Table 1. ERR of five different illuminance groups

Illuminance	Very low	Low	Medium	High	Very high
ERR	> 50%	46%	24%	48%	> 50%

Table 2. The parameters used by FIllum membership functions

Parameters	FIllum$_{high}$	FIllum$_{med}$	FIllum$_{low}$
a	128	64	$-\infty$
b	215	110	$-\infty$
c	$+\infty$	146	40
d	$+\infty$	192	128

Table 3. ERR of 5 different SNR groups

SNR (dB)	Very low	Low	Medium	High	Very high
FAR	16%	8.3%	7.8%	7%	6.5%

Table 4. The parameters used by SNR membership functions

Parameters	SNR$_{high}$	SNR$_{med}$	SNR$_{low}$
a	40	18	$-\infty$
b	50	22	$-\infty$
c	$+\infty$	40	16
d	$+\infty$	45	22

are shown in Table 3). We observe that utterance with higher SNR tends to have lower ERR. Based on this observation, we select parameters for SNR membership functions. The parameters are shown in Table 4:

PScore. PScore represents the password strength. In this paper, we measure this value using the method proposed by Jamuna KS, Karpagavalli S, and Vijaya MS in [4]. The strength of passwords ranges from 0 to 100 and it is categorized into 5 classes (see Table 5).

Based on this categorization, parameters used by PScore membership functions are selected and detailed in Table 6:

Table 5. Different classes of password strength

Class	Very weak	Weak	Good	Strong	Very strong
Score	< 20	21 - 39	40 - 59	60 - 79	80 - 100

Table 6. The parameters used by PScore membership functions

Parameters	PScore$_{high}$	PScore$_{med}$	PScore$_{low}$
a	60	20	$-\infty$
b	80	40	$-\infty$
c	$+\infty$	60	20
d	$+\infty$	80	40

3.3 Fuzzy Control Rules

The general form of fuzzy control rules which are used in the system is:

R_i IF(x is (Y/N)) and (y is (Y/N)) and (z is (Y/N)) then t is V_i, where x, y, z and t are linguistic variables representing the input variables and the output variable, respectively, and V_i is the linguistic value of t. If the condition in a rule specifies a Y concept, the input will be set equaling to the membership degree, β. For an N concept, the input will be set at $1 - \beta$. Fuzzy control rules for FIllum, SNR and PScore are shown in Table 7, Table 8, and Table 9 respectively.

Table 7. Fuzzy rules for FIllum

ID	Fuzzy Rules
R_1	(FIllum$_{high}$ is N) and (IF FIllum$_{med}$ is Y) and (FIllum$_{low}$ is N) then W_{Face} is High
R_2	(FIllum$_{high}$ is Y)and (IF FIllum$_{med}$ is Y) and (FIllum$_{low}$ is N) then W_{Face} is Med
R_3	(FIllum$_{high}$ is N) and (IF FIllum$_{med}$ is Y) and (FIllum$_{low}$ is Y) then W_{Face} is Med
R_4	(FIllum$_{high}$ is N) and (IF FIllum$_{med}$ is N) and (FIllum$_{low}$ is Y then W_{Face} is Low
R_5	(FIllum$_{high}$ is Y)and (IF FIllum$_{med}$ is N) and (FIllum$_{low}$ is N) then W_{Face} is Low

Table 8. Fuzzy rules for SNR

ID	Fuzzy Rules
R_1	IF(SNR$_{high}$ is Y) and (SNR$_{med}$ is N) and (SNR$_{low}$ is N) then W_{Voice} is High
R_2	IF(SNR$_{high}$ is Y) and (SNR$_{med}$ is Y) and (SNR$_{low}$ is N) then W_{Voice} is High
R_3	IF(SNR$_{high}$ is N) and (SNR$_{med}$ is Y) and (SNR$_{low}$ is N) then W_{Voice} is Med
R_4	IF(SNR$_{high}$ is N) and (SNR$_{med}$ is Y) and (SNR$_{low}$ is Y) then W_{Voice} is Med
R_5	IF(SNR$_{high}$ is N) and (SNR$_{med}$ is N) and (SNR$_{low}$ is Y) then W_{Voice} is Low

Table 9. Fuzzy rules for PScore

ID	Fuzzy Rules
R_1	IF(PScore$_{high}$ is Y) and (PScore$_{med}$ is N) and (PScore$_{low}$ is N) then W_{Pass} is High
R_2	IF(PScore$_{high}$ is Y) and (PScore$_{med}$ is Y) and (PScore$_{low}$ is N) then W_{Pass} is High
R_3	IF(PScore$_{high}$ is N) and (PScore$_{med}$ is Y) and (PScore$_{low}$ is N) then W_{Pass} is Med
R_4	IF(PScore$_{high}$ is N) and (PScore$_{med}$ is Y) and (PScore$_{low}$ is Y) then W_{Pass} is Med
R_5	IF(PScore$_{high}$ is N) and (PScore$_{med}$ is N) and (PScore$_{low}$ is Y) then W_{Pass} is Low

3.4 System Architecture

Fig. 2 shows the flow of *Fuzzy Logic Weight Estimation System*. Input of the system is numerical measurement of an external factor. First of all, this input factor is fuzzified. In detail, for each linguistic variable, the crisp value is converted to fuzzy value by evaluating the values of the corresponding membership functions. For example, if the input factor FIllum = 80, the degree of "medium illuminance" is 0.35. After fuzzification, the system will infer results from the logical rules (fuzzy rules) using the linguistic variables. The degree of the rule antecedents is then computed by taking the minimum of all present degrees. This degree is also chosen as the degree with which the rule is fulfilled. E.g. the FIllum = 80 fulfills the first rule with degree(R1) = min{1 - FIllum$_{high}$(80), FIllum$_{med}$(80), 1 - FIllum$_{low}$(80)} = min{1 - 0, 0.35, 1 - 0.55} = 0.35. The fuzzy outputs for all rules are then aggregated to one fuzzy set. The degree of a linguistic variable is computed by taking maximum of all rules describing this variable i.e. degree(medium) = max{degree(R2), degree(R3)}. Finally, to get the weight (degree of support) of the feature, defuzzification using standard centroid-of-area technique is performed. Details about fuzzy logic system can be found in [6].

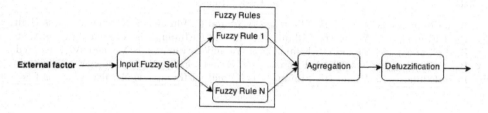

Fig. 2. Fuzzy logic weight estimation system

4   Experimental Results

We conduct four experiments to evaluate authentication performance of the proposed system as well as individual systems such as face-based authentication system and voice-based authentication. To perform these experiments, we use 110 face images and 110 utterances of 20 different people which are selected randomly from The Extended Yale Face Database B [5] and Voxforge [1] respectively.

4.1   Face-Based Authentication

Firstly, we use 60 images of 10 different people (6 images per person) to evaluate the False reject rate (FRR) of face-based authentication. The first image of one person is used for enrollment and the remaining 5 images are used for authentication. Then, in order to evaluate the False accept rate (FAR), we use 50 images of 10 other people to authenticate with the enrolled images. The FAR and FRR of face-based authentication are depicted in Fig. 3a. With the best distance threshold is 870, the FAR is 24% and the FRR is 20%.

4.2   Voice-Based Authentication

The settings to measure the FRR and FAR of this experiment are similar to the settings used in face-based authentication. The FAR and FRR of voice-based authentication are shown in Fig. 3b. The best distance threshold is 17.5, and with this threshold, the FAR and FRR are 13% and 10% respectively.

4.3 Co-authentication System Using Average Score Fusion

To begin, 60 test sets of 10 different people are used to estimate the FRR of the system. A test set of each person, which includes a face image, an utterance and a password, is used to enroll. The five other test sets are used for authentication. Next, to evaluate the FAR, 50 remaining test sets of 10 other people are used to authenticate with enrolled test sets. The FAR and FRR of the system are depicted in Fig. 3c. As can be seen, the FAR is 1.4% and the FRR is 2% at the score threshold of 50.

4.4 Co-authentication System Using Fuzzy Logic Fusion

The settings to measure the FRR and FAR of this experiment are similar to the settings used in co-authentication system using average score fusion. The FAR and FRR of the system are illustrated in Fig. 3d. With the best score threshold of 45, the FAR and FRR are 0.4% and 0% respectively.

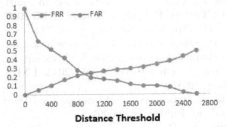

(a) FAR and FRR for face-base authentication

(b) FAR and FRR for voice-base authentication

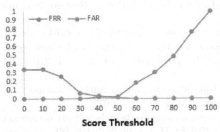
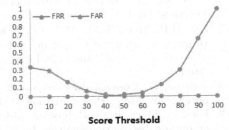

(c) FAR and FRR for co-authentication system using average score fusion

(d) FAR and FRR for co-authentication system using fuzy logic fusion

Fig. 3. Experimental results

5   Conclusions and Future Works

In this paper, we presented a co-authentication system that combines password-based, face-based and voice-based authentication. Co-authentication system using average score fusion produced relative FAR and FRR improvement of 22.6% and 18% compared with face-based authentication, 11.6% and 8% compared with voice-based authentication. We also proposed a *Fuzzy Logic Weight Estimation System* in order to accounted for external factors which affect authentication performance such as lightning conditions, noise and strength of passwords. As a result, the combination of co-authentication system and fuzzy logic weight estimation system generated further relative improvement of 1% and 2% on FAR and FRR compared with co-authentication system using average score fusion.

However, the proposed system accounted for only three external factors (lightning, noise and strength of passwords). Some additional factors such as user's head pose in face verification, quality of utterances in voice verification and other ones are need to be considered in the future.

References

1. Voxforge database, http://voxforge.org (accessed: November 26, 2013)
2. Conti, V., Milici, G., Ribino, P., Sorbello, F., Vitabile, S.: Fuzzy fusion in multi-modal biometric systems. In: Apolloni, B., Howlett, R.J., Jain, L. (eds.) KES 2007, Part I. LNCS (LNAI), vol. 4692, pp. 108–115. Springer, Heidelberg (2007)
3. Dang, T.T., Truong, Q.C., Dang, T.K.: Practical construction of face-based authentication systems with template protection using secure sketch. In: Mustofa, K., Neuhold, E.J., Tjoa, A.M., Weippl, E., You, I. (eds.) ICT-EurAsia 2013. LNCS, vol. 7804, pp. 121–130. Springer, Heidelberg (2013)
4. Jamunna, K.S., Vijaya, M.S., Karpagavalli, S.: In proceeding of International Journal of Recent Trends in Engineering. Academy Publishers (2009)
5. Georghiades, A.S., Belhumeur, P.N., Kriegman, D.J.: From few to many: Illumination cone models for face recognition under variable lighting and pose. IEEE Trans. Pattern Anal. Mach. Intelligence 23(6), 643–660 (2001)
6. Hellmann, M.: Fuzzy logic introduction. Epsilon Nought Radar Remote Sensing Tutorials (2001)
7. Hui, H.P., Meng, H.M., Mak, M.: Adaptive weight estimation in multi-biometric verification using fuzzy logic decision fusion. In: IEEE International Conference on Acoustics, Speech and Signal Processing, ICASSP 2007, vol. 1, pp. I-501–I-504 (2007)
8. Jonsson, E.: Co-authentication - a probabilistic approach to authentication. Supervised by Assoc. Prof. Christian D. Jensen, IMM, DTU (2007)
9. Kim, C., Stern, R.M.: Robust signal-to-noise ratio estimation based on waveform amplitude distribution analysis. In: INTERSPEECH, pp. 2598–2601. ISCA (2008)
10. Tiwari, Vibha: Mfcc and its applications in speaker recognition. International Journal on Emerging Technologies I(1), 19–22 (2010)
11. Turk, M., Pentland, A.: Eigenfaces for recognition. J. Cognitive Neuroscience 3(1), 71–86 (1991)
12. Plataniotis, K.N., Wang, Y.: Biometrics Symposium. Springer (2007)

A Real-Time Intrusion Detection and Protection System at System Call Level under the Assistance of a Grid

Fang-Yie Leu[1,*], Yi-Ting Hsiao[1], Kangbin Yim[2], and Ilsun You[3]

[1] Department of Computer Science, Tunghai University, Taichung, Taiwan
{leufy,g98357001}@thu.edu.tw
[2] Soonchunhyang University, South Korea
[3] Korean Bible University, Korea

Abstract. In this paper, we propose a security system, named the Intrusion Detection and Protection System (IDPS for short) at system call level, which creates personal profiles for users to keep track of their usage habits as the forensic features, and determines whether a legally login users is the owner of the account or not by comparing his/her current computer usage behaviors with the user's computer usage habits collected in the account holder's personal profile. The IDPS uses a local computational grid to detect malicious behaviors in a real-time manner. Our experimental results show that the IDPS's user identification accuracy is 93%, the accuracy on detecting its internal malicious attempts is up to 99% and the response time is less than 0.45 sec., implying that it can prevent a protected system from internal attacks effectively and efficiently.

Keywords: Forensic Features, Intrusion Detection and Protection, Data Mining, Identifying Malicious behaviors, Computational Grid.

1 Introduction

Currently, most computer systems use user IDs and passwords to authenticate their users. However, many users often share their login information with their coworkers and request them to assist co-tasks, thereby making the login information as one of the weakest points of computer security. Also, internal hackers, the legal users of a system who attack the system internally, are hard to detect. Shan et al. [1] claimed that OS-level system calls are much more helpful in detecting hackers and identifying a malicious internal user. In this paper, we propose a real time security system, named the Intrusion Detection and Protection System (IDPS for short) which detects malicious behaviors at system call level. The IDPS collects users' system-call-usage histories, and uses data mining and forensic techniques to mine typical system calls and their sequences (together named system call sequences (SC-sequences)), as a user's forensic features generated by the activities that the user often performs. The features are a kind of biological characteristics essential in identifying a user. When a user logs in a computer, the IDPS starts monitoring the user's input system calls so as to detect whether he/she is issuing an attack or not, and identify who the account owner

---

* Corresponding author.

Linawati et al. (Eds.): ICT-EurAsia 2014, LNCS 8407, pp. 375–385, 2014.
© IFIP International Federation for Information Processing 2014

is if IDPS discovers that this user is not the account holder. This system collects system call patterns for user operations, and identifies those system call attack patterns that hackers often use. By a long-term observation on user behaviors, user habits can be effectively identified. Further, The Longest Common Subsequence (LCS) algorithm [2] for pattern and profile mining and computational clustering are also employed to improve the performance of the IDPS.

2   Related Research

Computer Forensics science is one kind of computer security technologies that analyzes what attackers have done, like sending computer viruses, malware and malicious codes, or issuing Distributed Denial-of-Service (DDoS for short) attacks. O'Shaughnessy et al. [3] acquired particular network intrusion and attack patterns from a system log file. The datasets required are extracted from system log files, containing the traces of computer misuse. Therefore, there are obvious potentials for the use of synthetically generated log files that accurately present the traces or patterns of misuse. In this paper, IDPS adopts a similar method to establish attack patterns and evaluate the proposed algorithms. Mahony et al. [4] collected attack patterns and studied on-line systems, including various effective collaborative filtering algorithms, information filtering techniques and expert-system applications. In the previous work [5], we developed a security system to collect forensic features for users on the system command level, rather than on the system call level, by invoking the data mining and forensic techniques. However, if attackers use many sessions to issue attacks, named multi-stage attacks, or DDoS attacks, then due to system processing capability, the intrusion detection system (IDS) cannot thoroughly identify all attack patterns. Giffin et al. [6] provided another example of integrating computer forensics with a knowledge-based system. The system, adopting a predefined model which allows system call sequences to be normally executed, was employed by detection systems to restrict program execution so as to protect an underlying system. This is helpful to detect applications with a series of malicious system calls and automatically identify attack sequences having been collected in knowledge models. Other DoS/DDoS security systems can be found in [7, 8]. The IDPS uses data mining and profiling techniques to respectively analyze and identify user operation characteristics, which as a kind of biological patterns, are essential in identifying a user. This system can analyze and identify attack patterns that hackers often use as well.

3   System Framework

The IDPS as shown in Fig. 1 consists of a system call monitor & filter, mining server, detection server and local computational grid. The system call monitor & filter, as a loadable kernel module embedded in the kernel of the system being considered, collects the system calls submitted to the kernel and stores these system calls in the user's own log file. The mining server analyze users' log data with data mining techniques to identify a user's habit patterns, which are recorded in the user' profiles. Detection server compares users' current inputs with users' computer usage habits collected in their user profiles and attacker profile to, respectively, detect malicious behaviors and identify sources of attacks in a real-time manner. When an intrusion is discovered, the detection server notifies the system call monitor & filter to isolate the user from submitting system calls to the system kernel. Both the detection server and mining server are run on the local computational grid to respectively accelerate the IDPS's on-line detection and mining speeds, and enhance its detection and mining capability. If a user logs in the system by using other person's login user ID and password, the IDPS can identify who the underlying user is by computing the similarity score between the user's current inputs and the habit patterns collected in the account holders' user profile.

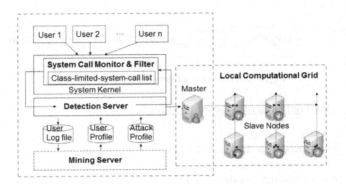

Fig. 1. The IDPS system architecture

3.1   System Call Monitor and Filter

Due to the possibility of submitting too many system calls to the kernel at the same time, the IDPS may not completely monitor all system calls generated by user-submitted jobs. In this study, we focus on those system calls produced by shell-commands, named shell-command system calls. The Class-limited-system-call list, a component of the system call Monitor & Filter, collects the shell-command system calls that the kernel has received. To know what the typical shell-command system calls are, we use the term frequency-inverse document frequency (TF-IDF, Zhang et al., 2005) algorithm and iData Analyzer [9] tool to analyze the intercepted system calls. Table 1 lists the four commands' representative system calls, which are also the members of the Class-limited-system-call list contained.

Table 1. A part of the Class-limited-system-call list

Command	The representative System call
chmod	fchmodat()
kill	kill()
date	clock_gettime()
rm	unlinkat()

3.2 Mining Server

A mining server extracts those system calls generated by a user from user's log file and counts the time that an SC-sequence appears in this file to produce the user's habit file. The SC-sequences collected in this habit file are then compared with those generated in all other users' habit files in the underlying system to identify the user's user-specific SC-patterns and those SC-patterns commonly used by all or most users. After that, the user profile is established by attaching a SC-pattern with the corresponding similarity weight. The calculation of the weight will be described later. Fig. 2 illustrates the corresponding control flow.

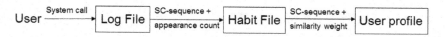

Fig. 2. Control flow of generating a user profile

Algorithm 1: the algorithm of generating a user habit file

```
Input: a user's log file
Output: the user's habit file
{
  u=|log file| − |sliding window| − 1;
  for(i=0; i < u; i++){₁ /* i: L-windows */
    for(j=i+1; j < u; j++){₂ /* j: C-windows */
      for (each of ∑ᵏ₌₂^|L-windows|(|L − windows| − k + 1) k-grams in cur-
          rent L-window) {₃
        for (each of ∑ᵏ'₌₂^|C-window|(|C − window| − k' + 1) k'-grams in
            current C-window) {₄
          Compare the k-gram and k'-gram with the LCS
          algorithm;
              if (the identified common pattern already ex-
                  ists in the habit file)
                  Increase the count of the common pattern
                  by one;
          else
              Insert the common pattern into the user's
              habit file with count=1;
        }₄}₃
      shift C-window one system call right as a new C-
      window;}₂
    shift L-window one system call right as a new L-win-
    dow;}₁}
```

3.2.1   Mining User and Attack Habits

The IDPS processes the system calls in user log file with a sliding window, named a Log-sliding window (L-window for short), to partition the system calls collected in user's log file along their submitted sequence into k-grams where k is the number of a series of consecutive system calls, $k = 2$, 3, 4... |sliding window|. In addition, another sliding window of the same size (i.e., the same number of system calls), named Compared-sliding window (C-window for short), is employed for another session in the same user log file. This time, k' consecutive system calls, preserving their submitted sequence, are extracted from a C-window to generate a total of (|sliding window| – k' + 1) k'-grams, $k' = 2$, 3, 4...|sliding window|. Mining server invokes Algorithm 1 to compares each of $\sum_{k=2}^{|L-windows|}(|L-windows| - k + 1)$ k-grams with $\sum_{k'=2}^{|C-window|}(|C - window| - k' + 1)$ k'-grams by using the LCS algorithm which can reveal the similarity between two strings by skipping noises. After that, the C-window shifts one system call right, and the above mentioned comparison is performed again.

> execve access getcwd getdents64 = 10
> open getdents64 getdents64 exit_group mkdir = 8
> execve access rename rename exit_group = 6
> access exit_group chdir = 21

Fig. 3. A part of a user habit file, in which a line is ended by its appearance count

Fig. 3 shows an example of a habit file in which a line is a habit, also a SC-sequence or an access pattern, ended by its appearance count. The more frequently a SC-sequence appears, the higher probability the sequence is one of the user's habits. Furthermore, we can apply this algorithm to process an attacker's log file so as to extract his/her usage habits. After legal operations are ripped off, what remains is attack patterns that form a signature file.

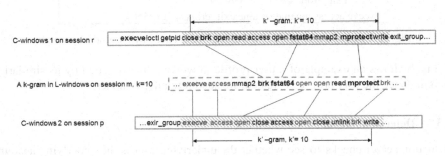

Fig. 4. An example of comparison between an L-window on session m and a C-window of 10 system calls on session p (10 system calls on session r) with the LCS algorithm [9]

Fig. 4 shows two examples. The dash-line rectangle contains an SC-sequence, i.e., a k-gram, extracted from an L-window on session m where k= 10. The solid-line rectangles list two compared sessions, sessions r and p. The shaded areas are C-windows. In session r, system calls that match those in the k'-gram when k' = 10, include brk, fstat64 and mprotect. The remaining system calls, including close, open, read, access, open, mmap2 and write, are noises, and thus are ignored. When k'=k=10, the longest common subsequence between the k-gram in session m and k'-gram in session p, includes execve, access, open, open and brk.

3.2.2   Creating User Profiles

A user profile is a habit file with the appearance counts of SC-patterns being substituted by the patterns' corresponding similarity weights. Given a set of user habit files $D=\{UP_1,UP_2...UP_N\}$ where N is the number of users and also the number of habit files in the system. Let $T=\{CS_1,CS_2...CS_k\}$ be the set of SC-patterns retrieved from D. Let $D_i=\{UP'_1,UP'_2...UP'_{Mi}\}$. Each D_i element consists of a set of habit files containing at least one element of T, e.g., CS_i, $CS_i \in T$, and $|D_i|=M_i$. The similarity weight W_{ij} of CS_i in UP_j is defined as

$$W_{ij} = \frac{sf_{ij}}{sf_{ij} + 0.5 + 1.5 \frac{ns_j}{AVG(ns)}} \times \frac{log\left(\frac{N+0.5}{M_i}\right)}{log(N+1)} \tag{1}$$

where $i=1,2,3...k$, $j=1,2,3...N$, sf_{ij} is the appearance count of CS_i in UP_j, ns_j is the total number of SC-patterns in UP_j, $AVG(ns)$ is the average number of SC-patterns an element of D has, and $log((N+0.5)/M_i)/log(N+1)$ is the inverse characteristics profile frequency (ICPF). We employ Eq. (1), which is commonly used to assign a weight to a term in the information retrieval domain [10], to calculate the similarity weight of CS_i in UP_j.

> open getdents64 getdents64 exit_group mkdir = 0.198390
> execve access getcwd getdents64 = 0.200543
> access exit_group chdir = 0.556029
> execve access rename rename exit_group = 0.135409

Fig. 5. A part of a user profile, in which a line is ended by its similarity weight

Fig. 5 shows an example of a user profile in which a line is ended by its similarity weight. Once the user profile is created, we send it to all grid nodes.

3.3   Detection Server

Detection server checks to see whether the underlying user is the underlying account holder j or not by calculating the similarity scores between these newly submitted system calls in the user's current session and the usage habits collected in the undering user profile by using the Okapi formula (Robertson et al., 1996), which is commonly used to define the similarity score between documents. Given an unknown user x's current input SC-sequences, denoted by SCSx, the similarity score, e.g., $SimS_{xj}$, between SCSx and user j's user profile UP_j, is defined as

$$SimS_{xj} = \sum_{i=1}^{p} F_{ix} W_{ij} \tag{2}$$

where p is the number of SC-sequences, i.e., a pattern, appearing in both the SCSx and UP_j, F_{ix} is user x's SC-sequence's appearance count in habit file, W_{ij} is the SC-sequence's similarity weight in UP_j. The higher the similarity score, the higher the probability that the user x is the person j who submitted the inputs. The concept of detection server in calculating the user habit is similar to that of the mining server. [5] showed a method to calculate the similarity scores between current session's system-command-sequences and each of the user profiles in the system. The similarity scores between the underlying user and the account holder's profile should be ranked high within the first x%. If not, the underlying user is recognized as hacker, meaning he/she is not the account holder.

3.3.1 Attack Types
In this study, there are three types of intrusions. Type 0 is defined as the situation where a member of a specific group submits a system call that the group members are prohibited to use. Type I attack is an attack that penetrates a system and submits a sensitive system call that will erase or modify sensitive data or attack the system. A type II attack consists of several attack patterns, each of which is considered as an attack stage. In fact, a hacker mixing specific system calls as noises with an attack pattern can sometimes successfully penetrate a security system. Type 0 and Type I attacks can be detected by the system call monitor & filter by comparing an input system call directly with Class-limited-system-call list. This detection in system call level can protect a system completely. The Type II attack will be identified by detection server.

3.3.2 Detection Multi-stage Attack
As stated above, attackers' common attack patterns are presented in the format of a profile. Given current input SC-sequences, we can make sure whether the SC-sequences contain hacker-specific attacks by checking the hacker j's ranking. If the similarity score between the input SC-sequences and hacker profile is within the first x%, the IDPS will issue an alert message, and reply an "unsafe" message accompanied by the user's ID to inform the system call monitor & filter which will isolate the user and prevent him from further use of the system.

4 Experiments

We first install the system call monitor & filter into the main computer, e.g., Redhat ES, of an enterprise system to obtain 10 different categories of user log files as the experimental data for the duration between November 1, 2012 and April 30, 2013. The testbed resources in this study are shown in Table 2.

Table 2. The specifications of the Computational grid (cluster) resources

Resource	No.	CPU Type	No. Core	BogoMips /each	Mem (GB)	Open-Mpi
Alpha (IDPS)	1	Intel(R) Xeon(R) E5645 @ 2.40GHz	12	4800	25	1.4.1
Beta	1	AMD Opteron(tm) 6174 @ 2.20GHz	48	4400	50	1.4.1
Gamma	1	Intel(R) Xeon(R) E5645 @ 2.40GHz	12	4800	25	1.4.1

4.1   User's Similarity Score Ranking Threshold

In this experiment, we define a paragraph size as 3 * |sliding window|. A typical paragraph size is 30 system calls, in which detection server ranks the similarity scores of all user accounts in a system. The purpose is to avoid continuously performing ranking when each system call is input.

logid=0, uid=1000, SCS length=30, attacker= 0.1347, account= 0.9578
logid=0, uid=1000, SCS length=60, attacker= 0.3124, account= 0.9634
logid=0, uid=1000, SCS length=90, attacker= 0.7003, account= 0.9284 -> alert
logid=0, uid=1000, SCS length=120, attacker= 0.9501, account= 0.9073 -> alert

Fig. 6. Detection server ranks for all user profiles when the paragraph size is 30

Fig. 6 shows an example, in which the IDPS detects the current input SC-sequence. If the rank of the profile of account holder is lower than the threshold 0.95 or if the rank of an attacker profile is higher than the threshold, the detection server alerts the system manager that the current user is suspected as a hacker.

4.2   Identifying Malicious Programs

A malicious program which is suspected as a Type II attack can be detected by the detection server by checking to see whether the hacker ranking is higher than the per-defined threshold.

setreuid32(), setuid32(), setregid32(), setgroups32() = 0.8531
fork(),ptrace(),execve(), ptrace() = 0.9854
socket(), setsockopt(), sendto(), close(), nanosleep() = 0.7638

Fig. 7. A part of a hacker profile, in which a line is ended by its similarity weight

During the experiment, we installed the attack patterns listed in Fig.7 as the hacker injection codes into a running process or issued a DDoS attack to the system. The detection server's attack recognition rate is 99%.

4.3   Detection Server Accuracy and Response Time

We use 75% of the user's historical data as the training data to test Algorithm 1 run on the mining server in parallel for creating user profiles. The remaining 25% as the test data is then given to the detection server to simulate the user online inputs. The threshold is set to 0.95. A total of 105400 system calls were collected from 1726 log files. The average length of the SC-sequence sliding window was 10. The user recognition rate of the IDPS is 93%.

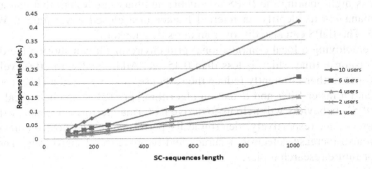

Fig. 8. The experimental response time of the detection server run on 1, 2, 4, 6 and 10 users on 60 processors in parallel

Fig. 8 shows the experimental result generated by the detection server which employs 60 processors in parallel. The maximum response time is less than 0.45 sec. This means that IDPS can detect malicious behaviors in a real-time manner.

4.4   Comparison with Other Host-Based Intrusion Detection Systems

In this experiment, we compare the IDPS with other host-based intrusion detection systems (HIDS for short). The results are shown in Table 3, in which "✓" means that the system has this function, "×" represents that the system does not have the function, "Δ" shows that the system has the function but not completely equivalent and ART is the average response time.

Table 3. The comparsion of IDPS with other HIDS under attack

System \ Attack	Identify User /ART(sec.)	Type 0 /ART(sec.)	Type I /ART(sec.)	Type II /ART(sec.)	DDoS /ART(sec.)
OSSEC	×	✓ / 60	✓ / 60	×	×
SAMHAIN	×	✓ / 60	✓ / 60	×	×
McAfee	×	×	×	×	×
Symantec CSP	×	✓ / 2	✓ / 2	Δ / 3	Δ / 3.5
IDPS	✓ / 0.45	✓ / 0	✓ / 0	✓ / 0.45	✓ / 0.45

5   Conclusions and Future Work

In this article, we proposed an approach to find users' habits by employing data mining techniques and profile features. The purpose is to identify the representative SC-sequences for a user. After that, the weight of SC-sequences is computed so that a user's profile can be established. To make sure whether a user is the current account holder or a hacker, the IDPS calculates the similarity scores between the SC-sequences in the current user's input session and each user' usage behaviors. The accuracy is high, making the IDPS a valuable auxiliary subsystem that can assist the system managers to identify an internal hacker in a closed environment. With this approach, The IDPS can also discover an out-side attacker.

Also, employing a local computational grid environment can shorten the detection server's response time which is less than 0.45 sec. Additionally, to effectively detect an attack and further efficiently reduce the response time, we need a cluster workload monitor and a faster filter and detection algorithm [11, 12]. A mathematical analysis on the IDPS's behaviors will help us to derive its formal performance and cost models so that users can, respectively, determine its performance and cost before using it. They can also increase detection accuracy and improve the decisive rate. Those constitute our future research topics.

References

1. Shan, Z., Wang, X., Chiueh, T., Meng, X.: Safe side effects commitment for OS-level virtualization. In: The ACM International Conference on Autonomic Computing, NY, USA, pp. 111–120 (2011)
2. Shyu, S.J., Tsai, C.Y.: Finding the longest common subsequence for multiple biological sequences by ant colony optimization. Computers & Operations Research 36(1), 73–91 (2009)
3. O'Shaughnessy, S., Gray, G.: Development and evaluation of a dataset generator tool for generating synthetic log files containing computer attack signatures. International Journal of Ambient Computing and Intelligence 3(2), 64–76 (2011)
4. O'Mahony, M.P., Hurley, N.J., Silvestre, G.C.M.: Promoting recommendations: An attack on collaborative filtering. In: Hameurlain, A., Cicchetti, R., Traunmüller, R. (eds.) DEXA 2002. LNCS, vol. 2453, pp. 494–503. Springer, Heidelberg (2002)
5. Leu, F.-Y., Hu, K.-W., Jiang, F.-C.: Intrusion detection and identification system using data mining and forensic techniques. In: Miyaji, A., Kikuchi, H., Rannenberg, K. (eds.) IWSEC 2007. LNCS, vol. 4752, pp. 137–152. Springer, Heidelberg (2007)
6. Giffin, J.T., Jha, S., Miller, B.P.: Automated discovery of mimicry attacks. In: Zamboni, D., Kruegel, C. (eds.) RAID 2006. LNCS, vol. 4219, pp. 41–60. Springer, Heidelberg (2006)
7. Choi, J., Choi, C., Ko, B., Choi, D., Kim, P.: Detecting web based DDoS attack using MapReduce operations in cloud computing environment. Journal of Internet Services and Information Security 3(3/4), 28–37 (2013)
8. Kang, H.-S., Kim, S.-R.: A new logging-based IP traceback approach using data mining techniques. Journal of Internet Services and Information Security 3(3/4), 72–80 (2013)

9. Roger, R.J., Geatz, M.W.: Data Mining: A tutorial-based primer. Addison-Wesley, New York (2002)
10. Zhu, D., Xiao, J.: R-tfidf, a variety of tf-idf term weighting strategy in document categorization. In: The IEEE International Conference on Semantics, Knowledge and Grids, Washington, DC, USA, pp. 83–90 (2011)
11. Angin, P., Bhargava, B.: An agent-based optimization framework for mobile-cloud computing 4(2), 1–17 (2013)
12. Ling, A.P.A., Kokichi, S., Masao, M.: Enhancing smart grid system processes via philosophy of Security -case study based on information security systems. Journal of Wireless Mobile Networks, Ubiquitous Computing, and Dependable Applications 3(3), 94–112 (2012)

A Hybrid System for Reducing Memory and Time Overhead of Intrusion Detection System

Zhi-Guo Chen and Sung-Ryul Kim

Division of Internet and Multimedia Engineering
Konkuk University, Seoul, Rep. of Korea
chenzhiguo520@gmail.com, kimsr@konkuk.ac.kr
http://www.konkuk.ac.kr

Abstract. With the growing use of the internet worldwide, internet security becomes more and more important. There are many techniques available for intrusion detection. However, there remain various issues to be improved, such as detection rate, false positive rate, memory overhead, time overhead, and so on. In this paper, a new hybrid system for network intrusion detection system using principal component analysis and C4.5 is presented, which has a good detection rate and keeps false positive and false negative rate at an acceptable level for different types of network attacks. Especially, this system can effectively reduce the memory overhead and the time overhead of building the intrusion detection model. These claims are verified by experimental results on the KDD Cup 99 benchmark network intrusion detection dataset.

Keywords: Intrusion Detection System, Principal Component Analysis Algorithm, C4.5 Algorithm, Time Overhead and Memory Overhead.

1 Introduction

With the rapid development and application of computing and communication technologies, more and more people solve problems or handle things with the internet, using such things as email, internet banking, video conference, save personal information and so on. Therefore, internet security becomes one of the key problems in the world. Traditionally, firewall is a widely used security measure but the firewall alone does not provide enough security. The protection of computer systems, network systems and the securities of information infrastructure usually depend on a kind of intrusion detection technology also [1].

So far, many techniques for intrusion detection have been proposed and intrusion detection systems [2] by these techniques are broadly classified into two categories: misuse-based IDS and anomaly-based IDS [3]. Misuse-based IDS is based on signatures for known attacks. If unknown attacks or known attacks which do not match any signatures appear, then these attacks may not be detected with misuse-based IDS. So, in order to detect new attacks, IDS need to revise the set of signatures frequently. Anomaly-based IDS is different from

Linawati et al. (Eds.): ICT-EurAsia 2014, LNCS 8407, pp. 386–395, 2014.

misuse-based IDS, Anomaly-based IDS is able to detect known and unknown attacks by building profiles of normal behaviors. If a new behavior is far from normal behaviors of the profiles, then the behavior will be treated as an attack. Anomaly based intrusion detection using data mining algorithms such as nave Bayesian classifier (NB), decision tree (DT), neural network (NN), k-nearest neighbors (KNN), support vector machine (SVM), and genetic algorithm have been widely used by researchers to improve the performance of IDS [4]. However, Anomaly detection suffers from low detection and high false positive rates and it incurs large memory and time overhead for the detection model.

In this paper, we present a new hybrid system for network intrusion detection using principal component analysis and C4.5 algorithm [5] which has good detection rate and keeps false positive and false negative rates at an acceptable level for different types of network attacks while having the benefit of lower the memory and the time overhead for building the detection model. PCA (principal component analysis) [6, 7] is used to reduce the dimension of original high dimensional data and remove noise effectively. Then we use new dataset which handled by PCA to make intrusion detection model by C4.5 algorithm. The experimental results show that the proposed method has acceptable detection rates (DR), false positive rate(FP), false negative rate(FN) and accuracy.

The rest of this paper is organized as follow: in section 2, we will introduce principal component analysis and C4.5 algorithm. Section 3, describes our proposed method. In section 4, we introduce experiment and result, performances estimation of IDS, experimental dataset and experimental analysis. Finally, in section 5, we conclude this paper.

2 Algorithm

2.1 PCA Algorithm

The performance of the intrusion detection model depends on the quality of dataset. So noise in the dataset is one of the challenges in data mining. The reason for dealing with noisy data is that it will avoid over-fitting the dataset. The irrelevant and redundant attributes of dataset may lead to complex classification model and reduce the classification accuracy. So we need to reduce noises, irrelevant and redundant attributes firstly. Principal component analysis algorithm have been widely used in dimension reduction; it can be effective to deal with complex data that have high dimensions. It can identify the main elements and structure of data, remove noise and redundant attributes, express the data with simple format.

The following procedure describes the PCA algorithm we use to deal with dataset S $(D \times N)$ where N is the number of data example and D is the number of dimension of original dataset S. Each column represents one data that have dimensionality D.

$$S = \begin{pmatrix} S_{11} & \cdots & S_{m1} & \cdots & S_{N1} \\ S_{12} & \cdots & S_{m2} & \cdots & S_{N2} \\ \vdots & \ddots & \vdots & \ddots & \vdots \\ S_{1D} & \cdots & S_{mD} & \cdots & S_{ND} \end{pmatrix}$$

1. Map discrete attributes to continuous attributes;
2. Calculate the mean value of all data examples $\bar{S}$;
3. Subtract mean vector for each data example;
4. Find covariance matrix $\sum$ of dataset S, and then calculate all eigenvectors and eigenvalues of $\sum$;
5. According the eigenvalues to select the dimension number d of biggest eigenvectors to make the new dataset. The eigenvectors are represented as $u_1, u_2, ..., u_d$ and then find its matrix transpose U;
6. Get new dataset $D = (US')^T (N \times d)$, where N is the number of the data examples and d is the dimension of the new dataset D. Add the original datasets class identity in new Dataset D and we have completed the transformed dataset D and with every record included with d attributes and one class identity.

2.2   C4.5 Algorithm

C4.5 algorithm has been widely used in classification and decision making. C4.5 algorithm is a later version of the ID3 algorithm [8] proposed by R. Quinlan [9]. The majority of this algorithm uses a descendent strategy from the root to the leaves. To ensure this procedure, the following generic parameters are required. The gain ratio (attribute selection measure) taking into account the discriminative power of each attribute over classes in order to choose the best one as the root of the decision tree. C4.5 decision tree divides data items into subsets, based on the attributes. It finds the one attribute that maximizes gain ratio and divides the data using that attribute.

Let us assume that D is a dataset and that A_i is one of attribute of the dataset. Let us also assume that the dataset has a set of classes $C_1, C_2, ..., C_m$. The information gain is calculated as the follows:

$$Gain(D, A_i) = Entropy(D) - \sum_{i \in Values(A_i)} \frac{|D_i|}{|D|} Entropy(D_i) \tag{1}$$

where,

$$Entropy(D) = -\sum_{i=1}^{m} \frac{freq(C_i, D)}{|D|} log_2 \frac{freq(C_i, D)}{|D|} \tag{2}$$

where $freq(C_i, D)$ denotes the number of examples in the dataset D belonging to class C_i and D_i is the subset of dataset D divided by the attribute $A_i's$ value a_m.

Then $SplitInfo(A_i)$ is defined as the information content of the attribute A_i itself [12]:

$$SplitInfo(D, A_i) = - \sum_{i \in Values(A_i)} \frac{|D_i|}{|D|} log_2 \frac{|D_i|}{|D|} \tag{3}$$

The gain ratio is the information gain calibrated by Split Info:

$$GainRatio(D, A_i) = \frac{Gain(D, A_i)}{SplitInfo(A_i)} \tag{4}$$

1. If A_i is a discrete attribute [10] then divide the dataset by discrete values of $A_i(a_1, a_2, ..., a_m)$.
2. If A_i is a continuous attribute then use information gain to efficiently find the best split point and disperse the dataset by this best split point [11]. If attribute A_i has values $(A_{i1}, A_{i2}, , A_{im}, , A_{ih})$ then firstly sort the continuous values (called candidate cut point) from small to large and then divide dataset with these candidate cut points with $> A_{im}$ and $\leqslant A_{im}(i \leqslant m < h)$. Then we calculate the information gain for each possible cut point. The cut point for which the information gain is maximized amongst all the candidate cut points is taken as the best split point. We divide the current dataset (subset dataset) according this point. Now we can build the tree by dividing the current dataset (subset dataset) by the selected attribute (discrete attributes according the attribute values, continuous attributes according to best split point).

3   Our Proposed Method

3.1   Using PCA Algorithm

To determine different types parameters of network attacks. Firstly, we need randomly select data in file "corrected" which is downloaded from KDD Cup 99 site to make training dataset and test dataset. The dataset is $S(N \times D)$, where N is the number of the data records and D is the dimension of the KDD data (41 dimension except for class identity). And then we use the PCA algorithm to reduce the dimension of the KDD data to get new Dataset $D(N \times d)$. Where N is the number of the new dataset and d is the dimension (the number of attributes) of new dataset D. We then add the original datasets class identity in the new Dataset D. After reducing the dimension by PCA we use the C4.5 algorithms to build the intrusion detection model.

3.2   Making Detection Model

After reducing the dimension by PCA, we get new dataset D where all of the attributes are continuous ones. So we should use the continuous attributes handling method of C4.5 algorithm that has been described earlier to make tree structure.

Dataset D contains attributes $A_1, A_2, ..., A_d$ and each attribute A_i contains the following continuous attribute values $(A_{i1}, A_{i2}, ..., A_{im}, ..., A_{ih})$. The training dataset also has a set of Class $C_1, C_2, ..., C_m$. Each data in the training data D have particular class C_j. We follow the next procedure.

1. Find the best split point of every attributes and calculate gain ratio in training dataset D with C4.5 continuous attribute handling method. Compare the gain ratio of every attribute. Select A_i among the attributes $A_1, A_2, ..., A_d$ which have maximize gain ratio to make the root attribute node, and then divide the training dataset D into subsets (D_1, D_2) depending on the best split point A_{im}.

2. Find the best split point of every attribute and calculate gain ratio in subset dataset D_i. Compare the gain ratio of every attribute. Select A_i among the attributes $A_1, A_2, ..., A_d$ which have maximize gain ratio to make the attribute node, Then divide the subset dataset D_i into subsets (D_{i1}, D_{i2}) depending on the best cut point A_{im}.

3. Continue this process until subset dataset's entropy is zero or all attributes have same maximizes gain ratio in the subset dataset D_s. If subset dataset's entropy is zero and we know that all of the Class C_i in subset dataset is same. In this case, a leaf node will be set up. And if all attribute's gain ratio is same, We use $freq(C_1, D_s), freq(C_2, D_s), ..., freq(C_m, D_s)$ to determine the class in dataset D_s.

When we test an example data X, we should use PCA algorithm to deal with this example. And then we use the tree structure to find the Class (leaf node).

Pseudo Code: Since after reducing the dimension by PCA, we get new dataset D where all of the attributes are continuous ones. So we just need use the continuous attributes handling method of C4.5 algorithm to build tree:

```
C4.5 (Dataset D, Attributes Sets A, Attributes values)
 Create a root node for the tree by Maximum (Gain Ratio (D,A))
  If Entropy of dataset is 0, we are sure that the Class of this
  dataset(subset dataset) is same. In this case we stop dividing
  the dataset
  If all attribute have same maximum gain ratio in the subset
  dataset Ds. We do not know which attribute we can select to
  divide dataset. Use freq(C1,Ds),freq(C2,Ds),...,freq(Cm,Ds)
  to determine the classes in dataset Ds.
  Otherwise Begin
     Ai -- The attribute that best classifies examples(select by
     Maximum Gain Ratio (D,A)).
     Decision Tree attribute for node = Ai
     For best split point Aim of Ai (best split point find by C4.5
     continuous attributes handling method)
        Add a new tree branch below node according > Aim and <= Aim
        Let dataset (> Aim) be the subset of Dataset that have the
        values > Aim for Ai
```

```
      If all attribute have same maximum gain ratio in the subset
      dataset (> Aim)
           Then below this new branch add a leaf node with label
           = most common type in the subset dataset
      If Entropy of subset dataset (> Aim) == 0
           Then all with the same value of the categorical att-
           ribute, return a leaf
      Else below this new branch add the subtree C4.5 (subset
      dataset (> Aim), Attributes Set A, Attributes values)
End
Return Root
```

4   Experiment and Result

4.1   Performances Estimation

Accuracy, detection rate (DR), false positive rate (FP) and false negative rate (FN) are basic parameters that are used for performance estimation [4] of intrusion detection models. We can accord the following simple confusion matrix for calculating the parameters.

Table 1. Confusion Matrix

	Predicted Class Positive	Predicted Class Negative
Actual Class Positive	a	b
Actual Class Negative	c	d

In the Intrusion Detection System(IDS), a detection rate(DR) is an instance which is normal is classified as normal or attack is classified as attack. False positive(FP) means no attack but IDS detect as attack and false negative(FN) means attack occurs but IDS detect as normal. Accuracy is also an important parameter that determines the percentage of correctly classified instance. Form the confusion matrix; we can get these parameters by following calculations.

$$DetectionRate = a/(a+b) \quad and \quad d/(d+c)$$
$$FP = b/(a+b) \quad FN = c/(c+d)$$
$$Accuracy = (a+d)/(a+b+c+d)$$

4.2   Dataset

The KDD Cup 1999 dataset [12] is used in this experiment, which is network connection data collected from the U.S Air Force LAN in nine weeks. KDD-CUP99 dataset have a set of inherent constructed features. Each record has 41 characteristic attributes and one more attribute assigns the record type. And 34 attributes are continuous data types, 7 attributes are discrete data types in the

Table 2. Input attributes in KDD99 Dataset

No	Input Attribute	Type	No	Input Attribute	Type
1	Duration	Con.	22	is_guest_login	Dis.
2	protocol_type	Dis.	23	Count	Con.
3	Service	Dis.	24	srv_count	Con.
4	Flag	Dis.	25	serror_rate	Con.
5	src_bytes	Con.	26	srv_serror_rate	Con.
6	dst_bytes	Con.	27	rerror_rate	Con.
7	Land	Dis.	28	srv_rerror_rate	Con.
8	wrong_fragment	Con.	29	same_srv_rate	Con.
9	Urgent	Con.	30	diff_srv_rate	Con.
10	Hot	Con.	31	srv_diff_host_rate	Con.
11	num_failed_logins	Con.	32	dst_host_count	Con.
12	logged_in	Dis.	33	dst_host_srv_count	Con.
13	num_compromised	Con.	34	dst_host_same_srv_rate	Con.
14	root_shell	Con.	35	dst_host_diff_srv_rate	Con.
15	su_attempted	Con.	36	dst_host_same_src_port_rate	Con.
16	num_root	Con.	37	dst_host_srv_diff_host_rate	Con.
17	num_file_creations	Con.	38	dst_host_serror_rate	Con.
18	num_shells	Con.	39	dst_host_serror_rate	Con.
19	num_access_files	Con.	40	dst_host_rerror_rate	Con.
20	num_outbound_cmds	Con.	41	dst_host_srv_rerror_rate	Con.
21	is_host_login	Dis.			

characteristic attributes. The list of the input attributes in KDD99 dataset for each network connections is shown below.

The data contains attack types (marked at last attribute) that can be classified into four main categories as follows:

1. Denial of Service (DOS): Denial of Service (DOS) attack makes some computing or memory resources too busy or too full to handle legitimate re-quests, or denies legitimate users access to a machine.

2. Remote to User (R2L): Remote to User (R2L) is an attack that a remote user gains access of a local user account by sending packets to a machine over a network communication.

3. User to Root (U2R): User to Root (U2R) is an attack that an intruder begins with the access of a normal user account and then becomes a root-user by exploiting various vulnerabilities of the system.

4. Probing: Probing (Probe) is an attack that scans a network to gather information or find known vulnerabilities. An intruder with a map of machines and services that are available on a network can use the information to look for exploits.

So, all the classes in KDD99 dataset can be categorized into five main classes and four attacks are recorded into different attacks which are shown in Table 3.

Table 3. Different Data Types in KDD99 Dataset

Data Type	Mark
normal	normal
Denial of Service (DOS)	apache2, mailbomb, processtable, udpstorm, back, land, neptune, pod, smurf, teardrop
Remote to User (R2L)	ftp_write, guess_passwd, multihop, phf, spy, warezclient, warezmaster, imap, named, sendmail, snmpgetattack, snmpguess, worm, xlock, xsnoop
User to Root (U2R)	buffer_overflow, loadmodule, perl, rootkit, httptunnel, ps, sqlattack, xterm
Probing	Satan, ipsweep, nmap, portsweep, mscan, saint

4.3 Experimental Analysis

The number of training and test data is shown in the following:

Table 4. Number of training and test examples

Types	Training data	Test data
Normal	5869	5781
Probing	429	384
DOS	22086	22297
U2R	20	21
R2L	1596	1517

In order to evaluate the performance of the proposed algorithm for different types of network attacks, we performed 5-Class classification using KDD99 dataset. We compared our method with C4.5 algorithm.

Table 5. Confusion matrix of our method   **Table 6.** Confusion matrix of C4.5 method

a	b	c	d	e	classified as	a	b	c	d	e	classified as
5469	9	12	3	288	a = normal	5491	7	5	9	269	a = normal
13	357				b = Probing	1	378				b = Probing
7		22274			c = DOS	1		22285			c = DOS
9			10		d = U2R	5			11		d = U2R
283				1226	e = R2L	299				1217	e = R2L

Our experimental results show that detection rates (DR) and accuracy of our proposed method and C4.5 algorithm almost identical. But from Figure 3, we can see that our method is effective to reduce the memory overhead and the time overhead of building the intrusion detection model.

There are not many examples of U2R, R2L and Probing to build the intrusion detection model. Thus, the C4.5 method and our method have lower detection rates for these types of network intrusions. For similar reasons, even if one example is not correctly detected the resulting rate will show considerable differences. Therefore, the detection rate of Probe and false negative of U2R have considerable difference between our proposed method and C4.5 method.

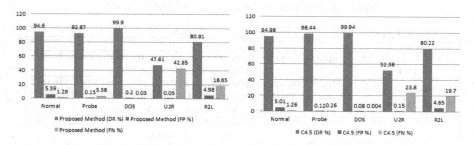

Fig. 1. Performance of our method and C4.5 algorithm

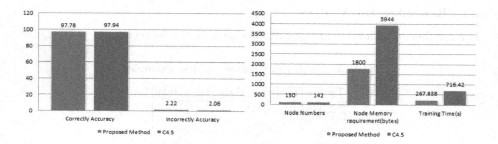

Fig. 2. Accuracy of two methods

Fig. 3. Node numbers, node memory requirement and training time

From figure 3, we can see that the number of nodes in our proposed method is almost similar to C4.5 method, but one node in our method occupies just 12bytes and it can be stored as $[x, y]$ (x is the selected attribute written as int format, y is best split value that can be written as $double$ format). If we use C4.5 algorithm to deal with the original dataset S. For continuous attribute, we also can store the node as $[x, y]$, but for discrete attribute, if it have lots of attribute values, we need to store a node as $[x, a_1, a_2, ..., a_i, ..., a_m]$ (x is the selected attribute written as int format, a_i is discrete attribute value that can be written as int format). In this case, the discrete attribute values requires more memory. So, we can conclude that our proposed method can effectively reduce the memory overhead of C4.5 method.

Because of we use PCA algorithm to reduce the dimension of the data, our proposed method just need 267.838 seconds to build the intrusion detection model. Therefore, after comparing the training time of two methods we can conclude that PCA algorithm can be effective to reduce the time overhead of building Intrusion Detection Model.

Overall consideration accuracy, detection rates, false positive rate, false negative rate, memory overhead and time overhead, we can conclude that our method has good performance for intrusion detection system and that our proposed method is effective to improve the performances of Anomaly-based intrusion detection system.

5   Conclusion

This paper introduced a new hybrid system for network intrusion detection using principal component analysis and C4.5 algorithm. The results show that it has acceptable detection rate, false positive and false negative to detect the 5 types of the KDD dataset. It also can be effective to reduce the memory overhead and the time overhead of building the intrusion detection model. But the false negative and false positive rates for R2L are high. The reason is there are not many examples of R2L to build detection model and the intrusion detection model has misclassified the data as normal. So the future work will focus on avoiding misclassified R2L, reducing the false positive and false negative rates of R2L and improving the detection rate of normal and R2L.

Acknowledgments. This research was supported by Next-Generation Information Computing Development Program through the National Research Foundation of Korea (NRF) funded by the Ministry of Science, ICT & Future Planning (2011-0029924).

References

1. Lu, H., Xu, J.: Three-level Hybrid Intrusion Detection System
2. http://www.sans.org/reading-room/whitepapers/detection/understanding-intrusion-detection-systems-337
3. Brown, D.J., Suckow, B., Wang, T.: A Survey of Intrusion Detection Systems
4. Hlaing, T.: Feature Selection and Fuzzy Decision Tree for Network Intrusion Detection. International Journal of Informatics and Communication Technology (IJ-ICT) 1(2), 2252–8776 (2012) ISSN: 2252-8776
5. Ben Amor, N., Benferhat, S., Elouedi, Z.: Naive bayes vs decision trees in intrusion detection systems. In: ACM Symposium on Applied Computing (SAC 2004), pp. 420–424, Nic-osia, Cyprus (2004)
6. Smith, L.I.: A tutorial on Principal Components Analysis, New York (2002)
7. Zhao, L., Kang, H.-S., Kim, S.-R.: Improved Clustering for Intrusion Detection by Principal Component Analysis with Effective Noise Reduction. In: Mustofa, K., Neuhold, E.J., Tjoa, A.M., Weippl, E., You, I. (eds.) ICT-EurAsia 2013. LNCS, vol. 7804, pp. 490–495. Springer, Heidelberg (2013)
8. Quinlan, J.R.: Induction of Decision Trees. Machine Learning 1, 81–106 (1986)
9. Quinlan, J.R.: Improved Use of Continuous Attributes in C4.5. Journal of Artifcial Intelligence Research 4, 77–90 (1996); Submitted 10/95; published 3/96
10. Jain, Y.K.: Upendra: An Efficient Intrusion Detection Based on Decision Tree Classifier Using Feature Reduction. International Journal of Scientific and Research Publications 2(1) (January 2012) ISSN 2250-3153
11. Ruggieri, S.: Efficient C4.5. IEEE Transactions on Knowledge and Data Engineering 14(2) (March/April 2002)
12. The third international knowledge discovery and data mining tools competition dataset KDD 1999-Cup (1999), http://kdd.ics.uci.edu/databases/kddcup99/kddcup99.html

LDFGB Algorithm for Anomaly Intrusion Detection

Shang-nan Yin, Zhi-guo Chen, and Sung-Ryul Kim

Division of Internet and Multimedia Engineering
Konkuk University, Seoul, Rep. of Korea
{yinshangnan,chenzhiguo520}@gmail.com, kimsr@konkuk.ac.kr
http://www.konkuk.ac.kr

Abstract. With the development of internet technology, more and more risks are appearing on the internet and the internet security has become an important issue. Intrusion detection technology is an important part of internet security. In intrusion detection, it is important to have a fast and effective method to find out known and unknown attacks. In this paper, we present a graph-based intrusion detection algorithm by outlier detection method which is based on local deviation factor (LDFGB). This algorithm has better detection rates than a previous clustering algorithm. Moreover, it is able to detect any shape of cluster and still keep high detection rate for detecting unknown or known attacks. LDFGB algorithm uses graph-based cluster algorithm (GB) to get an initial partition of dataset which depends on a parameter of cluster precision, then we use the outlier detection algorithm to further processing the results of graph-based cluster algorithm. This measure is effective to improve the detection rates and false positive rates.

Keywords: Graph-based clustering, outlier detection, Intrusion Detection.

1 Introduction

In modern society, we use internet at anytime and anywhere, so internet security becomes one of the hottest issues and we need to find an effective way to protect this network infrastructure. Intrusion detection system [1] is a useful method for detecting attacks. In 1987, Denning [2] introduced the first anomaly intrusion detection model, which is able to detect known and unknown attacks. After that research, many methods have been proposed for anomaly intrusion detection, such as machine learning [3], immunological [4] and data mining. Among these techniques, data mining has been widely used and it successfully solves the deficiencies of intrusion detection. The clustering algorithm is an important technology of data mining which can offset these deficiencies.

Clustering is the task of grouping a set of objects in such a way that objects in the same group (called a cluster) are more similar (same attributes) to each other than to those in other groups (clusters). K-means algorithm [5]

Linawati et al. (Eds.): ICT-EurAsia 2014, LNCS 8407, pp. 396–404, 2014.

is a popular clustering algorithm which is used in anomaly intrusion detection. This algorithm classifies similar data set into same clusters, and classifies dissimilar data set into different clusters. However, the user must set the number of clusters k, meaning that the user has to have some knowledge about the data. Other methods also have some disadvantages, for example, combining simulated annealing and clustering algorithm [6] requires a lot of training data and thus consumes excessive resource. In recent year, many researchers have proposed to avoid excessive resource consumption. One of effective methods is graph-based clustering. For example, PBS algorithm [7] introduces a measurement method of data points similarity which is based on an approximate function. But, this algorithm cannot achieve an exciting detection rate. LDC algorithm [8] improves the detection rate, but it doesnt accurately and comprehensively analysis the distribution situation of data nodes.

In this paper, we present LDFGB algorithm for intrusion detection which is one of the graph clustering algorithms. It is based on the LDC algorithm, uses local deviation factor to differentiate the distribution situation of data nodes and to identify outliers. The experimental results show that the proposed method is efficiently for anomalybased intrusion detection.

The paper is organized as follows. In section 2, we introduce the graph-based clustering. In section 3, we describe the LDFGB algorithm in detail. In section 4, we describe our evaluation methods and experimental results. Finally, we conclude this paper.

2   Graph-Base Cluster Algorithm

Graph-based clustering algorithm is a method commonly used in automatic partitioning of a data set into several clusters. It proceeds by setting a parameter of clustering precision to control the result of clustering. Records in dataset are packaged as a node. These nodes are treated as vertex of a complete undirected graph, and the distance values between these notes as weight of the edge. The distance is calculated by Euclidean distance function (Table 1).

$$d(i,j) = \sqrt{|x_i 1 - x_j 2|^2 + |x_i 2 - x_j 2|^2 + ... + |x_i p - x_j p|^2} \tag{1}$$

Table 1. Euclidean distance

	Id1	Id2	Id3	......	Idn
Id1	0	0.81	0.11	......	0.02
Id2	0.81	0	0.45	......	0.71
Id3	0.11	0.45	0	......	0.15
......	......	......	......	......	......
Idn	0.02	0.71	0.15	......	0

According these values of distance, we construct a distance matrix I. And the threshold δ is computed from a parameter of cluster precision α.

$$\delta = dismin + dismax - dismin * Clusterprecision \tag{2}$$

dismin and dismax represent the minimum and maximal value of matrix I respectively. So an edge is cut down from this graph if its value of weight greater than threshold δ as shown in Figure.1

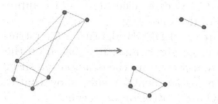

Fig. 1. GB Cluster

Finally, we transverse the whole graph, the nodes would be classified into the same cluster if there is an edge between them. Therefore, several sub-graphs are created. Each sub-graph represents a cluster. Finally, outliers are processed.

The Steps of GB Algorithm Are as Follows:

```
Input: Dataset (record set), Cluster Precision
Record I is packaged as a note
Put note I into Graph
Repeat {
    Calculate threshold (delta) by function
    Cut down all the edges whose value is greater than the
    threshold (delta)
    Transverse Graph, label all the sub-graphs.
    Outlier processing
} until the outlier is processed completely
```

GB algorithm has been used for clustering for decades. However, it mainly has two shortcomings when it is applied for intrusion detection: the first one is that it distinguishes the normal and abnormal cluster just by a value of threshold. So the clustering accuracy is far from enough. Second, it doesnt offer a reasonable method to address outliers, but it just throws them away. With this coarse granularity partition, it cannot achieve a satisfactory detection rate. On the other hand, the ability to detect any shape of cluster has made it very suitable for the dataset with complex shape from real network.

3   LDFGB Algorithm for Intrusion Detection

In order to achieve higher detection rate, we further propose an improved graph-based clustering algorithm by using outlier detection method based on local deviation factor in label process. This method mainly focuses on how to classify the data on the boundary to be classified more accurately and then augment the difference between normal and abnormal clusters. Firstly, we define some related definitions:

Definition 1: (Outlier). These can be objects that are outlying relative to their local neighborhoods, particularly with respect to the densities of the neighborhoods. These outliers are regarded as local outliers. (Figure 2)

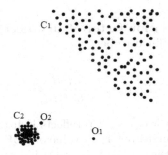

Fig. 2. O_1 and O_2 are outliers

Definition 2: (k distance of an object p). For any positive integer k, the k-distance of object p, denoted as k-distance (p), is defined to be the distance d (p, o) between p and an object o∈D such that:

For at least k objects o'∈D \ {p}, it holds that d(p,o')≤d(p,o)

For at most k-1 objects o'∈D \ {p}, it holds that d(p,o')<d(p,o)

Definition 3: (k-distance neighborhood of an object). Given the k-distance of p, the k-distance neighborhood of p contains every object whose distance from p is not greater than the k-distance.

$$N_{k-distance}(p) = \{q \in D \setminus \{p\} \,|\, d(p,q) \leq k - distance\,(p)\}$$

These objects q are called the k-nearest neighbors of p.

Definition 4: (local deviation rate of an object). Given the k-distance of p, and p is a center of circle with radius k. All objects in this circle are k-distance neighborhood of p. p is the Centre of mass of this circle. So the local deviation rate is defined to be:

$$LDR_{k(p)} = \frac{dis\,(p,p')}{|N_{k-distance(p)}|} \qquad (3)$$

The dis (p, p') is the distance between object p and Centre of mass of p'.

Definition 5: (local deviation influence rate of an object). Given the k-distance neighborhood of p and LDR, the local deviation influence rate is defined to be:

$$LDIR_{k(p)} = \frac{\sum_{o \in N_{k-distance}}^{LDR_{k(o)}}}{|N_{k-distance(p)}|} \qquad (4)$$

Definition 6: (local deviation factor of an object). Given LDR and LDIR, local deviation factor is defined to be:

$$LDF_{k(p)} = \frac{LDR_{k(p)}}{LDIR_{k(p)}} \qquad (5)$$

The local deviation factor of object p reflects k-distance neighborhood of object p within the dispersion degree. High value of LDF means higher probability of one object being an outlier; a low LDF value indicates that the density of an objects neighborhood is high. So its hardly to be an outlier.

The Steps of LDF Algorithm Are as Follows:

```
Step1: implement GB algorithm to cluster dataset and gain
       n clusters C1, C2...Cn, they are sorted in descending
       order according to the records they embraced.
Step2: initialize CN ={}, CS ={}, CA ={},
Step3: For i =1 to n
           IF (C1.num+C2.num...Ci.num> (lambda)2*M),
           THEN CN={C1,C2...Ci-1},
           IF (Cn+Cn-1...Cj+1 >(lambda)2*M)
           THEN CA = {Cj+1...Cn}.
       The remaining cluster is classified into CS {Ci...Cj}.
       End for.
Step4: compute LDF of every object p by the function (3) (4)
       and (5), p CS, sorted these values in descending order.
       The first k records are classified in CA, and the rest
       are classified in CN.
Step5: the data in CN are labeled as normal, while in CA, they
       are labeled as abnormal. After all data are labeled,
       the labeling process is over.
```

In this process, CN, CS and CA stand for the set of normal clusters, suspicious clusters and abnormal clusters respectively. CS is the set that need to be processed in next step. In step 3, M is the number of data set and $\lambda1$, $\lambda2$ ($\lambda1+\lambda2=1$) represent the percentage of normal and anomaly rate. They should meet the premise that the number of normal action is far greater than the number of intrusion action. So their values must satisfy $\lambda1\gg\lambda2$. Otherwise, the isolated points were classified in abnormal clusters rather than discard them away. In detecting phase, a new record d, calculate its distance to each data, it will belong to the cluster the same to the data that has nearest distance with it. If the cluster is normal, d is normal. Otherwise, d is an attack.

4   Experiments and Results

To evaluate the performance of LDFGB approach, a series of experiments was conducted on a 2-dimensional artificial dataset. (Figure 3)

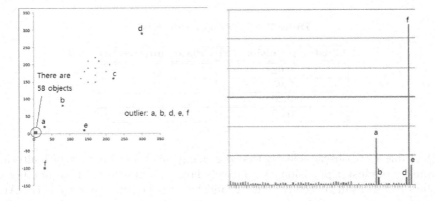

Fig. 3. 2-dimensional dataset and LDF values

Figure 4 shows that the data nodes distributed in two kinds of situations. Similar results are obtained by the LDC algorithm, so the LDC algorithm cant differentiate these kinds of situations. If we use the proposed method (LDFGB Algorithm) by adjusting K values that we can differentiate two situations. So the performance of LDFGB is the better than LDC algorithm.

KDDCup99 dataset is a dedicated test dataset established for intrusion detection assessment by Massachusetts Institute of Technology. It contains 24 kinds of attacks categorized into 4 types: Denial of Service, Remote to User, User to Root and Probing. In the dataset, a record has 7 classified attributes and 34 numeric attributes, and this belongs to the implementation of clustering in high-dimensional space. The In order to improve the detection efficiency of the experiment, we remove the attributes that is useless for this experiment. After careful analysis, we screen 20 properties as the objects of study, such as the lifetime of the TCP, window size and the length of the packet.

We randomly select 10000 samples for training data set. Besides, we randomly select 2500 samples of intrusion which types are different from the training dataset. It is aimed to evaluate ability of this algorithm on detecting unknown attacks. First, we alter the cluster precision of α. The result is shown in Table 2:

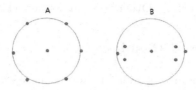

Fig. 4. Two kinds of distribution

Table 2. Clustering result of GB

Cluster precision (α)	Cluster number(n)
0.02	21
0.05	9
0.20	6
0.50	4

On Table 2, we observe clearly that the change of cluster number with altering parameter of cluster precision. A relatively large α will lead to small number of clusters. As a result, excessive data would be classified in one large class. And most of the abnormal behaviors cant be detected in this situation. On the other hand, with a small value of α, the partition will generate excessive clusters.

The next step, for the GB model, the best situation is that all data were divided into 9 subsets. So we fixed $\alpha= 0.05$. To meet the one of premise of anomaly intrusion detection that normal action is far greater than the number of intrusion action, we try the parameter of $\lambda 1$ and $\lambda 2$ in (0.9 , 1.0) and (0.0 , 0.1) respectively. Finally, we change the values of parameter K and testing these constructed models by group 3. We find that, when k=9, $\lambda 1$=0.95 and $\lambda 2$=0.05, the performance of this algorithm is the best. The output of detection rate and false positive rate showed in Table 3:

The LDC algorithm output of detection rate and false positive rate showed in Table4:

We discover the LDFGB algorithm achieves better detection rate than the LDC algorithm. Table 3 and Table 4 show that when there are the same K values, the performance of LDFGB algorithm is superior to the LDC algorithm. The experimental result shows that the parameter K is an important factor for

Table 3. The performance of LDFGB

K	Detection rate	False positive rate
5	94.30%	2.26%
8	96.14%	2.09%
12	97.25%	2.03%
15	96.52%	2.13%

Table 4. The performance of LDC

K	Detection rate	False positive rate
5	93.30%	2.24%
8	95.31%	2.08%
12	92.67%	2.14%
15	92.00%	2.11%

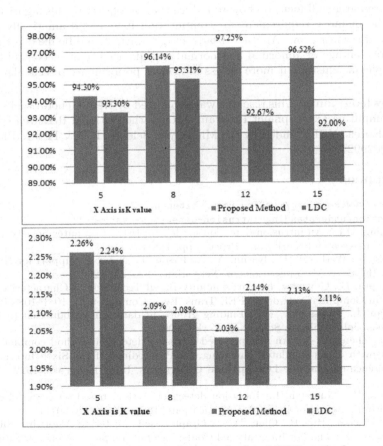

Fig. 5. The preferment of our method and LDC method

the performance of this algorithm. We should not set a value for K that is too large, because a large K value will cause many isolated points to be classified from normal classes. On the other hand, a relatively small value of K will lead to the most of records have a large LDF value. Therefore, we could not separate the abnormal records from suspicious cluster. Both of these situations would decrease cluster precision. Figure 5 shows that the proposed method always outperforms the LDC method.

5   Conclusions

Intrusion detection system based on data mining increases the safety and reliability of network. Obviously, by means of clustering method, intrusion detection may be carried out. The LDFGB algorithm presented in this paper may overcome some disadvantages of the traditional cluster algorithm for intrusion detection and can obtain comparative satisfactory performance of intrusion detection. However, there are still many deficiencies that need to be improved. Our further research will focus on how to reduce the complexity of this algorithm because the memory requirement for computation increases dramatically as the number of records grow. Another disadvantage which should be fixed is that the initial percentage of abnormal and normal records need manual control to find the suspicious clusters, it more or less influences performance of this algorithm.

Acknowledgments. This research was supported by Next-Generation Information Computing Development Program through the National Research Foundation of Korea (NRF) funded by the Ministry of Science, ICT & Future Planning (2011-0029924).

References

1. http://www.sans.org/reading_room/whitepapers/ detection/understanding-intrusion-detection-systems_337
2. Denning, D.E.: An intrusion-detection model. In: IEEE Computer Society Symposium on Research Security and Privacy, pp. 118–131 (1987)
3. Savage, S., Wetherall, D., Karlin, A., Anderson, T.: Network Support for IP traceback. IEEE/ACM Transactions on Networking, 226–237 (2001)
4. Dasgupta, D., Gonzalez, F.: An Immunity-Based Technique to Characterize Intrusions in Computer Networks. IEEE Trans. Evol. Comput. 6(3), 1081–1088 (2002)
5. Kaufan, L., Rousseeuw, P.J.: Finding groups in data: an introduction to cluster analysis. John Wiley & Sons, New York (1990)
6. Ni, L., Zheng, H.-Y.: An unsupervised intrusion detection method combined clustering with chaos simulated annealing. In: Proceedings of the Sixth International Conference on Machine Learning and Cybernetics, Hong Kong, vol. 1922 (August 2007)
7. Guohui, W., Guoyuan, L.: Intrusion detection method based on graph clustering algorithm. Journal of Computer Applications, 1888–1900 (July 2011)
8. Mingqiang, Z., Hui, H., Qian, W.: A Graph-based Clustering Algorithm Intrusion Detection. In: The 7th International Conference on Computer Science & Education (ICCSE), pp. 1311–1314 (2012)

Assets Dependencies Model in Information Security Risk Management

Jakub Breier[1,2] and Frank Schindler[3]

[1] Physical Analysis and Cryptographic Engineering, Temasek Laboratories@NTU
[2] School of Physical and Mathematical Sciences, Division of Mathematical Sciences,
Nanyang Technological University, Singapore
jbreier@ntu.edu.sg
[3] Faculty of Informatics, Pan-European University, Bratislava, Slovakia
frank.schindler@paneurouni.com

Abstract. Information security risk management is a fundamental process conducted for the purpose of securing information assets in an organization. It usually involves asset identification and valuation, threat analysis, risk analysis and implementation of countermeasures. A correct asset valuation is a basis for accurate risk analysis, but there is a lack of works describing the valuation process with respect to dependencies among assets. In this work we propose a method for inspecting asset dependencies, based on common security attributes - confidentiality, integrity and availability. Our method should bring more detailed outputs from the risk analysis and therefore make this process more objective.

Keywords: Information Security Risk Management, Asset Valuation, Asset Dependency, Risk Analysis.

1 Introduction

Information systems are subject to various threats that can have undesirable effects on them. As information technologies evolve, threats are more sophisticated and harder to detect. Great volumes of valuable data are stored in information systems that are connected to the Internet and therefore it is necessary to use security techniques for their protection.

Information security risk management [2] is a fundamental process conducted for the purpose of securing information assets in an organization. It usually involves asset identification and valuation, threat analysis, risk analysis and implementation of countermeasures. There are few standards that deliberate this process and provide recommendations for security specialists in organizations. The most popular are NIST Special Publication 800-39 [1] and ISO/IEC 27005:2011 standard [3], both provide a high-level overview of the risk management process.

The important part of the risk management process is the asset valuation that, if used properly, will tell us which assets are important for the organization in the meaning of price and necessity in business processes. Works that

Linawati et al. (Eds.): ICT-EurAsia 2014, LNCS 8407, pp. 405–412, 2014.

implement one of these standards usually use simple valuation methods, based on qualitative techniques of measurement. They express value on some discrete scale, consisting mostly of 3 to 5 degrees of precision, for example 'none', 'low', 'medium', or 'high' importance in a meaning of contribution to organization's business processes. Usually, they do not take asset dependencies into consideration, but it can significantly change the results of a risk analysis if two assets are strongly dependent. If is, for example, a storage server in a high risk resulting from its physical placement and the database server running on this physical server has only low level of risk, resulting from risk evaluation, we cannot consider these two entities as independent. The way how dependent are they should be an outcome from asset valuation sub-process.

In this paper we would like to introduce a model for asset valuation that involves inspection of asset dependencies. This inspection is based on examining dependencies from the security attributes point of view - confidentiality, integrity and availability. After evaluation of asset relations we consider risk values, acquired by the preliminary risk assessment, and assign new risk values deliberating the original values and the dependencies.

The rest of this paper is structured as follows. Section 2 provides an overview of a related work dealing with the problem of security risk management techniques with focus on asset dependencies. Section 3 proposes our approach and describes method used for examining dependencies among assets. Finally, section 4 concludes this paper and provides a motivation for further work.

2   Related Work

There exist a number of works in the field of information security risk management. These works implement mostly the ISO/IEC 27005:2011 standard and use various methods in order to automate this process. They usually follow process structure from the standard and propose own methods based on either quantitative or qualitative assessment techniques. We will examine these works from the asset valuation perspective.

Some works do not examine dependencies at all. For example, Vavoulas and Xenakis [9] use five dimensions in asset valuation - value, repair cost, reputational damage, operational damage, and legal or regulatory damage. The consequences of an attack are then equal to the sum of these values. Tatar and Karabacak [8] propose a hierarchy based asset valuation method that express the value in three terms - confidentiality, integrity and availability. Their method is straightforward and needs a security expert to determine these values for each asset. They do not deliberate asset dependence, buying price or operating costs.

Leitner [4] propose his own risk analysis approach called ARiMA (Austrian Risk Management Approach). It uses a configuration management database (CMDB) to identify relevant assets in accordance to the business processes. The assets are classified into five degrees according to the importance for the organization from 'very low' to 'very high'. The corresponding multiplicators that affect the risk value are numbers from 1 to 1.5, with 0.125 granularity. The risks are computed using standard matrices with impact values for the columns and probability values for the rows. The asset dependencies are modelled by using two logical connection types OR and AND that are used in evaluating asset's security attributes - confidentiality, integrity and availability. If OR is used, the values are computed as an average, if AND is used, the highest number among dependent entities is chosen. It is naturally better to implement at least some technique for examining dependencies, but this approach is very simple and does not provide desired complexity for asset analysis.

Loloei, Shahriari and Sadeghi [5] propose an asset valuation model, emphasizing dependencies between assets. They define dependencies in terms of security attributes and divide organization's assets into three layers - business, application and technical layer. They use a value propagation graph to represent how assets affect the value of each other, and how an asset value propagates through other assets. Authors claim that the well-known risk management methodologies, such as CRAMM, OCTAVE, or NIST 800-30 show limitations during risk assessment because of lack of considering dependencies among assets. However, the work is missing comparison between different asset valuation methods, therefore it cannot be decided whether the asset dependencies are modelled correctly and contribute in terms of more precise assessment, or not.

Suh and Han [7] propose a risk analysis method based on Analytic Hierarchy Process with more detailed view of asset identification and evaluation. They divided this phase into five sub-processes: asset identification, assignment of assets to business functions, determination of initial asset importance, asset dependency identification, and determination of final asset importance. The dependencies are expressed from the view of asset importance. If asset A depends on assets B,C and D, its importance is maximum of importances of these assets. This value can be then revised by a security analyst and can be further adjusted.

Mayer and Fagundes [6] design a model for assessing the maturity model of the risk management process in information security. This model is aimed to identify weaknesses or deficiencies in the risk management and improve its effectiveness. It examines all the processes measuring their quality. From our point of view, the main disadvantage is that the asset analysis is not deliberated as an individual process, just as a sub-process of risk analysis.

3   Methods

We can examine dependencies among assets on a simplified organization model, depicted in Figure 1. Dependencies are arranged in a tree-based hierarchy, with the building as a top-level node. If the building is destroyed, all the other assets would be lost, if we consider simple model without information backup and alternative information processing facilities in other building(s). As we can see, one entity can be dependent on multiple entities, the Exchange server is dependent both on Physical server 2 and on Active Directory server. If we look at Database server, there is a redundancy - company has one secondary backup server in a case of failure of the primary one. Therefore we have to differentiate a connection between the data stored on these servers.

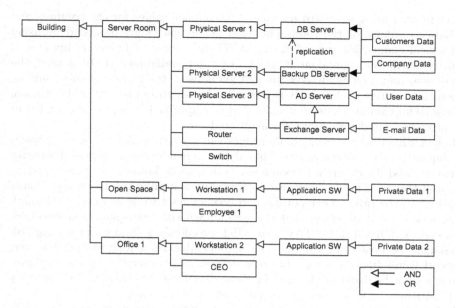

Fig. 1. Dependencies between assets

3.1 Model Assumptions

Now we can make following assumptions for our model:

- We can assume that the business goal of our model company is dependent on all the leaves, therefore we need to ensure confidentiality, integrity and availability of all the other components following the hierarchy. We will call this set of entities 'chain of dependence', for example User data in our picture has four entities in its chain of dependence, beginning with AD server and ending with the building.
- We have to assign dependency weights for each entity in the chain of dependence. These weights will be then used to adjust the process of a risk analysis - if entity N depends on other entity M that has high level of risk, this risk should be distributed on the entity N.
- If we have redundant entities, we will use the 'OR' type of connection. Normal type of connection, 'AND', means that the dependent entity depends exclusively on the superior entity in the hierarchy. The 'OR' connection lowers the risk, distributing it on two or more superior entities.
- Weights cannot be represented as a single value, since dependencies can have different character. For example, Customers data depends on Physical server 1 from the availability point of view mainly, but their confidentiality is strongly influenced by the Database server.

We will use 4x4 risk matrix [10] for demonstrational purposes. This matrix has threat probability for its columns and impact for its rows. We will define following risk values:

– in interval [1,5] as a *low* risk value,
– in interval [6,9] as a *medium* risk value,
– in interval [10,16] as a *high* risk value.

It is clear that we cannot assign some of these numbers by using the risk matrix below, but we will need the whole intervals in the latter phase.

Let us assume that we have already made the risk analysis using standard methodology. To save the space we will analyze only part of our model company, risk values for particular elements can be seen in Figure 2. These are the average risk values for threats, we will not examine dependencies among individual threats.

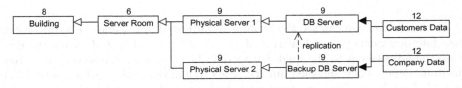

Fig. 2. Risk values

3.2   Model Construction

We can now construct our dependency valuation model based on previous assumptions. The valuation process consists of following steps:

1. Begin with the top level entity (building in our example).
2. Assign dependency component weight values of confidentiality (W_{con}), integrity (W_{int}) and availability (W_{ava}) to each relation in the hierarchy. These values are from interval [0,1] with the granularity of 0.1 points.
3. Adjust the risk value by using the dependency adjustment formula. If there is 'OR' connection between entities, compute the average of the adjusted risk values and divide it by the number of redundant entities. If one entity is directly dependent on more than one entity, we have to adjust the risk value considering all of the superior entities.
4. Continue with the lower level entities until the last level in the hierarchy.

We define an overall dependency weight value W_o as a sum of component weight values.

$$W_o = \sum_{i=con,int,ava} W_i \tag{1}$$

The dependency adjustment formula, used in step 3, is used for adjusting the risk value by examining dependency weight values:

$$W_o \times max(W_{con}, W_{int}, W_{ava}) \times RV \tag{2}$$

The formula depends on three factors. First, we sum the component weight values and multiply it with the maximal value among components. And finally we multiply this value with the RV, which is the simplified risk value of the upper level entity connected with the dependency relation. If the risk of the asset is low, this value would be 1, if medium, the value is 2 and for the high risk this value is 3.

Table 1. Dependency adjustment formula examples

Dependent Entity	W_o	$max(W_{con}, W_{int}, W_{ava})$	RV	Adjustment Value
Asset 1	0.5	0.2	1	**+1**
Asset 2	1.5	0.8	2	**+2.4**
Asset 3	2.4	1.0	3	**+7.2**

In the Table 1 we can see the example of adjusted risk values. The first asset has low dependency and low risk of the entity on which it depends, in this case the adjustment to the final value would be +1 point. The second asset has medium dependency and medium RV, the original risk will be adjusted by +2.4 points. Finally, we have an asset with high dependency and high RV, so the adjustment in this case will be +7.2 points.

3.3   Model Example

We will now examine our method on the provided example. In Figure 3 we can see part of our model company with assigned dependency component weight values. In Table 2 are listed adjusted risk values corresponding to dependency weights. Redundant entities are stated in one row, because their weights are equal. Notice that after the first assignment we take the adjusted risk values as an input, for example when considering Customers Data, we take high risk value of the DB Server as an input, not medium from the original risk assessment. Also notice that Data are adjusted just by +2.1 risk value because of the DB Server redundancy.

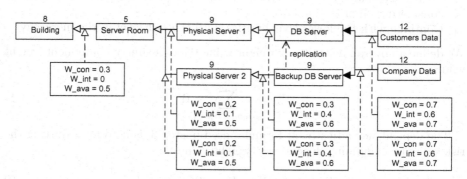

Fig. 3. Dependency component weight values

Table 2. Adjusted risk values

Dependent Entity	W_o	W_{max}	Original Risk Val.	RV	Adjusted Risk Val.
Server Room	0.8	0.5	5	2	**5.8**
Physical Server 1 & 2	0.8	0.5	9	1	**9.4**
DB Server & Backup Server	1.3	0.6	9	2	**10.56**
Customers Data	2	0.7	12	3	**14.1**
Company Data	2	0.7	12	3	**14.1**

Adjusted values in the whole organization model are listed in Figure 4. Building is the only entity that does not depend on any other entity, therefore its risk value remains the same. Minimal adjustments were made to physical servers, after considering dependencies they have +0.4 risk values. Maximal adjustments were made to both Private Data, their values were raised by +4 points. It is because of double dependency on both AD server and Physical server 3.

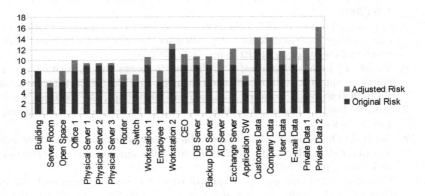

Fig. 4. Adjusted risks in the whole model

4 Conclusions

In this paper we proposed an asset dependency evaluation method that can be used in order to improve results of a risk analysis. Despite the fact that there are not many works dealing with this problem, we find it important to take it in the consideration when assessing risks in an organization.

The ISO/IEC 27005:2011 standard [3] recommends to encompass dependencies of assets in the asset analysis process. It suggests to take the degree of dependency and the values of other assets into account. In our work we inspect this degree from the confidentiality, integrity and availability perspective and instead of the value, we consider the risk value. The dependency valuation model also deals with the situation of dependency on more than one entity and with the dependency on redundant entities. The final risk value is adjusted with respect to these conditions.

It is easy to include our method into the complex risk analysis process, so that the risk values would be adjusted by the terms of asset dependencies. In the future, we would like to provide the whole risk management evaluation model based on quantitative measurement techniques, that would measure security state in an organization and output meaningful results.

References

1. NIST Special Publication 800-53 Managing Information Security Risk - Organization, Mission, and Information System View. NIST (2011)
2. Blakley, B., McDermott, E., Geer, D.: Information security is information risk management. In: Proceedings of the 2001 Workshop on New Security Paradigms, NSPW 2001, pp. 97–104. ACM, New York (2001)
3. ISO. ISO/IEC Std. ISO 27005:2011, Information technology – Security techniques – Information security risk management. ISO (2011)
4. Leitner, A., Schaumuller-Bichl, I.: Arima - a new approach to implement iso/iec 27005. In: 2nd International Logistics and Industrial Informatics, LINDI 2009, pp. 1–6 (2009)
5. Loloei, I., Shahriari, H.R., Sadeghi, A.: A model for asset valuation in security risk analysis regarding assets' dependencies. In: 2012 20th Iranian Conference on Electrical Engineering (ICEE), pp. 763–768 (2012)
6. Mayer, J., Lemes Fagundes, L.: A model to assess the maturity level of the risk management process in information security. In: IFIP/IEEE International Symposium on Integrated Network Management-Workshops, IM 2009, pp. 61–70 (2009)
7. Suh, B., Han, I.: The is risk analysis based on a business model. Inf. Manage. 41(2), 149–158 (2003)
8. Tatar, U., Karabacak, B.: An hierarchical asset valuation method for information security risk analysis. In: 2012 International Conference on Information Society (i-Society), pp. 286–291 (2012)
9. Vavoulas, N., Xenakis, C.: A quantitative risk analysis approach for deliberate threats. In: Xenakis, C., Wolthusen, S. (eds.) CRITIS 2010. LNCS, vol. 6712, pp. 13–25. Springer, Heidelberg (2011)
10. Williams, R., Pandelios, G., Behrens, S.: Software Risk Evaluation (SRE) method description (version 2.0). Software Engineering Institute (1999)

Creation of Assurance Case
Using Collaboration Diagram

Takuya Saruwatari[1] and Shuichiro Yamamoto[2]

[1] Graduate School of Information Science Nagoya University, Nagoya, Japan
saruwatari.takuya@e.mbox.nagoya-u.ac.jp
[2] Strategy Office, Information and Communications Headquarters,
Nagoya University, Japan
yamamotosui@icts.nagoya-u.ac.jp

Abstract. Recently, serious failures of complex IT systems are becoming social problems. Assurance case attracts an attention as a technique to assure the dependability of critical systems. We have proposed d* framework which is an extended assurance case notation based on the network of dependable actors. In this paper, The assurance case creation procedure that creates the assurance case from the collaboration diagram is proposed and the case study is performed using this procedure. In this case study, a result is described by d* framework.

Keywords: assurance case, dependability, d* framework, collaboration diagram.

1 Introduction

Recently, serious failures on complex IT systems are becoming social problems. A failure of critical system raises a significant loss. Therefore, assurance of dependability of such critical systems is an important issue. But, it is not an easy task. In such a situation, an assurance case attracts an attention as a technique to assure the dependability of critical systems. In the assurance case, the argument of dependability is described. GSN (Goal Structuring Notation) [1] is proposed as a graphical notation of assurance cases. d* framework (d*) which introduced the concept of actor to extend assurance case [2] is also proposed. In this paper, the assurance case creation procedure that creates the assurance case from a collaboration diagram is proposed and the case study is performed using it.

In section 2, some related works are described. In section 3, d* framework is described. It is used in the proposed procedure. In section 4, the assurance case creation procedure is descirbed. In section 5, the case study is described. Discussions and conclusions are described in section 6 and section 7.

2 Related work

The assurance case is a document that describes argument of system dependability. Such a document is needed for critical systems that require high assurance.

Linawati et al. (Eds.): ICT-EurAsia 2014, LNCS 8407, pp. 413–418, 2014.

Dependability is defined as an integrated concept including availability, reliability, safety, integrity, and maintainability [3]. The assurance case is proposed as the document that describes argument of system safety. This may be called safety case. GSN [1] and CAE (Claim, Argument Evidence) [4] are proposed as graphical notation to describe a safety case. In GSN, safety cases are described mainly by four types of nodes (goal, strategy, evidence, and context) and two types of relationships ("supported by" and "in context of"). Recently, target of assurance case is extended to dependability[5]. An assurance case for dependability may be called as dependability case. There are several definitions for the assurance case. One definition is shown as follows [6].

A documented body of evidence that provides a convincing and valid argument that a system is adequately dependable for a given application in a given environment.

There are many researches for the assurance case. In [7], a module concept of assurance case is researched. By using the module of the assurance case, there is an advantage that can manage and represent a large assurance case. Creation process of assurance case is also researched. In [1], six process steps are proposed to create safety cases based on GSN. Another assurance creation methods are also proposed [8]. Meanwhile, method for the decomposition of arguments as required when creating assurance cases is proposed [9], [10].

3   d* Framework (d*)

The d* framework (d*) is an extended assurance case notation [2]. In d*, an actor concept is introduced into assurance case. 5 types of node (actor, goal, strategy, context, and evidence) and 4 types of relationship ("supported by", "in context of", "depend on", and "belong to") of nodes are defined. An actor is a new element. Previous notations do not have it. A person, an organization, a system, a subsystem, and a component etc. can be defined as actor.

4   Assurance Case Creation Procedure

In this paper, an assurance case creation procedure is proposed. The assurance case is created from collaboration diagram in this procedure. It is consisted of 3 steps. They are shown below.

- Step 1 : Actor definition
  Actors of assurance case are defined. Objects in a collaboration diagram are defined as actors in an assurance case.
- Step 2 : Inter dependency definition
  Arguments (goal) between actors in an assurance case are defined using message relationships between objects in collaboration diagram.
- Step 3 : Actor merging
  Actors that should be merged into one actor are merged.

5   Case Study

5.1   Collaboration Diagram of Target System

The target system for case study is an "AP Download system". Using this system, user can select the application (AP) and download it from the system to his/her IC Card. The collaboration diagram of target system is shown in Fig. 1. In this diagram, 6 objects and 13 message relationships between them are represented.

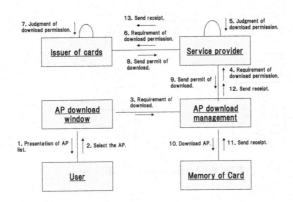

Fig. 1. Collaboration diagram of AP download system

5.2   Creation Experiment

In the case study, the assurance case creation experiment is performed. The created assurance case is described by d*. The result of experiment for each step in procedure is shown as below.

1. Step 1
   In this step, 6 objects are defined as assurance case's actor from collaboration diagram. The 6 actors are "Issuer of cards", "Service provider", "AP download window", "AP download management", "User", and "Memory of Card".
2. Step 2
   In this step, 8 dependability arguments (goals) are defined between actors. For example, "Sevice provider" requires the download permission to "Issuer of cards" and "Issuer of cards" permits the download to "Service provider" in the collaboration diagram. Therefore, it is considered that "Issuer of the card" depend on "Service provider". The dependum is that "only permitted AP can be downloaded". Created assurance case is shown in Fig. 2.

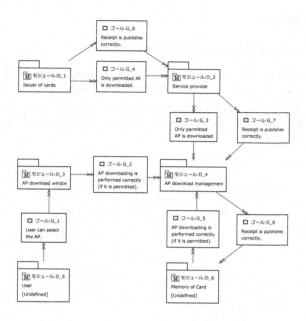

Fig. 2. Assurance case after Step 2

3. Step 3

   In this step, "AP download window" and "AP download management" are merged. The two actors are included in the same system. Therefore,they are merged. The new actor is "AP download system". Modified assurance case is shown in Fig. 3.

6   Discussions

6.1   Merits of Using Collaboration Diagrams

When creating assurance case, it is convenient if there is information that can be used. In this research, it is confirmed that collaboration diagram is useful for creating assurance case. 2 merits are shown as follows. 1) The actor of assurance case can be defined using collaboration diagram's object. 2) The dependability requirement between actors of assurance case can be considered using message relationships of collaboration diagram. In the case study, 6 actors are defined in the assurance case from 6 objects in the collaboration diagram directly (Step 1). Moreover, 8 dependability requirements between actors are defined from message relationships in the collaboration diagram (Step 2). In this definition, 13 message relationships in collaboration diagram are used. Thus, it can be say that collaboration diagram is useful, when assurance case is created by d*.

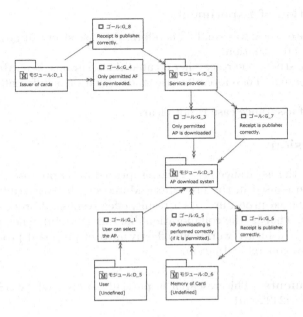

Fig. 3. Assurance case after Step 3

6.2 Dependability Propagation

By the case study, it is understood that assurance case of d* can represent the dependability propagation that passes between actors. Commonly, some dependability information is propagating between actors. In the case study, dependability requirement ("Only permitted AP is downloaded") is propagating between "Issuer of cards", "Service provider", and "AP download system." Two dependability requirements have same sentence. But, evidences of requirement may be different between them. This difference should become clear by continuous arguments. Thus, dependability propagation can be considered by using an assurance case of d*. Previous assurance case notation like the GSN does not have this characteristic. This is a one of the strong point of d*.

6.3 Granularity of the Actor

Deciding granularity of actor is one of the problems when creating assurance case by d*. Creating the assurance case from collaboration diagram is one of the solutions against this problem. Objects in collaboration diagram can be used directly to define actors in assurance case of d*. At this point, granularity of actor is decided. But, granularity may be not appropriate for actors in assurance case. Since, a purposes of creation is different between them. In the proposed creation procedure, granularity of actors is adjusted in Step 3.

6.4   Limitation of Experiments

- Scale of case study was small. Therefore, the case study situation is different from concrete situation.
- In the case study, one researcher created the assurance case. Real developers did not create it. Therefore, the case study situation is different from concrete situation.
- Validity of assurance case is not clear.

7   Conclusion

In this paper, the assurance case creation procedure is proposed. The collaboration diagram is used in the procedure. Moreover, the case study is perfomed using this proposed procedure. As a result, effectiveness of proposed procedure was confirmed. That is, the collaboration diagram is useful, when the assurance case is created. In future works, an effectiveness of proposed procedure has to be confirmed in concrete situation.

Acknowledgments. This research is partially supported by JSPS Research Project Number:24220001.

References

1. Kelly, T.: Arguing Safety - A Systematic Approach to Managing Safety Cases. PhD thesis, University of York (1998)
2. Yamamoto, S., Matsuno, Y.: d* framework: Inter-Dependency Model for Dependability. In: DSN 2012 (2012)
3. Avizienis, A., Laprie, J., Randell, B., Landwehr, C.: Basic Concepts and Taxonomy of Dependable and Secure Computing. Dependable and Secure Computing 1, 11–33 (2004)
4. Adelard, http://www.adelard.com/web/hnav/ASCE/
5. Despotou, G., Kelly, T.: Extending the Safety Case Concept to Address Dependability. In: Proceedings of the 22nd International System Safety Conference (2004)
6. Ankrum, T.S., Krombolz, A.H.: Structured Assurance Cases: Three Common Standards. Slides presentation at the Association for Software Quality (ASQ) Section 509 Meeting (2006)
7. Fenn, J., Hawkins, R., Williams, P., Kelly, T.: Safety case composition using contracts - refinements based on feedback from an industrial case study. In: Proceedings of 15th Safety Critical Systems Symposium (SSS 2007). Springer (2007)
8. Despotou, G., Kelly, T.: Dessign and Development of Dependability Case Architecture during System Development. In: Proceedings of the 25th International System Safety Conference (ISSC), Baltimore, USA (2007)
9. Bloomfield, R., Bishop, P.: Safety and assurance cases: Past, present and possible future - an Adelard perspective. In: Proceedings of 18th Safety-Critical Systems Symposium (2010)
10. Yamamoto, S., Matsuno, Y.: An Evaluation of Argument Patterns to Reduce Pitfalls of Applying Assurance Case. In: Proceedings of ASSURE 2013, co-located ICSE2013, San Francisco, CA, USA (2013)

Using Model Driven Security Approaches in Web Application Development

Christoph Hochreiner[1], Zhendong Ma[3], Peter Kieseberg[1],
Sebastian Schrittwieser[2], and Edgar Weippl[1]

[1] SBA-Research, Austria
{chochreiner,pkieseberg,eweippl}@sba-research.org
[2] St. Poelten University of Applied Sciences, Austria
sebastian.schrittwieser@fhstp.ac.at
[3] Austrian Institute of Technology
zhendong.ma@ait.ac.at

Abstract. With the rise of Model Driven Engineering (MDE) as a software development methodology, which increases productivity and, supported by powerful code generation tools, allows a less error-prone implementation process, the idea of modeling security aspects during the design phase of the software development process was first suggested by the research community almost a decade ago. While various approaches for Model Driven Security (MDS) have been proposed during the years, it is still unclear, how these concepts compare to each other and whether they can improve the security of software projects. In this paper, we provide an evaluation of current MDS approaches based on a simple web application scenario and discuss the strengths and limitations of the various techniques, as well as the practicability of MDS for web application security in general.

1 Introduction and Related Work

Model Driven Engineering (MDE) has gained a lot of attention during the past few years. The rise of modeling languages, especially UML, drove the development of MDE techniques as well as more and more sophisticated tool support for the automated generation of code. One of the most important motivations for applying MDE techniques is software correctness. Generally, software defects can result from two sources during the software development process: First, problems can originate from bad design decisions in the planning phase of the software development process. This type of defects, often referred as flaws, is fatal as elimination of the fundamental design misconceptions in later phases of the development process may require a general overhaul of the entire architecture. Modeling techniques can support development in this early design phase. The second type of defect is based on implementation errors (bugs). Even if the software was designed to work correctly, the actual implementation can introduce errors which led to the development of tools for automated code generation. In this case, the availability of automated tools that allow the translation of

Linawati et al. (Eds.): ICT-EurAsia 2014, LNCS 8407, pp. 419–431, 2014.

the abstract model into code that can be compiled or directly interpreted by a machine is of crucial importance. Furthermore, techniques such as model validation, checking and model-based testing can be used to support the reliability of a program in reference to its model.

With the success of MDE approaches the idea of bringing these concepts to the security domain was raised by the scientific community almost a decade ago [3,6]. The basic idea is similar to MDE: The process of modeling security aspects of a software project should enhance its quality - in this case related to security. The theoretical consideration is to deal with the same two categories like in MDE (flaws in the design and the implementation phase) by modeling the security requirements before the implementation. Design-based vulnerabilities can be addressed with model checking techniques and goal oriented system analysis and the number of implementation errors can be reduced by using automated code generation for sensitive, security-related parts of the software.

In the last years, a vast amount of different techniques for Model Driven Security (MDS) in software applications has been developed. The main purpose of this paper lies in providing a novel comparison of several major modeling approaches for designing secure software based on the example of a simple web application. In particular, we not only wanted to analyze how typical mistakes in web application scenarios could be described by security modeling techniques but also if these techniques actively push the developer towards a more secure implementation by incorporating security essential within the modeling process. In contrast to MDE, the modeling of security is heavily influenced by the open world assumption. Security aspects, as being non-functional requirements of a software project, can be left out of the model and the implementation without having direct influence on the functionality of the software. We strongly believe that the benefit of security modeling techniques is limited, if their sole purpose is to offer the possibility of modeling security aspects without actually enforcing them. In 2011 Kasal et al. [4] provided a taxonomy evaluation of different state-of-the-art approaches for model driven engineering. The taxonomy was proposed purely theoretically, still, to the best of our knowledge, there has not been a structured practical comparison of the actual techniques with respect to implementing a real-life scenario. Our work is focused towards the practical applicability and effectiveness of model driven engineering approaches such as Lloyd and Juerjens [5] did when they applied the UMLsec and JML approaches to practically evaluate a biometric authentication system. The main contributions of this paper can be defined as follows: We show what types of common threats in web application scenarios can be modeled and to what degree corresponding security measures are enforced by the different modeling techniques. Furthermore, we provide the analysis of our experimental assessment of current security modeling techniques based on a typical web application scenario. Additionally, we discuss the practicability of MDS for the secure development of web applications.

2 Methodology

2.1 Evaluation Scenario

For our evaluation we designed a typical basic web application scenario, which covers the threats outlined by the Open Web Application Security Project (OWASP) in their 2010 published version of their TOP 10 list [9]. This allows us to evaluate the modeling techniques and compare their functionality. In detail, the scenario consists of three machines: A client accesses a web server that is connected to a database server. On the web service, there exist two different user roles, normal user and administrator, which have different access permissions regarding the database server. Figure 1 shows the basic scenario. Please note that the model in the figure does not follow the concepts of any common modeling language in order to be formulated as neutral as possible before modeling the scenario with different MDS approaches. In this simple use case, the threats of the OWASP Top 10 can be identified (see [9]).

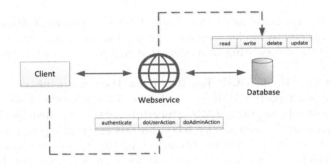

Fig. 1. Simple Web Application Scenario

3 Selection of Methods

In this section, we evaluate the possibility of modeling the threats of the OWASP Top10 with different MDS approaches. We give a short introduction on each concept and then model our web application use case with respect to the OWASP threats.

3.1 UML Based

UML [10] is a widely used model notation method for analyzing software system objects. Several diagrams are defined to express different aspects of the systems from an abstract to an implementation perspective. Original UML notations have been extended to integrate non-functional system properties such as security or the threat environment in an explicit way. The extended UML diagrams allow the developer to model threats as well as countermeasures.

Secure UML. Secure UML is an extension of the standard UML specification that encapsulates the modeling aspect of Role Based Access Control (RBAC) to include security aspects [11]. It is a single purpose extension and solely allows for modeling the access control aspects of the example by adding roles, permissions and constraints on the method level to the existing syntax. The authors of Secure UML created a prototypical tool to automatically transform the model into an EJB (Enterprise Java Beans) based architecture incorporating all standard access controls and primitive comparison functions (e.g. $<, >, \neq \emptyset$), all other functions have to be implemented by the user. With these additions, the model can be transferred automatically into executable code, thereby taking care of the first two OWASP entries (A1) and (A2). SecureUML derives input validation [2] through implementation of a separate validation class which takes care of input content. RBAC is a fundamental part of SecureUML, access control restrictions for objects, databases and files are ensured, thus covering (A3) and (A4), furthermore, RBAC relates to URL access restriction, thus (A8) can be modeled. The Secure UML specification does not provide the functionality to model the aspects of transport security or the required logging of queries.

UMLsec. As an extension to the classical UML standard, UMLsec provides additional methods to model security aspects of software systems based on so-called *secure guards* resulting in models that are compatible to standard UML diagrams.

When applying the OWASP Top 10 threats, there are some aspects that can be prevented with proper UMLsec modeling. The first two threats, Injection (A1) and Cross-Site Scripting (A2), concern the data provided by the user. To prevent attacks on the web service based on this external input, every external input has to be checked. The threats concerning the Broken Authentication and Session Management (A3) cannot be dealt with proper modeling, because the authentication mechanism is encapsulated within the authenticate method and the evaluation of this functionality was omitted, because they are not in the focus of UMLsec. It is possible to model countermeasures against Direct Object Reference (A4), Cross-Site Request Forgery (CSRF) (A5), Failure to Restrict URL Access (A8) and Unvalidated Redirects and Forwards (A10) with secure guards. There have to be secure guards for every possible attack scenario. One example is a special guard that checks the feasibility of the called method to prevent CSRFs.

The terminal aspect that can be modeled with UMLsec, thus covering the problem of Insufficient Transport Layer Protection (A9). With UMLsec it is possible to tag specific communication paths with security requirements like encryption. Beside the aspects that can be modeled with UMLsec, there are some that cannot be taken care of with this engineering technique, including Security Misconfiguration (A6) and Insecure Cryptographic Storage (A7). It is not feasible to handle these two types of errors with model engineering techniques, because these techniques only cover the architecture of the program and not the deployment environment.

Misusecase. The misusecase specification is an extension to the use case specification of the UML use case diagram. This extension was developed by Guttorm Sindre and Andreas L. Opdahl [12] to describe malicious acts against a system, which are added to the normal use case diagram with inverted colors. Because of the high level of abstraction it is not possible to provide any tool support to generate code out of the use case diagram.

When applying the OWASP Top 10, we can identify some problems that can be covered with the misusecase diagram. The misusease diagram can model any attack like injection (A1), cross-site scripting (A2) or the failure to restrict URL access (A8). The issue of broken authentication (A3) can be tackled with the modeling of unauthorized actions, but the use case diagram cannot model any temporal or causal dependencies. The configurational aspects like security misconfiguration (A6) or insecure cryptographic storage (A7) as well as technical requirements like insufficient transport layer protection (A9) can thus not be covered with misusecase diagrams.

3.2   Aspect Oriented Software Development

Aspect oriented software development (AOSD) is an emerging approach with the goal of promoting advanced separation of concerns. The approach allows system properties such as security to be analyzed separately and integrated into the system environment.

Aspect Oriented Modeling. The framework proposed by Zhu et. al. [15] is designed to model potential threats on a system in an aspect-oriented matter. These additions are designed to model an attacker-and-victim-relation in different types of UML diagrams. Due to page limitations, in the evaluation we only describe the class diagram that already shows most of the additional features compared to standard UML specifications. The basis of the class diagrams is an abstract *attacker class* that provides basic attributes and methods.

This framework is applicable in the context of risk oriented software development. After a risk analysis of the system, all high impact attacks have to be identified and can subsequently be model. These models can be transformed into aspect-oriented code that is weaved into the existing code base. The code generator published by Zhu et. Al. is capable of producing AspectJ and AspectC++ code. These extensions to the standard UML specification are not practical enough in order to model basic security aspects like RBAC or transport layer security, they are only useful for handling specific attack scenarios and adding specific countermeasures to a given system. Still, in general it is possible to model all aspects of the OWASP Top10 using aspect oriented modeling.

SAM. Besides UML-based modeling approaches, there exist also some modeling techniques based on Petri nets and temporal logic, like the AOD framework proposed by H.Yu et al. [14] This framework is designed to model complex workflows and join them with security aspects. Nodes in the petri net represent single steps of the workflow and the security aspects handle the transitions between these nodes. The constraints for the workflow are modeled in a temporal logic that allows a formal verification of the system.

Protocol Checker. The AVISPA Tool for automated validation of Internet security protocols and applications is mainly concerned with verifying (cryptographic) protocols with respect to known vectors like man-in-the-middle- or replay-attacks. At the heart of AVISPA lies a definition language for protocols called HLPSL (High Level Protocol Security Language), which is specifically designed for modeling protocol flows together with security parameters and requirements. Furthermore, AVISPA provides four different analysis engines that can either be targeted at a problem separately, or together.

Another tool for analyzing synchronous as well as asynchronous protocols is the Symbolic Model Verifier (SMV), which is based on temporal logic. Models are specified in the form of temporal logic formulas, the tool is able to specify and handle finite automata and to check temporal logic formulas for validity. A speciality lies in the ability to handle asynchronous protocols and distributed systems. Still it is not possible to model executable software systems using SMV.

The modeling language Alloy is based on a first-order relational logic, its primary goal lies in the realm of modeling software designs. The logical structures of the systems are modeled using relations, existing properties are modeled by relational operators. Furthermore, Alloy provides the user with means for typing, sub-typing as well as type-checking on runtime and the building of reusable modules. The actual analysis is done by using the tool Alloy Analyzer which is based on a SAT-solver, since due to the construction of the language, the analysis of a model is basically a form of constraint solving.

Since these techniques aim at providing a detailed security analysis on the protocol level, using them for modeling whole software applications is not practically feasible, especially since they are not concerned with architectural decisions, but with the execution of actual protocols using cryptographic primitives. Still, they can be useful for analyzing cryptographic primitives or transport layer protocols, thus being a good strategy for thwarting insufficient transport layer protection.

3.3   Goal Driven Approaches

Goals are the objectives, expectations and constraints of the system environment. Goal driven approaches address the problems associated with business goals, plans and processes as well as systems to be developed or to be evolved in order to achieve organizational objectives. Goals cover different types of issues - both functional and non-functional. Goal models demonstrate how the different goals contribute to each other through refinement links down to particular software requirements and environmental assumptions. Functional goals focus on the services to be provided while non-functional goals are inked with the quality of services like security or availability.

KAOS. The KAOS model originates from the requirements engineering domain and was designed by researchers at the University of Lauvain and the University of Oregon. The name of the methodology KAOS stands for "Knowledge Acquisition in autOmated Specification" [13] and it describes a framework to model and refine goals including the selection of alternatives. The framework is supported by a software solution called *Objectiver* [1], which supports the developer in designing the goal models and refining them, as well generating object or operation models, but does not provide any code generation functionality. This modeling approach allows the developer to model all OWASP Top 10 threats as goals that can be further used for the requirements generation.

Secure Tropos. The Tropos methodology [1] supports the software development process by describing the environment of the system and the system itself. It is used to model dependencies between different actors that want to achieve different goals by executing plans. There are four different abstraction layers defined that describe different stages of requirements and layers of design. Secure Tropos [8] is an extension to the original Tropos methodology by adding security constraints and secure entities as well as the concepts of ownership, trust and dependency. The Secure Tropos methodology does not allow the designer to model any OWASP TOP 10 threat directly within the model, still there are some software solutions, like ScTro [2], that support the software engineer during the design and requirements analysis phase.

4   Evaluation

Secure UML. Beside the intention to use the constraints only for access restrictions and preconditions to these access restrictions like the UserAuthenticated constraint, it is possible to add more complex requirements to provide input validation as the application of the framework to our use case shows. In Figure 2 we have added the InputValidated constraint, which assures that the parameters do not contain any strings that can be used for XSS or SQL injections. The additional functionality to cover XSS and SQL injection checks has to be implemented by the user, since the tool only covers primitive comparison functionality for constraints. The Secure UML specification does not provide the functionality to model the aspects of transport security or the required logging of queries to the database.

UMLsec. This evaluation focuses on the class and the deployment diagram, because these two diagrams cover all security requirements of our simple web application scenario.

---

[1] http://www.objectiver.com
[2] http://sectro.securetropos.org

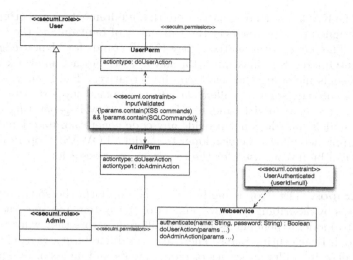

Fig. 2. Use case modelled with Secure UML

The aspect of transport security tangles the communication among the three components, as shown in Figure 1. The communication between the client machine and the application server is done over the Internet and therefore all service-calls and the resulting replies have to be encrypted. The communication between the application server and the database server is not that critical, especially because they are situated in the same local network. In this case it is enough to reduce the requirement to integrity instead of encryption. These two stereotypes are expressed with the UMLsec specification. The environments like Internet and LAN are added to the link between the systems and the calls are tagged with the required stereotypes. Although these transport requirements are easy to model, it is not feasible to automatically generate code ensuring compliance with these requirements, because these systems are too heterogeneous.

The two aspects *authentication* and *RBAC* are modeled within the class diagram. The UMLsec specification only supports class based access restrictions and it is necessary to extend the basic model with two additional classes (UserAction and AdminAction) to define user specific access control. These two classes are simple wrapper classes, which are annotated with two different guards. These two guards are called from the web service class and check if the current user has a specific role, which has been assigned to him by a successful authentication.

Due to this implicit mechanism, it is not necessary to model additional constraints, like that the user has to be authenticated. In [7] one can find a successful evaluation of how UMLsec properties can be transferred into actual code. The downside of this kind of modeling is that it does not scale well for additional roles and it increases the complexity of the model. The proper input validation is modeled with a secure dependency between the web service and the InputValidator which is called for every input, as shown in Figure 5. The model (Figure 4) that shows the usage of secure guards covers this scenario. These guards check, whether the users have enough privileges to perform actions.

The final aspect is the assertion that all queries get logged. This aspect is modeled with the secure dependency addition of UMLsec. By means of this addition it is possible to model the constraint that every call to a method that is provided by the database class is succeeded by the log method of the logger class. In this scenario every user could submit malicious input to the system, there has to be some input validation to prevent attacks like SQL-injection or XSS. This aspect is modeled using the secure dependency addition: Every input that is passed on to a method provided by the web service has to by checked for malicious input.

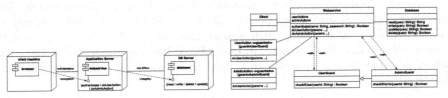

Fig. 3. Secure Links in UMLsec   **Fig. 4.** Secure Guards in UMLsec

Fig. 5. Secure Dependency in UMLsec   **Fig. 6.** Input Validation in UMLsec

Misusecase. The use case diagram (Figure 7) shows the modeling of different threats to the system. The threats are carried out by the attacker indicated with an ordinary use case actor that has the background color black. The same applies to the misusecases in the diagram, that are ordinary use case elements with a black background.

The misusecase diagram provides the functionality to model high level threats that are executed by different actors of the system, but is does not provide the functionality to model any countermeasures or mitigation approaches. The only possibility to model countermeasures is to extend the existing use cases to implement organizational countermeasures, like additional permission checks.

Aspect Oriented Modeling. In our example, the attacker tries to tamper with the authentication using invalid input. This attack is modeled as an aspect that provides some methods to execute checks to prevent this attack, the remaining part of the diagram is a simplified representation of our basic UML class diagram. In the context of this framework it is feasible to omit all classes or methods that are not used in this attack, every diagram that is modeled within this framework visualizes one single attack.

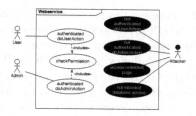

Fig. 7. Modeling of malicious acts with misusecase diagrams

Thus, the approach is only feasible for covering the most pressing topics like injections and XSS, since every possible attack needs to be modeled with respect to its effects on the system, which implies that all possible attacks need to be known beforehand. Furthermore, in case of real-life-size applications, the number of possible attack scenarios that need to be modeled separately will grow drastically.

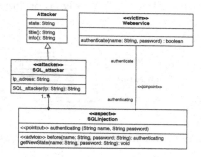

Fig. 8. Aspect Oriented Modeling

SAM. Due to the lack of complex workflows in our scenario, we omitted a detailed analysis of this framework. The single method calls do not trigger any workflows within the web service. Currently there is no tool support for this framework that provides automatic code generation, but this framework can be used in order to perform a detailed risk analysis of a complex workflow.

KAOS. The KAOS model itself starts at a high level that describes abstract requirements for the system, which are separated in functional and non-functional requirements, while the security requirements lie in the non-functional section as one can see in Figure 9 (i). Figure 9 (ii) shows a refinement of the secure system requirement, where most OWASP Top 10 issues can be modeled. Figure 9 (iii) shows a model for a concrete requirements model for the call of the method doAdminAction. This model already includes actors and specific requirements that are linked to the rather high level requirements like restricted access or authenticity. These goal models can be further used to generate object models, operation models or responsibility models to derive concrete software development requirements and restrictions.

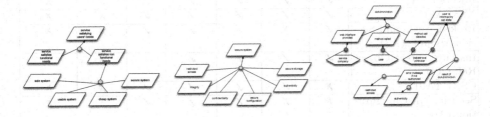

Fig. 9. Goal model: (i) Basic, (ii) refined, (iii) for a specific action

Secure Tropos. Figure 10 shows a simple dependency model with security constraints, which are modeled in the cloud shaped elements. It shows the three actors of the system, namely the user, admin and the service provider itself and the two plans that can be executed by the first two actors. The security constraints can be used to introduce requirements for actions between two actors, but none for systems, like a database server. This methodology is designed to model dependencies and trust relations within multiple stakeholders, but it is not feasible to apply this methodology to our evaluation scenario to improve the security of the system.

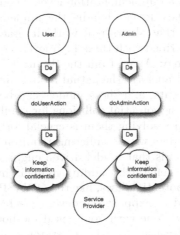

Fig. 10. Security constraints modeled with Tropos

Table 1. Summary of OWASP Top 10 mitigation coverage

OWASP Top 10	Secure UML	UMLsec	Misuse-case	Aspect Oriented	KAOS	Protocol Checker	Secure Troposker
Injection (A1)	✓	✓	✓	✓	✓	✗	✗
XSS (A2)	✓	✓	✓	✓	✓	✗	✗
Broken Auth. and Session Mgmnt. (A3)	✓	✗	✓	✓	✓	✗	✗
Insecure Direct Object Ref. (A4)	✓	✓	✓	✓	✓	✗	✗
CSRF (A5)	✗	✓	✓	✓	✓	✗	✗
Security Misconfiguration (A6)	✗	✗	✗	✓	✓	✗	✗
Insecure Cryptographic Storage (A7)	✗	✗	✗	✓	✓	✗	✓
Failure to Restrict URL Access (A8)	✓	✓	✓	✓	✓	✗	✗
Insufficient Transport Layer Protection (A9)	✗	✓	✗	✓	✓	✓	✓
Unvalidated Redirects and Forwards (A10)	✗	✓	✓	✓	✓	✗	✓
Toolsupport	✓	✗	✗	✓	✓	✗	✓

5   Conclusions

Most of the UML based modeling methodologies support the modeling of mitigation and countermeasures to the OWASP Top 10 threats, mostly by adding additional constraints on an implementation level. The misuse case diagram and the goal based approaches do not handle the implementation, they model a higher abstraction layer that shows real world interactions and requirements. Some threats can be described with these high level requirements, as can be see for the KAOS methodology. Apart from the Secure UML approach there is no feasible tool support to transform the actual models into source code that mitigates the mentioned threats, and these models can be rather used to identify potential security issues or potential collisions for conflicting goals. The aspect of detecting conflicts and resolving them is crucial for large systems that have several different stakeholders with conflicting requirements. The second major outcome of our evaluation is that model driven engineering does not make the software more secure in general by adding implicit mitigation procedures or checking the models for potential flaws, like the OWASP Top 10. These methodologies are only supposed to support the developers by indicating the location of conflicts, which can be done with goal based methodologies or the addition of standard mitigation features to existing systems, which can be done with the UMLsec and the Secure UML methodologies. Table 1 presents an overview about the capabilities of the evaluated methodologies. Overall it can be said that model driven engineering can reduce the occurrence of threats that are listed in the OWASP Top 10 by indicating them within the model, but this indication does not ensure that the software architect who designs the model, plans the appropriate countermeasures or mitigation features and that the actual implementation is compliant with the model.

Acknowledgements. This work has been supported by the Austrian Research Promotion Agency (FFG) under the Austrian COMET Program.

References

1. Bresciani, P., Perini, A., Giorgini, P., Giunchiglia, F., Mylopoulos, J.: Tropos: An agent-oriented software development methodology. Autonomous Agents and Multi-Agent Systems 8(3), 203–236 (2004)
2. Hayati, P., Jafari, N., Rezaei, S., Sarenche, S., Potdar, V.: Modeling input validation in uml. In: 19th Australian Conference on Software Engineering, ASWEC 2008, pp. 663–672. IEEE (2008)
3. Jürjens, J.: Umlsec: Extending UML for secure systems development. In: Jézéquel, J.-M., Hussmann, H., Cook, S. (eds.) UML 2002. LNCS, vol. 2460, pp. 412–425. Springer, Heidelberg (2002)
4. Kasal, K., Heurix, J., Neubauer, T.: Model-driven development meets security: An evaluation of current approaches. In: 2011 44th Hawaii International Conference on System Sciences (HICSS), pp. 1–9. IEEE (2011)
5. Lloyd, J., Jürjens, J.: Security analysis of a biometric authentication system using UMLsec and JML. In: Schürr, A., Selic, B. (eds.) MODELS 2009. LNCS, vol. 5795, pp. 77–91. Springer, Heidelberg (2009)
6. Lodderstedt, T., Basin, D., Doser, J.: SecureUML: A UML-based modeling language for model-driven security. In: Jézéquel, J.-M., Hussmann, H., Cook, S. (eds.) UML 2002. LNCS, vol. 2460, pp. 426–441. Springer, Heidelberg (2002)
7. Montrieux, L., Jürjens, J., Haley, C., Yu, Y., Schobbens, P., Toussaint, H.: Tool support for code generation from a umlsec property. In: Proceedings of the IEEE/ACM International Conference on Automated Software Engineering, pp. 357–358. ACM (2010)
8. Mouratidis, H., Giorgini, P.: Enhancing secure tropos to effectively deal with security requirements in the development of multiagent systems. In: Barley, M., Mouratidis, H., Unruh, A., Spears, D., Scerri, P., Massacci, F. (eds.) SASEMAS 2004-2006. LNCS, vol. 4324, pp. 8–26. Springer, Heidelberg (2009)
9. OWASP. Open web application security project top 10, https://www.owasp.org/index.php/Top_10_2010-Main (last access: January 15, 2013)
10. Rumbaugh, J., Jacobson, I., Booch, G.: The Unified Modeling Language Reference Manual, 2nd edn. Pearson Higher Education (2004)
11. Sandhu, R., Coyne, E., Feinstein, H., Youman, C.: Role-based access control models. Computer 29(2), 38–47 (1996)
12. Sindre, G., Opdahl, A.: Templates for misuse case description. In: Proceedings of the 7th International Workshop on Requirements Engineering, Foundation for Software Quality (REFSQ 2001), Switzerland. Citeseer (2001)
13. van Lamsweerde, A., Dardenne, A., Delcourt, B., Dubisy, F.: The kaos project: Knowledge acquisition in automated specification of software. In: Proceedings AAAI Spring Symposium Series, pp. 59–62 (1991)
14. Yu, H., Liu, D., He, X., Yang, L., Gao, S.: Secure software architectures design by aspect orientation. In: Proceedings of the 10th IEEE International Conference on Engineering of Complex Computer Systems, ICECCS 2005, pp. 47–55. IEEE (2005)
15. Zhu, Z., Zulkernine, M.: A model-based aspect-oriented framework for building intrusion-aware software systems. Information and Software Technology 51(5), 865–875 (2009)

An Evaluation of Argument Patterns Based on Data Flow

Shuichiro Yamamoto

Strategy Office, Information and Communications Headquarters Nagoya University
Nagoya, Japan
syamamoto@ acm.org

Abstract. In this paper, we will introduce some of the problem areas that software engineers are susceptible during the creation of assurance cases, based on the author's educational experience with assurance cases. To mitigate these problems, assurance case patterns are proposed based on Data flow diagrams that help engineers develop assurance cases by reusing those patterns. It is also shown an evaluation result of assurance case pattern application to develop an assurance case for a smart card application system.

Keywords: assurance case, argument pattern, data flow diagram, experimental evaluation, smart card application.

1 Introduction

The safety case, the assurance case, and the dependability case are currently the focus of considerable attention for the purpose of verifying that systems are safe. Methods have thus been proposed for representing these using Goal Structuring Notation (GSN)[1][2][3]. However, in order to facilitate the creation of assurance cases by engineers during real-world system development, it is not enough to simply provide them with an editor. They also need a more concrete creation method for assurance cases that has been adapted to suit the system-development process and documentation.

Against this backdrop, a number of methods have been developed for safety cases and dependability cases as part of research in the field of assurance cases: For example, Kelly has proposed the following six-step method for GSN creation: (1) Identify the goals to be supported; (2) define the basis on which the goals are stated, (3) identify a strategy to support the goals, (4) define the basis on which the strategy is stated, (5) evaluate the strategies, and (6) identify the basic solution[1][2]. The Safety Case Development Manual[4] established by the European Organization for the Safety of Air Navigation identifies the establishment of contexts for safety cases as being extremely important. This manual also proposes a checklist for the review of safety cases.

In terms of the development process for a system that itself comprises multiple systems (i.e., a system of systems), a technique involving system analysis, goal elicitation, identification of candidate design alternatives, and resolution of conflicts has been proposed for the creation of assurance cases in a structured fashion[5].

Linawati et al. (Eds.): ICT-EurAsia 2014, LNCS 8407, pp. 432–437, 2014.
© IFIP International Federation for Information Processing 2014

Meanwhile, methods for the decomposition of arguments as required when creating assurance cases have been arranged into categories such as architecture, functional, and set of attributes [6]. Goodenough, Lipson and others proposed a method to create Security Assurance case [7]. They described that the Common Criteria provides catalogs of standard Security Functional Requirements and Security Assurance Requirements. They decomposed Security case by focusing on the process, such as requirements, design, coding, and operation. The approach did not use the Security Target structure of the CC to describe Security case. Alexander, Hawkins and Kelly overviewed the state of the art on the Security Assurance cases [8]. They showed the practical aspects and benefits to describe Security case in relation to security target documents. However they did not provide any patterns to describe Security case using CC.

Kaneko, Yamamoto and Tanaka proposed a security countermeasure decision method using Assurance case and CC [9]. Their method is based on a goal oriented security requirements analysis [10-11]. Although the method showed a way to describe security case, it did not provide Security case graphical notations and the seamless relationship between security structure and security functional requirements. Yamamoto, Kaneko and Tanaka have proposed assurance case patterns based on security common criteria [12]. In addition, Yamamoto and Matsuno also evaluated the effectiveness of argument patterns for LAN device management system [13].

The diversity of these techniques is evidence of assurance-case creation methods being proposed on an individual basis for a range of different development processes and fields of application. However, in order that the assurance case may be used to verify that real-world systems are dependable, its specific correlation with the system development process and stage deliverables and its mode of use must be clear and consistent. In this regard, many improvements must still be made to today's methods for creating assurance cases.

This paper discusses the effectiveness of argument patterns of assurance case based on data flow diagram, DFD. Section 2 proposes argument patterns based on DFD. Section 3 shows the experiment of applying these argument patterns to assure dependability of a smartcard application. In section 4, we discuss the effectiveness of the proposed argument patterns. Section 5 concludes the paper and shows future work.

2   Argument Patterns Based on DFD

We will look briefly at the DFD level decomposition pattern.

2.1   DFD Level Decomposition Pattern

An assurance case must be created for a system analyzed using data flow diagrams (DFD). The assumed condition for application of DFD level decomposition is the system being clearly definable using data flow diagrams.

Claims are decomposed based on the hierarchical levels of DFD. Data flow diagrams take the form of (1) a top-level context diagram that defines data flow between the system and external agents; (2) lower-level data flow diagrams that are hierarchically decomposed from the context diagram for individual process; (3) process specifications for processes that cannot be decomposed any further; and (4) data stores for retaining data. Accordingly, assurance cases for DFD levels can be created using the following procedure.

Step 1:   The claim "The system is dependable" is decomposed in line with the process decomposition pattern and on the basis of the context diagram. Here, "Definition of data flow diagrams" is connected to this claim as an assumption.

Step 2:   If processes can be decomposed;
An assurance case is created for each process in line with the process decomposition pattern. Because the assurance case will contain a parent node corresponding to the upper-level process, the process structure definition is connected to the parent node as an assumption node at this time.

Step 3:   If processes cannot be decomposed, the following two options are available.

Step 3-1:   When the process specification has been defined;
An assurance case is created for the process specification. Because the process specification will describe the corresponding processing, risk can be analyzed for each processing step at this time and evidence of countermeasures for the identified risks can be displayed.

Step 3-2:   When the process specification has not been defined;
An undefined element is connected to the claim.

3   Evaluation of Argument Patterns

3.1   Design of Experiment

The experiment was conducted to evaluate the effectiveness of assurance case patterns for the real smartcard based security application. Examinee is two engineers who have several years of experience in the smartcard system development. 4 hour course of assurance case education was provided to the examinee.

The examinees, then, developed the assurance case for the target system described below.

3.2   Overview of the Target System

The Employee Attendance Management System (EAMS) consists of Server, Smartcard readers, Android terminals, Manager's PCs, and employee's PCs. These components are connected by intranet. The purpose of EAMS is to manage attendance information of employees with smartcards. Smartcards are monitored by readers that are controlled by Android terminals.

The Server gathers smartcard attendance information through Android terminals. Each terminal monitors smartcards of employees through readers in each location. The employees can register attendance schedule by user PCs in regional offices. Managers also execute employee management based on the attendance information of employees by Managers PCs.

3.3 Result of the Experiment

The examinee developed the assurance case in 280 man hours during 2 month. There were 5 work items, learn D-Case, understand specification, develop DFD, analyze risk, and develop D-Case. D-Case is an abbreviation of Dependability Case that means assurance case for assuring dependability. D-Case was described by D-Case editor [14] that was originally developed by Tokyo University and enhanced currently by Nagoya University.

43% of time was used to describe D-Case diagram. 35% of time was also used to analyze risk of EAMS. 11% and 8% of total time were consumed to understand specification and develop DFD. 3% of the application time was used to learn D-Case. The pattern application time was included in D-Case development.

3.4 Examples of Developed Assurance Case

Fig.1 shows the lower level assurance case example developed for the claim G_5 by using iteratively the DFD decomposition pattern according to the hierarchy of the DFD specifying EAMS.

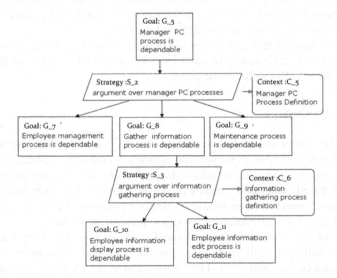

Fig. 1. Assurance case tree developed by using DFD decomposition pattern

3.5   Volume of the Assurance Case

There were 33 processes in DFD. There were 549 nodes of the assurance case in total. The ratio of claim and evidence are 46.6% and 26.4%. Although the number of context nodes was only 30, the numbers of risks corresponded to context nodes are 146.

4   Discussion

4.1   Effectiveness of Argument Patterns

As the examinee said, the architecture decomposition pattern was useful to analyze risk, although the decision to choose it from argument decomposition patterns needed time to understand appropriateness between the target system and argument patterns.

Pitfalls discussed in the paper [13] were not observed in the course of the experiment. This also showed the effectiveness of the argument patterns based on DFD. Without the knowledge of argument patterns, the examinee could not develop a large assurance case consists of 549 nodes in less than two weeks. Very little time, only 3%, was spent for learning D-Case, because the examinee studied the D-case development method from DFD very well. This showed the appropriateness of the proposed D-Case development method.

4.2   Limitation

The experimental evaluation treated only one application. It is necessary to show the effectiveness of the method by evaluating more number of applications. Patterns used in the experiment were also limited, although these were effectively applied to develop assurance cases. The developed assurance case is assuring the dependability of the target system as a product. The dependability of the development process of the target system is also necessary as mentioned in ISO 26262.

In addition, other argument patterns are needed to evaluate. For example, there are several number of argument patterns described in [6]. The applicability of these patterns for the EAMS can be investigated.

5   Conclusion

This paper introduced assurance case patterns for dealing with DFD. Evaluation of the pattern approach was also evaluated for assuring an employee attendance management system using smartcards. The experimental evaluation showed the effectiveness of the DFD based patterns of argument decomposition. The examinees developed assurance case contains more than 500 nodes systematically in two weeks, after learned assurance case introduction course and patterns in 4 hours.

Future work includes more experimental evaluation of the proposed approach, comparative analysis of different argument patterns, and consistency management between assurance case and DFD. The author plans to develop and evaluate argument patterns for operation phase [15] in the future.

Acknowledgment. This research was partially supported by JSPS Research Project No. 24220001 and the DEOS (Dependable Operating Systems for Embedded Systems Aiming at Practical Applications) project [16].

References

1. Kelly, T.P.: A Six-Step Method for the Development of Goal Structures. York Software Engineering (1997)
2. Kelly, T.: Arguing Safety, a Systematic Approach to Managing Safety Cases, PhD thesis, Department of Computer Science, University of York (1998)
3. Jackson, D., et al.: Software for dependable systems–sufficient evidence? National Research Council (2008)
4. European Organisation for the Safety of Air Navigation, Safety Case Development Manual, 2nd edn. EUROCONTROL (October 2006)
5. Despotou, G., Kelly, T.: Design and Development of Dependability Case Architecture during System Development. In: Proceedings of the 25th International System Safety Conference (ISSC). Proceedings by the System Safety Society, Baltimore (2007)
6. Bloomfield, R., Bishop, P.: Safety and assurance cases: Past, present and possible future– an Adelard perspective. In: Proceedings of 18th Safety-Critical Systems Symposium (February 2010)
   Goodenough, J., Lipson, H., Weinstock, C.: Arguing Security - Creating Security Assurance Cases (2007),
   https://buildsecurityin.uscert.gov/bsi/articles/knowledge/assurance/643-BSI.html
7. Alexander, T., Hawkins, R., Kelly, T.: Security Assurance Cases: Motivation and the State of the Art. CESG/TR/2011 (2011)
8. Kaneko, T., Yamamoto, S., Tanaka, H.: Proposal on Countermeasure Decision Method Using Assurance Case and Common Criteria. In: ProMAC 2012 (2012)
9. Kaneko, T., Yamamoto, S., Tanaka, H.: SARM – a spiral review method for security requirements based on Actor Relationship Matrix. In: ProMAC 2010, pp. P1227–P1238 (2010)
10. Kaneko, T., Yamamoto, S., Tanaka, H.: Specification of Whole Steps for the Security Requirements Analysis Method (SARM)-From Requirement Analysis to Countermeasure Decision. In: ProMAC 2011 (2011)
11. Yamamoto, S., Kaneko, T., Tanaka, H.: A Proposal on Security Case based on Common Criteria. In: Mustofa, K., Neuhold, E.J., Tjoa, A.M., Weippl, E., You, I. (eds.) ICT-EurAsia 2013. LNCS, vol. 7804, pp. 331–336. Springer, Heidelberg (2013)
12. Yamamoto, S., Matsuno, Y.: An Evaluation of Argument Patterns to Reduce Pitfalls of Applying Assurance Case. In: Assure 2013, pp. 12–17 (2013)
13. D-Case editor, http://www.dependable-os.net/tech/D-CaseEditor/
14. Takama, S., Patu, V., Matsuno, Y., Yamamoto, S.: A Proposal on a Method for Reviewing Operation Manuals of Supercomputer. In: ISSRE Workshops 2012, pp. 305–306 (2012)
15. DEOS, http://www.jst.go.jp/kisoken/crest/en/research_area/ongoing/area04-4.html

A Design of Web Log Integration Framework Using NoSQL

Huijin Jeong[1], Junho Choi[1], Chang Choi[1], Ilsun You[2], and Pankoo Kim[1,*]

[1] Department of Computer Engineering Chosun University,
375 Seoseok-dong, Dong-gu, Gwangju, Republic of Korea
{Jeonghuijin,enduranceaura}@gmail.com,
xdman@paran.com, pkkim@chosun.ac.kr
[2] School of Information Science Korean Bible University,
16 Danghyun 2-gil, Nowon-gu, Seoul, Republic of Korea
isyou@bible.ac.kr

Abstract. Webservice is a software technology as the representative method of information communication currently used to create a dynamic system environment that is configured to fulfill its users' needs. Therefore, analyzing log data that occurred at provision is being used as the significant basic data in webservice research. Thanks to development of Cloud computing technology, it has resulted in centralized points from which data is generated and data enlargement. A research is now implemented to create information from collecting, processing and converting flood of data and to obtain the new various items of information. Against this backdrop, it is justified that collection, storage and analysis of web log data in the existing conventional RDBMS system may be inadequate to process the enlarged log data. This research propose a framework which to integrate web log for storage using HBase, a repository of the Cloud computing- based NoSQL. In addition, data validation must be completed in the pre-process when collecting web log. The validated log is stored in the modeling structure in which takes features of web log into account. According to the results, introduction of NoSQL system is found to integrate the enlargement of log data in more efficient manner. By comparisons with the existing RDBMS in terms of data processing performance, it was proved that the NoSQL- based database had a superior performance.

Keywords: Big Data, Security Log aggregation, Cloud computing, NoSQL, HBase.

1 Introduction

Webservice can be the most representative service in which a business and customers communicate each other. Analysis of web log data from its operation allows for re-processing various information that include status of a system, popular service pages after being extracted into any contributing information to the operation [15].

---

* Corresponding author.

Linawati et al. (Eds.): ICT-EurAsia 2014, LNCS 8407, pp. 438–445, 2014.
© IFIP International Federation for Information Processing 2014

Nonetheless, as Smart Phone penetration increases in recent times, this has made it possible to access to the service regardless of time and place, constantly increasing the amount of log. Because of this, it brings about the newly-coined word of Big Data [3]. There have been vigorous research efforts in various fields to derive different type of information from Big Data by the process of understanding [1, 16, 4, 18, 19], analyzing and gathering. In general, the existing web log repository consists of RDBMS. However, due to data enlargement, there are many difficulties to manually analyze web log and efficiently manage the service. RDBMS is not enough to process such gigantic data completely. The most representative technology that overcomes the incompetence is referred to as a distributed database or NoSQL. The most comparative advantages with NoSQL include that it supports for the horizontal expansions which enable massive data to be processed to overcome the limitations. In addition, it has strength in not using schema that presents a relationship data hold. As a result, a web log with different structures can smoothly be replaced with a log of the new formation [2]. The propose framework is a formalized one that fulfills the objective for collecting, storing and analyzing the massive web log data using HBase, a repository of NoSQL data in effective manner. Under the assumption that different web logs are integrated, a Cloud computing environment was considered, and a web log which had little effect on the existing system at storage and at the same time was configured to function for collection in real time was through preprocessing for eliminating unnecessary data after taking field structures into account. Later, data modeling structure for NoSQL environment was designed in order to store data. To verify the framework that is being proposed, it checked whether the massive web log data was more speedily processed using Wikipedia Accesslog Dataset [8] than in the previously used RDBMS. the reminder of the research is organized as follows: Chapter 2 it describes NoSQL-based log integration with comparisons between its features and log repository. Chapter 3 describes a preprocessing in a way that efficiently integrate a web log with the propose web log integration framework as well as a HBase-based modeling structure for integration. In chapter 4 an experiment of data processing speed and its results, as a solution that is proposed in chapter 3 are described. In the final chapter 5 it ends with conclusions and future research directions.

2   Related Works

Log data refers to recording information that includes sequential events occurred in system operation as well as details of operation in system or on network [17]. Logs can be classified into operating system, network packet logs, and internet access record log. The existing RDBMS is designed with the standards of integrity and consistency of data, and it stores log data. RDBMS has an advantage in that it designs a table with normalized schema, proving join functions and with data expression opened. In contrast, the formalized schema structure has a significant difficulty in database expansions as it is not proper for the distributed processing environment. The supplementary database for expansions is developed and called as NoSQL(Not Only SQL) [5, 6]. Right off the bat, NoSQL databases are unique because they are usually independent from Structured Query Language (SQL) found in relational databases. Relational databases all use SQL as the domain-specific language for ad hoc queries, while non-relational databases have no such standard query language, so they can use whatever they want. That can, if need be, include SQL [14]. In addition, it promises no perfect data consistency as the distributed storage database, by its characteristics, is focused on system provision even though a few database with data storage fail to respond [7, 12]. There has been an ongoing research in which NoSQL is used as repository to effectively process the ever-growing data [13]. NoSQL repository is divided into 4 types of data storage structures. Out of the four structures, HBase which opts for Column Model is usefully employed as the non-formalized data repository since it is capable of configuring multi-dimensional data based on columns [9]. Additionally, with employment of multi-slave method when configuring data nodes, it can flexibly be used in log integration.

Choi et al. [10] had proposed security log analysis system with a NoSQL-based Mapreduce design that allowed firewall log data of this type with higher capacity to be collected and analyzed for integration, compared to RDBMS in terms of data processing performance and performed an analysis of the three attack patterns selected for evaluation.

WEI et al. [11] had proposed a system using MongoDB, a repository of NoSQL in order to integrate a large number of networks monitoring log data. The research included a system design that took respective features of hardware layers and application layers in Cloud environment into consideration, Mapreduce programming that worked for log integration processing of massive log data in effective manner, and the improvement of log integrated architecture compared to RDBMS.

3 Hbase-BASED Log Integration

3.1 Proposed Framework

The integration of security logs must not create any problems with the service, even if the security logs often occur such as, added, modified and deleted thing. Also, these security logs shall be no degradation in system performance through big security logs for detecting security incident. Therefore, this paper proposes an integrated system for good storage efficiency based on big log data. The Figure 1 is a framework of the proposed log integration system.

There are some preconditions for the configuration of log analysis system as follows:

(1) System operation and assuming that the attack happens.
(2) The web logs are created in the working service.
(3) Confirm to create the SSH Tunnel for transmission of web logs.
(4) Transfer the variety web log data through web log collector.
(5) Perform the preprocessing of transferred web logs.
(6) The web log data are stored in HBase after preprocessing.
(7) The Extraction of pattern and information using stored web log data.
(8) The extracted information is forwarded to the administrator.

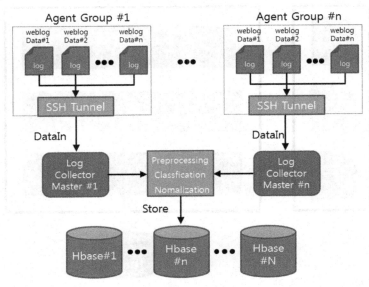

Fig. 1. Framework of the proposed log integration system

The first step is the collection of big logs for security logs integration. The security logs are transferred through SSH Tunnel and these are performed the preprocessing for removing of security threats. The reason of performing preprocessing are a step for removing unnecessary information after checking the data type of a heterogeneous logs. Also, there is needed for the model structure according to the type HBase after extracting necessary data. Finally, the integrated log storage when storing the common purpose is to integrate information.

3.2   Web Log Preprocessing

The second step is the preprocessing of big log data. The preprocessing is classified the format type after checking the contents of log data. Also, this step is reduced the waste of storage space by removing unnecessary data. The type classification is very important because the structure of log data is different in occurred log data of heterogeneous services. The figure 2 is a framework of the preprocessing.

There are some steps of preprocessing as follows:

(1) The variety web log data is occurred in service.
(2) To validate the input data as a web log.
(3) To classify through analysis of web log data.
(4) To format by administrator using the characteristics of classified web log.
(5) The purified data is stored.
(6) Repeat steps 1 to 6 times.

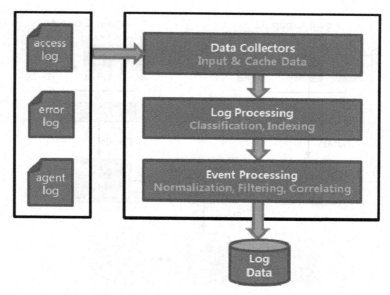

Fig. 2. Framework of the Preprocessing

3.3   Data Modeling for Log Integration

Amount of large scaled security logs which should be collected and stored under cloud computing environment is rapidly increasing. However, conventional collection method based on RDBMS storage can't afford the amount of security logs. In order to solve this problem, this paper proposes NoSQL-based method to collect and integrate security logs. NoSQL is more effective and rapid data storage than conventional RDBMS. Actually, data modeling based on relational database can performs freely queries through setting relation between tables. However, the design of data store model is needed because NoSQL does not support complex queries.

The Figure 3 is an example of the log integrated modeling framework. In figure 3, the Host table is entered 'Host' information using Row Key for data identification from LogData table in structure of the framework. Also, data is generated by the column such as, Log the type, log generation time, count and so on. The type of web log is classified by time in service. The time information is the most basic and important information for security incident or analysis of operational status because the data is stored by time sequentially. The Row key is defined 'DateTime' + 'Host' + 'Count' information in Log-Data table for log storage because of data query information such as, 'who', 'when', 'occurrence' and so on. DataLogInfo Column is classified Acceslog, Errorlog and Agentlog by log characteristics.

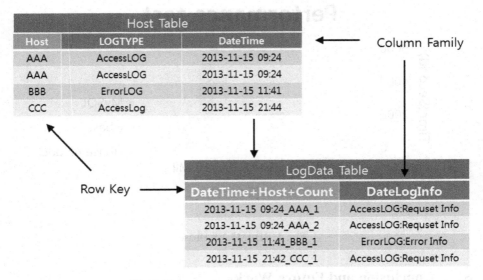

Fig. 3. Framework of log integration modeling

4   Performance Evaluation

4.1   Experimental Environment

The performance evaluation of data input is performed between NoSQL and RDMS. RDMS is MySQL-5.1.69 because the most widely used. NosQL is used HBase-0.92.12 and it consists of master node, 4 data nodes, 50 Thread. The experiment is performed the data input performance using Wikipedia AccessLog data set [8]. The AccessLog data set based on Wikipedia are consists of 2 million, 5 million and 10 million elements.

The Figure 4 is the result of performance test. This test is processed number per hour and integration available amount based on web log.

4.2   Evaluation

In the results, 2mil is not large difference count but 5mil and 10mil can be clearly confirmed large difference count between HBase and MySQL. Also, the performance can be improved by increasing Data Node. If number of DataNodes is ensured sufficient, it seems possible additional performance boost.

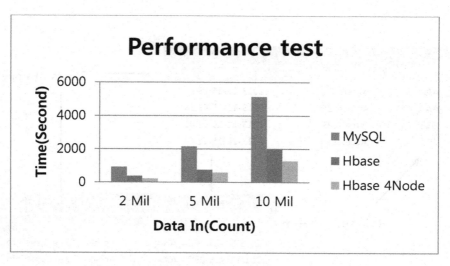

Fig. 4. RDBMS VS Hbase

5   Conclusion and Future Works

As cloud computing technologies are rapidly advancing, cloud environment is significantly expanding. Although cloud environment provides users with convenience, prevention and detection of possible security invasion accidents is still unsolved problems. The most intrinsic method to prevent security invasion accident is to collect security logs for each system and then analyze them.

This paper proposes NoSQL-based large capacity security log integration method for cloud security platform. Since cloud computing provides various services to users, a new web log that is different from existing one is likely to occur. Therefore, this paper proposes large scaled web log management to collect, store and integrate logs considering characteristics between heterogeneous machines. In the future, it needs the effective analysis methods based on heterogeneous web logs.

Acknowledgments. This research was supported by Basic Science Research Program through the National Research Foundation of Korea (NRF) funded by the Ministry of Education (No. 2013R1A1A2A10011667).

References

1. Choi, J., Choi, C., Ko, B., Choi, D., Kim, P.: Detecting Web based DDoS Attack using MapReduce operations in Cloud Computing Environment. Journal of Internet Services and Information Security 3(3/4), 28–37 (2013)
2. Oliner, A., Ganapathi, A., Xu, W.: Advances and challenges in log analysis. Communications of the ACM 55(2), 55–61 (2012)

 3. Yunhua, G.U., Shu, S., Guansheng, Z.: Application of NoSQL Database in Web Crawling. International Journal of Digital Content Technology and its Applications 5(6) (2011)
 4. Elkotob, M., Andersson, K.: Cross-Layer Design for Improved QoE in Content Distribution Networks. IT CoNvergence PRActice (INPRA) 1(1), 37–52 (2013)
 5. Srinivasan, V., Bulkowski, B.: Citrusleaf: A Real-Time NoSQL DB which Preserves ACID. In: The 37th International Conference on Very Large Data Bases, Proceedings of the VLDB Endowment, vol. 4(12), pp. 1340–1350 (2011)
 6. Yi, X., Wei, G., Dong, F.: A Survey on NoSQL Database. Communication of Modern Technology, 46–50 (2010)
 7. Zhou, W., Han, J., Zhang, Z., Dai, J.: Dynamic Random Access for Hadoop Distributed File System. In: 32nd International Conference on Distributed Computing Systems Workshops, pp. 17–22. IEEE (2012)
 8. http://www.wikibench.eu
 9. George, L.: HBase The Definitive Guide. O'ReillyMedia (2011)
10. Bomin, C., Jong-Hwan, K., Sung-Sam, H., Myung-Mook, H.: The Method of Analyzing Firewall Log Data using Map Reduce based on NoSQL. Journal of The Korea Institute of Information Security & Cryptology (JKIISC) 23(4), 667–677 (2013)
11. Yang, J., Leskovec, J.: Patterns of Temporal Variation in Online Media. In: ACM International Conference on Web Search and Data Mining, pp. 177–186 (2011)
12. Shvachko, K.V.: HDFS Scalability: The limits to growth. Login 35(2), 6–16 (2010)
13. Borthakur, D., Sarma, J.S., Gray, J.: Apache Hadoop goes realtime at Facebook. In: SIGMOD, pp. 1071–1080 (2011)
14. Proffitt, B.: When NoSQL Databases Are Yes Good For You and Your Company (2013)
15. Agosti, M., Crivellari, F., Nunzio, G.M.: Web log analysis: a review of a decade of studies about information acquisition, inspection and interpretation of user interaction. Data Mining and Knowledge Discovery 24(3), 663–696 (2012)
16. Choi, C., Choi, J., Ko, B., Oh, K., Kim, P.: A Design of Onto-ACM (Ontology based Access Control Model) in Cloud Computing Environments. Journal of Internet Services and Information Security 2(3/4), 54–64 (2012)
17. Herrerias, J., Gomez: Log Analysis Towards an Automated Forensic Diagnosis System. IEEE ARES, 15–18 (2010)
18. Han, S., Han, Y.: Meaning and Prospects of IT Convergence Technology in Korea. IT CoNvergence PRActice (INPRA) 1(1), 2–12 (2013)
19. Gonzalez-Miranda, S., Alcarria, R., Robles, T., Morales, A., Gonzalez, I., Montcada, E.: An IoT-leveraged information system for future shopping environments. IT CoNvergence PRActice (INPRA) 1(3), 49–65 (2013)

Motivation-Based Risk Analysis Process for IT Systems

Agata Niescieruk[1] and Bogdan Ksiezopolski[1,2]

[1] Polish-Japanese Institute of Information Technology
Koszykowa 86, 02-008 Warsaw, Poland
[2] Institute of Computer Science, Maria Curie-Sklodowska University,
pl. M. Curie-Sklodowskiej 5, 20-031 Lublin, Poland

Abstract. Information security management is one of the most important issues to be resolved. The key element of this process is risk analysis. The standards are (ISO/IEC 27000, ISO/IEC 31000) based on the complex and time consuming process of defining vulnerabilities and threats for all organisation assets. In the article we present a new approach to analysing the risk of an attack on information systems. We focus on human factor - motivation, and show its relation to hacker profiles, as well as impacts. At the beginning we introduce a new model of motivation-based risk analysis. Then we describe case study illustrating our approach for a simple set of organisation processes.

1 Introduction

The ISO/IEC 27001 standard, as the part of the growing ISO/IEC 27000 family of standards, brings information security under explicit management control. Being a formal specification, ISO/IEC 27001 provides requirements for establishing, implementing, maintaining and continuously improving an Information Security Management System. ISO/IEC 27001 requires a systematic examination of information security risks, taking into account threats, vulnerabilities, and impacts, designing and implementing a coherent and comprehensive suite of information security controls to address those risks, as well as adopting an overarching management process to ensure that the information security controls continue to meet the information security needs. Information security risks can be estimated according to the different approaches which can be categorised as the quality or quantity analyses, with deterministic or probabilistic methods. However, the most common methods (FRAP, STIR, CRAMM, CORAS, STIR - [10,13]) consist of the same three stages - risk identification, risk estimation and risk prioritization. All these methodologies have two significant limitations. The first is that while estimating the probability of an attack [12] the methods focus on vulnerabilities [3], threats, weaknesses of resources only in one dimension, treating elements as independent. The second limitation is that motivation as a human factor is neglected. The literature on the subject contains only brief discussions of motivation as a factor influencing risk [9,1,2,11].

Linawati et al. (Eds.): ICT-EurAsia 2014, LNCS 8407, pp. 446–455, 2014.
© IFIP International Federation for Information Processing 2014

The main contribution of the paper is introducing a new motivation-based risk analysis process which focuses on human motivation as the main factor which determines the decision of the attack on an IT system. Another contribution, as opposed to traditional risk analysis, which study individual assets in isolation, is that our method is multidimensional. We try to combine processes and assets involved in them.

2   The Model

In the article we propose a new model for motivation-based risk analysis process. Our modified model is presented in the figure 1. In the following sections all steps are described.

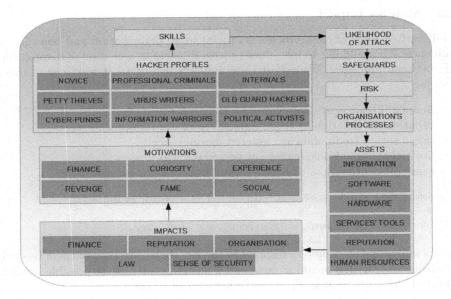

Fig. 1. The model of motivation-based risk analysis process

2.1   Step 1 - Organisation's Processes

In the first step we have to focus on all processes in the organisation. They are crucial in realisation of business objectives and require many different resources. In this step we create a set of processes for which the risk will be estimated: $P_1, ..P_n$.

2.2   Step 2 - Assets

In the second step we have to enumerate all assets which take part in the processes defined in the first step. All assets we will denote by A. Referring to ISO 27002 we have 6 groups of our assets, so $A = \{I, S, H, T, R, P\}$, where

1. $I = \{I_1, ..., I_n\}$ - information;
2. $S = \{S_1, ..., S_n\}$ - software;
3. $H = \{H_1, ..., H_n\}$ - hardware;
4. $T = \{T_1, ..., T_n\}$ - services' tools;
5. $R = \{R_1, ..., R_n\}$ - non-material assets - reputation;
6. $HR = \{HR_1, ..., HR_n\}$ - human resources.

For each type of processes n the number of assets can be different. Now for chosen processes we should identify their assets. We will ascribe assets for process P_j as A_j. All assets influence the performance and the development of a company. Each single asset is involved in at least one process, each process uses at least one asset.

2.3 Step 3 - Impact

Undisturbed work of each process is crucial to an organisation and has certain influence. We would like to introduce process impacts as a method of distinguishing between processes. We expect these impacts belong to at least one of these groups:

− finance (higher costs, lower profits, shares depreciation) $[fin]$;
− reputation (violation of trust, damage to brand reputation) $[rep]$;
− organisation (redundancies, lowered morale) $[org]$;
− law (legal obligations, leakage of personal data) $[law]$;
− sense of security (loss of control, awareness of a threat) $[sec]$.

Therefore each single asset a is represented as a vector of impacts:

$$imp_a = [fin_a, rep_a, org_a, law_a, sec_a]$$

where individual elements correspond to the list above and each of them has values from $[0..1]$ with 0 meaning none and 1 meaning the highest possible impact. Similarly for each process P_j, we have a vector of impacts:

$$imp_{P_j} = [fin_{P_j}, rep_{P_j}, org_{P_j}, law_{P_j}, sec_{P_j}]$$

Now we can calculate total impacts for each process and all its assets. Having process P_j and a set of all its assets A_j, the total impacts will be:

$$imp_{P_j, A_j} = [fin_{P_j, A_j}, rep_{P_j, A_j}, org_{P_j, A_j}, law_{P_j, A_j}, sec_{P_j, A_j}]$$

where each element of this vector is calculated as follows:

$$x_{P_j, A_j} = x_{P_j} \cdot [max_{a \in A_j} + (1 - max_{a \in A_j}) \cdot (median_{A_j \setminus max_{a \in A_j}})],$$

where: $x \in \{fin, rep, org, law, sec\}$. The reason why we take the maximum and add it to the median multiplied by 1 - maximum is the fact that we want to have total impacts as numbers from $[0..1]$.

2.4   Step 4 - Motivation

Different impacts for the assets determine certain types of motivation. These categories of motivation [8,1] that are related to attack on IT system could be one or combination of more of these listed below:

- finance [$finm$];
- curiosity [cur];
- experience/knowledge [exp];
- revenge/anger [rev];
- fame/notoriety [fam];
- social - membership of group (e.g. radical beliefs, political activists) or a desire to impress a group [soc].

The impacts and the motivations are strongly related. In [11] they are parts of sequential steps. However, we did not find this relation directly described in the literature. That is why we introduce 5 levels to describe it: 1 - very high, 0.75 - high, 0.5 - medium, 0.3 - low, 0.1 - very low. For each type of motivation various impacts have various meanings. Using levels above, the relation is illustrated by matrix:

$$
mot_{imp} = \begin{bmatrix}
finm_{fin} & finm_{rep} & finm_{org} & finm_{law} & finm_{sec} \\
cur_{fin} & cur_{rep} & cur_{org} & cur_{law} & cur_{sec} \\
exp_{fin} & exp_{rep} & exp_{org} & exp_{law} & exp_{sec} \\
rev_{fin} & rev_{rep} & rev_{org} & rev_{law} & rev_{sec} \\
fam_{fin} & fam_{rep} & fam_{org} & fam_{law} & fam_{sec} \\
soc_{fin} & soc_{rep} & soc_{org} & soc_{law} & soc_{sec}
\end{bmatrix} =
$$

$$
= \begin{bmatrix}
1 & 0.5 & 0.3 & 0.5 & 0.3 \\
0.3 & 0.75 & 0.5 & 0.1 & 0.75 \\
0.1 & 0.5 & 0.75 & 0.3 & 0.75 \\
0.75 & 0.75 & 0.1 & 0.5 & 0.3 \\
0.5 & 0.75 & 0.5 & 0.5 & 0.5 \\
0.5 & 1 & 0.5 & 0.3 & 0.3
\end{bmatrix}
$$

Each element of this matrix bind a certain type of motivation with a certain type of impact, i.e. for whichever x_y, x is a kind of motivation, y - type of an impact. E.g. fam_{org} is about fame motivation and organisation impact. To obtain exact values, the proper motivations for our process are:

$$
mot_{P_j} = [finm_{P_j}, cur_{P_j}, exp_{P_j}, rev_{P_j}, fam_{P_j}, soc_{P_j}]
$$

where each element of this vector is calculated in a similar way, e.g.:

$$
finm_{P_j} = max(fin_{P_j,A_j} \cdot finm_{fin}, rep_{P_j,A_j} \cdot finm_{rep},
$$

$$
org_{P_j,A_j} \cdot finm_{org}, law_{P_j,A_j} \cdot finm_{law}, sec_{P_j,A_j} \cdot finm_{sec})
$$

2.5   Step 5 - Hacker Profile

The next component of our model is a hacker profile. It is determined by his or her motivation [4]. According to article [8] we define the taxonomy of hackers. There are nine primary categories of hackers: Novices [No], Cyber-punks [CP], Internals [In], Petty Thieves [PT], Virus Writers [VW], Old Guard hackers [OG], Professional Criminals [PC], Information Warriors [IW] and Political Activists [PA]. We have to link these hacker profiles with motivation. Referring to the categories of motivation above and to the hacker profiles [8] we define the relationship between them which are presented in the tab. 1.

Table 1. The combination of hacker profile with motivation

Hacker profile	Motivation					
	$finm$	cur	exp	rev	fam	soc
No	no	no	yes	no	no	yes
CP	yes	no	no	no	yes	no
In	yes	no	no	yes	no	no
PT	yes	no	no	yes	no	no
VW	no	yes	no	yes	no	no
OG	no	yes	yes	no	no	no
PC	yes	no	no	no	no	no
IW	yes	no	no	no	no	yes
PA	no	no	no	no	yes	yes

In this step, having calculated values for all types of motivation for a chosen process j we will be able to determine hacker profile. Basing on [8] and [1] we propose matrix which will be used to represent levels of motivation for all types of hackers.

$$mot_{hac} = \begin{bmatrix} 0 & 0.5 & 0.3 & 0.7 & 0 & 0 & 1 & 0.5 & 0 \\ 0 & 0 & 0 & 0 & 0.5 & 0.5 & 0 & 0 & 0 \\ 0.5 & 0 & 0 & 0 & 0 & 0.5 & 0 & 0 & 0 \\ 0 & 0 & 0.7 & 0.3 & 0.5 & 0 & 0 & 0 & 0 \\ 0 & 0.5 & 0 & 0 & 0 & 0 & 0 & 0 & 0.5 \\ 0.5 & 0 & 0 & 0 & 0 & 0 & 0 & 0.5 & 0.5 \end{bmatrix}$$

Each column corresponds to a hacker profile (first to No, second to CP, etc.) and each row is for a different type of motivation ($finm, cur, exp, rev, fam, soc$). E.g. $mot_{hac}[1, 1] = finm_{No} = 0$ is finance motivation for Novices, $mot_{hac}[4, 4] = rev_{PT} = 0.3$ is revenge for Petty Thieves. Now we can multiply a vector of motivations for a process j (mot_{P_j}) by this matrix of hackers (mot_{hac}). As a result we obtain vector which has 9 elements, and each one corresponds to one hacker profile:

$$mot_{P_j,hac} = mot_{P_j} \cdot mot_{hac} =$$

$$= [No_{P_j}, CP_{P_j}, In_{P_j}, PT_{P_j}, VW_{P_j}, OG_{P_j}, PC_{P_j}, IW_{P_j}, PA_{P_j}]$$

2.6   Step 6 - Hackers' Skills

We have our processes, assets, impacts, motivation and hacker profiles. However, there is one more crucial factor - hackers' skills. Each group of hackers is at a certain level of knowledge and we need to include that factor to our analysis. According to [8] the least skilled group are No, the next are CP and PT, then In, VW, and the most skilled are OG, PC, IW and PA. We define the skills vector as:

$$skl_{hac} = [skl_{No}, skl_{CP}, skl_{In}, skl_{PT}, skl_{VW}, skl_{OG}, skl_{PC}, skl_{IW}, skl_{PA}] =$$

$$= [0.2, 04, 0.6, 0.4, 0.8, 1, 1, 1, 1]$$

2.7   Step 7 - Likelihood of Attack

Having a vector of hacker profiles and a vector of their skills we could now estimate which groups of hackers are highly probable to attack. We estimate it by the following multiplication.

$$att_{P_j} = mot_{P_j,hac} \cdot skl_{hac} =$$

$$= [att_{No,P_j}, att_{CP,P_j}, att_{In,P_j}, att_{PT,P_j},$$

$$att_{VW,P_j}, att_{OG,P_j}, att_{PC,P_j}, att_{IW,P_j}, att_{PA,P_j}]$$

All elements of this result vector are from $[0..1]$. For a number less than 0.1 we will talk about a small likelihood of an attack, for numbers from $[0.1..0.5]$ the likelihood will be at a medium level. Finally, values greater than 0.5 will mean the likelihood is high. Our method has just showed whether the process is critical and could be interesting for a hacker of a certain type - the likelihood of an attack. The question whether this attack will be successful or not could not be answered here as we did not analyse safeguards.

2.8   Step 8 - Safeguards

In the next step the safeguards for all analysed processes must be defined. We suggest using a scale: 1 - very high, 0.75 - high, 0.5 - medium, 0.25 - low, 0 - very low. That means, if there is a level 1, the safeguards are strong, so the assets are properly protected. At the same time, level 0 means that the assets are practically unsecured. We will denote the safeguard level as SF, and it is a number used for all assets taking part in the specific process. However the analysis could be extended to a version where we identify separate safeguard levels for each asset.

2.9 Step 9 - Risk

Finally, the risk of specific processes can be calculated - $Risk_{P_j}$ (Risk for the process j). The risk is estimated by the following formula.

$$Risk_{P_j} = (1 - SF^2)_{P_j} \cdot att_{P_j}$$

In our model the risk can be a value from 0..1 where 0 means no risk and 1 means that it is highly probable that potential attack will be successful. That is why, we multiply the likelihood by $1 - SF^2$. Results greater or equal 0.5 show a very high risk of a successful attack.

3   The Case Study

In the next section we demonstrate our new method for motivation-based risk analysis. Due to the space limitations we are prepare an analysis of a simple example where each component of our model will be described and final risk of an attack will be calculated.

3.1   Step 1 - Processes

In our example we define a small online store. Let $P_1, P_2, P3$ be our crucial processes in this chosen company. P_1 is registration of a new customer (standard form on the website and then an authentication mail sent to an address given), P_2 is a payment for an order (with finished shopping going to a bank webpage), P_3 is viewing archive orders (list of an user's previous orders with prices and products bought). As a result of this step we have a list of defined processes.

3.2   Step 2 - Assets

According to our model, now we have to present assets. There are many of them in this company, but those that are relevant to our processes are:

- I_1 (databases with personal data, orders, and products data);
- S_1 (web server), S_2 (mail authentication app.), S_3 (api to bank payments);
- H_1 (server), H_2 (router);
- T_1 (air conditioning), T_2 (power).
- R_1 (good reputation);
- HR_1 (administrator).

In process P_1 we have all assets except S_3, in P_2 all assets except S_2, in P_3 all assets except S_2 and S_3. Therefore:

$$A_1 = \{I_1, S_I, S_2, H_1, H_2, T_1, T_2, R_1, HR_1\}$$

$$A_2 = \{I_1, S_I, S_3, H_1, H_2, T_1, T_2, R_1, HR_1\}$$

$$A_3 = \{I_1, S_I, H_1, H_2, T_1, T_2, R_1, HR_1\}$$

3.3   Step 3 - Impact

Having processes and assets, we should define impacts for all of them. As it was presented in section 2.3, below we combine impacts with assets:

$$imp_{I_1} = [0.6, 0.5, 0.4, 0.4, 0.5], imp_{S_1} = [0.3, 0.8, 0.6, 0.5, 0.5],$$

$$imp_{S_2} = [0.1, 0.5, 0.7, 0.7, 0.4], imp_{S_3} = [1, 0.6, 0.5, 0.8, 1],$$

$$imp_{H_1} = [0.6, 0.5, 0.7, 0.4, 0.6], imp_{H_2} = [0.5, 0.5, 0.4, 0.3, 1],$$

$$imp_{T_1} = [0.6, 0.4, 0.75, 0.1, 0.4], imp_{T_2} = [0.6, 0.75, 0.6, 0.3, 0.4],$$

$$imp_{R_1} = [0.75, 1, 0.4, 0.4, 0.4], imp_{HR_1} = [0.5, 0.4, 0.75, 0.5, 0.75].$$

Similarly, impacts for processes are:

$$imp_{P_1} = [0.5, 0.8, 0.9, 0.4, 0.8], imp_{P_2} = [1, 0.7, 0.4, 0.5, 0.9],$$

$$imp_{P_3} = [0.3, 0.6, 0.3, 0.6, 0.5].$$

Next, we calculate vectors of total impacts for the three processes.

$$imp_{P_1, A_1} = [0.44375, 0.8, 0.81, 0.328, 0.8]$$

$$imp_{P_2, A_2} = [1, 0.7, 0.355, 0.44, 0.9]$$

$$imp_{P_3, A_3} = [0.27, 0.6, 0.27, 0.42, 0.5]$$

3.4   Step 4 - Motivation

The following step is to calculate vectors of motivation for each process. We do that by taking the maximum of the products from multiplying elements of mot_{imp} - matrix with $1, 0.75, 0.5, 0.3$ and 0.1 by already calculated elements of the impact vector, for each process imp_{P_i, A_i}.

$$mot_{P_1} = [0.44375, 0.6, 0.6075, 0.6, 0.6, 0.8]$$

$$mot_{P_2} = [1, 0.675, 0.675, 0.75, 0.525, 0.7]$$

$$mot_{P_3} = [0.3, 0.45, 0.375, 0.45, 0.45, 0.6]$$

3.5   Step 5 - Hacker Profile

Now we can multiply motivation vectors by hacker profile matrix (mot_{hac}) and we obtain three vectors that correspond to hacker profiles.

$$mot_{P_1, hac} = [0.7, 0.52, 0.55, 0.49, 0.6, 0.6, 0.44, 0.62, 0.7]$$

$$mot_{P_2, hac} = [0.69, 0.76, 0.82, 0.92, 0.71, 0.68, 1, 0.85, 0.61]$$

$$mot_{P_3, hac} = [0.49, 0.38, 0.40, 0.34, 0.45, 0.41, 0.30, 0.45, 0.52]$$

3.6   Step 6 - Hackers Skills

As we defined before, the skills vector is as follows:

$$skl_{hac} = [0.2, 04, 0.6, 0.4, 0.8, 1, 1, 1, 1],$$

where consecutive values correspond to No, CP, In, PT, VW, OG, PC, IW, PA.

3.7   Step 7 - Likelihood of Attack

Finally we will calculate the likelihood of an attack - multiplying $mot_{P_j,hac}$ by skl_{hac}:

$$att_{P_1} = [0.14, 0.208, 0.33, 0.196, 0.48, 0.6, 0.44, 0.62, 0.7]$$

$$att_{P_2} = [0.138, 0.304, 0.492, 0.368, 0.568, 0.68, 1, 0.85, 0.61]$$

$$att_{P_3} = [0.098, 0.152, 0.24, 0.136, 0.36, 0.41, 0.3, 0.45, 0.52]$$

All values are in range $[0..1]$. However the highest value is for process P_2 - we see that $att_{PC,P_2} = 1$. We may conclude that this process is alluring for Professional Criminals, which does not seem to be astonishing. What is also worth mentioning is that P_3 is safe, only the last value is for medium likelihood, but it is low.

3.8   Step 8 - Safeguards

The safeguards are in our method for all assets, so let our company be in the middle of a scale with $SF = 0.5$. That means there is some security but it could be not sufficient enough.

3.9   Step 9 - Risk

To obtain risk, we now calculate the likelihood of an attack by $1 - SF^2 = 0.75$. It gives us:

$$Risk_{P_1} = [0.105, 0.156, 0.2475, 0.147, 0.36, 0.45, 0.33, 0.465, 0.525]$$

$$Risk_{P_2} = [0.1035, 0.228, 0.369, 0.276, 0.426, 0.51, 0.75, 0.6375, 0.4575]$$

$$Risk_{P_3} = [0.0735, 0.114, 0.18, 0.102, 0.27, 0.3075, 0.225, 0.3375, 0.39]$$

During the analysis of results one can see that the risk vector for the second process has several values greater than 0.5. It means that there is a high probability of a successful attack on this process and a risk reduction method should be applied.

4   Conclusions

The risks analysis for IT systems is one of the major activities in the information security management. In the article we present motivation-based risk analysis which estimates the risk based on the attack motivation as the human factor. The presented approach is less complicated that the standard one which based on the vulnerabilities and threats analysis. Another feature of the presented approach is that the new method for risk analysis is multidimensional. Owing to that, the calculated risks of the a given process will take into account all assets taking part in the analysed process. In the article we present a case study for our methodology where risks of simple processes were calculated. The proposed risk analysis method can be used as part of Quality of Protection models [6,7] which introduce adaptable security [5] for IT Systems.

Acknowledgements. This work is supported by Polish National Science Centre grant 2012/05/B/ST6/03364.

References

1. Barber, R.: Hackers Profiled - Who Are They and What Are Their Motivations? Computer Fraud & Security 2(1), 14–17 (2001)
2. Gao, J., Zhang, B., Chen, X., Luo, Z.: Ontology-Based Model of Network and Computer Attacks for Security Assessment. Journal of Shanghai Jiaotong University 18(5), 554–562 (2013)
3. Gerber, M., Solms, R.: Management of risk in the information age. Computer & Security 14, 16–30 (2005)
4. Grunske, L., Juoyce, D.: Quantitative risk-based security prediction for component-based systems with explicit modeled attack profiles. Journal of Systems and Software 81(8), 1327–1345 (2008)
5. Ksiezopolski, B., Kotulski, Z.: Adaptable security mechanism for the dynamic environments. Computers & Security 26, 246–255 (2007)
6. Ksiezopolski, B.: QoP-ML: Quality of Protection modelling language for cryptographic protocols. Computers & Security 31(4), 569–596 (2012)
7. Ksiezopolski, B., Rusinek, D., Wierzbicki, A.: On the efficiency modelling of cryptographic protocols by means of the Quality of Protection Modelling Language (QoP-ML). In: Mustofa, K., Neuhold, E.J., Tjoa, A.M., Weippl, E., You, I. (eds.) ICT-EurAsia 2013. LNCS, vol. 7804, pp. 261–270. Springer, Heidelberg (2013)
8. Rogers, M.K.: A two-dimensional circumplex approach to the development of a hacker taxonomy. Digital Investigation 3(2), 97–102 (2006)
9. Rogers, M.K., Seigfried, K., Tidke, K.: Self-reported computer criminal behavior: A psychological analysis. Digital Investigation 3, 116–120 (2006)
10. Othmane, L., Weffers, H., Klabbers, M.: Using Attacker Capabilities and Motivations in Estimating Security Risk. In: SOUPS (2013)
11. NIST SP 800-30: Risk Management Guide for IT Systems (2008)
12. Sheyner, O., Haines, J., Jha, S., Lippman, R., Wing, J.M.: Automated generation and analysis of attack graphs. S&Pi (2002)
13. Vavoulas, N., Xenakis, C.: A Quantitative Risk Analysis Approach for Deliberate Threats. In: Xenakis, C., Wolthusen, S. (eds.) CRITIS 2010. LNCS, vol. 6712, pp. 13–25. Springer, Heidelberg (2011)

Formalizing Information Flow Control in a Model-Driven Approach[*]

Kurt Stenzel, Kuzman Katkalov, Marian Borek, and Wolfgang Reif

Institute for Software & Systems Engineering,
Augsburg University, Germany

Abstract. Information flow control is a promising formal technique to guarantee the privacy and desired release of our data in an always connected world. However, it is not easy to apply in practice. IFlow is a model-driven approach that supports the development of distributed systems with information flow control. A system is modeled with UML and automatically transformed into a formal specification as well as Java code. This paper shows how the this specification is generated and presents several advantages of a model-driven approach for information flow control.

1 Introduction

Smartphones are useful digital assistants that simplify our life. However, they store larger and larger amounts of private data. This data can and should be accessed by apps, but we would like to have control over the when and how, and what happens with the data afterwards. Information flow control (IFC) is an area of research to achieve this. IFC (e.g., [3,7,6]) is stronger than access control, and can be applied to a large number of systems and applications. However, it is not easy to use in practice because the theory is quite intricate, and it is easy to lose track of what information is released. IFlow is a model-driven approach designed specifically for IFC. The overall approach is fully implemented and explained in [4]. This paper briefly introduces an example (Sect. 2), and then describes the advantages of the model-driven approach for the formal specification: formal proofs become easier, and specification errors are avoided (Sect. 3). Sect. 4 concludes.

2 An Example Application

The *travel planner app* is a typical distributed application consisting of a smartphone app and web services. The user enters his travel details into the app. The app connects to a travel agency web service which in turn contacts an airline web service for suitable flights. The found flights are returned via the travel agency

---

[*] This work is part of the IFlow project and sponsored by the Priority Programme 1496 "Reliably Secure Software Systems - RS³" of the Deutsche Forschungsgemeinschaft.

Linawati et al. (Eds.): ICT-EurAsia 2014, LNCS 8407, pp. 456–461, 2014.

to the app. The user selects a flight and books it with his credit card (which is stored in a *credit card center* app) directly at the airline. Finally the airline pays a commission to the travel agency. Fig. 1 shows this behavior as a sequence diagram.

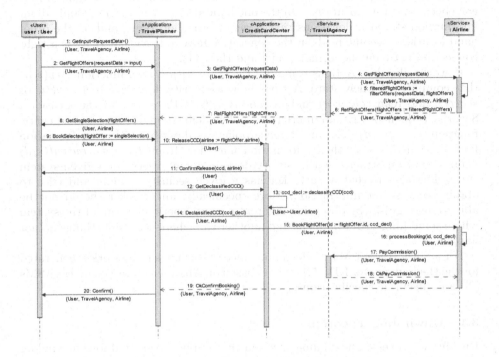

Fig. 1. Sequence diagram for the travel planner app

The lifelines represent the (real human) users, the apps, and the web services. Arrows denote message passing as in UML, but a domain-specific language is used that supports, e.g., assignments to provide more information. Additionally, every message is annotated with a security domain in curly brackets, e.g. {User TravelAgency, Airline}. They are used in the formal information flow framework.

Together with a class diagram (not shown), and a security policy (Fig. 2) the sequence diagram contains enough information and is precise enough to generate a formal specification as well as Java code.[1] Two information flow properties are of interest:

1. The user's credit card data does not flow to the travel agency.
2. The credit card data flows to the airline only after explicit confirmation and declassification.

---

[1] See our web page
   `http://www.informatik.uni-augsburg.de/lehrstuehle/swt/se/projects/iflow/`
   for the full model.

3   The Formal Model

As the formal framework we chose Rushby's intransitive noninterference [7] which is an extension of Goguen's and Meseguer's transitive noninterference [3], and specifically Rushby's *access control* instance of intransitive noninterference because it uses locations. On the one hand it is very natural to think about information stored in locations that flows to other locations, and on the other hand locations become fields in the generated Java code so that there is a tight connection between the formal model and the code.

It works like this: Actions a modify the state with a *step* function $step(s, a)$ that computes the new state. Actions have a security domain d (e.g., *public* or *secret*), and read (*observe*) and/or modify (*alter*) the values of the locations. Security is defined w.r.t. an interference policy defined on domains and a generic function $output(s, d)$. The interference policy $\rightsquigarrow$ describes allowed information flows, i.e., if $d_1 \rightsquigarrow d_2$ then information may flow from d_1 to d_2. $output(s, d)$ defines what an attacker with security domain d can observe in a given system state. The idea is that an attacker has a given security domain and tries to obtain some secret information. More specifically, an attacker should not be able to distinguish (by observing different outputs) between a run of the system where something secret happens and another run where the secret things do not happen.

For a given IFlow UML model an instance of Rushby's framework is generated for the theorem prover KIV [5,1] that is based on Abstract State Machines (ASMs [2]) and algebraic specifications.

3.1   Unwinding Theorem

Rushby [7] proves an unwinding theorem that implies security if four unwinding conditions hold. The second condition was later weakened by van der Meyden [8] (we show van der Meyden's version):

- RM1: $s_1 \approx_d s_2 \rightarrow output(s_1, d) = output(s_2, d)$
  If two states look alike to an attacker with domain d ($\approx_d$) then the attacker's output is the same in both states.
- RM2: $s_1 \approx_{dom(a)} s_2 \wedge s_1(l) = s_2(l) \wedge l \in alter(dom(a))$
     $\rightarrow step(s_1, a)(l) = step(s_2, a)(l)$
  If two states look alike to the security domain of an action a and this action is executed (with the *step* function) then every location that is altered by the domain and has the same value in the initial states has the same value in the two new states. (See [8] for a discussion.)
- RM3: $step(s, a)(l) \neq s(l) \rightarrow l \in alter(dom(a))$
  If the execution of an action modifies a location then this location is contained in the *alter* set for the action's domain.
- AOI: $alter(d_1) \cap observe(d_2) \neq \emptyset \rightarrow d_1 \rightsquigarrow d_2$
  Alter/observe respects interference: if a location is altered by one domain d_1 and observed by another domain d_2 then there is an information flow from d_1 to d_2. This must be allowed by the interference policy $\rightsquigarrow$.

Condition RM3 basically ensures that the definition of *alter* is correct: If an action *a* modifies a location *l* then *l* must be contained in the action's domain *alter* set. Similarly, RM2 ensures that the definition of *observe* is correct. RM2 and RM3 use the *step* function, i.e., here every action of the system must be executed (once in the case of RM3 and twice in RM2). Hence, they are the really expensive proof obligations for larger systems. On the other hand they only depend on *alter* and *observe* (since $\approx$ is defined with *observe*), but not on *output* or the interference policy $\rightsquigarrow$.

In IFlow the generation of the formal model from the UML guarantees that

- RM1 is always true because of the fixed definition of *output*.
- RM2 is always true because *observe* is computed correctly from the UML model.
- RM3 is always true because *alter* is computed correctly from the UML model.

Therefore, proving AOI

$$\text{AOI: } alter(d_1) \cap observe(d_2) \neq \emptyset \rightarrow d_1 \rightsquigarrow d_2$$

(which is trivial) already implies that a system is secure. This shows a great benefit of IFlow's model driven approach that cannot be achieved otherwise.

3.2 Automatic Declassification

Intransitive noninterference allows to model secure systems with controlled or partial information release. However, if used excessively or in an arbitrary manner the result may be a system that is secure in terms of the formal definition, but has cryptic or undesired information flows.

Again, the model-driven approach can be helpful because usage of intransitive domains can be controlled. This will be explained with the help of the travel planner example. In general the interference relation may be an arbitrary relation. In IFlow some restrictions apply. Fig. 2 shows the security policy for the example. An edge denotes a (direct) interference, i.e., {User, TravelAgency, Airline} $\rightsquigarrow$ {User, Airline}. The unmarked edges are transitive (i.e., {User, TravelAgency, Airline} also interferes {User}), and the relation is automatically reflexive. Intransitive edges may only be used for declassification (also called downgrading) as shown Fig. 2: Both edges to and from a declassification domain must be intransitive and inverse to the "standard" policy, and a declassification domain must have exactly one incoming and one outgoing edge. In effect, we have a usual transitive policy with possibly some declassification domains.

When a declassification domain is used (message 13) it must be contained in its own action to avoid undesired interferences. A program counter is introduced automatically to ensure that actions/messages 12, 13, and 14 are executed in the correct order. There is another complication. Generating the formal model results in an insecure system, i.e., the only remaining unwinding condition AOI does not hold. The problem are messages 15–17 in Fig. 1: The airline receives a booking message with the credit card details (message 15) that is labeled {User, Airline}, and processes the booking (message 16) at the same security level. However, in message 17 the airline pays a commission to the travel agency that is labeled {User, TravelAgency, Airline}. If messages 15–17 are contained in one action with domain {User, Airline} the action writes to domain {User, TravelAgency, Airline} (the mailbox containing the PayCommission message) which is an illegal information flow.

However, our desired property (*Credit card details never flow to the travel agency*) holds because the PayCommission message does not include the credit card details. The travel agency (or, to be more precise the {User, TravelAgency, Airline} domain) does learn that a booking took place (otherwise it would not receive a commission) but not the parameters of the booking message. This may or may not be seen as a problem, but is independent from the desired property. So we want to modify the formal system so that it is secure, but would still detect that the credit card data flows to the travel agency in a faulty model.

The solution is to introduce a new declassification domain from {User, Airline} to {User, TravelAgency, Airline} that leaks only the information that a booking took place but nothing more. Fig. 2 shows how this works.

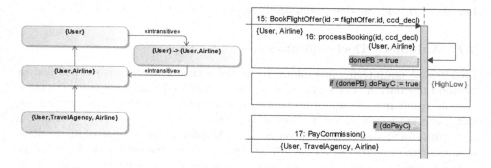

Fig. 2. Security policy and new actions

The original action is split into three actions, one that receives the booking and processes the booking (messages 15 and 16), but then sets a boolean flag to true (donePB) to indicate that it is finished. Then the declassification domain {HighLow} sets the flag doPayC to true to indicate that PayCommission can happen. The third action checks the flag and pays the commission. Both flags are reset after they are read (not shown in Fig. 2).

The action leaks only the information that donePB was true. This modified system is secure, i.e., the unwinding condition AOI holds. On the other hand, an illegal information flow will still be detected. Assume that the PayCommission message includes the credit card details as parameter (PayCommission(ccd_decl)). Then the third action in Fig. 2 observes ccd_decl (which must be a local variable), and the first action alters it (because it writes the credit card details to ccd_decl). In effect {User, TravelAgency, Airline} interferes {User, Airline} directly which is forbidden by the policy. And the {HighLow} domain obviously does not leak the credit card details either. So we have exactly the desired effect.

The main point is that all this (adding a new declassification domain and splitting the original action into three) is done automatically during generation of the formal model. This guarantees that the {HighLow} domain is not used anywhere else (by generating a new unique name) and that the new action only accesses the two flags, and nothing else. A user specifying this by hand could easily make mistakes. This again shows the benefits of a model-driven approach.

4 Conclusion

Information flow control is a promising technique, but difficult to use in practice. IFlow is a model-driven approach that supports the development of distributed applications with guaranteed and intuitive information flow properties. The resulting UML specification is automatically transformed into a formal model based on intransitive noninterference where IF properties can be proved, and into Java code with the same IF properties. To the best of our knowledge IFlow is the only work that uses a model-driven approach for IFC (a broader comparison with related work must be omitted due to lack of space). We showed that the model-driven approach has additional benefits for IFC: proofs become simpler because functions like *observe* and *alter* can be computed, and specification errors can be avoided by the automatic introduction of declassifications with guaranteed properties.

References

1. Balser, M., Reif, W., Schellhorn, G., Stenzel, K., Thums, A.: Formal system development with KIV. In: Maibaum, T. (ed.) FASE 2000. LNCS, vol. 1783, pp. 363–366. Springer, Heidelberg (2000)
2. Börger, E., Stärk, R.F.: Abstract State Machines—A Method for High-Level System Design and Analysis. Springer (2003)
3. Goguen, J.A., Meseguer, J.: Security Policy and Security Models. In: Symposium on Security and Privacy. IEEE (1982)
4. Katkalov, K., Stenzel, K., Borek, M., Reif, W.: Model-driven development of information flow-secure systems with IFlow. In: Proceedings of 5th ASE/IEEE International Conference on Information Privacy, Security, Risk and Trust (PASSAT). IEEE Press (2013)
5. KIV homepage, http://www.informatik.uni-augsburg.de/swt/kiv
6. Mantel, H.: Possibilistic definitions of security - an assembly kit. In: IEEE Computer Security Foundations Workshop. IEEE Press (2000)
7. Rushby, J.: Noninterference, Transitivity, and Channel-Control Security Policies. Technical Report CSL-92-02, SRI International (1992)
8. van der Meyden, R.: What, indeed, is intransitive noninterference? In: Biskup, J., López, J. (eds.) ESORICS 2007. LNCS, vol. 4734, pp. 235–250. Springer, Heidelberg (2007)

Security Assessment of Computer Networks Based on Attack Graphs and Security Events

Igor Kotenko and Elena Doynikova

Laboratory of Computer Security Problems
St. Petersburg Institute for Informatics and Automation (SPIIRAS)
39, 14 Liniya, St. Petersburg, Russia
{ivkote,doynikova}@comsec.spb.ru

Abstract. Security assessment is an important task for operation of modern computer networks. The paper suggests the security assessment technique based on attack graphs which can be implemented in contemporary SIEM systems. It is based on the security metrics taxonomy and different techniques for calculation of security metrics according to the data about current events. Proposed metrics form the basis for security awareness and reflect current security situation, including development of attacks, attacks sources and targets, attackers' characteristics. The technique suggested is demonstrated on a case study.

Keywords: cyber situational awareness, security metrics, security metrics taxonomy, attack graphs, SIEM-systems.

1 Introduction

Analysis and enhancement of the information security of the computer networks and systems is widely researched area. One of the essential aspects in this area is security evaluation that includes calculation of different security metrics. Calculation of security metrics is most relevant when it is solved in real-time (or near real-time) mode, which is specific to Security Information and Event Management (SIEM) systems [13]. Obviously these metrics should be clear and valuable for security decisions.

Currently there is a lot of investigations that consider different security assessment techniques and security metrics [1-6, etc.]. In the paper we aim to develop an approach intended for near real-time security metrics calculation. This approach should allow taking into account new security information and events that appear in the network operation process and fulfilling appropriate recalculation of security metrics. For this goal we developed the metrics taxonomy that considers the following aspects: recent research in the security metrics area; modeling of attacker steps as attack graphs; goals and characteristics of SIEM systems. For calculation of security metrics we use known and adopted techniques. On the base of these metrics, we determine current security situation, including existence of attacks, attacker skills and position, possible previous and future attacker steps and attack target. The main contribution of the paper is the developed metrics taxonomy and its application for security

Linawati et al. (Eds.): ICT-EurAsia 2014, LNCS 8407, pp. 462–471, 2014.

assessment of computer networks based on attack graphs. The key feature of the technique suggested is taking into account current security information and events.

The paper is organized as follows. *Section 2* outlines main related works. *Section 3* describes the common idea of the assessment technique and its stages. *Section 4* presents case study and experiments for evaluating the security assessment technique. Conclusion analyzes the paper results and provides insight into the future research.

2   Related Work

Currently there is a multitude of security metrics taxonomies. We analyzed some of them and concluded that these taxonomies are defined according to the goals of the security assessment. For example, in [9] three categories are outlined: technical, operational and organizational. In [22] two categories are considered: organizational and technical. Taxonomy suggested by NIST [21] includes three categories: management, technical and organizational, and 17 sub-categories. In [20] the information assurance metrics taxonomy is defined. It includes three categories (security, quality of service, availability) and technical, organizational and operational metrics.

From another hand, there are classifications of security metrics according to the way of their measurement and computation. In [6] the metrics are divided on primary and secondary. In [11] metrics are classified on the metrics that are calculated for the attack graph (used to define, for example, attacker skill level, attack potentiality) and for the service dependencies graph (implemented to determine, for instance, attack/response impact or response benefit). The Center for Internet Security divides metrics according to six business functions [4]: incident management, vulnerability management, patch management, application security, configuration management, and financial metrics. In [2] eight categories of metrics are differentiated according to the value type: existence (indicator of whether something exists); ordinal (subjective qualitative measure); score (numeric values for qualitative measure); cardinal (number); percentage; holistic (based on external data sources); value (consider value loss); uncertainty (include stochastic or probabilistic aspect).

Nevertheless, we have not found an appropriate taxonomy of metrics based on attack graphs applicable for security assessment in SIEM systems. Thus, we aimed to develop the appropriate taxonomy taking into account the next aspects: contemporary research in the security metrics area [9, 10, 16, etc.]; characteristics of the architecture of the security analysis component in the scope of the SIEM system (modeling of the attack sequences on the base of attack graphs [8, 12, 17, 19] and service dependencies [10, 11]); different stages of security analysis (static and dynamic). We outlined the following categories: topological, attack, attacker, integral (system).

Topological characteristics can be defined from the network topology and the description of hosts [4, 15]. They involve host parameters [15], application characteristics [4], features about service dependencies [10, 11], characteristics that consider information about the vulnerabilities and possible attacks [4]. Attack characteristics (such as attack potentiality/probability) are defined on the base of attack graphs [10]. Attacker parameters are related to possible attackers and are considered in [3, 5, 10, 18]. Integral (system) characteristics involve features that define common security estimations [5, 7, 13, 14]. From another hand, important aspects in our classification are cost-benefit analysis and analysis of zero-day attacks. Cost-benefit analysis is usually used for decision support and involves cost metrics that define costs of impacts and responses [8, 11]. For zero day attacks analysis, the metrics reflecting possible zero day attacks are used [1].

3   Security Assessment Technique

The component that implements the suggested security assessment technique is the part of the security evaluation system based on attack graphs [12]. The architecture of the component is presented in Fig. 1.

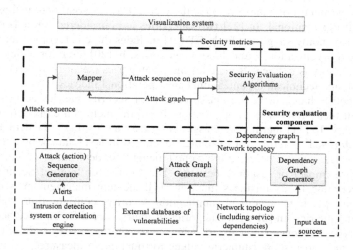

Fig. 1. Architecture of the security evaluation component

The core of the component is the set of security evaluation algorithms for calculation of metrics. Other important subcomponent - Mapper - allows detecting attacker position on the base of security events and attack graph structure. Security evaluation component gets input data from different sources including: attack graph generator that builds attack graphs for the analyzed network; dependency graph generator that provides graph of the dependencies between the network services; and attack sequences generator that generates steps of the current attack on the base of the security alerts. Output data includes different security metrics according to the suggested taxonomy. Further output data is provided to the visualization system.

To describe the security assessment technique the following *input details* are used: (1) Test network with host characteristics and values of the topological metrics: *Business Value, Criticality* (including propagated criticality via service dependencies), etc.; (2) Attack graph that contains system vulnerabilities as vertexes and transitions between the vulnerabilities as arcs (these paths constitute threats). Possibility of transition from one vulnerability to another is defined by pre- and post-conditions of the vulnerabilities exploitation according CVSS [16]; (3) Calculated unconditional probabilities for each node (in consideration that the attacker can implement all attack actions). Unconditional probabilities are defined on the base of the local conditional distributions for each node S_i, $i \epsilon [1, n]$: $Pr(S_1, ..., S_n) = \prod_{i=1}^{n} Pr(S_i | Pa[S_i])$, where $Pa[S_i]$ - set of all parents of S_i. Conditional probabilities of the transitions between nodes are defined on the base of CVSS access complexity of the vulnerability; (4) Calculated risk values for each critical host for attack graph level (considering attack probability and possible impact); (5) Security events that include information about the attacked host, privileges and/or impact on the host.

The *security assessment technique* includes the following stages:

1. Definition of the attacker position on the attack graph on the base of the information from the security event. It can be done on the base of the next steps: Define the list of the vulnerabilities for the host which is described in the security event; Select the vulnerabilities that lead to the privileges and\or impact described in the event; If only one vulnerability was selected, the next steps of the technique should be performed for the node that corresponds to the exploitation of this vulnerability; If multiple vulnerabilities were selected, the next steps of the technique should be performed for all possible nodes; If a vulnerability was not selected, then the event is defined as exploitation of the zero-day.

2. Determination of the attacker skill level on the base of information from the security event. The next steps should be performed for all nodes selected on the previous stage: Define the most probable path of the attacker to the current node (on the base of the Bayes theorem); In case of multiple paths with the same probabilities, consider them all in further calculations; Select vulnerabilities with the maximum CVSS access complexity [16] for this path; Define the attacker skill level according to the access complexity as "High"/"Medium"/"Low". Quantitative values are defined: 0.7 - "High", 0.5 - "Medium", 0.3 - "Low" *Attacker Skill Level*; Define the probability of skills as *(number of nodes with vulnerability with this access complexity)/(total number of steps in the path)*.

3. Calculation of the probabilities of the paths that go through the node that corresponds to the attacker position. On this step the next features should be considered: defined attacker skill level and that the probability of the compromise of this node is equal to 1.

4. Definition of the risks for the attack paths that go through the compromised node (based on the target asset criticality, attack impact and attack path probability).

5. Selection of the path with maximum value of risk. This path is selected as the most probable attack path and its end point should be selected as attacker goal.

As the result of the technique, we get the next output data: attacker skill level, attack path and attackers goal. Further this information is used for the decision support.

4   Case Study

4.1   Input Data Gathering

Let us consider the following input data used for the security assessment: topology of the test network (Fig. 2), values of the topological metrics, especially *Criticality* of the hosts (calculated on the previous assessment stage), attack graph, security events.

Host-1 and Host-2 are web-servers with critical web applications. External users of the local network are directed to the web-applications through Router-1 and Firewall-1 to Host-1 or Host-2. Authentication is needed to work with these applications. Authentication data is stored on the Authentication server. Critical data that the user get or add when working with applications is stored on Database server. Requests from Host-1 and Host-2 are handled by Web-server first. Internal users have access to Web-server via Router-2 and Firewall-3. The parameters of the hosts for the test network are as follows: (a) *External users* - Microsoft Windows 7 64-bit, Apple ITunes 9.0.3, Microsoft Office 2007 SP1, Microsoft Internet Explorer 7; (b) *Web-server* - Windows Ftp Server 2.3.0, Windows Server 2008 for 32-bit Systems; (c) *Database server* - Apache Software Foundation Derby 10.1.3.1, phpMYAdmin 3.5.2.2, Oracle MySQL 5.5.25, Linux Kernel 2.6.27.33; (d) *Host-1 and Host-2* - Red Hat JBoss Community Application Server 5.0.1, Windows Server 2008 R2 for x64-based Systems; (e) *Firewall-1, Firewall-3* - Linux Kernel 2.6.27.33, Citrix ICA Client; (f) *Firewall-2* - Novell SUSE Linux Enterprise Server 11 Service Pack 1 (with Netfilter),; (g) *Authentication server* - Novell SUSE Linux Enterprise Server 11 Service Pack 1, Novell eDirectory 8.8.1; *Internal users* - Apple Mac OS X Server 10.6.1, Apple iTunes 9.0.2 for Mac OS X, Microsoft Office 2008 Mac.

Fig. 2 depicts the values of the host *Criticality*. It is calculated on the base of the *Business Value* of the hosts for the system and the dependencies between the network services. *Criticality* is a vector that includes three scores <*Criticality of Confidentiality, Criticality of Integrity, Criticality of Availability*>.

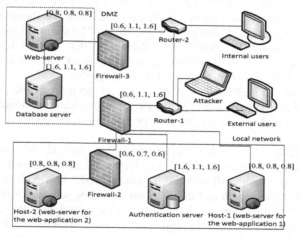

Fig. 2. Topology of the test network and *Criticality* values

The example of the user interface for the security evaluation system, which outlines the metrics values, is shown in Fig. 3 [12]. Common attack graph for the considered test case is presented in Fig. 4. Nodes of the attack graphs are defined as triple <Exploited vulnerability, Pre-conditions, Post-conditions>. Pre-conditions include privileges that are needed to exploit the vulnerability, Post-conditions are acquired privileges and impact. For each node of the attack graph the appropriate vulnerabilities (according to the NVD database) are represented. Color of the node is defined with vulnerability BaseScore according to the CVSS [16] (yellow color - for the Medium score, red color - for the High score). For each node the probabilities that attacker can reach the node are calculated.

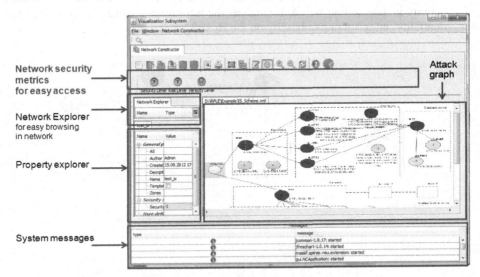

Fig. 3. Example of the user interface

For example, conditional probability on the node 1 in case of successful initialization of attack is equal to 0,61 (the access complexity of the CVE-2010-2990 is 0,61). Conditional probability on the node 6 in case of the success on the node 1 is equal to 0,71 (the access complexity of the CVE-2008-1436 is 0,71). Unconditional probability for the node 6 is defined as product of probabilities of successful states: $1 \cdot 0,61 \cdot 0,71 = 0,4331$.

As was defined above the description of the security event should include information about the attacked host and acquired privileges and/or impact.

To illustrate the experiments in the paper, two types of attackers were defined:

1. *Attacker with "Medium" attacker skill level.* He (she) has external access and some information on the network topology. This attacker can use exploits of known vulnerabilities with "Medium" access complexity. His (her) goal is to get data from the database. The sequence of such actions is represented with yellow color. We define the following events for this case as example: **event1** – malicious activity is detected on step 1, it contains the information on illegitimate admin access on the Firewall-3; **event2** – malicious activity on step 2, it contains the information on illegitimate admin access on the Web-server.

2. *Attacker with "High" attacker skill level.* He (she) has external access and no information about network topology. This attacker can exploit a zero-day vulnerability. His (her) goal is to compromise web-application on Host-2. The sequence of such actions is outlined with red color. We define the following events for this

case as example: **event1** - malicious activity is detected on step 1, it contains the information about illegitimate admin access on the Firewall-1; **event2** - malicious activity on step 2, it contains the information about illegitimate admin access on the Firewall-2; **event3** - malicious activity is detected on step 3, it contains the information about illegitimate admin access on the Host-2; **event4** - malicious activity is detected on step 4, it contains the information about violation of confidentiality, integrity or availability on the Host-2.

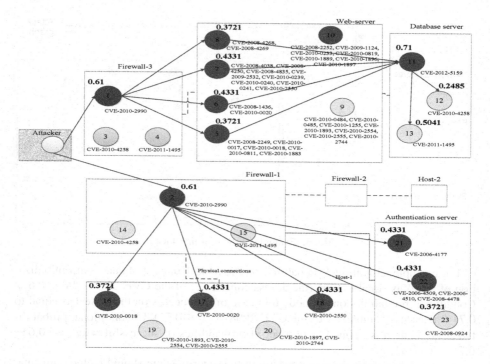

Fig. 4. Attack graph with calculated probabilities

4.2   Security Assessment Implementation

Let us go through the steps of the technique suggested for the described test case:

1. Definition of the node of the graph which corresponds to the attacker position. For example, for the first scenario to detect the attacked node after event1 we determine all vulnerabilities on the Firewall-3 defined in the event and then select vulnerabilities that provide privileges/impact described in the event. For the first scenario it is still node '1'.
2. Calculation of the attacker skill level on the base of the security event. For the nodes defined on the previous stage, the previous attacker steps are defined, i.e. the attack sequence on the attack graph with the maximum probability value. For the first scenario after event1 there is only one possible previous node – external

network, and only one exploited vulnerability – 1. On the base of the performed steps the attacker skill level is a maximum access complexity of them.

3. Determination of the probabilities of the attack sequences that go through the node with attacker and definition of the attacker goal. For the first scenario, according to event1, new probabilities are calculated: the probabilities on the nodes 5-8 are decreased, as from the one hand they were influenced by the new knowledge about the attacker position, but from another - by new knowledge about attacker skills. Also probabilities of the attacks on the nodes 2, 16-81, 21-23 are decreased, because of the new knowledge about attacker skills. Thus, after the first security event we can suppose that attack goal is Database Server, but additional information is needed. Fig. 5 depicts appropriate probabilities after each defined security event for the first scenario. Fig. 6 outlines the same calculations made for the second scenario.

4. Definition of the risks of the attack sequences. On this step the *Criticality* values are considered. Cumulative risk values for the graph nodes are represented in Fig. 6 (with new events the risk on the attacker goal node increases).

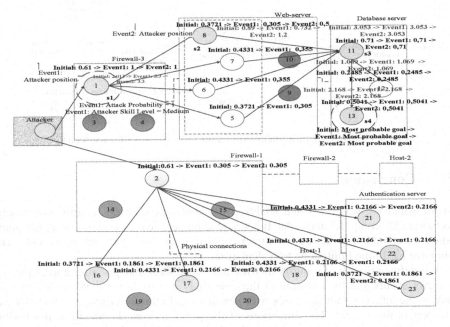

Fig. 5. Changes of attack probabilities after security events for the scenario 1

Output of the security assessment technique contains the following data: attack path with maximum risk value that defines the most probable attack sequence and attackers goal; the most probable previous attacker steps; attacker skills. These results allow making decision about the most efficient countermeasures. These experiments demonstrate the main possibilities of the suggested security evaluation system on security metrics calculation.

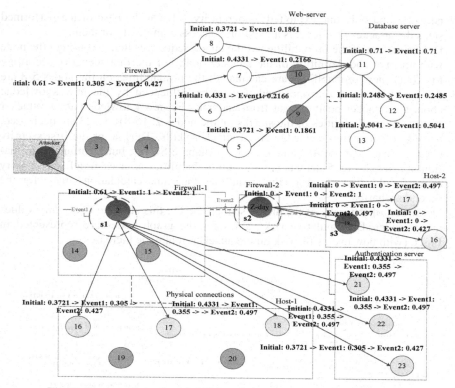

Fig. 6. Changes of attack probabilities after security events for the scenario 2

5   Conclusion

In the paper we suggested and analyzed the application of the security assessment technique for computer networks. It is oriented on near real time situation assessment, when we can monitor the current attacker position and his (her) path in the network, but have hard time limitations for calculations.

We defined the set of security metrics and traced their changes after appearance of security events. On the example of the case study it was shown that probability and risk of the attacker path increases with new data and allows defining the track of the attacker in the system. The limitations of the paper volume do not allow discussing proposed system of security metrics and techniques of their calculation in details.

The future research will be devoted to further specification of the technique and extension of the experiments.

Acknowledgements. This research is being supported by grants of the Russian Foundation of Basic Research (13-01-00843, 13-07-13159, 14-07-00697, 14-07-00417) and the Program of fundamental research of the Department for Nanotechnologies and Informational Technologies of the Russian Academy of Sciences (contract #2.2).

References

1. Ahmed, M.S., Al-Shaer, E., Khan, L.: A Novel Quantitative Approach for Measuring Network Security. In: INFOCOM 2008, pp. 1957–1965 (2008)
2. Axelrod, C.W.: Accounting for Value and Uncertainty in Security Metrics. Information Systems Control Journal 6, 1–6 (2008)
3. Blakely, B.A.: Cyberprints Identifying Cyber Attackers by Feature Analysis. Doctoral Dissertation: Iowa State University (2012)
4. The Center for Internet Security, The CIS Security Metrics (2009)
5. Dantu, R., Kolan, P., Cangussu, J.: Network Risk Management Using Attacker Profiling. Security and Communication Networks 2(1), 83–96 (2009)
6. Idika, N.C.: Characterizing and Aggregating Attack Graph-Based Security Metric. PhD Thesis, Purdue University, pp. 1–131 (2010)
7. ISO/IEC 27005: 2008, Information technology — Security techniques — Information security risk management (2008)
8. Jahnke, M., Thul, C., Martini, P.: Graph-based Metrics for Intrusion Response Measures in Computer Networks. In: IEEE Workshop on Network Security (2007)
9. Henning, R., et al.: Workshop on Information Security System, Scoring and Ranking ("Security Metrics"), MITRE, Williamsburg, Virginia (2002)
10. Kanoun, W., Cuppens-Boulahia, N., Cuppens, F., Araujo, J.: Automated Reaction Based on Risk Analysis and Attackers Skills in Intrusion Detection Systems. In: CRiSIS 2008, Toezer, Tunisia, pp. 117–124 (2008)
11. Kheir, N., Cuppens-Boulahia, N., Cuppens, F., Debar, H.: A Service Dependency Model for Cost-Sensitive Intrusion Response. In: Gritzalis, D., Preneel, B., Theoharidou, M. (eds.) ESORICS 2010. LNCS, vol. 6345, pp. 626–642. Springer, Heidelberg (2010)
12. Kotenko, I., Chechulin, A.: A Cyber Attack Modeling and Impact Assessment Framework. In: CyCon 2013, pp. 119–142. IEEE and NATO COE Publications (2013)
13. Kotenko, I., Saenko, I., Polubelova, O., Doynikova, E.: The Ontology of Metrics for Security Evaluation and Decision Support in SIEM Systems. In: RaSIEM 2013 (2013)
14. Manadhata, P.K., Wing, J.M.: An Attack Surface Metric. IEEE Transactions on Software Engineering, 371–386 (2010)
15. Mayer, A.: Operational Security Risk Metrics: Definitions, Calculations, Visualizations. Metricon 2.0. CTO RedSeal Systems (2007)
16. Mell, P., Scarfone, K., Romanosky, S.: A Complete Guide to the Common Vulnerability Scoring System Version 2.0 (2007)
17. Moore, A.P., Ellison, R.J., Linger, R.C.: Attack Modeling for Information Security and Survivability. Technical Note CMU/SEI-2001-TN-001. Survivable Systems (2001)
18. NMap reference guide, http://nmap.org/book/man.html
19. Poolsappasit, N., Dewri, R., Ray, I.: Dynamic Security Risk Management Using Bayesian Attack Graphs. IEEE Transactions on Dependable and Security Computing 9(1), 61–74 (2012)
20. Seddigh, N., Pieda, P., Matrawy, A., Nandy, B., Lambadaris, I., Hatfield, A.: Current Trends and Advances in Information Assurance Metrics. In: Proc. of the 2nd Annual Conference on Privacy, Security and Trust (PST 2004), Fredericton, NB (October 2004)
21. Swanson, M., Bartol, N., Sabato, J., Hash, J., Graffo, L.: Security Metrics Guide for Information Technology Systems. NIST Special Publication 800-55 (July 2003)
22. Vaughn, R., Henning, R., Siraj, A.: Information Assurance Measures and Metrics: State of Practice and Proposed Taxonomy. In: Proc. of 36th Hawaii Int. Conf. on System Sciences, HICSS 2003 (2003)

A Pipeline Optimization Model for QKD Post-processing System

Jianyi Zhou, Bo Liu, Baokang Zhao[*], and Bo Liu

School of Computer
National University of Defense Technology
Changsha, Hunan, China
zjy1024kb@gmail.com, {boliu,bkzhao}@nudt.edu.cn,
liuboyayu@163.com

Abstract. Quantum key distribution (QKD) technology can create unconditional security keys between communication parties, but its key generation rate can't satisfy high-speed network applications. As an essential part of QKD system, the design of post-processing system has a huge influence on its key generation rate. For the challenges of real-time and high-speed processing requirements, we propose a pipeline optimization model for QKD post-processing system. With the variable granularity division policies in our model, a high-speed pipeline QKD post-processing system can be designed with the constraints of limited computing and storage resources and security requirements. Simulation results show that for GHz BB84 protocol based QKD system, the security key generation rate of our post-processing system can reach to 600kbps with 25km distance. We believe that our work can provide useful guidance for the design of future QKD system.

Keywords: QKD, Post-processing, pipeline, performance optimization.

1 Introduction

Quantum key distribution [1] technology is currently the most feasible practical application of quantum information. Based on the laws of physics rather than computational complexity of mathematical problems, quantum key distribution can create information-theoretical security (ITS) keys between communication parties. The keys generated by QKD systems can be used for cryptographic applications with one-time-pad [2], AES or other security protection schemes.

QKD system involves two phases, quantum communication phase and classical post-processing phase. Due to its high complexity, the design and implementation of post-processing has a huge influence on the speed of security key generation. For high-speed QKD systems, most works utilize hardware for real-time post-processing [3-8]. However, hardware based methodology suffers from long design cycle, high complexity in realization and troublesome debugging. Therefore some researchers turn to

---

[*] Corresponding author.

Linawati et al. (Eds.): ICT-EurAsia 2014, LNCS 8407, pp. 472–481, 2014.

software based post-processing [9], in which the main challenge is how to design the software architecture to speed-up the processing procedures. Currently parallel computing technologies such as pipeline and multithreading have been adopted to improve processing efficiency [10-11].

As a consequence, how to divide the pipeline and design efficient multithread post-processing system has become a hotspot of research. In this paper, we propose a pipeline partition optimization model. To test the performance of our model, a multi-core parallel computing system was built on the basis of our previous works in literature [12-15]. Experimental results show that our pipeline design can reach a speed over 600kbps for BB84 protocol based GHz QKD system, which may prove useful for the future design and optimization of QKD post-processing system.

The rest of the paper is organized as follows. Section 2 provides the background of quantum key distribution and pipeline. Our pipeline optimization model for QKD post-processing system is in section 3. The experimental results and analysis are presented in section 4 while section 5 concludes the paper.

2   Preliminaries

2.1   Quantum Key Distribution

QKD protocols can be divided into preparation-measurement protocol and entanglements based protocol. The most mature in research and feasible protocol is BB84, which consists quantum communication phase and classical post-processing phase.

Security key rate is the most important performance indictor of QKD system. Secure rate R (bits/pulse) which is defined as the possibility that the security key drawing from the photon pulse sent by Alice, as expressed in equation (1).

$$R = I(A:B) - I(B:E) \tag{1}$$

$I(A:B)$ is the mutual information between Alice and Bob while $I(B:E)$ is the mutual information between eavesdropper and Bob. $I(A:B)$ can be further expressed as equation (2), in which q is determined by specific QKD protocol, Q_μ is the photon counting rate, E_μ is quantum bit error rate and $H_2(E_\mu)$ is Shannon entropy.

$$I(A:B) = qQ_\mu[1 - H_2(E_\mu)] \tag{2}$$

$I(B:E)$ can be represented as equation (3), in which Q_0 is count rate of vacuum quantum signals, Q_1 is single photon count rate, Q_{multi} is multi-photon count rate and e_1 is the quantum bit error rate caused by single photons.

$$I(B:E) = qQ_0 \cdot 0 + qQ_1 H_2(e_1) + qQ_{multi} \times 1 \tag{3}$$

Combining (1), (2) and (3), the final security key rate can be represented as equation (4), in which Δ_1 is the ratio of single photon signal in the signals detected by Bob and f is the frequency of QKD system.

$$B_{secure} = qQ_\mu \{-H_2(E_\mu) + \Delta_1[1 - H_2(e_1)]\} \cdot f \tag{4}$$

2.2   QKD Post-processing Procedures

The post-processing procedures of QKD system in which conducts BB84 protocol mainly include the following steps:

- **Key Sifting.** Through sifting, Alice and Bob can drop the signal bits which do not carry quantum state information and obtain sifted key.
- **Basis Sifting.** By comparing the basis, the different bits in the basis of Bob and Alice are deleted and the initial key is obtained.
- **Error Correction.** Alice calculates and transmits the error correction information to Bob via the public classical channel and Bob corrects the errors in sifted keys.
- **Key Confirmation.** Bob and Alice send information to each other to confirm their keys are identical after error correction procedure.
- **Privacy Amplification.** Alice randomly chooses a Hash function and sends the generation information of the function to Bob. Bob generates the Hash matrix, and then they can gain the security key after the privacy amplification.

2.3   Concurrency Analysis

The main procedures of post-processing have the characteristics of strict order requirement, rich interaction and huge data amount, but they are uncorrelated for difference data unit, which is suitable for pipeline structure. Performance, resource and security requirement have conflicted influence on the design of QKD post-processing system. For example, performance can be improved by increasing the number of stages in pipeline, but this will result in increased consumption of storage. Moreover, in order to guarantee the security of QKD system, the security key length must be long enough to eliminate the finite size effect [16]. Thus resource requirement will grow, which may consequently limit the number of stages when available resource is constrained. Therefore we need to maximize system performance under the constraints of security demand and resource, which is challenging yet meaningful problem.

3   A Pipeline Optimization Model for QKD Post-processing System

In this section we firstly provide the hypotheses of our model. Then the variable granularity division policies of pipeline are conducted. Finally, an optimization model for QKD post-processing system is formulated to solve the pipeline design problem.

3.1 Hypotheses

We assume that the tasks can be divided evenly which means the sub-tasks after partition has uniform time consumption. In each macro stage, the change of data length is relatively small. Thus, we assume that the data length remains the same in one macro stage. Moreover, only CPU core number and memory needs to be considered as the constraint of system resource.

3.2 VGDP Method for Stage Division

The performance of pipeline can be optimized if all operations in all stages are identical in processing time. Otherwise, the slowest stage will become the bottleneck. We proposed a method called variable granularity division of pipeline (VGDP). VGDP's idea is to conduct coarse division at first so that calculation and communication can be conducted in a parallel way and then conduct fine division for load balancing.

A Coarse Granularity Division
For the scenario depicted in Fig. 1, the entire process can be divided into five steps which consist of three calculation and two communication procedures.

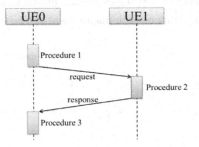

Fig. 1. Cooperative Computation

Our principle of division is to overlay calculation and communication procedures as much as possible with the purpose of utilizing delay hiding to the fullest. We denote the time consumption of the each macro stage on Alice and Bob as Ta_i and Tb_i correspondingly. Two situations may occur for Alice and Bob, one is that both of them are working, and the other is that one of them is working and one is idle. We define step function as:

$$\varphi(x) = \begin{cases} 1 & x \neq 0 \\ 0 & x = 0 \end{cases},$$ (5)

then the number of working macro stages on Alice and Bob are $\sum_{i=1}^{j} \varphi(Ta_i)$ and $\sum_{i=1}^{j} \varphi(Tb_i)$ respectively, and in which j is the number of macro stages.

The amount of error corrected key has to be accumulated for a few rounds before privacy amplification and we denote the number of rounds required as n. Key sifting is the first stage of post-processing and we denote the length of the data processed as l_{Raw}. We define ra_i and rb_i as the ratio of the length of data processed in the each macro stage compared with l_{Raw}. The initial macro stages need to be merged to make the number of macro stages not exceed CPU core number. The two stages which produce least time costing resulting stage should be chosen.

B Fine Granularity Division

After the coarse division, the time consumption of each stage still varies greatly. To further improve the performance of pipeline, we need to divide the macro stages into smaller sub-stages. The fine granularity division is only conduct for calculation procedures. T   he data interaction among subtasks will introduce additional delay. Let εa_i and εb_i be the data interaction delay, then we have:

$$\begin{cases} \varepsilon a_i = ra_i \cdot l_{Raw} \cdot n \cdot v \\ \varepsilon b_i = rb_i \cdot l_{Raw} \cdot n \cdot v \end{cases}, \tag{6}$$

in which v is the unit data transmit time between successive stages.

Assume that the number of sub-stages in each macro stage of Alice and Bob be Xa_i and Xb_i respectively. The delay of each macro stage can be expressed as equation (7).

$$t_i = \begin{cases} {Ta_i}/{Xa_i} + \varepsilon a_i & (Ta_i \neq 0 \ and \ Tb_i = 0) \\ {Tb_i}/{Xb_i} + \varepsilon b_i & (Ta_i = 0 \ and \ Tb_i \neq 0) \\ Max\left\{ {Ta_i}/{Xa_i} + \varepsilon a_i, {Tb_i}/{Xb_i} + \varepsilon b_i \right\} & (Ta_i \neq 0 \ and \ Tb_i \neq 0) \end{cases} \tag{7}$$

3.3   Model Formulation

There are some constraints in pipeline design. Firstly the number of stages should not exceed the number of computing cores (e.g. CPU). If the number of cores on Alice and Bob is Ca and Cb correspondingly, then the cores constraint can be expressed as (8).

$$\begin{cases} \sum_{i=1}^{j} Xa_i \leq Ca \\ \sum_{i=1}^{j} Xb_i \leq Cb \end{cases} \tag{8}$$

The next is the usage of memory. The memory needed for data storage is determined by the data length of each stage and the length of shared queen length m while it is determined by the specific algorithms adopted and the final key length l_{key} for computation. If we denote the available storage of Alice and Bob as Ma and Mb correspondingly, and λ as the amount of storage needed to compute key of unit length, then the memory constraints can be expressed as (9).

$$\begin{cases} m(\sum_{i=1}^{j-1} Xa_i \cdot ra_i \cdot l_{Raw} + Xa_j \cdot l_{key}) + \lambda \cdot l_{key} \leq Ma \\ m(\sum_{i=1}^{j-1} Xb_i \cdot rb_i \cdot l_{Raw} + Xb_j \cdot l_{key}) + \lambda \cdot l_{key} \leq Mb \end{cases} \tag{9}$$

As for security, Procedures such as key confirmation and authentication consume security keys, expressed as R_{cost}. System performance can be improved by increasing the number of stages in pipeline. However, this will cause degradation in the security level. Thus, a threshold P is needed to fulfill the minimal security requirement.

$$\frac{l_{key} - R_{cost}}{l_{key}} \geq P \tag{10}$$

The system performance is usually measured by throughput, which can be defined as the amount of data processed in unit time. The throughput of the system is (11).

$$Q_{parallel} = \frac{N}{\sum_{i=1}^{j} Max\{Ta_i + Xa_i \cdot \varepsilon a_i, \ Tb_i + Xb_i \cdot \varepsilon b_i\} + (N-1)Max\{t_1, t_2 \cdots t_j\}} \tag{11}$$

When the data length N is large enough, the time of filling the pipeline can be neglected. The final throughout is

$$Q_{parallel} = \frac{1}{Max\{t_1, t_2, \cdots, t_j\}}. \tag{12}$$

With the goal of optimizing system performance and constraints, the pipeline design problem can be expressed as (13) to (15).

$$Max \ \frac{1}{Max\{t_1, t_2, \cdots, t_j\}} \tag{13}$$

$$t_i = \begin{cases} Ta_i / Xa_i + \varepsilon a_i & (Ta_i \neq 0 \ and \ Tb_i = 0) \\ Tb_i / Xb_i + \varepsilon b_i & (Ta_i = 0 \ and \ Tb_i \neq 0) \\ Max\{Ta_i / Xa_i + \varepsilon a_i, \ Tb_i / Xb_i + \varepsilon b_i\} & (Ta_i \neq 0 \ and \ Tb_i \neq 0) \end{cases} \tag{14}$$

$$s.t. \begin{cases} \sum_{i=1}^{j} Xa_i \leq Ca \\ \sum_{i=1}^{j} Xb_i \leq Cb \\ m(\sum_{i=1}^{j-1} Xa_i \cdot ra_i \cdot l_{Raw} + Xa_j \cdot l_{key}) + \lambda \cdot l_{key} \leq Ma \\ m(\sum_{i=1}^{j-1} Xb_i \cdot rb_i \cdot l_{Raw} + Xb_j \cdot l_{key}) + \lambda \cdot l_{key} \leq Mb \\ l_{key} = ra_j \cdot l_{Raw} \cdot n \\ \frac{l_{key} - R_{cost}}{l_{key}} \geq P \\ \forall i \in \{1, \cdots, j\}, Xa_i \in N, Xb_i \in N \end{cases} \tag{15}$$

3.4   Model Solution Procedure

Algorithm 1. Feasible Direction Algorithm

Input: j , $Ta[1..j]$, $Tb[1..j]$, $ra[1..j]$, $rb[1..j]$, m , l_{Raw} , v , l_{key} , κ , Ca , Cb , Ma , Mb

Output: $t[1..j]$, $Xa[1..j]$, $Xb[1..j]$

1. $Xa[1..j]$, $Xb[1..j]$ Initialization
2.   **while** 1
3.   **do for** $i \leftarrow 1$ to j
4.   **do** calculate $t[i]$
5.   **if** $t[i]$ = max $t[1..j]$
6.   **then if** $t[i] = \dfrac{Ta[i]}{Xa[i]} + ra[i] \cdot l_{Raw} \cdot n \cdot v$
7.   **then** $Xa[i] \leftarrow Xa[i] + 1$
8.   **if** $\sum_{i=1}^{j} Xa[i] > Ca$ or
                            $m(\sum_{i=1}^{j-1} Xa[i] \cdot ra[i] \cdot l_{Raw} + Xa[j] \cdot l_{key}) + \lambda \cdot l_{key} \leq Ma$
9.   **then** $Xa[i] \leftarrow Xa[i] - 1$
10.   **break**
11.   **else** $Xb[i] \leftarrow Xb[i] + 1$
12.   **if** $\sum_{i=1}^{j} Xb[i] > Cb$ or
                            $m(\sum_{i=1}^{j-1} Xb[i] \cdot rb[i] \cdot l_{Raw} + Xb[j] \cdot l_{key}) + \lambda \cdot l_{key} \leq Mb$
13.   **then** $Xb[i] \leftarrow Xb[i] - 1$
14.   **Break**

Our model is a nonlinear programming problem with variable dimensions. If we use exhaustive search to solve our model with dimension j, the time complexity will be $O(n^j)$. We can adopt feasible direction algorithm to solve the problem, whose idea is choosing a direction that best optimizes the objective function locally. A near optimal solution can be obtained after sufficient iterations. As for our problem, we only need to increase the number of subtask of the most time consuming macro stage by one. Time complexity can be reduced to $O(n)$ if Algorithm 1 is utilized.

Algorithm 2. Solution to Variable Dimension Nonlinear Programming Model

Input: J , $Ta[1..J]$, $Tb[1..J]$, $ra[1..J]$, $rb[1..J]$, m , l_{Raw} , v , l_{key} , κ , Ca , Cb , Ma , Mb

Output: Tmin, XA, XB

1.   Tmin $\leftarrow \infty$
2.   **while** $j > 1$
3.   **do if** $\sum_{i=1}^{j} \varphi(Ta[i]) \leq Ca$ and $\sum_{i=1}^{j} \varphi(Tb[i]) \leq Cb$
4.   **then** use Algorithm 1 to solve problem with dimension j
5.   **if** max $t[1..j]$ < Tmin
6.   **then** Tmin $\leftarrow$ max $t[1..j]$
7.   Jmin $\leftarrow$ j
8.   XA $\leftarrow$ $Xa[1..j]$
9.   XB $\leftarrow$ $Xb[1..j]$
10.   Merge the macro stages
11. $j \leftarrow j - 1$

For each value of j, a local optimal solution can be obtained using algorithm 1. Then a global optimal can be chosen from the local optimal. If the system is divided into J macro stages, the overall solution of the model can be expressed as Algorithm 2.

4   Evaluation

4.1   Experiment Setting

We designed and constructed our multi-thread post-processing software. We also designed a quantum communication simulator based on our previous work in [12-15].

Our QKD system conducts BB84 protocol. The hardware platform of our system is Intel(R) Core(TM) i7@ 3.40 GHz, 1G. The system can be divided into 9 macro stages and the parameters such as ra_i, rb_i, Ta_i and Tb_i in our platform was measured. The default values of other experiment parameters are listed in Table 1.

Table 1. Default Parameter Values for QKD Post-processing System

Ca	4	Cb	4	m	20	l_{Raw}	1Mbits
Ma	1G	Mb	1G	v	3123MB/s	l_{key}	85kbits
Q_μ	1%	E_μ	2%	λ	576		

4.2   Quantum Communication Distance

If the quantum communication distance becomes very long, the count rate will decreased rapidly due to quantum channel loss. In this section, we focus on the influence of distance on the performance of post-processing system. We set the Q_μ as 0.5%, 1%, 2% and 5% respectively and the security key rates for both parallel and pipeline post-processing system are depicted in Fig. 3.(a).

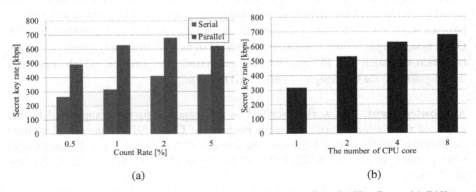

(a)   (b)

Fig. 2. (a) Security Key Rate under Different Count Rate; (b) Security Key Rate with Different CPU Core Number

Fig. 3.(a) shows that regardless of the quantum communication distance, our pipeline post-processing system can increase security key rate significantly compared with serial system. For example, our pipeline system can reach a security key rate above 600kbps which is 98% higher than serial system, proving the effectiveness of the model. Moreover, the raise in security key rate decreases with count rate, which can be explained by the fact that privacy amplification is the most time-consuming task. Thus, the increase in count rate merely shortens the time of the procedures before privacy amplification while privacy amplification becomes the bottleneck of the system. In this condition, the macro stage division may need to be redone according to pipeline design model and privacy amplification should be divided into different macro stages.

4.3   Post-processing System Resource

CPU core number is an important factor on pipeline performance. When tasks in different stages are allocated on different CPU core, the advantage of pipeline can be maximized. In this section we investigate the influence of CPU core number on system performance. The security key rates for post-processing systems with 1, 2, 4 and 8 cores are obtained and plotted in Fig. 3.(b).

As Fig. 3.(b) indicates security key rate increases with CPU core number. For example, the key rate for two-core platform reaches 500kbps which is 68% more than single core platform. This is because the task can be pipelined to more CPUs. But the increase in key rate gradually slows down with more CPU cores, which could be explained by the growth of synchronization cost with more stages. We can improve the system performance by stage division and using more cores. However, this methodology may reach its limit because of the increase in synchronization cost.

5   Conclusion

In this paper, we proposed an optimization model to maximize the thought of the pipeline under resource and security constraints. And flexible granularity division policies are conducted. Our model proves the ability to improve the performance of QKD system significantly compared to serial system. We also analyzed the influence of parameters such as CPU core number on system performance, which may offer useful guidance for the design of future QKD system.

Acknowledgment. The work described in this paper is partially supported by the grants of the National Basic Research Program of China (973 project) under Grant No.2009CB320503, 2012CB315906; the project of National Science Foundation of China under grant No. 61070199, 61103189, 61103194, 61103182, 61202488, 61272482.

References

1. Bennett, C.H., Brassard, G.: Quantum cryptography: Public key distribution and coin tossing. In: Proceedings of IEEE International Conference on Computers, Systems and Signal Processing, pp. 175–179. IEEE Press, Bangalore (1984)
2. Vernam, G.S.: Secret signaling system. U.S. Patent 1310719 (1919)
3. Xu-Yang, W., Zeng-Liang, B.A.I., Shao-Feng, W., et al.: Four-State Modulation Continuous Variable Quantum Key Distribution over a 30-km Fiber and Analysis of Excess Noise. Chinese Physics Letters 30(1) (2013)
4. Zhang, H.F., Wang, J., Cui, K., Luo, C.L., Lin, S.Z., Zhou, L., ... Pan, J.W.: A real-time QKD system based on FPGA. Journal of Lightwave Technology 30(20), 3226–3234 (2012)
5. Tanaka, A., Fujiwara, M., Yoshino, K.I., Takahashi, S., Nambu, Y., Tomita, A., ... Tajima, A.: High-speed quantum key distribution system for 1-Mbps real-time key generation. IEEE Journal of Quantum Electronics 48(4), 542–550 (2012)
6. Wang, J., Luo, C.L., Lin, S.Z., et al.: Research of hash-based secure key expansion algorithm for practical QKD. Optik-International Journal for Light and Electron Optics (2012)
7. Cui, K., Wang, J., Zhang, H.F., et al.: A real-time design based on FPGA for Expeditious Error Reconciliation in QKD system. IEEE Information Forensics and Security (2011)
8. Walenta, N., Burg, A., Caselunghe, D., et al.: A fast and versatile QKD system with hardware key distillation and wavelength multiplexing. arXiv preprint arXiv: 1309. 2583 (2013)
9. Wijesekera, S., Palit, S., Balachandran, B.: Software Development for B92 Quantum Key Distribution Communication Protocol. In: ICIS 2007: 6th IEEE/ACIS International Conference on Computer and Information Science, pp. 274–278. IEEE Press, New York (2007)
10. Lin, X., Peng, X., Yan, H., Jiang, W., Liu, T., et al.: An Implementation of Post-Processing Software in Quantum Key Distribution. In: 2009 WRI World Congress on Computer Science and Information Engineering, pp. 243–247. IEEE Press, New York (2009)
11. Li, Q., Le, D., Rao, M.: A Design and Implementation of Multi-thread Quantum Key Distribution Post-processing Software. In: Second International Conference on Instrumentation, Measurement, Computer, Communication and Control, pp. 272–275. IEEE Press, New York (2012)
12. Liu, B., Zhao, B., Wei, Z., Wu, C., Su, J., Yu, W., ... Sun, S.: Qphone: A quantum security VoIP phone. In: Proceedings of the ACM SIGCOMM 2013 Conference on SIGCOMM, pp. 477–478. ACM Press, New York (2013)
13. Liu, B., Liu, B., Zhao, B., Zou, D., Wu, C., Yu, W., You, I.: A real-time privacy amplification scheme in quantum key distribution. In: Mustofa, K., Neuhold, E.J., Tjoa, A.M., Weippl, E., You, I. (eds.) ICT-EurAsia 2013. LNCS, vol. 7804, pp. 453–458. Springer, Heidelberg (2013)
14. Zou, D., Zhao, B., Wu, C., Liu, B., Yu, W., et al.: CLIP: A Distributed Emulation Platform for Research on Information Reconciliation. In: 2012 15th International Conference on Network-Based Information Systems (NBiS), pp. 721–726. IEEE Press, New York (2012)
15. Sun, S.H., Ma, H.Q., Han, J.J., et al.: Quantum key distribution based on phase encoding in long-distance communication fiber. Optics Letters 35(8), 1203–1205 (2010)
16. Experimental Decoy State Quantum Key Distribution with Unconditional Security Incorporating Finite Statistics, http://arxiv.org/pdf/0705.3081.pdf

Aggregation of Network Protocol Data
Near Its Source

Marcel Fourné, Kevin Stegemann, Dominique Petersen,
and Norbert Pohlmann*

Institute for Internet Security,
Westfälische Hochschule, University of Applied Sciences,
Gelsenkirchen, Germany
{fourne,stegemann,petersen,pohlmann}@internet-sicherheit.de

Abstract. In Network Anomaly and Botnet Detection the main source
of input for analysis is the network traffic, which has to be transmitted
from its capture source to the analysis system. High-volume data sources
often generate traffic volumes prohibiting direct pass-through of bulk
data into researchers hands.

In this paper we achieve a reduction in volume of transmitted test data
from network flow captures by aggregating raw data using extraction of
protocol semantics. This is orthogonal to classic bulk compression algorithms. We propose a formalization for this concept called Descriptors
and extend it to network flow data.

A comparison with common bulk data file compression formats will
be given for full Packet Capture (PCAP) files, giving 4 to 5 orders of
magnitude in size reduction using Descriptors.

Our approach aims to be compatible with Internet Protocol Flow
Information Export (IPFIX) and other standardized network flow data
formats as possible inputs.

Keywords: Network Anomaly Detection, Botnet Detection, Network
Flow Data Formats, Data Compression.

1 Introduction and Background

For Network Anomaly Detection as well as network based Botnet and Malware
Detection (common umbrella term: NAD) the network traffic is their defining
input. Any findings rely on the availability of large volumes of network data. The
standard approach to get network data from Internet Service Providers (ISPs)
is to simply request them for research or security purposes under a contract.
A common problem emerges from the difference in bandwidth of big Internet
exchanges compared to the bandwidth of common research laboratories.

The most common format for network flow data is called NetFlow, which was
the basis for the more modern and standardized IPFIX. Since IPFIX is the future

---

* This work was supported by the German Federal Ministry of Economics and
Technology (Grant 16BY1201A iAID).

replacement for NetFlow, it can be expected to get widespread implementation in network routing equipment. The main target for this protocol is the transfer of data from an exporter to a collector.

When transmitting data for analysis, the most common formats in use today are NetFlow version 5 and raw PCAP files. Using NetFlow or IPFIX, the set of data to analyze is equally dependent on the supplier — ISPs etc. — so both have different problems. The first has — in its minimal form — only limited information for reliable detection of malicious activity and the second is not reasonable to transmit from live, high bandwidth data sources. A wider selection of records in NetFlow or IPFIX leads to more useful data, but in return raises the requirements for larger transmission bandwidth.

A possible workaround is compression of the bulk data using the DEFLATE or similar compression algorithms, but this only achieves modest improvements.

2   Related Work

There are projects using different approaches to NAD, including protocol headers [1], statistical detection [2] and others. We will only name a few as a primer for the interested [3, 4].

Bulk data compression was also demonstrated to lessen the strain on research ressources [5], but other works [6] could especially benefit from our proposal.

Most other research is done using already available NetFlow data using a minimal dataset [7–9] and sometimes also direct packet captures [10], but other flow data formats are also contestants for statistic approaches in finding anomalies. The main benefit of sampling flow data formats, by only transferring every N-th network packet is to be able to get information on Internet links which would otherwise saturate NAD systems is also their main disadvantage: Since not every packet gets reported, finding anomalies becomes a work of chance.

NetFlow [11] in itself is widely available in commercial routing hard- and software, so NetFlow data are easy to collect and many data are extractable from NetFlow records. The data available from NetFlow is variable, so the least common denominator is the only guaranteed information set, all other reportable records are optional. This may hamper NAD research if probabilistic analysis has to be inserted to find common higher level protocol usage without having detailed records available [12]. Standardization of the NetFlow format has led to IPFIX [13], which will see further adoption first in industrial use and therefore later in scientific literature using data in this format.

The general idea of Descriptors [14] has been mentioned earlier, but their approach was based on time intervals alone, thus not allowing to detect parties connected to anomalous activity in network flows. This is not needed for simple alarms, but for precise detection of attack sources.

3   Approach

We propose a security flow data transfer format with aggregate network protocol data to reduce the need for bandwidth compared to other formats containing the same information without aggregation. The aim of this format is to enable analysis of high bandwidth network data sources at smaller bandwidth sites. The security information content has to be maximized, of course, else a NAD system would be hampered in its workings. We define the security information (SI) of the data using P (Information at the Producer), D (Data at a sensor) and Y (Result of aggregation) as

$$SI(Y) \leq SI(D) \leq SI(P) \tag{1}$$

and

$$Y <<< P,\ SI(Y) \leq SI(P)\ (\text{ideally } SI(Y) = SI(P)) \tag{2}$$

The transport format Version 5 is structurally similar to common flow formats with the addition of so-called Descriptors, carrying the aggregate protocol data.

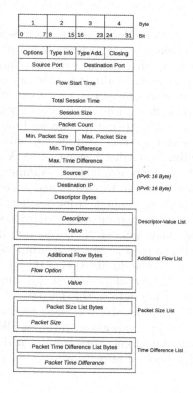

Fig. 1. Network Flow aware packet format v5 for Descriptor-Value pairs

Additional flow information can be added, e.g. labeling information, full packet size lists or the time distance of packets — called time difference list.

Of special note is the semantic approach in reducing the transferable network protocol data, since it relies on expert knowledge to implement aggregation plug-ins. They are as stable in their implementation details as the network protocol standards, so it would be combinatorically complex to implement all network protocols. It is in our best interest to implement a subset of most common network protocols instead of taking an "every last bit" approach, since very uncommon protocols only falsify the network view by very small and easily quantifiable percentages, so the Descriptors compress large amounts of data very well.

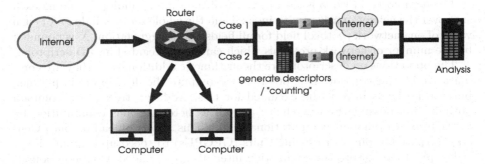

Fig. 2. Network setup comparing with and without Descriptor counting

We implemented the data aggregation not at a research laboratory, but on-site of the ISP to be able to extract network protocol data for detection right before transmitting the data to researchers. This can be seen as case 2 of Fig. 2, case 1 being the standard case, e.g. usage with plain IPFIX.

As seen on Fig. 2, the computer aggregating the network protocol data before the — ideally cryptographically secured — transmission is non-invasive to the core business of an ISP and can be fed with possibly filtered data coming from internal processes which are intended for data forwarding in other formats.

Our main input at the moment are raw PCAP files as well as direct network links, but structurally any well documented format (see Fig. 1) containing as much protocol data as possible is well suited for conversion.

3.1   Descriptors

The Descriptors are a subset of the transferable information, resulting in a big reduction of data by summation of occurrences of protocol data fields. The definition of a descriptor can be presented in a more exact manner over a larger set of formal languages each describing a unique data field in a network protocol.

Our set of values we want to transmit for further analysis is the data describing the network flow and a set of Descriptors defined as

$$\left\{ Descriptor(i) = \sum_{j=1}^{Y} V_j \right\}_{i=1}^{X} \tag{3}$$

where

$$V \in \Sigma_F, \Sigma_F = \text{ values of protocol field } i, \forall j \in \text{network packets} \tag{4}$$

Most protocol fields are single bit flags, so $\Sigma_F = \{0, 1\}$, but byte counters are also supported in the same fashion.

The main focus of Eq. 3 is the difference of the running indices, building each sum over the network packets with index j and the whole set over index i for each value of one network protocol field for all fields under aggregation. X is bounded by the number of network protocols which can be aggregated into Descriptors.

The operations on descriptors are the arithmetic addition +, so they are commutative by construction. It is practical to compute the descriptors in parallel, but special fields have to be excluded for this. Addition trees are a common optimization possible by this choice as well as heterogeneous computation by distribution to different computational units. This allows offloading onto General Purpose Graphics Processing Units (GPGPUs) to speed up computation.

For practical reasons the summation intervals are bounded. Common boundaries are network flows and time intervals. If a Descriptor is 0, it is omitted from the set of transferable data, so the set will be sparsely populated. Still, the sparse set of Descriptors is a map with many small values, resulting in a high number of 0x00-bytes in the data structure. This property allows for further compression of the data, as we will see.

3.2 Implementation

Our prototype was implemented during the course of a masters thesis and is in use locally and on-site at industry partners.

We define a network flow as unidirectional, since each bidirectional network flow can easily be recombined from the two complementary unidirectional flows. Using this approach, it is possible to identify malicious parties even using only aggregate protocol data.

Our implementation is a prototype based on a cost-benefit analysis. There were several ways to implement the count system for flows. The decision was given by the main requirements for a modular, maintainable, scalable system and a meaningful data caching. The system is in use locally and on-site at industry partners. There are different possibilities for recording and handling the flow data. The most important variant for testing is writing data into binary files. A tool for editing and implementation of privacy policy was also created, containing a buffered parser. It can print out datasets and a content summary, anonymize IP addresses (see Fig 3) and reset timestamps or label datasets.

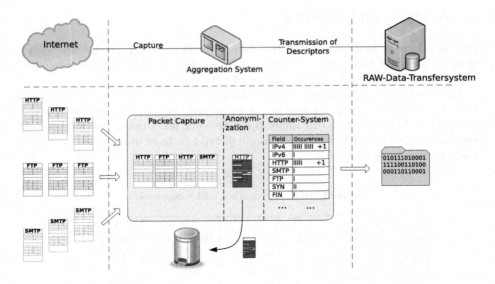

Fig. 3. Simplified overview of the aggregation process

The network protocol aware parts of the code-base have been split out into plug-ins for simple extensibility. These are also the most computationally critical parts of the implementation, limiting the aggregatable bandwidth. Currently over 50 plug-ins are implemented. Most of them represent a whole protocol aggregation and other ones search for defined incidents. If a new plug-in is needed it can be easily added to the system. It is also possible to define different aggregation processes that use only selected plug-ins.

A time memory trade-off in aggregation of data over a certain time interval in each flow results in better compression at the cost of more time in computation as well as necessary memory. To offset this trade-off, we use the independence of different network flows as well as the commutative quality of Descriptors to offload their generation onto different threads. Offloading onto GPGPUs would most certainly be beneficial due to the embarrassingly parallel nature of the computations, but the bandwidth of the memory bus is a limiting factor for high data rates, since the data is moved from a source — e.g. a network interface card — into the main memory, switching at least once to a GPGPU and again at least once back into the main memory, where the results reside ultimately. Another practical limit is thus the main memory bus transfer rate.

Computationally the emergence of cheaper parallel processing units makes a strong case for some form of compression before the transmission of captured network flow data. This is due to the fact that available processing power grew faster than the ratio between available bandwidth at research laboratories compared to that at ISPs.

4   Analysis and Results

For an effective measurement of the data reduction ability of Descriptors for network protocol data transfer we took an exemplary PCAP file with some very large network flows and a large number of very small ones.

Intuitively the larger network flows should be easier to reduce in size, since most protocol header data should be recurring and thus easy to aggregate in one Descriptor. In contrast to this many small network flows make the overheads of our format more visible, as Descriptors will tend to have only small number of packets for aggregation.

Table 1. Data aggregation and compression

Format	Raw data size	.tar.gz	.tar.xz
PCAP-testfile	2147483647 B	2034619265 B	2026200592 B
relative size	100 %	94.74 %	94.35 %
Flow-subversion5	274056 B	32067 B	17832 B
relative size	100 %	11.70 %	6.51 %
relative to full raw data	0.0128 %	0.00165 %	0.0009 %
compression factor 1/	7835.93	63449.01	113627.22

Numerically, our results are some orders of magnitude better than bulk compression of the raw data, but of course we omit network packet data which carry no protocol information, so the network flows get trimmed of their big payloads. This is not the only size reduction, since our format allows for better compression factors and can deliver interesting data during protocol handshakes even if the later payloads will be encrypted, which we expect to happen more routinely in the future.

Nonetheless, if we set the magnitudes in data size reduction into relation (again see Fig. 4) to the practicability of having the network protocol data or missing them entirely because of bandwidth saturation, we see huge benefits in our approach.

Please note the omission of large parts in the scale numbering in Fig. 4(a) to make the small differences from bulk file data compression more visible, since in Fig. 4(b) their differences are hardly visible at all on the logarithmic scale.

5   Problems Encountered

Our prototype does not honor packet ordering constraints and detects new flows by transport layer properties: If TCP or UDP, group flows by IP-addresses, network ports used and network interface source ID. The ordering of network packets in each flow is not important due to the nature of Descriptors. More agrregation protocols can be implemented via further protocol plug-ins and the percentage of network traffic with no implementation of Descriptor aggregating

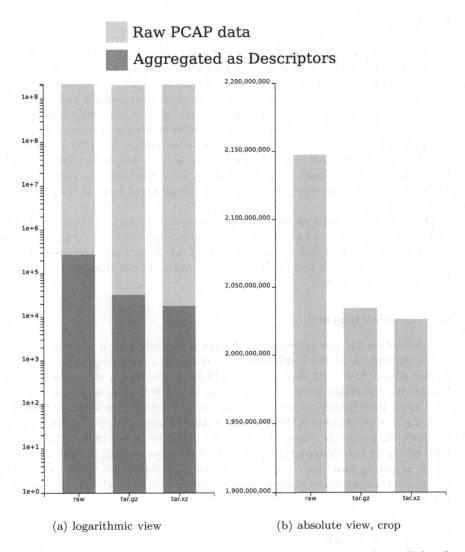

Fig. 4. Compression results compared logarithmically, to the right are the small details of the top in absolute values

plug-ins can be measured as the difference between the aggregated packet count and the unaggregated one.

The bottleneck in our implementation is the copying of network data during aggregation into Descriptors, so the compression on multi gigabit per second Internet links is not in real-time.

Since our prototype only works on unidirectional network flows and not directly on bidirectional ones, connection tracking is harder to implement.

6   Conclusion

We presented an efficient method to effectively reduce the bandwidth needed for transferring network flow protocol data for later analysis in NAD. Our approach can be used as an addition to standard ISP operating procedures producing flow data in different formats as long as these formats also contain higher protocol level data. Our aggregation of network protocol data is efficiently parallelizable and can be computed in a data pipeline fashion at high data rates on standard computing hardware. Since the aggregated data are grouped by network flow membership, single flows containing malicious activity can be detected by higher level analysis. Providing rich protocol data for researchers on slower Internet links allows analyzing network activity on the protocol level at larger ISPs for malicious activity.

Our approach compares favorably to common bulk data file compression formats and is itself a good pre-filter before their application, resulting in further compression at higher factors than on raw PCAP data. Using our approach it is much more practicable to pass full network protocol data through to researcher laboratories for NAD.

6.1   Lessons Learned

Parallelization for the aggregation of data is not effective if not planned from the beginning on, so the bottleneck for getting data from large ISPs takes place in this phase. Our next development will be optimized in its performance for bandwidth scalability from the ground up, so our solution can be used to make data acquisition from most sources viable even for smaller research organizations.

A minor unwieldiness is the implementation of aggregation plug-ins for different network protocols, since each Descriptor has to be selected by a developer with semantic knowledge of the protocol on implementation. This is mostly offset by targeting most major protocols in use on the Internet and measuring the difference between those implemented by Descriptors and the small percentage left over.

7   Future Work

Our main focus is re-engineering and optimizing the parallel aggregation pipeline to achieve optimal throughput in the order of 10 gigabit per second utilizing GPGPU if available.

More network protocol plug-ins will be developed to generate more Descriptors, giving an even more complete view of network protocol activity.

We will implement an IPFIX connector to get our input from IPFIX records. After pre-filtering of bulk data, our aim is to build efficient and therefore scalable network malware detection systems.

References

1. Ahmad, R., Ghani, M., Haris, S.H.C., Waleed, G.M.: Anomaly detection of ip header threats (2012)
2. Bykova, M., Shawn Ostermann, B.T.: Detecting network intrusions via a statistical analysis of network packet characteristics (2001)
3. Deri, L., Maselli, G., Suin, S.: Design and implementation of an anomaly detection system: An empirical approach (2003)
4. Rossow, C., Dietrich, C.J., Bos, H., Cavallaro, L., van Steen, M., Freiling, F.C., Pohlmann, N.: Sandnet: Network traffic analysis of malicious software. In: Proceedings of the First Workshop on Building Analysis Datasets and Gathering Experience Returns for Security, pp. 78–88. ACM (2011)
5. Politopoulos, P.I., Markatos, E.P., Ioannidis, S.: Evaluation of compression of remote network monitoring data streams. In: IEEE Network Operations and Management Symposium Workshops, NOMS Workshops 2008, pp. 109–115. IEEE (2008)
6. Palmieri, F., Fiore, U., Castiglione, A.: A distributed approach to network anomaly detection based on independent component analysis. Concurrency and Computation: Practice and Experience, n/a–n/a (2013)
7. Lakhina, A., Crovella, M., Diot, C.: Characterization of network-wide anomalies in traffic flows. In: Proceedings of the 4th ACM SIGCOMM Conference on Internet Measurement, pp. 201–206. ACM (2004)
8. Bilge, L., Kirda, E., Kruegel, C., Balduzzi, M.: Exposure: Finding malicious domains using passive dns analysis. In: Proceedings of NDSS (2011)
9. Bilge, L., Balzarotti, D., Robertson, W., Kirda, E., Kruegel, C.: Disclosure: Detecting botnet command and control servers through large-scale netflow analysis. In: Proceedings of the 28th Annual Computer Security Applications Conference, pp. 129–138. ACM (2012)
10. Tegeler, F., Fu, X., Vigna, G., Krügel, C.: Finding bots in network traffic without deep packet inspection. In: The 8th ACM International Conference on Emerging Networking EXperiments and Technologies (CoNEXT 2012), Nice, France (December 2012)
11. Claise, E.B.: Cisco systems netflow services export version 9 (2004)
12. Abt, S., Wener, S., Baier, H.: Performance evaluation of classification and feature selection algorithms for netflow-based protocol recognition. In: INFORMATIK 2013, pp. 2184–2197. Gesellschaft für Informatik (2013)
13. Network Working Group, Trammell, B.: Bidirectional Flow Export Using IP Flow Information Export (IPFIX), http://www.ietf.org/rfc/rfc5103.txt
14. Petersen, D., Himmelsbach, K., Bastke, S., Pohlmann, N.: Measuring and warning (2008)

The Mediating Role of Social Competition Identity Management Strategy in the Predictive Relationship between Susceptibility to Social Influence, Internet Privacy Concern, and Online Political Efficacy

Juneman Abraham[1] and Murty Magda Pane[2]

[1] Bina Nusantara University, Psychology Department, Jakarta, Indonesia
juneman@binus.edu
[2] Bina Nusantara University, Character Building Development Center, Jakarta, Indonesia
murty.pane@gmail.com

Abstract. There are few psychotechnological researches in political world in Indonesia, whereas Indonesia will enter "Year of Politics" by General Election which will be held in 2014. This research aimed at examining the hypothesis of predictive correlation, at the individual level, between susceptibility to social influence, internet privacy concern (as predictor variables) and online political efficacy (as the dependent variable). This research hypothesized that the relationship between the variables is mediated by online identity management strategy in the form of social competition. This research employed questionnaire to gain variables data. Participants of this research were 214 undergraduate students of Bina Nusantara University, Jakarta (106 males, 108 females). Result of this research shows that five of seven proposed hypotheses are supported by empirical data. Implications of the result of this research for online system development for political activities are discussed in the end of this article.

Keywords: Online efficacy, politics, identity management, social influence, privacy.

1   Introduction

By the rapid use of online social media to gain political purposes, today it becomes urgent to identify variables taking role in predicting online political efficacy. There are numbers of factors known influence online political efficacy. They are successful past experience (including satisfaction with the experience) in using internet as a political instrument, the nature (quantity and quality) of online interaction among members in a political group, type of social media use (information, entertainment, interaction), as well as quality of access (access location and years online) [1,2]. This research assumes that online political self-efficacy is influenced by identity management strategy in the form of social competition--defined as continued engagement in

Linawati et al. (Eds.): ICT-EurAsia 2014, LNCS 8407, pp. 492–499, 2014.

the conflict. The concept of identity management is borrowed from Niens and Cairns [3]. According to Tajfel, in: Niens and Cairns [3], identity management strategy is a self-identification strategy of an individual in his/her group "to cope with the perceived outcomes of social comparisons (with his/her out-group)" in order to maintain self-esteem and self-image. Political world is a world which is full of conflict dynamics related to identity, either conflicts among individuals, between individuals and groups, or among groups. Monroe, in: Bernstein [4], stated that conflicts reflect the existence of psychological assumptions concerning how social identity constructed, either actively or passively. Related to that case, referring to the theories of social conflict, conflict is an inherent part of politics [5]. Based on this idea, the author builds the first hypothesis (H1), "The higher an individual uses identity management strategy of social competition, the higher his/her online political efficacy will be".

Furthermore, the author hypothesizes that susceptibility to social influence and various aspects of information privacy concern influence individual's online political efficacy. Bobier had conducted a psychometric analysis and found out that there are two factors of susceptibility to social influence, i.e. principled autonomy and social adaptability [6]. An individual having high principled autonomy is a kind of individual who has less possibility to give conformity response, but has more possibility to give correct responses on critical trials. An individual having high social adaptability is an individual who has more possibility to give conformity response, but less possibility to give correct responses on critical trials. The author presumes that an individual who tends to conform to his/her in-group will exactly shows high social competition to his/her out-group; the other way around, individual who is more autonomous or independent will shows low social competition toward his/her out-group. Thus, second hypothesis (H2) of this research is "The higher principled autonomy of an individual, the lower identity management of social competition will be", and third hypothesis (H3) is "The higher social adaptability of an individual, the higher identity management of social competition will be".

Social competition can be limited by the individual's privacy concern. The ground idea is that social competition in politics is often accompanied with techniques containing ethical problems from light to heavy, such as the case of tapping the phones of Indonesian public officials, including the President of Indonesia done by intelligent agencies working for Australia [7]. Sims and Gehan through their empirical research also found that online competitions (in the field of economics) often have excesses of information misuse and privacy violation [8]. This reality means that individuals who are competitive and who have high online political efficacy are possibly individuals who have less attention (or: more tolerable) to privacy issues. The author employs three dimensions of contextual model of Internet Users' Information Privacy Concerns (IUIPC) by Malhotra, Kim, and Agarwal, i.e.: (1) Risk beliefs, (2) Perception of errors corrections of privacy practices, and (3) Perception of unauthorized secondary use of personal information [9].

Based on the aforementioned idea, the author hypothesizes (H4, H5), "The higher risk beliefs and perception of unauthorized secondary use of personal information, the lower identity management strategy in the form of social competition in the online world" also (H6) that "The higher perception of errors corrections of privacy practices, the higher identity management strategy in the form of social competition in the online world". By integrating H1 to H6, the author builds a hypothetical model as seen on Fig. 1. This model stated that (H7): "There is a nomological network among variables mentioned above which can explain high or low level of individual's online political self-efficacy".

2   Methods

Participants of this research were 214 undergraduate students of Bina Nusantara University, Jakarta (106 males, 108 females), whose mean of age is 19.35 years old and standard deviation of age is 1.678 years old. The data of this research was analyzed by using path analysis. This research used a questionnaire containing seven scales as an instrument to gain the data of the participants.

This research employed quantitative, predictive correlational design. The research data were processed with LISREL 8.8 program. Measurement specification is as show in Table 1. **Online Political Self-efficacy** scale consists of nine items. The guideline to fill this scale is as follows: *"Please rate how certain are you that you can do the things discussed below by choosing the appropriate response."* Examples of the items are: (1) Use social media applications to express your political views; (2) Express coherently your political ideas to other online. **Identity Management Strategy (Social Competition)** scale consists of four items. Examples of the items are: (1) I want my online community to demonstrate that it is the superior one; (2) I want my online community to demonstrate that it is culturally superior. **Principled Autonomy** scale consists of five items. Examples of the items are: (1) I am willing to stand up for what I believe, even if I lose some friends as a result; (2) I would be willing to take a public stand regarding my beliefs, even if it meant being dropped out or going to jail. **Social Adaptability** scale consists of nine items. Examples of the items are: (1) I have deliberately, falsely, agreed with someone because I knew I would have to work with them in the future; (2) I have publicly agreed with something I didn't really believe because it would make it easier to keep working with a person. **Risk Beliefs** scale consists of four items. Examples of the items are: (1) In general, it would be risky to give information to online companies; (2) There would be high potential for loss associated with giving information to online firms (including Facebook, Twitter, Google, etc). **Perception of Unauthorized Secondary Use of Personal Information** consists of four items. Examples of the items are: (1) Online companies should not use personal information for any purpose unless it has been authorized by the individuals who provided information; (2) When people give personal information to an online company for some reason, the online company should never use the information for any other reason. **Perception of Errors Corrections** scale consists of four items. Examples of the items are: (1) All the personal information in computer databases should be double-checked for accuracy, no matter how much this cost; (2) Online companies should have better procedures to correct errors in personal information.

Table 1. Measurement specification

Variable measured	Source of scale adaptation	Cronbach's Alpha (Reliability)	Response scales	Corrected item-total correlations (Validity)
Online political efficacy	Perilla [1]	0.895	Strongly Unsure (score of 1) to Strongly Sure (score of 6)	0.366–0.778
Social competition identity strategy	Niens and Cairns [3]	0.751		0.406–0.640
Principled autonomy	Bobier [6]	0.680	Strongly Disagree (score of 1) to Strongly Agree (score of 6)	0.397–0.550
Social adaptability		0.672		0.258–0.458
Risk belief		0.689		0.366–0.596
Perception of unauthorized secondary use of personal information	Malhotra et al. [9]	0.725		0.466–0.596
Perception of errors corrections		0.728		0.411–0.606

3   Results and Discussion

The result of this research shows that overall hypothetical model (H7) is supported by empirical data (Chi-Square = 7.83, df = 5, P-value > 0.05, GFI > 0.90, RMSEA < 0.10) (see Fig. 1). However, the second (H2) hypothesis is supported by the data in term of relationship statistical significance among variables, but not in term of relationship direction since the hypothesis asserts the occurrence of negative correlation, but in fact the author found a positive correlation. This research also found that there is no significant correlation among variables hypothesized in H4 and H5.

Based on the empirical data, path analysis shows that social adaptability (susceptibility to social influence/conformity) is able to indirectly predict online political efficacy through the mediation of social competition identity management strategy. This finding is in line with a study conducted by Kaplan, Brooks-Shesler, King, and Zaccaro entitled *"Thinking inside the box: How conformity promotes creativity and innovation"* [10]. The result of their analysis indicates that conformity is necessary to effectively implement creative ideas--of which creative idea is indeed hugely demanded in the political world. Conformity can facilitate team coordination, information exchange, conflict management, and collective efficacy. This proposition is different from common sense and many other results of researches saying that the success of an innovation can only be generated by the non-conforming team members or those who think divergently. What is often forgotten by the people in this context is that creative idea generations or originations is only a facet of the creative process, and that team's innovation does not only depend on creative ideas production but also depend on realization of the ideas [10]. The realization of the ideas needs conformity to in-group. Conformity does not need to mean stick to *any or all* group or organizational norms, but it means adhere to norms that promote and express team unity. At today's online political life in Indonesia, the finding of this research matches with everyday realities. Online volunteers for Jokowi-Ahok (Current Governor and Deputy Governor of DKI Jakarta, Indonesia) are an effective online team ("cyber troops"; [11]) who show conformity to group norms, although each of them is a creative individual and even has a high education [12,13].

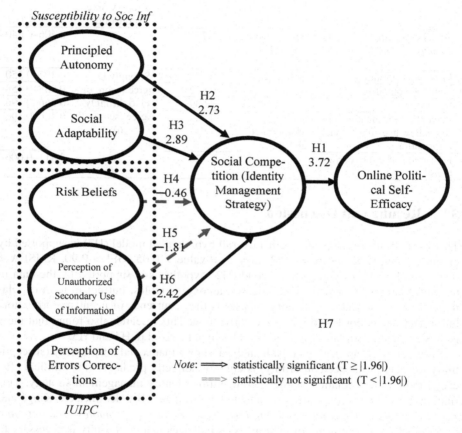

Chi-square = 7.83, df = 5, P-value = 0.16575, GFI = 0.99, RMSEA = 0.052

Fig. 1. Research hypotheses and results

This research also found that principled autonomy positively correlate with social competition which later influences online political efficacy. Individual's principled autonomy can be a valuable input for social identity of an individual through one's engagement process toward stories ("master narratives") growing in one's in-group [14]--in this case, his/her online political group. It seems to be enabled by lots of attribute diversities of individuals in Jakarta as a megapolitan city and moreover in the online world, which enables an online political group to build their social identity by considering and synthesizing expectation, aspiration, and principles of most of their members. This kind of appreciative thing can latter enhances individual's competitiveness in facing out-group, and next enhances individual's online political efficacy.

This research also found that risk beliefs and perception of unauthorized secondary use of personal data are not essential for participants in determining activities which are related to their identity in the virtual world. There are two explanations related to this matter. *First*, youth who becomes the participants of this research has undergone desensitization of privacy concern. The desensitization occurs since the individual is faced with the frequent dilemma between inevitable need for data sharing (including political interest) and awareness that there is compensation or trade-off that is the reduction of data privacy [15,16]. In the end, the urgent need for data sharing is prioritized, and at the same time people actively or passively monitor policies development concerning solutions to privacy problem. Shacklett added that younger workers are more relaxed about privacy [17]. *Second* explanation is that youth (who becomes participants of this research), in fact, has the need to move dynamically, back and forth, between risky experiences [18]. Nevertheless, this research found that Perception of Errors Corrections correlates positively with social competition. The author presumes that the positive correlation tends to be resulted by the fact that in political competition, there is a need to access accurate data from political opponents or out-groups. Data integrity is needed by people or party who conduct online political activities in order to be able to determine the precise strategy. It will activate measurable social competition and further will enhance an individual's online political efficacy.

4   Conclusion

This research concludes that there is a psychotechnological model which is able to explain an individual's online political efficacy. Online political efficacy can be predicted by (1) Principled autonomy, (2) Social adaptability, and (3) Perception of errors corrections, through the mediating role of social competition identity management strategy. However, internet privacy concerns (risk beliefs and perception of unauthorized secondary use of personal information) are not able to predict it.

In the context of enhancing political participation of the young generation, the result of this research has some important implications. *First*, since it has been known that online political efficacy is influenced by social competition identity management, thus certain online environments which are intended to be a political arena should be constructed in such a way so that it can facilitate a stimulating, engaging and fun as well as fair competition. This kind of online environment can support political education for the young generation. The author agrees with Priem et al. [19] who emphasize that online customers should be empowered. It has been already clear that online political world has its own customers who continuously grow as time goes by since Indonesia now is entering "Year of Politics" by General Elections 2014. In addition, smart phone and laptop which are usually used to do online activities become cheaper. The empowerment can be done by customization of the online system which embodies effective coordination among members of each political group so that members can align mission, strategy, and symbolic instruments before "fighting" by online in expressing political identity and winning online community's heart who become the target of political campaign. Customization of the online system can also be aimed at creating an express and quick profiling concerning constellation of aspiration and expectation of online political group's members. The resulting profiling can be used to encourage social competition in accordance with strength, weakness, and development opportunities of each member. *Second*, since it has been known that perception of errors corrections influences social competition, online system needs to be design in such a way so that the data accuracy precision reaches the maximum level. Defect in the online system which results in data inaccuracy will decrease healthy social competition and further will decrease online political efficacy.

Third, since it has been known that most of privacy concerns are not significant in influencing identity management strategy--and further online political efficacy, this knowledge should not be unethically used by online system providers as a chance to exploit individual information of online political player. As mentioned above, insignificant correlation is supposedly caused by a condition in which users experience such "helplessness" as they do not have another choice except accept that private information submission by online is a compensation for the service they use. Academicians and practitioners in psychotechnology fields play a role to design online system which is able to enhance bargaining power of online media services' user in such a way so that unnecessary information disclosure will be further minimized.

References

1. Perilla, A.A.V.: Social Media and Individual and Collective Activism: The Role of Interdependence and Online Political Efficacy. Unpublished PhD dissertation, Communication Arts and Sciences – Media and Information Studies, Michigan State University (2012)
2. Livingstone, S., Helsper, E.: Balancing Opportunities and Risks in Teenagers' Use of The Internet: The Role of Online Skills and Internet Self-efficacy. New Media Society 12(2), 309–329 (2010)
3. Niens, U., Cairns, E.: Identity Management Strategies in Northern Ireland. The Journal of Social Psychology 142(3), 371–380 (2002)
4. Bernstein, M.: Identity Politics. Annu. Rev. Sociol. 31, 47–74 (2005)
5. Acemoglu, D.: Why Not a Political Coase Theorem? Social Conflict, Commitment, and Politics. J. Comp. Econ. 31, 620–652 (2003)
6. Bobier, D.M.: A Measure of Susceptibility to Social Influence: Scale Development and Validation. Unpublished PhD dissertation, Graduate College of The University of Iowa (2002)
7. Akuntono, I.: Sadap Presiden SBY, DPR Tuntut Australia Minta Maaf (July 28, 2013), http://nasional.kompas.com/read/2013/07/28/1836235/Sadap.Pre siden.SBY.DPR.Tuntut.Australia.Minta.Maaf
8. Sims, A., Gehan, G.: Privacy and the Spam Act in Online Competitions. UABR 12(1), 1–7 (2010)

9. Malhotra, N.K., Kim, S.S., Agarwal, J.: Internet Users' Information Privacy Concerns (IUIPC): The Construct, the Scale, and a Causal Model. Inform. Syst. Res. 15(4), 336–355 (2004)
10. Kaplan, S., Brooks-Shesler, L., King, E.B., Zaccaro, S.: Thinking Inside the Box: How Conformity Promotes Creativity and Innovation. In: Mannix, E.A., Goncalo, J.A., Neale, M.A. (eds.) Creativity in Groups (Research on Managing Groups and Teams), vol. 12, pp. 229–265. Emerald Group Publishing Limited, Bingley (2009)
11. Andi, R.F.: Mencermati Fenomena Pasukan Dunia Maya Jokowi (November 4, 2013), http://nasional.inilah.com/read/detail/2043655/mencermati-fenomena-pasukan-dunia-maya-jokowi#.Ur-w9-KeaeY
12. Afifah, R.: Saat Anak Muda Berkarya Untuk Jokowi-Ahok (2012), http://olahraga.kompas.com/read/2012/06/10/06165790/function.fopen
13. Ichsan, A.S.: Forum Akademisi IT Menjadi Relawan Jokowi (August 11, 2013), http://www.republika.co.id/berita/nasional/jabodetabek-nasional/13/08/11/mrd2sk-forum-akademisi-it-menjadi-relawan-jokowi
14. Hammack, P.L.: Narrative and the Cultural Psychology of Identity. Pers. Soc. Psychol. Rev. 12, 222–247 (2008)
15. Bakken, D.E.: Data Obfuscation: Anonymity and Desensitization of Usable Data Sets. (IEEE) Security Privacy 2(6), 34–41 (2004)
16. CBSDC: Expert: Individuals 'Desensitized,' 'Numb' to Privacy Threats (June 10, 2013), http://washington.cbslocal.com/2013/06/10/expert-individuals-desensitized-numb-to-privacy-threats/
17. Shacklett, M.E.: Younger Workers More Relaxed About Privacy (July 18, 2012) , http://www.internetevolution.com/author.asp?section_id=562&doc_id=247574
18. Răcătău, I.-M.: Adolescents and Identity Formation in a Risky Online Environment: The Role of Negative User-Generated and Xenophobic Websites. Journal of Media Research 3(17), 16–36 (2013)
19. Priem, B., Leenes, R., Kosta, E., Kuczerawy, A.: The Identity Landscape. In: Camenisch, J., Leenes, R., Sommer, D. (eds.) Digital Privacy. LNCS, vol. 6545, pp. 33–51. Springer, Heidelberg (2011)

Formal Security Analysis and Performance Evaluation of the Linkable Anonymous Access Protocol

Rima Addas and Ning Zhang

School of Computer Science
University of Manchester
Manchester, UK

Abstract. The introduction of e-Health applications has not only brought benefits, but also raised serious concerns regarding security and privacy of health data. The increasing demands of accessing health data, highlighted critical questions and challenges concerning the confidentiality of electronic patient records and the efficiency of accessing these records. Therefore, the aim of this paper is to provide secure and efficient access to electronic patient records. In this paper, we propose a novel protocol called the Linkable Anonymous Access protocol (LAA). We formally verify and analyse the protocol against security properties such as secrecy and authentication using the Casper/FDR2 verification tool. In addition, we have implemented the protocol using the Java technology to evaluate its performance. Our formal security analysis and performance evaluation proved that the LAA protocol supports secure access to electronic patient records without compromising performance.

1   Introduction

Information security and privacy in the e-health domain are issues of growing concern. The adoption of electronic patient records, increased regulation, provider consolidation and the increasing need for information exchange between patients, providers and payers, all lead towards the need for a better information security and privacy [1].

The exponential growth of the Internet and electronic health brings not only benefits, but also risks. Numerous attacks pose a real challenge to different aspects of security techniques. Among these security techniques, security protocols play a significant role. They use cryptographic primitives as building blocks to achieve security goals such as authentication, confidentiality and integrity [2].

In [3], we have proposed a new method called 3LI2Pv2 method to support controlled access to electronic patient records (EPRs) with three levels of identity privacy reservations. In the method, we have identified three levels of patient identity privacy protection:

* *Level-1 (L1)- Linkable access:* At this level, multiple data objects of the same patient can be linked, and this set of objects can be linked to the patient's

Linawati et al. (Eds.): ICT-EurAsia 2014, LNCS 8407, pp. 500–510, 2014.

identity. L1 access should be limited to L1 users, i.e. users with linkable access privilege.

* *Level-2 (L2)- Linkable anonymous access:* At this level, multiple data objects of the same patient can be linked, but this set of objects cannot be linked to the patient's identity. L2 access should be limited to L1/L2 users, i.e. users with linkable anonymous access privilege.

* *Level-3 (L3)- Anonymous access:* At this level, multiple data objects of the same patient cannot be linked, nor the patient's identity be exposed. L3 access should be limited to L1/L2/L3 users, i.e. users with anonymous access privilege.

The 3LI2Pv2 method relied of cryptographic primitives to meet its goals. We have informally analysed the 3LI2Pv2 method against some security properties, and the result was positive. For future work, we suggested to include the design of the access protocol for the three levels. Therefore, in this paper, we introduce a secure and robust protocol for the Level-2 (Linkable anonymous access).

By and large, security protocols have been modelled and verified using informal verification tools. As a result, it is now very common that security protocols, which were previously proposed have found to be vulnerable later on. For example, the Needham-Schroeder public key protocol [4] succeeded in the informal analysis, but failed in the formal verification [5]. To address this problem, formal methods have been widely used to specify security protocols and verify security properties, such as confidentiality, authentication and non-repudiation, to ensure correctness [6].

In this paper, a formal method, Casper/FDR2 verification tool [7] [8], is used to model and verify the LAA protocol. Casper/FDR2 has proven to be successful for modelling and verifying several security protocols; it has been used to verify authentication, secrecy, and other security properties [9] [10]. Accordingly, we consider it also suitable for the verification of the LAA protocol. The Casper/FDR2 model checker is used to verify the security properties of the protocols. If the protocols do not fulfil the specified security properties, then the FDR2 checker shows a counterexample which represents the cause against vulnerability. After completing the formal verification of the protocol using Casper/FDR2, we implement the protocol using the Java technology [11] to test it against performance. JAVA is selected because it supports a set of standard security primitives such as the hash function SHA-256 [12], the symmetric cryptographic algorithm AES [13] and the asymmetric cryptographic algorithm RSA [14].

This paper is organized as follows; In Section 2, we introduce common security threats. In section 3, we describe, model and verify the LAA protocol. In addition, we set the security goals that the LAA protocol should fulfil. Then, we present the result of the verification. In Section 4, we present the implementation and performance evaluation of the LAA protocol. In Section 5, we conclude the paper and discuss future work.

2   Common Security Threats

Access to electronic patient records is subject to diverse types of security threats and attacks. In this paper, we will exclude threats of environmental origin such as fire or accidental ones such as user errors or software malfunction. The threats that we will consider are, confidentiality threats, integrity threats and authentication threats.

2.1   Confidentiality Threats

In this type of threat, an intruder may gain access to sensitive information. The attack consists in eavesdropping the communication links, without interfering with the transmissions, or in inspecting data stored in the system. Examples of this type of threat are Man in the middle attack, replay attack, credential forgery and impersonation.

2.2   Integrity Threats

In this type of threat, an intruder may alter the information exchanged between entities. The attack consists in interfering with the transmissions, so that the recipient receives data, which are different from those sent by the originator. An example of this type of threat is data tampering.

2.3   Authentication Threats

In this type of threat, an intruder may prepare false data and deceive the recipient into believing that they come from a different originator (which the recipient takes as the authentic originator). The attack consists in forging the part of the data where the originator is identified (usually in the identity credentials). An example of this type of threat is spoofing. Repudiation is also a variant of this type of threats that consists in denying authorship or the contents of data previously sent.

3   Formal Verification and Security Analysis of the Linkable Anonymous Access (LAA) Protocol

In this section, we first describe and model the LAA security protocol with Casper. Then, we introduce some important security requirements that the LAA protocol should fulfil. Finally, we verify the protocol using the FDR2 model checker, discuss the verification result of the protocol and analyse its security requirements.

3.1   The LAA Protocol Description

The purpose of the LAA protocol is to link multiple data objects of the same patient managed by a heath service provider (HSP), but this set of objects cannot be linked to the patient's real identity (e.g. NHS number). This type of access should be granted to users with higher privileges (L1 and L2 users) such as general practices (GPs) and specialist who need such information to proceed

Table 1. The LAA Protocol Notation and Meaning

Notation	Meaning
a	An identifier of an initiator/client
b	An identifier of a responder/server
ca	An identifier of a certification authority
nx	A random nonce of x
cr	A challenge response
PKx	A public key of x
SKx	A secret Key of x
ts	A time Stamp (an expiration time)
h	A hash function
msg	A message of data request
certa	A PK-certificate of a generated by ca
attr-certa	An attribute certificate of a generated by ca
veri1	An integrity verification of $certa$
ps3intra12	An L3 pseudonym Type-III
sigb	A signature of b
integrity1, integrity2	Used in attr-certa integrity verification

with the patient's treatment. Until now, no research has been conducted to analyse the vulnerability of the LAA protocol using a formal verification tool. Table 1 shows the basic notation of the LAA protocol. Figure 1 shows message sequences of the LAA protocol.

The communication channel in the LAA protocol, is based on the Secure Socket Layer (SSL) protocol [15] to ensure security for data transmission. For protocol analysis using Casper/FDR2, we assume the following.

- The underlying cryptographic algorithms used in SSL's public key and symmetric key ciphers are secure.

- All parties unconditionally trust the certification authority. The certification authority certifies the public key for clients.

- All parties unconditionally trust the attribute authority who issues the attribute certificates for clients.

- Patients' records have already been de-identified.

In the LAA protocol, ca is the certification authority who issues public-key (PK) certificates to legitimate users. Server, b is the health service provider (HSP) who provides patient data to the requesting client a, the initiator.

The PK-certificate includes two parts, {a, Pk(a), l2, ts} and {h(a, Pk(a), l2, ts}{SK(ca)}. The first part, contains information about the client, such as, identity a, public key of a PK(a), group membership $l2$ and timestamp ts. The second part, is the signature of the ca. ca signs subject a, public key of a, $PK(a)$, a group membership $l2$ and timestamp ts using its own private key $SK(ca)$, which is only known to the ca. Since it is encrypted with the private key of ca, any other user cannot spoof it. It provides confidence of certificate's information to a participant. The certificate can only be decrypted by the public key of ca, which is known to client a and HSP b. The following describes the message sequence of the LAA protocol depicted in Figure 1.

Message 1: ca issues and sends the PK-certificate, $certa$, to client a in order to authenticate client a and distribute $PK(a)$ safely.

```
Message 1. ca ──→a : certa
Message 2. b ──→a : attr-certa
Message 3. a ──→b : {na, msg}{SKey}
Message 4. a ──→b : certa
[b computes decryptable (certa, PK(ca)) & veri2==h(veri1)]
Message 5. b ──→a : cr1
[a computes decrypt(cr1, SK(a)==na,nb,b)]
Message 6. a ──→ b : cr2
[b computes dectypt (cr2, SK(b)==nb,a) & ga==l1 or ga==l2]
Message 7. a ──→b : attr-certa
[b computes decryptable (sigb, PK(b)) & decrypt(ps3intral2,SK(b)) == ps2 &
ts==now || ts+1==now & integrity1=h(integrity2)]
Message 8. b ──→ a : {a, ps3intral2, o1, o2}
```

Fig. 1. The LAA protocol description

Message 2: b issues and sends the attribute certificate, *attr-certa*, to a. This certificate includes the issuer name (b), the client name (a), an L3 pseudonym (ps3intral2), a timestamp (ts) and the issuer's signature on the certificate (sigb). The L3 pseudonym (ps3intral2), contains another pseudonym (ps2), a recovery token (w), issuer name (b) and the request (All) which indicates all objects of a patient managed by this HSP b.

Message 3: Client a sends his/her nonce (na) and a message containing the requested data encrypted with the shared symmetric key.

Message 4: a sends his/her PK-certificate (certa) to b. This certificates contains *veri1* and *veri2*. The variable *veri1* contains the plain content of the certificate. The variable *veri2* contains the deciphered b's signature on the certificate. Using *veri1* and *veri2* allows checking the integrity of the certificate. HSP b then validates the *ca's* public on the certificate and verifies the certificate's integrity.

Message 5: HSP b sends to client a the challenge response *cr1*, which contains the random nonces (na, nb) and his/her identity b, encrypted with a's public key. Client a checks if *cr1* is decryptable by SK(a) and contains the right nonce *na*. This step is essential to allow client a to authenticate verifier b.

Message 6: Client a sends to b the challenge response *cr2*, which contains *nb* and a. Recipient b checks if *cr2* is decryptable by SK(b) and contains the right nonce *nb*. This step is essential to allow b to authenticate a. Also, in this step, b checks a's group membership to ensure that s/he belongs to the right group and legitimate for this type of access.

Message 7: After successful authentication, a sends to b his attr-cert to check his authorisation. HSP b then checks the correctness of the certificate. It completes this by verifying the signature on the certificate and checks a's access credentials. That is to ensure that the certificate contains the right type of L3 pseudonym (ps3intral2). After that, it verifies the integrity of the lower-level pseudonym (ps2) to ensure that it has not been altered during transmission.

Message 8: Finally, after successful authorisation, b forwards to a the requested patient's data objects indexed with the right pseudonym and encrypted with the shared secret key.

3.2 Modelling the LAA Protocol Using Casper

Based on the LAA protocol's notation in Table 1, we model the LAA protocol in Casper script as shown in Figure 2.

```
#Protocol description
--ca issued and sends PK-certificate to client a
0. -> a : {{a,PK(a),{12}%ga,ts}%veri1,{{h(a,PK(a),{12}%ga,ts)}%veri2}{SK(ca)%skca}
%certa}{PK(a)}
--a wants to contact b
1. -> a : b
--a sends his original request message with a nonce
2a. a -> b : {msg, na}{PK(b)}
--a sends his PK-certificate to be verified by b
2b. a -> b :{veri1%{a,PK(a),ga%{12},ts},{certa%{veri2% {h(a,PK(a),ga%{12},ts)}}}}
{SK(ca)}} {SKey}
[decryptable(certa, PK(ca)) and veri2== h(veri1) and ts==now or ts+1==now]
--Mutual authentication and check user membership
3. b -> a : {{b, nb, na}{PK(a)} %cr1}{Skey}
[decryptable(cr1, SK(a))]
4. a -> b :{{a, nb}{PK(b)} %cr2}{Skey}
[decryptable(cr2, SK(b)) and ga==12 or ga==11]
-- b issues and sends an attribute certificate to a
5. b -> a :{{b,a,{ps2,w,b,ALL, nonce}%integrity2, {h(ps2, w, b, ALL, nonce)}%
integrity1}{PK(b)}% ps3intral2,ts, {h(b,a,ps3intral2,ts)} {SK(b)} %sigb} {SKey}
[ts==now or ts+1==now]
--a sends to b his attribute certificate for authorisation verification
6. a -> b :{{b,a, ps3intral2 %{integrity2%{ps2, w,b,ALL,nonce},integrity1%
{h(ps2,w,b,ALL,nonce)}}, ts}{PK(b)},sigb%{h(b,a,ps3intral2,ts)}{skb%SK(b)}} {SKey}
[decryptable(sigb, PK(b)) and integrity1== h(integrity2) and decrypt(ps3intral2,
SK(b))== (ps2, w, b, ALL) and ts==now or ts+1==now]
--b sends the response to client a
7. b -> a : {a, na, ps3intral2, o1, o2, ts}{SKey}
[ts==now or ts+1==now]
```

Fig. 2. The LAA protocol modelling using Casper

3.3 LAA Protocol Goals

In this section, we identify the LAA protocol security goals or properties.

(P1) Data Confidentiality: Confidentiality is a vital requirement that provides secrecy and privacy in e-health applications. An unauthorised party or an intruder should not be able to learn anything about any communication between two entities by observing or even tampering the communication lines.

(P2) Integrity Protection: A strong integrity mechanism should be deployed to protect against data tampering. The LAA protocol should detect any unauthorised alteration to data being transmitted between authorised entities.

(P3) Mutual Authentication: Or two-way authentication, refers to both entities of the protocol should authenticate each other to allow secure exchange of data between them.

(P4) Certificate Manipulation Protection: It should be guaranteed that certificates (i.e., PK-certificates) presented in the protocol by entities are valid and have not been corrupted or modified during transmission.

(P5) Credential Forgery Protection: It should be assured that users' credentials are not stolen or forged. This is because it can lead to elevation of privileges attack. That is when a user with limited privileges assumes the identity of a user with higher privileges to gain access to patient confidential data.

(P6) Data Freshness: There should be a proof that nonces, generated during protocols, are fresh and the integrity of the session key is preserved. Both entities should also have undeniable proof that the other party is in possession of a valid session key. Any previous compromised key should be easily detected, and the protocol run should terminate.

(P7) Anonymous Linkability: A user with L2 access credentials should be able to link multiple de-identified or anonymous objects of the same patient managed by an HSP but should not be able to link them to the patient's real identity.

3.4   Verification Result and Security Analysis of the LAA Protocol

The result of the verification using Casper/FDR2 tool confirms that the LAA protocol has fulfilled l the security properties identified in Section 3.3. The result of the verification is shown in Figure 3.

(P1) Data Confidentiality: was fulfilled by deploying cryptographic techniques such as symmetric cryptoystem, asymmetric cryptoystem, and hash functions.

(P2) Integrity Protection: was achieved by using digital signatures and hash functions that can detect any data modification during transmission.

(P3) Mutual Authentication: was met by integrating the challenge response protocol.

(P4) Certificate Manipulation Protection: was abided by including a timestamp in the certificate, which can spot any manipulation or sniffing.

(P5) Credential Forgery Protection: was met by adding the credential holder's identity in both types of certificates, the PK-certificate and the attribute certificate. So by checking that both certificates contain the same credential holder identity, we can detect any forgery.

```
Initialising Casper.... Done.
Initialising FDR.... Done.
Ready.

Casper version 2.0

Parsing...
Type checking...
Consistency checking...
Compiling...
Writing output...
Output written to /home/Rima/Download/casper-2.0/L2intra-
HSPAccessProtocol.csp
Done

Starting FDR
Checking /home/Rima/Download/casper-2.0/L2intra-
HSPAccessProtocol.csp

Checking assertion SECRET_M::SECRET_SPEC [T= SECRET_M::SYSTEM_S
No attack found

Checking assertion SECRET_M::SEQ_SECRET_SPEC [T=
SECRET_M::SYSTEM_S_SEQ
No attack found

Checking assertion AUTH1
_M::AuthenticateRESPONDERToINITIATORAgreement_na [T= AUTH1
_M::SYSTEM_1
No attack found

Checking assertion AUTH2
_M::AuthenticateINITIATORToRESPONDERAgreement_nb [T= AUTH2
_M::SYSTEM_2
No attack found

Done
```

Fig. 3. Verification result of the LAA protocol using Casper/FDR2

(P6) Data Freshness: was achieved by including a freshly random nonce with the transmitted data.

(P7) Anonymous Linkability: was fulfilled by integrating the L3 pseudonym-TypeIII in the user's access credential. This allows linkable anonymous access to patient data as it contains a lower-level pseudonym that can be used to link all the patient's objects.

4   Implementation and Performance Evaluation

This section illustrates the implementation and performance evaluation of the LAA security protocol.

Performance is measured by two metrics, minimising access delay and minimising server computation time. An access delay is the time elapsed from submitting an access request until the time the response is obtained. A server computation time is the time required for the server to complete the necessary operations from receiving the request until the response to the request is sent. Both metrics should be kept as low as possible.

To extract the access delay and server computational time resulted from the LAA protocol, we have measured the time taken to execute the protocol under two scenarios.
- The first scenario is called the L3 Scenario. In this scenario, we run the protocol without applying any extra security layer to the protocol. This scenario is the Level-3 access, which has been described in the introduction section.
- The second scenario is called the L2 Scenario. In this scenario, we run the protocol with applying our additional security solution.

The measurements are taken for 10 execution rounds for each scenario, and the averages are calculated. The results are depicted in Figure 4.

4.1 Implementation Hardware and Software

To implement the LAA protocol, we have used a desktop computer running Windows 8 with a 2.30 GHz Intel Core i3 and 8GB of RAM. The software used to implement the LAA protocol is JAVA 2 Platform, Standard Edition (J2SE).

4.2 Performance Evaluation Result and Analysis

Figure 4 shows that the time (Access delay) taken to execute the LAA protocol (L2 Scenario) is 111 milliseconds, which is approximately 30% more than the time taken in L3 Scenario, which is 85 milliseconds. The server computation time in L2 Scenario is 107 milliseconds, which is approximately 33% more than that in L3 Scenario, which is 81 milliseconds.

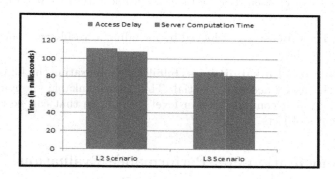

Fig. 4. Performance evaluation result of the LAA protocol

The extra cost in the L2 Scenario is caused by the following reasons.
- The extra communications between the client and the verifier.
- The extra computations in signature verifications by both the client and the verifier.
- The extra computation in the attribute certificate verification by the verifier.
- The extra computation in checking the timestamp in the attribute certificate.

- The extra computation in validating the pseudonym, PS3intral2 in the attribute certificate.
- The extra integrity check of the lower-level pseudonym (PS2) included in PS3intral2.

5 Conclusion

The focus of this paper was on two important aspects. The first aspect is designing a robust protocol to facilitate secure access to patient electronic records. The second aspect is providing an efficient access to electronic patient records.

The first aspect was achieved by relying on the formal verification tool, Casper/FDR2. The result of the verification showed that the protocol has fulfilled important security requirements. We have incorporated SSL protocol, which allowed communication channels to be confidentiality, integrity and authentication protected. Our protocol offers a wide range of significant features. It supports linkable anonymous access to patient data by deploying important cryptographic techniques. It ensures confidentiality of patient sensitive data. It supports data freshness by making use of timestamp and random nonces. It protects from certificate manipulation and credential forgery. Mutual authentication is also supported to obtain unforgeable proof of the participants in the protocol.

The second aspect was achieved by implementing the LAA protocol using the Java technology to evaluate its performance. The result from the protocol implementation showed that we had successfully balanced between security and performance. This is because the increase in performance was linear with the increase of security layer. In other words, the analysis proved that our LAA protocol is secure and efficient. For future work, we aim to extend the analysis of the LAA protocol to other security e-health protocols, considering security and performance as essential criteria.

Acknowledgments. This work is financially sponsored by the Ministry of Higher Education in Saudi Arabia.

References

1. Alvarez, R.C.: The promise of e-health - A canadian perspective. Ehealth International 1(1) (September 2002)
2. Pang, C., Hansen, D.: Improved record linkage for encrypted identifying data, Sydney, Austrailia, pp. 164–168 (2006)
3. Addas, R., Zhang, N.: An enhanced approach to supporting controlled access to eprs with three levels of identity privacy preservations. In: Holzinger, A., Simonic, K.-M. (eds.) USAB 2011. LNCS, vol. 7058, pp. 547–561. Springer, Heidelberg (2011)
4. Needham, R.M., Schroeder, M.D.: Using encryption for authentication in large networks of computers. Commun. ACM 21(12), 993–999 (1978)

5. Lowe, G.: An attack on the needham-schroeder public-key authentication protocol. Information Processing Letters 56(3), 131–133 (1995)
6. Kim, I.G., Choi, J.Y.: Formal verification of pap and eap-md5 protocols in wireless networks: Fdr model checking. In: 18th International Conference on Advanced Information Networking and Applications, AINA 2004, vol. 2, pp. 264–269 (2004)
7. Lowe, G.: Casper: A compiler for the analysis of security protocols, pp. 18–30 (June 1997)
8. Formal System (Europe) LTD.: Failure-divergences refinement fdr2 manual (2010)
9. Kim, I.G., Kim, H.S., Lee, J.Y., Choi, J.Y.: Analysis and modification of ask mobile security protocol. In: The Second IEEE International Workshop on Mobile Commerce and Services, WMCS 2005, pp. 79–83 (2005)
10. Kim, H.S., Oh, J.H., Choi, J.Y., Kim, J.W.: The vulnerabilities analysis and design of the security protocol for rfid system. In: The Sixth IEEE International Conference on Computer and Information Technology, CIT 2006, p. 152 (2006)
11. Chan, P., Lee, R., Kramer, D.: The Java Class Libraries, Volume 1: Supplement for the Java 2 Platform, Standard Edition, V 1.2., vol. 1. Addison-Wesley Professional (1999)
12. Gilbert, H., Handschuh, H.: Security Analysis of SHA-256 and Sisters. In: Matsui, M., Zuccherato, R.J. (eds.) SAC 2003. LNCS, vol. 3006, pp. 175–193. Springer, Heidelberg (2004)
13. Blömer, J., Seifert, J.-P.: Fault based cryptanalysis of the advanced encryption standard (aes). In: Wright, R.N. (ed.) FC 2003. LNCS, vol. 2742, pp. 162–181. Springer, Heidelberg (2003)
14. Rivest, R.L., Shamir, A., Adleman, L.: A method for obtaining digital signatures and public-key cryptosystems. Commun. ACM 21, 120–126 (1978)
15. Wagner, D., Schneier, B.: Analysis of the ssl 3.0 protocol. In: Proceedings of the Second Unix Workshop on Electronic Commerce, pp. 29–40. USENIX Association (1996)

On Safety of Pseudonym-Based Location Data in the Context of Constraint Satisfation Problems

Tomoya Tanjo[1], Kazuhiro Minami[1], Ken Mano[2], and Hiroshi Maruyama[1]

[1] Institute of Statistical Mathematics, Tokyo, Japan
[2] NTT Corporation, Kanagawa, Japan
{tanjo,kminami,hm2}@ism.ac.jp, mano.ken@lab.ntt.co.jp

Abstract. Pseudonymization is a promising technique for publishing a trajectory location data set in a privacy-preserving way. However, it is not trivial to determine whether a given data set is safely publishable against an adversary with partial knowledge about users' movements. We therefore formulate this safety decision problem based on the framework of constraint satisfaction problems (CSPs) and evaluate its performance with a real location data set. We show that our approach with an existing CSP solver outperforms a polynomial-time verification algorithm, which is designed particularly for this safety problem.

1 Introduction

Nowadays, a location data set, which is obtained by collecting GPS data from people's mobile devices, can be used for various analytic purposes, such as real-time traffic monitoring [5] and urban planning for future sustainable cities [13]. However, due to the significant concern about location privacy [1], the sharing of mobile users' location traces has largely been restricted to k-anonymized data sets [6], which degrade the granularity of location data to ensure that every location contains more than k people. Such a k-anonymized data set provides little information on trajectory patterns of mobile users.

We, therefore, consider a dynamic pseudonym scheme for constructing a location data set that retains users' path information while preserving their location privacy. The basic idea is to exchange multiple users' pseudonyms randomly when they meet at the same location to eliminate the linkability of their pseudonyms before and after that exchange. Roughly speaking, a user's location privacy is preserved if we can find enough number of plausible alternate paths for that user in the data set. We believe that such a dynamic pseudonym approach is effective enough to publish large segments of the users' whole trajectory paths in a privacy-preserving way if the data set involves a large number of users whose trajectory paths intersect with each other many times.

However, it is not trivial to count the numbers of users' alternate paths under the presence of an adversary who owns partial information on users' movements (e.g., a user's home location). Such an adversary can eliminate some of the

Linawati et al. (Eds.): ICT-EurAsia 2014, LNCS 8407, pp. 511–520, 2014.

Fig. 1. Pseudonymized location data publishing. The data publisher replaces a user's identity u_i with a pseudonym p_i before releasing location data to data set users.

users' alternate paths that are inconsistent with his external knowledge. We thus need to address the issue of multi-path inconsistencies among multiple users and formulate this problem in the context of constraint satisfaction problems (CSPs) [4].

A CSP is defined as a set of variables whose values must satisfy a number of constraints expressed with arithmetic and logical operators. We can declaratively define constraints on each user's pseudonym assignments considering the possibility of pseudonym exchanges at mix zones and consistency requirements with an adversary's external knowledge. Once we formulate all constraints on users' plausible trajectory paths, we can compute the number of possible alternate paths with an existing CSP solver; that is, the number of different pseudonyms that are possibly taken by the same user corresponds to the uncertainty about that user's possible destinations.

Although the time complexity of solving a CSP is exponential at the worst case, our experimental results with a real location data set show that our CSP-based approach outperforms a polynomial-time algorithm we previously developed for this problem [9]. Therefore, we believe that our CSP-based approach is effective in many realistic situations.

2   Privacy Model

We first define our system model for a psedonymized location data publishing service, and introduce a technique of dynamic pseudonym exchanges at a mix zone. Next, we establish our privacy metrics we consider in this paper. Figure 1 shows our system model. We assume that each user u_i carrying a GPS-enabled mobile device periodically reports a triplet (u_i, l_k, t_k), which indicates that user u_i is at location l_k at time t_k. The data publisher receives identifiable location data from multiple users, replaces their identities with pseudonyms, and provides a dataset user with a pseudonymized location data set. This data set is an output from the data publisher in Figure 1.

To replace a user's identity on a given moving path with a static pseudonym does not necessarily protect the user's location privacy. The danger is that if an adversary knowing that a target user u is at location l at time t finds a data point (p, l, t) where p is a pseudonym from the received data set, the adversary can associate p with the user's identity u. Furthermore, he also learns that all the data points with the same pseudonym p in the data set belong to the same user u; that is, the adversary can identify user u's whole trajectory path.

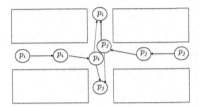

Fig. 2. Example pseudonym exchange. Two users exchange their pseudonyms p_i and p_j at the intersection. The solid lines denote each user's actual path while the dotted lines denote an alternate possible path.

To limit undesirable information disclosure from the above inference attack, we take an approach of changing each user's pseudonym dynamically when multiple users meet at the same location, which we call a *mix zone*. The basic idea is to divide a whole path of the same user into multiple segments with different pseudonyms such that the linkability of any neighboring segments is eliminated. Figure 2 shows an example of two users' exchanging their pseudonyms. Two users who own pseudonyms p_i and p_j, respectively, randomly exchange their pseudonyms when meeting at the intersection. Although the user who previously owned pseudonym p_i actually turns right at the corner, we consider that the alternate path of the users' turning left is also possible. The other user similarly has the two possible paths after passing the intersection.

If we consider the possible paths of a single user, whenever the user meets another user, we can add a new branch as a possible segment of the path. However, such a possible path must be consistent with an adversary's external knowledge. Suppose that the adversary knows users' home location and that every user starts its path with his home location and eventually returns home. We need to eliminate some possible branches if taking that direction makes it impossible for the user to return home. Furthermore, even if one user u_i is able to return home along a possible path, another user u_j who exchanged her pseudonym with u_i might lose a possible route to her home location. We thus need to consider possible pseudonym sequences for multiple users simultaneously. We call this requirement the *multi-path* consistency requirement, which is expressed as a set of constraints in a CSP in Section 3. We assume that an adversary learns a user u's location only at some mix zones; that is, the adversary observes user u where many people get together (e.g., a zebra zone on the street or a public space such as a hospital).

We consider the number of pseudonyms at a given time t on possible pseudonym sequences satisfying the multi-path consistency requirement as our location privacy metrics. Figure 3 shows such multiple pseudonym sequences of user u_i. If an adversary knows u_i's location at times t_0 and t^*, there is no uncertainty about a pseudonym taken by u_i at both times. However, user u_i is likely to have some uncertainty about his pseudonym in the middle of his trajectory after passing multiple mix zones. We now define the notion of (k, t)-pseudonym location privacy as follows.

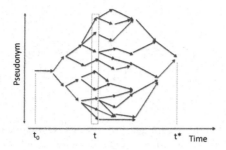

Fig. 3. Concept of (k, t)-pseudonym location privacy

Definition 1 ((k, t)-pseudonym location privacy). *If user u_i can take k or more pseudonyms at a given time t while satisfying the multi-path consistency requirement, we say that user u_i satisfies (k, t)-pseudonym location privacy.*

3   Background on Constraint Satisfaction Problems

We give a brief overview of a constraint satisfaction problem (CSP) [12], which is sufficient to formulate the safety problem of location data psuedonymization in the context of CSP in Section 4. A CSP is a problem of finding a solution satisfying all the given conditions on a set of variables. We define a CPS in a declarative way such that a CSP solver finds a solution in a computationally efficient way. Although solving a CSP is known as NP-hard, existing CSP solvers, which have been widely used in many areas (e.g., [2,8]), usually show good performance for practical purposes.

We first define a constraint network and a CSP as follows.

Definition 2 (Constraint network). *Constraint network (or Network) N is a tuple (X, D, C) where*

- *X is a finite set of integer variables,*
- *D is a mapping from X to a set of all possible finite subsets of integers which represents their possible values (domain), and*
- *C is a finite set of constraints over X which represents a conjunction of constraints ($\wedge$). Each constraint consists of:*
  - *Arithmetic operators (such as $+$, $-$)*
  - *Arithmetic comparisons (such as $=$, $\neq$, $\leq$)*
  - *Logical operators (such as $\wedge$, $\vee$, $\Rightarrow$)*
  - *Global constraints (such as **same**: described later)*

A global constraint is a constraint between non-fixed number of variables. For example, the **same** constraint takes two integer sequences $X =< x_1, x_2, \ldots, x_n >$ and $Y =< y_1, y_2, \ldots, y_n >$, and it represents X is a permutation of Y.

An *assignment* is a mapping from X to a set of integers and a *partial* assignment is a mapping from a subset of X to a set of integers.

Definition 3 (Constraint Satisfaction Problem). *Let $N = (X, D, C)$ be a constraint network. A constraint satisfaction problem (CSP) is a problem to find an assignment α such that*

- *α satisfies all the constraints $c \in C$ and*
- *$\alpha(x) \in D(x)$ holds for all integer variables $x \in X$.*

If there exists such assignment α, it is called a solution *of the CSP.*

An existing CSP solver typically finds a solution in the following way. First, it picks one variable x_i from X and defines a partial assignment to x_i. Second, the solver removes inconsistent values from the other domains by applying a constraint propagation algorithm. If another domain for a variable x_j becomes an empty set (i.e., the partial assignment cannot be extended to any solution), the solver picks a different value x_i' from $D(x_i)$ and repeats the same process to extend the partial assignment to variable x_j. This process is iterated until the solver finds a solution by extending the partial assignment to an assignment for all the variables.

4 Formalizing the CSP Safety Problem

We formalize the safety problem in Section 2 as the k-pseudonym decision problem and show how to solve that decision problem using a CSP solver.

4.1 The k-Pseudonym Decision Problem

We use letters u and $u_1, u_2, \ldots$ for users and p and $p_1, p_2, \ldots$ for pseudonyms respectively. We denote N_{t^*} as a finite set of integers $\{1, \ldots, t^*\}$.

Definition 4 (Mix Zone). *Let U be a finite set of users. A mix zone m over U is a subset of U whose size is greater than one. We denote by $\mathbb{M}_U$ all the set of mix zones over U.*

We next define the mix zone function that takes a time t as an input and outputs a finite set of mix zones, which occur at time t as follows.

Definition 5 (Mix zone function). *Let U be a finite set of users, t^* be a positive integer, and $\mathbb{M}_U$ be a set of all possible mix zones over U. The mix zone function $f_{U,t^*} : N_{t^*} \to 2^{\mathbb{M}_U}$ is a mapping from N_{t^*} to a finite subset of $\mathbb{M}_U$ where $\mathbb{M}_U$ is the set of all mix zones.*

To formulate a k-pseudonym decision problem, we express an adversary's external knowledge and each user u's security requirements as follows.

Definition 6 (External knowledge). *External knowledge is a finite set of pairs (u, t), which represents the fact that an adversary knows a user u's location at time t.*

Definition 7 (Security requirement). *A security requirement is a tuple (u, t, k) where $u \in U$ is a user and $1 \leq t \leq t^*$ and $k \geq 1$ are integers.*

This requirement represents the fact that a user u can possibly take more than k different pseudonyms at time t. We expect that each user specifies multiple security requirements on a given pseudonymized data set.

We next define the pseudonym function which returns a pseudonym for the user u at time t.

Definition 8 (Pseudonym function). *Let U be a finite set of users, $P = \{p_1, p_2, \ldots, p_{|U|}\}$ be a finite set of pseudonyms, and t^* be a positive integer. The function **pseudonym** $s : U \times N_{t^*} \rightarrow P$ maps a pair of a user u and time t to a pseudonym $p \in P$ such that a user u has a pseudonym p at time t.*

Finally, we define the k-pseudonym decision problem as follows.

Definition 9 (k-pseudonym decision problem). *Let U be a finite set of users, t^* be a positive integer, and E be an adversary's external knowledge. Let (u, t, k) be a security requirement. The k-pseudonym decision problem $(f_{U,t^*}, (u, t, k), E)$ is a problem to decide whether there exist k candidates for $s(u, t)$ that are consistent with the external knowledge E.*

4.2 Solving k-Pseudonym Decision Problem

We first represent the k-pseudonym decision problem as a constraint network and show how we solve it with a CSP solver in an incremental way. Figure 4 shows the function *generateCSP* that generates a constraint network from the given mix zone function. Quoted variables or constraints such as 's_u^t' in Figure 4 show the variables or constraints in the network. Here are the overview of the function *generateCSP*:

- We introduce an integer variable $s_u^t \in P$ which represents a pseudonym $s(u, t)$ for each user u and each time t. The domain of s_u^t is $\{1, 2, \ldots, i, \ldots, |U| - 1, |U|\}$ where each domain value i corresponds to the pseudonym p_i in the set of pseudonyms P.
- Without loss of generality, we add constraints for specifying the pseudonyms of users at time $t = 0$.
- For each time $t \in \{1..t^*\}$, we add the following constraints.
  - $s(u, t) = s(u, t - 1)$ holds if the user u is not included in any mix zones at time t.
  - **same**($< s(u_i, t - 1), s(u_j, t - 1), \cdots >, < s(u_i, t), s(u_j, t), \cdots >$) holds if there is a mix zone $\{u_i, u_j, \ldots\}$ at time t.

```
// U: a finite set of users, f: mix zone function, t*: maximum time
def generateCSP(U, f, t*)
  X = ∅
  C = ∅
  // introduce integer variables
  foreach u in U
    foreach t in 0..t*
      X = X ∪ {'s_u^t'}
    end
  end

  // pseudonyms at time t = 0
  i = 0
  foreach u in U
    C = C ∪ {'s_u^0 = i'}
    i = i + 1
  end

  foreach t in 1..t*
    // The same constraint should hold for each mix zone.
    foreach M in f(t)
      P = ∅
      foreach 's_u^t' in M
        P = P ∪ {'s_u^(t-1)'}
      end
      C = C ∪ {'same(P, M)'}
    end
    // If an user u is not included in any mix zones,
    // 's_u^t' is same as the pseudonym at the previous time.
    foreach u in U - ⋃ f(t)
      C = C ∪ {'s_u^t = s_u^(t-1)'}
    end
  end
  return (X, D, C) where D(s) = {1..|U|} for all s in X
end
```

Fig. 4. A pseudo code to generate a constraint network from the given mix zone function

In addition to the constraint network generated by the function $generateCSP$, we need to express extra constraints for the external knowledge. If an adversary knows only one external knowledge (u, t), she knows that one of the possible values in $D(s_u^t)$ corresponds to the user u. She cannot infer further information because she only knows the external knowledge at mix zones as described in Section 2. Therefore we do not need additional constraints in this case.

If the adversary knows two external knowledge $\{(u, t_1), (u, t_2)\}$ (i.e., she know the information about $s(u, t_1)$ and $s(u, t_2)$), she can infer more information from the external knowledge at the worst case where $s(u, t_1) = s(u, t_2)$ holds. To consider this worst case, we add an extra constraint $s_u^{t_1} = s_u^{t_2}$ to the generated constraint network. If there is more than two elements in the external knowledge, we add the corresponding constraints in the same way.

Let N be a constraint network which is generated with the function $generateCSP(U, f, t^*)$ and let us consider $(X_G, D_G, C_G) = \Phi_G(N)$ where $\Phi_G(N)$ is the function for removing all inconsistent values from the domains. Each domain value $d \in D_G(s_u^t)$ corresponds to a possible pseudonym which is computed with $s(u, t)$. Therefore, we can solve k-pseudonym decision problem by checking whether $|D_G(s_u^t)| \geq k$ holds for the security requirement (u, t, k).

However, many CSP solvers do not use Φ_G in practice because it requires too much computation time. Those solvers usually use the algorithms for other consistencies which are weaker but more reasonable with respect to execution time or memory consumption. Therefore, we propose an incremental solving method, which can be applicable to existing CSP solvers.

In the incremental solving method, we first generate a constraint network (X, D, C) from the given mix zone function, and check whether the network $(X, D, C \cup \{s_u^t = i\})$ has a solution for each domain value $i \in D(s_u^t)$.

5   Experimental Results

We develop the safety verification program for solving the k-pseudonym decision problem from a given mix zone function. It is written in Groovy with 409 lines using the Choco library [14] as an external CSP solver. Using this program, we further develop an optimization program based on dynamic programming that finds the minimum number of mix zones satisfying a given safety requirement.

We use the dataset [11] containing mobility traces of taxi cabs in San Francisco, USA. It contains GPS coordinates of approximately 500 taxis collected over 30 days in the San Francisco Bay Area. When we conduct our experiments with a given number of users, we randomly pick a specified number of users from the dataset.

Figure 5 shows performance results of finding the minimum set of mix zones satisfying all the security requirements changing the number of users in a dataset. We randomly define security requirements of up to five to randomly chosen users. We compare results with our safety verification program using the CSP solver with those using our previously developed polynomial-time algorithm[10]. Although the time complexity of the CSP solver is exponential at the worst

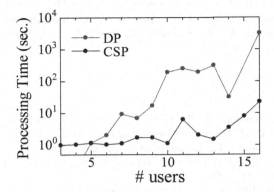

Fig. 5. Comparison of the processing time. *CSP* is the result with a CSP solver and *DP* is the results with our previously developed polynomial algorithm.

case, our safety versifier outperforms our previously algorithm. This results show that the CSP solver, which has been done with various performance turning, efficiently makes a safety decision with realistic location data sets.

6   Related Work

Using pseudonyms is a promising way to make location data unlinkable to a particular user. Beresford and Stajano [3] were the first to discuss the idea of dynamically changing pseudonyms in a mix zone where multiple people meet, in order to prevent an adversary from linking two pseudonyms of the same user. However, they only consider the situation where an adversary has just a local view of users' movements and observes pseudonyms of entering or leaving the same mix zone. Hoh and Gruteser [7] present a path perturbation algorithm that adds noises to original location data so that each user can construct alternate possible paths by exchanging his pseudonym with those of other users when they meet at the same place. However, their scheme does not consider an adversary's external knowledge that can associate each user with a particular location, as we assume in this paper.

7   Conclusions

In this paper, we introduce the safety definition of pseudonym-based location data and show how to represent the original safety problem in the context of constraint satisfaction problem. Our experimental results with a real location data set show that our approach with an existing CSP solver outperforms a polynomial-time verification algorithm, which is designed particularly for this safety problem.

Acknowledgments. This research is supported by the Strategic Joint Research Grant for NTT and Research Organization of Information and Systems (ROIS) and by the Grants-in-Aid for Scientific Research C, 11013869, of Japan Society for the Promotion of Science.

References

1. Anthony, D., Henderson, T., Kotz, D.: Privacy in location-aware computing environments. IEEE Pervasive Computing 6(4), 64–72 (2007)
2. Backofen, R., Gilbert, D.: Bioinformatics and constraints. In: Rossi, F., van Beek, P., Walsh, T. (eds.) Handbook of Constraint Programming, ch. 26, pp. 903–942. Elsevier Science Inc. (2006)
3. Beresford, A.R., Stajano, F.: Location Privacy in Pervasive Computing 2(1), 46–55 (January-March 2003)
4. Freuder, E.C., Mackworth, A.K.: Constraint satisfaction: An emerging paradigm. In: Rossi, F., van Beek, P., Walsh, T. (eds.) Handbook of Constraint Programming, ch. 2, pp. 11–26. Elsevier Science Inc. (2006)
5. Google maps, http://maps.google.com/
6. Gruteser, M., Grunwald, D.: Anonymous usage of location-based services through spatial and temporal cloaking. In: Proceedings of Mobisys 2003: The First International Conference on Mobile Systems, Applications, and Services. USENIX Associations, San Francisco (2003)
7. Hoh, B., Gruteser, M.: Protecting location privacy through path confusion. In: First International Conference on Security and Privacy for Emerging Areas in Communications Networks, SecureComm 2005, pp. 194–205 (September 2005)
8. Hooker, J.N.: Operations research methods in constraint programming. In: Rossi, F., van Beek, P., Walsh, T. (eds.) Handbook of Constraint Programming, ch. 15, pp. 525–568. Elsevier Science Inc. (2006)
9. Mano, K., Minami, K., Maruyama, H.: Privacy-preserving publishing of pseudonym-based trajectory location data set. In: Proceedings of the 2nd International Workshop on Security of Mobile Applications, IWSMA (2013)
10. Mano, K., Minami, K., Maruyama, H.: Protecting location privacy with k-confusing paths based on dynamic pseudonyms. In: Proceedings of the 5th IEEE International Workshop on SEcurity and SOCial Networking (SESOC), pp. 285–290 (2013)
11. Piorkowski, M., Sarafijanovic-Djukic, N., Grossglauser, M.: CRAWDAD data set epfl/mobility (v. 2009-02-24) (February 2009), http://crawdad.cs.dartmouth.edu/epfl/mobility
12. Rossi, F., van Beek, P., Walsh, T.: Handbook of Constraint Programming. Elsevier Science Inc., New York (2006)
13. Seike, T., Mimaki, H., Hara, Y., Odawara, R., Nagata, T., Terada, M.: Research on the applicability of "mobile spatial statistics" for enhanced urban planning. Journal of the City Planning Institute of Japan 46(3), 451–456 (2011)
14. The choco team: choco: An open source Java constraint programming library. In: Proceedings of the 3rd International CSP Solver Competition, pp. 7–13 (2008)

Advanced Techniques for Computer Sharing and Management of Strategic Data

Marek R. Ogiela, Lidia Ogiela, and Urszula Ogiela

AGH University of Science and Technology,
Cryptography and Cognitive Informatics Research Group
Al. Mickiewicza 30, PL-30-059 Krakow, Poland
{mogiela,logiela,ogiela}@agh.edu.pl

Abstract. In the paper will be presented some advances in the area of computer methods used for encryption and division of confidential data, as well as modern approaches for management of splitted information. Computer techniques for secret information sharing aim to secure information against disclosure to unauthorized persons. The paper will present algorithms allowing for information division and sharing on the basis of biometric or personal features. The development of computer techniques for classified information sharing should also be useful in the process of shared information distribution and management. For this purpose there will be presented a new approach for information management based on cognitive information systems.

Keywords: cryptographic protocols, bio-inspired cryptography, secret sharing algorithms.

1   Introduction

In the recent years there were developed many advanced cryptographic procedures for secure information splitting or sharing. Some of them are very intuitive and simple, but some others are more advanced and often dedicated for sharing of particular types of data e.g. visual information. Among such procedures we can also find some interesting examples of splitting procedures, which are based on using some special input data to the splitting algorithm. Such universal approach for information sharing may be very interesting, when as input values we can also put biometric or personal information for generation of particular shares or information shadows. In the next section we'll try to describe some important features of such crypto-biometric techniques, which may be used for secret sharing tasks. Additionally we'll also try to present some others procedures, especially oriented for performing management task, and allowing for intelligent information shares distribution using a new classes of cognitive information systems. Such systems may play a great role in future, developing the new areas of cognitive cryptography [12].

Linawati et al. (Eds.): ICT-EurAsia 2014, LNCS 8407, pp. 521–525, 2014.

2   Crypto-Biometrics Approach

A lot number of cryptographic methods for secret splitting or sharing are developed. Some of them may also use individual human information or biometrics during generation particular number of secret shares. For such purposes may be used different personal information, starting from the physical personal features, as well as standard biometrics or non-standard biometric features [13]. The most popular physical and biometric features are: iris features, fingerprints patterns, facial features, blood vessels layout or even DNA code. Among non-standard biometric we can find some personal information connected with any pathological changes observed on medical diagnostic visualization [1], obtained during medical examination of particular human body parts or internal organs. Examples of such non-standard personal biometrics can be found in [13], and it may be connected with coronary arteries structures, brain perfusion parameters or other similar values [3, 4].

The process of information splitting using biometrics or personal information can be executed by two different ways i.e. by a layer split and by a hierarchical split. The former means splitting the information between n secret holders and its reconstruction by n-m trustees of the secret. The latter case means that the secret is split between n holders of the secret, but the information can be reproduced by superior groups of secret holders within which the specific secret has been split into k parts (k < n). Thus the splitting methods depend on the purpose for which the information is split and concealed.

Using biometrics during sharing procedure is possible thanks to application of linguistic coding processes [14, 15, 16]. Those procedures are based on the mathematical linguistic formalisms, particularly sequence, tree and grammatical formalisms to record and interpret the meaning of the analysed biometric data. Linguistic coding processes are used because of the ability to execute generalized information coding as in DNA cryptography. In the traditional DNA coding model, one- or two-bit coding is used (utilizing one of the four nitrogen bases or nitrogen bonds). In DNA cryptography any personal information can be combined with biometric features. In linguistic coding, it is possible to code longer bit sequences containing more than two bits of information [17, 18, 19]. This coding is done using terminal symbols introduced in this grammar, and lengthening the coded blocks directly proportionally contributes to accelerating information splitting and reproduction, as well as to increasing the secret component containing information on the grammar used.

The coded biometric information recorded in the form of an n-bit representation is split using a selected information splitting algorithm. The (m, n)-threshold algorithm allows this information to be reproduced by combining at least m of all n shares of the secret. Combining m shares of the secret causes the information to be reproduced in a coded version which can be fully understood only after executing its semantic analysis consisting in a grammatical reasoning carried out for the coded data set.

3   Cognitive Systems for Strategic Information Management

Application of cryptographic procedures for secret sharing allow us to obtain particular number of secret shares. Having splitted information the main problem remains in distribution and intelligent management of generated information shares. In our research we've tried to introduce a new approach based on using cognitive information systems. Cognitive systems allow understanding the contents and the semantics of the data examined [2, 5, 6, 7, 8]. Such examination may be very important for secure information management. Cognitive systems during application performs cognitive resonance functions, which may be used to guarantee the security and safety features during management of strategic data, both in various management structures.

During application of cognitive systems an information may be divided within particular group of persons or institutions regardless of its type or the purpose. The significance of information splitting may depend on the method of its splitting, the purpose of splitting it, and the type of information. Regarding the accessing privileges for particular persons division of information can be hierarchical (for different accessing grants) or layered (similar privileges). The principal difference between these types of divisions concerns the method of introducing the division itself. When a division is made within homogenous, uniform groups of participants with similar privileges, then it is a layer division, whereas if the division is made regardless of the homogeneity of the group but by reference to several different groups it is a hierarchical division [12]. Hierarchical division presents some dependencies between several different structures.

Finally the division of information between the members of a given group in which everyone has the same privileges is a layer division. A hierarchical division is characterized by the ability to make any division of secret information in the way determined by the access rights at individual levels of a hierarchical structure.

There are various methods of information protecting in layered or hierarchical structures, from being accessed by persons not authorized to learn it. Based on such different approaches we can define two types of UBMSS (Understanding Based Management Support Systems) systems [9, 10, 11]. The first class may contain the procedures in which the secret information will be secured using some individual standard or non-standard biometrics, and the second one based on mathematical linguistic formalisms [6]. The first class of such systems are connected with biometric threshold schemes [13], which may use some important physical and biometric features like the iris, fingerprints, hand veins, face etc. [12].

The second class uses linguistic coding processes, which are based on mathematical linguistic formalisms, particularly grammatical formalisms to encode the meaning of the secured data. Linguistic coding processes are very efficient because they have ability to execute generalised information coding similar to DNA cryptography mentioned in previous section [17].

An illustrative example of application of cognitive information systems UBMSS for information sharing and management may be found in [12], but from security point of view we can note that such systems could guarantee the security and integrity of shared information, and also guarantee safety features during distribution of secret parts. Among many important features we can point out following the most important. Cognitive systems are enough suitable for dividing strategic data and assigning its shares to members of the authorized group. Such systems can handle any digital data (both in visual or text form) which needs to be intelligently distributed among authorized persons and then secretly reconstruct. Such systems may be used in different management structures i.e. hierarchical or divisional.

4   Conclusions

In this paper we have presented some advances in using biometric information and personal characteristics to develop new procedures for secret information sharing and spiltting. Processes of splitting or hiding data are currently used in many fields of life, science and research. Employing linguistic coding methods in the concealment and analysis processes offers the full capability of using personal information for such purposes. Concealing biometric or personal data constitutes a very important problem because it is highly probable that personal data will be taken over by unauthorised persons. The individual DNA code, fingerprints, iris features and many other biometrics may be used during sharing procedure.

Additionally we presented the cognitive systems designed for the secure information management in various management structures. Such systems have the ability to perform a semantic analysis of information which allow to classify it for different semantic categories. Such systems allow also to perform an intelligent information management for strategic data. There were defined two different classes of secure information sharing, especially based on linguistic approach as well as based on some personal biometric features. It seems that in near future such systems will play an increasing role in developing new solutions in areas of very special and strategic information management [20].

Acknowledgements. This work has been supported by the National Science Centre, Republic of Poland, under project number DEC-2013/09/B/HS4/00501.

References

1. Bodzioch, S., Ogiela, M.R.: New approach to gallbladder ultrasonic images analysis and lesions recognition. Comput. Med. Imaging Graph. 33, 154–170 (2009)
2. Cohen, H., Lefebvre, C. (eds.): Handbook of Categorization in Cognitive Science. Elsevier, The Netherlands (2005)
3. Hachaj, T., Ogiela, M.R.: A system for detecting and describing pathological changes using dynamic perfusion computer tomography brain maps. Computers in Biology and Medicine 41(6), 402–410 (2011)
4. Hachaj, T., Ogiela, M.R.: Framework for cognitive analysis of dynamic perfusion computed tomography with visualization of large volumetric data. Journal of Electronic Imaging 21(4), Article Number: 043017 (2012)
5. Meystel, A.M., Albus, J.S.: Intelligent Systems – Architecture, Design, and Control. Wiley & Sons, Inc., Canada (2002)

6. Ogiela, L.: Syntactic Approach to Cognitive Interpretation of Medical Patterns. In: Xiong, C., Liu, H., Huang, Y., Xiong, Y. (eds.) ICIRA 2008, Part I. LNCS (LNAI), vol. 5314, pp. 456–462. Springer, Heidelberg (2008)

7. Ogiela, L.: Cognitive systems for medical pattern understanding and diagnosis. In: Lovrek, I., Howlett, R.J., Jain, L.C. (eds.) KES 2008, Part I. LNCS (LNAI), vol. 5177, pp. 394–400. Springer, Heidelberg (2008)

8. Ogiela, L.: UBIAS Systems for Cognitive Interpretation and Analysis of Medical Images. Opto-Electronics Review 17(2), 166–179 (2009)

9. Ogiela, L.: Cognitive Informatics in Automatic Pattern Understanding and Cognitive Information Systems. In: Wang, Y., Zhang, D., Kinsner, W. (eds.) Advances in Cognitive Informatics and Cognitive Computing. SCI, vol. 323, pp. 209–226. Springer, Heidelberg (2010)

10. Ogiela, L., Ogiela, M.R.: Cognitive Techniques in Visual Data Interpretation. SCI, vol. 228. Springer, Heidelberg (2009)

11. Ogiela, L., Ogiela, M.R.: Advances in Cognitive Information Systems. COSMOS, vol. 17. Springer, Heidelberg (2012)

12. Ogiela, L., Ogiela, M.R.: Towards Cognitive Cryptography. Journal of Internet Services and Information Security 4(1), 58–63 (2014)

13. Ogiela, M.R., Ogiela, L., Ogiela, U.: Strategic Information Splitting Using Biometric Patterns. Journal of Internet Services and Information Security 2(3/4), 129–133 (2012)

14. Ogiela, M.R., Ogiela, U.: Linguistic Extension for Secret Sharing (m, n)-threshold Schemes. In: SECTECH 2008 – Proceedings of the International Conference on Security Technology, China, December 13-15, pp. 125–128 (2008)

15. Ogiela, M.R., Ogiela, U.: Security of Linguistic Threshold Schemes in Multimedia Systems. In: Damiani, E., Jeong, J., Howlett, R.J., Jain, L.C. (eds.) New Directions in Intelligent Interactive Multimedia Systems and Services - 2. SCI, vol. 226, pp. 13–20. Springer, Heidelberg (2009)

16. Ogiela, M.R., Ogiela, U.: The use of mathematical linguistic methods in creating secret sharing threshold algorithms. Computers and Mathematics with Applications 60(2), 267–271 (2010)

17. Ogiela, M.R., Ogiela, U.: DNA-like linguistic secret sharing for strategic information systems. International Journal of Information Management 32, 175–181 (2012)

18. Ogiela, M.R., Ogiela, U.: Linguistic Protocols for Secure Information Management and Sharing. Computers and Mathematics with Applications 63(2), 564–572 (2012)

19. Ogiela, M.R., Ogiela, U.: Secure Information Management using Linguistic Threshold Approach. Advanced Information and Knowledge Processing. Springer, London (2014)

20. Peters, W.: Representing Humans in System Security Models: An Actor-Network Approach. Journal of Wireless Mobile Networks, Ubiquitous Computing, and Dependable Applications 2(1), 75–92 (2011)

On the Modelling of the Computer Security Impact on the Reputation Systems

Bogdan Ksiezopolski[1,2], Adam Wierzbicki[2], and Damian Rusinek[1]

[1] Institute of Computer Science, Maria Curie-Sklodowska University,
pl. M. Curie-Sklodowskiej 5, 20-031 Lublin, Poland
[2] Polish-Japanese Institute of Information Technology
Koszykowa 86, 02-008 Warsaw, Poland

Abstract. Reputation systems are an important factor for building trust in virtual communities. In the article we introduce reputation module for Quality of Protection Modelling Language which allows to represent the reputation system as a part of the protocol, where all operations and communication steps can be consistently modelled. Owing to the proposed approach the reputation systems can be formally specified and computer security impact can be considered as a factor of the metrics in the reputation systems. Finally, we model and analyse the case study of the eBay reputation system with modification which will refer to the computer security impact.

1 Introduction

Reputation systems are one of the most successful and important forms of trust management in open communities. Sophisticated algorithms and system designs can be applied in order to increase the resilience of reputation systems to various forms of attacks, such as coalition attacks, whitewashing, Sybil attacks and many others. Attacks against reputation systems depend on the capabilities of the attackers and defence mechanisms that protect reputation systems which significant part are based on technical measures [1]. The complete analysis of the computer security impact for the distributed reputation systems is a very difficult task, which should nevertheless be performed, because only then we can be sure that a reputation system has been properly tested. The completeness of analysis can be achieved by means of a formal approach, where reputation system can be represented as a part of the protocol, where all operations and communication steps can be consistently modelled. In the article [4] B.Ksiezopolski introduced the Quality of Protection Modelling Language (QoP-ML) which provides the modelling language for making abstraction of cryptographic protocols that put emphasis on the details concerning quality of protection. The intended use of QoP-ML is to represent the series of steps which are described as a cryptographic protocol. Additionally, in the QoP-ML the security economics analysis can be performed which is named adaptable security in literature [2,3].

In this article we would like to present the syntax and semantics of a new structure for the QoP-ML which is required for analysing a reputation system.

Linawati et al. (Eds.): ICT-EurAsia 2014, LNCS 8407, pp. 526–531, 2014.

A major contribution of this work is introducing the ability of formally specifying distributed reputation systems together with other protocols and functions of information security that support the reputation systems. Owing to the introduced reputation module the reputation systems can be analysed from the technical and information security perspectives. The reputation values of agents are calculated according to the defined algorithms which are abstracted as a process in the operating system which is realized by means of the host. This host is defined as a part of the whole IT architecture by means of which distributed communities can be abstracted. In this infrastructure one can model defence mechanisms and analyse their impact on the reputation system. The reputation module proposed in this paper, which is a part of the QoP-ML, is the first modelling language which allows abstracting and analysing reputation systems from the technical and information security perspectives in a formal way.

2   Reputation in QoP-ML

In this article we introduce the new reputation module owing to which the reputation analysis can be prepared simultaneously with standard quality of protection analysis of used security mechanisms. The reputation analysis will be will be performed simultaneously with the QoP evaluation according to the methodology presented in the article [4].

For reputation modelling in the QoP-ML one has to use two structures which were introduced in the QoP-ML: functions and security metrics. Additionally, we would like to introduce a new structure which will be used for reputation modelling, the *modules* structure. The semantics of all structures which are required during the reputation modelling in the QoP-ML is presented in the next sections.

2.1   Functions

The function modifies the states of the variables and pass the objects by communication channels. The function with the reputation qop parameters is declared as follows:

```
fun post(id)[Reputation: par1, par2, par3, par4, par5]
```

This function is named **post** and includes two types of factors. The functional parameters, which are written in round brackets, they are necessary for the execution of the function. The additional parameters, which are written in square brackets, influence the system reputation.

2.2   Security Metrics

In the case of representing the reputation metrics, the structure **data*** will be used because the reputation can not be measured but can be modelled [4]. Below we present the example of the *metrics* structure used for reputation modelling.

```
metrics
{
}
data*()
  {
    primhead[function][reputation:algorithm]
    primitive[post][alg1]
  }
}
```

The body of the **data*** structures contains two operators: **primhead** and **primitive**. The **primhead** operator defines the required parameters for agent actions which influence its reputation. In the presented example for **data*** the two parameters were defined, the first one is the function name which describes the operation influencing the modelled reputation. The second one defines the name of the additional module (*reputation*) for the previously defined function with the name of the algorithm which calculates the value of the reputation of this function. Then, the **primitive** operator is used which defines the details about previously defined functions. In our example the **data*** operator defines that the **post** function will be calculated according to the algorithm defined in the module *reputation* and the name of this algorithm is *alg1*.

2.3   Modules

In this article we introduce a new structure which will be used for defining details for different analysis modules according to the base QoP-ML analysis. This structure is named *modules*. In the presented approach, the structure for the reputation analysis will be presented. The security metrics structure in the QoP-ML approach is based only on static values which are defined as the *primitive* structure. One of the main features of the *modules* structure is enabling the representation of the results in the dynamic way. It means that the results defined in this structure can be estimated by means of the algorithms define mathematics operations.

In the next part of this section the exemplary declaration of this structure will be presented. Afterwards, this structure will be described.

```
modules {
  reputation {
  # rep=0
      alg1(par1, par2, par3, par4, par5){
        if(rep<=100){
          extra = (par4 * par5)/2;
          rep = rep + (par1 * par2 * par3) + extra;
                  }
        if(rep>100 || rep <200){
          extra = (par4 * par5)/2;
          rep = rep + par1 + par2 + par3 + extra;
                    }
        else{
          rep = rep + (par1 + par2 + par3 + par4 + par5)/5
          }
      }
  }
}
```

The *modules* structure is started by the operator `modules`. Inside the body of the *modules* structure one can define different types of modules. In the presented example the *reputation* module is described. In the specific modules, the initial values of variables can be defined, they are precoded by the # operator. After this, the algorithm which estimates the reputation value is defined `alg1(par1, par2, par3, par4, par5){}`. The name of the algorithm is not restricted and in the presented example it is *alg1*. In the round brackets the parameters of the algorithm are defined. The values of these parameters are defined during the QoP-ML protocol modelling in the specific function which are taken into consideration during reputation modelling. The body of the `alg1` algorithm includes the arithmetic operations which define the algorithm of reputation value calculation. In the *modules* structure one can use condition statements. In this example, three possible calculations can be prepared and they are changed depending on the current value of *rep* variable. When the *rep* variable will be lower or equal to 100 (`rep<=100`), then the first conditional statement will be true and the relevant algorithm will be executed. When the *rep* variable will be higher than 100 and lower than 200 (`rep>100 || rep <200`), then the second conditional statement will be true. In other cases the *else* structure will be executed. In the *modules* structure one can use other operators which are the same as in the language C.

3   Case Study - Reputation in the eBay

In the article we would like to model the eBay reputation system [6] with modification which will refer to the computer security impact. In the QoP-ML one can model the reputation system where the mark will be modified depending on the security measures used. One can imagine the scenario where the rates of seller transaction will be modified by the attacker as the part of Men in the Middle Attack. That kind of attack can be easily performed when the rate will be submitted by means of non-encrypted channel. As the defence from this attack can be usage of TLS protocol, which first of all authenticates the eBay server and encrypts transmitted data. In this case study we would like to present the possibility of modelling the reputation systems with computer security impact and in the basic way the reputation of an agent (seller) a can be computed as:

$$r(a) = \sum_{m=1}^{n} (m \cdot s) \tag{1}$$

where:
$r(a)$ - the overall reputation value of the agent a;
m - the single rate for the transaction from the set $\{-1, 0, 1\}$;
s - the security impact value, $s \in R$;
n - the number of transactions.

In the case study we presented three scenarios which differ in the type of security technology used for rating the eBay transactions. We modelled the agents reputation system based on formula 1. The security impact s will be equal to 1.3 when the transaction rating is sent by the security channel (with the TLS protocol) and will be equal to 0.7 when the the security channel is not used. It means that the transaction rate will be increased by 30% when the rate is secured against technical attacks and will be decreased by 30% when it is not secured.

For all scenarios we assume that agents (sellers) have 100 transactions and these transactions are rated by other agents (buyers or reviewers). We assume that all of these transactions are good and only honest buyers can asses the transactions. In the first scenario (version 1) the buyers will send 100 reviews by means of the secured channel (with the TLS protocol). In the second scenario (version 2) the buyers will send 100 reviews by means of not secured channel (without the TLS protocol). In the third scenario (version 3) the buyers will send 50 reviews by means of the secured channel (with the TLS protocol) and 50 reviews by means of the not secured channel (without the TLS protocol).

4   QoP and Reputation Evaluation

The QoP evaluation investigates the influences of the security mechanisms for the ensuring security attributes. That kind of evaluation can be found in the articles [4,5]. In this article we would like to focus on the reputation evaluation which is a new type of evaluation introduced here. The QoP and reputation evaluation algorithms are implemented in the Automated Quality of Protection Analysis tool (AQoPA). The AQoPA tool can be downloaded from the web page of the QoP-ML Project [7]. In the QoP-ML models library (included in the AQoPA tool) one can find presented in this article eBay reputation model.

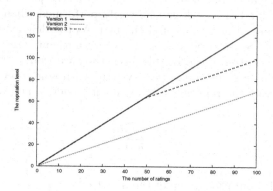

Fig. 1. The reputation evaluation for the modelled system

In the article we analysed a simple reputation algorithm based on the eBay reputation system where we added modification referring to the computer security impact. In Fig. 1 the results, which refer to the three analysed versions (scenarios) are presented. One can notice significant difference between the overall reputation level of the seller for versions 1 and 2. Version 1 refers to the rates, given by the secured channel, while in version 2 rates are not encrypted. The advantage of transaction rates which are submitted by secure channel is that we are sure that these rates were not modified as the results of one of technical attacks. In the second version we can not be sure that the transactions rates were not modified. This lower level of credibility of the submitted transactions reviews causes lower overall reputation level of the seller. The third version shows the combination of two earlier analysed behaviours of the transactions reviewer. In Fig. 1 one can notice that the last 50 rates submitted by means of not secure channel have less contribution to the overall reputation level of the seller.

5 Conclusions

The aim of this study was to present the new structure for the Quality of Protection Modelling Language (QoP-ML) which is required for analysing a reputation system. Owing to this module one can model and analyse the reputation systems from the technical and information security perspectives. In the article we modelled the case study in the QoP-ML where the eBay reputation systems were modified. In that system the transactions rates were modified depending on the fact of securing the transmission channel between the transaction reviewer and the eBay portal. We have shown that the reputation systems, taking into account factors related to information security, can provide protection against technical attacks on them.

Acknowledgements. This work is supported by Polish National Science Centre grant 2012/05/B/ST6/03364.

References

1. Hoffman, K., Zage, D., Nita-Rotaru, C.: A survey of attack and defense techniques for reputation systems. Journal ACM Computing Surveys 42(1) (2009)
2. Ksiezopolski, B., Kotulski, Z.: Adaptable security mechanism for the dynamic environments. Computers & Security 26, 246–255 (2007)
3. Ksiezopolski, B., Kotulski, Z., Szalachowski, P.: Adaptive approach to network security. In: Kwiecień, A., Gaj, P., Stera, P. (eds.) CN 2009. CCIS, vol. 39, pp. 233–241. Springer, Heidelberg (2009)
4. Ksiezopolski, B.: QoP-ML: Quality of Protection modelling language for cryptographic protocols. Computers & Security 31(4), 569–596 (2012)
5. Ksiezopolski, B., Rusinek, D., Wierzbicki, A.: On the efficiency modelling of cryptographic protocols by means of the Quality of Protection Modelling Language (QoP-ML). In: Mustofa, K., Neuhold, E.J., Tjoa, A.M., Weippl, E., You, I. (eds.) ICT-EurAsia 2013. LNCS, vol. 7804, pp. 261–270. Springer, Heidelberg (2013)
6. Schlosser, A., Voss, M., Brckner, L.: On the Simulation of Global Reputation Systems. Journal of Artificial Societies and Social Simulation 9(1) (2006)
7. The web page of QoP-ML project; link to the AQoPA tool: http://qopml.org/

Efficient Variant of Rainbow without Triangular Matrix Representation

Takanori Yasuda[1], Tsuyoshi Takagi[2], and Kouichi Sakurai[1,3]

[1] Institute of Systems, Information Technologies and Nanotechnologies
[2] Institute of Mathematics for Industry, Kyushu University
[3] Department of Informatics, Kyushu University

Abstract. Multivariate Public Key Cryptosystems (MPKC) is one of candidates for post-quantum cryptography. Rainbow is an MPKC digital signature scheme, with relatively efficient encryption and decryption processes. However, the size of MPKC key is substantially larger than that of an RSA cryptosystem for the same security level. In this paper, we propose a variant of Rainbow that has a smaller secret key. The smaller secret key is to the result of a different description of the quadratic polynomials appearing in the secret key from that of the original Rainbow. In addition, our scheme improves the efficiency of the Rainbow's signature generation. In particular, the secret key is reduced in size by about 40% and the signature generation is sped up by about 30% at the security level of 100 bits.

Keywords: Post-quantum cryptography, Multivariate public key cryptosystems, Rainbow.

1 Introduction

Multivariate public key cryptosystems (MPKC) [1,7] are candidates for post-quantum cryptography. Their security is based on the level of difficulty involved in finding solutions to a system of multivariate quadratic equations (MQ problem). Many MPKC schemes require secret and public keys that are larger than those of RSA and ECC. In recent years, a variety of MPKC schemes for encryption and for signatures, have been proposed. Unbalanced Oil and Vinegar (UOV) [5] is an MPKC signature scheme, whose signatures can be efficiently generated and verified. Rainbow [2] is a multilayer variant of UOV, with enhanced security. UOV and Rainbow both share the same problem of having large secret and public keys.

In this paper, we propose a variant of Rainbow that has a shorter secret key than the corresponding Rainbow key. In the case of the original Rainbow, the quadratic polynomials appearing in the secret key are expressed using triangular matrices. The non-zero parts of the triangular matrices coincide with coefficients of the quadratic polynomials. If we change the triangular matrices into general matrices, then the quadratic polynomials remain but, the correspondence of the matrix elements becomes more complicated. Conversely, if we utilize the

Linawati et al. (Eds.): ICT-EurAsia 2014, LNCS 8407, pp. 532–541, 2014.

complicated correspondence, then simple matrix operation like rotation of row vectors yields several quadratic polynomials which seem to have been chosen randomly. Our scheme uses this method to describe the quadratic polynomials appearing in the secret key. In Rainbow, we need the same number of triangular matrices as that of quadratic polynomials, whereas in our scheme, we need only one matrix to describe the secret key.

Our scheme also improves the efficiency of signature generation. Here, we use several rotations of row vectors in a matrix so that the same matrix computation appears several times.

This paper analayzes the security of our scheme. In particular, we investigate the effect to our scheme for famous attacks against Rainbow, including direct attacks, HighRank attack and UOV attack. Among these attacks, we show that the complexities of the HighRank attack and UOV attack against our scheme are the same as those against the original Rainbow. Furthermore, we verify that the there is no difference in security between our scheme and Rainbow against direct attacks.

Finally, we evaluate the security parameter of our scheme for several security levels on the basis of our security analysis and the results in [6]. We also compare the secret key length and efficiency of signature generation of our scheme with those of the corresponding Rainbow. In particular, the size of the secret key of our scheme is reduced by about 40% and signature generation is about 30% faster at the security level of 100 bits.

2   Original Rainbow

Ding and Schmidt proposed a signature scheme called Rainbow, which is a multilayer variant of Unbalanced Oil and Vinegar [2].

First, we define parameters that determine the layer structure of Rainbow. Let t be the number of layers in Rainbow. Let $v_1, \ldots, v_{t+1}$ be a sequence of $t+1$ positive integers such that $0 < v_1 < v_2 < \cdots < v_t < v_{t+1}$. For $i = 1, \ldots, t$, the set of indices of the i-th layer in Rainbow is defined by all integers from v_i to v_{i+1}, namely $O_i = \{v_i + 1, v_i + 2, \ldots, v_{i+1} - 1, v_{i+1}\}$. The number of indices for the i-th layer, O_i is then $v_{i+1} - v_i$, and this is denoted by $o_i = v_{i+1} - v_i$. Note that the smallest integer in O_1 is $v_1 + 1$. Upon defining $V_1 = \{1, 2, \ldots, v_1\}$, and for $i = 2, 3, \ldots, t+1$, we have

$$V_i = V_1 \cup O_1 \cup O_2 \cup \cdots \cup O_{i-1} = \{1, 2 \ldots, v_i\}.$$

The number of elements in V_i is exactly v_i for $i = 1, 2, \ldots, t+1$. The sets O_i and V_i are used for the respective indices of the Oil and Vinegar variables in Rainbow. We define $n = v_{t+1}$ as the maximum number of variables used in Rainbow.

Next, let K be a finite field of order q. Rainbow consists of t layers of n variables polynomials. For $h = 1, 2, \ldots, t$, the h-th layer of Rainbow contains the following system of o_h multivariate polynomials: For $k \in O_h$,

$$g_k(x_1,\ldots,x_n) = \sum_{i\in O_h, j\in V_h} \alpha_{i,j}^{(k)} x_i x_j + \sum_{i,j\in V_h, i\le j} \beta_{i,j}^{(k)} x_i x_j + \sum_{i\in V_{h+1}} \gamma_i^{(k)} x_i + \eta^{(k)}, \quad (1)$$

where $\alpha_{i,j}^{(k)}, \beta_{i,j}^{(k)}, \gamma_i^{(k)}, \eta^{(k)} \in K$. We call the variables x_i ($i \in O_h$) and x_j ($i \in V_j$) Oil and Vinegar variables, respectively. The central map of Rainbow is constructed according to $G = (g_{v_1+1}, \ldots, g_n) : K^n \to K^{n-v_1}$.

Note that a system of o_h equations, $g_k(b_1, \ldots, b_{v_h}, x_{v_h+1}, \ldots, x_{v_{h+1}}) = a_k$ ($k \in O_h$) becomes o_h linear equations in o_h variables for any $(a_{v_h+1}, \ldots, a_{v_{h+1}}) \in K^{o_h}$ and $(b_1, \ldots, b_{v_h}) \in K^{v_h}$. Therefore, once we know the values of the Oil variables in the h-th layer, we can then compute the values of the Vinegar variables in the $(h+1)$-th layer. This is the trapdoor mechanism of Rainbow.

2.1 Scheme

Now let us describe the key generation, signature generation, and verification processes of Rainbow.

Key Generation. The secret key consists of a central map G and two affine transformations $A_1 : K^m \to K^m$ ($m = n - v_1$), $A_2 : K^n \to K^n$. The public key consists of the field K and the composed map $F = A_1 \circ G \circ A_2 : K^n \to K^m$, which is a system of m quadratic polynomials of n variables over K. We denote the public key by $F = (f_{v_1+1}, \ldots, f_n)^{\mathrm{T}}$, where T denotes the transpose operation. In addition, we use f_k to denote the k-th public polynomial of F for $k = v_1 + 1, \ldots, n$.

Signature Generation. Let $\mathbf{M} \in K^m$ be a message. We compute $\mathbf{A} = A_1^{-1}(\mathbf{M})$, $\mathbf{B} = G^{-1}(\mathbf{A})$ and $\mathbf{C} = A_2^{-1}(\mathbf{B})$ in that order. The signature of the message is $\mathbf{C} \in K^n$. Note that the inverse of G can be efficiently computed. In fact, for any vector $w = (w_1, \ldots, w_m)^T \in K^m$, an element $G^{-1}(w)$ in the inverse image of w can be obtained as follows:

Step 1. Randomly choose $s_1', \ldots, s_{v_1}' \in K$.
Step 2. For $i = 1, \ldots, t$, do the following operations:
A system $g^{(v_i+1)}, \ldots, g^{(v_i+o_i)}$ can be regarded as a multivariate quadratic system with variables $x_1, \ldots, x_{v_i+o_i}$. Upon substituting $(x_1, \ldots, x_{v_i}) = (s_1', \ldots, s_{v_i}')$, set up a system of linear equations of o_i variables. Solve the system and obtain a solution $(x_{v_i+1}, \ldots, x_{v_i+o_i}) = (s_{v+1}', \ldots, s_n')$. (If the system is not regular, go back to Step 1.)
Result. $G^{-1}(w) = (s_1', \ldots, s_n')$.

Verification. If $F(\mathbf{C}) = \mathbf{M}$, the signature is accepted; it is rejected otherwise.

This scheme is denoted as Rainbow(K; $v_1, o_1, \ldots, o_t$), and we call $v_1, o_1, \ldots, o_t$ the parameters of Rainbow.

3   A Variant of Rainbow

In this section, we present our variant of Rainbow, called matrix-based Rainbow. Our scheme uses a special secret key to improve Rainbow's signature generation algorithm.

3.1   Basic Underlying Idea

We focus on the terms

$$\sum_{i,j \in S_h,\, i \le j} \beta_{i,j}^{(k)} x_i x_j \tag{2}$$

appearing in the components g_k of the quadratic polynomial map G that composes the secret key of Rainbow. Using a square matrix of size v_h,

$$B = \begin{pmatrix} \beta_{1,1}^{(k)} & \beta_{1,2}^{(k)} & \cdots & \beta_{1,v_h}^{(k)} \\ 0 & \beta_{2,2}^{(k)} & * & \vdots \\ \vdots & & \ddots & \vdots \\ 0 & \cdots & 0 & \beta_{v_h,v_h}^{(k)} \end{pmatrix},$$

the terms can be expressed as

$$\mathbf{x}.B.\mathbf{x}^T \quad (\mathbf{x} = (x_1, \ldots, x_{v_h})). \tag{3}$$

Let us see the change in (3) that is had by replacing the triangular matrix B with a general matrix. For a general matrix,

$$D = \begin{pmatrix} \delta_{1,1} & \cdots & \cdots & \delta_{1,v_h} \\ \vdots & \ddots & & \vdots \\ \vdots & & \ddots & \vdots \\ \delta_{v_h,1} & \cdots & \cdots & \delta_{v_h,v_h} \end{pmatrix},$$

$\mathbf{x}.D.\mathbf{x}^T$ is expressed by

$$\sum_{i,j \in S_h,\, i < j} (\delta_{i,j} + \delta_{j,i}) x_i x_j + \sum_{i \in S_h} \delta_{i,i} x_i^2. \tag{4}$$

Comparing this with (2), it is clear that the terms are more complicated. In addition, we will rotate down the row vectors in the matrix D by l rows; that is, for

$$D_l = \begin{pmatrix} \delta_{v_h-l+1,1} & \cdots & \cdots & \delta_{v_h-l+1,v_h} \\ \delta_{v_h-l+2,1} & \cdots & \cdots & \delta_{v_h-l+2,v_h} \\ \vdots & & & \vdots \\ \delta_{v_h-l,1} & \cdots & \cdots & \delta_{v_h-l,v_h} \end{pmatrix},$$

$\mathbf{x}.D_l.\mathbf{x}^T$ can be expressed as

$$\sum_{i,j \in S_h,\, i < j} (\delta_{i-l,j} + \delta_{j-l,i}) x_i x_j + \sum_{i \in S_h} \delta_{i-l,i} x_i^2. \tag{5}$$

Here, the indices are regarded as numbers modulo v_h.

Since number of the matrices in which row vectors are rotated is v_h, at most v_h quadratic polynomials of the form $\mathbf{x}.D_l.\mathbf{x}^T$ are obtained. As we can see from the coefficients of (5), it seems difficult to relate the coefficients in the form not appeared by $\delta_{i,j}$. In other words, from a general matrix D, we can construct up to v_h quadratic polynomials that look independent of each other.

The method is used to construct the terms (2) appearing in the secret key of our scheme. More concretely, for the h-th layer, we prepare a matrix D, and construct the terms (2) appearing in $g_{v_h+1}, \ldots, g_{v_{h+1}}$ by rotating the rows of D.

In the original Rainbow, $o_h (= v_{h+1} - v_h)$ triangular matrices are needed to describe the secret key, whereas in our scheme, only one matrix D is needed. Comparing these parts, we find that the number of elements in the base field of our scheme is reduced by $2/o_h$. Therefore, its secret key is shorter. We should remark that since the number of rows in D is at most v_h, for any h-th layer, the condition $v_h \geq o_h$ has to be satisfied for the design to be secure.

3.2   Construction of the Secret Key

In our scheme, we use the invertible map G used in the original Rainbow as a trapdoor. However, the choice of the coefficients of G in our scheme is different from that in the original Rainbow.

$t, v_1, \ldots, v_{t+1}, m, n$ are natural numbers satisfying the same condition as in § 2.1. In addition, for any $h = 1, \ldots, t$, it is assumed that $v_h \geq o_h$. For $i = 1, \ldots, t$, we write $S_i = \{1, \ldots, v_i\}$, $O_i = \{v_i + 1, \ldots, v_{i+1}\}$, and $o_i = v_{i+1} - v_i$.

First, for each $h = 1, \ldots, t$, we choose a square matrix $D^{(h)} = (\delta_{i,j}^{(h)})$, with a size v_h. Then, we create a map $G = (g_{v_1+1}, \ldots, g_n) : K^n \to K^m$ consisting of quadratic polynomials in the following form: For $h = 1, \ldots, t$, $l = 1, \ldots, o_h$, we write $k = v_h + l$, and

$$
\begin{aligned}
g_k(x_1, \ldots, x_n) = &\sum_{i \in O_h, j \in S_h} \alpha_{i,j}^{(k)} x_i x_j + \sum_{i \in S_h} \delta_{i-l+1,i}^{(h)} x_i^2 \\
&+ \sum_{i,j \in S_h, i<j} (\delta_{i-l+1,j}^{(h)} + \delta_{j-l+1,i}^{(h)}) x_i x_j + \sum_{i \in S_{h+1}} \gamma_i^{(k)} x_i + \eta^{(k)}. \quad (6)
\end{aligned}
$$

Here, $\alpha_{i,j}^{(k)}, \gamma_i^{(k)}, \eta^{(k)} \in K$.

3.3   Efficient Inverse Computation

Since the map G defined above can be expressed in the form used in the definition of Rainbow, we use the algorithm for computing the inverse map of G that is used in the signature generation of the original Rainbow. Moreover, we can improve the algorithm.

In the signature generation of the original Rainbow, the linear system appearing in the inverse map computation of G is described as $L.X = V$ where,

$$L = (\sum_{k=1}^{v_h} \alpha_{k,v_h+j}^{(v_h+i)} b_k + \gamma_{v_h+j}^{(v_h+i)})_{1 \leq i,j \leq o_h}, \tag{7}$$

$$V = \left(a_{v_h+i} - \sum_{1 \leq k \leq l \leq v_h} \beta_{k,l}^{(v_h+i)} b_k b_l - \sum_{1 \leq k \leq v_h} \gamma_k^{(v_h+i)} b_k - \eta^{(v_h+i)} \right)_{1 \leq i \leq o_h}, \tag{8}$$

$$X = (x_{v_h+1}, \ldots, x_{v_{h+1}})^T.$$

In our scheme, that is

$$\beta_{i,j}^{(v_h+l)} = \begin{cases} \delta_{i-l+1,j}^{(h)} + \delta_{j-l+1,i}^{(h)} & i \neq j \\ \delta_{i-l+1,i}^{(h)} & i = j. \end{cases}$$

Accordingly, $\sum_{1 \leq k \leq l \leq v_h} \beta_{k,l}^{(v_h+i)} b_k b_l$ appearing in V is expressed as $\mathbf{b}.D_{i-1}^{(h)}.\mathbf{b}^T$ ($\mathbf{b} = (b_1, \ldots, b_{v_h})$). Here, $D_{i-1}^{(h)}$ is a matrix whose row vectors are rotated down from those of $D^{(h)}$ by $i - 1$ rows. For any $i = 1, \ldots, o_h$, $D_{i-1}^{(h)}.\mathbf{b}^T$ coincides with a column vector rotated down from the components of $D^{(h)}.\mathbf{b}^T$ by $i - 1$ elements. Therefore, if we compute $D^{(h)}.\mathbf{b}^T$ once, $D_{i-1}^{(h)}.\mathbf{b}^T$ does not have to be computed. Computing the inner form of this and $\mathbf{b}$, $\sum_{1 \leq k \leq l \leq v_h} \beta_{k,l}^{(v_h+i)} b_k b_l$ can be computed. In our scheme, this method is used to compute the inverse of G is computed.

3.4   Our Scheme

Our scheme uses the invertible map G for the key generation, signature generation and verification as follows:

• **Key generation**

   Secret key. The secret key consists of the quadratic map G, and two randomly chosen affine transformations $L : K^m \to K^m$ and $R : K^n \to K^n$.
   Public key. The public key consists of the composite map $F = L \circ G \circ R : K^n \to K^m$.

• **Signature generation.** Let $\mathbf{M} \in K^m$ be a message. To generate a signature $\mathbf{S}$ from $\mathbf{M}$, first compute $\mathbf{M}' = L^{-1}(\mathbf{M})$. Next compute an element $\mathbf{S}' = G^{-1}(\mathbf{M}')$ in the inverse image of $\mathbf{M}'$, and finally compute $\mathbf{S} = R^{-1}(\mathbf{S}')$. $G^{-1}(\mathbf{M}')$ is computed using the improved algorithm described above. $L^{-1}(\mathbf{M})$ and $R^{-1}(\mathbf{S}')$ can be easily computed since L and R are affine transformations, .
• **Verification.** If $F(\mathbf{S}) = \mathbf{M}$, the signature is accepted. It is rejected otherwise.

We denote this scheme by NT-Rainbow$(K; v_1, d_1 * o_1', \ldots, d_t * o_t')$ and call $v_1, d_1, o_1', \ldots, d_t, o_t'$ the parameter.

4 Security Analysis for Our Scheme

Now let us analyze the security of our scheme against several attacks.

4.1 Security against Direct Attacks

We experimentally compared the time taken by direct attacks against our scheme NT-Rainbow($GF(256); v_1, o_1, o_2$) over against the time taken by the same attack against Rainbow($GF(256); v_1, o_1, o_2$). The experiment used the gröbner basis implemented in Magma. The table below lists the results: It shows that there is no significant difference between the times of those schemes.

Table 1. Comparison of Time Taken by Direct Attacks over $GF(256)$

(v_1, o_1, o_2)	(4,3,4)	(5,3,4)	(3,4,4)
Our scheme	5.32 s	11.70 s	13.80 s
Rainbow	5.34 s	11.70 s	13.84 s
Random system	5.36 s	11.72 s	13.88 s

4.2 Security against HighRank Attack

We can write $g_{v_1+1}^{(2)}, \ldots, g_n^{(2)}$ for the quadratic parts of the components of the central map $G = (g_{v_1+1}, \ldots, g_n)$. Each $g_i^{(2)}$ is expressed by $g_i^{(2)}(\mathbf{x}) = \mathbf{x}.T_i.\mathbf{x}^T$, ($\mathbf{x} = (x_1, \ldots, x_n)$) using a triangular matrix T_i of size n. The symmetric matrix S_i ($i = v_1 + 1, \ldots, n$) is defined by $S_i = T_i + T_i^T$, and we can write $\mathcal{A} = \mathrm{Span}_K\{S_{v_1+1}, \ldots, S_n\}$.

The HighRank attack finds a matrix in $\mathcal{A}$ with the maximal rank (not full rank), and it spends most of its times in this process. The computation has the following steps.

Step 1. Choose $M \in \mathcal{A}$ randomly.
Step 2. Determine whether M is regular. If M is regular, then return to Step 1
Output M.

The complexity of the computation for determining whether M is regular or not (which is equal to complexity of HighRank attack) is $q^{o_t} n^3 / 6$ field multiplication([3],[6]). If the $\alpha_{i,j}^{(k)}$'s are chosen randomly, the probability that M is not regular is equal to $1/q^{o_t}$. In our scheme, $\alpha_{i,j}^{(k)}$'s are chosen randomly as in the original Rainbow. Therefore, the complexity of the HighRank attack against our scheme is equivalent to that against the original Rainbow.

Security against UOV Attack. The space spanned by the variables $x_{v_t+1}, \ldots, x_n$ is a simultaneously isotropic space with respect to $g_{v_1+1}^{(2)}, \ldots, g_n^{(2)}$. Here, a subspace W of a vector space V with a quadratic form g is said to be isotropic if $v_1, v_2 \in V \Rightarrow g(v_1, v_2) = 0$.

The UOV attack finds the simultaneously isotropic space by using the following steps.

Step 1. Randomly choose $M_1, M_2 \in \mathcal{A}$ such that M_2 is regular.
Step 2. Compute a proper invariant subspace W of $M_{1,2} = M_1 M_2^{-1}$. If there is no invariant subspace, return to Step 1.
Output W.

The complexity of the UOV attack is $q^{n-2o_t-1}o_t^3$ field multiplication([4]). If the $\alpha_{i,j}^{(k)}$'s are chosen randomly, the probability that $M_{1,2}$ has an invariant subspace is equal to $1/q^{n-2o_t}$. In our scheme, the $\alpha_{i,j}^{(k)}$'s are chosen randomly similarly as in the original Rainbow. Therefore, the complexity of UOV attack against our scheme is equivalent to that against the original Rainbow.

5 Efficiency of Signature Generation

In this section, we compare the efficiencies of signature generation of our scheme and the original Rainbow. The respective schemes are fixed by setting NT-Rainbow($K; v_1, o_1, \ldots, o_t$) and Rainbow($K; v_1, o_1, \ldots, o_t$). The previous section shows these schemes have the same security level against direct attacks, the HighRank attack and the UOV attack.

5.1 Efficiency of Signature Generation

Now let us estimate the number of multiplications and additions of K in the signature generation in our scheme and the original Rainbow. We fix the schemes by setting Rainbow($K; v_1, o_1, \ldots, o_t$) and NT-Rainbow($K; v_1, o_1, \ldots, o_t$) and choose Gaussian elimination as the solver of the linear systems appearing in the signature generation. For both cases of the original Rainbow and our scheme, we consider to generate a signature corresponding to a message $\mathbf{M} \in K^m$. Then, we have to compute $\mathbf{A} = L^{-1}(\mathbf{M})$, $\mathbf{B} = G^{-1}(\mathbf{A})$ and $\mathbf{C} = R^{-1}(\mathbf{B})$ in this order and obtain a signature $\mathbf{C}$. The computation of $\mathbf{A} = L^{-1}(\mathbf{M})$ and $\mathbf{C} = R^{-1}(\mathbf{B})$ are common for both schemes.

The respective costs for computing $\mathbf{B} = G^{-1}(\mathbf{A})$ are described as follows:

Original Rainbow

Multiplication $\displaystyle\sum_{h=1}^{t} \left(\frac{o_h v_h^2}{2} + \frac{o_h^3}{3} + (v_h + 1)o_h^2 + \frac{3o_h v_h}{2} + \frac{v_h(v_h+1)}{2} - \frac{o_h}{3} \right),$

Addition $\displaystyle\sum_{h=1}^{t} \left(\frac{o_h v_h^2}{2} + \frac{o_h^3}{3} + (v_h + 1)o_h^2 + \frac{3o_h v_h}{2} - \frac{o_h}{3} \right).$

Our scheme

Multiplication $\displaystyle\sum_{h=1}^{t} \left(v_h o_h^2 + \frac{o_h^3}{3} + v_h^2 + 2o_h v_h + o_h^2 - \frac{o_h}{3} \right),$

Addition $\displaystyle\sum_{h=1}^{t} \left(v_h o_h^2 + \frac{o_h^3}{3} + v_h^2 + 2o_h v_h + o_h^2 - v_h - \frac{o_h}{3} \right).$

Comparison of Efficiencies. The term $v_h o_h^2$ appears in the cost computation of the original Rainbow, but not in our scheme. Moreover, the cubic terms with respect to v_h, o_h in the rest of the equation except for $v_h o_h^2$ are almost the same. This means the signature generation of our scheme is more efficient than that of the original Rainbow.

6   Examples

Our scheme NT-Rainbow$(K; v_1, o_1, \ldots, o_t)$ is valid if $v_h \geq o_h$ for all $h = 1, \ldots, t$. The security analysis of § 4 indicates that this scheme with this parameter must have same security level as that of Rainbow$(K; v_1, o_1, \ldots, o_t)$ against direct attacks, the HighRank attack and UOV attack. Petzoldt et al. [6] describe the corresponding parameters of the original Rainbow for several security levels. Since these parameters satisfy $v_h \geq o_h$ for all $h = 1, \ldots, t$, our schemes with the corresponding parameters exist. Table 2 lists the parameters of our schemes for security levels of 80, 90, 100-bits in correspondence with the parameters of Petzoldt et al. Our scheme NT-Rainbow$(K; v_1, o_1, o_2)$ is one with two-layers over $K = GF(256)$. Next, we compare the secret key lengths and the efficiencies of the signature generation of our scheme and the original Rainbow for these parameters. Table 3 compares the secret key lengths, and Table 4 compares the efficiencies of the signature generation. Table 4 shows the number of the multiplications and additions of $GF(256)$, and the time taken by a C-Language implementation. We used gcc and an Intel Core i5 2.67GHz CPU with 4GB RAM.

Table 2. Parameters of Our Scheme over $GF(256)$ and its Security Level

Parameter (v_1, o_1, o_2)	$(18, 14, 14)$	$(24, 17, 18)$	$(31, 21, 22)$
Security Level	80 bits	90 bits	100 bits

Table 3. Secret Key Lengths of Schemes over $GF(256)$

Parameter (v_1, o_1, o_2)	$(18, 14, 14)$	$(24, 17, 18)$	$(31, 21, 22)$
Security Level	80 bits	90 bits	100 bits
Secret Key Length of Our Scheme(Byte)	15284	29071	52709
Secret Key Length of Rainbow(Byte)	23680	47412	89776
Ratio	64.6%	61.3%	58.7%

Table 4. Efficiencies of Signature Generation of Schemes over $GF(256)$

Parameter (v_1, o_1, o_2)	$(18, 14, 14)$	$(24, 17, 18)$	$(31, 21, 22)$
Signature Generation Experiment(μs)	Mult:17660, Add:17536 144	Mult:33658, Add:33499 270	Mult:60966, Add:60766 475
Signature Generation Experiment(μs)	Mult:26097, Add:25324 189	Mult:52014, Add:50759 370	Mult:98112, Add:96121 695
Ratio	Mult:67.7%, Add:69.2% 76.2%	Mult:64.7%, Add:63.5% 73.0%	Mult:62.1%, Add:63.2% 68.3%

7 Conclusion

We presented a variant of Rainbow, that has a smaller secret key and faster signature generation process compared with the original. We analyzed the security of our scheme against known attacks such as direct attacks, HighRank attack, and UOV attack. In addition, we presented an explicit parameter of our scheme for several security levels. Our test proves that our scheme is 30% faster than Rainbow at generating the signatures and has a 40% smaller key at a security level of 100 bits.

Acknowledgments. This work was supported by gStrategic Information and Communications R&D Promotion Programme (SCOPE), no. 0159-0172h, Ministry of Internal Affairs and Communications, Japan. The first author is supported by Grant-in-Aid for Young Scientists (B), Grant number 24740078.

References

1. Ding, J., Gower, J.E., Schmidt, D.S.: Multivariate Public Key Cryptosystems. Advances in Information Security, vol. 25. Springer (2006)
2. Ding, J., Schmidt, D.: Rainbow, a New Multivariable Polynomial Signature Scheme. In: Ioannidis, J., Keromytis, A., Yung, M. (eds.) ACNS 2005. LNCS, vol. 3531, pp. 164–175. Springer, Heidelberg (2005)
3. Ding, J., Yang, B.-Y., Chen, C.-H.O., Chen, M.-S., Cheng, C.-M.: New Differential-Algebraic Attacks and Reparametrization of Rainbow. In: Bellovin, S.M., Gennaro, R., Keromytis, A., Yung, M. (eds.) ACNS 2008. LNCS, vol. 5037, pp. 242–257. Springer, Heidelberg (2008); Hu, Y.-H., Wang, L.-C., Chou, C.-Y., Lai, F.: Similar Keys of Multivariate Quadratic Public Key Cryptosystems. In: Desmedt, Y.G., Wang, H., Mu, Y., Li, Y. (eds.) CANS 2005. LNCS, vol. 3810, pp. 211–222. Springer, Heidelberg (2005)
4. Kipnis, A., Patarin, J., Goubin, L.: Unbalanced Oil and Vinegar Schemes. In: Stern, J. (ed.) EUROCRYPT 1999. LNCS, vol. 1592, pp. 206–222. Springer, Heidelberg (1999)
5. Patarin, J.: The Oil and Vinegar Signature Scheme. In: Dagstuhl Workshop on Cryptography (1997)
6. Petzoldt, A., Bulygin, S., Buchmann, J.: Selecting Parameters for the Rainbow Signature Scheme. In: Sendrier, N. (ed.) PQCrypto 2010. LNCS, vol. 6061, pp. 218–240. Springer, Heidelberg (2010)
7. Wolf, C.: Introduction to Multivariate Quadratic Public Key Systems and their Applications. In: YACC 2006, pp. 44–55 (2006)

Efficient Lattice HIBE in the Standard Model
with Shorter Public Parameters

Kunwar Singh[1], C. Pandu Rangan[2], and A.K. Banerjee[3]

[1] Computer Science and Engineering Department
NIT Trichy, Tiruchirappalli, India
kunwar@nitt.edu
[2] Computer Science and Engineering Department
IIT, Madras
rangan@cse.iitm.ac.in
[3] Mathematics Department
NIT Trichy, Tiruchirappalli, India
banerjee@nitt.edu

Abstract. The concept of identity-based cryptosystem was introduced by Adi Shamir in 1984. In this new paradigm users' public key can be any string which uniquely identifies the user. The task of Public Key Generator (PKG) in IBE is to authenticate identity of the entity, generate the private key corresponding to the identity of the entity and finally transmit the private key securely to the entity. In large network PKG has a burdensome job. So the notion of Hierarchical IBE (HIBE) was introduced in [11,12] to distribute the workload by delegating the capability of private key generation and identity authentication to lower-level PKGs. In Eurocrypt 2010 Agrawal et al [1] presented an efficient lattice based secure HIBE scheme in the standard model in weaker security notion i.e. selective-ID. Based on [1], Singh et al [18] constructed adaptive-ID secure HIBE with short public parameters and still the public parameters is very large (total $l'' \times h + 2$ matrices). In this paper, we have reduced the size of the public parameters from $l'' \times h + 2$ matrices to $l'' + 2$ matrices using Chatterjee and Sarkar's [8] and blocking technique [7], where h is the number of levels in HIBE.

Keywords: Lattice, Hierarchical Identity Base Encryption (HIBE), Learning With Error (LWE).

1 Introduction

The concept of identity-based cryptosystem was introduced by Adi Shamir in 1984 [16]. In this new paradigm, users' public key can be any string which uniquely identifies the user. For example, users' identifier information such as email, phone number and IP address can be public key. As a result, it significantly reduces cost and complexity of establishing public key infrastructure (PKI). Although Shamir constructed an identity-based signature scheme using RSA function but was not able to construct an identity-based encryption scheme and this remained open problem until 2001, when this open problem was independently solved by Boneh-Franklin [5] and Cocks [9].

The task of Public Key Generator (PKG) in IBE is to authenticate identity of the entity, generate the private key corresponding to identity of the entity and finally transmit the private key securely to the entity. In large network PKG has a burdensome job.

Linawati et al. (Eds.): ICT-EurAsia 2014, LNCS 8407, pp. 542–553, 2014.
© IFIP International Federation for Information Processing 2014

So the notion of Hierarchical IBE (HIBE) was introduced in [11,12] to distribute the workload by delegating the capability of private key generation and identity authentication to lower-level PKGs. However, lower level PKGs do not have their own public parameters. Only root PKG has some set of public parameters.

In 1994, Peter Shor in his seminal paper showed that prime factorization and discrete logarithm problem can be solved in polynomial time on a quantum computer. In other words, once quantum computer comes into reality all of the public-key algorithms used to protect the Internet [20] will be broken. It facilitated research on new cryptosystems that remain secure in the advent of quantum computers. Till now there is no polynomial time quantum algorithm for lattice based problems. Ajtai's seminal result on the average case / worst case equivalence sparked great interest in lattice based cryptography. Informally, it means breaking the lattice based cryptosystem in the average case is as hard as solving some lattice based hard problems in the worst case. So it gives strong hardness guarantee for the lattice hard problems. Recently Regev [15] defined the learning with errors (LWE) problem and proved that, it also enjoys similar average case / worst case equivalence hardness properties.

Related Work. Recently Cash et al [6] and Peikert [14] have constructed secure HIBE in the standard model using basis delegation technique. Their construction considers an identity as a bit string and then assign a matrix coresponding to each bit. Agarwal et al [1] constructed an efficient lattice based secure HIBE scheme in the standard model in weaker security notion i.e. selective-ID. They have considered identities as one block rather than bit-by-bit. Singh et al [18] appllied Waters's [19] idea to convert Agrawal et al [1] selective-ID secure lattice HIBE to adaptive-ID secure HIBE then they have reduced the public parameters by using Chatterjee and Sarkar's [7] blocking technique. Blocking technique is to divide an l'-bit identity into l'' blocks of l'/l'' so that size of the vector $\vec{V}$ can be reduced from l' elements of G to l'' elements of G. Still the public parameters is very large (total $l'' \times h + 2$ matrices).

Our Contributions. In this paper first, we apply Waters's [19] idea to convert Agrawal et al [1] selective-ID secure lattice HIBE to adaptive-ID secure HIBE. With this technique, for an h-level HIBE has public parameters as $A_{1,1}, \ldots, A_{1,l'}, A_{2,1}, \ldots, A_{2,l'}, \ldots, A_{h,1}, \ldots, A_{h,l'}$ and A_0, B. Here the public parameters is very large (total $l \times h + 2$ matrices). Similar to Chatterjee and Sarkar [8] we have used same public parameters $A_1, \ldots, A_{l'}$ for all levels. This way public parametrs is reduced from $l' \times h + 2$ matrices to $l' + 2$ matrices. Further we reduce the public parameters $(l' + 2)$ matrices to $l'' + 2$ matrices by using Chatterjee and Sarkar's [7] blocking technique. Size of the public parameter in Singh et al [18] scheme is $l'' \times h + 2$ matrices. In our present scheme we have reduced the public parameters to $l'' + 2$ matrices.

2 Preliminaries

2.1 Notation

We denote $[j] = \{0, 1, \ldots, j\}$. We assume vectors to be in column form and are written using bold letters, e.g. $\mathbf{x}$. Matrices are written as bold capital letters, e.g. $\mathbf{X}$. The norm $\|.\|$ here is the standard Euclidean norm in R^n.

Gram Schmidt Orthogonalization: $\widetilde{S} := \{\widetilde{s_1}, ..., \widetilde{s_k}\} \subset R^m$ denotes the Gram-Schmidt orthogonalization of the set of linearly independently vectors $S = \{s_1, ..., s_k\} \subset R^m$. It is defined as follows: $\widetilde{s_1} = s_1$ and $\widetilde{s_i}$ is the component of s_i orthogonal to $\text{span}(s_1, ..., s_i)$ where $2 \le i \le k$. Since $\widetilde{s_i}$ is the component of s_i so $\|\widetilde{s_i}\| \le \|s_i\|$ for all i.

2.2 Hierarchical IBE

Here definition and security model of HIBE are similar to [11,12,1]. User at depth l is defined by its tuple of ids : $(id/id_l) = (id_1, ..., id_l)$. The user's ancestors are the root PKG and the prefix of id tuples (users/lower level PKGs).

HIBE consists of four algorithms.

Setup(d, λ): On input a security parameter d(maximum depth of hierarchy tree) and λ, this algorithm outputs the public parameters and master key of root PKG.

Derive$(PP, (id/id_l), SK_{(id/id_l)})$: On input public parameters PP, an identity $(id/id_l) = (id_1, ..., id_l)$ at depth l and the private key $SK_{(id/id_{l-1})}$ corresponding to parent identity $(id/id_{l-1}) = (id_1, ..., id_{l-1})$ at depth $l - 1 \ge 0$, this algorithm outputs private key for the identity (id/id_l) at depth l.

If $l = 1$ then $SK_{(id/id_0)}$ is defined to be master key of root PKG.

The private key corresponding to an identity $(id/id_l) = (id_1, ..., id_l)$ at depth l can be generated by PKG or any ancestor (prefix) of an identity (id/id_l).

Encrypt$(PP, (id/id_l), M)$: On input public parameters PP, an identity (id/id_l), and a message M, this algorithm outputs ciphertext C.

Decrypt$(PP, SK_{(id/id_l)}, C)$: On input public parameters PP, a private key $SK_{(id/id_l)}$, and a ciphertext C, this algorithm outputs message M.

2.3 Adaptive-ID (Full) Security Model of HIBE

We define adaptive-ID security model using a game that the challenge ciphertext is indistinguisable from a random element in the ciphertext space. The game proceeds as follows.

Setup: The challenger runs Setup$(1^\lambda, 1^d)$ and gives the PP to adversary and keeps MK to itself.

Phase 1: The adversary issues a query for a private key for identity $(id/id_k) = (id_1, ..., id_k)$, $k \le d$. Adversary can repeat this multiple times for different identities adaptivly.

Challenge: The adversary submits identity id^* and message M. Identity id^* and prefix of id^* should not be one of the identity query in phase 1. The challenger choose a random bit $r \in \{0, 1\}$ and a random string C with the size of the valid ciphertext. If $r = 0$ it assigns the challenge ciphertext $C^* := Encrypt(PP, id^*, M)$. If $r = 1$ it assigns the challenge ciphertext $C^* := C$. It sends C^* to the adversary as challenge.

Phase 2: Phase 1 is repeated with the restriction that the adversary can not query for id^* and prefix of id^*.

Guess: Finally, the adversary outputs a guess $r' \in \{0, 1\}$ and wins if $r = r'$.

We refer an adversary $\mathscr{A}$ as an IND-ID-CPA adversary. Advantage of an adversary $\mathscr{A}$ in attacking an IBE scheme ξ is defined as

$$Adv_{d,\xi,A}(\lambda) = |Pr[r = r'] - 1/2|$$

Definition 1. *HIBE scheme ξ with depth d is adaptive-ID, indistinguishable from random if $Adv_{d,\xi,A}(\lambda)$ is a negligible function for all IND-ID-CPA PPT adversaries $\mathscr{A}$.*

2.4 Integer Lattices ([10])

A lattice L is defined as the set of all integer combinations

$$L(b_1,...,b_n) = \left\{ \sum_{i=1}^{n} x_i b_i : x_i \in Z \text{ for } 1 \le i \le n \right\}$$

of n linearly independent vectors $\{b_1,...,b_n\} \in R^n$. The set of vectors $\{b_1,...,b_n\}$ is called a lattice basis.

Definition 2. *For q prime, $A \in Z_q^{n \times m}$ and $u \in Z_q^n$, define:*

$$\Lambda_q(A) := \{e \in Z^m \ s.t. \ \exists s \in Z_q^n \text{ where } A^T s = e \ (mod \ q)\}$$
$$\Lambda_q^{\perp}(A) := \{e \in Z^m \ s.t. \ Ae = 0 \ (mod \ q)\}$$
$$\Lambda_q^u(A) := \{e \in Z^m \ s.t. \ Ae = u \ (mod \ q)\}$$

Theorem 1. *([2]) Let q be prime and $m := \lceil 6n\log q \rceil$.*
There is PPT algorithm TrapGen(q,n) that outputs a pair $(A \in Z_q^{n \times m}, T \in Z^{n \times m})$ such that statistically distance between matrix A and a uniform matrix in $Z_q^{n \times m}$ is negligible and T is a basis for $\Lambda_q^{\perp}(A)$ satisfying

$$\|\tilde{T}\| \le O(\sqrt{n\log q}) \ \text{ and } \ \|T\| \le O(n\log q)$$

with overwhelming probability in n.

2.5 The LWE Hardness Assumption ([15,1])

The LWE (learning with error) hardness assumption is defined by Regev [15].

Definition 3. *LWE: Consider a prime q, a positive integer n, and a Gaussian distribution χ^m over Z_q^m. Given $(A, As + x)$ where matrix $A \in Z_q^{m \times n}$ is uniformly random and $x \in \chi^m$.*
LWE hard problem is to find s with non-negligible probability.

Definition 4. *Decision LWE: Consider a prime q, a positive integer n, and a Gaussian distribution χ^m over Z_q^m. The input is a pair (A, v) from an unspecified challenge oracle O, where $A \in Z_q^{m \times n}$ is chosen uniformly. An unspecified challenge oracle O is either a noisy pseudo-random sampler O_s or a truly random sampler $O_\$$. It is based on how v is chosen.*

1. When v is chosen to be $As + e$ for a uniformly chosen $s \in Z_q^n$ and a vector $e \in \chi^m$, an unspecified challenge oracle O is a noisy pseudo-random sampler O_s.
2. When v is chosen uniformly from Z_q^m, an unspecified challenge oracle O is a truly random sampler $O_\$$.

Goal of the adversary is to distinguish between the above two cases with non-negligible probability.

Or we say that an algorithm A decides the (Z_q, n, χ)-LWE problem if $|Pr[A^{O_s} = 1] - Pr[A^{O_\$} = 1]|$ is non-negligible for a random $s \in Z_q^n$.

Above decision LWE is also hard even if s is chosen from the Gaussian distribution rather than the uniform distribution [3,13].

2.6   Inhomogeneous Small Integer Solution (ISIS) Assumption

Definition 5. Given an integer q, a matrix $A \in Z_q^{n \times m}$, a syndrome $u \in Z_q^n$ and real β, find a short integer vector $x \in Z_q^m$ such that $Ax = u \mod q$ and $x \leq \beta$.

3   Sampling Algorithms

Let A, B be matrices in $Z_q^{n \times m}$ and R be a matix in $\{-1, 1\}^{m \times m}$. Let matrix $F = (AR + B) \in Z_q^{n \times 2m}$ and suppose we have to sample short vectors in $\Lambda_q^u(F)$ for some u in Z_q^n. This can be done either a SampleLeft or SampleRight algorithm.

SampleLeft Algorithm (A, M_1, T_A, u, σ)([1]). On input matrix $A \in Z_q^{n \times m}$ of rank n , a matrix M_1 in $Z_q^{n \times m_1}$, a "short" basis T_A of $\Lambda_q^\perp(A)$, a vector $u \in Z_q^n$ and a Gaussian parameter $\sigma > \|\widetilde{T_A}\| \omega(\sqrt{(\log(m + m_1))})$, this algorithm returns a vector $e \in Z^{m+m_1}$ sampled from a distribution which is statistically close to $D_{\Lambda_q^u(F_1),\sigma}$, where $F_1 = A|M_1$.

SampleRight Algorithm $(A, B, R, T_B, u, \sigma)$([1]). On input a rank n matrix A in $Z_q^{n \times m}$, $B \in Z_q^{n \times m}$ where B is rank n, a matrix R in $Z_q^{k \times m}$, let $s_R := \|R\|$, a basis T_B of $\Lambda_q^\perp(B)$ and a vector $u \in Z_q^n$ and a Gaussian parameter $\sigma > \|\widetilde{T_B}\| s_R \omega(\sqrt{\log(m)})$, this algorithm returns a vector $e \in Z^{m+k}$ sampled from a distribution which is statistically close to $D_{\Lambda_q^u(F_2),\sigma}$ where $F_2 = (A|AR + B)$.

4   Adaptively Secure HIBE Scheme in Standard Model

Our new scheme is a variant of Agarwal et al HIBE [1], but with short public parameters. In our scheme, identity id/id_l is represented as $id/id_l = (id_1, ..., id_l) = ((b_{1,1}||...$
$||b_{1,l''}), ..., (b_{l,1}||...||b_{l,l''}))$ where id_i is l' bit string and $b_{i,j}$ is $l'/l'' = \beta$ bit string. In Agrawal et al [1] selective-ID secure lattice HIBE, encryption matrix

$$F_{id/id_l} = (A_0|A_1 + H(id_1)B|...|A_l + H(id_l)B) \in Z_q^{n \times (l+1)m}$$

We apply Waters's [19] idea to convert Agrawal et al [1] selective-ID secure lattice HIBE to adaptive-ID secure HIBE. With this technique, for an l-level HIBE has public parameters as $A_{1,1}, \ldots, A_{1,l}, A_{2,1}, \ldots, A_{2,l}, \ldots, A_{l,l}$ and A_0, B matrices. Now encryption matrix becomes

$$F_{id/id_l} = \left(A_0 \mid \sum_{i=1}^{l} A_{1,i} b_{1,i} + B \mid \ldots \mid \sum_{i=1}^{l} A_{l,i} b_{l,i} + B \right)$$

Here the public parameters is very large (total $l \times l + 2$ matrices). Similar to Chatterjee and Sarkar [8] we have used same public parameters $A_1, \ldots, A_l$ for all levels. This way public parametrs is reduced from $l \times l + 2$ matrices to $l + 2$ matrices. Further we reduce the public parameters $(l + 2)$ matrices to $(l'' + 2)$ matrices by using Chatterjee and Sarkar's [7] blocking technique. Finally encryption matrix in our scheme is

$$F_{id/id_l} = \left(A_0 \mid \sum_{i=1}^{l''} A_i b_{1,i} + B \mid \ldots \mid \sum_{i=1}^{l''} A_i b_{l,i} + B \right) \tag{1}$$

4.1 The HIBE Construction

Now we describe our adaptive secure HIBE scheme as follows.

Setup (d, λ): On input a security parameter λ and a maximum hierarchy depth d, this algorithm set the parameters $q, n, m, \overline{\sigma}, \overline{\alpha}$ as specified in the end of this section. Next we do the following.

1. Use algorithm TrapGen(q, n) to generate a matrix $A_0 \in Z_q^{n \times m}$ and a short basis T_{A_0} for $\Lambda_q^\perp(A_0)$ such that $\|\widetilde{T_{A_0}}\| \leq O(\sqrt{n \log q})$.
2. Select $l'' + 1$ uniformly random $n \times m$ matrices $A_1, A_2, \ldots, A_{l''}$ and $B \in Z_q^{n \times m}$.
3. Select a uniformly random n - vector $u \in Z_q^n$.
4. Output the public parameters and master key,
   PP $= A_1, A_2, \ldots, A_{l''}$ and $B, A_0 \in Z_q^{n \times m}$, MK $= T_{A_0} \in Z_q^{m \times m}$.

Derive $(PP, (id/id_l), SK_{(id/id_{(l-1)})})$: On input public parameters PP, a private key $SK_{(id/id_{l-1})}$ corresponding to an identity (id/id_{l-1}) at depth $l - 1$ the algorithm outputs a private key for the identity (id/id_l) at depth l.

From equation (1),

$$F_{id/id_l} = \left(A_0 \mid \sum_{i=1}^{l''} A_i b_{1,i} + B \mid \ldots \mid \sum_{i=1}^{l''} A_i b_{l,i} + B \right) \tag{2}$$

Or $F_{id/id_l} = \left(F_{id/id_{l-1}} \mid \sum_{i=1}^{l''} A_i b_{l,i} + B \right)$.

Given short basis $SK_{(id/id_{(l-1)})}$ for $\Lambda_q^\perp(F_{id/id_{l-1}})$ and F_{id/id_l} as defined in (1), we can construct short basis $SK_{(id/id_l)}$ for $\Lambda_q^\perp(F_{id/id_l})$ by invoking

$$S \longleftarrow \text{SampleLeft}\left(F_{id/id_{l-1}}, \sum_{i=1}^{l''} A_i b_{l,i} + B, SK_{(id/id_{(l-1)})}, 0, \sigma_l\right)$$

and output $SK_{(id/id_l)} \longleftarrow S$.

The private key corresponding to an identity $(id/id_l) = (id_1, \ldots, id_l)$ at depth l can be generated by PKG or any ancestor (prefix) of an identity (id/id_l) by repeatedly calling SampleLeft algorithm.

Encrypt (PP, Id, b)**:** On input public parameters PP, an identity (id/id_l) of depth l and a message $b \in \{0, 1\}$, do the following:

1. Build encryption matrix

$$F_{id/id_l} = \left(A_0 | \sum_{i=1}^{l''} (A_i b_{1,i} + B) || \ldots || \sum_{i=1}^{l''} (A_i b_{l,i} + B) \right) \in Z_q^{n \times (l''+1)m}$$

.

2. Choose a uniformly random vector $s \xleftarrow{R} Z_q^n$.
3. Choose l'' uniformly random matrices $R_j \xleftarrow{R} \{-1, 1\}^{m \times m}$ for $j = 1, \ldots, l''$. Define $R_{id}^1 = \sum_{i=1}^{l''} b_i R_i || \ldots || \sum_{i=1}^{l''} b_i R_i \in Z^{m \times l'' m}$
4. Choose noise vector $x \xleftarrow{\overline{\Psi}_{\alpha_l}} Z_q, y \xleftarrow{\overline{\Psi}_{\alpha_l}^m} Z_q^m$ and $z \leftarrow R_{id}^T y \in Z_q^{lm}$,
5. Output the ciphertext,

$$CT = \left(C_0 = u_0^T s + x + b \lfloor \tfrac{q}{2} \rfloor, C_1 = F_{id}^T s + \begin{bmatrix} y \\ z \end{bmatrix} \right) \quad \in Z_q \times Z_q^{(l+1)m}$$

Decrypt $(PP, SK_{(id/id_l)}, CT)$**:** On input public parameters PP, a private key SK_{id/id_l}, and a ciphertext CT $= (C_0, C_1)$, do the following.

1. Set $\tau_l = \sigma_l \sqrt{m(l+1)} w(\sqrt{log(lm)})$. Then $\tau_l \geq \|\widetilde{SK}\| w(\sqrt{log(lm)})$.
2. $e_{id} \longleftarrow SamplePre(F_{id/id_l}, SK_{(Id/id_l)}, u, \tau_l)$
   Then $F_{id} e_{id} = u$ and $\|e_{id}\| \leq \tau_l \sqrt{m(l+1)}$
3. Compute $C_0 - e_{id}^T C_1 \in Z_q$.
4. Compare w and $\lfloor \tfrac{q}{2} \rfloor$ treating them as integers in Z. If they are close, i.e., if $|w - \lfloor \tfrac{q}{2} \rfloor| < \tfrac{q}{4}$ in Z, output 1 otherwise output 0.

During Decryption:
$w_0 = C_0 - e_{id}^T C_1 = b \lfloor \tfrac{q}{2} \rfloor + x - e_{id}^T \begin{bmatrix} y \\ z \end{bmatrix}$.

Parameters and Correctness: We have during decryption, $w = C_0 - e_{id}^T c_1 = b \lfloor \tfrac{q}{2} \rfloor + x - e_{id}^T \begin{bmatrix} y \\ z \end{bmatrix}$. $x - e_{id}^T \begin{bmatrix} y \\ z \end{bmatrix}$ is called error term and for correctness it has to be less than $q/4$.

Lemma 1. *Norm of the error is less than* $[q 2^{\beta} l'' l^2 \sigma_l m \alpha_l \omega(\sqrt{\log m}) + O(2^{\beta} l'' l^2 \sigma_l m^{3/2})]$.

Proof: Lemma is essentially same as lemma 32 of [1] except now R_{id} is uniformly random matrix in $\{-2^{\beta} l'', 2^{\beta} l''\}^{m \times lm}$. So now $|R_{id}|$ will be equal to $2^{\beta} l'' R_{id}$. Hence error term will have extra factor $2^{\beta} l''$.

---

[1] In security proof, R_{id} is used to answer adversary's secret key query and also for valid challenge ciphertext, error vector has to be $\begin{bmatrix} y \\ R_{id}^T y \end{bmatrix}$.

For the scheme to work correctly, it is required that:

- the error is less than $q/4$ i.e. $\alpha_l < [2^\beta l'' l^2 \sigma_l m \omega(\sqrt{\log m})]^{-1}$ and $q = \Omega(2^\beta l'' l^2 \sigma_l m^{3/2})$
- that TrapGen can operate (i.e $m > 6n \log q$)
- That σ_l is sufficiently large for SimpleLeft and SimpleRight
  (i.e. $\sigma_l > \|\widetilde{T_B}\| s_R \omega(\sqrt{\log m})) = 2^\beta l'' \sqrt{lm} \omega(\sqrt{\log m})$
- that Regev's reduction applies (i.e. $(q2^\beta)^l > 2Q$), where Q is the number of identity queries from the adversary)

To satisfy these requirements we set the parameters $(q, m, \sigma_l, \alpha_l)$ as follows, taking n to be the security parameter:

$$m = 6n^{1+\delta}, \qquad\qquad \sigma_l = l'' \sqrt{lm} \omega(\sqrt{\log n})$$

$$q = max((2Q/2^\beta)^{1/l}, (2^\beta l'')^2 l^{2.5} m^{2.5} \omega(\sqrt{\log n})), \alpha_l = [(2^\beta l'')^2 l^{2.5} m^2 \omega(\sqrt{\log m})]^{-1} \quad (3)$$

From above requirements, we need $q = (2^\beta l'')^2 l^{2.5} m^{2.5} \omega(\sqrt{\log n})$.

4.2   Security Proof

Our proof of theorem will require an abort-resistant hash function defined as follows.

Abort-Resistant Hash Functions

Definition 6. *Let $H = \{\hbar : X \longrightarrow Y\}$ be family of hash functions from X to Y where $0 \in Y$. For a set of $Q+1$ inputs $\bar{x} = (x_0, x_1, ..., x_Q) \in X^{Q+1}$, non-abort probability of $\bar{x}$ is defined as*

$$\alpha(\bar{x}) = Pr[\hbar[x_0] = 0 \wedge \hbar[x_1] \neq 0 \wedge ... \wedge \hbar[x_Q] \neq 0]$$

where range of the probability is the random selection of $\hbar$ in H.

H is $(Q, \alpha_{min}, \alpha_{max})$ abort-resistance if $\forall \bar{x} = (x_0, x_1, ..., x_Q) \in X^{Q+1}$ with $x_0 \notin \{x_1, ..., x_Q\}$ we have $\alpha(\bar{x}) \in [\alpha_{min}, \alpha_{max}]$. we use the following abort-resistant hash family very similar to [1].
For a prime number q let $(Z_q^{l''})^* = Z_q^{l''} - \{0^l\}$ and the family is defined as

$$H : \{\hbar : ((Z_{2^\beta}^{l''})^* | ... | (Z_{2^\beta}^{l''})^*) \longrightarrow (Z_q | ... | Z_q)\}$$

$$\hbar(id) = \hbar(id_1 | ... | id_l) = \left(1 + \sum_{i=1}^{l''} h_i b_{1,i}\right) | ... | \left(1 + \sum_{i=1}^{l''} h_i b_{l,i}\right) \quad (4)$$

where h_i and $b_{k,i}$ are defined in section 4.1.

Lemma 2. *For prime number q and $0 < Q < q$. Then the hash family H defined in (3) is $(Q, \frac{1}{q^l}(1 - \frac{Q}{q^l}), \frac{1}{q^l})$ abort-resistant.*

Proof: The proof is similar to [1]. Consider a set of $\overline{id}$ of $Q+1$ inputs $id^0, ..., id^Q$ in $(Z_q^{l l''})^*$ where $id^0 \notin \{id^1, ..., id^Q\}$ and $id^i = \{id_1, ..., id_l\}$. Since number of functions in $H = q^{l''}(2^\beta)^{l''l}$ and for $i = 0, ..., Q+1$ let S_i be function $\hbar$ in H such that $\hbar(id^i) = 0$. Hence number of such functions $= |S_i| = \frac{q^{l''}(2^\beta)^{l''l}}{q^l}$. and $\frac{|S_0 \wedge S_j| \leq q^{l''}(2^\beta)^{l''l}}{q^{2l}}$ for every $j > 0$. Number of functions in H such that $\hbar(id^0) = (0|...|0)$ but $\hbar(id^i) \neq 0$ for $i = 1, ..., Q. = |S|$ and

$$|S| = |S_0 - (S_1 \vee ... S_Q)| \geq |S_0| - \sum_{i=1}^{Q} |S_0 \wedge S_i|$$

$$\geq \frac{q^{l''}(2^\beta)^{l''l}}{q^l} - Q\frac{q^{l''}(2^\beta)^{l''l}}{q^{2l}}$$

Therefore the no-abort probability of identities is atleast equal to $\frac{\frac{q^{l''}(2^\beta)^{l''l}}{q^l} - \frac{Qq^{l''}(2^\beta)^{l''l}}{q^{2l}}}{q^{l''}(2^\beta)^{l''l}} = \frac{1}{q^l}(1 - \frac{Q}{q^{2l}})$ Since $|S| \leq |S_0|$, so the no-abort probability is atmost $\frac{|S_0|}{q^{l''}(2^\beta)^{l''l}} = \frac{1}{q^l}$.

Theorem 2. *Our HIBE scheme is IND-ID-CPA secure provided that the* $(Z_q, n, \bar{\psi}_{\alpha_d})$-*LWE assumptions hold.*

Proof. Here proof is similar to [1,17]. We show that if there exist a PPT adversary A that breaks our *HIBE* scheme with non-negligible probability then there exists a PPT challenger B that answers whether an unspecified challenge oracle O is either a noisy pseudo-random sampler O_s or a truly random sampler $O_\$$ by simulating views of adversary A.

Setup: Challenger B generates uniformly random matrix A_0 in $Z_q^{n \times m}$ as follows. Challenger B obtains $m+1$ LWE samples i.e. $(u_i, v_i) \in Z_q^n \times Z_q$ $(0 \leq i \leq m+1$ from an unspecified challenge oracle, which get parsed as matrix $A_0 = (u_1, ..., u_m)$. Matrix B is generated by using algorithm TrapGen, which returns random matrix B in $Z_q^{n \times m}$ and a Trapdoor T_B for $\Lambda_q^\perp(B)$. Challenger also chooses l'' uniformly random matrices $R_i \in [-1, l]^{m \times m}, i \in [1, l'']$ and l'' random scalars $h_i \in Z_q, i \in [1, l'']$. Next it constructs the matrices A_i as

$$A_i \longleftarrow A_0 R_i + h_i B$$

By lemma 3, the statistical distance between distribution of A_i's and the uniform distribution is negligible.

Phase 1

$$F_{id/id_l} = \left(A_0 | \sum_{i=1}^{l''} A_i b_{1,i} + B || ... || \sum_{i=1}^{l''} A_i b_{l,i} + B \right) \tag{5}$$

Substituting the value of matrices A_i from equation (4)

$$F_{id/id_l} = \left(A_0 | A_0 \left(\sum_{i=1}^{l''} R_i b_{1,i} \right) + B \left(1 + \sum_{i=1}^{l''} h_i b_{1,i} \right) ||...||A_0 \left(\sum_{i=1}^{l''} R_i b_{l,i} \right) + B \left(1 + \sum_{i=1}^{l''} h_i b_{l,i} \right) \right)$$

Or $F_{id} = (A_0 | A_0 R_{id} + B h_{id})$ where $R_{id} = \sum_{i=1}^{l''} R_i b_{1,i} ||...|| \sum_{i=1}^{l''} R_i b_{l,i}$ and $B_{id} = B h_{id} = B(1 + \sum_{i=1}^{l''} h_i b_{1,i}) ||...|| (1 + \sum_{i=1}^{l''} h_i b_{l,i})$.

If $\hbar_{id}$ is not equal to zero then challenger responds the private key query of $id = (id^1, id^2, ..., id^l)$ by running

$$SK_{id} \longleftarrow \text{SampleRight}(A_0, B_{id}, R_{id}, T_B, 0, \sigma_l)$$

and sending SK_{id} to A. $\hbar_{id}$ is equal to zero will be part of abort resistant hash function.

Challenge: Adversary declares target identity $id^* = (id_1, id_2, ..., id_l)$ and bit message $b^* \in \{0, 1\}$. Simulator B creates challenge ciphertext for declared target identity as follows:

1. Set

$$v^* = \begin{pmatrix} v_1 \\ \vdots \\ v_m \end{pmatrix} \in Z_q^m$$

   where $v_1, \ldots, v_m$ be entries from LWE instance.
2. Blind the bit message by letting

$$C_0^* = v_0 + b^* \lfloor \frac{q}{2} \rfloor \in Z_q$$

3. Challenger also chooses l'' uniformly random matrices $R_i^* \in [-1, l]^{m \times m}, i \in [1, l'']$. Let

$$R_{id^*} = (R_1^* | ... | R_{l''}^*)$$

   and set

$$C_1^* = \begin{pmatrix} v^* \\ (R_{id^*})^T v^* \end{pmatrix} \in Z_q^{m + l'' m}$$

4. Randomly choose a bit $r \leftarrow \{0, 1\}$. If $r = 0$, send ciphertext $CT^* = (C_0^*, C_1^*)$ to the adversary. If $r = 1$ choose a random $(C_0, C_1) \in Z_q \times Z_q^{m + l'' m}$ and send (C_0, C_1) to the adversary.

Phase 2: Simulator repeats the same method used in Phase 1 with the restriction that the adversary can not query for id^* and prefix of id^*.

Artificial Abort: This artificial abort technique was introduced by Waters [19]. Chatterjee and Sarkar [7] presented a detailed exposition on artificial abort. Since probability of abort depends on the set of private key queries so it is possible that an adversary's success probability and simulator' abort probability are not independent. The purpose of the artificial abort step is to ensure that simulator aborts with almost same probability irrespective of any set of queries made by the adversary. This step increases the run time of the simulator.

We obtain the lower bound λ for the probability that challenger B does not abort. Let ab be the event that challenger B aborts and Σ' is the set of queries made by the adversary. Waters [19] has proved that probability challenger B does not abort is very close to λ for all adversarial queries.

$$|Pr[\overline{ab}|Y \in \Sigma'] - \lambda| \leq \frac{\varepsilon}{2}$$

From lemma 3 no-abort probability of identities is atleast equal to $\frac{1}{q^l}(1 - \frac{Q}{q^{2l}})$. With $Q \leq q^l/2$ no-abort probability of identities will be atleast equal to $\frac{1}{q^l}$.

Simulator requires an additional $\chi = O(\varepsilon^{-2}ln(\varepsilon^{-1})\lambda ln(\lambda^{-1}))$ time for artificial abort stage. Bellare and Ristenport [4] showed that artificial step can be avoided. They have provided following security reduction formula without artificial abort step.

$$Adv^{dbdh}(B) \geq \frac{\gamma_{min}}{2}Adv^{IND-CPA}_{Waters} + (\gamma_{min} - \gamma_{max})$$

From the above expression it is clear that Bellare and Ristenport's [4] proof will work when $\gamma_{min} - \gamma_{max}$ is negligible. But in our case $\gamma_{min} - \gamma_{max}$ is $-\frac{Q}{q^2}$ and it can be made negligible with large q which will affect the performance of the scheme. So we have used Waters [19] artificial abort.

When the LWE oracle is pseudorandom then $F_{id^*} = (A_0|A_0\overline{R}_{id^*})$ since $h_{id^*} = 0$ and

$$v^* = A_0^T s + y$$

for some uniform noise vector $y \in Z_q^m$ distributed as $\overline{\psi}_\alpha^m$. Therefore

$$C_1^* = \begin{pmatrix} A_0^T s + y \\ (A_0 R_{id^*})^T s + (R_{id^*})^T y \end{pmatrix} = (F_{id^*})^T s + \begin{pmatrix} y \\ (R_{id^*})^T y \end{pmatrix}$$

Above C_1^* is a valid C_1 part of challenge ciphertext. Again $C_0^* = u_0^T + x + b^*\lfloor\frac{q}{2}\rceil$ is also a valid C_0 part of challenge ciphertext. Therefore (C_0^*, C_1^*) is valid challenge ciphertext.

When LWE oracle is random oracle, v_0 is uniform in Z_q and v^* is uniform in Z_q^m. Therefore challenge ciphertext is always uniform in $Z_q \times Z_q^{l''m}$. Finally adversary A terminates with correct output, adversary B answers that an unspecified challenge oracle O is a noisy pseudo-random sampler O_s else an unspecified challenge oracle O is a truly random sampler $O_\$$ and terminates the simulation.

So probabilistic algorithm B solves the $(Z_q, n, \overline{\psi}_\alpha)$-LWE problem in about the time $= t_1 + O(\varepsilon^{-2}ln(\varepsilon^{-1})\lambda ln(\lambda^{-1}))$ and with $\varepsilon' \geq \varepsilon/4q^l$.

5 Conclusion

We have shown that by converting selective-ID HIBE to adaptive-ID HIBE security degradation is exponential in number of levels. The open problem is to construct adaptive-ID HIBE secure scheme without exponentialial degradation.

References

1. Agrawal, S., Boneh, D., Boyen, X.: Efficient Lattice (H)IBE in the Standard Model. In: Gilbert, H. (ed.) EUROCRYPT 2010. LNCS, vol. 6110, pp. 553–572. Springer, Heidelberg (2010)
2. Alwen, J., Peikert, C.: Generating Shorter Bases for Hard Random Lattices. In: International Symposium on Theoretical Aspects of Computer Science, STACS 2009, pp. 75–86. IBFI Schloss Dagstuhl (2009)
3. Applebaum, B., Cash, D., Peikert, C., Sahai, A.: Fast Cryptographic Primitives and Circular-Secure Encryption Based on Hard Learning Problems. In: Halevi, S. (ed.) CRYPTO 2009. LNCS, vol. 5677, pp. 595–618. Springer, Heidelberg (2009)
4. Bellare, M., Ristenpart, T.: Simulation without the Artificial Abort: Simplified Proof and Improved Concrete Security for Waters' IBE Scheme. In: Joux, A. (ed.) EUROCRYPT 2009. LNCS, vol. 5479, pp. 407–424. Springer, Heidelberg (2009)
5. Boneh, D., Franklin, M.: Identity Based Encryption From the Weil Pairing. In: Kilian, J. (ed.) CRYPTO 2001. LNCS, vol. 2139, pp. 213–229. Springer, Heidelberg (2001)
6. Cash, D., Hofheinz, D., Kiltz, E.: How to Delegate a Lattice Basis. In: IACR Cryptology ePrint Archive (2009)
7. Chatterjee, S., Sarkar, P.: Trading Time for Space: Towards an Efficient IBE Scheme with Short(er) Public Parameters in the Standard Model. In: Won, D.H., Kim, S. (eds.) ICISC 2005. LNCS, vol. 3935, pp. 424–440. Springer, Heidelberg (2006)
8. Chatterjee, S., Sarkar, P.: HIBE With Short(er) Public Parameters Without Random Oracle. In: Lai, X., Chen, K. (eds.) ASIACRYPT 2006. LNCS, vol. 4284, pp. 145–160. Springer, Heidelberg (2006)
9. Cocks, C.: An Identity Based Encryption Scheme Based on Quadratic Residues. In: Honary, B. (ed.) Cryptography and Coding 2001. LNCS, vol. 2260, pp. 360–363. Springer, Heidelberg (2001)
10. Micciancio, D., Goldwasser, S.: Complexity of Lattice Problems: A Cryptographic Perspective, vol. 671. Kluwer Academic Publishers (2002)
11. Gentry, C., Silverberg, A.: Hierarchical ID-Based Cryptography. In: Zheng, Y. (ed.) ASIACRYPT 2002. LNCS, vol. 2501, pp. 548–566. Springer, Heidelberg (2002)
12. Horwitz, J., Lynn, B.: Toward Hierarchical Identity-Based Encryption. In: Knudsen, L.R. (ed.) EUROCRYPT 2002. LNCS, vol. 2332, pp. 466–481. Springer, Heidelberg (2002)
13. Lindner, R., Peikert, C.: Better key sizes (and attacks) for LWE-based encryption. In: Kiayias, A. (ed.) CT-RSA 2011. LNCS, vol. 6558, pp. 319–339. Springer, Heidelberg (2011)
14. Peikert, C.: Bonsai trees (or, arboriculture in lattice-based cryptography). In: Cryptology ePrint Archive, Report 2009/359 (2009)
15. Regev, O.: On lattices, learning with errors, random linear codes, and cryptography. In: STOC, pp. 84–93. ACM (2005)
16. Shamir, A.: How to share a secret. Commun. ACM 22(11), 612–613 (1979)
17. Singh, K., Pandu Rangan, C., Banerjee, A.K.: Lattice based identity based proxy re-encryption scheme. Journal of Internet Services and Information Security (JISIS) 3(3/4), 38–51 (2013)
18. Singh, K., Pandurangan, C., Banerjee, A.K.: Adaptively secure efficient lattice (H)IBE in standard model with short public parameters. In: Bogdanov, A., Sanadhya, S. (eds.) SPACE 2012. LNCS, vol. 7644, pp. 153–172. Springer, Heidelberg (2012)
19. Waters, B.: Efficient identity-based encryption without random oracles. In: Cramer, R. (ed.) EUROCRYPT 2005. LNCS, vol. 3494, pp. 114–127. Springer, Heidelberg (2005)
20. You, I., Hori, Y., Sakurai, K.: Enhancing svo logic for mobile ipv6 security protocols. Journal of Wireless Mobile Networks, Ubiquitous Computing, and Dependable Applications (JoWUA) 2(3), 26–52 (2011)

Security Analysis of Public Key Encryptions Based on Conjugacy Search Problem

Akihiro Yamamura

Department of Mathematical Science and Electrical-Electric-Computer Engineering,
Akita University,
1-1, Tegata Gakuen-machi, Akita 010-8502, Japan

Abstract. We report a fatal flaw of CSP-ElG scheme, one of public key encryptions based on conjugacy search problem proposed in INSCRYPT 2010. It does not satisfy the security property claimed as it is. We also discuss imperfections of security proofs of the other proposals: CSP-hElG and CSP-CS schemes. Following the technique given by Gennaro et al. to smooth a distribution of DH transform outputs, we introduce a computational assumption related to monoid actions and fix the CSP-ElG scheme using a universal hash function and the leftover hash lemma.

Keywords: Conjugacy Search Problem, DDH Assumption, Monoid Action, Universal Hash Functions, Leftover Hash Lemma.

1 Introduction

Three generic designs, CSP-ElG, CSP-hElG and CSP-CS schemes, to construct a public key encryption using a conjugacy search problem are proposed by L.Wang, L.Wang, Z.Cao, E.Okamoto and J.Shao in Inscrypt 2010 [9]. The proposed schemes can be instantiated using any conjugacy search problem (CSP for short), which is used in [6,8]. Each scheme is claimed to have desired provable security provided that a computational assumption related to CSP holds. Their motivation of these proposals is to invent new schemes based on principles other than the ones suffering from attacks using quantum algorithms such as Shor's factoring or Glover's database search algorithm because most of the widely used schemes like RSA and ElGamal would confront such attacks if a quantum computer could be realized.

In this paper, we report fatal flaws in these schemes, in particular, we analyze the CSP-ElG scheme in detail. We also briefly discuss the security of the CSP-hElG and CSP-CS schemes and give circumstantial evidences that these schemes do not enjoy the claimed security property. In addition, we shall fix the CSP-ElG using the Gennaro, Krawczyk and Rabin's technique to smooth the distribution of outputs of DH transform over non-DDH group [5] using the leftover hash lemma [2,7]. For this purpose we show that both ElGamal and CSP-ElG are an instantiation of a generic scheme based on monoid actions. Then we prove such a generic scheme is indistinguishable against chosen plaintext attacks in the standard model under a reasonable computational assumption, that is, t-MA-DDH assumption.

Linawati et al. (Eds.): ICT-EurAsia 2014, LNCS 8407, pp. 554–563, 2014.

2 Flaws of Schemes Based on Conjugacy Search Problem

Let M be a (not necessarily commutative) monoid. Recall that a *monoid* is an algebraic system with an associative multiplication and the identity element "1". We denote the set of invertible elements x of M by $G(M)$, that is, $G(M) = \{x \mid \exists y \in M$ such that $xy = yx = 1\}$. The inverse of $x \in G(M)$ is the element y such that $xy = yx = 1$. Note that the inverse of x is uniquely determined. The *conjugacy search problem* is to find an element $g \in G(M)$ such that $f = gdg^{-1}$ for given $d, f \in M$ provided that such an element g exists.

Suppose that $d \in M$ and $g \in G(M)$ and the order of g is n. If the order of g is infinite, then n is specified to be a large enough. The *CSP-CDH problem* is to compute $g^{a+b}dg^{-(a+b)}$ for given $d \in M$, $g \in G(M)$, $g^a dg^{-a}$ and $g^b dg^{-b}$, where a and b are ramdomly and uniformly chosen from $\{1, \ldots, n\}$. We say that the *CSP-CDH assumption* holds for M if there is no efficient algorithm to answer correctly to a CSP-CDH problem instance.

The *CSP-DDH problem* is a decisional variant of the CSP-CDH problem, that is, it is to decide whether or not $f = g^{a+b}dg^{-(a+b)}$ for given $d \in M$, $g \in G(M)$, $g^a dg^{-a}$, $g^b dg^{-b}$ and $f = g^c dg^{-c}$, where a and b and are randomly chosen from $\{1, \ldots, n\}$ and either c is randomly chosen from $\{1, \ldots, n\}$ or $c = a + b$ with probability $\frac{1}{2}$. We say that the *CSP-DDH assumption* holds for M if there is no efficient algorithm to answer correctly to a CSP-DDH problem instance with probability non-negligibly larger than $\frac{1}{2}$.

2.1 CPS-ElG Scheme

The CSP-ElG scheme is defined as follows. Let $K = \{g^a dg^{-a} \mid 1 \leq a \leq \mathrm{Ord}(g)\}$, where $\mathrm{Ord}(g)$ stands for the order of the element g. Let P be the message space $\{0, 1\}^k$, C the ciphertext space $K \times P$. Suppose $H : K \to P$ is a cryptographic hash function. Alice picks a $(1 \leq a \leq \mathrm{Ord}(g))$ and publicizes $g^a dg^{-a}$. Bob picks b $(1 \leq b \leq \mathrm{Ord}(g))$ and encrypts a message $m \in P$ by

$$c = (g^b dg^{-b}, m \oplus H(g^b(g^a dg^{-a})g^{-b})).$$

Receiving the ciphertext $c = (c_1, c_2)$, Alice decrypts it by $m = c_2 \oplus H(g^a c_1 g^{-a})$.

Theorem 1 of [9] claims that the CSP-ElG scheme is indistinguishable against chosen plaintext attacks in the standard model under the CSP-DDH assumption. We note that if the monoid is instantiated by a braid group then the CSP-ElG scheme is exactly identical with the public key encryption proposed by Ko et al. [8], in which the function H is assumed to be an ideal hash function. The authors did not clearly describe what they mean by an "ideal hash function" and no precise security analysis of the scheme is given in [8].

We must not assume an random oracle in the standard model, and so H is not allowed to be a random oracle. We shall see that if H is a random oracle, the scheme is indistinguishable against chosen plaintext attacks and so a random oracle is vital in the CSP-ElG scheme and this disproves Theorem 1 of [9].

CSP-ElG is Not Indistinguishable in the Standard Model. We choose two messages m_1 and m_2 from P. One of them is chosen by coin toss and it is encrypted as c then we are asked to decide whether c is a ciphertext of m_1 or m_2. First, we define a cryptographic hash function H to be

$$H(m) = \text{SHA--1}(m)|0. \tag{1}$$

The value of H is the concatenation of the value of SHA-1(m) and a bit 0. Then H is a cryptographic hash function of hash size 161 bits and satisfies collision resistance, pre-image and second pre-image resistance, while it is not a random oracle because the last bit is always 0 and so the hash value is not random.

Let $P = \{0,1\}^{161}$. Take m_1 as any message with the last bit is 1, and m_2 as any message with the last bit is 0. Then the ciphertext of m_1 is given by

$$c = (g^b dg^{-b}, m_1 \oplus H(g^b(g^a dg^{-a})g^{-b})).$$

The last bit of the second entry is always 1 since the last bit of $H(g^b(g^a dg^{-a})g^{-b})$ is 0. The ciphertext of m_2 is

$$c = (g^b dg^{-b}, m_2 \oplus H(g^b(g^a dg^{-a})g^{-b})).$$

Similarly the last bit of the second entry is always 0 since the last bit of $H(g^b(g^a dg^{-a})g^{-b})$ is 0. Therefore an attacker can always distinguish the ciphertexts of m_1 and m_2 with probability 1. This shows that the CSP-ElG scheme is not indistinguishable in the standard model and disproves Theorem 1 of [9].

Error in Security Proof of CSP-ElG Scheme. We analyze the proof of Theorem 1 given in Appendix B of [9], where the authors assume an efficient adversary $\mathcal{A}$ that can distinguish ciphertexts of two distinct messages m_0 and m_1 and then construct an algorithm $\mathcal{B}$ for the CSP-DDH problem, which contradicts the CSP-DDH assumption. We may assume without loss of generality that the last bit of m_0 and m_1 are 0 and 1, respectively.

Given a CSP-DDH instance $Z = (d, g, g^a dg^{-a}, g^b dg^{-b}, g^c dg^{-c})$, $\mathcal{B}$ chooses randomly v and sets $g^{a+v} dg^{-(a+v)} = g^v(g^a dg^{-a})g^{-v}$ as a public key. $\mathcal{A}$ chooses two distinct messages m_0 and m_1. Receiving m_0 and m_1, $\mathcal{B}$ chooses randomly w and $\beta \in \{0,1\}$ and computes a ciphertext c_β^* by

$$c_\beta^* = (g^{b+w} dg^{-(b+w)}, m_\beta \oplus H(g^{c+v+w} dg^{-(c+v+w)})).$$

If $c = a + b$, then we have $c + v + w = (a + v) + (b + w)$. In this case c_β^* is a legitimate ciphertext of m_β since

$$c_\beta^* = (g^{b+w} dg^{-(b+w)}, m_\beta \oplus H(g^{b+w}(g^{a+v} dg^{-(a+v)})g^{-(b+w)})),$$

and so, $\mathcal{A}$ can answer correctly β with probability non-negligibly larger than $\frac{1}{2}$.

On the other hand, the authors of [9] claim that if c is chosen randomly, the distribution c_0^* is identical to that of c_1^* over all possible random choices of

v and w. In this case c_β^* is an illegitimate ciphertext and so $\mathcal{A}$ cannot behave differently depending on $\beta = 0$ or 1 to the input c_β^*. Repeating these tests, $\mathcal{B}$ can decide whether Z is a CSP-DDH instance or not because behavior of $\mathcal{A}$ is different according to whether $c = a + b$ or not. This contradicts to the CSP-DDH assumption. Then the authors conclude that the CSP-ElG scheme is indistinguishable in the standard model under the CSP-DDH assumption.

There is a pitfall in their discussion. One of the building blocks in the CSP-ElG scheme is a cryptographic hash function H. Since Theorem 1 of [9] is based in the standard model, H may not be a random oracle. Let us instantiate the CSP-ElG scheme by the hash function H defined in (1) which is intensionally designed to have correlation among output bits. The authors claim that if c is chosen randomly, the distribution c_0^* is identical to that of c_1^* over all possible random choices of v and w. This claim is incorrect as we explain next. Whatever c is chosen, the last bit of the second entry of c_0^* and c_1^* are 0 and 1, respectively, by the definitions of m_1, m_2 and H. It follows that the distribution c_0^* is completely different from that of c_1^*. As a matter of fact, we can construct the adversary $\mathcal{A}$ as follows. $\mathcal{A}$ chooses two messages m_1 of all 0 and m_2 of all 1. Given c_β^*, $\mathcal{A}$ outputs the last bit of the second entry of c_β^*. Then the algorithm $\mathcal{A}$ always correctly distinguishes the cipher texts of m_0 and m_1.

Our argument clarifies that the security of the CSP-ElG greatly depends on the randomness of hash values; hash values make the distribution of c_0^* indistinguishable from that of c_1^*. If H is a random oracle, the distributions c_0^* and c_1^* are indistinguishable. Thus, the proof of Theorem 1 of [9] is correct "in the random oracle model."

The CSP-ElG is different from ElGamal and its security requires a random oracle. The bits extracted from the underlying CSP problem do not necessarily have sufficient randomness and do not match plaintexts in size. The length of the element $g^a(g^b dg^{-b})g^{-a}$ is not equal to the length of a plaintext. The random oracle solves these two issues.

2.2   CSP-hElG and CSP-CS Schemes

The CSP-hElG and CSP-CS schemes are the other proposals. Theorem 4 of [9] claims the CSP-CS enjoys IND-CCA in the standard model using a target collision hash function H and a secure symmetric cipher Π under the CSP-DDH assumption. The CSP-CS scheme is a CSP-based variant of a Cramer-Shoup like encryption in [4]. The authors give no proof but claim that the proof of Theorem 4 in [9] is similar to the one of Theorem 13 of [4]. Surprisingly, Theorem 13 does not exist in [4]. We strongly believe Theorem 4 in [9] is incorrect. As a circumstantial evidence, we remark that the hashed DDH assumption, which is a computational assumption of hash values of Diffie-Hellman transforms, is required for the variant of Cramer-Shoup encryption given in [4], whereas no similar assumption is required for the CSP-CS scheme. On the other hand, Theorem 2 of [9] claims that the CSP-hElG scheme enjoys IND-CCA in the random oracle model. No proof is given but the authors claim that a proof is similar to that of Theorem 2 of [1] in which the proof is omitted. In the ElGamal scheme, a DH output is multiplied with a plaintext, on the other hand, the CSP-DH output must be filtered by a hash function and so we also suspect the security of the CSP-hElG scheme even though we have not completely analyzed.

3   Gennaro, Krawczyk and Rabin's Method

We recall Gennaro, Krawczyk and Rabin's method to obtain a uniform distribution over the set $\{0,1\}^s$ bit strings of length s from DH transform over non-DDH groups to fix the CSP-ElG scheme. The ElGamal encryption is indistinguishable against chosen plaintext attacks provided a generator g is chosen adequately and the base group enjoys the DDH assumption. However, g may be chosen inadequately and its order may be insufficient in length in real-life systems. For example, SSH and IPSec standards instantiate groups in which the DDH assumption does not necessarily hold. Even in such a case, the ElGamal scheme still enjoys provable security under the so-called t-DDH assumption introduced in [5].

We recall necessary terminology. Let $\mathcal{X}$ and $\mathcal{Y}$ be random variables with support contained in $\{0,1\}^n$. The *statistical distance* between $\mathcal{X}$ and $\mathcal{Y}$ is

$$\text{dist}(\mathcal{X}, \mathcal{Y}) = \frac{1}{2} \sum_{x \in \{0,1\}^n} |\text{Prob}(\mathcal{X} = x) - \text{Prob}(\mathcal{Y} = x)|.$$

Now suppose $\mathcal{X}_n$ and $\mathcal{Y}_n$ are probability ensembles. Let $\mathcal{D} = \{D_n\}$ be a family of circuits. Then $\mathcal{X}_n$ and $\mathcal{Y}_n$ are called *computationally indistinguishable* (by nonuniform distinguishers) if for every polynomial-size distinguisher family $\mathcal{D}$, for every polynomial $P(\cdot)$ and for sufficiently large n we have

$$|\text{Prob}_{x \in \mathcal{X}_n}(D_n(x) = 1) - \text{Prob}_{y \in \mathcal{Y}_n}(D_n(y) = 1)| \leq \frac{1}{P(n)}.$$

Let $\mathcal{X}_n$ be a probability ensemble over A_n. The *min-entropy* of $\mathcal{X}_n$ is defined to be

$$\text{min-ent}(\mathcal{X}_n) = \min_{x \in A_n : \text{Prob}_{x \in \mathcal{X}_n}(x) \neq 0}(-\log(\text{Prob}_{x \in \mathcal{X}_n}(x))).$$

Let $\mathcal{G} = \{G_n\}$ be a family of cyclic groups. We say that $t(n)$-*DDH assumption* holds over $\mathcal{G}$ if for all n there exists a family of probability distributions $\mathcal{X}_n(x^a, x^b)$ such that

1. $\text{min-ent}(\mathcal{X}_n(x^a, x^b)) \geq t(n)$
2. The probability ensemble

$$\mathcal{DH}_n = \{(x^a, x^b, x^{ab} \mid a, b \in_U \{1, \ldots, \text{Ord}(G_n)\}\}$$

is computationally indistinguishable from the ensemble

$$\mathcal{R}_n^* = \{(x^a, x^b, C \mid a, b \in_U \{1, \ldots, \text{Ord}(G_n)\} \text{ and } C \in_{\mathcal{X}_n(x^a, x^b)} G_n\},$$

where $\text{Ord}(G_n)$ stands for the order of the group G_n.

The notation $x \in_{\mathcal{D}} A$ is to be read as x is chosen from A according to the distribution $\mathcal{D}$, and $x \in_U S$ means choosing x uniformly from the set S. The probability distributions $\mathcal{X}_n(x^a, x^b)$ may be different for each triple x, x^a, x^b. Intuitive meaning of the assumption is that a DH output x^{ab} has some degree of unpredictability.

We also recall a universal hash function introduced in [3]. Suppose $h : \{0,1\}^n \times \{0,1\}^{l(n)} \to \{0,1\}^{m(n)}$ is a function. For each fixed $Y \in \{0,1\}^{l(n)}$ we have a function $h_Y(\cdot) = h(\cdot, Y)$ that maps n bits to $m(n)$ bits. Then h is called a *(pairwise independent) universal hash function* if for all $x_1, x_2 \in \{0,1\}^n$ $(x_1 \neq x_2)$ and for all $a_1, a_2 \in \{0,1\}^{m(n)}$, we have

$$\text{Prob}_{Y \in_U \{0,1\}^{l(n)}} (h_Y(x_1) = a_1 \text{ and } h_Y(x_2) = a_2) = \frac{1}{2^{2m(n)}}.$$

Leftover hash lemma is introduced and used to construct pseudorandom bit strings in [7]. It is also used to smooth distributions in [5]. See also [2] for a recent development of the leftover hash lemma.

Lemma 1 (Leftover hash lemma [7]). *Let $\mathcal{X}_n$ be a probability ensemble such that $\mathsf{min\text{-}ent}(\mathcal{X}_n) = m(n)$. Let $e(n)$ be a positive integer valued parameter. Let $h : \{0,1\}^n \times \{0,1\}^{l(n)} \to \{0,1\}^{m(n)-2e(n)}$ be a universal hash function. Let $X \in_{\mathcal{X}_n} \{0,1\}^n$, $Y \in_U \{0,1\}^{l(n)}$ and $Z \in_U \{0,1\}^{m(n)-2e(n)}$. Then we have*

$$\text{dist}(\langle h_Y(X), Y \rangle, \langle Z, Y \rangle) \leq \frac{1}{e(n)+1},$$

where $\langle X, Y \rangle$ stands for the concatenation of X and Y.

Using the leftover hash lemma, Gennaro et al. [5] show that if $\mathcal{G} = \{G_n\}_n$ is a group family in which the $t(n)$-DDH assumption holds and $h : \{0,1\}^{|G_n|} \times \{0,1\}^{l(n)} \to \{0,1\}^{t'(n)}$ is a universal hash function, where $t'(n) = t(n) - \omega(\log n)$, then the induced distribution of $h(g_n^{ab}, Y)$ for $a, b \in_U \{1, 2, \ldots, \text{Ord}(G_n)\}$ and $Y \in_U \{0,1\}^{l(n)}$ is computationally indistinguishable from the uniform distribution over $\{0,1\}^{t'(n)}$ even when h, g_n^a and g_n^b are given to the distinguisher. This implies that the ElGamal scheme using the hashed value $h(g_n^{ab}, Y)$ instead of g_n^{ab} to mask a plaintext is indistinguishable if the underlying group satisfies $t(n)$-DDH assumption. In this case the universal hash function is common knowledge between Alice and Bob and $Y(\in \{0,1\}^{l(n)})$ is a piece of a ciphertext.

4 Encryption Scheme Based on Monoid Action

Before fixing the CSP-ElG, we integrate the ElGamal and CSP-ElG encryption in a generic scheme using the terminology of monoid actions. Then we apply the Gennaro et al.'s technique to smooth distributions to prove the indistinguishability of the generic scheme. A generic scheme covers more instantiations based on many other principles and its proof gives a universal security proof. In particular, the security proof of the generic scheme is applicable to the revised CSP-ElG.

4.1 Monoid Action

We first define a *monoid action*. Let M be a monoid, and X be a nonempty set. The symbol "1" stands for the identity of the monoid M, that is, $m \cdot 1 = 1 \cdot m = m$ for every $m \in M$. Suppose that we have a mapping $\sigma : X \times M \to X$ satisfying:

1. $\sigma(\sigma(x,a),b) = \sigma(x,ab)$ for $x \in X$ and $a, b \in M$,
2. $\sigma(x,1) = x$ for $x \in X$.

Then we say that σ is an *action* of M on X or M *acts on* X without mentioning σ if the context is clear. A group action is a special case of monoid actions.

A monoid action is frequently used in cryptology (see [10,11]). For example, the mechanism of the Diffie-Hellman key exchange and the ElGamal encryption are explained in terms of the monoid action. Let p be a prime. Suppose a prime q divides $p - 1$. Take an element $g \in \mathbb{Z}_p^*$ such that $\mathrm{Ord}(g) = q$. We should note that $(\mathbb{Z}_q, \cdot)$ forms a monoid but not a group. Let $X = \langle g \rangle$ and $M = (\mathbb{Z}_q, \cdot)$. Then the mapping $\sigma : X \times M \to X$ given by $\sigma(g^i, s) = (g^i)^s = g^{is}$ is a monoid action of $(\mathbb{Z}_q, \cdot)$ on the cyclic group $\langle g \rangle$. The discrete logarithm problem is to compute s for given g and $\sigma(g,s) (= g^s)$. The Diffie-Hellman problem is to compute $\sigma(g,ab) (= g^{ab})$ for given $g, \sigma(g,a) (= g^a)$ and $\sigma(g,b) (= g^b)$, where $a, b \in (\mathbb{Z}_q, \cdot)$. These computational problems related to the monoid action play vital role in the security of the Diffie-Hellman key exchange and the ElGamal encryption. Furthermore, the RSA encryption is also explained in terms of monoid actions although we do not explain here due to lack of space (see [11]).

4.2 Computational Assumption Related to Monoid Actions

Suppose $\sigma : X \times M \to X$ is an action of commutative monoid M on a nonempty set X. A *monoid action search problem* (MA-SP for short) is to compute a for given $x, \sigma(x,a)$. A *monoid action computation Diffie-Hellman problem* (MA-CDH for short) is to compute $\sigma(x,ab)$ for given $x, \sigma(x,a)$ and $\sigma(x,b)$. A *monoid action decision Diffie-Hellman problem* (MA-DDH for short) is to decide whether or not $\sigma(x,ab) = \sigma(x,c)$ for given $x, \sigma(x,a), \sigma(x,b), \sigma(x,c)$.

The CSP related problems can also be characterized in terms of monoid actions. Suppose X is a monoid and $G(X)$ is the group of units of X. Suppose that $a \in G(X)$ and $\mathrm{Ord}(a) = n$ and if it is infinite then we set n large enough integer. An action $\sigma : X \times \langle a \rangle \to X$ is given by $\sigma(b, a^i) = a^i b a^{-i}$, where $b \in X$. We note that $M (= \langle a \rangle)$ is indeed a commutative group whereas the base monoid X is not necessarily commutative. Obviously, the conjugacy search, CSP-CDH and CSP-DDH problems are an instance of MA-SP, MA-CDH and MA-DDH problems, respectively. We should also note that the discrete logarithm, CDH and DDH problems are an instance of MA-SP, MA-CDH and MA-DDH, respectively.

We now give formal definition of the MA-CDH and MA-DDH. Suppose $\sigma_n : X_n \times M_n \to X_n$ is a family of actions of commutative monoid M_n on nonempty set X_n. Let us consider the following two ensembles

$$\mathcal{R}_n = \{(x, \sigma_n(x,a), \sigma_n(x,b), \sigma_n(x,c)) \mid x \in X_n, a, b, c \in_U M_n\},$$

$$\mathcal{MA\text{-}DH}_n = \{(x, \sigma_n(x,a), \sigma_n(x,b), \sigma_n(x,ab)) \mid x \in X_n, a, b \in_U M_n\}.$$

We say that the *MA-DDH assumption* holds over σ_n if $\mathcal{R}_n$ and $\mathcal{MA\text{-}DH}_n$ are computationally indistinguishable (with respect to non-uniform distinguishers).

Following [5], we introduce a $t(n)$-MA-DDH assumption. We say that $t(n)$-*MA-DDH assumption* holds over $\sigma_n : X_n \times M_n \to X_n$ if for all n there exists a family of probability distributions $\mathcal{X}_n(x, \sigma(x, a), \sigma(x, b))$ over X_n such that

1. $\mathsf{min\text{-}ent}(\mathcal{X}_n(x, \sigma(x, a), \sigma(x, b))) \geq t(n)$
2. The probability ensemble $\mathcal{MA\text{-}DH}_n$ is computationally indistinguishable from the ensemble

$$\mathcal{R}_n^* = \{(x, \sigma(x, a), \sigma(x, b), C \mid a, b \in_U M_n \text{ and } C \in_{\mathcal{X}_n(x, \sigma(x, a), \sigma(x, b))} \sigma(x, M_n)\}.$$

The probability distributions $\mathcal{X}_n(x, \sigma(x, a), \sigma(x, b))$ may be different for each triple $x, \sigma(x, a), \sigma(x, b)$. Intuitive meaning of the assumption above is that a MA-DH output $\sigma(x, ab)$ has some degree of unpredictability.

4.3   Public Key Encryption Based on Monoid Actions

Suppose $\sigma : X \times M \to X$ is an action of a commutative monoid M on a set X. Alice chooses $a \in M$ and Bob chooses $b \in M$. An element $x \in X$ is chosen and fixed and publicized. Alice sends $\sigma(x, a)$ to Bob, and Bob sends $\sigma(x, b)$ to Alice. Then $\sigma(x, ab)(= \sigma(x, ba))$ turns out to be a shared key between Alice and Bob. Recall that we assume M is commutative. If the shared key is indistinguishable from the uniform distribution over $\{0, 1\}^l$, where l is the size of representation of elements of X, then it can be used to mask a plaintext P of length l, where the ciphertext C is given by $P \oplus \sigma(x, ab)$. In the case of ElGamal scheme, the length of a plaintext is equal to that of a DH transform output and so it is unnecessary to operate a hash function if the DDH assumption holds.

In the case of the CSP based scheme, the length of a plaintext is not necessarily equal to that of the shared bit string $\sigma(x, ab)$ and so we need to match the length of plaintexts and that of the bit strings extracted from $\sigma(x, ab)$ and make it uniform distribution. We expect the resulting bit sequences $\sigma(x, ab)$ to have randomness to some extent. The MA-DDH assumption implies that the MA-DH transform outputs $\sigma(x, ab)$ distribute uniformly over the set $\sigma(x, M)$.

On the other hand, we should note that the range $\sigma(x, M)$ does not necessarily form the set $\{0, 1\}^{l(n)}$ of bit strings of fixed length $l(n)$. This is indeed the same case as the ElGamal scheme. We would like to obtain uniform distribution over the set $\{0, 1\}^{l(n)}$ of bit strings of some fixed length $l(n)$ using a MA-DH transform. In particular, if we apply it to encryption scheme by masking a plaintext of length n, we require the ensemble $\mathcal{X}$ of masking sequences to have $\mathsf{min\text{-}ent}(\mathcal{X}) = n$.

Applying the leftover hash lemma to MA-DH outputs from a family of monoid actions in which $t(n)$-MA-DDH assumption holds, we obtain the next theorem.

Theorem 1. *Let* $\mathcal{S} = \{\sigma_n : X_n \times M_n \to X_n\}$ *be a family of monoid actions in which the $t(n)$-MA-DDH assumption holds, and $h : \{0, 1\}^{|M_n|} \times \{0, 1\}^{l(n)} \to \{0, 1\}^{t'(n)}$ be a universal hash function; h_Y maps $\{0, 1\}^{|M_n|}$ into $\{0, 1\}^{t'(n)}$, where $Y \in \{0, 1\}^{l(n)}$ and $t'(n) = t(n) - \omega(\log n)$. Then the distribution of $h_Y(\sigma(m, ab))$ for $a, b \in_U M_n$ and $Y \in_U \{0, 1\}^{l(n)}$ is computationally indistinguishable from the uniform distribution over $\{0, 1\}^{t'(n)}$.*

Revised CSP-ElG Scheme. We revise the CSP-ElG scheme as follows. Suppose $t(n)$-CSP-DDH assumption (one of a concrete instance of the $t(n)$-MA-DDH assumption) holds for M, $d \in M$, $g \in G(M)$ and $h : \{0,1\}^{|M_n|} \times \{0,1\}^{l(n)} \to \{0,1\}^{t'(n)}$ is a universal hash function. A public key is a pair $(g, g^a dg^{-a})$. A plaintext $P \in \{0,1\}^{t'(n)}$ is encrypted as

$$(Y, g^b dg^{-b}, P \oplus h(Y, g^{a+b} dg^{-(a+b)})),$$

where $Y \in_U \{0,1\}^{l(n)}$. In this case, the universal hash function h is publicized and $Y (\in_U \{0,1\}^{l(n)})$ is a piece of a ciphertext. Decryption is obvious and we omit it.

Theorem 2. *The revised CSP-ElG scheme is indistinguishable against chosen plaintext attacks in the standard model under the $t(n)$-CSP-DDH assumption.*

Proof. One can prove the indistinguishability along the same line as the argument in Section 2.1. We replace the hash function H by a universal hash function h_Y $(Y \in_U \{0,1\}^{l(n)})$ here. We have to discuss the case that c is chosen randomly. In this case, we have $c_\beta^* = (g^{b+w} dg^{-(b+w)}, m_\beta \oplus h_Y(g^{c+v+w} dg^{-(c+v+w)}))$ Because c and $v + w$ are randomly chosen, the hash value $h_Y(g^{c+(v+w)} dg^{-(c+(v+w))})$ is uniformly distributed over $\{0,1\}^{t'(n)}$ by Theorem 1. It follows that both distributions c_0^* and c_1^* are computationally indistinguishable from the uniform distribution over $\{0,1\}^{t'(n)}$ and that c_0^* and c_1^* are computationally indistinguishable. Therefore, the original proof of Theorem 1 in [9] shows the indistinguishability of this revised CSP-ElG scheme in the standard model under the $t(n)$-CSP-DDH assumption holds. □

We can similarly construct an encryption scheme using any action of commutative monoid in which the t-MA-DDH assumption holds. Our scheme is generic as the one in [9], and therefore, it is necessary to study the underlying algebraic structures and determine whether a t-MA-DDH holds or not.

4.4   Direct Product of Submonoids

We can generalize Theorem 3 in [5] as follows. Suppose that M has a direct submonoid decomposition $M \cong L \times N$, that is, we have an isomorphism of $L \times N$ onto M by $(m_1, m_2) \mapsto m_1 m_2$, where $m_1 \in L$ and $m_2 \in N$. We should note that this is not always possible like groups. Note that we have naturally induced actions of L and N on X.

Theorem 3. *Let $\sigma : X \times M \to X$ be a monoid action. If MA-DDH assumption holds for the action $\sigma : X \times L \to X$ on the point $x \in X$ and $|Ord(L)| = t$, then t-MA-DDH assumption holds for $\sigma : X \times M \to X$ on the point $x \in X$.*

Proof. Given $\sigma(x,a), \sigma(x,b) \in X$, we define $\mathcal{X}(\sigma(x,a), \sigma(x,b))$ to be the uniform distribution over $\{\sigma(x,c) \,|\, c \in cL\}$. Then $\mathsf{min\text{-}ent}(\mathcal{X}(\sigma(x,a), \sigma(x,b))) = |Ord(L)| = t$ since $\mathcal{X}(\sigma(x,a), \sigma(x,b))$ has the same number of elements as L. Let $\mathcal{R}^* = \{(\sigma(x,a), \sigma(x,b), y) \,|\, a, b \in_U M, y \in_{\mathcal{X}(\sigma(x,a), \sigma(x,b))} X\}$. Suppose t-MA-DDH does not hold for the action σ on M on the point x and so we have a distinguisher D between $\mathcal{MA}\text{-}\mathcal{DH}_M$ and $\mathcal{R}^*$. Using D, we construct a distinguisher D_1 between $\mathcal{MA}\text{-}\mathcal{DH}_L$ and $\mathcal{R}_L$. Given y_1, y_2, y_3 where $y_1 = \sigma(x, a_L), y_2 = \sigma(x, b_L)$ and y_3 is either $\sigma(x, a_L b_L)$ or $\sigma(x, c_L)$ for $c_L \in_U L$, the distinguisher D_1 does the following. First, choose $a_N, b_N \in_U N$. Second, set $x_1 = y_1 a_N, x_2 = y_2 b_N, x_3 = y_3 a_N b_N$. Third, pass D the triple (x_1, x_2, x_3). Lastly, output the same bits as does D. Note that $x_1 = y_1 a_N = \sigma(x, a_L) a_N = \sigma(x, a_L a_N)$ and $x_2 = y_2 b_N = \sigma(x, b_L) b_N = \sigma(x, b_L b_N)$. If $y_3 = \sigma(x, a_L b_L)$ then we have $x_3 = y_3 a_N b_N = \sigma(x, a_L b_L) a_N b_N = \sigma(x, a_L b_L) a_N b_N = \sigma(x, a_L a_N b_L b_N)$ and so the triple (x_1, x_2, x_3) is a member of $\mathcal{MA}\text{-}\mathcal{DH}_M$. If $y_3 = \sigma(x, c_L)$ then we have $x_3 = y_3 a_N b_N = \sigma(x, c_L) a_N b_N = \sigma(x, c_L a_N b_N)$. Then (x_1, x_2, x_3) is a member of $\mathcal{R}^*$ since $c_L(a_N b_N) = c_L(a_L b_L)^{-1}(a_L b_L a_N b_N)$ and $c_L(a_L b_L)^{-1} \in_U L$. $\square$

Theorem 3 implies we can strengthen an encryption scheme just by taking a direct product of several monoid actions. We do not know whether or not a concrete monoid can be factorized into a direct product of submonoids and do not guarantee the theorem is always applicable.

References

1. Abdalla, M., Bellare, M., Rogaway, P.: The oracle Diffie-Hellman assumptions and an analysis of DHIES. In: Naccache, D. (ed.) CT-RSA 2001. LNCS, vol. 2020, pp. 143–158. Springer, Heidelberg (2001)
2. Barak, B., Dodis, Y., Krawczyk, H., Pereira, O., Pietrzak, K., Standaert, F.-X., Yu, Y.: Leftover hash lemma, revisited. In: Rogaway, P. (ed.) CRYPTO 2011. LNCS, vol. 6841, pp. 1–20. Springer, Heidelberg (2011)
3. Carter, L., Wegman, M.N.: Universal classes of hash functions. J. Computer and System Sciences 18(2), 143–154 (1979)
4. Cash, D., Kiltz, E., Shoup, V.: The twin Diffie-Hellman problem and applications. In: Smart, N. (ed.) EUROCRYPT 2008. LNCS, vol. 4965, pp. 127–145. Springer, Heidelberg (2008)
5. Gennaro, R., Krawczyk, H., Rabin, T.: Secure hashed Diffie-Hellman over non-DDH groups. In: Cachin, C., Camenisch, J.L. (eds.) EUROCRYPT 2004. LNCS, vol. 3027, pp. 361–381. Springer, Heidelberg (2004)
6. Grigoriev, D., Shpilrain, V.: Authentication from matrix conjugation. Groups, Complexity and Cryptology 1(2), 199–205 (2009)
7. Hastad, J., Impagliazzo, R., Levin, L., Luby, M.: Construction of a pseudo-random generator from any one-way function. SIAM J. Computing 28(4), 1364–1396 (1999)
8. Ko, K.H., Lee, S.-J., Cheon, J.H., Han, J.W., Kang, J.-S., Park, C.-S.: New Public-Key Cryptosystem Using Braid Groups. In: Bellare, M. (ed.) CRYPTO 2000. LNCS, vol. 1880, pp. 166–183. Springer, Heidelberg (2000)
9. Wang, L., Wang, L., Cao, Z., Okamoto, E., Shao, J.: New Constructions of Public-Key Encryption Schemes from Conjugacy Search Problems. In: Lai, X., Yung, M., Lin, D. (eds.) Inscrypt 2010. LNCS, vol. 6584, pp. 1–17. Springer, Heidelberg (2011)
10. Yamamura, A.: A functional cryptosystem using a group action. In: Pieprzyk, J., Safavi-Naini, R., Seberry, J. (eds.) ACISP 1999. LNCS, vol. 1587, pp. 314–325. Springer, Heidelberg (1999)
11. Yamamura, A., Kurosawa, K.: Generic algorithms and key agreement protocols based on group actions. In: Eades, P., Takaoka, T. (eds.) ISAAC 2001. LNCS, vol. 2223, pp. 208–218. Springer, Heidelberg (2001)

Cryptanalysis of Unidirectional Proxy Re-Encryption Scheme

Kunwar Singh[1], C. Pandu Rangan[2], and A.K. Banerjee[3]

[1] Computer Science and Engineering Department
NIT Trichy, Tiruchirappalli, India
kunwar@nitt.edu
[2] Computer Science and Engineering Department
IIT, Madras
rangan@cse.iitm.ac.in
[3] Mathematics Department
NIT Trichy, Tiruchirappalli, India
banerjee@nitt.edu

Abstract. At Eurocrypt 1998, Blaze, Bleumer and Strauss [7] presented a new primitive called Proxy Re-Encryption (*PRE*). This new primitive allows semi trusted proxy to transform a ciphertext for Alice (delegator) into a ciphertext for Bob (delegatee) without knowing the message. Ateniese et al [6] introduced *master secret security* as another security requirement for unidirectional *PRE*. *Master secret security* demands that no coalition of dishonest proxy and malicious delegatees can compute the master secret key (private key) of the delegator. In this paper, first we have shown that Aono et al's scheme [4] is not secure under *master secret security* model. In other words if proxy and delegatee collude they can compute the private key of the delegator. Second, based on Aono et al's paper [4] we have constructed unidirectional *PRE* which is also secure under *master secret security* model. Like [4], our scheme is also multi-use.

Keywords: Lattice, Proxy Re-encryption, Learning With Error (LWE).

1 Introduction

At Eurocrypt 1998, Blaze, Bleumer and Strauss [7] presented a new primitive called Proxy Re-Encryption *PRE*. This new primitive allows semi trusted proxy to transform a ciphertext for Alice (delegator) into a ciphertext for Bob (delegatee) without knowing the message. A natural application of *PRE* is to forward encrypted e-mail to others. For example, Director (delegator) can authorize his secretary (proxy) to convert encrypted mail for Director into encrypted mail for Dean (delegatee) whenever he is on leave. Then Dean can decrypt the encrypted mail using his secret key. Blaze et al gave first *PRE* scheme which was bidirectional and multi-use. Bidirectional means proxy can transform a ciphertext for Alice to a ciphertext for Bob and vice-versa without knowing the message. In multi use, proxy can transform a ciphertext from Alice to Bob, then from Bob to Carol and so on. Ateniese et al [6] presented a first unidirectional *PRE* scheme. In unidirectional, proxy can transform a ciphertext for Alice to a ciphertext for Bob but does not allow vice-versa.

Lattice based cryptogrphy have bloomed in recent years because of the following advantages.

Linawati et al. (Eds.): ICT-EurAsia 2014, LNCS 8407, pp. 564–575, 2014.

- Number-theoretic hard problems like prime factorization and discrete logarithm problem can be solved in polynomial time by Shor's algorithm [11]. But till now there is no polynomial time quantum algorithm for lattice hard problems.
- Ajtai [2] in his seminal result on the average case / worst case has shown that lattice based cryptosystem in the average case is as hard as solving some lattice based hard problems in the worst case. So lattice problems give strong hardness guarantee in the average case. Lattice based cryptosystems are also efficient and parallelizable.

Recently Regev [10] defined the Learning With Error (LWE) problem and showed that it also enjoys similar average case / worst case equivalence hardness properties through a quantum reduction.

Combining these two concepts Xagawa [14] presented bidirectional lattice based proxy re-encryption scheme under LWE assumption. Singh et al [13] gave bidirectional identity based lattice based proxy re-encryption scheme. Recently Aono et al [4] presented first unidirectional lattice based proxy re-encryption scheme.

Our Contribution: Ateniese et al [6] introduced *master secret security* as another security requirement for unidirectional *PRE*. *Master secret security* demands that no coalition of dishonest proxy and malicious delegatees can compute the master secret key (private key) of the delegator. Ateniese et al [6] gave following motivation for *master secret security*.

1. Some PRE may define two or more type of encryption schemes. In one encryption scheme ciphertext may be decrypted by only master secret (private key) of the delegator. Other encryption scheme re-encrypted ciphertext may be decrypted by private key of the delegatee.
2. Delegator may want to delegate decryption rights to delegatee but may not want to delegate signing rights to delegatee. With this security it is possible.

In this paper, first we have shown that Aono et al's scheme [4] is not secure under *master secret security* model. In other words if proxy and delegatee collude they can compute the private key of the delegator. Second, based on Aono et al's paper [4] we have costructed unidirectional *PRE* which is also secure under *master secret security* model. Like [4], our scheme is also multi-use.

2   Preliminaries

2.1   Notation

We denote $[j] = \{0, 1, ..., j\}$. We assume vectors to be in column form and are written using bold letters, e.g. $\mathbf{x}$. Matrices are written as bold capital letters, e.g. $\mathbf{X}$. The norm $\|.\|$ here is the standard Euclidean norm in R^n. We denote probabilistic polynomial time as PPT.

2.2   Unidirectional Proxy Re-Encryption Scheme(PRE)

PRE consists of seven algorithms.

PublicParameters(n): On input a security parameter n, this algorithm outputs public parameters.

KeyGeneration(n): On input a security parameter n, this algorithm outputs a secret key sk and the corresponding public key pk of the user.

Encrypt(pk, M): This algorithm takes input as a public parameters, a public key and a message, and outputs ciphertext C.

Re-Encryption Key(sk_i, pk_i, pk_j): This algorithm takes input as a secret key sk_i, a public key pk_i and a public key pk_j, and outputs unidirectional reencryption key $rk_{i,j}$.

Re-Encryption($rk_{i,j}, C_i$): On input a ciphertext C_i and re-encryption key $rk_{i,j}$, this algorithm outputs a re-encrypted ciphertext C_j.

Decrypt(sk_j, C_j): This algorithm takes input as public parameters PP, a private key sk_j and a ciphertext C_j, and outputs message m.

Correctness. Unidirectional Proxy Re-encryption is correct if suppose $C_i \leftarrow Encrypt(pk_i, m)$, $rk_{i,j} \leftarrow$ Re-Encryption Key(sk_i, pk_i, pk_j) and $C_j \leftarrow$ Re-Encryption($rk_{i,j}, C_i$), following equation holds.

- Decrypt $(sk_i, C_i) = m$.
- Decrypt $(sk_j, C_j) = m$.

2.3   Security Model for Unidirectional Proxy Re-En cryption Scheme

Here security model is adapted from [6]. Security of *PRE* is defined using two properties: semantic security (IND-p-CPA) and master secret security.

2.3.1   Semantic Security (IND-p-CPA)

Following security model captures the idea that when a group of polynomially bounded adversarial users and proxy collude against target delegator B, they can not get any bit of information with the condition that target delegator B never gives delegation rights to any adversarial users (including delegatee). We define security model using the following game that is played between the challenger and adversary.

Setup: The challenger C runs Setup(1^k) and gives the public parameters PP to the adversary. Challenger C runs the KeyGeneration algorithm n_u times to obtain a list of public/private keys PK_{good}, SK_{good}, and runs the KeyGeneration algorithm for n_c times to obtain a list of corrupted private/public keys PK_{corr}, SK_{corr}. Adversary gets PP, SK_{corr}, and $PK = (PK_{good} \cup PK_{corr})$.

Phase 1: The adversary can make following queries.

- The adversary can issue re-encryption key query $rk_{i,j}$ corresponding to the public keys pk_i and pk_j such that either $pk_i, pk_j \in PK_{good}$ or $pk_i, pk_j \in PK_{corr}$ or $pk_i \in PK_{corr}$ and $pk_j \in PK_{good}$. Adversary can repeat this query polynomial times for different pair of public keys adaptivly.
- The adversary can issue re-encryption query $rk_{i,j}$ corresponding to public keys pk_i and pk_j such that either $pk_i, pk_j \in PK_{good}$ or $pk_i, pk_j \in PK_{corr}$ or $pk_i \in PK_{corr}$ and $pk_j \in PK_{good}$. Challenger runs $RKGen$ algorithm to obtain $rk_{i,j}$ corresponding to public keys pk_i and pk_j then challenger generates ciphertext C_2 by running $Re-encryption$ algorithm.

Challenge: The adversary submits target public key pk_{i^*} and message m with the conditions that pk_{i^*} should belong to PK_{good}. Challenger randomly choose a bit $r \in \{0,1\}$ and a random string C with the size of valid ciphertext. If $r = 0$ it sets the challenge ciphertext to $C^* := \text{Encrypt}(PP, pk^{i^*}, m)$. If $r = 1$ it assigns the challenge ciphertext $C^* := C$. It sends challenge ciphertext C^* to the adversary.

Phase 2: Phase 1 procedure is repeated.

Guess: Adversary finally outputs a answer $r' \in \{0,1\}$ and wins the game if $r = r'$.

Adversary A is referred as an IND-p-CPA adversary. The advantage of the adversary A in attacking a PRE scheme ξ is defined as

$$Adv_{\xi,A}(n) = |Pr[r = r'] - 1/2|$$

Definition 1. *PRE scheme is IND-p-CPA if for all PPT algorithm A and negligible function ε, $Adv_{\xi,A}(n) \leq \varepsilon$.*

2.3.2 Master Secret Security

Security model captures the idea that no coalition of dishonest proxy and malicious delegatees can compute the master secret key (private key) of the delegator. We define security model using a game that is played between the challenger and adversary. The game proceeds as follows.

Setup: The challenger C runs Setup(1^k) and gives the public parameters PP to adversary.

Challenge: The adversary submits target delegator B.

Query Phase

1. The adversary can issue re-encryption key query $rk_{i,j}$ corresponding to any public keys pk_i and pk_j.
2. The adversary can issue re-encryption query $rk_{i,j}$ corresponding to any public keys pk_i and pk_j.

Guess: Adversary finally outputs a guess x for private key sk_B of target delegator B and wins if $x = sk_B$.

We define the adversary's advantage in winning this game as $AdvMSS_{\xi,A}(n) = |Pr[x = sk_B]|$

Definition 2. *PRE scheme is secure if for all PPT algorithm A and negligible function ε, $Adv_{\xi,A}(n) \leq \varepsilon$ and $AdvMSS_{\xi,A}(n) \leq \varepsilon$.*

2.4 Integer Lattices ([8])

A lattice is the set of all integer combinations

$$L(b_1,...,b_n) = \left\{ \sum_{i=1}^{n} x_i b_i : x_i \in Z \text{ for } 1 \leq i \leq n \right\}$$

of n linearly independent vectors $\{b_1,...,b_n\} \in R^n$. The set of vectors $\{b_1,...,b_n\}$ is called a lattice basis.

Definition 3. *For q prime, $A \in Z_q^{n \times m}$ and $u \in Z_q^n$, define:*

$$\Lambda_q(A) := \{e \in Z^m \ s.t. \ \exists s \in Z_q^n \text{ where } A^T s = e \ (mod \ q)\}$$

$$\Lambda_q^{\perp}(A) := \{e \in Z^m \ s.t. \ Ae = 0 \ (mod \ q)\}$$

$$\Lambda_q^u(A) := \{e \in Z^m \ s.t. \ Ae = u \ (mod \ q)\}$$

Theorem 1. *([2,3]) Let q be prime and $m := \lceil 6n\log q \rceil$.*

There is PPT algorithm TrapGen(q,n) that outputs a pair $(A \in Z_q^{n \times m}, T \in Z^{n \times m})$ such that statistically distance between matrix A and a uniform matrix in $Z_q^{n \times m}$ is negligible and T is a basis for $\Lambda_q^{\perp}(A)$ satisfying

$$\|\widetilde{T}\| \leq O(\sqrt{n \log q}) \ \text{ and } \ \|T\| \leq O(n \log q)$$

with overwhelming probability in n.

2.5 The LWE Hardness Assumption ([10,1])

Regev [10] proposed the LWE (learning with error) assumption.

Definition 4. *LWE: Consider a prime number q, a positive integer n, and a Gaussian distribution χ^m over Z_q^m. Given $(A, As + x)$ where matrix $A \in Z_q^{m \times n}$ is uniformly random and $x \in \chi^m$.*

LWE hard problem is to find s with non-negligible probability.

Definition 5. *Decision LWE: Consider a prime number q, a positive integer n, and a Gaussian distribution χ^m over Z_q^m. The input is a pair (A, v) from an unspecified challenge oracle O, where $A \in Z_q^{m \times n}$ is chosen uniformly. An unspecified challenge oracle O is either a noisy pseudo-random sampler O_s or a truly random sampler $O_\$$. It is based on how v is chosen.*

1. When v is chosen to be $As + e$ for a uniformly chosen $s \in Z_q^n$ and a vector $e \in \chi^m$, an unspecified challenge oracle O is a noisy pseudo-random sampler O_s.
2. When v is chosen uniformly from Z_q^m, an unspecified challenge oracle O is a truly random sampler $O_\$$.

Goal of the adversary is to distinguish between the above two cases with non-negligible probability.

Or we say that an algorithm A decides the (Z_q, n, χ)-LWE problem if $|Pr[A^{O_s} = 1] - Pr[A^{O_\$} = 1]|$ is non-negligible for a random $s \in Z_q^n$.

Above decision LWE is also hard even if s is chosen from the Gaussian distribution rather than the uniform distribution [5,9].

2.6 Small Integer Solution (SIS) Assumption ([2])

SIS and ISIS hard problems were proposed by Ajtai [2] in 1996.

Definition 6. *Given an integer q, a matrix $A \in Z_q^{n \times m}$ and real β, find a short nonzero integer vector $x \in Z_q^m$ such that $Ax = 0 \bmod q$ and $\|x\| \le \beta$.*
OR find a nonzero integer vector $x \in Z_2^m$ such that $Ax = 0 \bmod q$.

2.7 Inhomogeneous Small Integer Solution (ISIS) Assumption

Definition 7. *Given an integer q, a matrix $A \in Z_q^{n \times m}$, a syndrome $u \in Z_q^n$ and real β, find a short nonzero integer vector $x \in Z_q^m$ such that $Ax = u \bmod q$ and $\|x\| \le \beta$.*
OR find a nonzero integer vector $x \in Z_2^m$ such that $Ax = u \bmod q$.

3 Cryptanalysis of the Aono et al's Unidirectional Proxy Re-Encryption Scheme

3.1 Aono et al's Unidirectional Proxy Re-Encryption Scheme

In Indocrypt 2013, Aono et al [4] presented key private unidirectional proxy re-encryption scheme. First, we describe Aono et al's scheme [4]. Before that we describe functions **Bits()** and **Power2()** used in [4].

Let $v = (v_1, \ldots, v_n) \in Z_q^n$, $k = \lceil lg\ q \rceil$ and $(b_{i,1}, \ldots, b_{i,k})$ be the bit representation of v_i such that $v_i = \sum_{j=0}^k 2^j b_{i,j}$. Then **Bits()** is defined as

$$Bits(v) = [b_{1,1} \ldots b_{n,1} | b_{1,2} \ldots b_{n,2} | \ldots | b_{1,k} \ldots b_{n,k}] \in \{0,1\}^{1 \times nk}$$

(First n bits are first bit of $v_1, \ldots, v_n$ and next n bits are second bit of $v_1, \ldots, v_n$ and so on).

Let $X = [X_1 | \ldots | X_l] \in Z_q^{n \times l}$ where X_i are columns. Then

$$Power2(X) = \begin{bmatrix} X_1 \ldots X_l \\ 2X_1 \ldots 2X_l \\ \vdots \quad \vdots \\ 2^{k-1}X_1 \ldots 2^{k-1}X_l \end{bmatrix} \in Z_k^{nk \times l}$$

It can be shown that

$$Bits(v)Power2(X) = vX \in Z_q^{1 \times l}$$

Setup (n): On input a security parameter n, set the parameter $q = poly(n)$ and randomly choose matrix $A \in Z_q^{n \times n}$.

KeyGeneration (n): Let $s = \alpha q$ for $0 < \alpha < 1$. Choose Gaussian noise matrices $R, S \in \psi_s^{n \times l}$ and $E \in \psi_s^{nk \times l}$ where l is message length. Compute $P = R - AS$.
So private key is S and public key is P.

Proxy Key Gen (PP, S_A, P_B): On input of Alice's private key S_A and Bob's public key P_B, do the following.

1. Bob chooses matrices $X \in \psi_s^{nk \times l}$ $(k = \lceil lg\ q \rceil)$ randomly and noise Matrix $E \in \psi_s^{nk \times l}$ where ψ_s is a gaussian distribution. Bob computes $-X S_B + E$ and sends $X, -X S_B + E$ secretly to the Alice.
2. Alice compute proxy re-encryption key $rk_{A,B} = (P_B, Q)$ where

$$Q = \begin{bmatrix} X & -X S_B + E + Power2(S_A) \\ 0_{l \times n} & I_{l \times l} \end{bmatrix}$$

Above three algorithm is enough for our cryptanalysis. Complete scheme is given in [4].

3.2   Attack on Aono et al's Unidirectional Proxy Re-Encryption Scheme

In Aono et al's scheme, if proxy and delegatee collude they can compute delegator's private key. It works as follows.

Let $S = [S_1|...|S_l] \in Z_q^{n \times l}$ where S_i are columns. Then Power2(S) is defined as

$$Power2(S) = \begin{bmatrix} S_1 \ldots S_l \\ 2S_1 \ldots 2S_l \\ \vdots \quad \vdots \\ 2^{k-1}S_1 \ldots 2^{k-1}S_l \end{bmatrix} \in Z_k^{nk \times l}$$

Here first n rows are S. So if we know Power2(S) then we can find S. (Here k is number of bits required to represent q).

Now let us see the expression of proxy key Q

$$Q = \begin{bmatrix} X & -X S_B + E + Power2(S_A) \\ 0_{l \times n} & I_{l \times l} \end{bmatrix},$$

where S_B is private key of Bob (delegatee). Bob (delegatee) creats X, E and securely sends $X, -X S_B + E$ to Alice. Basically Bob knows $X, -X S_B + E$. Both Bob (delegatee) and proxy know Q, X and $-X S_B + E$ and they can compute Power2(S_A). So they can compute private key of Alice (delegator) S_A which is first n rows of the Power2(S_A).

4 Lattice Based Unidirectional Proxy Re-Encryption Scheme

We describe our scheme to avoid the above attack. Our scheme is variant of Aono et al [4].

Setup (n): On input a security parameter n, we set the parameters $q = poly(n)$ and $m = O(nlg\ n)$ accordingly. We choose a matrix $A \in Z_q^{n \times n}$ and matrix $X \in Z_q^{nk \times n}$ randomly, where $k = \lceil lg\ q \rceil$. Public parameters (PP) are matrix A and matrix X.

KeyGeneration (n): Let $s = \alpha q$ for $0 < \alpha < 1$. We choose noise matrices $R, S \in \psi_s^{n \times l}$ and $E \in \psi_s^{nk \times l}$ where l is message length. We compute $P_1 = R - AS$ and $P_2 = -XS + E$. So private key is S and public key $P = (P_1, P_2) \in (Z_q^{n \times l}, Z_q^{nk \times l})$.

Encrypt (PP, m, P_1, P_2): To encrypt a message $m \in \{0,1\}^l$, we do the following.

1. We choose noise vectors $e_1, e_2 \in \psi_s^{1 \times n}$ and $e_3 \in \psi_s^{1 \times l}$ where ψ_s is a gaussian distribution.
2. Compute $c_1 = e_1 A + e_2 \in Z_q^{1 \times n}$, $c_2 = e_1 P_1 + e_3 + m \lfloor \frac{q}{2} \rfloor$.
3. Output the ciphertext $C = (c_1, c_2) \in Z_q^{1 \times (n+l)}$.

RKGen (PP, S_A, P_B): On input of Alice's private key S_A and Bob's public key P_B, we do the following.

1. We choose noise vectors $e_4 \in \psi_s^{nk \times nk}$ and $e_5 \in \psi_s^{nk \times l}$ where ψ_s is a gaussian distribution.
2. We compute proxy re-encryption key $rk_{A,B} = Q$ where

$$Q = \begin{bmatrix} e_4 X & e_4 P_2 + e_5 + Power2(S_A) \\ 0_{l \times n} & I_{l \times l} \end{bmatrix}$$

Re-Encrypt $(PP, rk_{A,B}, C_A)$: On input of re-encryption key $rk_{A,B}$, proxy transforms Alice'ciphertext C_A to Bob's ciphertext C_B by the following equation.

$$C_B = (c_{1B}, c_{2B}) = [Bits(c_1)|c_2].rk_{A,B} \in Z_q^{1 \times (n+l)}$$

Decrypt (PP, S_B, C_B): To decrypt $C_B = (c_1, c_2)$, we do the following.

1. We compute

$$m = [c_1\ c_2] \begin{bmatrix} S_B \\ I_{l \times l} \end{bmatrix}$$

2. Let $m = (m_1, \ldots, m_l)$. If m_i is less than $\lfloor \frac{q}{4} \rfloor$ mod q than $m_i = 0$ otherwise $m_i = 1$.

Correctness: First we decrypt the normal ciphertext

$$c_1 S_A + c_2 = e_2 S_A + e_3 + m\lfloor \frac{q}{2} \rfloor,$$

which will yield m if $e_2 S_A + e_3$ is less than $\lfloor \frac{q}{4} \rfloor$. Now we decrypt the re-encrypted ciphertext

$$
\begin{aligned}
[Bits(c_1)|c_2].rk_{A,B}.\begin{bmatrix} S_B \\ I_{l\times l} \end{bmatrix} &= [Bits(c_1)|c_2].\begin{bmatrix} e_4 X & e_4 P_2 + e_5 + Power2(S_A) \\ 0_{l\times n} & I_{l\times l} \end{bmatrix}\begin{bmatrix} S_B \\ I_{l\times l} \end{bmatrix} \\
&= [Bits(c_1)|c_2].\begin{bmatrix} e_4 E + e_5 + Power2(S_A) \\ I_{l\times l} \end{bmatrix} \\
&= Bits(c_1)e_4 E + Bits(c_1)e_5 + Bits(c_1)Power2(S_A) + c_2 \\
&= Bits(c_1)e_4 E + Bits(c_1)e_5 + c_1 S_A + c_2 \\
&= Bits(c_1)e_4 E + Bits(c_1)e_5 + e_2 S_A + e_3 + m\lfloor \frac{q}{2} \rfloor
\end{aligned}
$$

which will yield m if $Bits(c_1)e_4 E + Bits(c_1)e_5 + e_2 S_A + e_3$ is less than $\lfloor \frac{q}{4} \rfloor$.

Since e_2, e_3, e_4, e_5, S_A are from Gaussian distribution ψ_s so with some $s = \alpha q$ it is possible that $Bits(c_1)e_4 E + Bits(c_1)e_5 + e_2 S_A + e_3$ is less than $\lfloor \frac{q}{4} \rfloor$.

Theorem 2. *Lattice based unidirectional PRE scheme is IND-p-CPA (semantic) secure assuming the $LWE_{q,\chi}$ is hard or $Adv_{B,LWE_{q,\chi}}(n) = Adv_{\chi,A}(n)$.*

Proof: Here proof has similar structure as in the proof of [4,14,12]. Now we show semantic security (IND-p-CPA) of *PRE*. Suppose there is a PPT adversary $\mathscr{A}$ with non-negligible probability breaks *PRE* scheme. Then we construct PPT algorithm $\mathscr{B}$ (challenger) that solves LWE hard problem with non-negligible probability. Here CU denotes set of corrupted users and HU denotes set of honest users.

Challenger $\mathscr{B}$ obtains the $n+l$ LWE samples from LWE oracle, which is parsed as $(A, c_1 = e_1 A + e_2)$ and $(P_1, c_2 = e_1 P_1 + e_3)$. Now challenger $\mathscr{B}$ sets the master public key $mpk = A$ and public key of target delegator $PK^* = P_1$.

Re-Encryption Queries: Challenger $\mathscr{B}$ answers re-encryption key queries and re-encryption queries of the adversary $\mathscr{A}$ in following way.

- Whenever $\mathscr{A}$ submits a re-encryption key query for the the identities u_j and u_k such that $u_j, u_k \in HU$, challenger $\mathscr{B}$ randomly choose matrices $X_1, X_2 \in Z_q^{nk\times l}$ and returns

$$Q = \begin{bmatrix} X_1 & X_2 \\ 0_{l\times n} & I_{l\times l} \end{bmatrix}$$

  to the challenger $\mathscr{B}$.
- Whenever $\mathscr{A}$ submits a re-encryption query for the the public keys u_j and u_k such that $u_j, u_k \in HU$, Challenger $\mathscr{B}$ returns a random vector in $Z_q^{1\times(n+l)}$.
- Whenever $\mathscr{A}$ submits a re-encryption key query or a re-encryption query for the the public keys u_j and u_k such that $u_j, u_k \in CU$. Since private key is known to corrupted users so adversary himself can compute re-encryption key or re-encrypted ciphertext. (This query may not be required)

Challenge Ciphertext: Now adversary $\mathscr{A}$ submits a message m. Now challenger $\mathscr{B}$ computes $c_1^* = c_1$ and $c_2^* = c_2 + m\lfloor \frac{q}{2} \rfloor$ and sends $C^* = (c_1^*, c_2^*)$ to adversary $\mathscr{A}$.

Phase 2: Adversary can ask query with some restriction same as in phase one.

Now adversary $\mathscr{A}$ outputs that challenged ciphertext is a valid ciphertext, then challenger will output that oracle O as pseudo-random LWE oracle. If adversary $\mathscr{A}$ outputs random ciphertext then adversary will output random LWE oracle. In other words if adversary $\mathscr{A}$ terminates with some output then challenger $\mathscr{B}$ outputs the same. So if adversary $\mathscr{A}$ breaks the scheme then one can construct challenger $\mathscr{B}$ which solves LWE.

$Adv_{B,LWE_{q,\chi}}(n) = Adv_{\chi,A}(n)$. Hence our scheme is semantically secure.

Theorem 3. *Lattice based unidirectional PRE scheme is* master secret security *assuming the* $LWE_{q,\chi}$ *is hard or* $Adv_{B,LWE_{q,\chi}}(n) = AdvMSS_{\chi,A}(n)$.

Proof: Here proof has similar structure as in the proof of [4,14]. We now show master secret security of *PRE*. Suppose there is a PPT adversary $\mathscr{A}$ that can compute private key of the delegator D in our *PRE* scheme with non-negligible probability then we construct a PPT algorithm (challenger $\mathscr{B}$) that solves LWE hard problem with non-negligible probability. Here CU denotes set of corrupted users and HU denotes set of honest users.

For $i = 1$ to $i = l$,

- Challenger $\mathscr{B}$ obtains the $nk + n$ LWE samples from LWE oracle, which is parsed as $(-A, P_{1,i} = -AS_i + R_i)$ and $(-X, P_{2,i} = -XS_i + E_i)$.

Now challenger $\mathscr{B}$ sets the master public key $mpk = A$ and public key of the target delegator $P = (P_1, P_2)$, where

$$P_1 = (P_{1,1}, \ldots, P_{1,l}) \text{ and } P_2 = (P_{2,1}, \ldots, P_{2,l}).$$

$\mathscr{B}$ does not know about private key $S = (S_1, \ldots, S_l)$.

Re-encryption Queries: Challenger $\mathscr{B}$ answers re-encryption key queries and re-encryption queries of the adversary $\mathscr{A}$ in following way.

- Whenever $\mathscr{A}$ submits a re-encryption key query for the the public keys u_j and u_x such that $u_j \in HU$, $u_k \in CU$, challenger $\mathscr{B}$ randomly choose matrices $X_1, X_2 \in Z_q^{nk \times l}$ and returns

$$Q = \begin{bmatrix} X_1 & X_2 \\ 0_{l \times n} & I_{l \times l} \end{bmatrix}$$

to the challenger $\mathscr{B}$. Here X_1 is random because $X_1 = e_4 X$, where e_4 is random and X is public key of corrupt user. But in [4] $X_1 = X$, so $\mathscr{B}$ can not return random X_1 as one part of Q in [4].

- Whenever $\mathscr{A}$ submits a re-encryption query for the the public keys u_j and u_x such that $u_j \in HU$, $u_k \in CU$, challenger $\mathscr{B}$ returns a random vector in $Z_q^{1 \times (n+l)}$.

Now adversary $\mathscr{A}$ outputs private key of the target delegator, challenger $\mathscr{B}$ outputs the same as the solution for LWE problem. So if adversary $\mathscr{A}$ can compute private key of the delegator D in our PRE scheme then one can construct challenger $\mathscr{B}$ which solves LWE.

$Adv_{B,LWE_{q,\chi}}(n) = Adv_{\chi,A}(n)$. Hence our scheme is secure under *master secret security*.

5 Conclusion

We have shown that Aono et al's [4] scheme is not secure under *master secret security*. We have also shown that our scheme is not only semantically secure but also secure under *master secret security* model. Lattice based *PRE* in identity based setting is an open problem.

References

1. Agrawal, S., Boneh, D., Boyen, X.: Efficient Lattice (H)IBE in the Standard Model. In: Gilbert, H. (ed.) EUROCRYPT 2010. LNCS, vol. 6110, pp. 553–572. Springer, Heidelberg (2010)
2. Ajtai, M.: Generating hard instances of lattice problems (extended abstract). In: STOC, pp. 99–108. ACM (1996)
3. Alwen, J., Peikert, C.: Generating Shorter Bases for Hard Random Lattices. In: International Symposium on Theoretical Aspects of Computer Science, STACS 2009, pp. 75–86. IBFI Schloss Dagstuhl (2009)
4. Aono, Y., Boyen, X., Phong, T.L., Wang, L.: Key-private proxy re-encryption under LWE. In: Paul, G., Vaudenay, S. (eds.) INDOCRYPT 2013. LNCS, vol. 8250, pp. 1–18. Springer, Heidelberg (2013)
5. Applebaum, B., Cash, D., Peikert, C., Sahai, A.: Fast Cryptographic Primitives and Circular-Secure Encryption Based on Hard Learning Problems. In: Halevi, S. (ed.) CRYPTO 2009. LNCS, vol. 5677, pp. 595–618. Springer, Heidelberg (2009)
6. Ateniese, G., Fu, K., Green, M., Hohenberger, S.: Improved Proxy Re-encryption Schemes with Applications to Secure Distributed Storage. In: 12th Annual Network and Distributed System Security Symposium. LNCS, pp. 29–35. Springer (2005)
7. Blaze, M., Bleumer, G., Strauss, M.: Divertible protocols and atomic proxy cryptography. In: Nyberg, K. (ed.) EUROCRYPT 1998. LNCS, vol. 1403, pp. 127–144. Springer, Heidelberg (1998)
8. Micciancio, D., Goldwasser, S.: Complexity of Lattice Problems: A Cryptographic Perspective, vol. 671. Kluwer Academic Publishers (2002)
9. Lindner, R., Peikert, C.: Better key sizes (and attacks) for LWE-based encryption. In: Kiayias, A. (ed.) CT-RSA 2011. LNCS, vol. 6558, pp. 319–339. Springer, Heidelberg (2011)
10. Regev, O.: On lattices, learning with errors, random linear codes, and cryptography. In: STOC, pp. 84–93. ACM (2005)
11. Shor, P.W.: Polynomial-time algorithms for prime factorization and discrete logarithms on a quantum computer. SIAM Journal on Computing, 1484–1509 (1997)
12. Singh, K., Pandu Rangan, C., Banerjee, A.K.: Lattice based efficient threshold public key encryption scheme. Journal of Wireless Mobile Networks, Ubiquitous Computing, and Dependable Applications (JoWUA) 4(4), 93–107 (2013)

13. Singh, K., Pandu Rangan, C., Banerjee, A.K.: Lattice based identity based proxy re-encryption scheme. Journal of Internet Services and Information Security (JISIS) 3(3/4), 38–51 (2013)
14. Xagawa, K.: Cryptography with Lattices. PhD Thesis. Department of Mathematical and Computing Sciences Tokyo Institute of Technology (2010)

An Algorithm to Analyze Non-injective S-Boxes

Leandro Marin[1] and Ludo Tolhuizen[2]

[1] Department of Applied Mathematics,
Computer Sciences Faculty, University of Murcia,
Reg. Campus of Int. Excellence Campus MareNostrum, Murcia, Spain
leandro@um.es
[2] Philips Group Innovation, Research
High Tech Campus 34, 5656AE Eindhoven, The Netherlands
ludo.tolhuizen@philips.com

Abstract. We present an algorithm for constructing pairs of an invertible mapping A and an affine mapping B such that $AS = SB$ for a given S-box. For doing we so, we introduce and analyse the link graph of an S-box. We apply the algorithm to the eight DES S-boxes. All obtained pairs (A, B) are those reported in previous work, in which it was required that both A and B are invertible affine mappings. In particular, the relaxation that A need not be affine does not yield new pairs.

Keywords: Security, DES, S-Box, Non-injective maps, Link Graph, Link Path, Self Equivalences.

1 Introduction

The study of invariant properties of cryptographic maps under actions of linear or affine groups is a well-known cryptanalysis tool [1]. In many cases, we can deal with bijective maps $S : \mathbb{F}_2^k \to \mathbb{F}_2^k$. This can be helpful to make an extensive search with computers, because we can take an affine transformation $A : \mathbb{F}_2^k \to \mathbb{F}_2^k$, compute $B = S^{-1} \circ A \circ S$ and check if B is also affine. It is also possible to have an early abort strategy to check the affine properties of B, see [1].

When S is not injective we have an extra difficulty, that is the exponential amplification that appears when we have not a unique B, but multiple choices for the values $B(p)$ such that $AS(p) = SB(p)$. The problem is even more complicated if we look for non-bijective affine maps B.

In this paper, we present an algorithm for constructing pairs of an invertible mapping A and an affine mapping B such that $AS = SB$ for a given S-box. Note that we do not require that A be affine, and therefore we may find more such pairs than in [1, Section 4.2], where for the seven of the eight DES S-boxes, we only can have A and B equal to the identity mapping, while for S_4, there is only one more choice. This work adds to the further analysis of the DES S-boxes, although the technique can be applied to any surjective map $S : \mathbb{F}_2^t \to \mathbb{F}_2^k$.

We are going to use the affine properties of B to reduce the number of options to a quantity that allows exhaustive look up.

Linawati et al. (Eds.): ICT-EurAsia 2014, LNCS 8407, pp. 576–585, 2014.

Let $S : \mathbb{F}_2^t \to \mathbb{F}_2^k$ be a map, we are going to consider pairs $A : \mathbb{F}_2^k \to \mathbb{F}_2^k$ and $B : \mathbb{F}_2^t \to \mathbb{F}_2^t$ such that the following diagram commutes:

$$
\begin{array}{ccc}
\mathbb{F}_2^t & \xrightarrow{\;\;S\;\;} & \mathbb{F}_2^k \\
\downarrow{\scriptstyle B} & & \downarrow{\scriptstyle A} \\
\mathbb{F}_2^t & \xrightarrow{\;\;S\;\;} & \mathbb{F}_2^k
\end{array}
$$

We will consider the case when B is affine; there are no requirements on A, except that it should be chosen such that $AS = SB$.

2   Link Paths

For any $p \in \mathbb{F}_2^k$ we are going to consider the set $S^{-1}(p)$ and the affine subspace of $\mathbb{F}_2^t$ generated by these points, this affine subspace will be called $L(p)$.

We will use barycentric coordinates for the affine space $\mathbb{F}_2^t$, therefore for all $v \in L(p)$ we can find values $\lambda_w \in \mathbb{F}_2$, called the barycentric coordinates of v, such that $\sum_{w \in S^{-1}(p)} \lambda_w = 1$ and $v = \sum_{w \in S^{-1}(p)} \lambda_w \cdot w$. These values are unique if and only if the points are independent. A general reference about barycentric coordinates can be found in [2, pp. 216–221].

Definition 1. *Let $p, q \in \mathbb{F}_2^k$, we will say that p links q, and we will write $p \to q$, if $S^{-1}(q) \cap L(p) \neq \emptyset$.*

Proposition 1. *Let $A : \mathbb{F}_2^k \to \mathbb{F}_2^k$, and let $B : \mathbb{F}_2^t \to \mathbb{F}_2^t$ be affine, such that $AS = SB$. Let $p, q \in \mathbb{F}_2^k$ such that $p \to q$, then the values $\{B(w) : w \in S^{-1}(p)\}$ determine the value of $S(B(v'))$ for all $v' \in S^{-1}(q)$.*

Proof. We know that $p \to q$, therefore $S^{-1}(q) \cap L(p) \neq \emptyset$ and we can take a point v in this set.

This value v satisfies that $S(v) = q$ and $v = \sum_{w \in S^{-1}(p)} \lambda_w \cdot w$ for some values λ_w that satisfy $\sum_{w \in S^{-1}(p)} \lambda_w = 1$.

The map B is affine, therefore it preserves the barycentric combinations and we have $B(v) = \sum_{w \in S^{-1}(p)} \lambda_w \cdot B(w)$, which is a known value if the values $\{B(w) : w \in S^{-1}(p)\}$ are known.

For any $v' \in S^{-1}(q)$ we have that $S(v') = q = S(v)$, therefore $SB(v') = AS(v') = AS(v) = SB(v)$.

Definition 2. *Let $p_0 \to p_1 \to \cdots \to p_n$ be a path of links for the map $S : \mathbb{F}_2^t \to \mathbb{F}_2^k$. We will say that this path is exhaustive if the points $\cup_{i=0}^n S^{-1}(p_i)$ generate the whole affine space $\mathbb{F}_2^t$.*

The algorithm for constructing mappings A and B such that $AS = SB$ is the following:

1. Find an exhaustive link path $p_0 \to p_1 \to \cdots \to p_n$
2. Choose a value for $A(p_0)$
3. For every $v \in S^{-1}(p_0)$ choose an image $B(v)$ in $S^{-1}(A(p_0))$
4. Fix the value of $A(p_1)$ and at least the image by B of one point of $S^{-1}(p_1)$
5. Choose the other images in $S^{-1}(A(p_1))$
6. This process should continue until p_n is reached, then enough images will be chosen and the value of B fixed under these conditions
7. Check if $AS = SB$
8. If not, make new choices until all the possible values of B are checked

This algorithm, given in very general terms, will be applied to the DES S-Boxes.

3 Application to DES S-Boxes

Let $S_i : \mathbb{F}_2^6 \to \mathbb{F}_2^4$ be a DES S-box. We are going to apply the method described previously to study the existence of maps $A : \mathbb{F}_2^4 \to \mathbb{F}_2^4$ (general) and $B : \mathbb{F}_2^6 \to \mathbb{F}_2^6$ (affine) such that the following diagram commutes:

$$
\begin{array}{ccc}
\mathbb{F}_2^6 & \xrightarrow{\ S_i\ } & \mathbb{F}_2^4 \\
{\scriptstyle B}\big\downarrow & & \big\downarrow{\scriptstyle A} \\
\mathbb{F}_2^6 & \xrightarrow{\ S_i\ } & \mathbb{F}_2^4
\end{array}
$$

Notice that the existence of these kind of maps is trivial if we accept general maps for B, and the algorithm proposed is not applicable because it is based on the affiness of B.

Suppose that for S_i we can find an exhaustive path $p \to q$ with length 1. Then we choose a value for $A(p)$ (we have 2^4 choices) and then for each of the values in $S_i^{-1}(p)$ we choose the image of B in $S_i^{-1}(A(p))$. We have $4^4 = 2^8$ possible choices if we do not require injectivity of B.

The link relation $p \to q$ forces the value of $A(q)$ and the value for the point in $S_i^{-1}(q) \cap L_i(p)$. The other three values of $S_i^{-1}(q)$ can be chosen in $4^3 = 2^6$ different ways.

As $p \to q$ is exhaustive, these choices fix the value of B, and then we can check if the diagram commutes. The number of choices that we have is $2^4 \cdot 2^8 \cdot 2^6 = 2^{18}$, which is not a small number, but can be reached with a simple PC.

This can be done if the S-box has an exhaustive link $p \to q$. We are going to see that this is possible for all S-boxes but S_4, that will require an exhaustive path of length two.

Although in the analysis, any map A can be considered, we have imposed the extra condition of bijectivity of A. If this is not the case, a lot of options arise, for example constant maps $B : \mathbb{F}_2^6 \to \mathbb{F}_2^6$, that are not interesting for cryptographical purposes. Nonbijective maps B that could have generated bijective maps A are accepted, but none of them appear, as we can see in the following proposition:

Proposition 2. *Suppose A is invertible, B is affine such that $AS = SB$. If x_1, x_2 are such that $Bx_1 = Bx_2$, then for all y, we have $S(y + x_1 + x_2) = S(y)$.*

Proof. We are in characteristic 2, and $Bx_1 = Bx_2 = -Bx_2$, thus $Bx_1 + Bx_2 = 0$. We also know that B is affine, therefore for each y we have that $B(y + x_1 + x_2) = B(y) + B(x_1) + B(x_2) = B(y)$. As $AS = SB$, this implies that $AS(y + x_1 + x_2) = AS(y)$, and so, as A is invertible, $S(y + x_1 + x_2) = S(y)$.

We know from [1, Section 4.2] that the for all DES S-boxes S_j $(j = 1, \cdots, 8)$, if $S_j(x+a) = S_j(x)$ holds then $a = 0$. Thus it follows from the above proposition that if $AS_j = S_j B$ with A invertible and B affine, then B is invertible as well.

In the following sections, we will show the graphs with the exhaustive links of the different DES S-Boxes. The vertices of the graphs will be the vectors written in decimal representation. An arrow between p and q is drawn if and only if we have an exhaustive link path $p \to q$.

4   The S-Box S_1

The graph with the exhaustive links of S_1 is

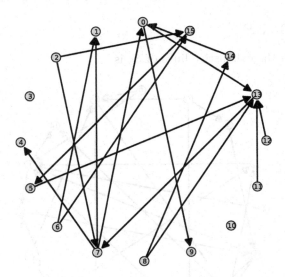

We have used for our analysis the values $p = 0$, $q = 9$. It turned out that the only choice for A and B are the identity maps on $\mathbb{F}_2^4$ and $\mathbb{F}_2^6$, respectively.

5   The S-Box S_2

The graph with the exhaustive links of S_2 is

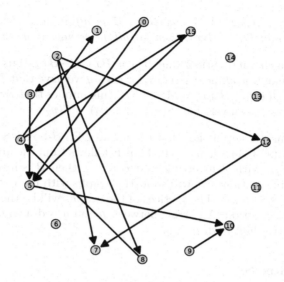

We have used for our analysis the values $p = 0$, $q = 3$. It turned out that the only choice for A and B are the identity maps on $\mathbb{F}_2^4$ and $\mathbb{F}_2^6$, respectively.

6   The S-Box S_3

The graph with the exhaustive links of S_3 is

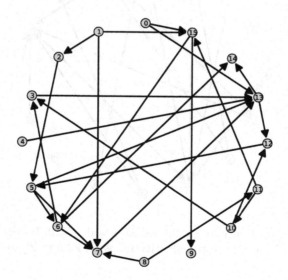

We have used for our analysis the values $p = 0$, $q = 13$. It turned out that the only choice for A and B are the identity maps on $\mathbb{F}_2^4$ and $\mathbb{F}_2^6$, respectively.

7   The S-Box S_4

The graph with the exhaustive links of S_4 is

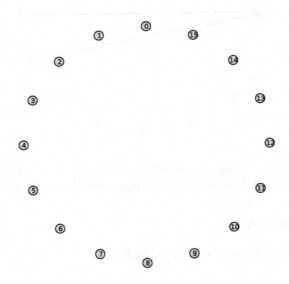

This means that we have not any exhaustive link path of length 1, but this is not a big problem, because we can find link paths of length two, for example $0 \to 10 \to 2$.

This search gave no example out of the identities and the already known affine transformation, that is obtained when the set $S_4^{-1}(0)$ is sent to $S_4^{-1}(6)$. The affine map B in this case is $B(v) = v + (1, 0, 1, 1, 1, 1)$ and $A(w) = w + (0, 1, 1, 0)$. This is already metioned in the literature several times (see [1,3]).

The existence of S-Boxes without exhaustive link paths is not common, although a definition of the probability is not simple because S-Boxes are not taken randomly, this makes very difficult to define the sample space.

8   The S-Box S_5

The graph with the exhaustive links of S_5 is

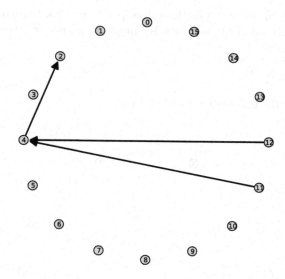

We have used for our analysis the values $p = 4$, $q = 2$. It turned out that the only choice for A and B are the identity maps on $\mathbb{F}_2^4$ and $\mathbb{F}_2^6$, respectively.

9   The S-Box S_6

The graph with the exhaustive links of S_6 is

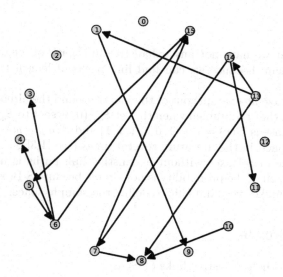

We have used for our analysis the values $p = 1$, $q = 9$. It turned out that the only choice for A and B are the identity maps on $\mathbb{F}_2^4$ and $\mathbb{F}_2^6$, respectively.

10   The S-Box S_7

The graph with the exhaustive links of S_7 is

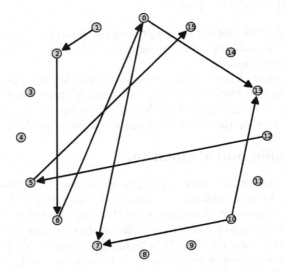

We have used for our analysis the values $p = 0$, $q = 7$. It turned out that the only choice for A and B are the identity maps on $\mathbb{F}_2^4$ and $\mathbb{F}_2^6$, respectively.

11   The S-Box S_8

The graph with the exhaustive links of S_8 is

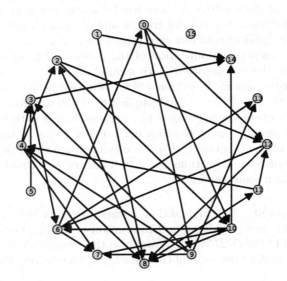

We have used for our analysis the values $p = 0$, $q = 9$. It turned out that the only choice for A and B are the identity maps on $\mathbb{F}_2^4$ and $\mathbb{F}_2^6$, respectively.

12   The Bijectivity of A

Although it is not interesting for cryptographic pourposes, this algorithm can give us also the possibilities for non bijective maps $A : \mathbb{F}_2^4 \to \mathbb{F}_2^4$. Think for example all constant maps.

As an application of the method, we have computed the pairs (A, B) for S_4, and we have obtained 74658 affine maps B, most of them constant or with only one independent vector. When B is chosen, the value of A can be determined for some values and for the others we have a complete freedom.

13   Conclusion and Evaluation

The existence of linear and affine equivalences between invertible S-boxes (permutations) have been considered and analyzed with general algorithms, for example in [1]. The exponential amplification that appears when S is non-bijective makes an exhaustive search much more difficult. In this paper we introduced the notion of link graph of an S-box. This technique focus the search of candidates for equivalences to a small set of choices, that compensate the exponential amplification and therefore let us develop an algorithm to find pairs of a bijective mapping A and an affine mapping B such that $AS = SB$.

We applied this algorithm to the eight DES S-boxes, and found that all such pairs were already obtained before under the condition that both A and B are bijective affine mappings. In particular, the relaxation of the requirement that A should be affine, as in [1], to the very general requirement of being bijective, does not yield new pairs of mappings.

The problem of nonbijective S-boxes has been considered in [1] with a different approach, because they require that A and B both should be affine. Their algorithm is not applicable to our case that is more general, and we both compensate the exponential amplification of the problem, but we can make some comments about the complexity of both methods.

The complexity given in [1, Section 4.2] for affine equivalences of noninvertible S-boxes is $n^3 \cdot 2^n \cdot (2^{n-m}!)^{\frac{n}{2^{n-m}}}$ that applied to $n = 6$ and $m = 4$ gives around 2^{20}. The number of choices in our case (for exhaustive link paths) is 2^{18}, but each choice generate an affine map B and a map A. For those we have to check the commutativity of the diagram and previously compute the link path, therefore the complexity of both algorithms for $n = 6$ and $m = 4$ could be similar, but our search is much more general.

Acknowledgement. The first author wishes to thank the financial support given by the Ministry of Science and Innovation of Spain, through the Walkie-Talkie project (TIN2011-27543-C03) and also the *Fundación Séneca*.

The authors wish to thank Paul Gorissen for the interesting discussions about this topic.

References

1. Biryukov, A., De Cannière, C., Braeken, A., Preneel, B.: A toolbox for cryptanalysis: Linear and affine equivalence algorithms. In: Biham, E. (ed.) EUROCRYPT 2003. LNCS, vol. 2656, pp. 33–50. Springer, Heidelberg (2003)
2. Coxeter, H.: Introduction to geometry, 2nd edn. John Wiley and Sons (1969)
3. Hellman, M., Merkle, R., Schroppel, R., Washington, L., Diffie, W., Pohlig, S., Schweitzer, P.: Results on an initial attempt to cryptanalyze the nbs data encryption standard. Technical report, Stanford University (September 1976)

Attribute-Based Fine-Grained Access Control with User Revocation

Jun Ye[1,2,*], Wujun Zhang[2], Shu-lin Wu[1], Yuan-yuan Gao[1], and Jia-tao Qiu[3]

[1] School of Science
Sichuan University of Science & Engineering, Sichuan, 643000, China
yejun@suse.edu.cn, wushulin_sh@163.com, gaoyuanyuan@iie.ac.cn
[2] School of Telecommunication Engineering
Xidian University, Shanxi, 710071, China
yejun@suse.edu.cn, wjzhang@xidian.edu.cn
[3] School of Automation and Electronic Information
Sichuan University of Science & Engineering, Sichuan, 643000, China
yhuiqiu@126.com

Abstract. Attribute-based encryption brings a lot of convenience for access control. But it introduces several challenges with regard to the user revocation. In this paper, we propose an access control mechanism using new key update technology to enforce access control policies with efficient user revocation capability. The access control can be achieved by efficient key update technology which takes advantage of the attribute-based encryption and key distribution. We demonstrate how to apply the proposed mechanism to securely manage the cloud data. The analysis results indicate that the proposed scheme is efficient and secure in user revocation.

Keywords: Attribute-Based Encryption, Security, Efficient Revocation.

1 Introduction

In cloud computing, data owner outsources sensitive data to cloud server, which is shared with the users whose attributes satisfy the specific access privilege. It is widely applied to the Internet of Things. In the field of access control system, especially under the background of cloud computing, in order to optimize resources and management, more and more businesses and individuals store the data resources in third-party servers. So to provide effective access control [8,16] of data resources is very necessary. The basic security requirement is to provide the data resources confidentiality. Attribute encryption system has many advantages compared with the traditional method in access control system, but access control has a new challenge in cloud environment.

In this case attribute-based encryption [11,12,14] (ABE) offers many convenient. ABE allows for a encrypter to encrypt a message to series of users who have such attributes, without access to a public key certificate. In ABE all the

---

* Corresponding author.

Linawati et al. (Eds.): ICT-EurAsia 2014, LNCS 8407, pp. 586–595, 2014.

entities are uniformly described in the same way, but the attribute authority of different entities may be different from each other. This makes the decision function of access control may be able to adopt a uniform treatment according to the basis of determination. The ability to do public key encryption without certificates has many practical applications.

1.1   Related Work

Sahai proposed an private key-policy attribute-based encryption scheme by using secret sharing scheme. Goyal [5] proposed a key-policy scheme with a tree access structure where the interior nodes consist of AND and OR gates and the leaves consist of different parties. This scheme can be used to construct fine-grained access control. subsequently, Ostrovsky [13] proposed a non-monotonic ABE. The first ciphertext-policy ABE scheme is proposed by Bethencourt [2]. The ciphertext-policy is defined through the tree access structure and can deal with And an OR gates. On the construct of ABE scheme key-policy scheme is not convenient with the ciphertext-policy scheme, and scalability cannot be achieved. So most attribute-based encryption schemes are ciphertext-policy scheme. Many ABE scheme are proposed in different application fields. Sometimes besides the confidentiality of documents we also need to protect attribute in the ciphertext and the related policy. Anonymous ABE [11,6,7] is proposed to solve this problem. In order to disperse the right of authorized center, Chase and Lin [4,9] proposes an multi-authority ABE scheme. For the purpose of improve the efficiency of user management in broadcast encryption based on public key encryption, Lubicz [10] proposes attribute-based broadcast encryption system. Recently, some ABE schemes with attributes and user revocation [3] have been proposed. And there are two main problems comes out, the backward security and the key updating.

Attribute revocation and user revocation is an essential mechanism in many applications. Attrapadung and Imai [1] proposed an user revocable ABE schemes, but to enable the direct user revocation, the data owner should take charge of all the membership. But the data owner can not directly control the data distribution when the data is outsourced. An efficient user revocation scheme is needed.

1.2   Our Contributions

An attribute-based access control scheme with efficient user revocation is proposed in this paper. An improved ABE model is established, in which the users has two classed of keys. One is the attribute keys and the other is private keys. Attribute keys can be used to get the part of deception key, K. The decryption key is generated by K and the users private keys. This scheme can easily to add and remove users. At last we give the rigorous security proof of our schemes.

The organization of this paper is as follows. Some preliminaries are given in Section 2. The improved attribute-based encryption model is given in Section 3.

Table 1. Notations

k:	security parameters
ω':	set of attributes needed for decryption
ω:	set of user's attributes
$E(\cdot)$:	encryption algorithm
$D(\cdot)$:	decryption algorithm
sk:	private key
pk:	public key
$R(\cdot, \cdot)$:	matching relation of tow elements
f:	key generation algorithm
s:	side information

The secure ABE scheme with efficient user revocation and the security analysis is given in Section 4. Finally, conclusion will be made in Section 5.

2 Preliminaries

2.1 Bilinear Maps

Let $\mathbb{G}_1, \mathbb{G}_2$ be the cyclic groups of prime order p, let g be a generator of $\mathbb{G}_1$, and $e : \mathbb{G}_1 \times \mathbb{G}_1 \to \mathbb{G}_2$ be a map with the following properties.

1. Bilinearity: $e(g^a, g^b) = e(g, g)^{ab}$, $a, b \in \mathbb{Z}_p$.
2. Non-degeneracy: There exist $x, y \in \mathbb{G}_1$ such that $e(x, y) \neq 1$.
3. Computable: For all $x, y \in \mathbb{G}_1$, $e(x, y)$ has to be computable in an efficient manner.

2.2 Complexity Assumption

Decisional Modified Bilinear Diffie-Hellman (MBDH) Assumption.
Given $g, g^x, g^y, g^z \in \mathbb{G}_1$ for unknown random $x, y, z, r \in \mathbb{Z}_p^*$. The MDBDH assumption is that no polynomial-time adversary is to be able to distinguish the tuple $(g^x, g^y, g^y, e(g, g)^{\frac{xy}{z}})$ from a random tuple $((g^x, g^y, g^y, e(g, g)^r)$ with more than a negligible advantage.

$$|Pr[\mathcal{A}(g^x, g^y, g^y, e(g, g)^{\frac{xy}{z}}) = 1] - Pr[\mathcal{A}((g^x, g^y, g^y, e(g, g)^r))] = 1| \leq \epsilon$$

3 Improved ABE Model

Some notations are list in table 1.

Setup: Encrypter generates different private key $sk^{(2)}$ for every user, and sends to every user by a secure channel. Then generates a secret key x which is used to encrypt the message, and another private key $sk^{(1)}$ which satisfies $x = f(sk^{(1)}, sk^{(2)})$ for every different $sk^{(2)}$.

Authority generates pk, and for every user, generates different $sk^{(3)}$ and s, user's attributes ω. Then sends to users.

Encryption: Encrypter encrypts the message M with x by computing $C = E(M, x)$, and encrypts $sk^{(1)}$ with pk, then gets a new key $sk^{(4)} = E(sk^{(1)}, s, pk)$. So the ciphertext is $\{\omega', C = E(M, x), s, sk^{(4)}\}$.

Decryption: If $R(\omega, \omega') = 0$, then $sk^{(1)} \neq D(sk^{(4)}, sk^{(3)}, s, pk)$, $x \neq f(sk^{(1)}, sk^{(2)})$. If $R(\omega, \omega') = 1$, user can get $sk^{(1)}$ by computing $sk^{(1)} = D(sk^{(4)}, sk^{(3)}, s, pk)$. Then user computes $x = f(sk^{(1)}, sk^{(2)})$, and recovers message $M = D(M, x)$. Where

$$R(\omega, \omega') = \begin{cases} 1 \text{ , the relation of } \omega \text{ and } \omega' \text{ satisfies decryption conditions} \\ 0 \text{ , else} \end{cases}$$

A schematic diagram of our model are as Fig. 1.

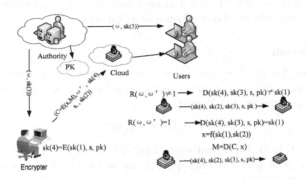

Fig. 1. Improved ABE Model

In this improved ABE model, to achieve user revocation efficiently, the key to encrypt M is divided into tow parts. One part is as a part of user's private key, the other part is used in the attributes policy.

4   Secure ABE Scheme with Efficient User Revocation

We now informally specify an improved threshold Attribute-Based Encryption system as a collection of four algorithms:

Setup (k): Authority generates an algorithm1 which takes a threshold value d as input and outputs a master key MK and a set of public parameters PK. Encrypter chooses a secret key K_1, and generates tow algorithms. One is a key generation algorithm2 with the security parameter k. The other is algorithm3 with which the private keys generated from algorithm2 achieve K_1.

Key Generation (S, MK): The authority executes the Key-Gen algorithm for the purpose of generating a new secret key SK. The algorithm takes as input the user's identity S, as a set of strings representing a user's attributes and the master-key MK and outputs the secret key SK related to S. And encrypter run algorithm3 generates different secret private key K_2 for users and K_3, then sends the different K_2 to every user through a secure channel and publish algorithm3. And sends K_3 to authority.

Encryption (M, S', PK, K_1, K_3): Encrypter to encrypt a message M with K_1, outputs a ciphertext C. Encrypter encrypts K_3 with a target set S', out put K^*, and sends K^*, C and public parameters to users.

Decryption (C, S', S, SK, K^*, K_2): The decrypt algorithm is run by a user with identity S and secret key SK to attempt to decrypt K^* that has been encrypted with S'. If the set overlap $|S \bigcap S'|$ is greater than or equal to d the algorithm can decrypt K^* and output K. Along with K_3, users can compute the secret key K_1 with his/her own secret private key K_2 to recover M.

Here we give a secure ABE scheme in the improved ABE model. In this scheme authority can not recover M and it is easy to add and remove users.

A detailed description of our scheme is as follows.

4.1   Description

Initialization. Assume there are n users in this system, authority chooses $m \times m$ full rank matrix A $(m > n)$ and a random number $y \in \mathbb{Z}_p^*$. Authority generates a new m-dimensional vector Y with y,

$$Y = (y, y, \ldots, y)^T$$

and computes X from the linear equations $AX = Y$.

In this way y is used to encrypt the message M. X is as a part of private key. And athority chooses n vectors $\{a_1, a_2, \ldots, a_n\}$ from matrix A ($a_i = (a_{i1}, a_{i2}, \ldots, a_{im})$)as the secret private keys of n users, and sends a_i to each user U_i. (For the security of our scheme, we will give a method to generate X an Y, see the proof of Proposition 2 in this section).

We now create an scheme for authority in which a encryption of X created using attributes ω, can be decrypted only by users whose attributes ω' satisfied $|\omega \bigcap \omega'| \geq d$.

Let $\mathbb{G}_1$ be a bilinear group of prime order p, let g be a generator of $\mathbb{G}_1$, and let $e : \mathbb{G}_1 \times \mathbb{G}_1 \to \mathbb{G}_2$ denote the bilinear map.

We also define the Lagrange coefficient $\Delta_{i,s}$ for $i \in \mathbb{Z}_p$ and a set S of elements in $\mathbb{Z}_p$:

$$\Delta_{i,s(x)} = \prod_{j \in S, j \neq i} \frac{x - j}{i - j}.$$

Identities will be element subsets of universe μ, of size $|\mu|$. And the attributes will be associated with the elements of μ. Our construction is as follows:

Setup(d). For simplicity, we can take the first $|\mu|$ elements of $\mathbb{Z}_p^*$ to be the universe of elements. Then authority chooses $t_1, \ldots, t_{|\mu|}$ and r uniformly from $\mathbb{Z}_p^*$. The published public parameters are:

$$T_1 = g^{t_1}, \ldots, T_{|\mu|} = g^{t_{|\mu|}}, Y = e(g, g)^r.$$

The master key is:

$$t_1, \ldots, t_{|\mu|}, r.$$

Key Generation. A $d-1$ degree polynomial q is randomly chosen by autyority such that $q(0) = r$. The private key consists of components, $(D_i)_{i \in \omega}$, where $D_i = g^{q(i)/t_i}$ for every $i \in \omega$.

Encryption. First, a random value $a, t, s \in \mathbb{Z}_p^*$ is chosen by encrypter, and encrypter computes b satisfies $ab = 1 \mod p$. The ciphertext is the published as:

$$E = (\omega', C = tyM, (tX)^a = ((tx_1)^a, (tx_2)^a, \ldots, (tx_m)^a)^T, E' = bY^s, \{E_i = T_i^s\}_{i \in \omega'}).$$

Decryption. Some parts of ciphertext E is encrypted with a key associated with ω', where $|\omega \bigcap \omega'| \geq d$. User chooses an arbitrary subset of $\omega \bigcap \omega'$ with d elements. Then, the ciphertext can be decrypted as follows:

First, user U_j computes $E'/\prod_{i \in S} e(D_i, E_i)^{\Delta_{i,s}(0)}$ and gains b.

$$E'/\prod_{i \in S} e(D_i, E_i)^{\Delta_{i,s}(0)} = be(g, g)^{sy}/\prod_{i \in S} (e(g^{q(i)/t_i}, g^{st_i}))^{\Delta_{i,s}(0)}$$

$$= be(g, g)^{sy}/\prod_{i \in S} (e(g, g)^{sq(i)})^{\Delta_{i,s}(0)}$$

$$= b.$$

Second, user U_j computes

$$tX = (tX)^{ab} = ((tx_1)^{ab}, (tx_2)^{ab}, \ldots, (yx_m)^{ab})^T \mod p$$

and gets $tX = (tx_1, tx_2, \ldots, tx_m)^T$. Then U_j can get ty by the equation

$$ty = a_i tX \mod p$$

Last, user U_j can recover the message M by computing $M = C/ty$.

4.2   Security Analysis

Proposition 1. *The adversary whose attributes are not satisfied $|\omega \bigcap \omega'| \geq d$, can get y with the probability $\frac{1}{p} + \epsilon$. (ϵ is negligible).*

Proof. From the security of Decisional Modified Bilinear Diffie-Hellman (DMBDH) Assumption in [15], we know the probability with which the adversary can get the vector X which is used to compute ty is ϵ_1 (ϵ_1 is negligible).

The other way, adversary can just to guess ty. For ty is randomly chosen in $\mathbb{Z}_p$ by encrypter, the only information of ty adversary can get is ty is different from the other data which is used before. So the probability which adversary can guess ty is $\frac{1}{p} + \epsilon_2$, where ϵ_2 is negligible.

Therefore, the adversary whose attributes are not satisfied $|\omega \bigcap \omega'| \geq d$, can get ty with the probability $\frac{1}{p} + \epsilon_1 + \epsilon_2 = \frac{1}{p} + \epsilon$, where $\epsilon = \epsilon_1 + \epsilon_2$.

Proposition 2. *The probability which curious user can get other user's secret private key is at most $\frac{1}{p}$.*

Proof. With out loss of generality we assume U_1 is curious. When U_1 recover enough M, he/she would get enough pairs of X and Y. The original linear equations are

$$A_{m \times m} X_{m \times 1} = Y_{m \times 1} \mod p.$$

If there are m vectors of X which are linearly independent, U_1 can construct the following equations with the corresponding vectors of Y.

$$A(X_1, X_2, \ldots, X_m) = (Y_1, Y_2, \ldots, Y_m) \mod p$$

Generation of X and Y: Here we give a method to generate X and Y, which leads the curious user can not get other user's secret private key. By using this generation of X, encrypter would not reveal the private key a_i.

Encrypter can generate small amounts of X, i.e.$(X_1, X_2, \ldots, X_l), l \ll m$, and use the linear combination of vectors $(X_1, X_2, \ldots, X_l)$ to generate other X_j and get corresponding Y_j $(l \leq j \leq m)$.

$$X_j = k_{1j} X_1 + k_{2j} X_2 + \cdots + k_{lj} X_l \mod p (k_{ij} \in \mathbb{Z}_p^*, 1 \leq i \leq l)$$

and corresponding m-dimensional vector

$$Y_j = (\sum_{i=1}^{l} k_{ij} y_i, \sum_{i=1}^{l} k_{ij} y_i, \ldots, \sum_{i=1}^{l} k_{ij} y_i) \mod p.$$

Correctness of Operation: X_j and Y_j generate from this way can make our scheme execute correctly. The correctness is as follows.

$$AX_j = \left(a_1, a_2, \ldots, a_m \right)^T (k_{1j} X_1 + k_{2j} X_2 + \cdots + k_{lj} X_l)$$
$$= \begin{pmatrix} k_{1j} a_1 X_1 + k_{2j} a_1 X_2 + \cdots + k_{mj} a_1 X_m \\ k_{1j} a_2 X_1 + k_{2j} a_2 X_2 + \cdots + k_{mj} a_2 X_m \\ k_{1j} a_m X_1 + k_{2j} a_m X_2 + \cdots + k_{mj} a_m X_m \end{pmatrix}$$
$$= \begin{pmatrix} k_{1j} y_1 + k_{2j} y_2 + \cdots + k_{mj} y_m \\ k_{1j} y_1 + k_{2j} y_2 + \cdots + k_{mj} y_m \\ k_{1j} y_1 + k_{2j} y_2 + \cdots + k_{mj} y_m \end{pmatrix}$$
$$= \left(\sum_{i=1}^{l} k_{ij} y_i, \sum_{i=1}^{l} k_{ij} y_i, \ldots, \sum_{i=1}^{l} k_{ij} y_i \right) \mod p.$$

In this way the rank of the matrix which is consist of any combination of m vectors is less than l, so there are at least p^{m-l} vectors satisfies $AX = Y$. So the probability U_1 can get other user's secret private key is at most $\frac{1}{p^{m-l}}$.

Every user's secret private key (a m-dimensional vector) a satisfies $aX = Y$ mod p. There are P^{m-1} m-dimensional vectors a satisfies $aX = Y$ in $\mathbb{Z}_p$, but there are p^m m-dimensional vectors in $\mathbb{Z}_p$. So the probability U_1 can get other user's secret private key is $\frac{1}{p}$.

Hence, the probability the other user's key a_i can be gained is at most $\frac{1}{p}$.

4.3   User Addition and Revocation

User Addition: When U_{n+1} join in, encrypter will give him/her a_{n+1} as the secret private key from the matrix $A_{m \times m}$ through a secure channel, and authority give him/her the corresponding private key according to his/her attributes. It is very easy to implement. Because a_{n_1} is the n_1th vector of A, so for all X used before, U_{n+1} can compute $a_{n+1}X = y$. In this way U_{n+1} can recover the message which encrypt before his/her join.

User Revocation: When U_i is removed, the secret private key a_i is not available and the message M which is recovered by U_i should be re-encrypted by encrypter. Encrypter use a new vector a'_i which is the linear combination of vectors in A to instead of a_i, and get the new matrix A'.

$$a'_i = h_1 a_1 + h_2 a_2 + \cdots + h_i a_i + \cdots + h_m a_m \quad \bmod p$$

Where $h_j \in \mathbb{Z}_p, (1 \le j \le m)$, $\sum_{j=1}^{m} h_j \neq 1$ (If $\sum_{j=1}^{m} h_j = 1$, then $a'_i X = y$ and $a_i X = y$, so U_i can recover M). A is still full rank, X is uniquely determined.

    U_j re-encrypt M, and computes the new $y' = a_j X'$ from the equation $A'X' = Y$ (where the vector a_i is replace by a'_i), then $C' = y'M \bmod p$.

Proposition 3. *The probability the removed user can get the new y' is $\frac{1}{p}$.*

Proof. Even the new X' is gained, the removed user U_i uses his/her original secret private key a_i can not get y' yet. We assume $y' = a'_i X'$, here

$$a'_i = h_1 a_1 + h_2 a_2 + \cdots + h_i a_i + \cdots + h_m a_m \quad \bmod p,$$

and $\sum_{j=1}^{m} h_j \neq 1$. So

$$y' = \sum_{j=i}^{m} h_j a_j X' = \sum_{j=1, j \neq i}^{m} h_j a_j X' + h_i a_i X' = \sum_{j=1, j \neq i}^{m} h_j y' + h_i a_i X'.$$

If $a_i X' = y'$, then

$$y' = \sum_{j=i}^{m} h_j a_j X' = \sum_{j=1, j \neq i}^{m} h_j y' + h_i y' = \sum_{j=1}^{m} h_j y'$$

but $\sum_{j=1}^{m} h_j \neq 1$, then $a_i X' \neq y'$. So U_i can not get the new y'.

    The another way to get y' is that U_i guess it from $\mathbb{Z}_p$. For y' is chosen form $\mathbb{Z}_p$ randomly, so the probability is $\frac{1}{p}$.

    Therefore, the probability which the removed user can get the new y' is $\frac{1}{p}$.

Efficiency: When some member is removed, sever should update other members' secret private keys, which is efficient for small group by using the above technology.

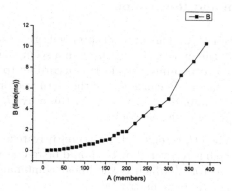

Fig. 2. Time Cost of User Revocation

The time cost of secret private keys update is as Fig. 2. We implement our mechanism using MATLAB language with a version of R2012b. The process is conducted on a computer with Intel(R) Core(TM)i3-3230 CPU processor running at 2.60 GHz, 4 GB RAM.

The time cost is related to the number of members, has nothing to do with the number of deleted members.

5   Conclusion

In order to easily achieve user revocation, an improved ABE model is proposed in this paper. The improved scheme building on the proposal of fuzzy IBE from [15] is as examples of schemes in our model. The method that the keys which can recover messages are divided into tow parts are very effective to achieve user revocation. And a key updating method and a re-encryption method are proposed for the security of user revocation. The security of our schemes are strictly proved.

Acknowledgements. The work described in this paper is supported by the Science Founding of Artificial Intelligence Key Laboratory of Sichuan Province (2014RYJ06, 2012RYJ05); The Scientific Research Fund Project of Sichuan University of Science & Engineering (2013KY02); NSFC (No.11301362); Project of Innovative Research Team in University of Sichuan (NO.13TD0017); The talent project of Sichuan University of Science & Engineering (2013RC13).This work was supported by the high-quality goods resource sharing courses "mathematical modeling" of Sichuan province (2012-57); Science Founding of Science School of Sichuan university of science & engineering(10LXYB05); "mathematical modeling teaching group" of Sichuan University of Science & Engineering (2009-142-01).

References

1. Attrapadung, N., Imai, H.: Conjunctive broadcast and attribute-based encryption. In: Shacham, H., Waters, B. (eds.) Pairing 2009. LNCS, vol. 5671, pp. 248–265. Springer, Heidelberg (2009)
2. Bethencourt, J., Sahai, A., Waters, B.: Ciphertext-policy attribute-based encryption, vol. 3494, pp. 321–334. Springer (May 2007)
3. Boldyreva, A., Goyal, V., Kumar, V.: Identity-based encryption with efficient revocation, pp. 417–426 (October 2008)
4. Chase, M., Chow, S.S.M.: Privacy-aware attribute-based encryption with user accountability, pp. 121–130. Springer (November 2009)
5. Goyal, V., Pandey, O., Sahai, A., Waters, B.: Attribute-based encryption for fine-grained access control of encrypted data, vol. 3494, pp. 89–98 (October 2006)
6. Kapadia, A., Tsang, P.P., Smith, S.W.: Attribute-based publishing with hidden credentials and hidden policies, pp. 179–192 (2007)
7. Li, J., Ren, K., Zhu, B., Wan, Z.: Privacy-aware attribute-based encryption with user accountability. In: Samarati, P., Yung, M., Martinelli, F., Ardagna, C.A. (eds.) ISC 2009. LNCS, vol. 5735, pp. 347–362. Springer, Heidelberg (2009)
8. Li, J., Li, J., Chen, X., Jia, C., Liu, Z.: Efficient keyword search over encrypted data with fine-grained access control in hybrid cloud. In: Xu, L., Bertino, E., Mu, Y. (eds.) NSS 2012. LNCS, vol. 7645, pp. 490–502. Springer, Heidelberg (2012)
9. Lin, H., Cao, Z., Liang, X., Shao, J.: Secure threshold multi-authority attribute based encryption without a central authority. Information Sciences 180(13), 2618–2632 (2010)
10. Lubicz, D., Sirvent, T.: Attribute-based broadcast encryption scheme made efficient. In: Vaudenay, S. (ed.) AFRICACRYPT 2008. LNCS, vol. 5023, pp. 325–342. Springer, Heidelberg (2008)
11. Nishide, T., Yoneyama, K., Ohta, K.: Attribute-based encryption with partially hidden encryptor-specified access structures. In: Bellovin, S.M., Gennaro, R., Keromytis, A., Yung, M. (eds.) ACNS 2008. LNCS, vol. 5037, pp. 111–129. Springer, Heidelberg (2008)
12. Okamoto, T., Takashima, K.: Adaptively attribute-hiding (hierarchical) inner product encryption. In: Pointcheval, D., Johansson, T. (eds.) EUROCRYPT 2012. LNCS, vol. 7237, pp. 591–608. Springer, Heidelberg (2012)
13. Ostrovsky, R., Sahai, A., Waters, B.: Attribute-based encryption with non-monotonic access structures, pp. 195–203 (October 2007)
14. Parno, B., Raykova, M., Vaikuntanathan, V.: How to delegate and verify in public: Verifiable computation from attribute-based encryption. In: Cramer, R. (ed.) TCC 2012. LNCS, vol. 7194, pp. 422–439. Springer, Heidelberg (2012)
15. Sahai, A., Waters, B.: Fuzzy identity-based encryption. In: Cramer, R. (ed.) EUROCRYPT 2005. LNCS, vol. 3494, pp. 457–473. Springer, Heidelberg (2005)
16. Xie, X., Ma, H., Li, J., Chen, X.: New ciphertext-policy attribute-based access control with efficient revocation. In: Mustofa, K., Neuhold, E.J., Tjoa, A.M., Weippl, E., You, I. (eds.) ICT-EurAsia 2013. LNCS, vol. 7804, pp. 373–382. Springer, Heidelberg (2013)

A Full Privacy-Preserving Scheme for Location-Based Services

Fei Shao, Rong Cheng, and Fangguo Zhang*

School of Information Science and Technology,
Sun Yat-sen University, Guangzhou 510006, China
{tianxin0120,chengrongada}@163.com, isszhfg@mail.sysu.edu.cn

Abstract. Location based services(LBS) pose risks to user's privacy, as they have access to user's identity, location and usage profile. Many approaches have been made up to deal with the privacy problems. But few of them meet the requirement of full privacy. In this paper, we propose a protocol that does not require a trusted third party and provides full privacy. We use group anonymous authentication to fulfill identity privacy, while using program obfuscation to satisfy the privacy requirement of usage profile. And we assume that there exist some geography or geometry methods to form a cloaking region to meet location privacy.

Keywords: privacy, location based service, anonymous credential system, program obfuscation.

1 Introduction

Location based services involve the collection, using, and sharing of location data[6]. Which may pose a great risk to user's privacy[4]. The malicious location services providers(LP) may do something against the users' willing. Users may have the feeling of being followed up and queries may disclose sensitive information about individuals. So privacy issue is something that must be concerned[1].

All the exiting privacy preserving techniques can be divided into three categories, that is two-tier spatial transformations, three-tier spatial transformations and cryptographic transformations[6]. Methods in Category 1 do not require any trusted third party, and the query anonymization is performed by the mobile user itself. [12,5] are all of that category. Those methods offer an amount of privacy, however, none of them can prevent re-identification of the query source if an attacker has knowledge about specific users' locations. Category 2 assumes the presence of a trusted third-party anonymizer server, and offers better protection against background knowledge attacks. [10,9,11] are all of that category. They offers a better privacy guarantee, but has several drawbacks: (i) The anonymizer is a single point of attack. (ii) A large number of cooperating, trustworthy users are needed. (iii) Privacy is guaranteed only for a single snapshot, users are not protected against correlation attack. Category 3 offers a stronger privacy guarantees, and protects user's privacy even against powerful adversaries. A novel

---

* Corresponding author.

Linawati et al. (Eds.): ICT-EurAsia 2014, LNCS 8407, pp. 596–601, 2014.

LBS privacy approach based on Private Information Retrieval (PIR) was introduced in [8].It can resists the correlation attack, but can hardly protect user's identity privacy. It occupies a large computational and communication cost even for a small databases.

In this paper, we propose a full privacy LBS scheme without the anonymizer. We use the anonymous credentials system to protect user's identity privacy, while we use obfuscation of a program to protect user's usage profiles. We assume that there exists some geography or geometry methods to form a CR, in which all users are indistinguishable.

The rest of this paper is organized as follow: section 2 gives some basic preliminaries, section 3 provides the system architecture and presents our scheme, the security and privacy properties are considered in section 4, and the paper concludes in section 5 finally.

2 Preliminaries

In this section, we present the building blocks we are using to construct the proposed scheme.

The Anonymous Credentials System. Anonymous credentials system consists of users and organizations. Organizations know the users by pseudonyms. It allows users to authenticate themselves in a privacy-preserving manner. There are many protocol of that kind [3]. In this paper, we propose a anonymous credentials system based on Jan Camenisch and Anna Lysyanskaya (CL) signature scheme [3].

Program Obfuscation. An obfuscation $\mathcal{O}$ can obfuscate a code or program to create an obfuscated code, which is difficult for humans to understand. Recently in [7,2], they use multilinear map and fully homomorphic encryption to realize security confusion of arbitrary polynomial circuit. That is, any function that can be realized using polynomial circuit can be obfuscated into an obfuscation $\mathcal{O}$. The obfuscation $\mathcal{O}$ will not reveal anything about what the function is.

3 Full Privacy-Preserving LBS Scheme

In this section, we describe the details of the system architecture and the proposed scheme of our full privacy-preserving LBS scheme.

3.1 The System Architecture

Fig.1 depicts the architecture of our proposed scheme. It consists of two parts, the mobile user(Bob) and LP. LP has a database(DB), the data stores in DB in the form of ($attribute, coordinate, content$) short for ($att, coo, con$). The attribute of the data includes hospital, school and so on. The coordinate of data is a location in the form of (longitude, latitude), while the content is the detail of the data. Typically a user asks NN queries in the form of $query(attribute, coordinate, \theta)$

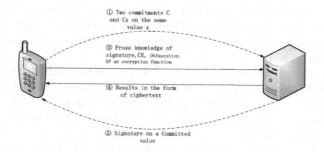

Fig. 1. The System Architecture

short for $q(att, coo, \theta)$. The message flow in that architecture can be divided into three phases: System Setup, User Join, Getting services. The Fig.1 shows only the last two phases.

- System Setup: LP and Bob generate the system public keys and secret keys, LP manages DB in the form of (att, coo, con).
- User Join: Bob joins the system and obtains an anonymous credential from LP.
- Getting services: Bob first proves knowledge of the anonymous credential to LP, then sends his query and cloking area CR to LP. After verifying Bob's credential, LP feeds back Bob's query according to its database.

3.2   The Proposed Scheme

The target of this paper is to propose a full privacy LBS scheme. Our approach is twofold. One is to use the anonymous credentials system to hide the user's identity and the other is to use the obfuscation of a program to protect user's usage profile. The scheme is shown below in detail.

System Setup Phase: In this phase, LP does the things: Generate two safe primes p, q, and calculate a special RSA modulus $n = pq$. The length of p, q is $l_n = 2k$, k is a system parameter; Randomly choose $a, b, c \in \mathbf{QR}_n$; Set $PK = (n, a, b, c)$ and $SK = p$; Manage the database DB in the form of (att, coo, con). Bob does the following things: Generate a number $h_c \in \mathbf{QR}_n$ as a generator of group $< h_c >$; Randomly choose a number g_c from group $< h_c >$. Sets (n_c, g_c, h_c) as commitment public key; Generate $ElGamal$ public key $pk = (\mathbb{G}, q, g, h)$ and secret key $sk = x$.

User Join Phase: In this phase, Bob randomly chooses a value, and makes commitments on that value. LP signs on that committed value, and knows nothing about it. The detail is shown in Figure.2.

Getting Services Phase : The getting services phase starts, when Bob wants to make a service query to LP. Bob does the following things: Contacts LP

User: Bob($pk = (n_c, g_c, h_c)$)	Signer: LP($pk = (n, a, b, c), sk = p$)

Bob selects x, r_c, r
Computes $C = g_c^x h_c^{r_c}$ and $C_x = a^x b^r$

$$\xrightarrow{\begin{array}{c} C, C_x \text{ proves } C, C_x \\ \hline are\ commited\ to\ x \end{array}}$$

LP selects r' and e

Computes $v = (C_x b^{r'} c)^{1/e}$

$$\xleftarrow{(r', e, v)}$$

Let $s = r + r'$, output a signature
(s, e, v) that satisfies $v^e = a^x b^s c$

Fig. 2. *User Join* Protocol

through proof knowledge of the signature to make LP believe he is a legal user. It goes like the phase of proof knowledge of the signature in [3], you can go to [3] for detail, thus it is omitted here; Gets himself located and generates a CR; Generates the following program F in figure 3; Uses obfuscation method to obfuscate F into an obfuscated code $\mathcal{O}$; Lastly sends $\mathcal{O}$ and CR to LP.

Input: $T = Sizeof DB'$, $data_i(1 \le i \le T)$.
$data_i$ means the ith data in DB'.
Output:$Enc(data_i)$.

1. for $1 \le i \le T$;
2. if $data_i(att) = q(att) \wedge d(data_i(coo), q(coo)) \le \theta$;
3. output $Enc(data_i)$;
4. else output $Enc(ans)$.

$d(a, b) = \sqrt{(x_2 - x_1)^2 + (y_2 - y_1)^2}$ is a simple function to compute the distance between bivector $a(x_1, y_1)$ and $b(x_2, y_2)$; ans is an initial random number known to Bob, unknown to LP; $Enc(data)$ is an El Gamal encryption scheme

Fig.3. Program of *Getting Service*

LP first verifies the zero knowledge proof. If passed, he does the things: Searches DB according to CR and θ to find all the available data DB'; Sets all the data as inputs of the obfuscated code $\mathcal{O}$; Sending all the outputs of $\mathcal{O}$ to Bob.

Bob uses the *ELGamal* decryption function decrypt the results to obtain the results in the form of plaintext. If none of the data satisfies Bob's query, $\mathcal{O}$ may give a result of $Enc(ans)$. Bob decrypts the $Enc(ans)$ will get ans, Bob will know that there is no place satisfying his requirement.

4   Security

The proposed scheme has the property of full privacy. The full privacy includes location privacy, identity privacy and usage profiles privacy. Following we analyze the full privacy from three aspects.

Theorem 1. The location privacy preserved if the user is indistinguishable from $K - 1$ other users in the CR.

Proof: The location privacy of our scheme is based on the property of CR. If the user is indistinguishable from $K - 1$ other users in that CR, So LP won't know the exact location of the user and the user's location privacy has been protected.

Theorem 2. The identity privacy preserved if CL signature-based authentication is anonymous.

Proof: The identity privacy property means that LP are conceived to forestall the re-identification of anonymous users. In CL signature, it allows users to authenticate themselves in a privacy-preserving manner. He can prove to LP that he has a right credential without revealing anything else about his identity. So LP won't know who the user is, and the anonymous property holds in a snapshot. CL signature makes the user capable to prove knowledge of signature as mangy time as possible even to the same verifier. So users can make continuous services queries while LP won't know that the queries came from the same user. Therefore our scheme can resist correlation attack and keep identity privacy in single or continuous services queries.

Theorem 3 . The usage profiles privacy preserved if program obfuscation $\mathcal{O}$ satisfies virtual black-box property.

Proof: From the virtual black-box property of obfuscation $\mathcal{O}$, LP won't know anything about the function. The outputs of $\mathcal{O}$ are ciphertexts of $ElGamal$ encryption, LP won't know what results are they. When no data in DB matches, $\mathcal{O}$ outputs an encryption of an initial random number ans, so LP won't know that no data matches and get nothing from the execution of $\mathcal{O}$. The $ElGamal$ encryption is a scheme of CPA security, the same data encrypts twice will get different results. So LP cannot use the $\mathcal{O}$ as random oracle to test which result the user has got. The usage profiles have been preserved.

5   Conclusion and Comparison

In this paper we proposed a full privacy LBS scheme. We assume that there exist geographical or geometrical methods to form a CR. The efficiency of our scheme may be low, but we proposed the first scheme to fulfil full privacy. We use anonymous credentials system to hide the user's identity and use obfuscation of a program to protect user's usage profiles. The security of our scheme is based on the security of CL signature, CR, $obfuscation$ and so on. To find other efficient and useful function families which can provide anonymous property is our future work.

Acknowledgment. This work is supported by the National Natural Science Foundation of China (No. 61379154 and U1135001) and the Specialized Research Fund for the Doctoral Program of Higher Education.

References

1. Kofod-Petersen, A., Cassens, J.: Proxies for Privacy in Ambient Systems. JoWUA 1(4), 62–74 (2012)
2. Brakerski, Z., Rothblum, G.N.: Virtual Black-Box Obfuscation for All Circuits via Generic Graded Encoding. IACR Cryptology ePrint Archive (2013)
3. Camenisch, J., Lysyanskaya, A.: A Signature Scheme with Efficient Protocol. In: Cimato, S., Galdi, C., Persiano, G. (eds.) SCN 2002. LNCS, vol. 2576, pp. 268–289. Springer, Heidelberg (2003)
4. Damiani, M.L.: Privacy Enhancing Techniques for the Protection of Mobility Patterns in LBS: Research Issues and Trends. European Data Protection: Coming of Age (2013)
5. Damiani, M., Bertino, E., Silvestri, C.: PROBE: An Obfuscation System for the Protection of Sensitive Location Information in LBS, Technique Report 2001-145, CERIES (2008)
6. Ghinita, G.: Understanding the Privacy-Efficiency Trade-off in Location Based Queries. In: ACM APRINGL 2008, pp. 1–5 (2008)
7. Garg, S., Gentry, C., Halevi, S.: Candidate multilinear maps from ideal lattices. In: Johansson, T., Nguyen, P.Q. (eds.) EUROCRYPT 2013. LNCS, vol. 7881, pp. 1–17. Springer, Heidelberg (2013)
8. Ghinita, G., Kalnis, P., Khoshgozaran, A., Shahabi, C., Tan, K.: Private Queries in Location Based Services: Anonymizers are not Necessary. SIGMOD 2008, pp. 121-132 (2008)
9. Kalnis, P., Ghinita, G., Mouratidis, K., Papadias, D.: Preserving Location-based Identity Inference in Anonymous Spatial Queries. IEEE TKDE 19(12), 1719–1733 (2007)
10. Mokbel, M.F., Chow, C.Y., Aref, W.G.: The New Casper: Query Processing for Location Services without Compromising Privacy. In: Proceedings of VLDB, pp. 763–774 (2006)
11. Dahl, M., Delaune, S., Steel, G.: Formal Analysis of Privacy for Anonymous Location Based Services. In: Mödersheim, S., Palamidessi, C. (eds.) TOSCA 2011. LNCS, vol. 6993, pp. 98–112. Springer, Heidelberg (2012)
12. Yiu, M.L., Jensen, C., Huang, X., Lu, H.: SpaceTwist: Managing the Trade-Offs Among Location Privacy, Query Performance, and Query Accuracy in Mobile Services. In: International Conference on Data Engineering (ICDE), pp. 366–375 (2008)

Implementation of Efficient Operations over $GF(2^{32})$ Using Graphics Processing Units

Satoshi Tanaka[1,2], Takanori Yasuda[2], and Kouichi Sakurai[1,2]

[1] Kyushu University, Fukuoka, Japan
{tanasato@itslab.inf,sakurai@csce}.kyushu-u.ac.jp
[2] Institute of Systems, Information Technologies and Nanotechnologies,
Fukuoka, Japan
yasuda@isit.or.jp

Abstract. Evaluating non-linear multivariate polynomial systems over finite fields is an important subroutine, e.g., for encryption and signature verification in multivariate public-key cryptography. The security of multivariate cryptography definitely becomes lower if a larger field is used instead of $GF(2)$ given the same number of bits in the key. However, we still would like to use larger fields because multivariate cryptography tends to run faster at the same level of security if a larger field is used. In this paper, we compare the efficiency of several techniques for evaluating multivariate polynomial systems over $GF(2^{32})$ via their implementations on graphics processing units.

Keywords: Efficient implementation, multivariate public-key cryptography, GPGPU.

1 Introduction

1.1 Background

The security of the public-key cryptography depends on the complexity of math problems. Of course, the public-key cryptography uses well-known hard problems, however, some of them will be insecure in the future. For example, the security of RSA public-key cryptosystem[5] is based on the complexity of integer factorization. However, quantum computers can solve it in polynomial time[6]. Hence, RSA public-key cryptosystem is going to be insecure in the future.

Therefore, some researchers study post-quatum cryptosystemsas, none of the known quantum algorithms can solve the problem in polynomial time.. The multivariate public-key cryptosystem (MPKC) is expected a candidate of post-quatum cryptosystems. Starting from the seminal work on MPKCy [3], researchers have provided efficient signature scheme [2] and provably secure symmetric-key cipher [1]. The security of MPKC is based on the complexity of solving non-linear multivariate quadratic polymial equations over a finite field (MP), which is known as NP-complete.

Evaluating non-linear multivariate polynomial systems over a finite field is an important subroutine in MPKC. The core operations in evaluating a multivariate

Linawati et al. (Eds.): ICT-EurAsia 2014, LNCS 8407, pp. 602–611, 2014.

polynomial system are additions and multiplications over a finite field. Therefore, accelerating these operations will accelerate all multivariate cryptosystems. On the other hand, the security of a MPKC depends on the numbers of unknowns and polynomials, as well as the order of the finite field.

1.2 Related Works

Typically, $GF(2)$ and its extension fields are used in many multivariate cryptosystems, as additions over them only need cheap XOR operations. In the past, uses of $GF(2)$, $GF(2^4)$ and $GF(2^8)$ have been considered for multivariate cryptosystems [1]. For $GF(2^{16})$, multiplications are implemented by using intermediate fields of $GF(2^{16})$ on CPU and GPU[7]. Figure 1 shows the result of [7].

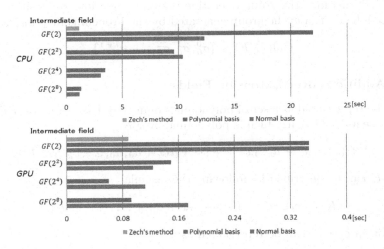

Fig. 1. The result of multiplications over $GF(2^{16})$[7]

1.3 Our Contribution

In this paper, we have simply extended to $GF(2^{32})$ case from $GF(2^{16})case$[7]. We study arithmetic operations over $GF(2^{32})$ and their implementation because we expect that they will be used for MPKC in the future.

In the following, we compare four methods for multiplications over $GF(2^{32})$ with CPU and graphics processing units (GPU) implementations.

2 Operations over Extension Fields

2.1 Extension of Finite Field

Let p be a prime, and $F = GF(p^m)$, $K = GF(p^n)(m, n \geq 1)$. Then K is an extension field of F, where $m \mid n$. We asuume that $k = n/m$, $q = p^m$. Then the Frobenius map σ_0 of K/F is defined as:

$$\sigma_0(a) = a^q.$$

σ_0 is a map from K to K. It satisfies:

1. $\sigma_0(a + b) = \sigma_0(a) + \sigma_0(b) \ \forall a, b \in K$;
2. $\sigma_0(ab) = \sigma_0(a)\sigma_0(b)$; and
3. $\sigma_0(\alpha) = \alpha \ \forall \alpha \in F$.

The Galois group $\mathrm{Gal}(K/F)$ is given by:

$$\mathrm{Gal}(K/F) = \{\sigma : K \mapsto K : automorphism | \sigma(\alpha) = \alpha \ (\forall \alpha \in F)\}.$$

The elements of a Frobenius map σ_0 are the elements of the Galois group $\mathrm{Gal}(K/F)$, in which the group operation is simply function composition. Moreover, $\mathrm{Gal}(K/F)$ is a cyclic group generated by the Frobenius map σ_0, i.e.,

$$\mathrm{Gal}(K/F) = \{\sigma_0^0, \sigma_0^1, \sigma_0^2, \ldots, \sigma_0^{k-1}\}.$$

2.2 Additions over Extension Fields

K can be represented as a set of polynomials of degrees less than k over F. Now, we choose a degree-k irreducible polynomial over F:

$$f_0(x) = x^k + a_{k-1}x^{k-1} + \cdots + a_1 x + a_0, a_0, \ldots, a_{k-1} \in F. \tag{1}$$

Then, K can be described by following the formula:

$$K = \{c_{k-1}x^{k-1} + \cdots + c_1 x + c_0 | c_0, \ldots, c_{k-1} \in F\}.$$

Addition $e_1 + e_2$ can be represented as:

$$e_1 + e_2 := e_1(x) + e_2(x) \mod f_0(x),$$

where $e_1, e_2 \in K$. Therefore, we can compute addtions over extension fields by summations of coefficients of polynomials over the base field.

2.3 Multiplications over Extension Fields

Polynomial Basis. Let K be a set of polynomials over F. Then, we can compute multiplication $e_1 * e_2$, where $e_1, e_2 \in K$, by:

$$e_1 * e_2 := e_1(x) * e_2(x) \mod f_0(x), \tag{2}$$

Zech's Method. $K^* := K \setminus \{0\}$ is a cyclic group. Therefore, K^* has a generator $\gamma \in K^*$, and $K = \langle \gamma \rangle$. Then we can represent any element in K^* as γ^ℓ, where ℓ is an integer. In particular, $\gamma^\ell \neq \gamma^{\ell'}$, $0 \leq \ell \neq \ell' \leq p^n - 2$. In this way, K^* can be represented by $[0, p^n - 2]$. Then, multiplications over K^* can be computed by integer additions modulo $p^n - 1$.

Normal Basis. There exists an $\alpha \in K$ for a finite Galois extension K/F such that $\{\sigma(\alpha)|\sigma \in \mathrm{Gal}(K/F)\}$ is an F-basis of K, which is called a normal basis of K/F. A normal basis of K/F can thus be denoted by:

$$\{\alpha, \alpha^q, \alpha^{q^2}, \ldots, \alpha^{q^{k-1}}\}. \tag{3}$$

Then, an element $a \in K$ can uniquely be written as:

$$a = c_0\alpha + c_1\alpha^{p^m} + \cdots + c_{k-1}\alpha^{p^{(k-1)m}}, \quad c_0, \ldots, c_{k-1} \in F. \tag{4}$$

Let $a = [c_0, c_1, \ldots, c_{k-1}]_n \in K$ be defined in Eq. (4). Then Frobenius map $\sigma_0(a)$ as:

$$\sigma_0(a) = a^q = [c_{k-1}, c_0, c_1, \ldots, c_{k-2}]_n. \tag{5}$$

In other words, $\sigma_0(a)$ is simply a right circular shift [4].

Furthermore, let $a = [c_0, c_1, \ldots, c_{k-1}]_n$, $b = [c'_0, c'_1, \ldots, c'_{k-1}]_n \in K$, and the result of the multiplication $a * b$ be $[d_0, d_1, \ldots, d_{k-1}]_n$. Then, every d_i, where $0 \leq i < k$, can be computed by evaluating the quadratic polynomials of $c_0, c_1, \ldots, c_{k-1}, c'_0, c'_1, \ldots, c'_{k-1}$ over F. Let $d_i = p_i(c_0, \ldots, c_{k-1}, c'_0, \ldots, c'_{k-1})$, $\forall 0 \leq i < k$. According to Eq. (5), we can compute $\sigma_0(a * b)$ by:

$$\begin{aligned}
\sigma_0(a * b) &= [d_{k-1}, d_0, d_1, \ldots, d_{k-2}]_n \\
&= \sigma_0(a) * \sigma_0(b) \\
&= [c_{k-1}, c_0, \ldots, c_{k-2}]_n * [c'_{k-1}, c'_0, \ldots, c'_{k-2}]_n \\
&= [p_0(c_{k-1}, c_0, \ldots, c_{k-2}, c'_{k-1}, c'_0, \ldots, c'_{k-2}), \ldots, \\
&\qquad p_{k-1}(c_{k-1}, c_0, \ldots, c_{k-2}, c'_{k-1}, c'_0, \ldots, c'_{k-2})]_n.
\end{aligned} \tag{6}$$

By comparing coefficients, d_{k-2} can be computed by:

$$d_{k-2} = p_{k-1}(c_{k-1}, c_0, c_1, \ldots, c_{k-2}, c'_{k-1}, c'_0, c'_1, \ldots, c'_{k-2}),$$

with Eq. (6). In the same way, we can compute $\sigma_0^2(a * b), \ldots$, for all i by doing right circular shifts and computing all the d_r's by evaluating p_{k-1}.

Multiplication Tables. We create a multiplication table by offline precomputing all combinations of multiplications over K. Then, we can compute multiplications by looking up the multiplication table.

2.4   Analysis of Multiplication Algorithms

Polynomial Basis. Let $e_1, e_2 \in K$ be $c_{k-1}x^{k-1} + \cdots + c_1x + c_0$ and $c'_{k-1}x^{k-1} + \cdots + c'_1x + c'_0$, respectively, and an irreducible polynomial f_0 be defined as Eq. (1). Then, the addition $e_1 + e_2$ needs k additions over F. On the other hand, the multiplication $e_1 * e_2$ can be computed by:

$$e_1 * e_2 = c_{k-1}c'_{k-1}x^{2k-2} + \cdots + c_0c'_0 \mod f_0(x).$$

In this method, we need compute multiplications $c_i c'_j$ for $0 \le i, j < k$ and summations $\sum_{i+j=t,i,j\ge 0} c_i c'_j$ for $0 \le t \le 2(k-1)$ over F. The summation $\sum_{i+j=t,i,j\ge 0} c_i c'_j$ needs t and $2k - t - 2$ additions for $0 \le t < k$ and $k \le t \le 2(k-1)$ respectively. Therefore, it needs $(k-1)^2$ additions and k^2 multiplications over F if schoolbook multiplication is used. Moreover, $e_1 * e_2$ takes $k\lceil \log_2 p^m \rceil \simeq n\lceil \log_2 p \rceil$ bits of memory.

Zech's Method. In this method, a multiplication over K needs one integer addition modulo $k - 1$. On the other hand, addition is not simple. Therefore, we convert it to the polynomial basis for additions and convert it back to the cyclic group representation for multiplications. Therefore, a multiplication needs three such conversions. One is for converting from polynomial to cyclic group representation, while the other is the opposite. Therefore, an addition takes k additions over F, similar to the polynomial basis representation, and a multiplication needs one integer addition modulo $k - 1$ plus three conversions between polynomial and cyclic group representations. Moreover, since the tables represent maps from K to itself, Zech's method needs $2p^n \lceil \log_2 p^n \rceil$ bits of memory.

Normal Basis. Let $a, b \in K$ be $[c_0, \ldots, c_{k-1}]_n$ and $[c'_0, \ldots, c'_{k-1}]_n$, respectively. An addition over K takes k additions over F, similar to the polynomial basis method. On the other hand, a multiplication $a * b$ takes $2(k-1)$ right circular shift operations and k evaluations of a fixed (quadratic) polynomial $p_{k-1}(c_0, \ldots, c_{k-1}, c'_0, \ldots, c'_{k-1})$. An evaluation of a quadratic polynomial takes $k^2 - 1$ additions and $2k^2$ multiplications over F. We can further speed up such an evaluation by precomputing common multiplications $c_i c_j$ over F, where $0 \le i, j \le k - 1$. Moreover, we can modify formula for c_i, c_j, c'_i, c'_j to :

$$p_{k-1}(c_0, \ldots, c_{k-1}, c'_0, \ldots, c'_{k-1})$$
$$= c_0 c'_0 + \sum_{0 \le i < j < k} s_{i,j}(c_i + c_j)(c'_i + c'_j) \; \forall (i,j), s_{i,j} \in F,$$

where $i \ne j$. Therefore, a multiplication over K needs $k(k-1)(k+2)/2$ additions and $k(k^2+1)/2$ multiplications over F plus $2(k-1)$ right circular shift operations. Moreover, the normal basis method needs $(k^2 - k + 2)\lceil \log_2 p^m \rceil/2$ bits of memory.

Multiplication Tables. An addition over K can be computed using k additions over F. On the other hand, a multiplication over K needs only one table look-up. Since the entire multiplication table needs to store every possible combination of multiplications over K, this method requires $p^{2n} \lceil \log_2 p^n \rceil$ bits of memory.

3 GPGPU via CUDA

A graphics processing unit (GPU) is a special-purpose processor for accelerating computer graphics computations. Due to the nature of its computational tasks, GPUs can handle many operations in parallel in a high speed.

General-purpose GPU (GPGPU) computing is a technique that uses GPUs for general-purpose computation. Since GPUs are designed for single instruction multiple data (SIMD) operations, they are quite efficient for parallel processing. On the other hand, they are not so efficient when there is limited amount of parallelism. Therefore, the most important task in GPGPU is to identify or manufacture parallelism in the algorithms to be implement.

3.1   CUDA API

CUDA is a development environment for NVIDIA's GPUs [8]. Before CUDA, GPGPU must have been done via hacking OpenGL or DirectX. These tools are not easy to use for non-experts of graphics programming, which was changed by the introduction of CUDA.

In CUDA, hosts correspond to computers, whereas devices correspond to GPUs. In CUDA, a host controls one or more devices attached to it. A kernel is a function that the host uses to control the device(s). In earlier CUDA, only one kernel can run at a time, and a program launches a kernel whenever parallel processes is needed. A kernel handles several number of blocks in parallel. A block also handles multiple threads in parallel. Therefore, a kernel can handle many threads simultaneously.

3.2   Parallelization for CUDA Implementations

In CUDA API, we should consider how parallelize algorithms on GPUs. Especially, the number of threads in each block is important. This number is defined by GPUs. For example, NVIDIA GeForce 580 GTX can use 1,024 threads in each block registers. On the other hand, this number is alsor confined by the number of registers in blocks. Every thread use different registers for variables in kernels. When the total number of registers in every thread is greater than the number of registers in blocks, GPUs shows unexpected behavior (e.g. GPUs are halted). Therefore, we should parallelize algorithms for threads lest numbers of threads is greater than these GPU limitations.

4   Multiplications over $GF(2^{32})$

We can use XOR operations for computing additions over $GF(2)$. Moreover, multiplications over $GF(2)$ can be computed by the logical conjunctions AND.

4.1   Costs of Multiplications over $GF(2^{32})$

Table 1 shows the costs of multiplications over $GF(2^{32})$.

The polynomial basis method and the normal basis method need a lot more computational cost. On the other hand, Zech's method and using multiplication table are impractical, as it needs 32 GBytes and 64 EBytes of memory space, respectively.

Table 1. Costs of multiplications over $GF(2^{32})$

Methods	Computational cost	Memory space
Polynomial basis method	961 XOR + 1,024 AND + 1 MOD	4 Byte
Zech's method	1 ADD + 1 MOD + 3 LOOKUP	32 GByte
Normal basis method	16,864 XOR + 16,400 AND + 2 SHIFT	125 Byte
Multiplication table	1 LOOKUP	64 EByte

4.2   Using Intermediate Fields

Although the multiplication table method is impractical for $GF(2^{32})$, it is possible for $GF(2^8)$, as the table there requires only 256 KByte. Also, Zech's method over $GF(2^{32})$ needs just 256 KByte. Here, we consider a method using an intermediate field $GF(2^l)$ for $GF(2^{32})/GF(2)$, where $l = 2, 4, 8, 16$. In this method, we can compute multiplications over $GF(2^{32})$ by considering it as an extension field over $GF(2^l)$ and by using the polynomial basis method or the normal basis method. For example, since the extension degree $k = 4$ for $GF(2^{32})/GF(2^8)$, we can compute multiplication over $GF(2^{32})$ by 9 additions over $GF(2^8)$(72 XORs), 16 table look-ups, and one modulo over $GF(2^8)$ with the polynomial basis method, or 288 XORs and 34 table look-ups with the normal basis method.

Similarly, we estimate the computational costs of multiplications over $GF(2^{32})$ using $GF(2^2)$, $GF(2^4)$ or $GF(2^{16})$. We show the computational costs of multiplications over $GF(2^{32})$ using these intermediate fields in Table 2.

Table 2. Costs of multiplications over $GF(2^{32})$ using intermediate fields

Intermediate field $GF(2^l)$	Computation method		Computational cost				Memory space
	$GF(2^l)/GF(2)$	$GF(2^{32})/GF(2^l)$	XOR	LOOKUP	MOD	ADD	
$GF(2^2)$	Multiplication table	Polynomial basis	450	512	1	-	6B
		Normal basis	4,320	4,112	-	-	35B
$GF(2^4)$		Polynomial basis	196	256	1	-	132B
		Normal basis	1,120	1,040	-	-	143B
$GF(2^8)$		Polynomial basis	72	128	1	-	64kB+4B
		Normal basis	288	272	-	-	64kB+4B
$GF(2^{16})$	Zech's method	Polynomial basis	16	12	4	4 + 1	256kB+4B
		Normal Basis	64	15	5	5	256kB+4B

5   Experimentation

We implement the three basic multiplication methods, namely, polynomial basis, Zech's method, and normal basis, over $GF(2^{32})$ on CPU and GPU. We evaluate and compare the running time of 67,108,864 multiplications with random elements over $GF(2^{32})$ for each methods. Similarly, we also implement and perform the same experiment using intermediate fields as follows:

1. Multiplication table + polynomial basis method:
   $GF(2^{32})/GF(2^k)/GF(2)$ $(k = 1, 2, 4, 8)$
2. Multiplication table + normal basis method:
   $GF(2^{32})/GF(2^k)/GF(2)$ $(k = 1, 2, 4, 8)$
3. Zech's method + polynomial basis method:
   $GF(2^{32})/GF(2^{16})/GF(2)$
4. Zech's method + normal basis method:
   $GF(2^{32})/GF(2^{16})/GF(2)$

Moreover, we describe primitive polynomials for each field extensions.

1. $GF(2^{32})/GF(2)$:
   $Y^{32} + Y^{22} + Y^2 + Y + 1 = 0$
2. $GF(2^{32})/GF(2^2)/GF(2)$:
   $Y^{16} + Y^3 + Y + X = 0$
3. $GF(2^{32})/GF(2^4)/GF(2)$:
   $Y^8 + Y^3 + Y + X = 0$
4. $GF(2^{32})/GF(2^8)/GF(2)$:
   $X^4 + Y^2 + (X + 1)Y + (X^3 + 1) = 0$
5. $GF(2^{32})/GF(2^{16})/GF(2)$:
   $Y^2 + Y + X^{13} = 0$

5.1 Environment of Implementation

All the experiments are performed on Ubuntu 10.04 LTS 64bit, Intel Core i7 875K and NVIDIA GeForce 580 GTX with 8 GBytes of DDR3 memory.

Table 3 shows constructions of parallelizations of 67,108,864 multiplications on NVIDIA GeForce 580 GTX for each multiplication method.

Table 3. Constructions of parallelizations on NVIDIA GeForce 580 GTX

Intermediate field $GF(2^l)$	Polynomial basis			Normal basis		
	Block	Thread	Iteration	Block	Thread	Iteration
$GF(2)$	32,768	32	64	32,768	32	64
$GF(2^2)$	32,768	128	16	32,768	128	64
$GF(2^4)$	32,768	512	4	32,768	512	4
$GF(2^8)$	32,768	512	4	32,768	512	4
$GF(2^{16})$	32,768	512	4	32,768	512	4

5.2   Experiment Results

We show the result of implementations in Figure 2.

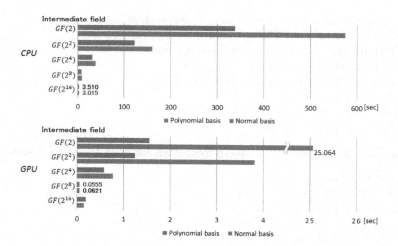

Fig. 2. Experimental result of multiplications over $GF(2^{32})$

In CPU implementations, the normal basis method using $GF(2^{16})$ is the fastest, possibly because it needs the fewest computations among every method.

On the other hand, in GPU implementations, the polynomial basis method using $GF(2^8)$ for the intermediate field is the fastest. We believe that the GPU cannot efficiently access the tables in Zech's method over $GF(2^8)$, as these tables are too large to fit into the fast memory on GPU.

6   Conclusions

In this work, we have implemented and compare of several multiplication methods over $GF(2^{32})$. In CPU implementations, the normal basis method using $GF(2^{16})$ is the fastest. The second fastest is the polynomial method over $GF(2^{16})$. On the other hand, for GPU implementations, it seems that $GF(2^8)$ is a very efficient intermediate field for building extension fields over it. Comparing CPU and GPU implementations, the fastest GPU implementation is about 49 times faster than the fastest one on the CPU. However, our GPU implementations are just parallelized CPU ones. We expect our research makes enables to enhance the security of MPKC by converting small finite fields (like $GF(2^8)$) to $GF(2^{32})$.

In future work, we would like to discuss optimizing multiplication methods for both CPU and GPU. Moreover, we would like to evaluate MPKCs using our implementaions.

Acknowledgement. This work is partly supported by "Study on Secure Cryptosystem using Multivariate Polynomial System," no. 0159-0172, Strategic Information and Communications R&D Promotion Programme, the Ministry of Internal Affairs and Communications, Japan, Grants for Excellent Graduate Schools, the Ministry of Education Culture, Sports, Science and Technology, Japan and "The Constitutive Theory of Non-Interactive Zero-Knowledge Proof based on Probability Certification and Practical Enhancement to the Cryptography," no. 25540004, Grant-in-Aid for Challenging Exploratory Research, Japan Society for the Promotion of Science. The authors are grateful to Xavier Dahan for his valuable comments on our proposal.

References

1. Berbain, C., Gilbert, H., Patarin, J.: QUAD: A Practical Stream Cipher with Provable Security. In: Vaudenay, S. (ed.) EUROCRYPT 2006. LNCS, vol. 4004, pp. 109–128. Springer, Heidelberg (2006)
2. Ding, J., Schmidt, D.: Rainbow, a new multivariable polynomial signature scheme. In: Ioannidis, J., Keromytis, A.D., Yung, M. (eds.) ACNS 2005. LNCS, vol. 3531, pp. 164–175. Springer, Heidelberg (2005)
3. Matsumoto, T., Imai, H.: Public quadratic polynomial-tuples for efficient signature-verification and message-encryption. In: Günther, C.G. (ed.) EUROCRYPT 1988. LNCS, vol. 330, pp. 419–453. Springer, Heidelberg (1988)
4. Menezes, A.J., van Oorschot, P.C., Vanstone, S.A.: Handboook of Applied Cryptography. CRC Press (1997)
5. Rivest, R.L., Shamir, A., Adleman, L.: A method for obtaining digital signatures and public-key cryptosystems. Communications of the ACM 21(2), 120–126 (1978)
6. Shor, P.W.: Algorithms for quantum computation. In: Discrete Logarithms and Factoring (1994)
7. Tanaka, S., Yasuda, T., Yang, B.-Y., Cheng, C.-H., Sakurai, K.: Efficient Computing over $GF(2^{16})$ using Graphics Processing Unit. In: The Seventh International Workshop on Advances in Information Security (2013)
8. NVidia Developer Zone,
https://developer.nvidia.com/category/zone/cuda-zone

M-SRS: Secure and Trustworthy Mobile Service Review System Based on Mobile Cloudlet

Tao Jiang[1], Xiaofeng Chen[1,*], Jin Li[2], and Jianfeng Ma[1]

[1] State Key Laboratory of Integrated Service Networks (ISN),
Xidian University, Xi'an, P.R. China
jiangt2009@gmail.com, {xfchen,jfma}@xidian.edu.cn
[2] School of Computer Science, Guangzhou University, China
lijin@gzhu.edu.cn

Abstract. The scope of services has skyrocketed to such an extent that it is necessary for the service consumers to quickly understand the quality of a service provided by different vendors through Service Review Systems (SRS). In this paper, we consider the trustworthyness of a SRS without a trusted review management center in location-based Service-oriented Mobile Social Networks (S-MSNs). Firstly, we broach some review statistic modification attacks, which are very important for service consumers to review a service. Secondly, the M-SRS network model based on Mobile Cloud Computing (MCC) is constructed, which could protect the security and reduce the communication and computation overhead. Also, data entanglement and verifiable service utilization tickets are adopted to prevent proposed attacks in existing SRS and guarantee the trustworthyness of the statistic SRS. Final results show that M-SRS could effectively resist the existing service review attacks, and it is efficient in terms of review submission and review authenticity verification for the whole system.

Keywords: cloud computing, mobile social networks, location-based service, service review, security, trustworthyness.

1 Introduction

Service review system (SRS) is designed to identify potential service delivery improvements, which contains the feedback of users such as compliments and complains about the services or products from service consumers. Typically, SRS is maintained by a trusted part in some popular Internet based social network such as Facebook. Unlike those global wide service whose service reviews are maintained by a trusted third part, the local service providers are interested mainly in their geographic vicinity and maintain a SRS by themselves.

Service-oriented Mobile Social Networks (S-MSNs) are composed of static service providers (vendors) and mobile service consumers (users). The vendors, such as restaurants and grocery stores, can provide Location-Based Services (LBSs)

---

* Corresponding author.

Linawati et al. (Eds.): ICT-EurAsia 2014, LNCS 8407, pp. 612–621, 2014.
© IFIP International Federation for Information Processing 2014

for mobile users. The LBSs can be embedded into various kinds of networks to obtain different applications [7, 8, 13, 14]. The security and privacy problems of LBSs in MSN have been widely discussed [1, 3, 11, 15]. On the contrary, in this paper, we mainly consider the security and privacy of SRSs managed by a selfish vendor, in which the vendor may be incented to conduct malicious activity on the reviews. Aiming at this problem, Liang et al. [10] designed a scheme SEER to protect against a selfish vendor from rejecting or deleting negative reviews or inserting forged positive ones to increase its reputation.

Based on SEER, we further study the fundamental security challenges of the SRSs without trust review managers.Correlation analysis of SEER shows that it is impossible for the vendor to drop or modify a review according to the ring structure, and the scheme has high submission rate and low submission delay. However, we find that, in SEER, a malicious vendor could always do the selective review deletion of rings that provide the negative effect, and there is no mechanism to check whether the reviews of some rings submitted before are deleted by the vendor. Also, the SRS that provides general ratings is not secure against the review statistical results forgery attack.

In this paper, we present general framework for secure and efficient SRS based on data entanglement. In our framework, mobile cloudlet, identity based aggregate signature could be adopted to improve the efficiency of our schemes, and the pseudonym technology is a secretive module for protecting the privacy of users in the SRS. It is shown that our entangled review submission method provides a strong protection on all reviews. The malicious activity of a vendor will be found with a very high probability, even if a small fraction of the reviews is destroyed. Specially, when each user provides an entanglement of 10 reviews, about 40 users, who submit reviews, will detect the malicious behavior of the vendor with 99% probability, when only 1% reviews are destroyed. The probability that a vendor conducts malicious activity on users' reviews, without being detected, decreases with the increase of new reviews submission.

2   Preliminaries

Let k be the security parameter and H be a cryptographic hash function. In addition, we make use of a pseudo-random permutation (PRP) π with the following parameters: $\pi : \{0,1\}^k \times \{0,1\}^{log_2(n)} \to \{0,1\}^{log_2(n)}$. We write $\pi_k(x)$ to denote π keyed with key k applied on input x.

Bilinear Maps: Let $\mathbb{G}_1$ and $\mathbb{G}_2$ be two cyclic groups of some large prime order q. We write $\mathbb{G}_1$ additively and $\mathbb{G}_2$ multiplicatively. We will call $\hat{e}$ an admissible pairing if $\hat{e} : \mathbb{G}_1 \times \mathbb{G}_1 \to \mathbb{G}_2$ is a map with the following properties:

1. Bilinear: $\hat{e}(aQ, bR) = \hat{e}(Q, R)^{ab}$ for all $Q, R \in \mathbb{G}_1$ and all $a, b \in \mathbb{Z}$.
2. Non-degenerate: $\hat{e}(Q, R) \neq 1$ for some $Q, R \in \mathbb{G}_1$.
3. Computable: There is an efficient algorithm to compute $\hat{e}(Q, R)$ for any $Q, R \in \mathbb{G}_1$.

Since $\hat{e}$ is bilinear and $\mathbb{G}_1$ is a cyclic group, it means that $\hat{e}$ is also symmetric. Then, we get $\hat{e}(Q, R) = \hat{e}(R, Q)$ for all $Q, R \in \mathbb{G}_1$.

3   Network Model and Attacks

In this section, the network model of S-MSN is described, over which we further propose our M-SRS.

3.1   Network Model

S-MSN is a network consists of multiple vendors that provide services to users, in which vendors maintain an SRS independently for themselves to provide public servers reviews for the services they provide. The vendor is equipped with a static wireless communication device and it has a large storage space and computational capabilities. Each user has a hand-held device with smaller communicational transmission range and computational capabilities than that of the vendor.

Users spontaneously form different social groups according to their common interests in an S-MSN. We suppose that there are v social groups $\{G_1, ..., G_v\}$ and denote I_u the universal interest set. Also, we denote the interest set of a social group G_i by $I_i(I_i \subseteq I_u)$ for $1 \leq i \leq u$. Each user u_j belongs to at least one social group and it inherits the interests of those social groups. Thus, the interest set of u_j is $S_j = \cup_i I_i$, where u_j is a member of G_i. The vendors, tagged by interests, periodically disseminate their up-to-date service information including service description and reviews to users. The integrity and unforgeability of such service information will be ensured by using a public/private key pairs of the vendors.

The membership management of every group $G_i(1 \leq i \leq u)$ is relied on an offline trusted authority TA. It has a public/private key pair (pk, sk), and publishes the public key to all users. Every user u_j has a unique identity ID_j and it is used for the TA to verify the validity of u_j when u_j joins group G_i.

In our network model, there are four entities, namely the users, the vendors, the mobile cloudlet (MC) composed of users and a trusted authority (TA).

3.2   Attack Model

The vendor will be able to conduct the following statistical review attacks:

- **Colluded Review Injection Attack:** Colluded review injection attack is launched by the vendor, where the selfish vendor conspires with some malicious users and submits some positive reviews without being detected.
- **Selective Review Delete Attack:** Selective review delete attack is conducted by a malicious vendor by deleting one or a set of target reviews in the service review system, where a vendor could find out and delete those negative reviews without being detected.

– **Review Statistical Results Forgery Attack:** Review statistical results forgery is an attack conducted by malicious vendors. In the attack, a malicious vendor will just provide a false statistical result of its service when the number of reviews in the SRS is too large and the users are not able or unwilling to calculate.

4 The M-SRS System

In this section, we elaborate on review entanglement based on mobile cloudlet and then describe the detail processes of the review generation and submission in M-SRS.

4.1 Reviews Entanglement and Mobile Cloudlet

In our M-SRS, to prevent from a lucrative opportunity in altering or simply neglecting to keep the negative review result in M-SRS, we adopt review entanglement to link the fate of reviews. Thus, according to the definition of *entangled* in [2], the fate of a review will be linked to at least t other reviews that a malicious vendor cannot hope to offend them all with impunity.

We adopt mobile cloudlets [12] to serve users, which is one network structure of the mobile cloud computing (MCC) [4, 5, 9]. It is a small cloud composed through the cooperation of mobile users and vendors nearby. The mobile cloudlet will assist the users to transmit or verify the message of users and vendors in our network. We assume that the public users are justice and it is difficult for a vendor to bribe all the users in the cloudlet. Thus, we consider that the cloudlet will always provide trusted activity in the processes of reviews submission of users in our M-SRS.

4.2 Constructions

The details of the construction of our M-SRS are elaborated as follows.

System Setup. The system setup phase initializes the necessary parameters in the following two steps:

Step1: The member management of a group relies on the offline trusted authority TA. TA initializes its public/private key pair (pk_{TA}, sk_{TA}) and publishes the public key pk_{TA} to all users in the network.

Step2: Every user u_j has a unique identity ID_j when an identity based signature scheme [6] is adopted to implement the membership of the system. When u_j joins the G_h, TA will verify the validity of the identity ID_j of u_j. We will identify the user as $ID_{h,j}$, when user ID_j joins a group G_h.

Review Generation and Submission. After being served by a vendor V, a user u_j will get a ticket TK as an evidence to prove that the user does enjoy the service and has the right to submit its review for the service. When u_j wants to generate a review for the service, it conducts a review generation process in the following steps.

Step1: The user u_j generates a random seed s. On inputting s, u_j computes coefficients $a_i = \pi_s(i)$ where $1 \leq i \leq t$.

Step2: When the vendor is within the communication range,

1. u_j will directly send the seed s to the vendor V in a verifiable message $Msg_{h,j} = ID_{h,j}|ID_V|\ TK_{h,j}|s_{h,j}|T_{h,j}|\sigma_{h,j}$ where $T_{h,j}$ is current time stamp and $\sigma_{h,j} = Sign_{sk_{h,j}}(ID_{h,j}\ ID_V|TK_{h,j}|s_{h,j}|T_{h,j,1})$ is the signature of the content of the message using its secret key $sk_{h,j}$. Otherwise, the seed s will be sent to the vendor through the mobile cloudlet around the vendor in an indirect way as shown in Step 3.

2. When V receives $Msg_{h,j}$, it will check the validity of the$Msg_{h,j}$ and $TK_{h,j}$. If both of the $Msg_{h,j,1}$ and $TK_{h,j}$ pass the validity test, V will compute coefficients $a_i = f_s(i)$ where $1 \leq i \leq t$ and send the review set $REV_{a_i}(1 \leq i \leq t)$, and the last review REV_N in the system to the u_j as shown bellow.

$$REV_{a_i} = KID|ID_{u,j}|ID_V|TK_{a_i}|s_{a_i}|T_{a_i}|Com_{a_i}|Rat_{a_i}|E_{a_i}|GRat_{KID-1}|$$
$$GRat_{KID}|\sigma_{h,*} \tag{1}$$

In the REV_{a_i}, $KID = a_i$ is the unique identity of a review, Com_{a_i} is the comment of the user with pseudonym $ID_{h,*}$, $Rat_{h,*}$ is the score for the service of the user, $E_{h,*}$ is the entangled message of t other reviews, $GRat_{KID}$ is the general rating of the SRS provided by the vendor. When review REV_{a_i} is submitted to the vendor, $\sigma_{h,*}$is the signature of the review content from a user of the group, which is used to verify the authenticity of the review.

$$\sigma_{h,*} = Sign_{sk_V}(KID|ID_{h,*}|ID_V|TK_{h,*}|s_{h,*}|T_{h,*}|Com_{h,*}|Rat_{h,*}|E_{h,*}|$$
$$GRat_{KID-1}|GRat_{KID}) \tag{2}$$

For example, $GRat$ is the average of all review Rats in the system which is used for rating a service in different aspects, and the value ot $GRat_{KID}$ is

$$GRat_{KID} = \frac{GRat_{KID-1}(KID-1) + Rat_{KID}}{KID}, \tag{3}$$

when all the general ratings are correctly computed.

3. When u_j receives the t reviews according to the seed $s_{h,j}$, it will verify the correctness of the $t + 1$ reviews. If they pass the validity test, then u_j computes $e_{a_i} = H(REV_{a_i})(1 \leq i \leq t)$ and entangled data $E_{h,j} = \oplus_{i=1}^t e_{a_i}$ and then generates its review REV_{N+1} as show in (2):

$$REV_{N+1} = N + 1|ID_{h,j}|ID_V|TK_{N+1}|s_{N+1}|T_{N+1}|Com_{N+1}|Rat_{N+1}|E_{N+1}|$$
$$GRat_N|GRat_{N+1}|\sigma_{N+1}. \tag{4}$$

In REV_{N+1}, we have $Tk_{N+1} = TK_{h,j}$ and $s_{N+1} = s_{h,j}$ as sent in message $Msg_{h,j}$.

Step3: In the indirect seed submission phase, the message $Msg_{h,j}$ is sent to MC, which will verify the validity of the message and forward $Msg_{h,j}$ to the vendor V. Since the mobile is considered as a trusted part in our network model, the verification of t random reviews as shown in Step 2.2 and the generation of the entangled data as shown in Step2.3 are conducted by MC instead of u_j. After generating $E_{h,j}$, MC will designate a valid user u_* of the MC to send $E_{h,j}$ to u_j in a message $Msg_{u_*} = ID_{u,*}|ID_{u,j}|s_{N+1}|T_{u,*}|E_{N+1}|GRat_N|\sigma_{u,j}$. Then, the only thing u_j needs to do is to verify the integrity of $E_{h,j}$ and generate its review $Msg_{h,j}$.

Review Submission

u_j submits its review $Msg_{h,j}$ to the vendor V. When V receives the review, it will firstly verify the validity of $Msg_{h,j}$ and $TK_{h,j}$. Then, it assigns a unique identity KID for $Msg_{h,j}$ and computes the general rating $Grat$ of the service according to the review of u_j. If the review is legitimate, u_j will store and publish the review in its local repository. Review submission may be conducted directly between the vendor and users when they are in the communication range of each other. However, when the vendor is out of a user's communication range, the MC will cooperate with users and help them to verify the authenticity of vendor's activity and forward the review of users.

4.3   Efficient and Privacy Preserve M-SRSs

Notice that it is important to improve the efficiency of the system and protect the privacy of users in our M-SRS. The identity based aggregate signature and pseudonyms could be adopted.

Efficient M-SRS Based on Aggregate Signature(EM-SRS). The detail of EM-SRS will be instantiated as bellow.

Setup: The Private Key Generator (PKG) generates parameters and keys essentially as bellow. Specifically, the TA:

1. generates groups $\mathbb{G}_1$ and $\mathbb{G}_2$ of prime order q and an admissible pairing $\hat{e} : \mathbb{G}_1 \times \mathbb{G}_1 \to \mathbb{G}_2$;
2. chooses an arbitrary generator $P \in \mathbb{G}_1$;
3. picks a random $s \in \mathbb{Z}/q\mathbb{Z}$ and sets $Q = sP$;
4. chooses a cryptographic hash functions $H_1, H_2 : \{0,1\}^* \to \mathbb{G}_1$ and $H_3 : \{0,1\}^* \to \mathbb{Z}/q\mathbb{Z}$.

The published system parameters are $params = (\mathbb{G}_1, \mathbb{G}_2, \hat{e}, P, Q, H_1, H_2, H_3)$. The root PKG's secret is $s \in \mathbb{Z}/q\mathbb{Z}$.

User Private Key Generation: The user u_j with identity ID_j receives from the TA the secret key $sk_j = sP_{j,i}$ for $i \in \{0,1\}$, where $P_{j,i} = H_1(ID_j, i) \in \mathbb{G}_1$.

Individual Signing: The vendor chooses a random string Str that has never been used before and publishes it to its group members. When u_j wants to sign the review content $\alpha_j = ID_{h,j}|TK_{h,j}|s_{h,j}|T_{h,j}|Com_{h,j}|Rat_{h,j}|E_{h,j}$, ID_j will:

1. computes $P_{Str} = H_2(Str) \in \mathbb{G}_1$;
2. computes $c_j = H_3(m_j, ID_j, Str) \in \mathbb{Z}/q\mathbb{Z}$;
3. generates a random number $r_j \in \mathbb{Z}/q\mathbb{Z}$;
4. computes the signature $\sigma_j = (Str, S'_j, T'_j)$, where $S'_j = r_j P_{Str} + sP_{j,0} + c_j sP_{j,1}$ and $T'_j = r_j P$.

When a user requires t random reviews from the vendor, it could conduct the signature aggregation as follows.

Aggregation: Every user in the group can aggregate a collection of individual signatures that uses the same string Str. For example, individual signatures (Str, S'_j, T'_j) for $1 \leq j \leq t$ can be aggregated into $\sigma = (Str, S_t, T_t)$, where $S_t = \sum_{j=1}^{t} S'_j$ and $T_t = \sum_{j=1}^{t} T'_j$.

Verification: Let σ be the identity-based aggregate signature. The user could check the validity of the t reviews from the vendor, as shown in the following formula.

$$\hat{e}(S_t, P) \stackrel{?}{=} \hat{e}(T_t, P_{Str})\hat{e}(Q, \sum_{j=1}^{t} P_{i,0} + \sum_{j=1}^{t} c_j P_{j,1}) \tag{5}$$

Privacy Preserve M-SRS Based on Pseudonyms (PPM-SRS). In the identity based pseudonyms, pseudonyms can be used for vendors and other users to verify the message of the user. Thus, if the reviews are associated with pseudonyms, the vendors and other users are able to check the authenticity of the reviews and TA is able to trace the reviews generated by their group members.

5   Security Analysis

In this section, we show that M-SRS is secure with respect to the following security analysis.

5.1   Security against Selective Review Delete Attack

In the situation that some users synchronously submit their reviews, they could entangle the reviews of other users and submit the entangled review IDs for other user to verify.

The following theorem indicates that the selective review delete attack can be detected with high probability.

Theorem 1. *The vendor is able to delete reviews without being detected with high probability if and only if the reviews are not entangled by other reviews stored in the SRS.*

Proof. Suppose that the vendor deletes a set of reviews in the SRS and there are still a set of valid reviews SET containing the entangled data of those deleted reviews stored in the system. Then, since the signature scheme adopted in our scheme is secure, a malicious vendor could not modify the content of the reviews stored in the system. The malicious activity of the vendor will be detected by the users who submit a review that requires to check the correctness of the reviews in SET. The probability that some user detects the selective review delete relies on the probability that a user needs to generate entangled data using a reviews in SET. According to the more detailed detection probability of selective review delete attack below, even a small fraction of reviews is deleted by the vendor, the users will be able to detect this malicious behaviour with high probability when those deleted reviews are entangled by some other reviews stored in the system. It means that a malicious vendor needs to delete all the entangled reviews in the system to avoid being detected, and this completes the proof.

We now analyse the probabilistic guarantees offered by our scheme. According to the construction of our scheme, each review $REV_i (1 \leq i \leq N)$ stores an entangled data E_i generated from t random previous reviews according to a random seed s_i. Even if one of the t review is deleted or modified, a user would not be able to generate a validate entangled data E_i' with $E_i' = E_i$. Therefore, we assume that there are N reviews stored in the SRS of a vendor. The vendor V deletes c out of N reviews in its SRS. Let t be the number of different reviews a user U asks for entangling in its review. Let X be a discrete random variable that is defined to be the number of reviews chosen by U that matches the reviews that deleted by the vendor. We compute P_X, the probability that at least one of the reviews picked by the user matches one of the reviews deleted by the vendor. We have:

$$P_X = P\{X \geq 1\} = 1 - P\{X = 0\} = 1 - \frac{n-c}{n} \cdot \ldots \cdot \frac{n-t+1-c}{n-t-1} \qquad (6)$$

Because we have $\frac{n-i-c}{n-i} \geq \frac{n-i-1-c}{n-i-1}$. It follows that:

$$1 - (\frac{n-c}{n})^t \leq P_X \leq 1 - (\frac{n-t-1-c}{n-c-1})^t \qquad (7)$$

P_X indicates the probability that, if V deletes c blocks of the file, then U will detect vendor misbehaviour after a review submission in which it asks proof for t blocks. Fig. 1 plots P_X for different values of N, t, c. When c is a fraction of the file, U can detect vendor misbehaviour with a certain probability by asking proof for a constant amount of reviews, independently of the total number of file blocks: e.g., if $c = 1\%$ of N, then u asks for 460 blocks and 300 blocks in order to achieve P_X of at least 99% and 95%, respectively.

We assume that P_Y is the probability that at least one of the reviews picked by v different users matches one of the reviews deleted by the vendor. Also, we assume that the vt randomly selected reviews are different from each other. Then, we have:

$$1 - (\frac{n-c}{n})^{tv} \leq P_Y \leq 1 - (\frac{n-t-1-c}{n-c-1})^{tv} \qquad (8)$$

It is obvious that, the communication and computation overhead of users (in M-SRS) and the mobile cloudlet (in EM-SRS) increase with t. Formula (8) shows

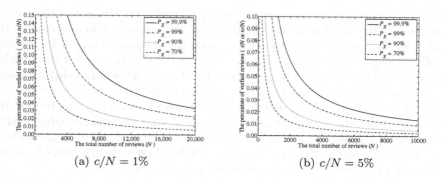

(a) $c/N = 1\%$ (b) $c/N = 5\%$

Fig. 1. The detection probability of review deletion

The figures show that our scheme could provide a very high selective review deletion attack detection probability, when the review number is significantly large and only a small fraction of reviews are deleted by the malicious vendor.

that the high detection probability could be realized according to the contribution of different users. Meanwhile, assuming that the vt reviews are different, we could also detect selective review deletion attack with high probability as show in Fig. 1.

5.2   General Review Results Security

According to the above analysis, our scheme is secure against the review modification, injection and deletion attack. Therefore, the security of the general review results of our scheme can be analyzed through the following two aspects when a user provides a review with wrong general review results.

First, when a user provides a wrong negative review, the vendor will detect the malicious of the user and then reject the review or ask the user to calculate a new review with right general review results.

Second, when a user provides a wrong positive review, a selfish vendor may accept and store the reviews in its system. However, the general review results are public verifiable, the new review submitter and the users in the mobile cloudlet will find the malicious activity of the vendor. The probability for users to detect this malicious activity of vendor is the same as the probability analysis shown in section 5.1.

6   Conclusion

The mobile cloudlet assisted SRS is introduced in this paper, in which the review entanglement and some identity based signature schemes are adopted to guarantee the security and improve the efficiency. The solutions provide a verification of the vendor's malicious activity with high probability for the whole reviews in the SRS. Also, it shows that our efficient schemes will significantly reduce the computational and communicational overhead of users by adopting mobile cloudlet.

Acknowledgement. This work is supported by the National Natural Science Foundation of China (Nos. 61272455 and 61100224), Doctoral Fund of Ministry of Education of China (No. 20130203110004), Program for New Century Excellent Talents in University (No. NCET-13-0946), and China 111 Project (No. B08038).

References

1. Aspnes, J., et al.: A critical evaluation of location based services and their potential. Journal of Location Based Services 1(1), 5–45 (2007)
2. Aspnes, J., et al.: Towards a theory of data entanglement. Theoretical Computer Science 389(1-2), 26–43 (2007)
3. Dhar, S., Varshney, U.: Challenges and business models for mobile location-based services and advertising. Communications of the ACM 54(5), 121–128 (2011)
4. Dinh, H., et al.: A survey of mobile cloud computing: architecture, applications, and approaches. Wireless Communications and Mobile Computing 1(1), 1–25 (2011)
5. Fernando, N., Loke, S., Rahayu, W.: Mobile cloud computing: a survey. Future Generation Computer Systems 29(1), 84–106 (2013)
6. Gentry, C., Ramzan, Z.: Identity-based aggregate signatures. In: Yung, M., Dodis, Y., Kiayias, A., Malkin, T. (eds.) PKC 2006. LNCS, vol. 3958, pp. 257–273. Springer, Heidelberg (2006)
7. Ghinita, G., et al.: Private queries in location based services: anonymizers are not necessary. In: Proc. ACM International Conference on Management of data (SIGMOD 2008), NY, USA, pp. 121–132 (April 2008)
8. Hengartner, U.: Location privacy based on trusted computing and secure logging. In: Proc. ACM International Conference on Security and Privacy in Communication Netowrks (SecureComm 2008), Waterloo, Canada, pp. 22–25 (September 2008)
9. Khan, A., et al.: Towards secure mobile cloud computing: A survey. Future Generation Computer Systems 29(5), 1278–1299 (2013)
10. Liang, X.: et al.: Seer: A secure and efficient service review system for service-oriented mobile social networks. In: Proc. IEEE International Conference on Distributed Computing Systems (ICDCS 2012), Macau, China, pp. 647–656 (June 2012)
11. Pan, X., Xu, J., Meng, X.: Protecting location privacy against location-dependent attacks in mobile services. IEEE Transactions on Knowledge and Data Engineering 24(8), 1506–1519 (2011)
12. Satyanarayanan, M., et al.: The case for vm-based cloudlets in mobile computing. IEEE Pervasive Computing 8(4), 14–23 (2009)
13. Tsai, H., Chen, T., Chu, C.: Service discovery in mobile ad hoc networks based on grid. IEEE Transactions on Vehicular Technology 58(3), 1528–1545 (2009)
14. Zhang, Y., Wu, Z., Trappe, W.: Adaptive location-oriented content delivery in delay-sensitive pervasive applications. IEEE Transactions on Mobile Computing 10(3), 362–376 (2011)
15. Zhu, Z., Cao, G.: Towards privacy-preserving and colluding-resistance in location proof updating system. IEEE Transactions on Mobile Computing 12(1), 51–64 (2011)

High-Quality Reversible Data Hiding Approach Based on Evaluating Multiple Prediction Methods

Cheng-Hsing Yang, Kuan-Liang Liu, Chun-Hao Chang,
and Yi-Jhong Jhang

Department of Computer Science, National Pingtung University of Education, Pingtung,
Taiwan 900
chyang@mail.npue.edu.tw,
{tony3161515,chanangsmj5210,at20021006}@gmail.com

Abstract. Reversible data hiding based on prediction methods is a good technique that can hide secret bits into cover images efficiently. In this paper, we propose a reversible data hiding method based on four candidates of prediction methods and local complexity for enhancing stego-image quality. In our proposed method, before we embed the secret message in one level, we evaluate the four prediction methods by calculating their efficiency ratios to decide which prediction method will be used. When the selected prediction method is applied, a threshold based on local complexity is used to determine which pixel should join the shifting and embedding process. Therefore, more pixels will avoid executing the process of pixel shifting. It results in stego-images with lower distortion. The experimental results show that our image quality is superior to that of other approaches at the same capacity.

Keywords: Reversible Data Hiding, Variance, Image Quality, Prediction.

1 Introduction

Reversible data hiding is a branch of data hiding. A reversible data hiding approach indicates that the original digital content can be completely recovered after the data extracting process is executed [1-2]. So far, many applications adopt the technique of reversible data hiding, such as military map, medical image [3, 4], law text, and so on.

Several reversible data hiding schemes have been proposed [5-23]. According to those literatures, the techniques in reversible data hiding could be divided into three categories. One is the difference expansion (DE for shorting) [8-10], another is histogram-based [11, 12], and the other is a hybrid. Here, the hybrid reversible data hiding indicates that the developer takes the combination of DE and predicted error (PE for shorting) or histogram-based and PE into consideration, and creates other views in the reversible data hiding scheme [13-23]. The hybrid reversible data hiding scheme is an improvement of DE or Histogram-based. The key point of hybrid reversible data hiding is prediction-based. Unlike in DE where only relation with two adjacent pixels is considered and Histogram-based where no relation is considered, prediction-based methods exploit the local relation between the current pixel and its predicted value.

Linawati et al. (Eds.): ICT-EurAsia 2014, LNCS 8407, pp. 622–632, 2014.
© IFIP International Federation for Information Processing 2014

Meanwhile, many valuable hybrid approaches have been proposed, such as Lin et al.'s multilevel scheme [13], Tsai et al.'s predictive coding scheme [14], Yang and Tsai's interleaving prediction scheme [15], and Li et al.'s general scheme [22]. On the other hand, some authors provided some different kind of data hiding methods, such as the one proposed in [24].

In this paper, we propose a reversible data hiding scheme based on four prediction methods and local complexity. Secret data is embedded into the cover image level by level [13]. In each level, the interleaving grouping approach is applied to divide the cover image into four groups [15]. Besides, one of the four prediction methods is chosen to apply to each group of the level. When a pixel of each group is processed, the predicted error is computed between the current pixel value and its predicted pixel value. Then, the local complexity, i.e. pixel variance, is adopted to determine whether the predicted error will join the process of pixel shifting and data concealing or not. After the process of pixel shifting and data embedding has been executed in one level, the difference between a cover pixel and a stego-pixel remains within ± 1.

The rest of this paper is organized as follows. In Section 2, the interleaving prediction method proposed by Yang and Tsai in 2010 is introduced [15]. In Section 3, our reversible data hiding with high image quality is presented in detail. The experimental result of our scheme is demonstrated in Section 4. Finally, the conclusion is given in the last section.

2   Related Works

In this section, we introduce Yang and Tsai's reversible data hiding scheme, which is based on interleaving prediction and histogram shifting [15]. The interleaving prediction method is used to promote the altitude of the peak point in histogram. Similar to a black-and-white chessboard, an image is partitioned into two groups with black and white pixels. In the first stage, white pixels are processed and predicted by their neighbor black pixels. Then, in the second stage, black pixels are processed and predicted by their neighbor white pixels.

The detailed steps of the first stage, which processes white pixels, are as follows. Let $P_{i,j}$ be a white pixel, where (i, j) is the location, and $D_{i,j}$ be the predicted error between $P_{i,j}$ and its predictive value. All predicted errors are collected to generate a histogram $HS(D)$. Then, the following steps are executed.

Step 1: Find two pairs of peak and zero points ($Peak_A$, $Zero_B$) and ($Peak_B$, $Zero_B$) from the histogram $HS(D)$, such that $Zero_B < Peak_B < Peak_A < Zero_A$.
Step 2: Shift the value of the predicted error $D_{i,j}$ by 1 in the following cases.

Case A: Change all values in the range of [$Zero_B$ +1, $Peak_B$ -1] to the left by 1 unit. This indicates that $D'_{i,j}$ is set to $D_{i,j}$-1 as $D_{i,j} \in$ [$Zero_B$ +1, $Peak_B$ -1].
Case B: Change all values in the range of [$Peak_A$+1, $Zero_A$-1] to the right by 1 unit. This shows that $D'_{i,j}$ is set to $D_{i,j}$ +1 as $D_{i,j} \in$ [$Peak_A$+1, $Zero_A$-1].

Step 3: Conceal a secret bit when the predicted error $D_{i,j}$ is equal to $Peak_A$ or $Peak_{Bc}$ as the following two cases.

Case A: If the to-be-embedded bit is 0, predicted error $D_{i,j}$ is unchanged. It indicates that $D'_{i,j}$ is set to $D_{i,j}$.

Case B: If the to-be-embedded bit is 1,

$$D'_{i,j} = \begin{cases} D_{i,j} + 1, & \text{if } D_{i,j} = Peak_A \\ D_{i,j} - 1, & \text{if } D_{i,j} = Peak_B \end{cases}$$

Step 4: Transform all the predicted errors into pixel values by running the inversed interleaving prediction. Then, output the stego-image.

After the first stage, its outputted stego-image is used as the input image of the second stage, which processes black pixels. After the second stage is processed, another two pairs of peak and zero points ($Peak_A$, $Zero_A$) and ($Peak_B$, $Zero_B$) are created and the final stego-image is obtained.

3   Our Proposed Methods

Our method takes four different prediction methods and a variance strategy into consideration. Firstly, the cover image is divided into four groups, Group1, Group2, Group3, and Group4, by the interleaving grouping method. Fig. 1 shows a grouping result, where each cell indicates a pixel and the number in the cell indicates the group number of the cell. Then, four stages are used to process the four groups, respectively. At each stage, four different prediction methods are evaluated and the one with the largest efficiency ratio R is chosen and used in this stage. Finally, all predicted error values and variance values are calculated by the chosen prediction method. Besides, a threshold TH is determined by variance values to decide whether a pixel would join the shifting and embedding process or not. The detail of the data hiding algorithm and extracting-restoring algorithm is given in following subsections.

1	2	1	2	1
3	4	3	4	3
1	2	1	2	1
3	4	3	4	3
1	2	1	2	1

Fig. 1. Interleaving grouping with four groups

3.1   Data Hiding Algorithm

We take the first stage, which processes Group1, to describe our data hiding method. As shown in the gray part of Fig 1, one Group1 pixel, says $P_{i,j}$, is surrounded by eight neighboring pixels which belong to the other groups. The detailed algorithm is as follows.

Algorithm Data_Hiding_of_the_First_Stage
Input: Cover Image I, Secret message S, Proportional relationship C.
Output: Stego Image I', the couple data $(Peak_A, Zero_A)$ and $(Peak_B, Zero_B)$, a variance
value TH_{first}.

Step 1: For each pixel $P_{i,j}$ in Group1, a predicted error $D_{i,j}$ is calculated by each of four
following prediction methods:

- Chessboard prediction:
  Case A: If $P_{i,j}$ has only two neighbor pixels P_1 and P_2 belonging to Group2 and
  Group3, the predicted error $D_{i,j}$ is given as

  $$D_{i,j} = P_{i,j} - \left\lfloor \frac{P_1 + P_2}{2} \right\rfloor.$$

  Case B: If $P_{i,j}$ has only three neighbor pixels P_1, P_2 and P_3 belonging to Group2
  and Group3, the predicted error $D_{i,j}$ is given as

  $$D_{i,j} = P_{i,j} - \left\lfloor \frac{P_1 + P_2 + P_3}{3} \right\rfloor.$$

  Case C: If $P_{i,j}$ has four neighbor pixels P_1, P_2, P_3 and P_4 belonging to Group2
  and Group3, the predicted error $D_{i,j}$ is given as

  $$D_{i,j} = P_{i,j} - \left\lfloor \frac{P_1 + P_2 + P_3 + P_4}{4} \right\rfloor.$$

- Edge prediction:
  Case A: If $P_{i,j}$ has only two neighbor pixels belonging to Group2 and Group3,
  the predicted error $D_{i,j}$ is given as

  $$D_{i,j} = P_{i,j} - \left\lfloor \frac{P_1 + P_2}{2} \right\rfloor.$$

  Case B: If $P_{i,j}$ has only three neighbor pixels belonging to Group2 and Group3,
  the predicted error $D_{i,j}$ is given as

  $$D_{i,j} = P_{i,j} - \left\lfloor \frac{P_1 + P_2 + P_3}{3} \right\rfloor.$$

  Case C: If $P_{i,j}$ has two neighbor Group2 pixels P_1 and P_2 and two neighboring
  Group3 pixels P_3 and P_4, the predicted error $D_{i,j}$ is given as

  $$\text{If } |P_1\text{-}P_2| > |P_3\text{-}P_4|, \quad D_{i,j} = P_{i,j} - \left\lfloor \frac{P_3 + P_4}{2} \right\rfloor ;$$

  $$\text{else, } \quad D_{i,j} = P_{i,j} - \left\lfloor \frac{P_1 + P_2}{2} \right\rfloor.$$

- Squared prediction:
  Case A: If $P_{i,j}$ has only three neighbor pixels P_1, P_2 and P_3, the predicted error
  $D_{i,j}$ is given as

  $$D_{i,j} = P_{i,j} - \left\lfloor \frac{P_1 + P_2 + P_3}{3} \right\rfloor.$$

Case B: If $P_{i,j}$ has only five neighbor pixels P_1, P_2, P_3, P_4 and P_5, the predicted error $D_{i,j}$ is given as

$$D_{i,j} = P_{i,j} - \left\lfloor \frac{P_1 + P_2 + P_3 + P_4 + P_5}{5} \right\rfloor .$$

Case C: If $P_{i,j}$ has eight neighbor pixels P_1, P_2, P_3, P_4, P_5, P_6, P_7 and P_8, the predicted error $D_{i,j}$ is given as

$$D_{i,j} = P_{i,j} - \left\lfloor \frac{P_1 + P_2 + P_3 + P_4 + P_5 + P_6 + P_7 + P_8}{8} \right\rfloor .$$

- Max-min-omitted prediction:

Case A: If $P_{i,j}$ has only two neighbor pixels P_1 and P_2 belonging to Group2 and Group3, the predicted error $D_{i,j}$ is given as

$$D_{i,j} = P_{i,j} - \left\lfloor \frac{P_1 + P_2}{2} \right\rfloor .$$

Case B: If $P_{i,j}$ has only three neighbor pixels P_1, P_2 and P_3 belonging to Group2 and Group3, the predicted error $D_{i,j}$ is given as

$$D_{i,j} = P_{i,j} - \left\lfloor \frac{P_1 + P_2 + P_3}{3} \right\rfloor .$$

Case C: If $P_{i,j}$ has four neighbor Group2 and Group3 pixels P_1, P_2, P_3 and P_4, with $P_1 \leqq P_2 \leqq P_3 \leqq P_4$, the predicted error $D_{i,j}$ is given as

$$D_{i,j} = P_{i,j} - \left\lfloor \frac{P_2 + P_3}{2} \right\rfloor .$$

Step 2: For each pixel $P_{i,j}$ in Group1, a variance value $V_{i,j}$ is calculated by each of the four prediction methods. The calculations of the four methods are similar, here only the chessboard prediction's calculation is shown below:

Case A: If $P_{i,j}$ has only two neighboring pixels P_1 and P_2 belonging to Group2 and Group3, the variance value $V_{i,j}$ is given as

$$V_{i,j} = 2 \cdot \left[\left(P_1 - \left\lfloor \frac{P_1 + P_2}{2} \right\rfloor \right)^2 + \left(P_2 - \left\lfloor \frac{P_1 + P_2}{2} \right\rfloor \right)^2 \right] .$$

Case B: If $P_{i,j}$ has only three neighboring pixels P_1, P_2 and P_3 belonging to Group2 and Group3, the variance value $V_{i,j}$ is given as

$$V_{i,j} = \left\lfloor \frac{4}{3} \cdot \left[\left(P_1 - \left\lfloor \frac{P_1 + P_2 + P_3}{3} \right\rfloor \right)^2 + \left(P_2 - \left\lfloor \frac{P_1 + P_2 + P_3}{3} \right\rfloor \right)^2 + \left(P_3 - \left\lfloor \frac{P_1 + P_2 + P_3}{3} \right\rfloor \right)^2 \right] \right\rfloor .$$

Case C: If $P_{i,j}$ has four neighboring pixels P_1, P_2, P_3 and P_4 belonging to Group2 and Group3, the variance value $V_{i,j}$ is given as

$$V_{i,j} = \left(P_1 - \left\lfloor \frac{P_1 + P_2 + P_3 + P_4}{4} \right\rfloor \right)^2 + \left(P_2 - \left\lfloor \frac{P_1 + P_2 + P_3 + P_4}{4} \right\rfloor \right)^2 + \left(P_3 - \left\lfloor \frac{P_1 + P_2 + P_3 + P_4}{4} \right\rfloor \right)^2 + \left(P_4 - \left\lfloor \frac{P_1 + P_2 + P_3 + P_4}{4} \right\rfloor \right)^2 .$$

Step 3: Collect all predicted error $D_{i,j}$ and generate their histogram. Then, select two pairs of peak and zero points $(Peak_A, Zero_A)$ and $(Peak_B, Zero_B)$, such that $Zero_B < Peak_B < Peak_A < Zero_A$.

Step 4: For each prediction method, its efficiency ratio R is calculated as follows: Let the numbers of pixels falling in $Peak_A$, $Peak_B$, $[Peak_A+1, Zero_A]$, and $[Zero_B, Peak_B-1]$ be J_1, J_2, I_1 and I_2, respectively.

$$R = \frac{J_1 + J_2}{I_1 + I_2}$$

Step 5: Select the prediction method with the maximal R value. Name the selected prediction method as M_{first}. Then, this level, including Group1, Group2, Group3 and Group4, will use the selected prediction method M_{first} to embed the secret data.

Step 6: We use Group1 as an example of embedding secret data by method M_{first}. Let all predicted errors $D_{i,j}$, variance values $V_{i,j}$, two peak points $Peak_A$ and $Peak_B$, and two zero points $Zero_A$ and $Zero_B$ have been calculated. Count the number of pixels with predicted errors equal to $Peak_A$ and $Peak_B$ and with variance values equal to r, and store the number in $V_{first}[r]$. The numbers of pixels with variance values equal to r and predicted errors falling into $[Peak_A+1, Zero_A]$ and $[Zero_B, Peak_B-1]$ are stored in $V_{positive\_shift\_first}[r]$ and $V_{negative\_shift\_first}[r]$, respectively. With the given proportional relationship C, find a maximal value $P_{first} \geqq 0$ satisfying

$$\frac{V_{positive\_shift\_first}[r] + V_{negative\_shift\_first}[r]}{V_{first}[r]} < C, 0 \leq r \leq P_{first}.$$

If P_{first} dose not exist, go to Step 10.

Step 7: Add values of $V_{first}[0], V_{first}[1], \ldots, V_{first}[t]$ to capacity until Capacity $\geqq |S|$ or $t = P_{first}$. Set a variance threshold $TH_{first} = t$.

Step 8: Use TH_{first} to distinguish whether a Group1's pixel $P_{i,j}$ will join the shifting and embedding process or not by setting the following flag:

$$Flag_{i,j} = \begin{cases} 1, & \text{if } V_{i,j} \leq TH_{first}. \\ 0, & \text{if } V_{i,j} > TH_{first}. \end{cases}$$

If $Flag_{i,j} = 0$, it means that the pixel $P_{i,j}$ in Group1 will not join the shifting and embedding process; If $Flag_{i,j} = 1$, it means that the pixel $P_{i,j}$ in Group1 will join the shifting and embedding process.

Step 9: Run the following cases for each predicted error $D_{i,j}$ and its variance $V_{i,j}$.

Case A: If $Flag_{i,j} = 1$ and the predicted error $D_{i,j}$ is equal to $Peak_A$ or $Peak_B$, fetch a secret bit from S and do the following two cases:
Case A1: If to-be-embedded-bit is 0, $D'_{i,j}$ is set to $D_{i,j}$.
Case A2: If to-be-embedded-bit is 1,

$$\begin{cases} \text{If } D_{i,j} = Peak_A, \ D'_{i,j} = D_{i,j} + 1 \\ \text{If } D_{i,j} = Peak_B, \ D'_{i,j} = D_{i,j} - 1. \end{cases}$$

Case B: If $Flag_{i,j} = 1$ and the predicted error $D_{i,j}$ falls into the range of $[Zero_B + 1, Peak_B - 1]$ or $[Peak_A + 1, Zero_A - 1]$, shift predicted error $D_{i,j}$ by one unit as follows:

$$\begin{cases} \text{If } D_{i,j} \in [Peak_A + 1, Zero_A - 1], \ D'_{i,j} = D_{i,j} + 1 \\ \text{If } D_{i,j} \in [Zero_B + 1, Peak_B - 1], \ D'_{i,j} = D_{i,j} - 1. \end{cases}$$

Case C: If $Flag_{i,j} = 0$, do nothing, that is, $D'_{i,j}$ is set to $D_{i,j}$.

Step 10: Transform each predicted error $D'_{i,j}$ into pixel value $P'_{i,j}$ by the inverse of the prediction method M_{first}. Finally, all pixel values $P'_{i,j}$ form the stego-image I'.

Step 11: Output two pairs $(Peak_A, Zero_A)$ and $(Peak_B, Zero_B)$, a variance threshold TH_{first}, and a prediction method M_{first}.

Step 12: If Capacity $< |S|$, repeat Step 1 to Step 12 until all secret S have been embedded. Else, output stego-image I'.

Note that the outputted parameter data in Step 11 can be seen as secret data and be embedded firstly in the next stage. So, only the outputted parameter data of the last stage cannot be embedded.

3.2   Overflow/Underflow

In our Histogram-based reversible data hiding method, each pixel will change ±1 at most in every level. Therefore, before embedding secret data into the image in one level, we pre-modify pixels with values 0 and 255 into pixels with values 1 and 254, respectively, to prevent overflow and underflow as follows:

$$P_{i,j} = \begin{cases} 1, & \text{if } P_{i,j} = 0 \\ 254, & \text{if } P_{i,j} = 255. \end{cases}$$

Also, to judge those modifications, the location map is created before those modifications as follows:

$$L[k] = \begin{cases} 0, & \text{if } P_{i,j} = 1 \text{ or } P_{i,j} = 254 \\ 1, & \text{if } P_{i,j} = 0 \text{ or } P_{i,j} = 255, \end{cases}$$

where L is the location map and k is an index for those recorded pixels. Therefore, in each level, the size of the location map is k bits if there are k pixels with values equal to values 0, 1, 254, or 255.

4   Experiments

In this section, we provide the resultant of embedding capacity and image quality to demonstrate the performance of our proposed scheme. In our experiment, five gray-level images with size 512×512, which are depicted in Fig. 2, are used, and the secret message is obtained by pseudo-random generation. To estimate the image quality, we applied the function of peak-signal-to-noise-ratio (PSNR), which is defined as Eq. (1). To estimate the embedding capacity, the function of ER (Embedded Ratio; bpp) is adopted, where ER = Total Embedded bits / Size of Cover image. In the experiment, the proportional relationship C is set to 20 at the first level. Then, the C value is added by 0.5 at each of the following levels.

$$PSNR = 10 \times \log_{10}(\frac{255^2}{MSE}), \tag{1}$$

where MSE is the mean square error between the cover image and the stego-image.

(a)   (b)   (c)   (d)   (e)

Fig. 2. The cover images with size 512×512; (a) Airplane; (b) Baboon; (c) Boat; (d) Lena; (e) Peppers

Table 1 shows the comparison among Weng et al.'s method, Yang-Tsai method, and our proposed scheme. From this table, our scheme has better image quality than that of Weng et al.'s method, and the Yang-Tsai method when the sizes of the embedded bits of these two methods are similar. The reason is that our approach forbids some prediction errors entering the process of pixel shifting and we use four different prediction methods. The threshold TH strategy in our proposed scheme has efficiently eliminated the distortion caused by pixel shifting. It therefore has good performance of PSNR than the previous work.

Table 1. The compared resultant between our approach and Yang and Tsai's scheme

	Weng et al.'s scheme[23]		Yang and Tsai's scheme [15]		Our approach	
	Payload (Bits)	PSNR	Payload (Bits)	PSNR	Payload (Bits)	PSNR
Airplane	31,142	60.41	30,013	52.70	31,142	60.41
Baboon	30,000	50.82	30,030	48.39	30,000	58.67
Boat	30,010	60.58	30,007	51.85	30,010	60.58
Lena	30,119	60.36	30,066	52.52	30,119	60.43
Peppers	30,148	60.44	30,005	52.23	30,148	60.42
Average	30,284	58.52	30,024	51.54	30,284	60.102

In addition, we also compared the resultant with some other previous works. As shown in Fig. 3, our scheme has better image quality than previous works [13, 15, 18, 23] with the same embedding capacities.

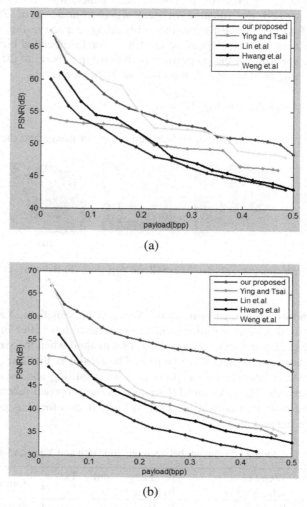

(a)

(b)

Fig. 3. Comparison results among our proposed scheme and other reversible schemes for images: (a) Lena; (b) Baboon

5   Conclusion

In this study, we propose a reversible data hiding method based on four candidates of prediction methods and local complexity for enhancing stego-image quality. We evaluate the four prediction methods by calculating their efficiency ratios to decide which prediction method will be used, and used the variance strategy to find out a threshold *TH* for selecting which prediction pixel should join the process of pixel shifting and data concealing. The variance strategy has efficiently improved histogram-based approaches to obtain high image quality. The experimental resultant shows that our method owns higher image quality than that of previous works when the embedding capacities are the same.

Acknowledgment. This research was partially supported by the National Science Council of the Republic of China under the Grant NSC-101-2221-E-153-002-MY2.

References

1. Feng, J.B., Lin, I.C., Tsai, C.S., Chu, Y.P.: Reversible watermarking: Current status and key issues. International Journal of Networks and Security 2(3), 161–170 (2006)
2. Shi, Y.Q., Ni, Z., Zou, D., Liang, C., Xuan, G.: Lossless data hiding: Fundamentals, algorithms, and applications. In: Proc. IEEE ISCAS, pp. 33–36 (2004)
3. Lou, D.C., Hu, M.C., Li Liu, C.: Multiple-layer data hiding scheme for medical image. Computer Standards and Interfaces 31(2), 329–335 (2010)
4. Al-Qershi, Q.M., Khoo, B.E.: High capacity data hiding schemes for medical images based on difference expansion. Journal of Systems and Software 31(4), 787–794 (2011)
5. Chang, C.C., Nguyen, T.S., Lin, C.C.: A reversible data hiding scheme for VQ indices using locally adaptive coding. Journal of Visual Communications and Image Representation 22(7), 664–672 (2011)
6. Yang, C.H., Wang, W.J., Huang, C.T., Wang, S.J.: "Reversible steganography based on side match and hit pattern for VQ-compressed images. Information Sciences 181(11), 2218–2230 (2011)
7. Wang, J.X., Lu, Z.M.: A path optional lossless data hiding scheme based on VQ joint neighboring coding. Information Sciences 179(19), 1016–1024 (2009)
8. Tian, J.: Reversible data embedding using a difference expansion. IEEE Trans. on Circuits Systems for Video Technology 16(3), 890–896 (2003)
9. Alttar, A.M.: Reversible watermark using the difference expansion of a generalized integer transform. IEEE Trans. on Image Processing 13(8), 1147–1156 (2004)
10. Lee, C.C., Wu, H.C., Tsai, C.S., Chu, Y.P.: Adaptive lossless steganography with centralized difference expansion. Pattern Recognition 141(6), 2097–2106 (2008)
11. Ni, Z., Shi, Y.Q., Ansar, N., Su, W.: Reversible data hiding. IEEE Trans. on Circuits Systems for Video Technology 16(3), 354–362 (2006)
12. Yousefl, S., Rablee, H., Yousefl, E., Ghanbarl, M.: Reversible data hiding using histogram sorting and integer transform. In: Proc. IEEE DEST, pp. 487–490 (2007)
13. Lin, C.C., Tai, W.L., Chang, C.C.: Multilevel reversible data hiding based on histogram modification of difference images. Pattern Recognition 41(12), 3582–3591 (2008)
14. Tsai, P., Hu, Y.C., Yeh, H.L.: Reversible image hiding scheme using predictive coding. Signal Processing 89(6), 1129–1143 (2009)
15. Yang, C.H., Tsai, M.H.: Improving histogram-based reversible data hiding by interleaving prediction. IET Image Processing 4(4), 223–234 (2010)
16. Lee, C.F., Chen, H.L., Tso, H.K.: Embedding capacity raising in reversible data hiding based on prediction of difference expansion. Journal of Systems and Software 83(10), 1864–1872 (2010)
17. Zhao, A., Luo, H., Lu, Z.M., Pan, J.S.: Reversible data hiding based on multilevel histogram modification and sequential recovery. AEU-International Journal of Electronics and Communication 65(10), 814–826 (2011)

18. Hwang, H.J., Kim, H.J., Sachnev, V., Joo, S.H.: Reversible watermarking method using optimal histogram pair shifting based on prediction and sorting. KSII Trans. on Internet and Information Systems 4(4), 555–670 (2010)
19. Li, X., Yang, B., Zeng, T.: Efficient reversible watermarking based on adaptive prediction-error expansion and pixel selection. IEEE Trans. on Image Processing 20(12), 3524–3533 (2011)
20. Tai, W.L., Yeh, C.M., Chang, C.C.: Reversible data hiding based on histogram modification of pixel differences. IEEE Trans. on Circuits Systems for Video Technology 19(6), 906–910 (2009)
21. Zhao, Z., Luo, H., Lu, Z.M., Pan, J.S.: Reversible data hiding base on multilevel histogram modification and sequential recovery. International Journal of Electronics and Communications (AEU) 65(10), 814–826 (2011)
22. Li, X., Li, B., Yang, B., Zeng, T.: General framework to histogram-shifting-based reversible data hiding. IEEE Transactions on Image Processing 22(6) (2013)
23. Weng, C.Y., Yang, C.H., Fan, C.I., Liu, K.L., Sun, H.M.: Histogram-Based Reversible Information Hiding Improved by Prediction with the Variance to Enhance Image Quality. In: The 8th Asia Joint Conference on Information Security, Seoul, Korea, July 25-26 (2013)
24. Catiglione, A., De Santis, A., Soriente, C.: Taking advantages of a disadvantage: Digital forensics and steganography using document metadata. Journal of Systems and Software 80(5), 750–764 (2007)

Steganalysis to Data Hiding of VQ Watermarking Upon Grouping Strategy

Ya-Ting Chang[1], Min-Hao Wu[2], and Shiuh-Jeng Wang[1]

[1] Department of Information Management, Central Police University,
Taoyuan, 33304, Taiwan
[2] Department of Computer Science and Information Engineering, National Central University,
Taoyuan, 32001, Taiwan
bowrose@gmail.com,
mhwu@csie.ncu.edu.tw,
sjwang@mail.cpu.edu.tw,

Abstract. This paper present a steganalysis method for the data hiding scheme based on VQ-compression. This data hiding algorithm divides the codebook into groups which contain two codewords each. The Euclidean Distance of the group is used instead of a codeword in traditional VQ-compression. A PoV-like effect of Chi-square attack is observed and used as a feature of detection. In the proposed steganalysis, we detect whether an unknown image is a VQ-compressed image or not, and then the target detection of codewords grouping type data hiding methods is proposed. We apply proposed scheme to Yang et al.'s watermarking scheme. A large amount test image database UCID (Uncompressed Colour Image Database) is utilized as various conditions, such as cover imaged, traditional VQ-compressed images, and stego images. The experimental shows that the proposed steganalysis method is able to identify the stego images among others, and the accuracy rate reaches over 90 %.

Keywords: Steganalysis, data hiding detection, vector quantization, group strategy.

1 Introduction

Steganography is developed to guarantee the confidentiality of the information which is aimed to protect. One of the steganography method is to hide some information into a particular media, such as an image, a video clip, or an audio file. The algorithms are designed not to be discovered the existence of the information hidden inside.

On the opposite side, steganalysis is a novel research area which aims the opposite goal to steganography. Steganalysis is an art of identify the suspected items, in other words, detect the embedding information inside the carrier. The types of steganalysis could be classified into blind steganalysis and targeted steganalysis according to objectives [7]. Blind steganalysis techniques detect the existence of secret messages when the steganography embedding algorithm is unknown. On the other hand, targeted Steganalysis are designed for a particular steganography algorithm.

Linawati et al. (Eds.): ICT-EurAsia 2014, LNCS 8407, pp. 633–642, 2014.

Certain detection tools to the steganography in spatial domain are developed. One of the well-known attack to steganography, Chi-square attack [13], is proposed for LSB steganography technique [13][4]. Histogram-based and PVD-based steganography techniques are also attacked by analysis the statistical distribution of the pixel values' histogram [5][2]. But there is no research about detect the VQ-based steganography so far.

One of the VQ-based information hiding method is to re-encode the index value according to the secret bit to be embedded [10][15][6][14]. The targeted steganalysis of the method is proposed in this paper. The rest of this paper is organized as follows. Related background knowledge such as vector quantization, VQ-based steganography method, and Chi-square detection are introduced in Section 2. Our scheme is presented in Section 3. Section 4 shows the experimental results compared with related work. Conclusions are given in Section 5.

2   Related Works

2.1   Vector Quantization

Vector quantization (VQ) was proposed by Linde, Buzo, and Gray (LBG) in 1980 [3]. A codebook is used for VQ-compression generated by the LBG algorithm [3]. A codebook is composed of these featured blocks, or called codewords. The first step of VQ divides the cover image into several non-overlapping blocks and each block size is $m \times m$. Let k be $m \times m$, and $u_1, u_2, \ldots, u_k$ represent the pixel values of a block. The second step encodes the blocks by u_i and the codewords in codebook, for $1 \leq i \leq k$. If a codeword CW_x has size k, for a block in an input image, Euclidean distance is calculated by Eq. (1) comparing with every codewords in the codebook.

$$d(u, CW_x) = \sum_{j=1}^{k} (u_j - v_j)^2 , \tag{1}$$

where $v_1, v_2, \ldots, v_k$ represent the component values of the codeword CW_x which its index value is x.

For every non-overlapping blocks of the cover image, find the closest codeword with the smallest Euclidean distance. The corresponding index value of the nearest distance codeword will be the output while VQ encodes an image block. The output will be an index table. Fig. 1 shows the procedure of VQ image compression. The compressed image can be reconstructed from the index table by referencing the codewords.

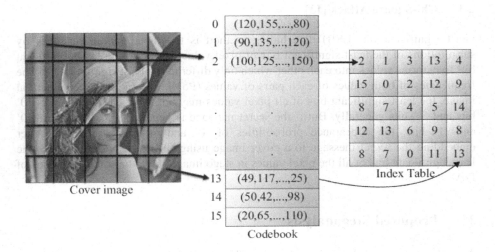

Fig. 1. The procedure diagram of VQ-compression

2.2   Yang et al.'s Data Hiding Method

Lu et al.'s method [6] and Wu-Chang's method [14] use codebook division to embed watermark bits. Yang et al. [15] enhanced the steganography of the algorithm of codebook division. The embedding method will be briefly presented as follows.

Codebook-Sorting Grouping: Before the embedding phase, a codebook is generated by the LBG algorithm [3], and the codebook division is processed. If a codebook size is CS, The division results are $CS/2$ groups G_x, where x is an integer from 1 to $CS/2$. For each codewords in the codebook, compute the KEY values by summing up the elements. For the codeword with the smallest KEY value, find another codeword matched to it such that their Euclidean distance is the least. The two codewords are labeled as CW_x and CW_x', forming the group G_x, The rest codewords in the codebook are divided as the same method above.

Shortest-Group Encoding: All the codewords are labeled as CW_x or CW_x', where x is from 1 to $CS/2$. While processing VQ-compression on a block C, compute the Euclidean Distance D between C and each group G_x. D is the summation of Euclidean Distance from C to all the elements in G_x. Extract one bit b from the secret message S. If G_y has the least D, CW_y and CW_y' are used instead of traditional VQ-compression. If b is '0', output the index value of CW_y; otherwise if b is '1', output the index value of CW_y'.

2.3   Chi-Square Attack [13]

Least significant bit (LSB) data hiding method is to embed secret messages by substitutions of the least significant bits of pixel values. Overwriting least significant bits transforms values into each other which only differ in the least significant bit. The frequencies of both values of each pairs of values (PoV), become equal. In a natural image, the least significant bits of all pixel values may not show close amount of '0' bits and '1' bits generally. But if the secret message is generated randomly with '0' and '1' bits, the appearance probabilities of '0' and '1' bits are equal. After embedding the secret message to a cover image using LSB data hiding method, the least significant bits of all the pixel values in stego image show the equal frequency of PoV.

3   Proposed Steganalysis

An inference could be inducted from Chi-square attack. According to Yang's embedding method, an index of the codewords is chosen to embed a secret bit. In other words, if the group G_y is selected to embed a secret bit, either CW_y or CW_y' is chosen according to the value of the secret bit. In the presupposition that the secret message S is a bit-stream generated randomly, the composition of '0' bits and '1' bits should be similar amounts. That is, the frequency of chosen CW_x and CW_x' should be similar, too, where x is from 1 to $CS/2$.

The flowchart of proposed steganalysis method is shown in Fig. 2.

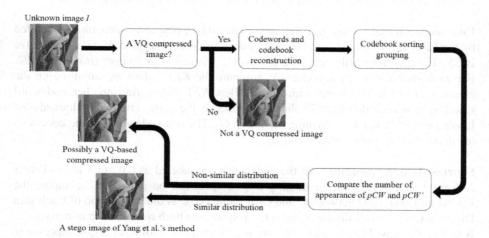

Fig. 2. The flowchart of proposed steganalysis method

3.1   Detection of VQ-Compression

The first step is to estimate an unknown image be a VQ-compression image or not. During the process of VQ-compression, all the non-overlapping blocks have the same size and are non-overlapping, we can inference that in a VQ-compression image, pixel values may have extent of diversity on the edge of non-overlapping blocks.

We first calculate the absolute difference values in vertical and horizontal directions. We can infer that a column or a row which has more intense changes of pixel values may be the edge of non-overlapping blocks of VQ-compression. We set a threshold T_F to be 1/3. If there are more than T_F of the total number of a column or a row have absolute difference values greater than its neighboring, then it is considered to be the possible edge of non-overlapping blocks. The position of the possible edges, such as i-th row or j-th column, are recorded, and their distances are calculated, dr_i and dc_j, for rows and columns, respectively. For example, if the possible edges are the 4-th, the 8-th, the 12-th, and the 20-th rows, then their edge distances are $dr_1 = 8 - 4 = 4$, $dr_2 = 12 - 8 = 4$, and $dr_3 = 20 - 12 = 8$.

If there are p edge distances between rows $dr_1, dr_2, ..., dr_p$, and q edge distances between columns $dc_1, dc_2, ..., dc_q$, the standard deviation of dr_i and dc_j, σ_R and σ_C, are calculated. In a natural image, σ_R and σ_C would be great values because pixel values should change smoothly in a small area and hence the "edges" do not exist. On the contrary, a small value of standard deviation represent higher centralization of the edge distances. If the non-overlapping blocks are sized 4×4, the ideal situation is that dr_i and dc_j would be all the same value 4, and σ_R and σ_C would be 0. Threshold T_s is set to be 5, and if σ_R or σ_C is greater than 5, then it is possible not compressed by VQ method.

If an unknown image is detected to be a VQ-compressed image by σ_R and σ_C, then the next step is to predict the possible non-overlapping block size. The most possible block size is the edge distance which shows up most frequently. The predicted block size wxh is defined as following Eq. (2):

$$w = Mo(dc_j), \quad j = 1, 2, ..., q,$$
$$h = Mo(dc_i), \quad i = 1, 2, ..., p, \tag{2}$$

where "Mo" denotes the function which returns the mode, the value that appears most often.

3.2   Detection of Stego Images of Yang et al.'s Method

We can reconstruct the codebook by copying the pixel values of every block. The blocks of the stego image are scanned from left to right and top to down, copied to the predicted codebook pCB. Pixel values of blocks form predicted codeword pCW_1, $pCW_2, ..., pCW_k$, and the index values are 1, 2, ..., k. The duplicated blocks would not create new codewords.

According to Chi-square attack, if the secret message is a random generated bit stream, the number of least significant bits of a stego image of '0' bits and '1' bits should be similar. The same concept in Yang et al.'s shortest-group encoding method, the number of times choosing CW_x and CW_x' to encode should be similar for a stego image. Predicted codewords are input to Yang et al.'s codebook-sorting grouping. The output of applying Yang et al.'s codebook-sorting grouping method to pCB are groups pG_x which each one contains two predicted codewords, pCW_x and pCW_x'.

Correlation coefficient R is used as judgment. If the number of appearance of pCW_y and pCW_y' are close, then the value of R would approach to 1. On the other hand, if the number of appearance of pCW_y and pCW_y' vary a lot, then the value of R would approach to 0. A threshold T_R is set to be 0.7. If $R \leq T_R$, the unknown image I is not a stego image using Yang et al.'s method. If $R > T_R$, then I is probably a stego image using Yang et al.'s method. If there are u groups of pG_x, the number of appearance of all pCW_x (pCW_1, pCW_1, ..., pCW_u) are X_1, X_2, ..., X_u, and the number of appearance of all pCW_x' (pCW_1', pCW_1', ..., pCW_u') are Y_1, Y_2, ..., Y_u, the correlation coefficient R is defined as Eq. (3):

$$R = \frac{\sum_{i=1}^{u}(X_i - \mu_X)(Y_i - \mu_Y)}{\sqrt{\sum_{i=1}^{u}(X_i - \mu_X)^2} \times \sqrt{\sum_{i=1}^{u}(Y_i - \mu_Y)^2}}, \tag{3}$$

where $\mu_X = \frac{1}{u}\sum_{i=1}^{u}X_i$ and $\mu_Y = \frac{1}{u}\sum_{i=1}^{u}Y_i$.

4   Experimental Results

We implement our scheme using the software Marlab 2013a. Traditional VQ-compression and Yang et al.'s method are coded by following their algorithms. Different sizes of codebooks, 128, 256, 512, and 1024 are generated using the LBG algorithm [3]. The UCID (Uncompressed Colour Image Database) [17] provides a benchmark dataset for image retrieval, containing over 1,300 images. Several of them are shown in Fig. 3. The images are size 384x512 or 512x384, and are all converted to 8-bit gray level images. The non-overlapping blocks of VQ-compression and Yang et al.'s method are sized 4x4. Various conditions of images are inputted to our scheme:

Condition A: Original pure images without any processing.
Condition B: Images compressed by traditional VQ coding.
Condition C: Images applied Yang et al.'s method with full embedding.

The expected output results corresponding to the different conditions above are:
Result A: The unknown image is not a VQ-compressed image.
Result B: The unknown image may be a VQ-compressed image.
Result C: The unknown image is a stego image of Yang et al.'s method.

All the images are categorized to Condition A, B, and C as following rules: 400 images are selected as cover images, which are not processed by any compression or data hiding; other 469 images are compressed by traditional VQ with randomly selected codebook size; and the rest 469 images are applied Yang et al.'s method, also with randomly selected codebook size and full embedding. The secret message is composed of '0' bit and '1' bit generated randomly. The output result of applying our steganalysis method for each image is either Result A, Result B, or Result C. The number of various results for the UCID test images are shown in Table 1.The thresholds are set to be $T_F = 1/3$, $T_S = 5$, and $T_R = 0.7$.

Fig. 3. Examples from UCID for testing

Table 1. The number of various results of the UCID test images

Results / Input	Result A (Cover image)	Result B (VQ-compressed image)	Result C (Stego image)
Condition A (400 images)	400	0	0
Condition B (469 images)	17	372	80
Condition C (469 images)	0	50	419

True positive (*TP*), true negative (*TN*), false positive (*FP*), and false negative (*FN*) are statistical measures for sensitive and specificity of our steganalysis scheme. Here stego images represent "Positive", and cover images and traditional VQ-compressed images represent "Negative". According to Table 1 above, the measure values of *TP*, *FP*, *FN*, and *TN* could be calculated as follows:

TP = Result C under Condition C = 419,
FP = Summation of Result C under Condition A and Condition B = 0 + 80 = 80,
TN = Summation of Result A and Result B under Condition A and Condition B = 400 + 17 + 372 = 789,
FN = Summation of Result A and Result B under Condition C = 0 + 50 = 50.

The accuracy rate *Acc* and error rate *Err* could be obtained by the following Eq. (4) and Eq. (5):

$$Acc = \frac{TP + TN}{TP + FP + TN + FN}. \tag{4}$$

$$Err = \frac{FP + FN}{TP + FP + TN + FN} \tag{5}$$

Substitute values of *TP*, *FP*, *FN*, and *TN*, *Acc* reaches 90.28 % but also errors occurred with *Err* 9.72 %. Error often occurs on complex image, which has many sharp lines on it, or the pixel values vary a lot from the adjacent ones. This may confuse the prediction of non-overlapping block size, which causes the wrongly reconstruction of predicted codewords and codebook. Incorrect predicted codewords and codebook lead codebook sorting grouping meaningless, and decrease the reliability of correlation coefficient.

Conclusions

There are many studies in respect of digital media steganalysis except for VQ-based steganography. In this paper, we take Yang et al.'s method as an example of steganalysis. We design the procedures to detect the existence of secret message in Yang et al.'s stego image. For other similar VQ-based data hiding methods such as Lu et al.'s method and Wu-Chang's method, the procedure of steganalysis in Fig. 2 is also suitable, only have to apply different algorithm of "Codebook sorting grouping". We observe the non-overlapping blocks of VQ-compression cause horizontal and vertical lines which make the pixel values change not continuously or smoothly. Hence, the proposed scheme is able to determine if an unknown image is VQ-compressed or not. Further, the PoV-like effect exists because of the same probability of '0' and '1' method of secret message, and Yang's shortest-group encoding choses either CW or CW' in a group. The distribution of predicted codewords appearance show high correlation if the unknown image is truly a stego image of Yang et al.'s method. In our experimental results, the accuracy rate reaches over 90 %. Most of the stego image could be indicated, and cover images and traditional VQ-compressed images are also classified.

Acknowledgments. This research was partially supported by the National Science Council of the Republic of China under the Grant NSC 100-2221-E-015-001-MY2- and NSC 102-2221-E-015-001-.

References

[1] El-Alfy, E.S.M., Al-Sadi, A.A.: High-capacity image steganography based on overlapped pixel differences and modulus function. Networked Digital Technologies 294(1), 243–252 (2012)

[2] Li, X., Li, B., Luo, X., Yang, B., Zhu, R.: Steganalysis of a PVD-based content adaptive image steganography. Signal Processing 93(9), 2529–2538 (2013)

[3] Linde, Y., Bruzo, A., Gray, R.M.: An algorithm for vector quantizer design. IEEE Transactions on Communications 28(1), 84–95 (1980)

[4] Lou, D.C., Hu, C.H.: LSB steganographic method based on reversible histogram transformation function for resisting statistical steganalysis. Information Sciences 188(1), 346–358 (2012)

[5] Lou, D.C., Chou, C.L., Tso, H.K., Chiu, C.C.: Active steganalysis for histogram-shifting based reversible data hiding. Optics Communications 285(10-11), 2510–2518 (2012)

[6] Lu, Z.M., Pan, J.S., Sun, S.H.: VQ-based digital image watermarking method. Electronics Letters 36(14), 1201–1202 (2000)

[7] Luo, X.Y., Wang, D.S., Wang, P., Liu, F.L.: A review on blind detection for image steganography. Signal Processing 88(9), 2138–2157 (2008)

[8] Ni, Z., Shi, Y.Q., Ansari, N., Su, W.: Reversible data hiding. IEEE Transactions on Circuits and Systems for Video Technology 16(3), 354–362 (2006)

[9] Noda, H., Niimi, M., Kawaguchi, E.: High-performance JPEG steganography using quantization index modulation in DCT domain. Pattern Recognition Letters 27(5), 455–461 (2006)

[10]   Qin, C., Chang, C.C., Chen, Y.C.: Efficient reversible data hiding for VQ-compressed images based on index mapping mechanism. Signal Processing 93(9), 2687–2695 (2013)

[11]   Sachnev, V., Kim, H.J.: Ternary data hiding technique for JPEG steganography. Digital Watermarking 6526(1), 202–210 (2011)

[12]   Tsui, S.R., Huang, C.T., Wang, W.J.: Image steganography using gradient adjacent prediction in side-match vector quantization. Advances in Intelligent Systems and Applications 2(1), 121–129 (2013)

[13]   Westfeld, A., Pfitzmann, A.: Attacks on steganographic systems. In: Pfitzmann, A. (ed.) IH 1999. LNCS, vol. 1768, pp. 61–76. Springer, Heidelberg (2000)

[14]   Wu, H.C., Chang, C.C.: A novel digital image watermarking scheme based on the vector quantization technique. Computers & Security 24(6), 460–471 (2005)

[15]   Yang, C.H., Weng, C.Y., Wang, S.J., Sun, H.M.: Grouping strategies for promoting image quality of watermarking on the basis of vector quantization. Journal of Visual Communication and Image Representation 21(1), 49–55 (2010)

[16]   S-Tools, a steganography software that allows audio and image files to be hidden within other audio and image files,
        http://www.cs.vu.nl/~ast/books/mos2/zebras.html

[17]   Uncompressed Colour Image Database (UCID), provides a benchmark dataset for image retrieval,
        http://homepages.lboro.ac.uk/~cogs/datasets/ucid/ucid.html

Experimental Evaluation of an Algorithm for the Detection of Tampered JPEG Images

Giuseppe Cattaneo[1], Gianluca Roscigno[1], and Umberto Ferraro Petrillo[2,*]

[1] Dipartimento di Informatica
Università degli Studi di Salerno, I-84084, Fisciano, SA, Italy
{cattaneo,giroscigno}@unisa.it
[2] Dipartimento di Scienze Statistiche
Università di Roma *"La Sapienza"*, I-00185, Roma, Italy
umberto.ferraro@uniroma1.it

Abstract. This paper aims to experimentally evaluate the performance of one popular algorithm for the detection of tampered JPEG images: the algorithm by Lin *et al.* [1]. We developed a reference implementation for this algorithm and performed a deep experimental analysis, by measuring its performance when applied to the images of the CASIA TIDE public dataset, the *de facto* standard for the experimental analysis of this family of algorithms. Our first results were very positive, thus confirming the good performance of this algorithm. However, a closer inspection revealed the existence of an unexpected anomaly in a consistent part of the images of the CASIA TIDE dataset that may have influenced our results as well as the results of previous studies conducted using this dataset. By taking advantage of this anomaly, we were able to develop a variant of the original algorithm which exhibited better performance on the same dataset.

Keywords: Digital Image Forensics, JPEG Image Integrity, Double Quantization Effect, Evaluation Datasets.

1 Introduction

Nowadays, the manipulation of digital images is simpler than ever thanks to solutions like sophisticated photo-editing software or photo-sharing social networks. Indeed, one of the key characteristics of digital images is their pliability to manipulation. As a consequence, we can no longer take the authenticity of digital photos for granted. This can be a serious problem in situations where the reliability of the images plays a crucial role, such as when conducting criminal investigations. This has led, in the recent years, to the development of the Digital Image Forensics, a discipline that is responsible for the acquisition and the analysis of images found on digital devices for investigation purposes (see, e.g., [2,3,4,5,6,7]).

---

* Corresponding author.

Linawati et al. (Eds.): ICT-EurAsia 2014, LNCS 8407, pp. 643–652, 2014.
© IFIP International Federation for Information Processing 2014

One of the problems faced by this discipline is to verify if a digital image is authentic or has been manipulated after the acquisition (*image tampering*). Several algorithms have been proposed in the scientific literature for solving this problem, such as [1], [4], [5]. It is a common practice to accompany these contributions with an experimental analysis devoted to prove the viability of the proposed approach in the real practice. A popular dataset that is widely used for these experimentations is the CASIA TIDE dataset [8]. In this paper, we focus our attention on a particular algorithm for the detection of tampered JPEG digital images: the algorithm by Lin *et al.* [1]. Despite its popularity, this algorithm has never been tested on the CASIA TIDE dataset. We decided to close this gap, by developing an implementation of this algorithm and testing it over several different variants of this dataset. The results are contrasting. On a side, they confirm the good performance of the Lin *et al.* algorithm. On the other side, we experimented an anomaly in a consistent number of images forming the CASIA TIDE dataset which is likely to partially influence the results of the experiments conducted using these images. By taking advantage of this anomaly, we were able to further improve the performance of the original algorithm.

Organization of the Paper. In Section 2 we provide some details about the JPEG standard. In Section 3, we review some of the main contributions in the field of the JPEG image integrity. The aim of this work is illustrated in Section 4. Then, in Section 5, we focus on the Lin *et al.* algorithm. Section 6 describes the experiments we have conducted and their results. Finally, in Section 7 we draw some concluding remarks for our work.

2   The JPEG Standard

The JPEG [9] is a very popular standard for the encoding of digital images. It uses several techniques to guarantee very high compression rates at the expense of a small degradation in the image quality. The core of this standard is a lossy-compression technique based on the discrete cosine transform (*DCT*). In a few words, this technique assumes that an input image is encoded in the YCbCr format, where the Y channel holds the luminance component of the image, and the Cb and Cr chrominance channels hold, respectively, the blue minus luminance component of the image and the red minus luminance component of the image. The DCT operation works by logically splitting each image channel into blocks of 8×8 pixels and by converting them from the spatial domain into the frequency domain, producing blocks of 8×8 *DCT coefficients*, for a total of 64 frequencies. Once in the frequency domain, these coefficients are compressed by drastically reducing the amount of information provided by the high frequencies (i.e., quantization). This is done by dividing for a fixed constant (*quantization step*) each component of the 8×8 block of the DCT coefficient matrix and, then, by rounding the resulting values. The quantization steps can be chosen according to the amount of information to leave out from the frequencies, thus influencing the quality and the size of the compressed image (*quality factor*,

QF). For different frequencies and channels, the quantization steps are saved in quantization matrices which can be extracted from the JPEG image. In general, there is a luminance quantization matrix for the luminance channel and a chroma quantization matrix for the two chrominance channels. At the end of this step, quantized coefficients are sequenced and losslessly compressed. The quality factor of a JPEG image (see [10]) can vary in the range $[1, 100]$, where smaller values result in a lower quality of the compressed image and a higher compression degree.

3   JPEG Image Integrity

The digital image integrity research field concerns with the problem of assessing if a digital image is the result of some *forging* operation. By this term, we mean all the techniques used to alter the contents of an authentic image, such as painting new objects in a portrayed scene or copying the region of an image over another image (*splicing* operation). Detecting the forgery of a JPEG image can be harder than for other formats because the compression steps employed by this encoding may delete the forgery traces left in a tampered image. However, an algorithm could also try to discover new traces caused by recompression of a tampered image and use these traces to detect the forgeries. In fact, the artifacts introduced by JPEG compression (so said *JPEG blocking artifacts*) can be seen as an inherent "watermark" for compressed images. These artifacts result to be modified when a JPEG image is altered by means of forging operations.

Many image integrity algorithms follow this approach (see, e.g., [1], [4], [5]). These algorithms use some of the statistical properties of the DCT coefficients to detect inconsistencies in the blocking artifacts of a target JPEG image. One of the first detection technique is described in [11]: it is a method that estimates the primary quantization matrix from a doubly compressed JPEG image using the histograms of the individual DCT coefficients. A similar approach has been proposed by Ye *et al.* in [4]. First, they used the histogram of the DCT coefficients to estimate the quantization step size and, then, they measured the inconsistency of quantization errors between different image regions for estimating local compression blocking artifacts measure. A major drawback of this algorithm is that it requires a preliminary human intervention to select a suspicious region of the image to analyze. Farid [5] proposed a technique, based on the detection of *JPEG ghosts*, to establish whether a region of an image was originally compressed at quality factor different than others regions of the same image. The disadvantage of this technique is that it only works when the tampered region has a lower quality than the surrounding image. Lin *et al.* presented in [1] a method for detecting and locating doubly compressed blocks in a JPEG image. This is done by examining the *double quantization* (DQ) effect contained in the DCT coefficients, and computing the Block Posterior Probability Map (BPPM) using a Bayesian approach.

4   Aim of This Work

The aim of this work is to experimentally assess the effectiveness of the Lin
et al. algorithm for detecting the tampering of JPEG images. The authors of
this algorithm already conducted an experimental evaluation of its performance.
However, this evaluation was conducted using a proprietary dataset, thus limiting the possibility to compare the performance of their algorithm with other
alternative approaches. As recognized by the authors of the algorithm, such a
choice was motivated by the difficulty in assembling a large set of images that
have not been (or that have been) tampered for sure. Nowadays, this problem
seems to be partially solved. The arising interest toward this topic has led to
the development of public datasets of images, to be used for evaluating digital
tampering detection algorithms. This fact marks an important opportunity for
the scientific community working in this field, as it allows to compare the different algorithms proposed so far according to a common benchmark. Moreover, it
becomes possible to evaluate the performance of an algorithm in a neutral way.

5   The Algorithm by Lin *et al.*

The algorithm by Lin *et al.* [1] detects tampered images by examining the *double
quantization* (DQ) effect contained in the DCT coefficients. This effect occurs
when the DCT coefficients histogram of an image has periodically missing values
or some periodic pattern of peaks and valleys. According to Lin *et al.*, this
effect can be used for image authentication. To this end, they show that the
image regions (i.e. 8×8 blocks) that do not exhibit the DQ effect are probably
tampered. Namely, in a tampered image, untampered blocks will exhibit the DQ
effect, while tampered blocks (also called *doctored* blocks) will not.

The algorithm works as follows. As a preliminary step, if the input image
I is not a JPEG image, it is converted to this format at highest quality. The
first step of the algorithm is the extraction from I of the DCT coefficients and
of the quantization tables for each of the three YCbCr channels. As second
step, the algorithm builds one DCT coefficients histogram for each of the three
YCbCr channels and for each of the 64 frequencies. The computed histograms
are used for determining a probability value which indicates if a particular 8×8
block of the input channel image is doctored, by checking the DQ effect. In
turns, in the third step, these probabilities are combined together to produce the
Block Posterior Probability Map (BPPM). The resulting BPPM is thresholded to
distinguish between (probably) doctored parts and undoctored parts. In details,
for each image and for each channel, the values of the corresponding BPPM are
classified, according to a threshold T, into two classes: tampered blocks (C_0) and
untampered blocks (C_1). The fourth step is the extraction of a four-dimensional
feature vector for each of the three YCbCr channels. The first feature is the
sum of the variances of the probabilities in C_0 and C_1. The second feature is
the squared difference between the mean probabilities of C_0 and C_1. The third
feature, T_{opt}, is a threshold that maximizes the ratio between the second feature

and the first feature. When using T_{opt}, we expect that the blocks in the class C_0 (i.e. those that have lower probability of T_{opt}) correspond to the doctored blocks. The last feature, K_0, is a measure of the connectivity of C_0 blocks: more is connected C_0, then smaller is K_0. In the last step of the algorithm, a trained Support Vector Machine (SVM) dichotomous classifier is run to decide, starting from the previously extracted features, whether the image is doctored or not.

6   Experimental Analysis

In this section we detail the results of the experimental analysis we conducted on the Lin *et al.* algorithm. To begin, we developed a Java-based implementation of this algorithm[1]. This implementation, here named DQD, includes two core modules:

- The **Feature Extractor** module is in charge of extracting the features used for the classification by the Lin *et al.* algorithm from a batch of input images. The extraction is performed with the help of the libjpeg library [12]. If the input image is not in the JPEG format, we apply the JPEG compression algorithm at the maximum quality factor.
- The **SVM Manager** module is in charge of managing the SVM classifier to be used for detecting tampered images or not. It uses the SVM implementation available with the Java Machine Learning library [13], using the LIBSVM module. To get more accurate decisions, our classifier uses the *Cross Validation (CV)* and the *Grid Search (GS)* techniques. The *CV* technique is a method of sampling used to divide the original sample into two subsets: in the first subset we estimate the parameters of a model, while in the second subset we measure the predictive ability of the estimate. The *GS* technique is a search technique used to identify the parameters that optimize the performance of the classifier exploiting the cross validation.

The next step has been to assess the performance of the developed implementation by analyzing its experimental behavior on several datasets. In the following, we introduce the datasets used in our experimentations, then we describe the experimental setting and discuss the outcoming results.

6.1   Dataset

In the recent years, several public datasets have been released for evaluating tampered image detection algorithms. If we restrict our interest to JPEG-based datasets, there is only one choice that has become the *de facto* standard for these experimentations: the CASIA TIDE dataset[2] [8]. It is available in two

---

[1] A copy of the source code of our implementation is available upon request.

[2] Credits for the use of the CASIA Tampered Image Detection Evaluation Database (CASIA TIDE) v2.0 are given to the National Laboratory of Pattern Recognition, Institute of Automation, Chinese Academy of Science, Corel Image Database and the photographers. http://forensics.idealtest.org

versions: v1.0 and v2.0. The v1.0 version is a small-scale dataset of low resolution images. The v2.0 version is a large-scale dataset containing 7, 491 authentic and 5, 123 tampered color images. The images have different resolutions, varying from 240 × 160 to 900 × 600 pixels, and different formats (i.e., BMP, TIFF, JPEG). Tampered images included in this dataset are the result of a splicing that has been dissimulated, sometimes, by using a *blur* operation over the tampered image.

We have chosen for our experiments the v2.0 of the dataset because it contains a large number of high resolution images, tampered using more sophisticated techniques. In addition, this dataset has been widely used in the scientific literature for evaluating tampered images detection algorithms. Thus, its adoption would simplify the comparison of the performance of the Lin *et al.* algorithm with other detection algorithms.

Starting from the original CASIA TIDE v2.0 dataset, we extracted a subset of images, called *SC_ALL*, containing 2, 000 random training photos divided into 1, 000 authentic (990 JPEG and 10 BMP) and 1, 000 tampered (633 TIFF and 367 JPEG). The remaining 6, 491 authentic (44 BMP and 6, 447 JPEG) and 3, 875 tampered images (2, 426 TIFF and 1, 449 JPEG) were used for SVM testing. Notice that some tampered images were left out of our experiments because they originated from non-JPEG images and, thus, they could not exhibit the DQ effect on which relies the Lin *et al.* algorithm. A second dataset, called *SC_JPEG*, has been obtained by filtering only the JPEG images of *SC_ALL*. A third dataset, called *DC_ALL*, was obtained by considering all images of *SC_ALL* and performing a JPEG recompression on authentic images using a quality factor randomly chosen in the set {100, 99, 95, 90, 85, 80, 75, 70}. Finally, we introduced a fourth dataset, *DC_JPEG*, obtained by filtering only the JPEG images existing in *DC_ALL*.

6.2   Preliminary Experimentations

In this section, we present the results of a first round of experimentations of the Lin *et al.* algorithm. To begin, we conducted a preliminary test to evaluate the optimal number of frequencies to be used for building the DCT coefficients histograms required by the algorithm. In theory, for each color channel, these coefficients are related to an overall number of 64 frequencies. However, since the high frequencies DCT coefficients are often quantized to zero, we will use only the lower frequencies histograms for each channel. To this end, we ran the algorithm on our datasets using, respectively, the 32, the 48 and the 64 lower frequencies. The outcoming results show that the best setting, in terms of *recognition rate* (RR, i.e. the percentage of testing images correctly recognized as authentic or tampered), is reached when using 32 frequencies. Therefore, in subsequent experiments, we will always use this value.

Table 1 shows the percentage of testing images correctly recognized as authentic or tampered (RR) when we ran DQD on the datasets defined in Section 6.1 using the 32 lower frequencies. These numbers confirm the good performance of the Lin *et al.* algorithm. We observe that the algorithm was able to correctly

Table 1. Recognition rates, in percentage, of the Lin *et al.* algorithm on different variants of the CASIA TIDE v2.0 dataset using different features

Algorithm	SC_ALL	DC_ALL	SC_JPEG	DC_JPEG
DQD	71.00	69.55	84.32	85.08
DQD_R	71.92	71.29	84.79	85.51
DQD_F	71.74	70.85	85.76	86.41
DQD_Q	86.01	74.41	85.37	85.79
DQD_FQ	88.78	78.72	87.46	89.30
DQD_QR	86.13	75.10	85.45	85.93
DQD_FR	73.06	72.25	86.36	87.30
DQD_FQR	89.15	80.17	89.25	90.10

recognize as original or tampered about the 70% of the images belonging to the *SC_ALL* and *DC_ALL* datasets. This percentage increases by, approximately, a 15% when considering the variants of these datasets including only JPEG images. This seems to indicate that, differently from TIFF tampered images, JPEG tampered images are able to retain some statistical artifacts useful for the classifier to detect their forgery. This is confirmed by the improvement of the performance of the algorithm on doubly compressed images (recall that the algorithm has been designed for dealing with doubly compressed JPEG images) while the inclusion of TIFF images (*DC_ALL*) leads to a small degradation of the overall performance of the algorithm.

A deeper analysis of the images of the CASIA TIDE dataset revealed a sort of anomaly. The luminance quality factor of the majority of the JPEG tampered images is always the same (i.e., either set to about 90 or to about 100), while authentic images have more variable quality factors, ranging mostly in the interval [70, 100]. This fact may compromise the quality of this dataset since it introduces a separation criteria between authentic and tampered images that is relatively easy to verify.

6.3   Experimenting with New Features

Starting from the observations made in Section 6.2, we explored the possibility to improve the performance of the Lin *et al.* algorithm, by enriching the SVM classifier with three additional groups of features.

The first feature is an estimation of the image luminance quality factor. This feature has been chosen for two reasons. First, we noticed that some of the Lin *et al.* algorithm features are influenced by the applied JPEG compression rate, i.e. quality factor. Second, we are interested in exploiting the anomaly found in the CASIA TIDE dataset, about the luminance quality factors being always the same for tampered images, to see how much it could influence the performance of the classification. In our experiments, we extracted this feature starting by the luminance quantization table embedded in each JPEG image. Namely, we apply an estimate of the inverse formula of [10] that, given a JPEG image quantization table and the standard quantization table, returns an estimation of the quality factor used to determine the image quantization matrix.

The second feature is the relative frequency of doctored blocks existing in authentic and tampered images on each channel. We noticed that both tampered and authentic images contain blocks that have been considered doctored by the Lin *et al.* method. However, if we consider only the chrominance channels, the average number of doctored blocks for tampered images clearly differs from the average number of doctored blocks for authentic images. Therefore, this information can improve the separation of these two classes.

The third feature we introduce is the spatial resolution of the input image (i.e., width and height). We consider this feature because we noticed that some of the features used by the Lin *et al.* algorithm in part depend on the resolution of the input image.

After introducing these new features, we have trained and tested the SVM classifier using the original features of the Lin *et al.* algorithm plus different combinations of the new ones. The results are presented in Table 1. Here, the R capital letter marks the inclusion of the image resolution feature (i.e, width feature and height feature), the F capital letter marks the inclusion of the relative frequencies of tampered blocks for each color channel feature and the Q capital letter marks the inclusion of the luminance quality factor estimation feature.

According to these results, it seems that the introduction of the feature related to the image resolution (DQD_R) brings only a slight advantage on the performance of the DQD algorithm on all considered datasets. An improvement is also achieved when considering the features related to the relative frequencies of tampered blocks (DQD_F), especially for the case of JPEG images. This is a further confirmation of the ability of the algorithm to detect the DQ effect on doubly compressed JPEG tampered images.

A completely different behavior is the one we observed with the introduction of the feature related to the image luminance quality factor. On the *SC_ALL* dataset, the inclusion of this feature led to a consistent performance improvement over DQD. On the *DC_ALL* dataset the improvement was consistent ye,t but smaller than on the *SC_ALL* dataset. On the *SC_JPEG* and *DC_JPEG* datasets, we measured only a slight performance improvement. To explain this we recall the observation made in Section 6.2 about the JPEG tampered images belonging to the CASIA TIDE datasets. These images are always saved using fixed quality factors, whereas their non-tampered counterparts are saved using variable quality factors. In addition, TIFF tampered images are automatically converted by our algorithm into JPEG images with a quality factor fixed to 100. These two facts provide the classifier with a clear distinction between tampered and non-tampered images, thus justifying the performance boost of DQD_Q on *SC_ALL*. If we leave out from the comparison the TIFF images, like in the *SC_JPEG* case, the improvement is still present but is smaller. Here the gap between the quality factor of authentic images (87, in the average) and tampered images (90, in the average) is smaller, thus preventing a clear separation between these two sets. The anomaly of the CASIA TIDE dataset is weakened when considering authentic images that have been recompressed using random quality factors, such as in DC_ALL. Here, the performance boost of DQD_Q is much smaller than in the SC_ALL case. Instead, the recompression of the input images brings a little benefit to DQD_Q when dealing with only JPEG images. In this case, the performance loss due to the absence of a clear distinction between the quality factor of tampered and authentic images is balanced by the ability of the algorithm to perform better when dealing with the DQ effect of doubly compressed images. According to our experiments, even the mixing of these new features improves the overall quality of the detection. This is especially the case of DQD_FQR algorithm, which is the variant of the Lin *et al.* algorithm exhibiting the better performance, by considering all the features of the original algorithm plus all the features we introduced in our experiments.

7   Conclusions and Future Work

In this paper, we analyzed the experimental performance of the algorithm by Lin *et al.* [1], a popular technique for the detection of tampered JPEG images. The experiments have been conducted on several variants of the v.2.0 CASIA TIDE dataset, a collection of images developed for the experimental evaluation of this family of algorithms. The final aim of this experimentation was to facilitate the comparison of the Lin *et al.* algorithm with other alternative approaches by measuring its performance on a widely-used testbed.

On a side, the results we obtained confirmed the good performance of this algorithm. On the other side, we were able to detect a sort of anomaly in the way the CASIA TIDE dataset has been built (i.e., many of the tampered images have been saved using almost-fixed quality factors) that could facilitate the detection activity. The relevance of this anomaly has been confirmed by a further experimentation, where we added to the original Lin *et al.* algorithm the ability to detect whether an image is tampered or not by looking also at this anomaly. As a matter of fact, the revised version of the algorithm exhibited a significant performance boost on a dataset featuring almost all the images of the CASIA TIDE dataset.

These observations pose the question about the full statistical soundness of the CASIA TIDE dataset while suggesting the opportunity to reconsider the results of all the experimental studies that have been conducted so far using this dataset. As a future direction, it would be useful to fix the anomaly we found in the CASIA TIDE dataset or, as an alternative, to introduce of an improved testbed for the experimentation of image integrity detection algorithm able to solve the problems existing in the CASIA TIDE dataset. Concerning the Lin *et al.* algorithm, a future direction for this work would be to extend our experimental analysis to other relevant contributions existing in the field of algorithms for assessing the integrity of JPEG images.

References

1. Lin, Z., He, J., Tang, X., Tang, C.-K.: Fast, Automatic and Fine-grained Tampered JPEG Image Detection via DCT Coefficient Analysis. Pattern Recognition 42(11), 2492–2501 (2009)
2. Lukáš, J., Fridrich, J., Goljan, M.: Digital Camera Identification from Sensor Pattern Noise. IEEE Transactions on Information Forensics and Security 1, 205–214 (2006)
3. Khanna, N., Mikkilineni, A.K., Chiu, G.T.C., Allebach, J.P., Delp, E.J.: Scanner Identification using Sensor Pattern Noise. In: Proceedings of the SPIE International Conference on Security, Steganography, and Watermarking of Multimedia Contents IX, vol. 6505(1), pp. 1–11 (2007)
4. Ye, S., Sun, Q., Chang, E.-C.: Detecting Digital Image Forgeries by Measuring Inconsistencies of Blocking Artifact. In: IEEE International Conference on Multimedia and Expo 2007, pp. 12–15 (2007)
5. Farid, H.: Exposing Digital Forgeries from JPEG Ghosts. IEEE Transactions on Information Forensics and Security 4(1), 154–160 (2009)
6. Cattaneo, G., Faruolo, P., Petrillo, U.F.: Experiments on improving sensor pattern noise extraction for source camera identification. In: 2012 Sixth International Conference on Innovative Mobile and Internet Services in Ubiquitous Computing (IMIS), pp. 609–616 (July 2012)
7. Castiglione, A., Cattaneo, G., Cembalo, M., Petrillo, U.F.: Experimentations with Source Camera Identification and Online Social Networks. Journal of Ambient Intelligence and Humanized Computing 4(2), 265–274 (2013)
8. Institute of Automation, Chinese Academy of Sciences (CASIA). CASIA Tampered Image Detection Evaluation Database (CASIA TIDE) v2.0 (2013), http://forensics.idealtest.org/
9. Wallace, G.K.: The JPEG Still Picture Compression Standard. Communications of the ACM, 30–44 (1991)
10. Independent JPEG Group code library (December 2013), http://www.ijg.org/
11. Lukáš, J., Fridrich, J.: Estimation of Primary Quantization Matrix in Double Compressed JPEG Images. In: Proc. Digital Forensic Research Workshop, pp. 5–8 (2003)
12. Tom Lane and the Independent JPEG Group (IJG). libjpeg (2013), http://libjpeg.sourceforge.net/
13. Abeel, T., de Peer, Y.V., Saeys, Y.: Java-ML: A Machine Learning Library. Journal of Machine Learning Research 10, 931–934 (2009)

A Semantic-Based Malware Detection System Design Based on Channels

Peige Ren, Xiaofeng Wang, Chunqing Wu, Baokang Zhao, and Hao Sun

School of Computer Science
National University of Defense Technology
Changsha, Hunan, China
renpeige@163.com, {xf_wang,chunqingwu,bkzhao}@nudt.edu.cn,
sunhao4257@gmail.com

Abstract. With the development of information technology, there are massive and heterogeneous data resources in the internet, as well as the malwares are appearing in different forms, traditional text-based malware detection cannot efficiently detect the various malwares. So it is becoming a great challenge about how to realize semantic-based malware detection. This paper proposes an intelligent and active data interactive coordination model based on channels. The coordination channels are the basic construction unit of this model, which can realize various data transmissions. By defining the coordination channels, the coordination atoms and the coordination units, the model can support diverse data interactions and can understand the semantic of different data resources. Moreover, the model supports graphical representation of data interaction, so we can design complex data interaction system in the forms of flow graph. Finally, we design a semantic-based malware detection system using our model; the system can understand the behavior semantics of different malwares, realizing the intelligent and active malware detection.

Keywords: Malware detection, interactive coordination model, semantic.

1 Introduction

With the rapid development of Internet technology, the data types and data amount in the internet is growing in amazing speed, and more and more malwares with different types are appearing, such as virus, worm and Trojan horse. So it is becoming a great challenge to accurately detect the various malwares from massive and heterogeneous internet data resources.

Traditional malware detection methods are based on text-based feature codes matching [1, 2], they cannot realize semantic-based similarity matching. And the malwares are appearing in different forms, it is difficult to accurately detect the various malwares from massive and heterogeneous internet data resources. This paper presents an intelligent and active data interactive coordination model based on channels, and we designed a semantic-based malware detection system using our model. Specifically, the contributions of this paper are fourfold: (1) Abstract the behaviors of

Linawati et al. (Eds.): ICT-EurAsia 2014, LNCS 8407, pp. 653–662, 2014.

data transmission, organization and processing as coordination channel, coordination atom and coordination unit respectively, which can support the understanding of semantic and data initiatively push, realize diverse data interactions; meanwhile define complex control functions during the data interaction, supporting the modeling of intelligent, initiative and flexible data interaction systems. (2) Support graphical representation of data interactions, which can be used to explicitly and visually design complex data interaction systems in the form of flow graph. (3) Accurately define the behavioral semantics of coordination channels and coordination atoms with logical mathematical formulas, which can be used to strictly verify the consistency between the system model design and the system realization. (4) Design a semantic-based malware detection system using the proposed model, which can realize semantic-based intelligent malware detection.

The remainder of the paper is organized as follows. Section 2 introduces the related work. Section 3 presents the intelligent and active data interactive coordination model based on channels. Then we present the coordination channels and coordination atoms, introducing their classification, operations and behavior semantics in section 4 and section 5. Followed the coordination unit are presented, and we design several special coordination units in section 6. In section 7, we design a semantic-based malware detection system using our model and conclusion can be found in Section 8.

2   Related Works

Future data interaction system should have the characteristics of intelligence, initiative and flexibility. However, for the theoretical modeling, we have not found a special data interactive coordination model to design data interaction system effectively. The related research works about interactive coordination mainly pay attention to the fields of multi-Agent and software coordination.

Multi-Agent interaction is the kernel of the research of distributed artificial intelligence and Multi-Agent Systems (MAS) [3], it realized the capability of autonomic group interaction between multiple Agent, can solve a complicated problem coordinately in a distributed environment. Early researches about Multi-Agent interaction include typical distributed problem solving system such as Actor [4], DVM [5], and MACE [6], these works emphasize the compact group cooperation between the Agent, and data interaction is in the form of tight coupling between entities. Researchers later recognized that the tight coupling interaction collaborative cannot meet the demand of increasingly complex network environment and the reality needs, which prompting a variety mode of interaction between agents. A BDI language called MAL is presented in [7], it overcomes the misunderstanding of the concepts of belief, desire and intention, supporting multi-agent interaction more effectively.

On the other hand, the coordination between software entities has been a hotspot problem. Software coordination [8] means that establishing connections between software entities, constraining the interaction behaviors between them to make them work together in harmony in an open environment. Farhad Arbab divided the software coordination models into data driven coordination model [10] and control driven coordination model [9]. The data driven coordination model mainly focused on the data exchange between coordination entities, realizing the shared space-based anonymous communication between them, the coordination entities need to call coordination primitives to exchange information with outside. The control driven coordination model, such as Manifold [11], Darwin [12], IWIM [13] and Reo [14], mainly focused on the status change of coordination entities and the control flow between them. The coordination entities were seen as black boxes with well-defined interfaces. They can perceive the change of external environment by accepting the messages through interfaces, which then caused their status change; meanwhile send messages to external environment to change surrounding environment. The control driven coordination model realized the separation of computation and coordination, helping to realize the maintenance and reuse of computing and coordination module.

3   The Overview of the Model

For realizing the intelligent, active and flexible data interaction in the internet, we abstracted the functions of data interaction, proposed a kind of intelligent and active data interactive coordination model.

In the model, the functional modules of data transmission, organization and control are defined abstractly as the coordination channel, coordination atom and coordination unit respectively. The coordination channels are the basic construction unit of this model, which can realize various data transmissions. The coordination atoms are the management units of the coordination channels as well as the data organization units in the network, which can be divided into syntax and semantic coordination atoms. The coordination atoms can find the useful data resources intelligently, and connect the corresponding channels together to form a data channel, realizing intelligent data aggregation, organization and distribution. The coordination units are formed by some coordination atoms and coordination channels connected in a certain topological structure, they can realize some specific data control function during data interaction.

4   Coordination Channels

A coordination channel can be seen as a point-to-point medium of communication between two interactive interfaces, it can transmit data resources. Every channel has two channel ends, which can be divided as three types: send ends, receive ends and bidirection ends. A send end accepts data into channel and sends data to the receive end along the channel; a receive end accepts data from channel and send data outside; a bidirection end can realize the functions of both send channel and receive channel.

The coordination channels are the basic functional unit in the model. They can be assigned by different functions according to the actual requirements. The synchronous channel supports the synchronous data transmission between its ends, can realize the real-time synchronous data interaction between users; while the asynchronous channel can cache the data inside the channel, can realize the loosely coupled asynchronous interaction between users, avoiding the interdependence between the users.

4.1   Coordination Channel Types

The coordination channels can be divided into data flow channels and control channels. The data flow channels include: Sync channel, SyncWrite channel, AsyncWrite channel, FIFO channel, RAW channel, etc. The control channels transmit only the control messages, mainly used to realize the remote procedure call between the entities connected the channel. Every channel has two ends of the same type or not. The behavior of a channel depends on its synchronizing properties, the types and numbers of its ends, the size of buffer inside the channel, and the loss policy, etc. Table 1 shows the types and the behavior description of channels. Certainly, we can present more new channels according to our requirement.

Table 1. Coordination channel types

Channel Type		Channel Behavior Description
	Sync	The channel has a send and a receive end, the I/O operations on the ends must succeed at the same time.
	SyncLossy	The channel has a send and a receive end, the send end can accepts data resources from outside at any time, if the operations on the receive end cannot take the data simultaneously, the data is lost.
	SyncWrite	The channel has two send ends, the write operations on its two ends must succeed simultaneously, and the accepted data objects are lost.
	AsyncWrite	The channel has two send ends, the write operations on its two ends must succeed asynchronously, and the accepted data objects are lost.
Data Flow Channel	Filter(pat)	The channel has a send and a receive end, when the data written to the send end does not match with the pattern pat, the data is lost; or else the channel behaves the same way as a Sync channel.
	FIFO	The channel has a send, a receive end and an unbounded buffer, the receive end can accept data at any time and the data are stored in the buffer, the operations on the receive end can obtain the data in the FIFO order.
	nFIFO n	The channel has a send, a receive end and a bounded buffer with capacity n, it operate in the same way of the FIFO channel until the buffer is full.
	RAW A B	The channel has two bidirection ends, the operation on end A can only obtain data from B when the data written to A is obtain by the operation on B simultaneously.
Control		The channel has a send and a receive end, the user connected to send end can send control command to realize the remote procedure call between the users.

4.2   Behavior Semantics of Coordination Channels

This section tries to describe the behavior semantics of coordination channels in formula. For a channel c, whose send and receive end are c_i and c_o, we have:

recv(c_i, d) denotes that the data object d is successfully written to the channel end c_i. Particularly, **syn_recv(c_i, d)** means that the data d is successfully written to the sync coordination channel end c_i. While **offer(c_o, p)** denotes the multi-set of pairs (c_o, d), d is a data object that taken from the channel end c_o and match with the pattern p.

We use * denotes a channel end of any other channel, $\hat{e}$ denote the unique coordination atom on which the channel end e coincides, $d \ni p$ means data d matches with the pattern p, recv($\hat{e}$,d) and offer($\hat{e}$,p) express the data operating on coordination atom $\hat{e}$ (see section 5.3). So we can define the behavior semantics of coordination channels with logical mathematical formulas, the following are some examples:

Sync channel behavior semantic: For a Sync channel c, c_i and c_o are its send and receive end, the behavior semantic of Sync channel can be defined by (1) and (2).

$$\text{syn\_recv}(c_i, d) = \text{syn\_recv}(\hat{c}_o, d) \wedge (d \ni p) \tag{1}$$

$$\text{offer}(c_o, p) = \{(c_o, d) \mid (*, d) \in \text{offer}(\hat{c}_i, p)\} \tag{2}$$

AsyncWrite channel behavior semantic: The behavior semantic of AsyncWrite channel c whose send ends are c_{i1} and c_{i2} can be defined by equations (3) and (4).

$$\text{recv}(c_{i1}, d_1) = \text{recv}(c_{i2}, d_2) = \text{true} \tag{3}$$

$$|\text{offer}(\hat{c}_{i1}, p_1)| \neq |\text{offer}(\hat{c}_{i2}, p_2)| \tag{4}$$

Filter(pat) channel behavior semantic: The behavior semantic of a Filter(pat) channel c whose send and receive end are c_i and c_o can be defined by (5) and (6).

$$\text{recv}(c_i, d) = d \not\ni \text{pat} \vee \text{recv}(\hat{c}_o, d) \tag{5}$$

$$\text{offers}(c_o, p) = \{(c_o, d) \mid (*, d) \in \text{offers}(\hat{c}_i, p) \wedge d \ni \text{pat}\} \tag{6}$$

5   Coordination Atoms

Coordination atoms are the organization function module of channels, as well as the data management module in the network. The coordination atoms can accurately find the right data resources and actively connect the correlative channels together to form data transmission path, without the requirements of the address of interaction parties, realizing the space decoupling between the interaction parties.

5.1   Coordination Atom Types

The coordination atoms can be divided into syntactic atoms and semantic atoms.

The syntactic atoms organize the channels according to the data description forms, realizing the aggregation, organization and forwarding of data resources in the same representation form. We denote a syntactic atom by the symbol $\bigcirc$, as shown in Figure 1. The syntactic atoms are divided into several types. Here, we define the set of all channel ends coincident on an atom N as $[N] = \{x \mid x \rightarrow N\}$, and divide the $[N]$ into the sets Sed(N), Rev(N) and Bir(N), respectively denoting the sets of send, receive and bidirection ends that coincide on N. If Sed(N)≠∅ ∧Rev(N)=∅ , N is called a send coordination atom, such as A1 and A2 in Figure 1; if Sed(N)=∅ ∧Rev(N)≠∅ , N is called a receive coordination atom, such as A5 and A6; if Bir(N) ≠∅ , N is a called bidirection coordination atom; and if Sed(N)≠∅ ∧Rev(N)≠∅ , N is called mixed coordination atom, such as A3 and A4.

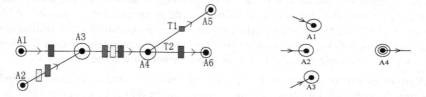

Fig. 1. Syntactic coordination atom   **Fig. 2.** Semantic coordination atom

The semantic coordination atom, denoted by the symbol ◎ (as shown in Figure 2), can extract the semantic information from various data resources. The semantic coordination atom first abstract the semantic features of data resources to construct a high-dimensional feature space, and the data resources and user request are expressed as high-dimensional points in the feature space, then use similarity search methods to find the data resources that have similar semantic to the user request, and forward them to the users. In Figure 2, the semantic coordination atom A4 can distinguish the semantic of the data resources from A1, A2 and A3, select the data resources with similar semantic to the user request and forward them.

5.2   Coordination Atom Operations

The main coordination atom operations are shown in Table 2. The parameter t indicates a time-out value, the operations fail if it does not succeed within the time t.

Table 2. Coordination atom operations

Operations	Behavior Description
a_create(A)	Create a coordination atom A for the connected channels
a_merge(A1, A2, A)	Merge the coordination atoms A1 and A2 to form a new atom A
a_split(A, A1(pat))	Produce a new atom A1 according to the data pattern pat, the channel ends matched with pat are split from A and connected to A1.
a_syn_write([t], A, d)	The operation succeeds as soon as having written the data object d to every channel end $x \in [A]$ simultaneously
a_write([t], A, d)	The operation succeeds when the data d is written to every channel end $x \in [A]$
a_read([t], A, v, p)	Read a data compatible with the pattern p from any one channel ends $x \in [A]$ into the variable v.
a_take([t], A, v, p)	Take a data compatible with the pattern p from any one channel ends $x \in [A]$ and read it into the variable v.
a_alert(A, p, f)	Register the function f as the callback function of the data compatible with pattern p in coordination atom A

5.3   Behavior Semantics of Coordination Atoms

The coordination atom manages the channel ends coinciding on it, and the behavior semantic of a coordination atom is the integration of the behavior semantics of all the channel ends on it, describing the data distribution on it.

For coordination atom A and a data pattern p, and the predicate $\int(O)$ designates an operation O is pending on its respective coordination atom if it is true, we define:

$$\text{offer}(A, p) = \begin{cases} \bigcup_{\int (a\_syn\_write(A,d))\vee(a\_write(A,d))} \{\langle \varepsilon, d \rangle \mid d \ni p\} & A \text{ is send atom} \\ \bigcup_{c_o \in Rev(A)} \text{offer}(c_o, d) & \text{otherwise} \end{cases} \quad (7)$$

If offer (A, p) is empty, we cannot obtain data from A; if offer (A, p) is not empty, that is, $\exists \langle x, d \rangle \in \text{offer}(A, p)$, then we can obtain data from A. The symbol ε represents "no channel end", means that when A is a send coordination atom, the data can only be obtained from the write operations pending on A.

For a coordination atom A and a data d, we define:

$$\text{recv}(A, d) = \begin{cases} \bigcap_{\int (a\_take(A,v,p))\vee(a\_alert(A,p,f))} d \ni p & A \text{ is receive atom} \\ \bigcap_{c_i \in Sed(A) \wedge d \ni p} \text{recv}(c_i, d) & \text{otherwise} \end{cases} \quad (8)$$

From the equation (8), we can find that when A is a receive coordination atom, it accepts the data d only if d matches with the pattern p of all a_take and a_alert operations pending on A; otherwise, A accepts d only when all send ends in [N] accept d.

For a coordination atom A that connected channels are all Sync channels, we have:

$$\text{syn\_recv}(A, d) = \begin{cases} \bigcap_{\int (a\_take(A,v,p))\vee(a\_alert(A,p,f))} d \ni p & A \text{ is receive atom} \\ \bigcap_{c_i \in Sed(A) \wedge d \ni p \wedge c \ni Sync} \text{syn\_recv}(c_i, d) & \text{otherwise} \end{cases} \quad (9)$$

The equation (9) has the similar behavior semantic as equation (8), except that the operations on A must be done simultaneously.

For a mixed atom A, we have:

$$\tau(A) = \{<c_x, d> \mid <c_x, d> \in \text{offer}(A, p) \wedge \text{recv}(A,d) \wedge (d \ni p)\} \quad (10)$$

In the equation (10), $\tau(A)$ means the data objects that are eligible for transfer at the mixed coordination atom A.

6   Coordination Units

A coordination unit is formed by a set of coordination channels organized in special topology to realize specific control function during the data interaction in the network. With coordination units, the actors of data interaction do not need to think about how to control the data flow reasonably, realizing intelligent and flexible data interaction. Here we list several coordination units with special functions as follows. Besides, we can design more various flexible coordination units according the system requirement.

Data Flow Controller: This kind of coordination units can monitor and control the data flow in the network. As shown in the left of Figure 3, the unit is formed by the FIFO channels T1, T2, T3 and a synchronous channel T4. The data flow from channel ends a and b to end c is controlled by the channel T4, only when a data item is taken from end d synchronously, a data item can flow into channel T3 from A. The taking operation on end d can monitor and control the data flow from A to end c. While in the right of Figure 3, T4 is an nFIFO channel with a buffer of size n. Operations on the channel end d can monitor, back up the data flow to the end c, and the channel T4 can be seen as a leaky bucket policer to adjust the transmission rate of the data flow.

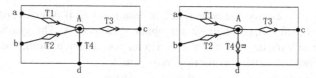

Fig. 3. Data Flow Controller

Semantic Aggregator: There have been many different data resources with similar semantic but of different representations, traditional syntactic-based matching methods cannot discover the data resources of user requirement efficiently. For realizing the accurately and efficiently discovery of data resources, we proposed the semantic aggregator. As shown in Figure 4, the semantic aggregator are formed by three Sync channels, one RAW channel, three syntactic coordination atoms and one semantic coordination atom. The data resources input from the channel ends a, b and c may have different types, to realize the semantic-based data retrieval, the semantic coordination atom D abstracts the semantic features of data resources and the user request from channel end d to map the data resources and user request to a high-dimensional feature space, then use similarity search methods to find the data resources that have similar semantic to the user request, and answer the user with the data resources through channel end d.

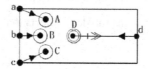

Fig. 4. Semantic Aggregator

7   Semantic-Based Malware Detection System

With the development of information technology, there are various malware in the internet, such as worm, Trojan horse and zombie. They are in different types, but all are harmful to the internet environment. Traditional text-based feature codes matching cannot detect all the malwares in different types. To realize semantic-based malware detection, we can use the semantic aggregator to distinguish the malware from normal data resources according to their semantics.

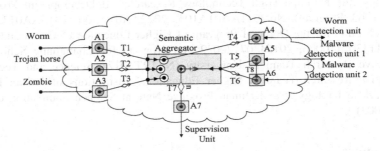

Fig. 5. The Semantic-based Malware Detection System

As shown in Figure 5, we design a semantic-based malware detection system. The worm, Trojan horse and zombie are different in data type, but all belong to the malware. The system built the data path between worm and worm detection unit according to syntactic-based accurate matching; the data resources flowed in the path are of the same type. The system built the data path connected to malware detection unit 1 and 2 using the semantic aggregator, the semantic aggregator can distinguish malware in this system, and the worm, Trojan horse and zombie can flow to malware detection unit 1 and 2 automatically. The coordination channel between coordination atom A5 and A6 is a SyncWrite channel, it provides that the malware detection unit 1 and 2 must obtain the malware synchronously. Besides, the coordination channel T7 is an nFIFO channel connected to the supervision unit, realizing the adjustment of the data transmission rate, and the supervision unit can monitor and back up the data resources flowed to the malware detection unit 1 and malware detection unit 2.

8   Conclusion

In order to realize semantic-based malware detection and data interaction efficiently, we propose an intelligent, active and flexible interactive coordination model based on channels. We present the coordination channels, coordination atoms, and coordination units in the model. The model can describe the process of the data organization, transmission and processing in network clearly, and support the graphical expression of data interaction. And we accurately define the behavioral semantics of coordination channels and coordination atoms, which can strictly verify the consistency between the system model design and the system realization. Finally, a semantic-based malware detection system instant is designed using the model. The model can efficiently organize, transmit and process the data resources in open, dynamic and heterogeneous network environment, which can promote the development of the advanced data interaction mechanisms.

Acknowledgment. The work described in this paper is partially supported by the grants of the National Basic Research Program of China (973 project) under Grant No.2009CB320503, 2012CB315906; the project of National Science Foundation of China under grant No.61070199, 61103189, 61103194, 61103182, 61202488, 61272482; the National High Technology Research and Development Program of China (863 Program) No.2011AA01A103, 2012AA01A506, 2013AA013505, the Research Fund for the Doctoral Program of Higher Education of China under Grant No.20114307110006, 20124307120032, the program for Changjiang Scholars and Innovative Research Team in University (No.IRT1012), Science and Technology Innovative Research Team in Higher Educational Institutions of Hunan Province ("network technology"); and Hunan Province Natural Science Foundation of China (11JJ7003).

References

1. Filiol, E., Helenius, M., Zanero, S.: Open problems in computer virology. J. Comput. Virol. 1, 55–66 (2006)
2. Szor, P.: The art of computer virus research and defense. Addison-Wesley Professional (2005)
3. Genesereth, M.R., Ketchpe, S.: Software Agents. Communications of the ACM 37(7), 48–96 (1994)
4. Hewitt, C.: Viewing Control Structures as Patterns of Passing Messages. Artificial Intelligence 8(3), 264–323 (1977)
5. Lesser, V., Corkill, D.: Functionally accurate: Cooperative distributed systems. IEEE Transactions on Systems, Man, and Cybernetics part C 11(1), 81–96 (1981)
6. Durfee, E.H., Montogomery, T.A.: MICE: A flexible testbed for intelligent coordination experiments. In: Proceedings of Distributed Artificial Intelligence Workshop (1988)
7. Kang, X.Q., Shi, C.Y.: Multi-agent interaction based on Bdi. Chinese Journal of Computers 22(11), 1166–1171 (1999) (in Chinese)
8. Lv, J., Ma, X.X., Tao, X.P., Xu, F., Hu, H.: The research and development of the Internetware. Science in China (Series E: Information Sciences) 36(10), 1037–1080 (2006) (in Chinese)
9. Papadopoulos, G.A., Arbab, F.: Coordination models and languages. Software Engineering (SEN) SEN-R9834, Centrum voor Wiskunde en Informatica (CWI), Amsterdam, Netherlands (December 1998)
10. Kielmann, T.: Objective Linda: A Coordination Model for Object-Oriented Parallel Programming [Ph.D. Thesis]. Germany, University of Siegen (1997)
11. Arbab, F., Herman, I., Spilling, P.: An overview of manifold and its implementation. Concurrency and Computation: Practice and Experience-Concurrency 5(1), 23–70 (1993)
12. Magee, J., Dulay, N., Eisenbach, S., Kramer, J.: Specifying distributed software architectures. In: Botella, P., Schäfer, W. (eds.) ESEC 1995. LNCS, vol. 989, pp. 137–153. Springer, Heidelberg (1995)
13. Arbab, F.: IWIM: A communication model for cooperative systems. In: Proceedings of the 2nd International Conference on the Design of Cooperative Systems (1996)
14. Arbab, F.: Reo: a channel-based coordination model for component composition. Mathematical Structures in Computer Science - MSCS 14(3), 329–366 (2004)

An Efficient Semantic-Based Organization and Similarity Search Method for Internet Data Resources

Peige Ren, Xiaofeng Wang, Hao Sun, Baokang Zhao, and Chunqing Wu

School of Computer Science
National University of Defense Technology
Changsha, Hunan, China
renpeige@163.com, {xf_wang,bkzhao,chunqingwu}@nudt.edu.cn,
sunhao4257@gmail.com

Abstract. A large number of data resources with different types are appearing in the internet with the development of information technology, and some negative ones have done harm to our society and citizens. In order to insure the harmony of the society, it is important to discovery the bad resources from the heterogeneous massive data resources in the cyberspace, the internet resource discovery has attracted increasing attention. In this paper, we present the iHash method, a semantic-based organization and similarity search method for internet data resources. First, the iHash normalizes the internet data objects into a high-dimensional feature space, solving the "feature explosion" problem of the feature space; second, we partition the high-dimensional data in the feature space according to clustering method, transform the data clusters into regular shapes, and use the Pyramid-similar method to organize the high-dimensional data; finally, we realize the range and kNN queries based on our method. At last we discuss the performance evaluation of the iHash method and find it performs efficiently for similarity search.

Keywords: feature space, high-dimensional index, similarity search.

1 Introduction

With the rapid expansion of information technology and the popularization of the Internet throughout the world, the data type and amount in the internet is growing in amazing speed, there are more and more data resources with different type appearing in the cyberspace, such as videos, digital images, text documents, etc. But some negative resources are harming our society and citizens, such as violent videos, pornographic pictures, reactionary remarks or bad public sentiments. To insure the harmony and development of the society, monitoring and discovering negative data resources from the heterogeneous massive data resources have become more and more important. To organize and mine internet data resources effectively, semantic-based similarity search has been advocated; while for the massiveness and heterogeneity of the internet data resources, it's difficult to discovery the negative data resources quickly and accurately.

The data resources in the internet may contain thousands of features, for discovering all resources that are semantic-similar to a given query, traditional methods represent

Linawati et al. (Eds.): ICT-EurAsia 2014, LNCS 8407, pp. 663–673, 2014.

the data objects as points in a high-dimensional feature space and use a distance function to define the similarity of two objects. But the data presented by high-dimensional feature space led to the "curse of dimensionality" problems. These problems are mainly in the following aspects [1-3]: 1. The data in the high dimensional feature space is very sparse, so it is difficult to organize and manage the data during the similarity search in the high dimensional feature space; 2. In the high dimensional feature space there is a tendency for data objects to be nearly equidistant to a given query object, so it's not easy to find the data objects which are have similar semantic to a given query data; 3. In high dimensional space, the overlap degree of classic high-dimensional index methods proposed before usually became large with the increase of the dimension, which increased the access path and the query cost during the similarity search.

So far, there is a long stream of research on realizing the semantic-based similarity search in high dimensional feature space, and people have present a number of high-dimensional index techniques, such as R-tree [4], KD-tree [5], VP-tree [6], M-tree [7], Pyramid-Technique [8], iDistance [9], etc., but most of them cannot meet people's needs of realizing semantic-based similarity search in the internet environment very well. First of all, the features of internet data objects are various and massive, showing the phenomenon of "explosion of the features", so it is difficult to manage the data objects in a uniform feature space. Secondly, exiting techniques are usually proposed for special purpose, such as the pyramid technique is efficient for window queries over uniform data, but inefficient for clustered data or kNN queries; while the iDistance method is usually efficient for kNN queries, but inefficient for window or range queries; moreover, multi-dimensional indexes such as R-trees and M-trees are inefficient for range queries in high-dimensional feature space, and are not adaptive to data distributions. Besides, traditional kNN query is realized by processing a sequence of range queries $R(q, r)$ with a growing radius r, which is costly and cannot meet the needs of users.

Motivated by the above disadvantages of exiting indexing technologies for high-dimensional feature space, we developed the iHash method, a semantic-based data management and similarity search method. The key contributions of our work are: 1.By normalizing the internet data objects to a feature space of fixed dimension, our method can solve the "explosion of the features" problem of the feature space; 2.By clustering the data objects according to their distribution, and transforming the data clusters into regular shapes, we can use Pyramid-similar method to map high-dimensional data into 1-dimensional values; 3.We realize the range query and kNN query for semantic-based similarity search based on the iHash method. Besides, to improve the performance of kNN queries, we employ a low-cost heuristic to find an estimated distance, and transform the kNN query to a range query with the estimated distance, which can reduce the query cost significantly.

The rest of the paper is organized as follows. Section 2 provides an overview of related work. Section 3 introduces the preliminaries of this paper. Section 4 give an overview of our method-iHash. In Section 5, we realize the range query and kNN query using the iHash. The experimental results are presented in Section 6, and finally we conclude in Section 7.

2   Related Work

Semantic-based similarity search has attracted a lot of attention recently. To speed up similarity searches, a number of high-dimensional indexes were developed in previous studies, such as R-tree, KD-tree, VP-tree, M-tree, X-tree [12] and their variations. High-dimensional indexes aims to accelerate the querying efficiency on multidimensional data, the basic idea of this indexes is to organize the underlying data from a global view, and all the dimensionality should be considered synthetically, the nature function of them is pruning-cutting away a lot of useless searching paths. However, most of the existing indexes suffer from the curses of dimensionality, that is, their similarity search performance degrades dramatically with the increasing of the dimensionality, which cannot meet our needs.

Stefan Berchtold et al. proposed the Pyramid-Technique for similarity search in high-dimensional data spaces. The basic idea of Pyramid-Technique is to partition the hypercube-shaped high-dimensional data space into subspaces, the subspaces are pyramid shaped, the center point of the high-dimensional space is the common top of the pyramids, and the surfaces of data space are bottoms of the pyramids. According to the space partition, the data objects in high-dimensional space can be mapped to 1-dimensiona values and the B+-tree [14] can be used to manage the transformed data. The Pyramid-Technique is effective for uniformly distributed data set. But in actual life, the data objects are usually irregular distributed, and the Pyramid-Technique cannot process irregular distributed data effectively.

Jagadish et al. presented the iDistance method for k-nearest neighbor (kNN) query in a high-dimensional metric space. The basic idea of this method is to cluster data objects firstly and find a reference point (cluster center) for each cluster; each data object is assigned a one-dimensional value according to the distance to its cluster's reference object, and the one-dimensional values are indexed in a B+-tree. The iDistance method is effective for uniformly distributed and irregular distributed data sets, but it cannot support the window query. Besides, according to the analysis in [10, 13], the most efficient method for similarity search in very high dimensional uniformly distributed data space may be the sequential scan method.

Additionally, with respect to the k-nearest neighbor (kNN) query, traditional methods [9] usually execute a series of range queries iteratively until finding k answers, which is costly. The X-tree [15] and SS-tree [16] use different node size to improve the query efficiency, and GHT* [17] method use a hyperplane to divide the data space ad use a heuristic to improve the efficiency of similarity query.

3   Preliminaries

In this section we present a brief introduction of similarity searching in the metric spaces and describe the K-means clustering method, further, we present the Pyramid-Technique, since our method will take advantage of these technologies.

3.1   Similarity Search in Metric Space

More formally, a metric space can be described as a pair M= (D, dist), where D is the domain of feature values and dist is a distance function with the following properties for all objects x, y, z∈D:

dist(x, y)≥0 (non negativity);
dist(x, y)=dist(y, x)(symmetry);
dist(x, y)≤dist(x, z)+dist(z, y)(triangle inequality);
d(x, y)=0 if x=y (identity).

Here we refer to the data objects in the feature space and two main types of similarity queries:

1) Range query Range (q, r) retrieve all elements that are within distance r to q, that is, $\{x \in I: \text{dist } (q, x) \leq r\}$;

2) k-nearest neighbor query kNN(q, k) retrieve the k closest elements to q, that is, retrieve a set $A \subseteq D$ such that $|A| = k$ and $\forall x \in A, \forall y \in D - A, \text{dist } (q, x) \leq \text{dist}(q, y)$.

3.2   The Pyramid-Technique

The basic idea of the Pyramid-Technique is to map the high-dimensional data objects in high-dimensional data space into 1-dimensional values, and then use the traditional index structure B+-tree to manage the 1-dimensional values, which is aimed to eliminate the effects of "curse of dimensionality" during similarity search in high-dimensional data space. The Pyramid-Technique first divide hypercube shaped data space into a series of pyramids and ensure a pyramid number for each pyramid. The pyramids share the center point of the high-dimensional data space as their common top, and the bottoms of pyramids are the surfaces of the data space. Then any one high-dimensional data in a pyramid can be mapped to a 1-dimensional value pv_v according to the pyramid number i and height from the high-dimensional data to the pyramid top h_v, that is, $pv_v=i+h_v$ (as shown in Figure 1), and all the 1-dimensional values transformed from the high-dimensional data are indexed by the B+-tree.

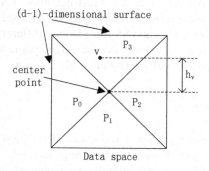

Fig. 1. The Pyramid technique

4   The Overview of the iHash

4.1   The Normalization of the High-Dimensional Data

To solve the problem of the variousness of the data objects and the inconsistent of the feature's number of different objects, we use a hash function to normalize the data objects, mapping the data objects of different features to a fixed feature space.

First, we express the high-dimensional data object with a feature array, such as a data object A= {A0, A1, ..., An-1}, Ai (0≤i≤n-1) denotes a feature of the data object A, Ai.attr denotes the name of the feature Ai, Ai.val denotes the value of Ai. Since the internet data object has its unique feature types and feature values, every data object has exclusive feature array and is mapped to different feature space from others, so it is hard to maintain and manage the mass of data objects in the internet. To map different data objects to the same feature space, here we define a hash function iHash1(Ai.attr), mapping the data object A to a normalized feature array B of M elements according to names of the data object features, and returning the specific locations of the A's features in feature array B. The main purpose of the function iHash1 is to map different kinds of internet data objects into a same feature array structure of a fixed size M, so the internet data objects can be mapped into a same M-dimensional feature space. Specifically, the iHash1 function inputs the name strings of the features, and gets values of range [0, M-1] after several operations, further, we can select an appropriate size of M to avoid the collision during the hash. Besides we define the other hash function iHash2(Ai.val) to map the feature values in A into a set of N-bit values, and store them to corresponding locations in the feature array B. The hash process can be formalized as $B = \text{iHash1}(A_i.\text{attr}) \oplus \text{iHash2}(A_i.\text{val})$, where B is an array of M elements; each element size is N bits; the element values represent the features in A. In this paper, we choose SHA-1algorithm as the iHash2 function, it inputs the values of every feature, gets 160-bit summaries after encoding, then maps the summary into N-bit values and stores them to the corresponding locations in B. The iHash function can map different internet data objects into a same feature space, which is convenient for the operations on the data objects. Figure 2 shows the process of the data normalization.

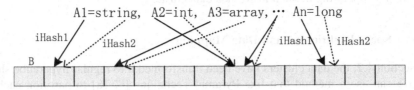

Fig. 2. Data normalization

4.2   Data Clustering and Transformation

In real life the data objects in feature space distribute irregularly, they are often clustered or correlated in the space, so space-based partitioning makes the high-dimensional index

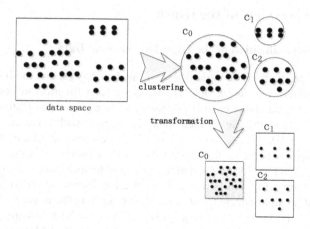

Fig. 3. Data clustering and transformation

inefficient (such as the Pyramid Technique). To address the deficiency, a more appropriate data-based partitioning strategy would be used to identify clusters from the space. In our method, we adopted the K-means clustering algorithm to divide the data objects in the high-dimensional data space, ensuring the data objects of similar semantic to be in a same cluster as far as possible. The number of the data clusters K is defined as a tuning parameter, can vary according to specific data distribution and applications.

The data clusters obtained by K-means methods are hypersphere shaped, but the Pyramid-Technique are based on the data spaces are hypercube shaped. To use the Pyramid-similar method to manage the high-dimensional data, we need to transform the data clusters into hypercube shaped. Figure 3 shows the process of data clustering and transformation. After the transformation, the data clusters are a series of hypercube-shaped data subspaces, the value of each side length is 1. And the cluster center is transformed into the center of hypercube, that is, its coordinate is [0.5, 0.5... 0.5]. The transformation is a one-to-one mapping, and as proved in [13], we can get the right answers by operating in the transformed data clusters.

4.3   Space Partitioning and Data Mapping

In section 4.2, the data clusters have been transformed into regular hypercube shaped, so we can use a method that like Pyramid-Technique [8, 18] to partition each data cluster and map the high-dimensional data objects into 1-dimensional values.

For each n-dimensional data cluster, we first take the cluster center as a common top and the surfaces of the data cluster as the bottoms to partition the data cluster into 2n hyper-pyramids, and define pyramid-index i for each pyramid p_i. Next, in each hyper-pyramid, we map the high-dimensional data objects to 1-dimensional values based on the deviations from data objects to the top of the pyramid and the pyramid-index i. The 1-dimensional value of a high-dimensional data object v can be expressed as $p_v = i + h_v$, where h_v is the deviation of v to the pyramid top.

We can observe that the pyramid-index i is an integer and the deviation h_v is a real number in the range [0, 0.5], so all high-dimensional data objects in pyramid p_i will be mapped into the interval [i, i+0.5] and different intervals are disjunct. Besides, we can note that there may be more than one high-dimensional data objects are mapped to a same 1-dimensional value, that is because different data objects with a pyramid may have a same deviation from the pyramid top, so the map is not a one-to-one transformation(As shown in Figure 4).

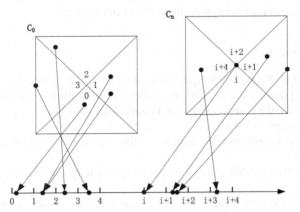

Fig. 4. Space partitioning and data mapping

4.4   Index Creation

To facilitate speedy semantic-based similarity query, we use the B+-tree to manage the transformed 1-dimensional values. Since having got the pyramid value p_v of any high-dimensional data object v, we can easily manage all the high-dimensional data objects with a B+-tree using their pyramid values as keys. The high-dimensional data are stored in the leaf nodes of the B+-tree, and leaf nodes of the B+-tree are linked to the left and right siblings, so when the search region is changed during a similarity search, it is easy to search the neighboring nodes. Besides, the B+-tree data structure can efficiently realize the insert, delete and update operations of data objects during the similarity search.

5   Semantic-Based Similarity Searching

5.1   Range Query

The Range (q, r) query algorithm is usually the base algorithm for more sophisticated similarity queries. In this paper, the query can be processed in several logical phase. Let R (q, r) be a range query, in the first phase, we determine the data clusters which are overlapped with the query range. Firstly, we transform the query R to T(R), and map the query range to a one-dimensional interval [q_{low}, q_{high}] using the pyramid technique, so we can easily get the clusters that are overlapped with the query range by comparing the query interval [q_{low}, q_{high}] and the intervals of each cluster in the B+-tree, and filter out clusters that do not intersect with the query. In the second phase, we determine the query subspaces. Specifically, we can get the subspaces by computing the intersected regions of the query interval and the pyramid interval in the B+-tree, and mapping the intersected regions to the transformed feature space. In the third phase, we determine the final query answers. The data objects in the query subspaces are the set of candidate data objects, thus we scan the data set and determine the final answers for the query T(R). Since the relationship of the transformed data objects and the original data objects are bijection, so we can easily get the final answers.

5.2   kNN Query

The traditional kNN query $NN_k(q)$ is realized by processing a sequence of range queries R(q, r) with a growing radius r, but the execution of multiple range query iterations is costly. To reduce the response time and query cost, the kNN query can be realized by the following steps:

(1) estimate an approximate distance of the k-th nearest data object from the query point q;

(2) transform the kNN query to a range query R(q, r_k) where r_k is the estimated distance;

(3) perform the range query R(q, r_k) to retrieve the k closest data objects to query point q.

To obtain the estimated distance r_k, we employ a low-cost heuristic to find k data objects that are near the query point q. The heuristic algorithm can be described as followed.

Firstly, compute the 1-dimensional pyramid value p_q of the query point q and determine the location of p_q in the B+-tree, traverse through the B+-tree leaves alternately, add the first found k data objects to the answer set randomly (for a pyramid value may map to more than one data objects), and compute the r_k value; secondly, examine the data objects x while its pyramid value $p_x \in I$, $I = [\ p_q - r_k, p_q + r_k]$, if the distance d(q, x)<r_k, remove the k-th data object from answer set, add x into answer set, and update r_k and I; thirdly, iterate the second step until the whole interval I has been searched and we will get the final estimated distance r_k. So we can obtain the k nearest neighbors of the query point by processing the range query R(q, r_k).

6   Performance Evaluation

In this section, we analyze the performance of our method by studying the experimental results. All the experiments were performed on a computer with Intel(R) Core (TM) 2 Quad CPU Q8300 2.5GHz and 4GB RAM, each index page is 4kB. The operating system is CentOS 5. In the experiment, we generated 8, 16, 32, 64, 128-dimensional synthetic clustered datasets following a Gaussian distribution with variance of 0.05. Besides, a real data collections was used, we abstracted the color image features from 68040 pictures to form a feature space using our method. During each experiment, for every experiment result we run 20 times and compute the average value as the final result.

6.1   Range Query

In the range query experiment, we observe the effect of the dimension of the dataset on the response time. We choose synthetic clustered datasets as input data, the input datasets are respectively 8, 16, 24, and 32-dimensional data objects, and the dataset size is 1000000. Besides, we choose the sequential scan and Pyramid-Technique as the references of our method. As shown in Figure 5, we can observe that the response time of three methods increases with the dimensionality, meanwhile Pyramid-Technique and the iHash can overcome the adverse effects of the "curse of dimensionality" in some extent, since they have less response time than the sequential scan method; moreover, the iHash is more efficient than the Pyramid Technique with the increase of the dimensionality, that is because with the increase of the dimensionality of the high-dimensional data space, the data objects in the high-dimensional space will get sparser, and the Pyramid technique will access more useless space. The result show that the iHash method scales well with the change of dimensionality of high-dimensional data space.

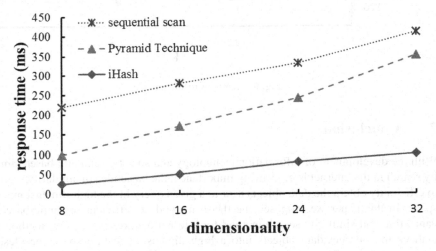

Fig. 5. Effects of dimensionality

6.2   kNN Query

For k-Nearest Neighbor (kNN) query, we use a real data collection that consist of 68040 pictures, we first abstracted the color image features from these pictures to form a 32-dimensional feature space using the hash function presented in section 3.1, and we took the iDistance technique and sequential scan method as the references of our method. In the kNN query experiment, we mainly study the influence of the result set size k on the query response time. As shown in Figure 6, we can observe that the query response time of the three techniques increase with the increasing of the result set size k, and the iDistance and the iHash methods have much better performance compared to the sequential scan method, that is because that during the kNN queries using the two methods, many irrelevant data points to the query point can be excluded from the search range. Besides, the iHash method can do better than the iDistance method in some extend. We can conclude that by efficient space division and estimating the distance of the k-th nearest data point, the iHash can achieve good performance during kNN query.

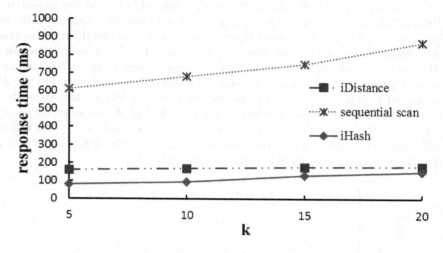

Fig. 6. Effects of result set size

7   Conclusion

With the development of information technology and society, semantic-based similarity search in the internet is of growing importance; the basic idea of similarity search is to efficiently obtain the data objects near to a given query in the high-dimensional data space. In this paper we proposed the iHash method, an efficient semantic-based organization and similarity search method for internet data resources. Our method normalizes the internet data objects into a high dimension feature space; besides, we partition and transform the feature space into hypercube-shaped subspaces so that the Pyramid-similar technique can be applied to index the high-dimensional data objects; finally, we realize the range and kNN queries based on our method. Our experimental evaluation employs synthetic and real data collections and the experimental result shows that our approach performs efficiently both in range queries and kNN queries.

Acknowledgment. The work described in this paper is partially supported by the grants of the National Basic Research Program of China (973 project) under Grant No.2009CB320503, 2012CB315906; the project of National Science Foundation of China under grant No. 61070199, 61103189, 61103194, 61103182, 61202488, 61272482;the National High Technology Research and Development Program of China(863 Program) No. 2011AA01A103, 2012AA01A506, 2013AA013505, the Re-search Fund for the Doctoral Program of Higher Education of China under Grant No.

20114307110006, 20124307120032, the program for Changjiang Scholars and Innovative Research Team in University (No.IRT1012), Science and Technology Innovative Research Team in Higher Educational Institutions of Hunan Province("network technology"); and Hunan Province Natural Science Foundation of China (11JJ7003).

References

1. Böhm, C., et al.: Searching in High-Dimensional Spaces—Index Structures for Improving the Performance of Multimedia Databases. ACM Computing Surveys 33(3), 322–373 (2001)
2. Chàvez, E., et al.: Searching in Metric Spaces. ACM Computing Surveys 33(3), 273–321 (2001)
3. Zezula, P., Amato, G., Dohnal, V., Batko, M.: Similarity Search: The Metric Space Approach. Advances in Database Systems (2006)
4. Guttman, A.: R-trees: a dynamic index structure for spatial searching. In: SIGMOD, pp. 47–57 (1984)
5. Bentley, J.L.: Multidimensional Binary Search Trees Used for Associative Searching. Communications of the ACM 18(9), 509–517 (1975)
6. Fu, A.W., Chan, P.M., Cheung, Y.L., Moon, Y.S.: Dynamic vp-Tree Indexing for n-Nearest Neighbor Search Given PairWise Distances. In: VLDB (2000)
7. Ciaccia, T., Patella, M., Zezula, P.: M-tree: An Efficient Access Method for Similarity Search in Metric Spaces. In: VLDB, pp. 426–435 (1997)
8. Berchtold, S., Böhm, C., Kriegel, H.P.: The Pyramid-Technique: Towards Breaking the Curse of Dimensionality. In: SIGMOD, pp. 142–153 (1998)
9. Jagadish, H.V., Ooi, B.C., et al.: iDistance: An Adaptive B$^+$-tree Based Indexing Method for Nearest Neighbor Search. ACM Transactions on Database Systems, 1–34 (2003)
10. Zhang, R., Ooi, B.C., Tan, K.-L.: Making the Pyramid Technique Robust to Query Types and Workloads. In: Proceeding of the 20th International Conference on Data Engineering, ICDE 2004 (2004)
11. Jain, A.K., Murty, M.N., Flynn, P.J.: Data Clustering: A Review. ACM Computing Surveys 31(3), 264–323 (1999)
12. Berchtold, S., Keim, D.A., Kriegel, H.-R.: The x-tree: An index structure for high-dimensional data. In: VLDB (1996)
13. Zhang, R., Ooi, B.C., Tan, K.-L.: Making the pyramid technique robust to query types and workloads. In: Proceedings of the 20th International Conference on Data Engineering. IEEE (2004)
14. Comer, D.: The Ubiquitous B-tree. ACM Computing Surveys 11(2), 121–138 (1979)
15. Berchtold, S., Keim, D.A., Kriegel, H.-P.: The X-tree: An index structure for high-dimensional data. Readings in Multimedia Computing and Networking, 451 (2001)
16. White, D.A., Jain, R.: Similarity indexing with the SS-tree. In: Proceedings of the Twelfth International Conference on Data Engineering. IEEE (1996)
17. Batko, M., Gennaro, C., Zezula, P.: Similarity grid for searching in metric spaces. In: Türker, C., Agosti, M., Schek, H.-J. (eds.) P2P, Grid, and Service Orientation . . . . LNCS, vol. 3664, pp. 25–44. Springer, Heidelberg (2005)
18. Berchtold, S., Boehm, C., Kriegel, H.-P.: High-dimensional index structure. U.S. Patent No. 6,154,746 (November 28, 2000)

Efficient DVFS to Prevent Hard Faults
for Many-Core Architectures

Zhiquan Lai[1], Baokang Zhao[1], and Jinshu Su[2,1]

[1] National University of Defense Technology, China
[2] National Key Laboratory of Parallel and Distributed Processing (PDL), China
{zqlai,bkzhao,sjs}@nudt.edu.cn

Abstract. *Dynamic Voltage and Frequency Scaling (DVFS)* is a widely-used and efficient technology for *Dynamic Power management (DPM)*. To avoid hard faults caused by voltage and frequency scaling, some overhead always be imposed on the performance of applications due to the latency of DVFS. Besides, on many-core architectures, the design of multiple voltage domains has made the latency of DVFS a much more significant issue. In this paper, we propose an efficient DVFS scheme to prevent hard faults, meanwhile eliminating the impact of latency of DVFS as possible. The main idea is applying *Retroactive Frequency Scaling (RFS)* where the latency of DVFS might be introduced. Based on the analysis, our approach is expected to achieve noticeable performance improvement on many-core architectures.

Keywords: efficient, DVFS, hard fault, many-core, retroactive frequency scaling (RFS).

1   Introduction

Low power has become a first-class design requirement in large-scale data centers and high performance computing systems. *Dynamic Voltage and Frequency Scaling (DVFS)* is a widely-used and efficient technology for *Dynamic Power management (DPM)* [1-3]. DVFS makes use of voltage scaling and frequency scaling to accomplish a trade-off between high performance and energy efficiency. Both of voltage scaling and frequency scaling take some latency to wait for voltage/frequency reach to given levels. However, the magnitudes of latency for voltage scaling and frequency scaling are much different. A frequency scaling only needs several CPU clock cycles, whereas a voltage scaling always needs tens, sometimes hundreds, of millisecond. Due to this difference, power state (voltage and frequency settings) could be in dangerous states (e.g. current voltage can't support the frequency) under some impropriate operations. In these cases, hard faults will happen and cause the CPUs to stop operating permanently [4].

Figure 1 shows the relationship between voltage and frequency during DVFS. As each CPU frequency setting has a least voltage value supporting the CPU operating in theory, we can draw a "Safe Boundary" in the frequency-voltage space. With this boundary, all the voltage/frequency states could be classified into three categories.

Linawati et al. (Eds.): ICT-EurAsia 2014, LNCS 8407, pp. 674–679, 2014.

All the states above the boundary are dangerous because the voltages are not enough to support the frequency settings. The states just under the boundary are energy-efficient as the least voltages promise that no additional power is wasted. The states far below the boundary are non-power-efficient as some unnecessary voltage is wasted. For example, if we want to scale from $s0$ to $s4$ and scale up the frequency firstly, the frequency will reach $F1$ from $F0$ quickly. However, as the voltage can't scale up as soon as the frequency, the power state will be in dangerous state (like $s3$ state). In this dangerous state, a hard fault will occur and the CPUs will stop operating permanently [4].

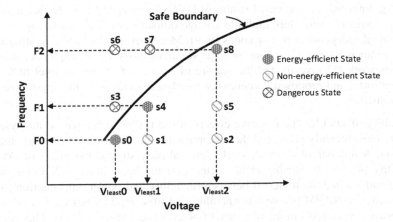

Fig. 1. Dangerous states causing hard faults during DVFS

To avoid hard faults caused by voltage and frequency scaling, some overhead always be imposed on the performance of applications due to the latency of DVFS. For example, as discussed in [5], in the cases of scaling up voltage and frequency, voltage is scaled firstly and the frequency will be not scaled until the voltage has reach the given level. And during voltage scaling, the application is stalled waiting the voltage scaling to finish. Although preventing hard faults, this type of DVFS schemes will cause some performance lost due to busy waiting within the latency of voltage scaling.

Besides, on many-core architectures, the design of multiple voltage domains has made the latency of DVFS a much more significant issue. As investigated in [5], the latency of voltage scaling could be up to 195ms in Intel SCC [6] many-core chip. The long latency of DVFS in many-core architectures could makes the DVFS scheme much more inefficient.

In this paper, we focus on the problem of inefficiency of DVFS due to latency of voltage scaling, especially for many-core architectures. We propose an efficient DVFS scheme to prevent hard faults, meanwhile eliminating the impact of latency of DVFS as possible. The main idea is applying *Retroactive Frequency Scaling (RFS)* where the latency of DVFS will be introduced. Instead of scaling frequency after stalling the application during voltage scaling, we make the frequency scaling retroactive and keep the application running during voltage scaling.

The rest of the paper begins with an overview of related work in Section 2. Then we will introduce our efficient DVFS scheme with RFS methodology in Section 3. As we have not evaluated our approach using experiments yet, we analyze the benefit of our approach in Section 3.3. Section 4 summaries our work.

2   Related Work

DVFS on Many-Core. DVFS technique is widely used for dynamic power management. However, in many-core architectures with tens or hundreds of cores in a single chip, e.g. Intel SCC, some new features of DVFS show up [5, 7, 8]. Rather than single voltage domain in one chip, multiple voltage domains are designed to separate cores into several independent power zones [6, 9]. Moreover, the latency of scaling voltage become much longer if scaling voltage simultaneously on multiple domains. Our previous work [5] investigated the feature of latency of DVFS on Intel SCC many-core platform, and proposed a latency-aware algorithm to avoid the aggressive power state transitions.

Reliability of DVFS. The negative effects of the DVFS technique on the system reliability have recently promoted the research on *reliability-aware power management (RAPM)*. A number of research works have already studied the effect of DVFS on reliability [4, 10-12]. Rosing et al. focused on the hard faults of *Systems on Chip (SoCs)* and studied the trade-off between reliability and power consumption [4]. Guo et al. study the RAPM problem for parallel real-time applications for shared memory multiprocessor systems in the presence of precedence constraints [11]. This paper will focus on the problem of inefficiency of DVFS due to latency of voltage scaling introduced for reliability. And the reliability in the paper focuses on the hard faults caused impropriate operation of DVFS.

3   Efficient DVFS with RFS

Considering the non-negligible latency of DVFS on many-core architectures, we propose an efficient DVFS using retroactive frequency scaling in this Section.

3.1   Case Study

Firstly, let us consider a case of scaling up voltage and frequency. As shown in Figure 2, it's the execution trace of a program running from T_0 to T_3[1]. At T_1, it decides to make a DVFS operation to scaling up the voltage and frequency. Assume the power state at from T_0 to T_1 is power efficient state (with frequency and its least voltage). As it needs to scale up frequency, it has to scale up the voltage firstly to avoid hard faults. However, the voltage scaling cost a non-negligible latency of T_2-T_1 so that it becomes

---

[1]   In this paper, T_i, i.e. T_1, T_2, T_3 and et al., denote specific timestamps in the execution trace of programs.

safe to scale up the frequency. Thus, the execution of this program takes run time of T_3-T_0, including the latency of voltage scaling.

This is the traditional handling of voltage scaling and frequency scaling during DVFS. Obviously, this method is not efficient enough, especially when the latency of voltage scaling is non-negligible (e.g. the latency of voltage scaling on Intel SCC as investigated in [5]).

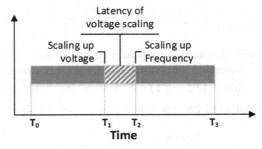

Fig. 2. Traditional voltage and frequency scaling up

3.2   Retroactive Frequency Scaling (RFS)

To eliminate the impact of latency of DVFS and improve the efficiency, we propose a novel DVFS scheme, named retroactive frequency scaling (RFS). As shown in Figure 3, let us review the case in last sub-section, RFS keeps the program running after scaling up voltage at T_1. Instead of stalling the program waiting for the voltage scaling up to given level, RFS makes the program running at the previous frequency setting during the latency of voltage scaling. When the voltage has reached the given level, we conduct the frequency scaling retroactively. By making use of the time slack during voltage scaling (from T_1 to T_2), RFS is capable to improve the performance of the program.

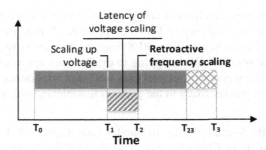

Fig. 3. Efficient voltage and frequency scaling up with retroactive frequency scaling

3.3   Analysis of Benefit

The benefit of RFS is obvious. With RFS, the program could keep running without any stall. As the latency of frequency scaling is in the scale of clock cycle, we don't consider it in this analysis. Thus, in the case shown in Figure 2 and Figure 3, the performance improvement (speedup) of RFS could be estimated by:

$$Speedup = 1 - \frac{(T1-T0)+(T2-T1)+(T3-T2)-(T2-T1)\cdot\frac{F_s}{F_d}}{(T1-T0)+(T2-T1)+(T3-T2)} \tag{1}$$

In Equation 1, the F_s denotes the frequency before scaling, and F_d denotes the frequency after scaling. Assuming the runtime performance ($1/execution\text{-}time$) is linearly with the frequency setting, $(T2 - T1) \cdot \frac{F_s}{F_d}$ denoted the rough estimate of execution time saving due to applying RFS. The Equation 1 can be simplified into:

$$Speedup = \frac{T2-T1}{T3-T0} \cdot \frac{F_s}{F_d} \tag{2}$$

In Equation 2, T_2-T_1 means the latency of voltage scaling ($T_{latency\_volt}$), and T_3-T_0 means the whole execution time of the program under traditional DVFS ($T_{program}$). Hence, the equation can be denoted as:

$$Speedup = \frac{T_{latency\_volt}}{T_{program}} \cdot \frac{F_s}{F_d} \tag{3}$$

From the Equation 3, we can find that larger the latency of voltage scaling is, more speedup will be achieved from RFS methodology. In many-core architectures, as the latency of DVFS is non-negligible, our efficient DVFS scheme with RFS is expected to achieve noticeable performance speedup.

4   Summary and Future Work

In this paper, we propose an efficient DVFS scheme to prevent hard faults, meanwhile eliminating the impact of latency of DVFS as possible. Through our analysis, by applying Retroactive Frequency Scaling (RFS) methodology, we expect to achieve noticeable performance speedup. We are going to evaluate our approach on the Intel SCC many-core platform. According our previous work and experience done on this platform, we expect that our approach in the paper is feasible and efficient.

Acknowledgement. Special thanks to Intel China Center of Parallel Computing (ICCPC) in Wuxi City of China for providing the SCC hardware platform to support this research work. The work of this paper is also supported by the Program for Changjiang Scholars and Innovative Research Team in University (PCSIRT, No.IRT1012), and the Aid Program for Science and Technology Innovative Research Team in Higher Educational Institutions of Hunan Province.

References

1. Grunwald, D., Morrey III, C.B., Levis, P., Neufeld, M., Farkas, K.I.: Policies for dynamic clock scheduling. Presented at Proceedings of the 4th Conference on Symposium on Operating System Design & Implementation, San Diego, California, vol. 4 (2000)
2. Weiser, M., Welch, B., Demers, A., Shenker, S.: Scheduling for reduced CPU energy. In: Proceeding of the 1st USENIX Conference on Operating Systems Design and Implementation, Monterey, California (1994)
3. Qingyuan, D., Meisner, D., Bhattacharjee, A., Wenisch, T.F., Bianchini, R.: CoScale: Coordinating CPU and Memory System DVFS in Server Systems. In: Proceeding of the 45th Annual IEEE/ACM International Symposium on Microarchitecture (MICRO), pp. 143–154 (2012)
4. Rosing, T.S., Mihic, K., De Micheli, G.: Power and Reliability Management of SoCs. IEEE Transactions on Very Large Scale Integration (VLSI) Systems 15, 391–403 (2007)
5. Lai, Z., Lam, K.T., Wang, C.-L., Su, J., Yan, Y., Zhu, W.: Latency-Aware Dynamic Voltage and Frequency Scaling on Many-core Architectures for Data-intensive Applications. Presented at International Conference on Cloud Computing and Big Data, CloudCom-Asia (2013)
6. Howard, J., Dighe, S., Vangal, S., Ruhl, G., Borkar, N., Jain, S., et al.: A 48-Core IA-32 message-passing processor in 45nm CMOS using on-die message passing and DVFS for performance and power scaling. IEEE Journal of Solid-State Circuits 46, 173–183 (2011)
7. Borkar, S.: Thousand core chips: a technology perspective. In: Proceedings of the 44th Annual Design Automation Conference, San Diego, California, pp. 746–749 (2007)
8. Ma, K., Li, X., Chen, M., Wang, X.: Scalable Power Control for Many-Core Architectures Running Multi-threaded Applications. In: Proceeding of ACM/IEEE International Symposium on Computer Architecture (ISCA), San Jose, California, USA (2011)
9. Gamell, M., Rodero, I., Parashar, M., Muralidhar, R.: Exploring cross-layer power management for PGAS applications on the SCC platform. In: Proceedings of the 21st International Symposium on High-Performance Parallel and Distributed Computing, Delft, The Netherlands, pp. 235–246 (2012)
10. Haase, J., Damm, M., Hauser, D., Waldschmidt, K.: Reliability-Aware Power Management of Multi-Core Processors. In: Kleinjohann, B., Kleinjohann, L., Machado, R., Pereira, C., Thiagarajan, P.S. (eds.) From Model-Driven Design to Resource Management for Distributed Embedded Systems, vol. 225, pp. 205–214. Springer, US (2006)
11. Guo, Y., Zhu, D., Aydin, H.: Reliability-Aware Power Management for Parallel Real-time Applications with Precedence Constraints. In: The Second International Green Computing Conference (IGCC), Orlando, FL (2011)
12. Guo, Y., Zhu, D., Aydin, H.: Efficient Power Management Schemes for Dual-Processor Fault-Tolerant Systems. In: The First Workshop on Highly-Reliable Power-Efficient Embedded Designs (HARSH), Shenzhen, China (2013)

Improving Availability through Energy-Saving Optimization in LEO Satellite Networks

Zhu Tang, Chunqing Wu, Zhenqian Feng, Baokang Zhao, and Wanrong Yu

College of Computer, National University of Defense Technology
Changsha, Hunan, China
{tangzhu,chunqingwu,bkzhao,wryu}@nudt.edu.cn, z_q_feng@163.com

Abstract. Recently, satellite networks are widely used for communication in areas lack of network infrastructures, and will act as the backbones in the next generation internet. Therefore, the availability of satellite networks is very important. In space, the energy is always limited for satellites, and highly efficient energy utilization would certainly improve the availability of satellite systems. In this paper, we consider the energy-saving optimization for the LEO satellite network instead of a single satellite. We modify and extend the multi-commodity flow model [3] to switch off satellite nodes and links as much as possible in LEO satellite networks. Taking advantage of the multi-coverage scheme and traffic distribution patents in satellite networks, we improve the heuristic algorithms in [3] to turn off the unnecessary satellites, up-down links and inter-satellite links respectively up to 59%, 61% and 72% under the constraints of link utilization and routing hops increase ratio, and the total energy saving ratio can be up to 65%. Finally, the availability of LEO satellite networks has been deeply developed.

Keywords: Reliability, energy-aware, low earth orbit (LEO) satellite network, snapshot routing algorithm, minimal cost multi-commodity flow model.

1   Introduction

Since the inherent large range broadcast and rapid deployment property of satellites, satellite networks are widely applied in the emergent communication regions, oceans, desserts, and many other places lack of network infrastructures. Besides, satellite network will become an integral part of next generation internet in the future, so the availability of satellite networks is becoming more and more important. In space, satellites can only convert the solar power or nuclear power into electricity to support the control, maintaining and communication system as well as charging the battery. For the energy limitation of satellites, decreasing the energy consumption would certainly improve the availability of the satellite systems.

There are some researches focusing on the satellite energy-saving problems [7] [8], however, most of them aim at the energy and resource allocation of the single satellite, not the whole satellite network or satellite constellation. Compared to the durative solar-coverage of geostationary orbit (GEO) satellite, the low earth orbit (LEO) satellite would move into the shadow behind earth almost in every orbit cycle, and

Linawati et al. (Eds.): ICT-EurAsia 2014, LNCS 8407, pp. 680–689, 2014.

then only the battery can be available, which is the same condition as the wireless sensor networks [2]. For the satellite moving problem, we use the classic snapshot routing algorithm [9] to keep the network topology changing stably.

The idea of switching off devices as many as possible in terrestrial networks is provided in [3]. The network energy saving problem is concluded as an integer linear programming (ILP) problem under the constraints of connectivity and QoS, which is NP-hard and cannot be solved in polynomial time. The authors propose some heuristic algorithms to obtain the switching off ratio of nodes and links. For the LEO satellite network, the energy-saving can be achieved by distributing the traffic in proper routing paths and switching off the unnecessary satellite nodes and links. However, the tradeoff between routing hops, computational cost and energy-saving should be considered as well.

In this paper, we learn the idea of the link capacity constrained minimal cost multi-commodity flow model in [3]. By modifying and extending the model based on the special architecture of LEO satellite networks, we propose new heuristic algorithms, which can gain the switching off ratio of the satellite nodes, UDLs and ISLs up to 59%, 61% and 72% under the link capacity constraints, and the total energy saving ratio can be up to 65%.

The rest of the paper is organized as follows: the next section gives the brief overview of the researches on network energy-saving methods; the satellite network model is described in section 3; the energy-saving problem is formulated in section 4; the proposed heuristic algorithm is presented in section 5; section 6 gives the experiments design and simulation results; finally, the conclusions and future work are summarized in section 7.

2   Related Work

The idea of saving the whole network energy by keeping the least necessary devices and links is firstly proposed in [4]. The authors use the standard minimal cost multi-commodity flow model (CMCF) to formalize the problem, but the complexity of the algorithms proposed increases rapidly with the devices adding in. Beside switching off nodes and links for energy-saving, many researchers take advantage of the low power mode and sleeping mode of network devices, such as [5][6], when there is no packets to send, the devices are set into the these modes to save energy.

However, the studies above are mainly focused on the terrestrial wired and wireless network, but for the special network topology and link characteristics in satellite network, direct deployment of current energy-saving methods cannot be efficient enough.

The energy allocation and admission control problem of single satellite is discussed in [7], and the authors use the dynamic programming methods to obtain the optimal transmission requests selection strategies for the maximum system profile. In [8], the authors send the multimedia broadcast flow in high bit rate burst instead of the continuous low bit rate mode, and turn off the RF elements to save energy in the spare time. However, these methods mainly discuss the energy allocation of the single satellite, not the whole satellite network or satellite constellation.

Since a large portion of satellite energy is consumed by wireless interface, such as up-down link (UDL) and inter-satellite link (ISL)[1], the method of switching off satellite nodes and links for energy-saving should be perspective in the global multi-coverage LEO satellite network in future.

3   Satellite Network Model

The satellite network model considered here is the iridium-like polar orbit constellation. As is shown in **Fig. 1**, the satellites constitute the Manhattan networks and are able to route data through ISLs. Every satellite has four ISLs: the up and down intra-orbit links are constant, and the left and right inter-orbit links are dynamic, which exist only between -60~60 degrees in latitude. For the predictable and periodic movements of satellites, every satellite network topology in each snapshot can be determined in advance. Meanwhile, we assume the traffic matrix in each snapshot is known in advance.

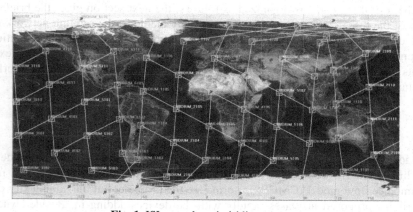

Fig. 1. ISLs topology in iridium system

To simplify the analysis, we assume that the satellite uses the single-beam transceivers, and each ground station is equipped with only one antenna, which connects to only one nearest satellite at one time. The ground station can see more than one satellite at anytime and anywhere, so we can lead the distributed traffic to the neighbor satellites under the UDL and ISL capacity constraints, and then close the redundant UDLs. Further, the ISLs with no traffic can be switched off, too.

The corresponding relationship between satellites and ground stations are one-to-multiple relationship. Each station is assigned with some channels of the big UDL. So switching off part of the up-down channel could only save the onboard processing cost, not the UDL energy of the satellite. Only when all the channels are closed, the UDL can be switched off.

However, switching off the satellite nodes and links would certainly increase the average routing paths and routing latency, leading to the computation cost and transmission times increase. But considering the communication components are always in effective work mode when power on, we simply assume that the device's energy consumption is independent of the transmission times.

3.1   Link Capacity Model

Since the network flow is used in our model, setting a practical link capacity could not indicate the link utilization of satellite network. We employ the initial maximal traffic values of all the UDLs and ISLs, represented by f_{max}^{UDL} and f_{max}^{ISL}, as the base capacity factor and its β times as the upper-bound capacity of UDLs and ISLs, i.e.:

$$c^{UDL} = \beta * f_{max}^{UDL}$$
$$c^{ISL} = \beta * f_{max}^{ISL}$$

Obviously, current link capacity can meet the network traffic demands, but when part of the satellite nodes, UDLs and ISLs are switched off, the remaining UDLs and ISLs' capacities will be the limiting factors for traffic aggregation.

3.2   Network Traffic Model

The predict traffic distribution in 2005 [10] is shown in **Fig. 2**, and the original traffic in each cell is represented by f_{cell}. We use this data sheet for reference to generate our own traffic model. It is assumed that a ground station stays at the center of each cell. Let t^{sd} be the traffic factor between cell s and cell d. t^{sd} is in direct proportion to f_{cell}, and in inverse proportion to cell distance d(s, d), i.e.:

$$t^{sd} = \frac{f_s f_d * \gamma}{(d(s,d))^\delta} \quad \forall s, \ d \in V_{sat}$$

where $\gamma = U[0,1]$ is the random number obeying the uniform distribution. Through adjusting distance coefficient δ, we can adjust the traffic distribution range between cells. d(s, d) represents the surface distance on earth between cell s and cell d, which is calculated as follow:

$$d(s, d) = \begin{cases} R * \theta_{sd} & s \neq d \\ \frac{R * \theta_{s(s+1)}}{2} & s = d \end{cases}$$

where the θ_{sd} represents the geocentric angle between cell s and cell d, and R is the radius of earth. When the traffic exists inside the cell, i.e. s=d, we use the distance between cell s and its right neighbor cell s+1 for calculation.

To adapt the generated traffic model to practical wideband mobile IP satellite network, we use the t^{sd} as the proportional coefficient for obtaining the simulated traffic values T^{sd} between cell s and d, i.e.:

$$T^{sd} = \frac{t^{sd}}{\sum_{s=1}^{N_{sat}} \sum_{d=1}^{N_{sat}} t^{sd}} * T_{total}$$

where T_{total} represents the total traffic values in the whole network (units: Mbps).

Intensity level and Corresponding Expected Traffic (2005)

Intensity level	1	2	3	4	5	6	7	8
Traffic (million minutes/year)	1.6	6.4	16	32	95	191	239	318

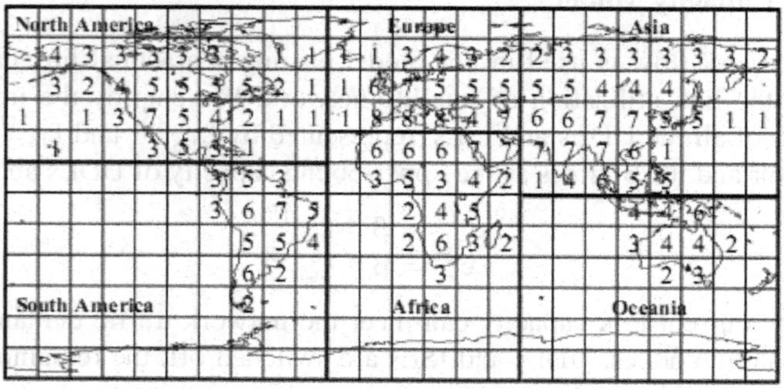

Fig. 2. Predict traffic distribution in 2005 (Millions of Minutes per Year) [10]

4   Problem Formulation

More formally, we use the integer linear programming (ILP) method to define this energy-saving problem as same as [3], and also present the distinction between them, especially the up-down link broadcast communication characteristics between the satellites and ground stations.

The network infrastructure is represented as a di-graph G= (V, E), where the vertex set V represents the network nodes (including satellite nodes and ground station nodes), and the edge set E represents the UDLs and ISLs. The number of network nodes is N=|V|, and the $N_{ground}=|V_{ground}|$, $N_{sat}=|V_{sat}|$ represent the number of ground station nodes and satellite nodes respectively, and let the L=|E| be the number of UDLs and ISLs.

In the aspect of network traffic, we let T^{sd}, s, d= 1…N_{ground}, represent the total traffic between ground station nodes s and d; let $f_{ij}^{sd} \in [0, t^{sd}]$, i, j=1… N, s, d=1…$N_{ground}$ be the traffic flowing through link (i, j) between node s and d. Let f_{ij}, i, j =1…N_{sat} be the total traffic flowing through the link (i, j), let $f_i^{UDL} \in [0, t^{sd}]$, i=1…$N_{sat}$ be the total traffic flowing through the UDL of sat i, let f_i^{ISL} represent the sum of the ISL traffic flowing through satellite node i, i.e.:

$$f_i^{ISL} = \sum_{j=1}^{N_{sat}} f_{ij}^{ISL} + \sum_{j=1}^{N_{sat}} f_{ji}^{ISL}$$

Let $x_{ij}^{ISL} \in \{0,1\}$, i=1…N_{sat}, j=1…N_{sat} be binary variables that take the value of 1 if the ISL from sat i to sat j is present and power on. Similarly, let $y_i \in \{0,1\}$, i=1…N_{sat} be binary variables that take value of 1 if sat i is powered on. Let PL_{ij}^{ISL} be the power consumption of ISL between sat i and sat j, PL_i^{UDL} be the power consumption of UDL of sat i, and PN_i be the power consumption of sat i. PN_i contains the power consumption of OBP without UDLs and ISLs.

However, we should also consider about the bad impact for the routing hops and routing latency increase along with the satellites and links switching off. Let the $hop_{routing}$ denote the proportion of the number of all end-to-end routing hops in current static network routing to the one in initial state, and let hop_{flow} denotes the proportion of the number of all routing hops with flow passed by to the one in initial state. To keep the satellite network's latency performance in system level, we confine hop_{flow} should be smaller than $\eta \in [1, 2]$.

Given the definitions above, the problem can be formalized as follow:

Minimize:

$$P_{tot} = \sum_{i=1}^{N_{sat}} \sum_{j=1}^{N_{sat}} x_{ij}^{ISL} PL_{ij}^{ISL} + \sum_{i=1}^{N_{sat}} x_i^{UDL} PL_i^{UDL} + \sum_{i=1}^{N_{sat}} y_i PN_i \qquad (1)$$

Subject to:

$$\sum_{j=1}^{N} f_{ij}^{sd} - \sum_{j=1}^{N} f_{ji}^{sd} = \begin{cases} T^{sd}, & \forall s, d, i = s \\ -T^{sd}, & \forall s, d, i = d \\ 0, & \forall s, d, i \neq s, d \end{cases} \qquad (2)$$

$$f_i^{UDL} = \sum_{s=1}^{N} \sum_{d=1}^{N} (\sum_{j=1}^{N_{ground}} f_{ij}^{sd} + \sum_{j=1}^{N_{ground}} f_{ji}^{sd}) \leq \alpha c^{UDL}, i = 1 \dots N_{sat} \qquad (3)$$

$$f_{ij}^{ISL} = \sum_{s=1}^{N} \sum_{d=1}^{N} f_{ij}^{sd} \leq \alpha c^{ISL}, i = 1 \dots N_{sat}, j = 1 \dots N_{sat} \qquad (4)$$

$$x_i^{UDL} + \sum_{j=1}^{N_{sat}} x_{ij}^{ISL} + \sum_{j=1}^{N_{sat}} x_{ji}^{ISL} \leq My_i, \ i = 1 \dots N_{sat}, j = 1 \dots N_{sat} \qquad (5)$$

$$hop_{flow} \leq \eta \qquad (6)$$

Equation (1) minimizes the total energy consumption of the satellite network. Equation (2) states the classic flow conservation constraints, and the traffic can travel through the intermediate nodes in many paths without consumption until reaching the destination. Constraints (3) and (4) forces the link load to be smaller than maximum link utilization ratio $\alpha \in [0.4, 1]$, while constraint (5) states that a satellite node can be turned off only if UDL and all incoming and outgoing ISLs are actually turned off, taking $M \geq 2N_{sat}+1$. Constraint (6) forces the total hop counts increase should be under the maximum increase ratio η.

According to these equations above, this formulation falls into the class of link capacity constraint minimal cost multi-commodity flow problems as [3]. It is NP-hard, and cannot obtain the optimal solution in polynomial time. Therefore, a simple heuristic algorithm is provided to obtain the approximate optimal solutions.

5   Heuristic Algorithms

We modify and consummate the heuristic algorithms proposed in [3], which is mainly used in terrestrial wired networks, and do not consider the special broadcast property of up-down links in satellite networks. In our algorithm, the full coverage of ground stations is checked at each node switching step, and the nodes and links are sorted every iteration to keep the selection greedy enough. The heuristic algorithm we proposed is shown as follows:

1. **Initial stage:** assume all the satellites, UDLs and ISLs are powered on, i.e. $x_i^{UDL}=1$, $x_{ij}^{ISL}=1$ ($i=1...N_{sat}$, $j=1...N_{sat}$). Then we use the dijkstra algorithm to calculate the satellite to satellite routing paths with the minimal hop counts, and distribute the traffic to the whole satellite network along these paths.
2. **Pretreatment stage:** switch off the UDLs and ISLs whose traffic equals zero and the satellite nodes whose UDL and ISLs both have been switched off.
3. **Satellite nodes switching off stage:**

   — Firstly, sort the satellite nodes in UDL traffic values f_i^{UDL} (UDLorder) or ISL traffic values f_i^{ISL} (ISLorder) ascending order. We do not sort the nodes by the incoming and outgoing degrees of satellite nodes because of its regular Manhattan network topology structure.
   — Secondly, iteratively switch off the satellite nodes and redistribute the traffic to the whole network. If the network flow can meet the flow conservation constraint (2), capacity constraints (3), (4), node switching off constraints (5) and the hop count increase constraint (6), the satellite node keeps off; or else, the satellite node should be switched on again, which gives the chance to the next satellite node.

4. **Links (UDLs and ISLs) switching off stage:** this stage is similar with the satellite nodes switching off stage. Because the satellites should cover all the terrestrial traffic demand, part of the UDLs could not be off even though the multi-coverage exists. Therefore, we optimize the UDL configurations before than the ISL configurations.
5. **Final check:** the algorithm checks whether there exists satellite nodes whose UDLs traffic and ISLs traffic equal zero, and it should be switched off, too.

6   Performance Analysis

6.1   Experiment Results

The energy-saving performance of proposed heuristic algorithms is evaluated in five different snapshots at different times, where the traffic is random with factor γ. The default values for all parameters are set as $\alpha = 0.5$, $\beta = 3$, $\delta = 1$, $\eta = 1.6$.

The energy-saving ratio is shown in **Fig. 3**. For the reasons of multi-coverage, 45% of the UDLs can be switched off in the pretreatment stage, and the traffic has been distributed throughout the whole network, so there are no satellite nodes that could be closed, and also only 2% ISLs could be closed. Compared to ISLorder heuristic algorithm, UDLorder performs better with the ratio of closed satellite node, UDLs and ISLs as 59%, 61% and 72%, respectively. Assuming that every satellite nodes, UDLs and ISLs have the same power consumption values, i.e. $PL_i^{UDL}=PL_{ij}^{ISL}=100$, $PN_i=50$, and the total energy saving can be up to 65%.

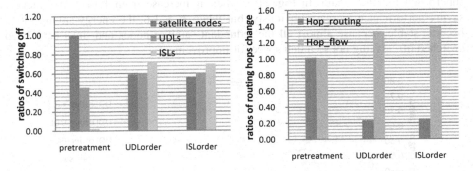

Fig. 3. Energy-saving ratio of satellite network   **Fig. 4.** Routing hops changes

As the satellite nodes and links switched off, the routing paths between each ground station pairs have been changed, along with the traffic distributions. The routing hops variations are shown in **Fig. 4**.

After pretreatment, the hop$_{routing}$ and hop$_{flow}$ stay almost unchanged, because the satellite node, UDLs and ISLs are not switched off. After the UDLorder algorithm executes, satellite node switching off leads to the decrease of network nodes, and the routing path is simpler than before, so the hop$_{routing}$ decreases to 23% of the initial state. However, the switching off of satellite nodes and links obviously increases the average length of routing paths, so hop$_{flow}$ increases rapidly up to 133% of the initial state, which means the average routing latencies increase largely.

The performance of ISLorder is also evaluated, and its increase ratios as hop$_{routing}$ and hop$_{flow}$ are 25% and 140% of the initial state. Thus it can be seen that UDLorder is superior to ISLorder, partially because UDL is more important than ISL in satellite network.

6.2   Parameters Impact

The impact of parameters to our energy-saving performance is studied as well. The link utilization ratio α and link capacity coefficient β mainly affect the switching off of satellite nodes and ISLs, as well as the UDLs traffic aggregation under multi-coverage, while distance coefficient δ is related to the traffic generation and distribution of the whole network.

Fig. 5(a) reports the switching off ratios for different δ values. As δ increase, the ratios increase slowly, however, UDLorder increases distinctly than ISLorder. And the curves of UDLorder-UDL and ISLorder-UDL are superposed together, since there are no changes in the terrestrial traffic aggregation while δ changes. **Fig. 5**(b) shows the variation of the ratios of nodes and links switching off versus α values. When α increase from 0.4 to 0.6, the energy-saving performance increase obviously, but when $\alpha > 0.6$, the energy-saving ratios become stable, because the link capacity is not the limiting factor anymore. In addition, the change of α values does not affect the terrestrial traffic aggregation, so the curves of UDLorder-UDL and ISLorder-UDL superposed together again. In **Fig. 5**(c), when η increase from 1 to 2, the energy-saving performance increase obviously, but when η > 1.6, the energy-saving ratios become stable, because almost all the redundant satellite nodes and links have been switched off, leaving not so much space for improvement.

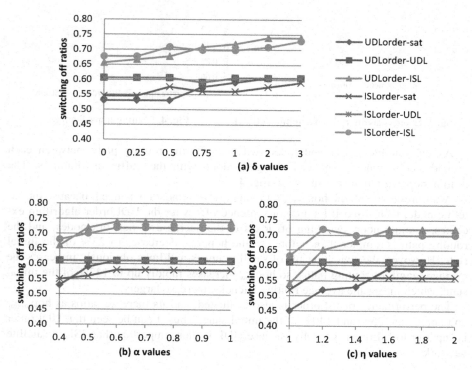

Fig. 5. Ratios of satellite nodes and links switched off versus δ, α and η

7   Conclusions and Future Work

In this paper, we discussed the availability improvement problem focused on energy-saving in satellite networks. Based on snapshot routing, we formulated this problem as a set of link capacity constrained minimal cost multi-commodity flow problems. We proposed simple heuristic algorithms to aggregate the distributed traffic in multiple satellites to a single satellite, and switch off the unnecessary satellite nodes, UDLs and ISLs, under the constraints of link utilization and routing hops increase. Results show that the total energy saving ratio can be up to 65% with the switching off ratios of satellite nodes, UDLs and ISLs being up to 59%, 61% and 72%.

As future work, we plan to consider the impact of variation of network traffic, which could be caused by satellite movements and the alternation of day and night. During the night, the traffic demand reduced largely, so more nodes and links could be switched off for energy-saving.

Acknowledgement. The work described in this paper is partially supported by the grants of the National Basic Research Program of China (973 project) under Grant No.2009CB320503, 2012CB315906; the project of National Science Foundation of China under grant No.61070199, 61103189, 61103194, 61103182, 61202488, 61272482; the National High Technology Research and Development Program of China (863 Program) No.2011AA01A103, 2012AA01A506, 2013AA013505, the Research Fund for the Doctoral Program of Higher Education of China under Grant No.20114307110006, 20124307120032, the program for Changjiang Scholars and Innovative Research Team in University (No.IRT1012), Science and Technology Innovative Research Team in Higher Educational Institutions of Hunan Province ("network technology"); and Hunan Province Natural Science Foundation of China (11JJ7003).

References

1. Alagoz, F.: Energy Efficiency and Satellite Networking: A Holistic Overview. Proc. IEEE 99(11), 1954–1979 (2011)
2. Pantazis, N.A., Vergados, D.D.: Energy efficiency and power control. In: Zheng, J., Jamalipour, A. (eds.) Wireless Sensor Networks: A Networking Perspective, pp. 307–341. Wiley, New York (2009)
3. Chiaraviglio, L., Mellia, M., Neri, F.: Reducing power consumption in backbone networks. In: Proc. IEEE ICC, Dresden, Germany, pp. 1–6 (2009)
4. Barford, P., Chabarek, J., Estan, C., Sommers, J., Tsiang, D., Wright, S.: Power Awareness in Network Design and Routing. In: IEEE INFOCOM 2008, pp. 1130–1138 (2008)
5. Nedevschi, S., Popa, L., Iannaccone, G., Ratnasamy, S., Wetherall, D.: Reducing network energy consumption via sleeping and rate-adaptation. In: Proc. USENIX/ACM NSDI, San Francisco, CA, pp. 323–336 (2008)
6. Gupta, M., Singh, S.: Dynamic Ethernet Link Shutdown for Energy Conservation on Ethernet Links. In: IEEE ICC 2007, pp. 6156–6161 (2007)
7. Fu, A.C., Modiano, E., Tsitsiklis, J.N.: Optimal energy allocation and admission control for communications satellites. IEEE/ACM Trans. Netw. 11(3), 488–500 (2003)
8. Hefeeda, M., Hsu, C.: On burst transmission scheduling in mobile TV broadcast networks. IEEE/ACM Trans. Netw. 18(2), 610–623 (2010)
9. Gounder, V., Prakash, R.: Routing in LEO-based satellite networks. In: Proceedings of IEEE Emerging Technologies. Symposium on Wireless Communications and Systems, pp. 91–96 (1999)
10. Chen, C.: Advanced Routing Protocols for Satellite and Space Networks. PhD thesis, Georgia Institute of Technology, p. 53 (2005)

An Effective Cloud-Based Active Defense System against Malicious Codes

Zhenyu Zhang, Wujun Zhang*, Jianfeng Wang, and Xiaofeng Chen

State Key Laboratory of Integrated Service Networks (ISN),
Xidian University, Xi'an, P.R. China
yijiedao@sina.com, {wjzhang,xfchen}@xidian.edu.cn, wjf01@163.com

Abstract. With the rapid development of cloud computing technique, network security has attracted more and more attention. Of all the network threats, malicious code is the major one. Due to the surge of number and species diversity of the malicious code, it is intractable for the existing antivirus techniques to defense all of the attacks. In this paper, we construct an effective cloud-based active defense system against malicious code. The constructed system utilizes the honey-pot subsystem to collect threaten data, and multiple behavior analysis engines work in parallel to generate a comprehensive program behavior analysis report. Furthermore, there are intelligent algorithms running on several computing servers to achieve automatic intelligent analysis on the reports. Associated with the multiple scan engines form a comprehensive, reinforced and more intelligent active defense system.

Keywords: Cloud computing, Honey-pot, Behavior analysis, Active defense.

1 Introduction

With the development of Internet technology, computer viruses and hacker techniques combined with more variants and other development trends. Traditional AV(Anti-Virus) modes are not available to defense malicious codes, the reasons are as follows: Hysteresis and limitations of the traditional stand-alone defense; high cost of the sample collection and low effectiveness; longer upgrade cycle, more consumption of resources, poor user experience.

The emergence of cloud computing provide the ideas to resolve these problems, such as "Cloud AV" [1,2] , "Cloud AV" moves the complex computing components from client to cloud computing server. However, some of the existing implements only combine the AV engines together, profit-driven make the detection with one-sidedness, moreover, some others deploy their server in the cloud, but still using signature-matching which cannot detect unknown viruses. Oberheide proposed a multiple antivirus engines work in parallel residing on cloud system called "CloudAV" [2], CloudAV does enhance the detection rate

---

* Corresponding author.

Linawati et al. (Eds.): ICT-EurAsia 2014, LNCS 8407, pp. 690–695, 2014.

but lack of discussing the sample analysis and collection parts. Some other systems like "MIDeA" [14] and "GrAVity" [15] utilize the same idea that make the security services or tools work in parallel to get better efficiency and data processing rate. In [12] Peter and Robin et al. show that how diversity AV(Anti-Virus) engines may help improve detection gains. Xu et al. proposed an on cloud collaborative security services composing system called "CloudSEC" [13] which is a dynamic peer-to-peer overlay hierarchy with three architectural components. Cristian and Gustavo et al. proposed an ontology based malware detection system deploy in the cloud named "nCLAVS" [1] which is specifically on Web service applications.

Our Contributions. We propose an active defense system with enhanced malware detection ability and can do actively defense against unknown virus.

- We deploy a hierarchy honey-farm system on cloud platform to collect malicious attacks in large scale. The honey-farm system combines "Potemkin" [9] with TCP conversation migrate technology.
- We deploy multiple behavior analysis engines work in parallel in cloud. Multiple engines ensure the analysis to be comprehensive.

2   Preliminaries

Cloud Computing. Cloud Computing distributed computing tasks into resource pool which is consisted of a large number of computers. This resource pool called "Cloud" [3]. The core of cloud computing is parallel computing which separates task into several parts, each part can be allocated to a separate processor. Parallel computing system can be specifically designed and contain supercomputers with more than one processor or clusters based on a number of stand-alone computers interconnected, the parallel computing cluster can process data and return the results to the user after treatment.

Honey-Pot. Honey-pot is a kind of computer on the Internet and with no defense policy, its internal runs variety data recorders and special self-expose programs to tempt network intrusion behaviors. Honey-pot aims to collect threat data. There are two types of honey-pot system in practice:Low-interaction honey-pots that offer limited services to the attacker like Nepenthe [4] honeyd [5]. High-interaction honey-pots that offer the attacker a real system to interact with. Such as Gen-III honey-net [6].

Behavior Analysis. Behavior analysis engine like CWSandbox [8], is based on the "sandbox" [7] which makes the suspicious program running in a virtual "sandbox" in the full show, "sandbox" will record all its actions. Once the program fully exposed its viral properties,"sandbox" will erase the traces of the virus and restore the system to its original normal state.

3 Active Defense System Architecture

In the proposed system, we deploy the LSSC (large scale sample collection) subsystem and VIA (virtual isolate analysis) subsystem on the cloud platform to master diversity threat behaviors. The skeleton of the proposed defense system architecture as shown in Fig. 1.

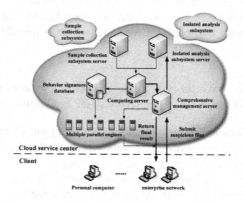

Fig. 1. Architecture of active defense system

3.1 Key System Components

Sample Collection Subsystem. We deploy LSSC in a hierarchical way to make two types of honey-pot cooperate. Low interactive honey-pot would possibly unable to response some of the malicious requests, we use the TCP conversation migration to redirect data stream to the high interaction honey-pot to offer for higher level of capture.The LSSC structure as shown in Fig. 2.

Isolated Analysis Subsystem. Since it's difficult for a single engine to capture comprehensive behaviors of a suspicious program, VIA integrates virtual monitors from different vendors work in parallel to perform a comprehensive monitoring.

Computing Server. Computing server mainly process the data reported from the two subsystems using intelligent detect algorithms. Suspicious malicious codes will be given a weighted value, so behavior characteristics meet certain threshold will be stored in special format to form a behavior characteristic database.

Integrated Scheduling Management Server. Integrated scheduling management server is responsible for components scheduling. Once received a request,the management server initiate multi-engine in a combination of optimized configuration to do a full scan of the file. If the file can not be judged, this server is responsible for submit it to VIA to do further analysis.

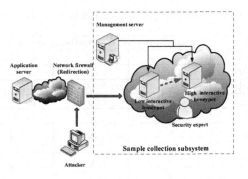

Fig. 2. Sample collection subsystem

4 Performance Analysis

Multiple Antivirus Engines. We deploy multiple AV engines work in parallel the same as proposed in [2]. We select several popular AV engines and collect 2718 old virus samples offered by "www.Bioon.com", and a new virus sample set of 283 offered by "bbs.kafan.cn" . Table 1 shows the detection rate of each engine when them work respectively on these samples.

Table 1. Detection rate of each engine

	Engine 1	Engine 2	Engine 3	Engine 4	Engine 5
2718 old samples	26.3%	49.42%	51.69%	51.06%	97.42%
283 new samples	10.03%	27.36%	43.45%	43.47%	56.53%

We also do the test of detecting the samples with different AV engines combinations. Make U denote the virus sample data set. If engine A can detect U_A samples out of U while engine B can detect $U_B(|U_A| \geq |U_B|)$, so the sum detect samples are

$$U_{SUM} = U_A \cup U_B$$

Even if $U_A \cap U_B = U_B$, the U_{SUM} is no less than either U_A or U_B. So we can conclude that multiple engines work concurrently will surely improve the detection rate. There is one thing that we should be concern: certain engine may did a false alarm. Its easy to realize that if we introduce more engines and the false alarm will be reduce accordingly.

Multiple Behavior Analysis Engines. The proposed VIA subsystem is consist of several analysis engines. Table 2 demonstrate their report details of each engine. The empty cells do not indicate that tools do not have the coordinate

Table 2. The main analysis items for each engine

	Threat Expert	CW Sandbox	Anubis	Joe sandbox	Cuckoo
File system modification	√	√	√	√	√
Registry modification	√	√	√	√	√
Memory modification	√	√	√	√	√
Process creation	√	√	√	√	√
DLL injection		√	√	√	√
API call	√	√		√	√
IP involved	√			√	
Network traffic	√	√		√	√
Source trace	√			√	

functions but show the inadequacy of tools. multiple engines work in parallel will surely enhance the analysis efficiency and the analysis report will be more comprehensive.

Hierarchical Honey-Pot System. We deploy the honey-pot system in cloud center in a hierarchy construction by traffic redirection and migrate technology, make the low and high interactive honey-pot cooperate. So the LSSC we proposed in this paper will sure be more efficient and comprehensive. Artail [10] and Bailey [11] implemented such a hybrid honey-pot system and proved its' efficiency.

5   Conclusion

The proposed system overcame the high cost and low efficiency of deploying honey-pot system under traditional antivirus mechanism and can collect network threats in large scale. On the other side, multiple behavior analysis engines work concurrently, avoid one-sidedness caused by single engine, ensure the reliability and practicability of analysis results from various aspects. The proposed system can deal with severe situation on network security.

Acknowledgement. This work is supported by the National Natural Science Foundation of China (Nos. 61272455), Doctoral Fund of Ministry of Education of China (No. 20130203110004), Program for New Century Excellent Talents in University (No. NCET-13-0946), and China 111 Project (No. B08038).

References

1. Martínez, C.A., Echeverri, G.I., Sanz, A.G.C.: Malware detection based on cloud computing integrating intrusion ontology representation. In: IEEE Latin-American Conference on Communications (LATINCOM), Bogota, pp. 1–6 (2010)

2. Oberheide, J., Cooke, E., Jahanian, F.: CloudAV: N-version antivirus in the network cloud. In: Proc. of the 17th USENIX Security Symposium, San Jose, Calofornia, USA, pp. 91–106 (2008)
3. Armbrust, M., Fox, A., Griffith, R.: A view of cloud computing. Communications of the ACM 53(4), 50–58 (2010)
4. Baecher, P., Koetter, M., Holz, T., Dornseif, M., Freiling, F.C.: The nepenthes platform: An efficient approach to collect malware. In: Zamboni, D., Kruegel, C. (eds.) RAID 2006. LNCS, vol. 4219, pp. 165–184. Springer, Heidelberg (2006)
5. Niels, P.: A Virtual Honeypot Framework. In: Proceedings of 13th USENIX Security Symposium, San Diego, CA, USA, pp. 1–14 (2004)
6. Balas, E., Viecco, C.: Towards a third generation data capture architecture for honeynets. In: Proceedings from the Sixth Annual IEEE SMC, Information Assurance Workshop, pp. 21–28. IEEE, NY (2005)
7. Wright, W., Schroh, D., Proulx, P.: The sandbox for analysis: concepts and Eevaluation. In: Proceedings of the 2006 Conference on Human Factors in Computing Systems, CHI 2006, Quebec, Canada, pp. 801–810 (2006)
8. Willems, C., Holz, T., Freiling, F.: Toward Automated Dynamic Malware Analysis Using CWSandbox. Security & Privacy 5(2), 32–39 (2007)
9. Vrable, M., Ma, J., Chen, J.: Scalability, fidelity, and containment in the potemkin virtual honeyfarm. In: Proceedings of the 20th ACM Symposium on Operating Systems Principles 2005, SOSP, Brighton, UK, pp. 148–162 (2005)
10. Artail, H., Safa, H., Sraj, M.: A hybrid honeypot framework for improving intrusion detection systems in protecting organizational networks. Computers & Security 25(4), 274–288 (2006)
11. Bailey, M., Cooke, E., Watson, D.: A hybrid honeypot architecture for scalable network monitoring. Technical Report CSE-TR-499-04, U. Michigan (2004)
12. Peter, G.B., Robin, E.B., Ilir, G., Vladimir, S.: Diversity for Security: A Study with Off-the-Shelf AntiVirus Engines. In: IEEE 22nd International Symposium on Software Reliability Engineering, ISSRE 2011, Hiroshima, Japan, pp. 11–19 (2011)
13. Xu, J., Yan, J., He, L., Su, P., Feng, D.: CloudSEC: A Cloud Architecture for Composing Collaborative Security Services. In: Proceedings of the Second International Conference on Cloud Computing, CloudCom 2010, Indianapolis, Indiana, USA, November 30-December 3, pp. 703–711 (2010)
14. Giorgos, V., Michalis, P., Sotiris, I.: MIDeA: a multi-parallel intrusion detection architecture. In: Proceedings of the 18th ACM Conference on Computer and Communication Security, CCS, Chicago, Illinois, USA, pp. 297–308 (2011)
15. Vasiliadis, G., Ioannidis, S.: GrAVity: A Massively Parallel Antivirus Engine. In: Jha, S., Sommer, R., Kreibich, C. (eds.) RAID 2010. LNCS, vol. 6307, pp. 79–96. Springer, Heidelberg (2010)

Erratum to: Acceptance and Use of Information System: E-Learning Based on Cloud Computing in Vietnam

Thanh D. Nguyen, Dung T. Nguyen, and Thi H. Cao

Erratum to:
Chapter "Acceptance and Use of Information System:
E-Learning Based on Cloud Computing in Vietnam" in:
Linawati et al. (Eds.): *Information and Communication*
Technology, **LNCS 8407,**
https://doi.org/10.1007/978-3-642-55032-4_14

The affiliation of Thanh D. Nguyen and Dung T. Nguyen was incorrectly rendered as "HCM University of Technology, Vietnam". The correct designation is "HCMC University of Technology, Vietnam".

The updated online version of this chapter can be found at
https://doi.org/10.1007/978-3-642-55032-4_14

Linawati et al. (Eds.): ICT-EurAsia 2014, LNCS 8407, p. E1, 2014.
© IFIP International Federation for Information Processing 2018
https://doi.org/10.1007/978-3-642-55032-4_72

Author Index

Printed in the United States
By Bookmasters